Distribution

Planning and Control

Distribution

Planning and Control

Managing In The Era Of Supply Chain Management

Second Edition

David Frederick Ross

Library of Congress Cataloging-in-Publication Data

Ross, David Frederick, 1948-
   Distribution: planning and control : managing in the era of supply chain management /
   David Frederick Ross.—2nd edition
      p. cm.
   ISBN: 1-4020-7686-X
   1. Marketing—Management. 2. Export marketing. 3. Business logistics.
   I. Title.

HF5415.13.R649 2004
658.7—dc22   2003062058

Printed in the United States of America.

9 8 7 6 5 4 3 2   SPIN 11399179

springeronline.com

TABLE OF CONTENTS

PREFACE

When work began on the first volume of this text in 1992, the science of distribution management was still very much a backwater of general management and academic thought. While most of the body of knowledge associated with calculating EOQs, fair-shares inventory deployment, productivity curves, and other operations management techniques had long been solidly established, new thinking about distribution management had taken a definite back-seat to the then dominant interest in Lean thinking, quality management, and business process reengineering and their impact on manufacturing and service organizations. For the most part, discussion relating to the distribution function centered on a fairly recent concept called *Logistics Management*. But, despite talk of how logistics could be used to integrate internal and external business functions and even be considered a source of competitive advantage on its own, most of the focus remained on how companies could utilize operations management techniques to optimize the traditional day-to-day shipping and receiving functions in order to achieve cost containment and customer fulfillment objectives. In the end, distribution management was, for the most part, still considered a dreary science, concerned with expediting and the tedious calculus of transportation rates and cost trade-offs.

Today, the science of distribution has become perhaps one of the most important and exciting disciplines in the management of business. In the space of a decade or so the management of supply and distribution channels has catapulted to world-wide prominence as the central fulcrum in the search for competitive advantage. Since the early 1990s, a host of critical trends, events, and ideas have intervened that have dramatically altered the theory and practice of logistics management and opened fresh areas for research and practical application. Much of the dialogue is the result of the maturation of a number of radically new marketplace dynamics such as the growth in power of the "voice of the customer," demands for the *mass customization* of products and services, a veritable explosion in globalization and outsourcing, a heavy focus on reengineering, cost control, and cash conservation, the end of the vertically integrated enterprise, and several order-of-magnitude breakthroughs in information and communications technologies. But of all the dynamics impacting today's business environment, perhaps the two most important are the rise of the concept of *Supply Chain Management* (SCM) and the birth of the Internet.

In 1992 SCM and the Internet were not even on the radar screen of logistics practitioners and theorists. Simply put, the Internet did not exist and was totally in the realm of odd pockets of "computer geeks" and very academic scientists. As for SCM, while a few visionaries began talking about it as early as 1990, it was really not until the middle of the decade that the concept began to gain traction as a new management science evolving out of the logistics concept.

Today, SCM and the Internet have come to dominate all thinking and it has become hard to talk about one without reference to the other. The literature on the topic has grown astronomically. Literally hundreds of articles and books have generated countless pages of perspectives on SCM/Internet theory and practice over the last few years. The discipline has its own journal - *Supply Chain Management Review* (founded 1996) - and trade magazines with evocative titles, such as *e-Supply Chain Management, Supply Chain Technology News*, and others, continue to emerge. College courses and business seminars discussing just about every aspect of channel management abound. Most consulting firms have whole practice areas devoted to SCM. The concept has actually engendered a whole genus of computer software.

The rise to dominance of the convergence of SCM and the Internet has not happened by chance. It has evolved as a response to the very real requirements that companies must now act through their supply chains if they expect to be capable of providing the market-winning value demanded by the customer; they must be agile and scalable to bring new products to market faster, flexible in the design of production and distribution processes, and capable of quick supply channel redesign; and they must be capable of engineering dazzlingly fast flow order-to-delivery cycles utilizing Internet technologies that eliminate channel costs and redundancies while increasing customer convenience. While the rise and fall of the Internet economy gave witness to the relative immaturity of the dot-com e-business revolution, the dramatics were an unfortunate side-show to the slow, but real changes being engineered by savvy executives who were coming to understand that the emerging vernacular of idioms like *connectivity, interoperability, networking, e-business,* and *collaboration* were more than just the newest management buzzwords but were, in reality, the kernels of new paradigms of how business in the twenty-first century would be conducted.

The changes to the concept and practice of distribution management brought about by the SCM/Internet manifold (termed *e-SCM* in the pages to follow) is the main driver for the redrafting of this text. While the word "supply chain management" appeared in the original 1996 edition, it was given scant attention. In its place, the concept of *Integrated Enterprise Manage-*

ment had been coined to compensate for the lack of a more robust definition. This construct has been eliminated in the revision in favor of e-SCM. In fact, the importance and recognition of the impact of e-SCM had become so critical in the intervening years since publication that the relevance of the first edition to today's student of distribution and logistics was in serious doubt. In addition, the footprint of the e-SCM body of knowledge had expanded so quickly, that every chapter in the original text had grown in many places seriously out of date and in need of drastic revision. Because of the importance of SCM, the author even considered changing the title to *Supply Chain Management: Planning and Control*. After much thought the original and all-inclusive title was retained with the phrase "Managing in the Era of Supply Chain Management" added as the subtitle.

The second edition of *Distribution: Planning and Control* follows the original structure of the first edition. Based on the assumption that, like all organizations, the distribution function is driven by purposes or goals and is composed of people working together to achieve common objectives, the most effective organizations are best managed through an interactive method of *planning* and *control*. At its highest level, enterprise *planning* seeks to develop comprehensive strategies that define clearly company goals while enabling operations functions to quick response to changing marketplace needs. *Control*, on the other hand, is a continuous management activity that strives to have in place the operational skills and performance measurements necessary, first of all, to direct the flow of energy and materials into executing business functions in support of strategic plans, and, second, to collect and communicate information to ensure processes are focused on achieving the best marketplace opportunities. Without purposeful planning and control, today's enterprise cannot hope to survive, much less achieve competitive superiority.

Unit 1 of the text attempts to set the background and define the terms necessary to understand today's distribution environment. The objective is twofold. To begin with, the Unit seeks to explore the origins, opportunities, and challenges confronting SCM and logistics management at the dawn of the twenty-first century. Particular importance is paid to the evolution of the body of management knowledge surrounding SCM and logistics, concluding with a concise definition and detailed dissection of contributing features and concepts. The second objective is to describe in detail the nature and functions of the distribution industry and its place next to manufacturing and retail in the supply chain. The unit provides a full review of the various types of distributor, ranging from wholesalers, brokers and agents, and manufacturers' and retailers' branches and offices, to exporting and importing distributors. Special attention is paid to the rise of new forms of distribution brought about by the Internet.

Once the goals and nature of SCM and distribution management have been defined, Unit 2 begins the discussion of the enterprise planning and control process. The Unit opens with a review of *business and strategic planning*. Business plans are formulated by top management to achieve enterprise goals. The objective of the entire process is to architect the strategies detailing the firm's growth, asset, revenue, and capital management goals in light of the political, economic, demographical, technological, and competitive challenges of the marketplace. Finally, business objectives define the culture of the enterprise, its competitive posture, and its perception of itself in the marketplace.

The second area considered in Unit 2 is *demand, operations, and channel planning*. These plans are the culmination of the enterprise planning process that began with the formulation of the business plan. The goal of this process is the creation of a set of highly integrated business functional plans that ensure that the five critical plans constituting the core of the executive planning process – the marketing plan, the sales plan, the production plan, the logistics plan, and the supply chain plan – are in balance. Individually, each of these plans attempts to define the strategies and operations decisions that must occur if the overall business mission is to be achieved. In detail, these plans center on strategic operations issues, such as determining the overall rates of product family sales and production, aggregate inventories, supply chain value delivery, and logistics capacities. Once each of these aggregate plans has been developed, they can be then integrated together to provide corporate decision makers with a medium- to long-range "rough-cut" window into how well individual enterprises and whole supply chains are responding to meet the overall business plans.

Unit 3 centers on the translation of strategic plans into the detailed operations plans that will guide the organization in the calculation of inventory requirements, detailed logistics capacity plans, and distribution channel resource deployment. One of the most important challenges facing the logistics organization is the effective control of inventory. Channel planners must seek effective techniques to minimize inventory carrying costs while at the same time continuously improving customer service levels. Inventory planners can utilize two broad methods of planning and controlling inventories: *statistical inventory replenishment* and *Distribution Requirements Planning* (DRP), or a combination of both. Statistical replenishment attempts to utilize historical usages and item planning data to calculate reorder points and optimal order quantities. DRP is a computerized technique encompassing two distinct processes. The first consists of the time phased calculation of the inventory requirements of each warehouse in the distribution network. This calculation is based on the difference between gross requirements and on-hand inventory, scheduled receipts and in-transit shipments. Gross requirements are attained by compiling the total demand placed on each distribution center. The second process passes the net requirements of each warehouse to the supplying source. Statistical planning methods are classically associated with *push* systems of channel replenishment, whereas DRP is associated with *pull* systems.

The effective control of inventory requires detailed *logistics resource planning*. This area of planning attempts to measure key resource capacities required for the realization of the inventory acquisition plans necessary to execute the marketing and sales strategies. Detailed logistics planning is focused on the management of four possible capacity resource constraints. The first capacity constraint is concerned with determining whether the organization has the financial ability to maintain the necessary inventory levels detailed in the inventory acquisition plan. The second capacity constraint involves reviewing the availability, cost, dispatching, and selection of transportation to support the inventory acquisition and delivery plans. The third capacity is concerned with individual warehouse stocking capacities, storage space, and equipment requirements. Finally, logistics planning provides a tool to gauge the need for staffing to receive, stock, and ship products as well as for requirements caused by seasonality or other factors. Logistics planning enables planners to keep demand and capacity in alignment by providing a window into the events occurring out in the distribution channel. Corrective action, such as adding overtime, temporary storage, or subcontracting, can then be taken effectively. When logistics capacities are insufficient, inventory planners must work with sales and marketing to align anticipated marketplace demands with the resources of the enterprise.

Unit 4 of the text is concerned with the execution of the strategic and operations planning processes. The Unit begins with a discussion of the focal point of the enterprise: customer relationship management. Superior customer service in the twenty-first century requires order processing and customer service functions that provide for the speedy and accurate transference of goods, value-added services, and order information. Among the topics discussed are the generation of effective demand management strategies, utilization of the Internet to facilitate customer ordering and service management, the development of the *customer-centric organization*, fulfillment management, establishing responsive customer service, and identifying performance gaps.

Following customer management, the Unit focuses on three areas traditionally considered at the heart of logistics management: purchasing, warehousing, and transportation. The performance of purchasing and value-added processing functions resides at the very core of supply channel management. Procurement is responsible for ensuring the availably of product throughout the channel network and, because of its impact on revenues, costs, and operational efficiencies, has become a key enabler of supply chain strategy. Procurement is also the establishment of collaborative relationships with suppliers, termed *supplier relations management* (SRM). Similar to CRM, SRM seeks to utilize integrative technologies, like the Inter-net and trading exchanges, to leverage the supply chain landscape to architect agile supplier relationships capable of collaborative product design, infor-mation transfer, mutual responsibility for quality, and close computerized linkages for replenishment planning.

Whereas the central focus of inventory acquisition function is to have inventory ready at the time and place required by the customer, the role of warehousing is to ensure the smooth flow of goods through the distribution pipeline. In today's "Lean" and highly interoperable supply chains, the concept of the warehouse as a static repository for product storage has been replaced by a more dynamic view that considers the warehouse as a high-velocity customer service center. Instead of an inflexible, lumbering giant accounting for the bulk of a typical distributor's costs and manpower requirements, today's *distribution center* utilizes computerization, automation, Lean concepts of quality and elimination of wastes to provide the channel network with a source of competitive differentiation and marketplace leadership.

Whereas procurement and warehousing focus on product and place utilities, transportation attempts to solve the issue of time utility by providing inexpensive, efficient, and easily accessed methods of moving product through the channel pipeline. By providing for the swift and uninterrupted flow of products, transportation provides companies with the ability to compete with other businesses in distant markets on an equal footing. Transportation also permits wider and deeper penetration of new markets far from the point of production. In addition, by maximizing vehicle and materials handling capacities and cargo requirements, effective transportation permits enterprises to leverage economies of scale by lowering the per-unit cost of transporting product. Efficient transportation enables firms to reduce the selling price by holding costs down, thereby providing for more competitive product positioning. Finally, transportation provides other business functions with essential information concerning products, marketing place and time utilities, and transit costs and capabilities necessary for effective supply chain planning and operational execution.

Unit 5 concludes the text with an analysis of two of the most important developments in today's distribution industry. The first, the emergence of international distribution, relates to the explosion in global trade, the integration of the world's economic activities, and the growth of world trading blocks. Among the topics discussed are international material and product sourcing, the nature and functions of international distribution, and managing international distribution channels. The final chapter in the text provides an overview of the impact of the computer revolution on the distribution industry and how enterprise distribution management can search and implement information technologies effectively from automation to enterprise information systems.

FEATURES

This text was written primarily for use by practitioners, instructors, students, and consultants involved in Supply Chain Management, logistics and distribution channel management courses, seminars, and internal company development programs, as well as professionals seeking to improve their knowledge concerning logistics topics. Although the text is broad enough to encompass all the management activities found in today's logistics and distribution channel organizations, it is detailed enough to provide the reader with a thorough understanding of essential planning and control processes, as well as problem-solving techniques that can be applied in everyday operations. Although the text deals largely with concepts, a concerted effort has been made to ground them by including examples from various industries. Each chapter provides the following features to facilitate the learning process.

- The contents of each chapter are provided on the first page of each new chapter. This assists readers in quickly gaining insight as to the key points of discussion in each chapter.
- Case studies and topical information are provided in the form of inserts into each chapter. These inserts help to broaden the discussion through real-world examples.
- Each chapter is concluded with a detailed summary. The goal is to provide a forum for concept summary and transition to the next chapter.
- Summary questions and problems are provided at the end of each chapter. The goal is to challenge readers as to their knowledge of topics presented in each chapter and to offer a tool for learning reinforcement.

ANCILLARIES

An instructor's manual is available for the text containing chapter outlines, transparency masters/PowerPoint slides covering the text, and additional multiple choice, essay, and case studies per chapter. These materials can be attained from the author in CD format through the author's Web-site or email david.ross@intentia.com.

ACKNOWLEDGEMENTS

The author is greatly indebted to the many individuals and companies that have provided the insight and understanding of logistics and manufacturing functions fundamental to the writing of this text. Of particular importance are the comments of the many students gleaned from countless hours spent in the classroom in a variety of settings. I am particularly grateful to the American Production and Control Society (APICS) for their support and sponsorship of the book. It has been a gratifying experience to have the text selected for use in the CPIM certification program. The author would also like to especially thank Mr. L. Eugene Magad who was responsible for shepherding the first edition through to completion. I would also like to thank the staff at Kluwer Academic Publishers for their keen support in drafting the second edition and finishing it through to completion. Finally, I would like to express my loving thanks to my wife Colleen and my son Jonathan who had to bear yet again another period of lost afternoons and long evenings but who receive little of the rewards.

ABOUT THE AUTHOR

A distinguished educator and consultant, **David Frederick Ross**, Ph.D., CFPIM, has spent over 25 years in the fields of production and distribution management. During his 13 years as an operations management professional, he held several line and staff positions in a number of manufacturing and distribution companies. For the past 16 years Dr. Ross has been involved in ERP, project management, and e-business education and consulting for several software companies. Currently, he is Education Business Group Manager for Intentia-Americas and is located in the corporate offices in Schaumburg, IL (e-mail: david.ross@intentia.com). He has also taught production and operations management courses at Eastern Illinois University and Oakton Community College. He is a long-time instructor in the APICS practitioner education program. Finally, he also offers supply chain management education, training, and consulting to companies through his own consulting company. Dr. Ross's degree is from the University of Chicago.

Besides numerous articles, Dr. Ross has published three books in the field of distribution and supply chain management. His first book, *Distribution: Planning and Control* (Kluwer Academic), first appeared in 1996 and has been used as a standard logistics management text by several universities and is a cornerstone book for the APICS CPIM certification program. The book has been updated and released in a new edition (Kluwer Academic, 2003). His second book, *Competing Through Supply Chain Management* (Kluwer Academic, 1998), was one of the very first complete texts on the science of supply chain management. The book has also been placed on the reading lists at several universities for courses in logistics and operations management. His third book, *Introduction to e-Supply Chain Management* (St. Lucie, 2003), explores the concepts, techniques, and vocabulary of the convergence of supply chain management and the Internet to help companies optimize their customer management planning, scheduling, engineering, manufacturing, and inventory management functions.

UNIT 1

DEFINING THE SUPPLY CHAIN
MANAGEMENT ENVIRONMENT

CHAPTERS:

1. The Rise of Supply Chain Management
2. Components of Distribution Management

The objective of Unit 1 is to squarely position the student of logistics and distribution channel management in the business environment found at the dawn of the twenty-first century. As discussed in the Preface, the pace of change brought about by the power of the customer, information technology, and globalization have forced all companies toady to critically reexamine the operating values and cultures of their organizations, the way their businesses and processes are structured, and the strategies and tactics by which they compete in the marketplace. The ability of supply chain strategists to continuously align their enterprises to meet these changes constitutes the foremost challenge before their organizations. Companies that can leverage the dramatic breakthroughs in information technologies and global trade will be those who gain market share and thrive in the new millennium.

Unit 1 begins by defining Supply Chain Management (SCM), modern logistics, and the organization of the distribution function. In Chapter 1, the nature and functions of SCM and logistics are examined. The chapter begins by exploring six critical dynamics that are reshaping the face of business on a global basis. Responding to each of these dynamics has required companies to look outward to their supply chain systems to gain quick access to critical competencies and resources in order to remain competitive. Building these networks is the objective of the new science of Supply Chain Management (SCM). This chapter seeks a definitive definition of SCM which traces the concept from its origins up to today's Internet-enabled "virtual" supply chain organization. The chapter concludes with a full definition of logistics management and its relationship to SCM.

Whereas Chapter 1 attempts to describe the organizational, operational, and philosophical foundations guiding the management of today's supply chain, Chapter 2 focuses on defining the meaning of "distributor" and the scope of the distribution industry. After detailing the operational characteristics and marketplace role of the distributor, the chapter offers a detailed analysis of the various types of distributor, ranging from manufacturers who distribute their own products, to wholesalers, brokers, retailers, and global importers and exporters. Among the topics covered are understanding the need for distribution, the channel functions performed by the distributor, and the inbound and outbound materials and information flows found within the typical distribution organization. The chapter concludes with a brief overview of the challenges facing the distribution industry in the business climate of the first decade of the twenty-first century.

1

THE RISE OF SUPPLY CHAIN MANAGEMENT

In the Preface it was stated that the accelerating pace of change is the single most important factor shaping all aspects of contemporary business from economics to technology, from the way products are produced to the way they are bought. Whereas it is true that technology has revealed exciting new methods of designing and producing products and communicating them to the customer, it is through the activity of distribution that products reach the marketplace and the exchange process is determined. Throughout history, businesses have been faced with the problem that demand for goods often extended far beyond the locations where they were made and that products were not always available at the time when customers wanted them. Where the capabilities of distribution have been limited, people must live close to the source of production and will have access to a limited range of goods and services. On the other hand, societies that possess highly complex and inexpensive distribution systems are marked by production efficiencies, a wide spectrum of available products, the rapid exchange of goods, and accelerating standards of living. Efficient and constantly developing supply chain systems enable enterprises to leverage and focus productive functions while extending the reach of their products to meet national and international demand. In today's marketplace, supply chain management provides the bridge linking products to distant markets separated by global time and distance.

Chapter 1 is focused on exploring the opportunities and challenges confronting supply chain and logistics management at the dawn of the twenty-first century. The chapter begins by defining six critical marketplace forces that are dramatically transforming today's global business environment. Responding effectively to these challenges has required corporate strategists to search for solutions outside of their internal organizations to gain quick access to core competencies and resources in the race for competitive survival. Next, the evolution of *supply chain management* (SCM) is explored. The argument is that SCM is the product of five distinct management stages, beginning first with logistics operations decentralization and progressing to today's Internet-driven supply chains. Once the foundations of SCM have been established, the discussion proceeds to a concise definition of SCM in the Internet Age. Full attention is given to exploring the distinct components of the SCM model and their merger with today's expanding Web-based capabilities. The chapter concludes with a full definition of logistics management and its relationship to SCM.

ADVENT OF SUPPLY CHAIN MANAGEMENT

Over the past decade, companies have become increasingly aware that to remain competitive in an era of accelerating change and intensified competition they can no longer depend solely on their own inventive and productive strengths but must look to the core competencies of supply chain partners to enhance and accelerate customer-winning products and services. In the past, companies sought to architect complex vertical organizations that provided them with access to unique competencies, physical resources, and marketplace value. Today, the myth of the self-sufficient corporation has been largely exploded. In reality, companies have always been interconnected and have survived more because of the relationships they have established with their supply chain partners than any particular internal strength. Once considered a strategic prohibition, creating chains of supporting channel network partners has become one of a successful company's most powerful competitive objectives.

Today's Business Environment

What has caused this concern with the development of channel alliances? What forces have obsoleted long-practiced methods of en-suring corporate governance, structuring businesses, and developing strategies? What will be the long-term impact on the fabric of business ecosystems of an increasing dependence on channel partnerships, increased outsourcing, and the establishment of virtual organizations? What computerized and business management tools should be utilized that will enhance supply channel integration and provide for new sources of market-winning product and service value? How will executives and workforces adapt long-standing models of business management and workplace structures that permit them to remain competitive and on the cutting-edge while retaining organizational continuity and purpose?

Answering these and other questions requires that strategic planners understand the following six dynamics that are reshaping the nature of both corporate governance and work life in the twenty-first century [1].

The Power of the Customer. Without a doubt, the expanding power of the customer to influence the dynamics of the marketplace has altered forever previous customer service paradigms. In the past, it was the producer and distributor who determined product and service offerings, pricing, methods of transaction, fulfillment, and information transfer. In contrast, today's customers are exerting an ever-expanding influence over the terms of fulfillment management, demanding to be treated as unique individuals, and expecting their supply partners to provide configurable, solutions-oriented bundles of products, services, and information that meet a specific want or need. In addition, with their expectations set by "world class" companies across global marketplaces, customers are demanding that their supply channels provide the highest quality for the lowest price, computerized ordering tools that empower them to design product and service content, speedy fulfillment, robust information content, ease of search, ordering, and self-service follow-up, and increased digitization of all processes.

These new marketplace values have dramatically altered the balance of power between customer and producer/distributor. Past business models assumed that each company was an island and that collaboration with other organizations, even direct customers and suppliers, was self-defeating. At the dawn of the twenty-first century, it is apparent that market-leading enterprises will increasingly depend on the creation of closely integrated supply chains to remain competitive. Such collaborative channel networks would possess the flexibility to merge supporting productive resources and core competencies to enable the joint development of new products, the acceleration of the time-to-market life cycle, the implementation of unifying information technologies like the Internet, and the structuring of radically new forms of partner-based vertical integration. As the pressures of the marketplace intensify, companies will have to become more capable of responding to requirements for increased customer product and service customization, more willing to engage in supplier, customer, even competitor value-creating relationships, and more agile and scalable in the design of internal and supply chain partner production and distribution processes and information flows. Today's most successful and revolutionary companies, such as Wal-Mart, Amazon.com, Intel, W.W. Granger, and others, know that continued market dominance will go to those who know how to harness the core competences and resources of channel partners to provide unsurpassed customer value.

Globalization. The growth of business and industry throughout the globe at the start of the twenty-first century has already made a profound and dynamic impact on the course of the industrial market system. The end of the Cold War, the growth of new markets in eastern Europe and Asia, Internet technology, the speed of transportation, and the integration of the world's economic activities have propelled companies large and small at a dizzying pace into the global marketplace. This explosion in internationalism is the result of four trends. The first can be found in the maturing of the economies of the world's industrialized nations. This reality has forced companies to look to foreign markets as a source of competitive advantage, as well as of basic materials, cost-effective components, and low-cost labor. This tightening of markets has generated the second global trend: increased competition. The emergence of China and Japan and the formation of trading blocks in North America, Europe, and Asia have altered the balance of trade established at the conclusion of the Second World War. Third, the connectivity power of the Internet, the growth in incomes worldwide, the development of distribution channel infrastructures, the formation of global strategic alliances and joint ventures, and the speed of communications have also increased global demand for products and services. Finally, the goal of competitive global distribution requires the integration of entire supply channels into single marketing systems focused on attaining the best cost and customer service possible.

Some economists have argued that business has become so "internationalized" that it is meaningless to speak of companies as if they belonged to a single country. The enabling power of the Internet has made it possible for businesses large and small to market and sell their products and services directly to any customer, at any time on the earth. Supplier search, comparison shopping, and ordering can be executed on a real-time basis without clumsy paper catalogues or direct contact with sales people. This expansion in global trade can be easily demonstrated by such facts as the following [2]:

- Almost 25 percent of the output of U.S. companies is produced globally.
- Almost 25 percent of U.S. imports occur between U.S. parent companies and global affiliates.
- 61 percent of manufacturers have moved production to lower cost geographical regions.
- Of these companies, most have spread supply chain and other operations worldwide, in some cases leaving them with more assets in foreign lands than in their own countries.
- Global sales account for almost 50 percent of the sales for the 100 largest U.S. companies.

In addition, globalization is also being impacted by governmental issues. The influence of domestic and foreign governments can be seen in two critical areas. The first relates to free trade and the formation of continental trading blocks. Economic embargoes, tariff barriers, and monetary policies are seen as critical elements of strategy and tactics in the new era of international global trade. A second area that governments are impacting global trade is internally through transportation, commerce restrictions, and other types of regulation.

Finally, environmental issues can be expected to play a much larger role both internally and externally. During the last decade, American presidents and their administrations have focused on a strong commitment to the environment in regard to clean air and water, the safe transport of toxic and hazardous materials, the repair of basic transportation infrastructures such as roads and waterways, and urban congestion and gridlock. Environmental issues can be expected to play a greater role in the trading negotiations between nations. One of the newest environmental issues is the concept of *reverse logistics*. This involves the reclamation of packaging materials and other wastes, and backhaul to a central collection point for recycling. Reverse logistics, however, is not just the collection of used, damaged or outdated products and packaging from end users, nor simply reducing wastes. The objective of reverse logistics is the effective coordination of both the forward and reverse processes necessary to fully utilize products and materials throughout their life cycles.

Supply Chain Structure. The requirement that today's businesses be agile as well as efficient in order to be responsive to customer demands for shorter cy-

Conservation Music

Over the past several decades, Yamaha Music Manufacturing, Inc. have found their environmental efforts are creating beautiful music when it comes to their financial statement. Yamaha Corp., which includes Yamaha Music Manufacturing (YMM), has made it a mission to be a good environmental citizen since 1974 when the company established the Environmental Management Division.

Since earning ISO14001 certification (the international environmental standard) in December 2000, Yamaha has been realizing the benefits accompanying a successful recycling and reusing program. YMM has reduced hazardous waste and air emissions by 26%, non-hazardous waste by 21%, and scrap by 44%. Additionally, it reduced energy consumption by 15% in 2001 and another 7% in 2002.

In total, it has recycled 3.8 million pounds of wood products, 360,000 pounds of metals, and 485,000 pounds of cardboard. The cost savings for YMM has reached $109,000, or 1% of its total annual costs.

Some of the reverse logistics initiatives were easy to come by. For example, instead of dumping tons of sawdust from piano manufacturing into landfill, YMM found channel partners willing to take the waste and use it to make other kinds of material such as particleboard.

Source: Purdum, Traci, "Conservation Music," *Industry Week*, May, 2003, pp. 57-58.

cle times regarding services, product mixes, and volume and variety changes has spawned the engineering of virtual organizations and interoperable processes performed by channel partners. As vertical integration declines as a strategy, businesses are increasingly migrating to outsourcing, contract manufacturing, service fulfillment, and third party logistics to counter ever shortening product life cycles, increasing costs, and tight profit margins. By divesting themselves of labor and capital intensive assets not central to their businesses, companies feel that they can much better focus on core strengths while retaining or even increasing market presence. Today's most successful companies, such as Wal-Mart, Intel, and others, depend on collaborative strategies with their channel partners to generate networked organizational structures capable of merging unique capabilities for the development of new products, productive processes, and service delivery.

There are a number of key advantages to outsourcing. To begin with, companies can reduce costly assets, like personnel, warehousing, transportation, non-core manufacturing, and other functions, thereby enhancing return on current assets and capital expenditure. Second, by eliminating non-core functions, employee productivity will increase. Third, outsourcing provides companies with the flexibility to access new markets and build new products without shouldering completely the associated costs. Fourth, by leveraging third party companies to handle non-core functions, customer service can actually be improved without changing the business. Finally, as requirements for computerized toolsets focused on increasing collaboration and data transfer grows, companies can outsource functions to realize EDI or Internet capabilities without the need to acquire or develop them in-house.

Logistics as a Competitive Weapon. In the past, logistics was seen primarily as an operational activity, consisting of a series of independent warehouse, transportation, and inventory management functions focused on delivery and cost performance. For the past two decades this narrow perception of the role of logistics has been gradually replaced by a growing understanding that logistics can provide today's dynamic, global organization with the capabilities to span geographical barriers, deliver product in as quick and cost effectively a manner as possible, and weld together channels of trading partners. Corporate strategists have actually defined logistics as a key competitive weapon whose mission is to plan and coordinate all activities necessary not only to achieve delivered service and quality at the lowest cost but also to enable today's enterprise to realize new avenues of competitive advantage. In fact, the effective positioning of the logistics function has the potential to create new value for customers, drive down operational costs, enable the marketing and sales effort, and facilitate operations flexibility. Logistics and supply chain management are concomitant strategies: the former provides the operational structure for the realization of the strategic objectives set by the latter.

Cost and Process Improvement. Over the past decade, companies have begun to extend the theories of cost reduction and business process improvement encapsulated in such management philosophies and techniques as *Enterprise Resource Planning* (ERP), *Total Quality Management* (TQM), and *Business Process Reengineering* (BRP) outside their organizations into the supply chain in search of additional sources of cost reduction and business process improvement. The objective is to relentlessly eradicate all forms of waste where supply channel entities touch, such as logistics, channel inventory management, procurement, customer management, product development, and financial functions. The goal is to architect performance metrics and organizational models that optimize channel productive capabilities and activate highly agile, lean supply networks capable of providing superlative customer value.

Information Technology. Finally, the development of radically new information and communication technologies driven by the Internet have enabled companies to deploy revolutionary methods of building levels of competitive advantage virtually impossible just a decade ago. Before the Internet, businesses used their channel partners to realize tactical advantages, such as shortening cycle times by integrating logistics functions or using EDI to pass documents between channel members. With the advent of e-commerce, entirely new business models could now be architected that leveraged supply chains to create dazzlingly new regions of strategic advantage and marketplace value. In place of logistics channels, the Internet has permitted companies to develop "value networks" consisting of the following three elements:

- High performance networks of supply chain partnerships and information flows capable of capturing customer requirements for customized product and service solutions and transmitting them in "real-time," digitally to the trading partners best able to respond.
- Highly agile and scalable supply chains capable of being rapidly assembled to provide targeted resources to respond to new product development and roll-out, flexible manufacturing, distribution, and information processes, and fast flow fulfillment before the competition.
- Utilization of Internet tools providing interactive pathways that enable the allocation of customer fulfillment tasks to specialist channel partners while presenting to the customer the appearance of dealing with a single, seamless enterprise dedicated to total customer service.

The ability of today's enterprise to respond effectively to these challenges will determine competitive survival in the twenty-first century. As the needs and expectations of customers and the information technologies available continuously change in the decade of the 2000s, the demand for low-cost, efficient distribution services will significantly expand. The explosion in global trade, product proliferation and customization, pressures to reduce inventories, and a growing spectrum of value-added services will dramatically increase the need for supply channel functions to develop complex, yet affordable solutions to meet tomorrow's customer services expectations. In this light, the strategic advantages afforded by flexible distribution functions necessary to meet the requirements of the virtual supply chain will increasingly be recognized as the competitive edge of marketplace leadership.

EVOLUTION OF SUPPLY CHAIN MANAGEMENT [3]

While the concept of *supply chain management* (SCM) is little more than a decade old, it has its roots in the ages old struggle of producers and distributors to overcome the barriers of space and time to deliver products and services as close as possible to the desires and needs of the customer. In fact, the origins of SCM can be traced back to the evolution of the logistics function. Logistics has always been about managing the synchronization of product and service availability with the time and place requirements speci-fied by the customer. Over the past half century, logistics has progressed from a purely operational function to become a fundamental strategic component of today's leading manufacturing and distribution companies. As logistics has evolved through time, the basic features of SCM can also be recognized: first in their embryonic state as an extension of integrated logistics management, and then, as a full-fledged business philosophy encompassing and directing the pro-ductive efforts of whole supply chain systems. A comprehensive understanding of SCM, therefore, requires a thorough understanding of the evolution of logistics management.

From the beginning of history, producers have been faced with the funda-mental problem of the dispersion of goods and services to the marketplace. Traditionally, it had been the role of logistics functions to satisfy this funda-mental need by providing for the efficient and speedy movement of goods and services from the point of manufacture to the point of need. Economies pos-sessed of complex and inexpensive logistics systems are marked by elaborate and enriching market systems, a wide spectrum of available products, the rapid exchange of goods, and accelerating standards of living. What is more, enterprises that have been able to effectively utilize supply channel partners to deliver products and services have been able to more profitably operate and focus their productive functions while extending their reach to capture marketplaces and generate demand beyond the compass of their physical lo-cations. When considered from this perspective, the supply chain concept can be described as not only an operational facilitator for satisfying market-place demand, but also as a strategic operator that provides more competitive advantage and more robust customer value the more the supply channel is used. In this sense the supply chain can be described as a network of inter-dependent partners who not only supply the necessary products and services to the channel system but who also stimulate demand and facilitate the syn-chronization of the competencies and resources of the entire supply network to produce capabilities enabling a level of operational excellence and market-place leadership unattainable by each business operating on its own.

STAGES OF SUPPLY CHAIN DEVELOPMENT

While as far back as the beginning of the twentieth century economists considered the activities associated with the effective management of the supply channel to be crucial to the smooth functioning of marketplace exchange, this concept, first termed *logistics*, was slow to develop. Most business executives considered their channel management functions to be of only tactical importance and, because of the narrow scope and lack of integration among channel trading partners, virtually impossible to manage as an integrated function. In fact, it was not until the late 1960s when cost pressures and the availability of computerized information tools enabled forward-looking companies to begin to dramatically revamp the nature and function of the supply chain that the strategic opportunities afforded by logistics began to emerge.

As portrayed in Figure 1.1, the SCM concept can be said to have evolved through five distinct stages. The first can be described as the era of logistics decentralization. In the second stage, logistics began the evolution from functional decentralization to organizational centralization driven by new attitudes associated with cost optimization and customer service. Stage three witnessed the dramatic expansion of logistics from a narrow concern with internal cost management to embrace new concepts calling for the linkage of internal operations with analogous functions performed by channel trading partners. As the concept of channel collaboration grew, the old logistics concept gave way in stage four to full-blown SCM. Today, with the application of Internet technology to the SCM concept, SCM can be described as entering into stage five, e-SCM.

STAGE 1: DECENTRALIZED FUNCTIONS

Historically, the first stage of SCM occurred in the period extending from the late 19th century to the mid-1960s. During this era logistics was not perceived as a source of significant competitive advantage. Viewed essentially as an intermediary function concerned with warehousing and transportation, it was felt that logistics could not make much of a contribution to profitability and, therefore, was not worthy of much capital investment, accorded little management status, and assigned less qualified staff. For the most part, companies fragmented logistics activities, often dividing them among different departments. It was not uncommon to find transportation functions reporting to sales and inventory to finance (since inventory appeared on the ledger sheet as a current asset). Not only were activities that were natural extensions of the same process, such as procurement management, inbound transportation, and inventory management, separated from one another, but narrow depart-

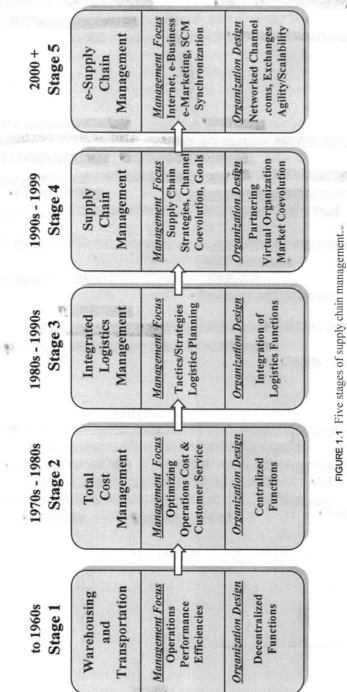

FIGURE 1.1 Five stages of supply chain management.

mental performance measurements actually pitted logistics functions against each other. What is more, the whole field of logistics was woefully ill-defined as a management science. The result was a rather disjointed, relatively uncoordinated, and costly management of logistics activities.

In an era when process and delivery cycle times were long, global competition practically non-existent, and the marketplace driven by mass production and mass distribution, logistics decentralization was a minor problem for most companies. By the early 1960's, however, changes in the economic climate were forcing corporate strategists to re-think the role of their logistics functions. To begin with, expanding product lines, demand for shorter cycle times, and growing competition had begun to expose the dramatic wastes and inefficiencies of logistics decentralization. Second, executives were finding themselves handcuffed by the lack of a unified logistics planning and execution strategy. Logistics responsibilities were scattered throughout the organization and no single manager was responsible for the development of a coherent logistics plan supportive of the business mission. Finally, logistics decentralization had made it impossible to pursue a comprehensive program to reduce costs and improve productivity. Logistics was often caught in a performance measurement paradox. For example, transportation might seek to reduce delivery costs by requiring a higher payload-to-cost ratio. Such an initiative, however, would require warehousing to stock more inventory while increasing cycle times.

Despite the gross inefficiencies of the decentralized logistics system, by even the late-1960s academics and practitioners had not yet begun to tackle the task of broadening the science of modern logistics. Much work needed to be done. Logistics suffered from a lack of standardized definitions and vocabulary. Questions regarding organizational structure needed to be answered. There was a distinct lack of professionalism, training, and skills among logistics managers, most of who had emerged out of operations roles in purchasing or warehousing. The true aggregate costs of logistics in the U.S. had never been accurately assessed, and there was little known about likely future trends. Should logistics be part of the marketing function? Should it be associated with manufacturing or perhaps with finance? Should it be a department on its own? How would the implementation of new information technologies impact logistics? What was the relationship between the budding research on logistics occurring in academic circles and practical application in the field [4]?

STAGE 2: TOTAL COST MANAGEMENT

The second stage in the evolution of SCM can be said to have emerged out of two critical management initiatives. The first can be described as the de-

cision of companies to centralize logistics functions into a single departmental organization. By merging what previously had been a series of fragmented functions into a single management system, it was reasoned that it
would be possible to decrease individual costs associated with transportation,
inventory, and physical distribution while simultaneously increasing the productivity of the logistics system as a whole. By the 1970's, companies had
begun the process of moving logistics functions formally under a single manager who was not only accountable for all functions, but also was now expected to possess the ability to make decisions in terms of the whole logistics
system and not just local departmental optimization. Achieving such a synergy would involve reengineering the entire organization to leverage productivity opportunities, charting the impact of logistics cost decisions on sales
volume and profits, and determining the required and probable return on investment.

In *Stages 1* and *2,* logistics was perceived as internally and externally
neutral in providing the enterprise with competitive advantage. The role of
logistics in such environments was defensive in nature and was concerned
purely with the effective management of inventories and delivery and cost-
containment. Management objectives revolved around detailed measurements of and control over performance in order to ensure that logistics as a
cost center functioned optimally. When making logistics decisions, the goal
of planners was to enable strategies that would keep logistics flexible and reactive. The objective of logistics functions was to have the product and value-added services available so that customer-facing functions could respond
to any type of customer demand. In business environments where companies
could dominate a particular market niche or where the competition was weak,
such as characterized the 1960s and 1970s, companies could ignore
considering logistics as critical to competitive advantage.

By the end of the period, however, logistics managers had become aware
that to assist in sustaining competitive advantage they needed not only to optimize the flow of goods occurring within the boundaries of the company but
also the flow through the entire supply chain right up to the customer's receiving dock. This also meant thinking about the flow of materials backward
to the source of supply. Such thinking cut across traditional company departmental boundaries and supply chain systems. Logistics was on the merge of
its next evolutionary step.

STAGE 3: INTEGRATED FUNCTIONS

During the 1980s, corporate strategists became increasingly aware that focusing solely on total cost management, although critical in aligning logistics

costs with customer service levels, represented a passive approach to channel management. In place of a preoccupation with minimizing logistics costs in isolation from other corporate performance targets, managers began to understand that integrating logistics with other business departments could result not just in minimizing enterprise costs but also actively enhancing customer value. Operational factors, such as speed of delivery, value-added services, and product availability realized when enterprise functions worked closely together, could in themselves provide a powerful facilitator significantly assisting the entire organization in sustaining competitive advantage. Past organizational strategies neither sought to activate the potential of their logistics functions nor to leverage the close links existing between logistics and other enterprise business areas. As firms began to search for new avenues of gaining competitive advantage, it became apparent that an integrated logistics system could be used as a powerful marketing tool, capable of generating additional value beyond product and price leadership.

In addition to the changes in executives' perception of the strategic role of logistics, powerful organizational and management processes were further fueling the growth of the integrated logistics model. If the 1980's could be compressed into two quintessential catchwords, they would be *competition* and *quality management*. Competition came in the form of global companies, often deploying radically new management philosophies and organizational structures that were realizing unheard of levels of productivity, quality, and profitability. The second driver of change came from the deployment of new management concepts, driven by JIT and *total quality management* (TQM) philosophies, that were providing competitors with tools to compress time out of development cycles, engineer more flexible and "lean" processes, tap into the creative powers of the workforce, and generate entirely new forms of competitive advantage.

Businesses responded to these challenges by focusing, first of all, on revamping their organizations by pursuing both cost/operational and service/value advantages through continuous process improvement and closer integration with channel partners. Second, companies began to understand that logistics and other channel management functions could be leveraged as a dynamic force capable of winning customers beyond the execution of logistics functions. Instead of being considered an isolated department, logistics capabilities and strategies could be integrated with the strategic plans of other enterprise departments. In this sense logistics could serve as an active catalyst derived from and in support of the firm's overall competitive strategy. Rather than simply a function to handle day-to-day fulfillment activities logistics could be perceived as having an long-term, strategic impact.

Stage 3 distributors recognized the strategic value of their logistics functions and sought to draft plant charters and mission statements to guide logistics development and ensure alignment with other enterprise functions. The concept of integrated logistics also afforded the logistics function an equal position alongside marketing, sales, and operations in the formulation of strategic plans, determining the allocation of enterprise resources, and defining the scope of customer service objectives. By closely aligning logistics capabilities and marketing, sales, and operations objectives, the enterprise could present customers with a unified approach, guaranteeing product, price, and delivery competitiveness.

STAGE 4: SUPPLY CHAIN MANAGEMENT

By the 1990's, companies began to understand that the integrated logistics concept was insufficient to tackle the new realities of the marketplace. The acceleration of globalization, the explosion in new information technology enablers, business process reengineering, increased outsourcing, and the growing power of the customer were forcing companies to look beyond the boundaries of their own core competencies to the capabilities and resources of their supply channel partners to remain competitive. The necessity of responding to these new challenges compelled companies to implement what can only be called a dramatic paradigm shift from *Stage 3* logistics to *supply chain management* (SCM).

In the past companies had sought to integrate operational channel functions, such as transportation and warehousing, with supply network partners in an effort to increase pipeline velocities and cut costs. By the 1990's it had become apparent that this early attempt at channel integration needed to be dramatically expanded and elevated to a strategic level. In place of the informal, short-term, tactical use of supply chain partners, corporate planners were now advocating strategies that sought the development of close collaborative relationships between channel constituents with the objective of optimizing and synchronizing the productive competencies of each trading partner. Logistics channels were to be replaced by "value networks."

SCM can be broken down into four main components.

- *Strategy.* While *Stage 3* logistics functions sought to interface activeties with channel partners, the focus was still primarily inward-looking. Logistics planners were mainly concerned with the execution of daily distribution processes, internal performance measurements, and parochial business strategies. In contrast, the SCM paradigm requires logistics managers to be transformed from internal keepers of cost and channel operations to strategists responsible for the development of "value chains." Building collaborative relationships, optimizing and synchronizing the total resources of the chain to achieve high-value customer service, and activating the potential for productivity to be found in the deployment of the collective competencies of trading partners dominates the thinking and planning of companies operating according to SCM principles.

- *Sourcing and Procurement.* *Stage 3* logistics sought to integrate internal demand, production, and purchasing functions in order to facilitate sourcing and planning, cut inbound logistics and warehousing costs, and ensure timely product delivery. SCM, in contrast, not only seeks to reduce sourcing, procurement, and delivery cycle times and costs, it also strives to develop close relationships with suppliers. Instead of focusing on competitive pricing and adversarial negotiations, SCM has opened exciting new vistas for the interactive, real-time sharing of product designs and costing, synchronization of channel product roll-out, application of procurement savings and efficiencies down the length of the supply chain, and the engineering of truly collaborative partnerships where core competencies can be merged to generate a common competitive vision.

- *Production.* Traditional companies focus on making standardized, "one -size-fits-all" products pushed sequentially from one network node to another. Such organizations resist sharing product design and process technologies with their channel partners. They are slow to respond to changing customer needs, slow to change configurations to accommodate new products and alternating product mixes, and are concerned only with internal performance metrics. Manufacturing functions driven by SCM, on the other hand, treat collaborative design planning and scheduling with their supply chains as a fundamental issue. When possible, they seek to closely integrate their ERP systems with those of their trading partners to eliminate time and cost. SCM production facilities are "customer-centric" and capable of responding to shrinking product life cycles and increasingly configurable products. Finally, SCM-driven firms also understand that speedy product design and release to market occurs when they leverage the competencies and resources of channel partners to generate "virtual" manufacturing environments capable of being as agile and scaleable as necessary to take advantage of every marketplace opportunity.

- *Delivery.* Customer management in *Stage 3* companies is squarely focused on making internal sales functions more efficient. Heavy priority is placed on available-to-promise functionality, finished goods management, and determining the proper timing of product differentiation in the channel. Specific information on market segments and customers is rarely communicated to channel partners, databases are considered proprietary, and pricing data is never shared. In contrast, SCM-driven customer functions are concerned with reducing logistics costs and channel redundancies and increasing customer service by converging channel partner warehouse space, transportation equipment, and delivery capabilities. SCM regards computerized avenues to engage with the customer, no matter where in the supply chain, as critical. SCM customer management looks toward automation tools to facilitate field sales, capability to promise tools, *customer relationship management* (CRM) software, mass customization, and availability of general supply chain repositories of joint trading partner market and customer data.

SCM-driven organizations possess the capability to move beyond a narrow focus on internal logistics optimization to a strategy that identifies and leverages the best core competencies and collaborative relationships among their supply chain partners to architect "value networks" capable of realizing continuous breakthroughs in product design, manufacturing, delivery, customer service, cost management, and value-added services before the competition. This strategic, channel-building attribute of SCM revolutionizes everyone in the supply chain and provides all network trading partners with the capability to view themselves and their channel partners as extended, "virtual organizations" possessed of radically new methods of responding in unique ways to provide total customer value.

STAGE 5: e-SUPPLY CHAIN MANAGEMENT

While SCM provided companies with the ability to escape from the four-wall boundaries of their own businesses and view the supply chains in which they participated in as a fertile new source for competitive advantage, by the turn of the twenty-first century it had become apparent that vertically integrated SCM was too brittle a concept to respond effectively to three major channel dynamics: accelerated global outsourcing, ever more ruthless competition, and demand and supply mismatches in the channel network. Several critical problems had arisen to the surface [5].

- *Information visibility, velocity, and timeliness.* It simply was taking too long to register and communicate important changes occurring in customer demand and supply to the channel network. Information, in fact, cascaded serially through the supply channel, with the result that trading partners located far from the channel event did not receive the information until it finally was passed to them by their immediate trading partners. In the meantime, companies continued to plan and build to what had become an increasingly obsolete plan. The problem was the lack of information systems that permitted all levels of the channel to be in touch with actual customer demand, and the absence of decision-support and analytical tools providing for rapid analysis and concurrent response among all affected trading partners.

- *Information variability and accuracy.* The traditional practice of creating long-range forecasts, generating large production lots, and pushing inventory downstream was often compromised by abrupt, unplanned changes in channel demand and supply patterns. Without timely and accurate information, the planning practices of even closely interlocked trading partners often became atomized. As the plan slowly spun out of control, planners begin increasingly to rely on second-guessing, intuition, and rule-of-thumb solutions, all of which simply further degraded the credibility of channel plans.

- *Analytics and control.* Regardless of the commitment to channel integration, traditional SCM depends on historical data to calculate trends, determine critical metrics, and guide decision-making for individual companies, and by extension, the entire supply chain. In such an environment, control and exception management tends to be centralized, proprietary, and prone to stand-alone point solutions.

- *Expense.* The lack of timely information about real demand and supply forced supply network nodes to shelter themselves from possible channel variances by stocking safety inventories. The impact of this problem becomes apparent when it is considered that excess inventory costs tend to compound as the number of channel partners expands.

- *Flexibility and scalability.* The SCM model is limited by what is termed the "chained-pairs trading model" [Figure 1.2]. The foundation of this model resides on the fact that channel members normally focus their efforts on one channel partner at a time. These one-to-one relationships consist of linear handoffs of goods and information from a company to its immediate channel partner. The problem with the model is its lack of responsiveness to the value chain needs of clusters or multiple tiers of channel business relationships. Information in the chained-pairs model is limited by system interoperability and its architecture inhibits the synchronization of data from multiple sources.

- *Company-centricity.* Despite the desire to participate in supply chain collaboration, *Stage 4* SCM companies view their strategic and operational plans primarily from the inside-out. The result is that marketplace and channel decisions are made primarily to benefit the company, often at the expense of the supply chain. This problem of supply chain suboptimization results in suppliers and customers being left out of the process. When compounded with the lack of a formal and closed-loop feedback process to capture and communicate execution exceptions, the

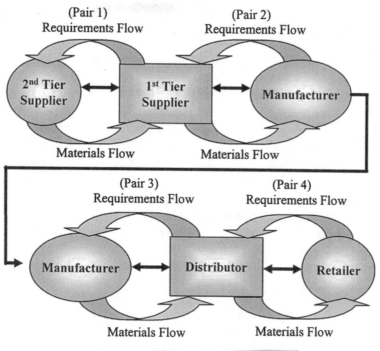

FIGURE 1.2 Chained-pairs trading model.

promise of the SCM concept begins to breakdown into disparate, often irreconcilable components.

Solving the problems residing at the core of SCM revolves around developing supply chain networks capable of possessing the highest visibility, the greatest information velocity, and the best analytical tools to manage channel variability. Obviously, the common thread permeating each of the above deficiencies in traditional SCM is the inability of whole supply chains to receive simultaneously and in real-time *information* regarding the interplay of actual demand and supply as it occurs through time in the channel network. Previous attempts at inter-channel data communication, such as EDI, were plagued by expensive equipment, transmission standards, and delays caused by the batch transfer of data up and down the supply chain.

By the opening of the twenty-first century, the application of the Internet to the SCM concept provided the necessary mechanism for SCM to escape from previous technology and operations limitations and move to the next level in the history of channel management: *e-SCM*. In place of rigid supply chains, the Internet enabled the establishment of more "adaptive" supply chains that were capable of truly leveraging the integrative and collaborative network to manage channel demand/supply variability and provide the necessary information visibility and velocity for each network node to execute decisions concurrently with a resulting minimal loss of operational and financial efficiency [6]. The application of the Internet to each of the above problem dynamics of classical SCM have been summarized in Table 1.1.

TABLE 1.1. Elements of e-SCM

Channel Issue	SCM	e-SCM
Information visibility, velocity, and timeliness	Slow, sequential, poor visibility across the supply chain	Dynamic, parallel, concurrent, responsive to change, Web-based central nervous system
Information variability, and accuracy	Batch driven, inaccurate through time, inconsistent, rule-of-thumb response	Real-time, synchronized, networked, reliable and predictable data
Analytics and control	Historical, proprietary, centralized, local performance metrics	Real-time, data sharing, concurrent/distributed decision making
Expense	Buffer inventories and capacities	Continuous cost reduction and process improvement
Flexibility and Scalability	"Chained-pairs" model, proprietary standards, stand-alone point solutions	Multiple tiers model, open systems, functional interoperability
Company-centricity	Strategies benefit company, channel sub-optimization, irreconcilable plans	Strategies benefit supply chain, channel optimization, supporting plans

Implementing e-SCM requires a radical evolutionary step in channel process and management design. To make the transition to e-SCM companies must pass through three stages. Enterprises begin first with the integration of supply chain functions within the enterprise. As described above in *Stage 3* logistics, the goal is to improve internal operational visibility and productivity. An example would be integrating sales and logistics through the implementation of a warehouse and transportation system. By linking the new system to the ERP backbone, increased visibility to delivery, cost, and other execution activities could be provided to the entire customer and supplier order process. The next step would be to integrate and synchronize inbound and outbound order management activities with channel partners. In this step companies are willing to share important information with immediate trading partners, but the information is normally restricted to tactical functions and are focused on short-term cost savings and operational efficiencies. Finally, the highest level would be achieved by utilizing Internet connectivity to synchronize the channel functions of the entire supply network into a single, scaleable "virtual" enterprise capable of optimizing core competencies and resources from anywhere at any time in the supply chain to enhance business processes and strategic development and optimize each component of the value network.

At the beginning of the twenty-first century most companies and their supply chains have not moved much beyond *Stage 3* or even *Stage 2* logistics. While increasing attention is being paid to collaborating with customers, many business strategists still see their supply chains as a minefield where predatory habits and short-term cost savings dominate. While companies would like to leverage common strategies, product and demand information, and deploy event-management and alert notification applications that would illuminate actual channel requirements and enable high velocity "value net" logistics, too many are simply at the beginning stages of the SCM evolutionary process.

As this section concludes, it is clear that channel management is no longer the loose combination of business functions characteristic of the early stages of logistics. New Internet-enabling technologies and management models have not only obscured company internal functional boundaries, they have also blurred the boundaries that separate supply chain partners, transforming once isolated channel functions into unified, "virtual" supply chain systems. Today's top companies are using Internet connectivity to reassemble and energize supply chain management processes that span trading partners to activate core competencies and accelerate cross-enterprise processes. They are also using Web technologies to enable new methods of providing customer value by opening new sales channels as they migrate from pure "bricks-and-mortar" to "clicks-and-mortar" business architectures. The next section will continue this discussion by offering a detailed definition of e-SCM that will serve as the cornerstone for the rest of the book.

DEFINING e-SCM [7]

SCM can be approached from several perspectives. Like most management philosophies, definitions of SCM must take into account a wide spectrum of applications incorporating both strategic and tactical objectives. As illustrated in Figure 1.3, SCM can be divided into four regions. The first, *internal optimization*, is the simplest, and consists of the integration of the *internal* channel functions of the enterprise. The goal of this region is *logistics optimization*. If technology is applied at all, it consists of local *intranets* that link only logistics functions. The second region, *external integration*, focuses on integrating day-to-day internal operations activities with the analogous inbound and outbound functions performed by channel trading partners. The goal is to streamline process flows, reduce network costs, and optimize productivity and delivery resources centered on conventional channel relationships. If technology is applied, EDI or intranet capabilities are used to link operations and transaction information transfer.

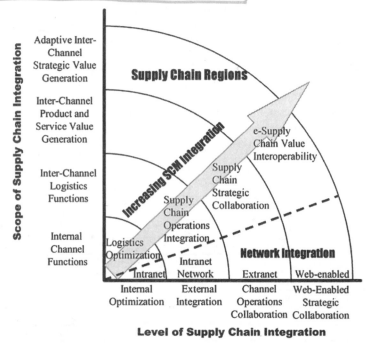

FIGURE 1.3 Phases of SCM

In the third region, *supply chain strategic collaboration,* the impact of SCM is dramatically enhanced as it moves from integrating inter-channel operations functions to the generation of *strategically integrated* supply chains. The mission of SCM is the establishment of collaborative partnerships characterized by the architecting of cross-channel correlative processes that create unique sources of value by unifying the resources, capabilities, and competencies of the entire network ecosystem to enhance the competitive power of the supply channel as a whole and not just an individual company. The technologies necessary to achieve this objective require channel partners to use *extranet* enablers that provide the capability to work in a real-time, interoperable information environment.

Finally, in the fourth region, *e-supply chain value interoperability*, the enabling power of the Internet is merged with strategic SCM. The application of the Internet is such a radical enhancement to the SCM concept that it deserves to be relabeled *e-SCM*. This new view of SCM is so radical because it enables companies to use the Internet to develop new methods of integrating with their customers, suppliers, and support partners. As is illustrated in Figure 1.4, e-SCM extends channel management systems beyond traditional boundaries to integrate in real-time the customer/product information and productive competencies to be found in customers' customers and suppliers' suppliers channel systems. What had been missing in *Stage 4* SCM was an effective mechanism to enable the intense networking of commonly shared strategic visions and mutually supportive competencies among channel partners. The architecture of technologies such as ERP and EDI imposed severe barriers to the range of information communication and erected unscaleable barriers limiting participation. The merger of the Internet and SCM, on the other hand, offers whole supply chains the opportunity to create value for their customers through the design of agile, flexible systems built around dynamic, high performance networks of Web-enabled customer and supplier partnerships and critical information flows.

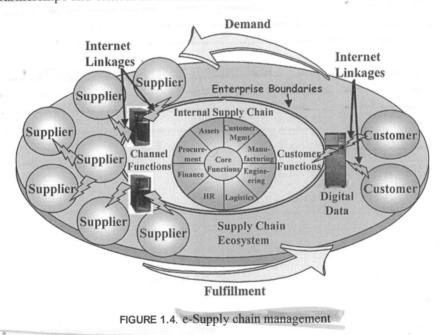

FIGURE 1.4. e-Supply chain management

e-SCM Definition

Since e-SCM is perhaps the central theme to be found in this text, a concise definition is necessary to guide the student through the various topics to come. The definition is as follows: [8]

> e-SCM is a supply chain operational and strategic management philosophy that utilizes Internet-enabling technologies to effect the continuous regeneration of networks of supply channel partners empowered to execute superlative, unique customer-winning value at the lowest cost through the collaborative, real-time synchronization of product/service transfer, demand priorities, vital marketplace information, and logistics delivery capabilities.

The critical components of this definition are revealing. To begin with, e-SCM is a *supply chain operational and strategic management philosophy* driven by the enabling power of the Internet. This defines the *scope* of e-SCM. The concept, *continuous regeneration of networks of supply channel partners,* implies that companies succeed in the twenty-first century by generating constantly evolving chains of channel partners capable of respond to the dynamic nature of today's ceaseless demand for new forms of customer/supplier collaboration and scaleable product and information delivery flows. This element defines how supply channels will organize to compete. *Unique customer-winning value* refers to the ability of companies to assemble agile, scalable production/distribution systems capable of continuously reinvent unique product and service configurations and value-creating relationships. This element defines the mission of the channel. And finally, *collaborative, real-time synchronization* refers to the application of technology process enablers that network internal enterprise systems, decision support tools, and data warehouses to merge, optimize, and effectively direct supply channel competencies. This element describes the mechanics of how Internet-enabled supply chains will compete.

COMPONENTS OF e-SCM

The evolution of adaptive, Internet-enabled supply chains has required a transvaluation of the former principles of supply channel management. Past definitions of SCM were more or less preoccupied with attempts to extend the concepts of channel integration to the performance of operations activities associated with optimizing manufacturing and logistics processes and accelerating the flow of inventory and information through the network system. With the emergence of Internet technologies, channel management was freed from the constraints of the past. The e-SCM model provides for the interlocking of information connectivity between channel systems. Today's Web applications provide whole supply chains with the capability to instantaneously share data bases, forecasts, inventory and capacity plans, product information, financial data, and just about anything else companies may need for effective decision making. And the integration can be global, 24/7/365, with 100 percent accuracy. Enabling the full power of e-SCM requires an understanding of the following principles [Figure 1.5].

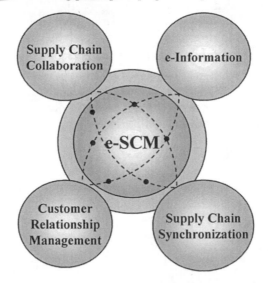

FIGURE 1.5 Components of e-SCM.

e-Information. If it can be said that the prime driver of SCM is information, then the faster information can be gathered, analyzed, and defused through the channel network, the more competitive will be the channel's trading partners. The application of Internet technology tools has created a new form of information–*e-information*–that has the power to dramatically enhance the capabilities for SCM information collaboration. The spread of technology tools for the networking of disparate channel systems and the nascent development of global standards for Internet operations have enabled forward-looking companies to be able to effectively accumulate, track, monitor, and harness e-information from anywhere in the supply chain in real-time and use it for effective decision-making.

Internet technology provides supply chains with an almost unlimited opportunity to apply e-information to not only link the complex processes of channel-wide demand management, logistics, manufacturing, and storage, it also provides the necessary insight and understanding so that trading partners can harmonize the main interacting components of supply chain design and execution. On the marketing side, e-information enables companies to integrate customers directly into their fulfillment systems thereby assisting in executing a perfect order every time, including the performance of all value-added services and billing. On the shop floor, e-information improves planners' backward visibility into supplier resources to smooth capacity spikes and improve throughput. In the supply channel, e-information provides the bridge

Fed Ex, Cisco and e-Information

Today's best companies are able to capitalize on the Internet to provide exciting new ways of servicing the customer. Federal Express, for example, uses e-information to manage in real-time the daily routing and tracking of 2.5 million packages. Fed Ex utilizes such applications as remote bar-code scanning that updates a centralized database, transmission bandwidth enabling concurrent rather than serial processing of transaction events driven by nearly 400,000 daily service calls, the evolution of new e-businesses as in the case of FedEx's alliance with Proflowers .com (a .com company operating a portal for ordering fresh flowers), and a total company dedication to continuously accelerating the speed of e-information and logistics flows.

Cisco Systems applies e-information as the critical driver in their efforts to continuously reengineer processes to achieve a truly global networked organization. Each critical node in Cisco's supply chain, from Web-enabled order entry (fifty percent of orders received) and customer service (inquiry, pricing, configuration, validation, product catalog) to software distribution download, is executed through Internet-based processes. In addition, Web-enabled *collaborative planning, forecasting, and replenishment* (CPFR) applications permit Cisco to communicate demand changes with suppliers and distributors. Finally, Cisco's e-procurement programs provide online access to purchasing/ marketplaces exchanges. Cisco's e-strategy has enabled the company to reduce costs by $560 million per year during the late 1990's, while spearheading an annual growth rate of 400 percent for the past five years.

between company-level optimization planning and the global demand pull of the entire business network. e-Information enables the generation of what one writer has described as "a portfolio of triggerable decisions with options to proceed or abandon by milestone [9]." As detailed below, these knowledge-driving components can be broken down into five areas [10].

- *Customer e-information.* Understanding and responding effectively to the needs of the customer pose as the first challenge to e-SCM. Marketplace intelligence is centered on gathering information relating to three channel areas providing insight into the customer. The first is the use of e-information to gather demand management intelligence regarding the validity of forecasts, the impact of out-of-bounds events, and actual product/service mix usage occurring at any point in the channel. Such intelligence can be accumulated by leveraging Internet-linked point-of-sale, collaborative forecast sharing, or event-management SCM software. The second area seeks to unearth data regarding the impact of pricing and promotions decisions governing channel fulfillment. e-Information tools in this area need to provide intelligence as to the velocity of sales and the timely reporting of revenues, costs, and profits. Finally, in the last area, Internet intelligence needs to detail the status of channel inventories, optimize the trade-off between capacity utilization and customer service, and enable replenishment visibility and rapid redeployment of channel inventories.

- *Logistics e-information.* The role of channel logistics functions is to utilize demand intelligence to determine the optimal application of transportation and warehouse resources that maximizes customer fulfillment value. Accomplishing this objective requires channel members to gain insight into the capacities of internal and external logistics functions in order to determine the optimal allocation of resources along a specific channel flow that best meets a specific demand flow. Such a process depends on real-time intelligence capable of providing logistics planners with the ability to configure unique value networks where the best channel partner is assigned the responsibility for customer fulfillment as the order moves through the distribution pipeline. To be successful, planners will require e-information applications that enable cross-channel system interoperability to provide insight into the status and velocity of production capacities, storage capabilities, inventory availability and replenishment processes, and transportation resources at each node in the supply network.

- *Channel network resource alignment e-information.* Critical to the cost-efficient management of the supply chain is timely intelligence as to the positioning and planned allocation of products and services as they exist in the channel network at any given point in time. Ensuring the optimal location of demand-satisfying resources requires an intimate knowledge of the total cost to serve a single customer using a specific channel configuration as well as re-aligning those resources to match changes in demand behavior. Channel partners would need to leverage e-information tools that enable the utilization of models such as activity-based costing, the balanced scorecard, or the *supply chain operations reference model* (SCOR) to identify in a graphical manner pools of costs residing at the points were the processes of trading partners intersect. The models deployed must be capable of determining such critical channel fulfillment values as reliability, responsiveness, flexibility, cost, and efficiency of asset utilization while communicating the metrics in real-time to other channel constituents.

- *Product and process e-information.* Because of the sheer size, scope, and complexity of manufacturing methods and databases, manufacturing has always been considered a prime area for computerization. MRP, MRP II, MES, ERP, and a host of other acronyms bear witness to the many information technologies applied over several decades to manufacturing. While all of these tools focused on optimizing the *internal* functions associated with production, increasingly companies today have become aware of the need for greater connectivity with customers and suppliers and have turned to the Internet for assistance.

  Three major areas come to mind. The first is the use of Web-based toolsets to execute design product content synchronization. Today's design teams are linked together by real-time, concurrent *peer-to-peer* (P2P) technologies that provide for the construction of interoperable knowledge repositories linking CAE/CAM systems, direct customer configuration feeds, *design collaboration software* (DCS), and product lifecycle management (PLM). The second area is associated with the slow but steady growth in *business-to-business* (B2B) supplier management which uses the Web to build trading communities that facilitate product and supplier search, order status/tracking, product catalogs, and buyer/supplier back-end integration. The final area of e-information used by manufacturers is the application of cross-channel *advanced planning and scheduling* (APS) systems that not only enable them to more effectively run production processes, but which also permit planners to be more proactive to impending changes in channel demand and supply by permitting them to more effectively synchronize and optimize channel resources and capacities.

- *e-Procurement information.* Working with suppliers today requires two types of information: intelligence about collaborative relationships and intelligence about supplier capabilities. Both are focused on a single objective: *to reduce supply chain risk.* While many companies in the past attempted to utilize EDI or merge ERP output, the results were inward-facing and did little to enhance the integration and collaborative relationships necessary to enhance the speed of transfer and depth of information needed by sales and manufacturing management. With the application of the Internet this gap in supplier intelligence is rapidly disappearing. e-Supplier management is permitting today's cutting edge companies for the first time to assemble a complete picture of their supply relationships and apply Web technologies to enhance traditional buyer functions, such as supplier product sourcing, e-RFQs, auctions, trading exchanges, logistics interfaces, and automated shopping applications, and Web-enabled services such as strategic sourcing, fulfillment, collaborative design, and finance and billing.

Customer Relationship Management. As was discussed earlier in this chapter, the central focus of today's e-supply chain is unparalleled *customer service*. e-SCM utilizes the enabling power of the Internet not only to find radically new ways of servicing the customer, but also of generating new forms of collaborative relationships that permit companies to design channel fulfillment systems that meet the individual needs of each customer. The goal is to align the core capabilities of unique configurations of channel partners to provide unique customer solutions any-where, at any time in the channel network. Bovet and Martha [11] have termed such an organization a "value net" and characterize the customer-supplier relationships that emerge as "symbiotic," in that customer choices trigger a cross-channel reaction in supply network sourcing, manufacturing, delivery, and information transfer to meet the requirement, "interactive," in that the customer owner can assign aspects of customer demand to the partner best able to perform the requirement, and "value-enhancing," in that both the customer and the entire supply channel ecosystem receive total value either through the streamlining of costs or flawless execution of customer product and service needs.

e-SCM enables companies to enhance the concept of *customer relationship management* (CRM). By implementing such Internet-enabled applications as Web sites for marketing and catalog information, entering orders, reviewing pricing, configuring orders, and participating in on-line auctions, self-service capabilities ranging from training, to order review and payment, and analytical tools providing business intelligence regarding marketing and sales information, the Internet provides the depth of information to provide the 360-degree view of the customer required by CRM. e-SCM provides supply networks with the ability to respond to three critical customer requirements [12]:

1. *Superior service.* The goal of the supply chain is to provide the customer with an unbeatable buying experience that not only meets but dramatically exceeds price, product availability, delivery and service expectations. Creating such a level of service requires two critical attributes possessed only by "world class" value chains: *speed of response* and a tireless *attention to reliability.* Speed means providing the critical values customers want at the highest velocity of response possible. Superior supply chains utilize the Internet to achieve such goals by passing demand information not serially, but simultaneously and automatically to supporting network partners through advanced shipping notices, bar coded shipments, on-line transportation tracking, and real-time fulfillment information. Reliability means executing the *perfect order* each and every time. This attribute is attained when each order is shipped complete and on time, received at the customer's site when desired, and is ready for use. In addition, reliability requires sup-

ply chains to be flexible enough to respond to last minute changes while never compromising high service levels.

2. *Convenient solutions.* In today's marketplace customers are searching for supply chains capable of providing them not just products and services but rather *solutions* to their business needs. In addition, customers should be able to define, configure, order, and review the progress of demand fulfillment in as convenient a manner as possible. Effective supply chains are able to leverage technologies that provide for the rapid deployment and synchronization of high performance networks capable of responding to each customer touch-point. Visibility to customer requirements in turn provides each channel partner with the opportunity to integrate core competencies that ensure each customer can realize their choice of product and/or service solution.

3. *Customization.* With the rise of the concept of *mass customization*, customers are no longer willing to purchase standardized goods and services, but instead require the ability to configure solutions to meet their own particular needs. Meeting this challenge can be accomplished in several ways. To begin with, supply chains may define strategies that postpone and place actual product differentiation at the points in the channel that actually touch the end-customer. Another strategy is to utilize Internet-driven order entry systems that permit customers to configure their own solutions from an extensive but controlled menu of choices. The order is then communicated directed to the ERP planning system for order manufacture. Often, the product is sent to other channel partners who complete the work of final assembly and delivery to the customer. Companies such as Dell, Sun Microsystems, IBM, and Gateway, for example, treat their reseller channels as extensions of their own manufacturing processes, expecting them to complete the final configuration based on the actual customer order. Channel synchronization is crucial: customization requires direct linkage of demand and supply at all points in the channel with the goal of minimizing cost and accelerating total channel throughput.

Supply Chain Synchronization. Utilizing e-information to respond to the requirements of the customer constitutes only two of the four components of e-SCM. The ability to simply transmit and share demand and supply information has always been present with tools like EDI. The real challenge is not only to send information in real-time but also to present it concurrently so that all points in the supply chain can receive it at the same time. The value of such synchronization is obvious: intelligence concerning actual demand and supply dynamics can be broadcast in real-time to all channel constituents so that effective planning and operations decisions can be made. The benefits are equally as obvious: minimization of work-in-process and finished good inventories up and down the channel, dampening of the channel "bullwhip effect" as products are pulled through the distribution pipeline, overall reduced costs, and the perfect matching of customer requirements with available products.

While supply chain synchronization provides channel trading partners with radically new opportunities for competitive advantage, the concept is very much at the beginning stage of development. In today's environment supply chain synchronization is limited by current interchannel information technologies and the level of their adoption. Networked computer systems are expensive to implement and have as yet to reach a critical mass. In addition, the economic conditions of the early 2000s have caused companies to heighten their focus on managing internal inventory, service, and costs. When they have sought to utilize their trading partners it has been more to pressure them into collaborative behaviors where one side wins and the other side complies just to retain the business.

To be of value, supply chain synchronization requires all members of a channel ecosystem to engage in partnerships that collectively optimize resources and reduce costs. Such a channel system will require the creation of highly integrated channel structures, cross-channel planning and control, and information architectures capable of promoting continuous channel synchronization through collaborative design. A synchronized supply chain will consist of the following key components:

- *Unified business strategy.* The development of a single, focused strategy to gain channel-wide marketplace success is a critical starting-point. In reality, most channel partners have always enjoyed a fair degree of cooperation that enabled them to structure mutually supportive resources in pursuit of common customer-winning objectives. No company, especially today, can say that it possesses all the strengths necessary to remain competitive. As such, the creation of business strategies rightfully extends beyond a company's boundaries and should be folded within an inter-channel effort. Such an effort should result in the formulation of joint strategies that foster the use of optimal methods of cost-effectively designing, building, and delivering unique, customer-winning value to the marketplace by leveraging the capabilities of the entire supply chain.

- *Common measurements for channel excellence.* Effective supply chain synchronization requires all channel members to collectively achieve superlative levels of operations excellence. Such an effort, however, means more than establishing electronic transaction transfer or sharing forecasts for joint planning and decision-making: it requires synchronizing the performance of each channel member and blending them into a total supply chain balanced scorecard. A quick view of these measurement goals is provided in Table 1.2. A measurement methodology that is growing in popularity that will assist with model development is the Supply Chain Council's *Supply Chain Operations Reference* (SCOR). The model includes a cross functional framework, standard terminology, common metrics, and best practices that can be applied to entire supply chains.

TABLE 1.2. Synchronized Performance Elements

Channel Function	Function	Measurement
Channel Management	ERP data integration EDI and Web-driven processing Collaborative customer/ supplier efforts Utilization of outsourcing	Reductions in inbound and outbound total costs Levels of channel resource alignment with demand Cycle time metrics Velocity of product/ service transfer
Product and Service Processing	Product/service development CPFR initiatives Manufacturing Procurement Channel physical distribution	Speed of new product design and roll-out Cross-channel capacity optimization Changes produced by event notification and exception management Levels of channel inventories
Channel Customer Management	CRM Service/Call centers Marketing	Channel sales and profits Channel customer service levels Order management costs Fulfillment objectives
Channel Support Assets	Logistics Warehousing Administration	Channel asset utilization ROA Outsourcing costs

- *Selection of enabling technologies.* The foundations for effective channel synchronization rest on the ability of trading partners to synchronize their internal business systems. Companies have always deployed the latest technologies to link themselves with channel members. First it was the telephone, the fax, and EDI that provided an information outlet. Today, companies are equipping themselves with powerful Internet applications that span intranets and extranets to enable participating partners access to the applications and content objectives of each supply network node. The goal is the development of interoperable process components that enable whole supply chains to encapsulate the databases and processes of both member ERP backbones and front- and back-end application such as CRM, HTML/XML document integration, data warehouses, and various forms of trading exchange.

Supply Chain Collaboration. The last, and perhaps, most critical component of e-SCM is to be found in the willingness of channel members to engage in and constantly enhance collaborative relationships with other chan-nel trading partners. What many companies have come to realize is that short-term benefits brought about by logistics optimization and technology automation are incapable of producing the radical competitive breakthroughs that can be attained when channel partners strive to build long-term, collaborative relationships. While the term "collaboration" has become today's newest buzzword and is subject to the same level of hype that accompanied JIT and TQM when they first appeared, when linked to the other three components of e-SCM it provides a powerful competitive force. As a supply web, e-SCM is composed of two things – collaboration and synchronization. Collaboration is really an ability to share. Synchronization is possessing the channel intelligence to be able to know how the right product and the right service can be accessed in the supply chain to satisfy the customer. Such statements reinforce the view that e-SCS is not just enabling trading partners to employ e-information and synchronization tools: it is demanding that companies up and down the supply chain embrace the accompanying cultural and organizational changes as well.

The application of collaboration to configure e-supply chains can have a wide meaning. As stated in another work,

> While the term describes an activity pursued jointly by two or more entities to achieve a common objective, it can mean anything from transmitting raw data by the most basic means, to the periodic sharing of information through Web-based tools to the structuring of real-time technology architectures that enable partners to leverage highly interdependent infrastructures in the pursuit of complex, tightly integrated functions ensuring planning, execution, and information synchronization [13].

One group of experts [14] divided the concept of collaboration into two spheres of ascending collaboration intensity. In the first can be found *technical* collaboration. Collaboration here ranges from no electronic connectivity to EDI and extranet, to server-to-server links, and finally to Internet applications providing real-time information and transaction synchronization. In the other sphere can be found *business* collaboration. On the low end, collaboration practices are at a bare minimum. As the level of collaboration intensifies so does the requirements for business-to-business integration and synchronization as it migrates from facilitating joint operations, to efforts focused on the coordination of network partner competencies, to joint visioning where partners cooperate and compete as if they were a single channel entity. According to Prahalad and Ramaswamy [15], each level of collaboration generates value through four critical drivers:

- The collaborative capacity of intra-company management teams grows in proportion to the level of collaboration intensity.
- As collaborative intensity grows there is an exponential growth in the need for more complex technical and business infrastructures to create and extract value.
- While unifying intra-channel business processes are critical in effecting collaborative value, they are just the beginning of the possible collaborative opportunities.
- Strategic planners must constantly search for and implement new technologies and management methods if supply network collaboration is to continue to provide useable knowledge and new competitive insights.

While no one can disagree on the efficacy of collaboration, there are many barriers inhibiting implementation. Perhaps one of the biggest impediments is overcoming existing corporate cultures. Long-tradition and internal performance silos often pose an almost insurmountable barrier to espousing an environment encouraging openness, communication, and mutual-dependence. Another barrier is *trust*. Companies fear that proprietary information will be broadcast to partners who will in turn pass it on to competitors or use it for unfair advantage. Collaborative relationships normally take years of good will, investment in resources, and proof of mutual benefit. In addition, collaboration has often been confused with process reengineering. In reality, while collaboration will increase *efficiencies*, such a short-term understanding misses the real advantages found in the leveraging of channel competencies, utilization of cross-channel best practices, and innovation. Finally, today's technology presents real barriers. The incompatibility of channel computer systems pose a serious deterrent to shared communications.

SCM AND LOGISTICS

As discussed earlier in the chapter, the science of logistics has evolved from a purely operation function to a competitive weapon capable of providing goods and services to the farthest regions of the supply chain. Originally, the role of logistics was to provide cost effective warehousing and transportation functions capable of meeting the day-to-day requirements of customer order fulfillment and channel inventory resupply. By the mid-1990s, logistics had risen to such a position of competitive importance that the concept required reformulation, the *strategic* side morphing into *supply chain management* and the *tactical* side focused on logistics operations execution. This section is concerned with a discussion of logistics as a operations function.

DEFINING LOGISTICS

When referencing current literature, a number of adequate definitions of logistics can be found. Perhaps the most popular describes logistics as consisting of the *Seven R's*: that is having the *right product*, in the *right quantity* and the *right condition*, at the *right place*, at the *right time*, for the *right customer*, at the *right price*. This common sense definition covers most of the value-added functions performed by logistics operations. Logistics provides *place* utility by moving goods from the producer through each node in the supply network to the demand origin. Logistics provides *time* utility by ensuring that the goods are at the proper place to meet the occasion of customer requirement. Logistics provides *possession* utility by facilitating the exchange of goods. Finally, logistics provides *form* utility through the use of value-added processing and light manufacturing. Time and place utilities, product movement and storage, and price and customer service are all specified.

The most often quoted formal definition of logistics is the one composed by the Council of Logistics Management. Logistics is defined as

> the process of planning, implementing and controlling the efficient, cost-effective flow and storage of raw materials, in-process inventory, finished goods, and related information from point of origin to point of consumption for the purpose of conforming to customer requirements.

Equally as concise is the definition found in the *APICS Dictionary* (9th edition). Logistics is defined as

> The art and science of obtaining, producing and distributing material and product in the proper place and in proper quantities.

These and other definitions imply that logistics creates competitive value by optimizing operations cost and productivity, the efficient utilization of assets, facilitating internal business fulfillment functions, integrating external channel suppliers, and achieving conformance to performance standards. All definitions characterize logistics as serving three central functions. To begin

with, logistics is concerned with the *storage* of inventory. Activities occur-
ing in this function are inventory control, replenishment and procurement,
and the number, design, type, and location of storage areas and warehouses.
The second function focuses on the *movement* of inventory from the supplier
through the manufacturing and distribution channel, ending with delivery to
the end user. Pivotal to this function is the effective selection and use of
modes of transportation. The final, and most important, function found in the
above definitions is the capability of logistics to satisfy *customer requirements*.

FUNCTIONAL DEFINITION

Another way of defining *logistics* is to separate it into two separate, yet closely integrated operations regions as illustrated in Figure 1.6. A definition of
these two regions is as follows:

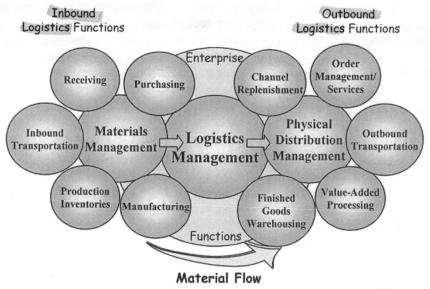

FIGURE 1.6 Logistics management functions.

- *Materials Management.* This component has been classically identified with the *incoming flow* of materials, components, and products into
  the enterprise. Materials management can be defined as the group of
  operation functions supporting the cycle of materials flow from the purchase, receipt, and control of production inventories, to the manufacture and delivery of finished goods to the channel system.

- *Physical Distribution Management.* This function is normally associated with the *outbound flow* of finished goods and supporting services through the distribution channel necessary to satisfy customer requirements. Often logistics is associated with the execution side of marketing and sales management, as it is concerned with the warehousing and movement of finished goods and service parts through the distribution channel to meet customer delivery demand. Detail activities encompass warehousing, transportation, finished goods handling and control, value-added processing, customer order administration, shipping, service, and return goods processing.

It can be argued that breaking down logistics into the above two categories is somewhat artificial, and to a large extent, the argument is justified. Although materials management and physical distribution management have defined functions, it is clear that there are many shared activities. In fact, many of the same skills, knowledge, and management control processes necessary to manage incoming and outgoing inventories, traffic, materials handling, and warehousing are identical and are to be found in each area. Most distribution organizations normally have a single department called "materials management" or "logistics" that manages the matrix of distribution activities. Rather than describing an organizational structure, the objective of establishing the logistics concept is to communicate regions of discrete business functions in order to facilitate understanding.

THE MAGNITUDE OF LOGISTICS

The sheer size of financial size of the logistics function bears witness to its central place in the business economy. According to Delaney [16], the cost of logistics for the year 2002 in the U.S. amounted to $910 billion. This expenditure was equivalent to 8.7 percent of U.S. gross domestic product in the same year. A breakdown of the detail can be seen in Figure 1.7.

LOGISTICS OPERATIONS

The daily activities of logistics are concerned with the management of the following five operational elements: (1) network design, (2) operations planning and execution, (3) logistics partnership management, (4) application of information technologies, and (5) logistics performance measurement. Each of these critical areas will be reviewed in succession.

Network design. The network of manufacturing plants, distribution warehouses, and retail stores provides the physical pipeline by which products

	$ Billions
Carrying Costs - $1.444 Trillion All Business Inventory	

Interest...	23
Taxes, Obsolescence, Depreciation, Insurance..........	197
Warehousing	78
Subtotal	298

Transportation Costs
Motor Carriers:

Truck – Intercity...	300
Truck – Local...	162
Subtotal	462

Other Carriers:

Railroads..	37
Water..........(International 21, Domestic 6)...........	27
Oil Pipelines...	9
Air..............(International 7, Domestic 20)..........	27
Forwarders...	9
Subtotal	109

Shipping Related Costs.......................................	6
Logistics Administration......................................	35
Total Transportation Costs	910

FIGURE 1.7 Total logistics costs - 2002

find their way to the customer and information relating to marketing and channel transaction events makes its way back to channel origins. The number, size, and geographical location of distribution facilities can be said to have a direct impact on a company's ability to provide the levels of service and cost demanded by the customer. Determining how many each of the different types of facility are needed, where they should be geographically located, and the nature of the fulfillment functions performed is the starting point in determining logistics strategy. Operationally, the logistics channel strategy is concerned with finding answers to several critical questions. What is the level of inventory to be stored at each location? How is inventory replenishment planning to be performed? How are customer orders going to be allocated for fulfillment? How are transportation costs to be measured? Are logistics partners to be involved, and at what point in the logistics network? In addition, marketing campaigns, new product introduction as well as product phase-out, actions of competitors, changes in technology, capabilities of channel partners, and others all will impact the viability of network strategies over time. Logistics planners must continually review network strategies to ensure they are providing optimal levels of customer service and competetiveness.

Operations Planning and Execution. Logistics is charged with the daily execution of a number of critical business functions. The overall goal of these activities is the optimization of internal resources and their application to effectively respond to material management and customer fulfillment needs. These functions can be separated into the following five operations areas:

- *Order management.* Perhaps the most important function performed by logistics, this activity is concerned with the navigation of the customer order through the inventory allocation, picking, pick relief, and back-order cycles. The fundamental performance target is always ensuring product shipment based on quoted lead times and order quantities and quality specifications.

- *Production and procurement.* While normally the reserve of other departments, the production and acquisition of inventories is fundamental to effective logistics. As the number of product families and distribution sites grow, many of today's firms have found that optimization of product across multi-channels requires close coordination with logistics or actual control by logistics planners.

- *Freight cost and service management.* The main functions in this area consist of managing inbound/outbound freight, carrier management, total cost control, operations outsourcing decisions, and execution of administrative services. Effective fulfillment planning in this area requires the architecting of fulfillment functions that can optimize inbound materials and outbound product movement, warehousing, and administrative services that utilize the most cost effective yet efficient transportation partners and carriers.

- *Warehouse management.* The effective management of inventory in the supply chain requires efficient and well-managed warehousing techniques. Among the activities found in this area of traditional logistics management can be found inventory storage, material handling, equipment utilization, receiving, putaway, and returns.

- *Transportation routing and scheduling.* The movement of product is a primary function of logistics. Areas to be considered are optimization of shipping capacity utilization, decreasing less-than-truckload shipments, and applying postponement strategies that assign actual end-product differentiation to the optimal channel node. Another important function is selection of third-part transportation providers. An often overlooked area is shipment documentation and compliance. Key points are concerned with ensuring accurate documentation regarding country quotas, tariffs, import/export regulations, product classification, and letters of credit.

- *Fleet management.* When companies maintain their own fleets, it is the responsibility of logistics to ensure the effective utilization of physical transportation assets. Critical areas revolve around equipment utilization and maintenance, and total cost. The goal is to determine the optimum use of transportation assets, whether internal or through a third party supplier, without compromising service levels.
- *Load planning.* Utilizing transportation assets to achieve maximum fulfillment optimization requires detailed load planning. Critical functions in this area are concerned with packaging and labeling, load building and consolidation, and possible third party transfer point or cross-docking functions.
- *Special functions.* Often logistics must develop strategies and policies to deal with several miscellaneous functions. Among these can be found managing service parts inventories and working with return goods. A grow area is handling *reverse logistics.* This process involves the reclamation of packaging materials and other wastes, and backhaul to a central collection point for recycling. The object of the process is the effective coordination of both the forward and reverse processes necessary to fully utilize products and materials throughout their life cycles.

While the effective management of each one of these areas is essential to organizational success, their benefits dramatically increase when the entire logistics channel network is integrated together in the pursuit of supply chain optimization and development of robust, flexible sourcing, warehousing, transportation, and delivery capabilities that unify total logistics capabilities.

Logistics partnership management. Providing agile and flexible fulfillment to meet customer demands often requires logistics planners to utilize a *third party logistics* (3PL) service provider. Over the past decade 3PL support partners have become more valuable as they utilize new technologies and expand services that permit them to integrate into the supply chain systems of their customers. Instead of being engaged merely to perform delivery functions on a spot basis, logistics planners have come to depend on the close collaboration of their 3PLs to execute strategic objectives. Besides the core services of motor cartage, transportation and warehouse leasing, warehouse operations, small package delivery, customs and export management, brokerage, and value-added processing, the utilization of Internet applications have enabled 3PLs to offer a variety of advanced services. Among these can be found track and trace, rate negotiation/carrier selection, freight payables, reverse logistics, order fulfillment utilizing Web and EDI interfaces to customers and suppliers, compliance consulting, and advanced information and material handling technologies. Some companies have even turned over the entirety of their logistics functions to *fourth-party* (4PL) or *lead logistics providers* (LLP) that deliver a comprehensive logistics solution to their customers through a single point of contact.

Application of information technologies. Increasingly, logistics management is turning to new forms of information technologies that utilize the Internet to assist them in channel management. One of the most critical is expanding *shipment visibility.* While it is critical that customers possess real-time "track and trace" data regarding their shipments, it constitutes the very first layer of service management. Of increasing importance is visibility to information about products and fulfillment capabilities found not just between immediate buyer and supplier, but also among all network trading partners. This requirement has become even more critical as the complexity of the supply chain has deepened, caused by the increase in contract manufacturing, raw material providers extending several levels upstream, global sourcing efforts requiring overcoming geographic boarders and language barriers, and the establishment of often separate Internet sales functions. Lack of shipment visibility simply increases fulfillment time delays, proliferates inventory safety stocks, and amplifies the "bull-whip effect," especially in complex supply channels. Supply chain visibility is about being able to access accurate infor-mation about inventory and shipments anywhere, anytime in the supply net-work so logistics planners can respond quickly and intelligently.

Another critical area where information technologies tools are being applied is *fulfillment event management.* The goal of these applications is to provide logistics planners with a window into the impact of events occurring at different points in the supply chain. These tools provide several channel fulfillment event information drivers such as

- *Monitoring*: Providing real-time information about supply network events such as the current status of channel inventory levels, open orders, production, and fulfillment.
- *Notifying*: Providing real-time exception management through alert messaging that will assist supply channel planners to make effective decisions as conditions change in the supply pipeline.
- *Simulating*: Providing tools that permit easy and fast supply channel modeling and "what-if" scenarios that recommend appropriate remedial action in response to an event or trend analysis.
- *Controlling*: Provides channel planners with capabilities to quickly and easily change a previous decision or condition, such as expediting an order or selecting less costly delivery opportunities.

- *Measuring:* Provides essential metrics and performance objectives or KPIs to assist supply chain strategists to assess the performance of existing channel relationships and to set realistic expectations for future performance [19].

Event management applications provide logistics planners with functions such as order and shipment tracking, workflow, alert messaging/notification, escalation processes, and performance/compliance management that alert them when an event violating predetermined fulfillment or channel stocking parameters has occurred requiring planner intervention. Altogether, the benefits of applying the latest computerized techniques that seek to automate logistics functions and increase the accuracy of logistics decisions can produce enormous benefits not only for individual companies, but for entire supply chains.

Performance measurement. Effective logistics performance requires the successful execution of those values deemed essential by the customer. Essentially, logistics performance is composed of three key metrics. The first, *logistics productivity,* provides meaningful productivity standards, optimization of logistics costs, integration of quality management processes, and broadening of logistics service levels. The second metric, *logistics service performance,* tracks the ability of logistics functions to meet customer service goals, such as product availability, order cycle time, logistics system flexibility, depth of service information, utilization of technologies, and breadth of postsales service support. The final performance component, *logistics performance measurement systems,* details the content of the actual metrics and how performance is to be tracked. Often this means working closely with trading partners to ensure the proper data is being gathered from channel SCM systems, ERP systems, and data warehouses [19].

Overall, logistics can be said to possess the following seven critical operating performance objectives [20]:

- *Service.* Today's supply chain is about creating *value* as determined by the customer. A *value chain* is about constructing agile, flexible operations that permit customers to configure the mix of product/service solutions they need. Effective channel operations imply that the customer-satisfying elements of manufacturing, product/service availability, fulfillment, and service can be constructed to meet the unique requirements of every customer.
- *Fast flow response.* This performance value refers to the ability of the supply chain to fulfill the delivery requirements of each customer in a timely manner. Rapid response requires the architecting of highly agile and flexible channels where all forms of processing time are collapsed

or eliminated. Besides accelerating the order-to-delivery cycle, this attribute also means migrating the supply chain away from stagnant pools of buffer inventory driven by forecasts to an environment capable of rapidly responding to each customer order on a shipment-by-shipment basis.

- *Reduction of operating variance.* In a Lean manufacturing and distribution environment variance in any sphere, from production, to quality, to inventory balances, is not permitted. Operating variances can occur both internally and externally out in the supply chain. Since logistics productivity is directly increased when variances are minimized, one of the most important duties of logistics management is the establishment of processes for the continuous elimination of all forms of variance.

- *Minimum inventories.* The levels of inventory necessary to support company sales and revenue objectives are part of the entire supply chain's commitment to customer service. The operating goal of logistics is to continuously reduce inventory to the lowest level as part of the process of achieving lowest overall logistics costs. Achieving this operating goal means pursuing inventory minimization and turn velocity for the entire supply chain and not merely one trading partner.

- *Transportation reduction.* The movement of products across the channel network constitutes one of the most important supply chain costs. Reduction in transportation costs can be achieved by closer inter-channel inventory planning and replenishment, utilization of larger shipments over longer distances to achieve movement economies of scale, and the effective use of third party service providers.

- *Quality management.* *Total quality management* (TQM) is not just an operating philosophy to be applied to manufacturing, but rather to the whole supply chain. In fact, it can be argued that the requirement for absolute quality is even more essential for logistics than anywhere else in the company. Logistics transactions often deal with transporting inventories and services over large geographical areas. Once set in motion, the cost of solving a quality problem, ranging from incorrect inventories to invalid orders and late shipments, require lengthy and costly processes to be reversed.

- *Product life-cycle support.* As stated above, environmental laws and popular opinion has mandated an increase in *reverse logistics* functions. Some of the critical challenges posed by recalls and returns are that they often involve a complex paper and product trail from worldwide sources, they can mean re-manufacturing, repairing, or destroying the return, and they can influence just about every link within the supply chain. Responding to this operational need requires logistics planners to develop detailed return, recycle, and repair programs that enable the efficient management of product life-cycles that can actually provide companies with a wealth of information on product performance, ease of use, defects, and consumer expectation.

THE ORGANIZATION OF LOGISTICS

The logistics function provides the *physical* aspect of channel management. The activities of the marketing function are to manage the channel and facilitate customer transactions by coordinating product, price, and promotional objectives. In contrast, logistics, regardless of the type of distributor, serves three central functions: the storage and management of inventories, the movement of inventory from the supplier through the distribution channel, ending with delivery to the end user, and the realization of the *place* and *time utilities* defined in the firm's marketplace strategy.

Logistics functions are generally structured around a combination of the following three organizational models [21]:

- *Strategic versus Operational.* This organizational model refers to the position of logistics relative to other enterprise functions. In the past logistics was treated as purely an operational function and considered of minimal strategic importance. In contrast, in today's business climate successful companies have learned that logistics must occupy an equal place alongside marketing, manufacturing, and finance. The strategic importance of logistics has, furthermore, required a close coupling of traditional logistics activities (warehousing, transportation, customer service, and inventory) with corporate management.
- *Centralized versus Decentralized.* Logistics functions can be administered from a centralized location, or authority can be decentralized throughout the distribution channel. In a centralized logistics system, activities are normally performed only at a corporate facility, managed by a single department or individual. Firms using this organizational model attempt to exploit economies of scale in transportation and storage, order processing, and information systems by managing them from a central location. Companies, on the other hand, with decentralized logistics systems are normally characterized as offering a diverse set of products to a heterogeneous marketplace. The most important argument for using a decentralized structure is positioning products and services close to the customer location.
- *Line versus Staff.* Finally, logistics functions can be oriented around line, staff, or a combination of line and staff. In a line organization, the activities of logistics (warehousing, customer service, transportation,

etc.) are centralized into a department, similar to sales, accounting, and production, and placed under the responsibility of a single manager. Logistics in this environment is centered on the performance of daily operational responsibilities. In contrast, in a staff organization logistics functions are divided up among marketing and sales, production, and finance. Various staff activities serve to coordinate and administer the line functions. Logistics in this model acts mostly in an advisory role to the responsible departments. Most companies combine elements of these two organizational models in order to optimize, coordinate, and integrate enterprise logistics strategies and operations.

As is illustrated in Figure 1.8, organizational structures can take various

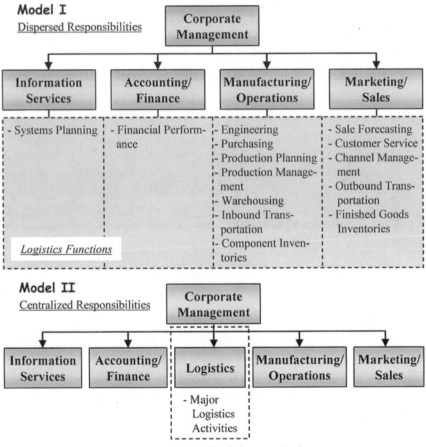

FIGURE 1.8 Types of logistics organizations.

forms based on the three organizational models detailed above. For the most part, traditional methods of viewing the logistics structure have focused either on a structure of dispersed responsibilities (Model I) or of consolidated responsibilities (Model II). Some may argue, however, that each possesses inherent weaknesses. In dispersed organizations, for example, logistics activeties tend to be performed in isolation from related activities, resulting in less than optimal overall performance. Consolidated organizations, on the other hand, tend to focus narrowly on departmental budgets, performance measurements, and defense of departmental "turf." One approach has been to combine the two models into what is called a *matrix organization* (Figure 1.9). This structure is based on the simple premise that logistics activities are encountered in various business departments and are spread throughout the enterprise in basically a *horizontal* manner. As local responsibility presents the optimal method of executing logistics functions, they should remain under their functional departments. However, the management of costs and overall direction is the responsibility of the logistics manager. In this sense, logistics line managers are subject to both the functional departmental manager and the logistics manager.

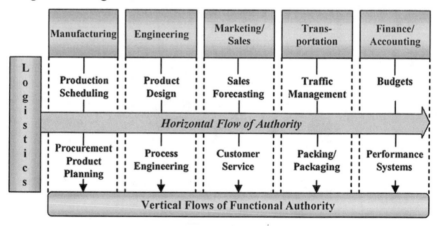

FIGURE 1.9 Matrix Organization

The advantages of a matrix organization can be found in its flexibility in adapting to most companies, its ability to provide enterprise-wide functional integration and coordination on a strategic level, rather than just solving tactical problems, and its placement of logistics as a responsibility center, enabling management by objective techniques. Despite the apparent benefits, matrix management models suffer from a critical fault stemming from the fact that lines of authority tend to become confused by making some functions responsible to two different managers. Issues can arise over conflicting management directives and differing performance targets.

TEAM-BASED ORGANIZATIONAL STRUCTURES

Since the early 1990s, companies have been exploring *team-based* management techniques as an alternative to the traditional organizational models detailed above. In the past, hierarchical structures of management were necessary to ensure that essential information was collected and summarized, work optimally designed and allocated, and execution activities supervised, monitored, controlled, and checked as work was performed and moved from one operator or function to the next. In today's fast-paced marketplace, the shift to total customer service, and the availability of interoperable computer networking have rendered this model obsolete. It has become increasingly clear that the focus of the organization must shift from a concern with managing internal operational performance measurements to an integrated supply chain perspective. Today's customer wants extremely rapid delivery, instantaneous answers to price and product availability, and immediate response to changing requests all without incurring penalties in cost or quality. Customer-based organizational strategies, therefore, must be based on optimizing both internal capabilities as well as channel partner competencies to react flexibly and quickly to the needs of the customer rather than on actualizing company-bound performance metrics. Over the past decade, corporations large and small have been "delayering" themselves in an effort to remove needless structure that simply clogs the velocity of product and information throughput and renders the organization unresponsive to the marketplace. Two features have facilitated this process: the growing power of computerized networking infrastructures and the rise of team-based management.

As was discussed in Chapter 1, the revolution in information technology has provided companies with exciting new opportunities for working with the supply channel. Organizationally, the most important facet of this revolution is the ability of a variety of computer systems to be linked together by Internet technologies to form an information network. Today, Web applications move information freely across departmental functions, empowering users to make decisions and perform activities that not only impact their own business areas but also those of their channel trading partners simultaneously. Take, for instance, advanced planning software that pulls inventory planning information from the database server and, through the use of simulation tools that include graphs and pie charts, enables planners to formulate several different production capacity and order release sequencing plans. Once the optimal choice has been decided on, the information is loaded back to the database server for the use of planners in other departments. The more sophisticated can also take these planning "events" and pass them through the Web to channel suppliers for input into their planning systems.

The ability of Web-based technologies to network people enables the creation of focused virtual teams. As is illustrated in Figure 1.10, instead of an organization structured around mutually exclusive tasks (jobs) and departmental assignments (charters), team-based management views the organization as a skills repository where individuals can be formed into teams horizontally within a function or vertically across departments. *Natural work teams* (composed of people who naturally work together) and *cross-functional teams* (composed of members from several business functions in the enterprise) have distinct advantages over traditional methods when it comes to accelerating daily activities as well as problem solving.

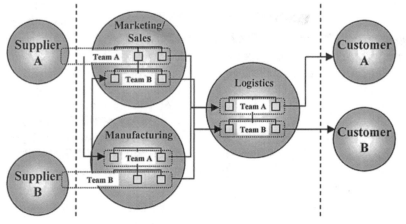

FIGURE 1.10 Team Networking

- Teams have a much wider range of expertise, knowledge, and facts at their disposal than do narrowly defined departmental task forces.
- Teams have a broader perspective and therefore can consider a broader range of approaches and alternative solutions.
- Teams promote company-wide ownership of critical issues, thereby enabling a quick solution and facilitating implementation.
- Teams are synergistic. The knowledge of individual team members mutually stimulate collective thinking and the generation of solutions unattainable by individuals or departments acting on their own.
- Teams develop individual member capabilities by providing opportunities to lead, facilitate, manage tasks, and implement solutions beyond their normal departmental functions.

When utilizing Internet-based SCM as an organizational model, companies must depart radically from traditional structures and the way work is organized. Hierarchical management styles lack the flexibility and adaptability to meet the constantly changing requirements of today's customer. In contrast, organizations characterized by flat hierarchies and virtual teams management styles have the ability to focus their resources into targeted teams to respond quickly and decisively to business issues as they occur. To be successful, these *virtual organizations* will require the following:

1. *Multifunctional management specialists.* In the past, managers needed to be experts in their own departments. In today's environment of virtual teams, managers need to have a wide functional understanding of manufacturing, finance, scheduling, marketing, and customer service, as well as warehousing and transportation. This is particularly true of logistics management who must be able to assemble cross-functional and cross-channel focused teams capable of linking logistics strategies with the strategies of other business functions, and to work effectively with supply chain partners to resolve conflicts and to actualize opportunities.

2. *Technology-literate personnel.* As information technology provides new interoperability tools that automate functions and provide for the closer peer-to-peer networking of professionals within the enterprise and outside in the supply channel, companies will increasingly be dependent on personnel who can leverage the power of technology to achieve targeted business results. In addition, it is the responsibility of the firm's personnel to continually search for new ways to utilize existing systems, as well as to search for newer technologies that will accelerate the velocity of information transfer and network system constituents closer together.

3. *Culture of continuous change and improvement.* Traditional organizations were organized around optimizing functional roles in response to static conditions. The business climate of the 2000s, however, requires that enterprises be flexible and adaptable to meet changing marketplace needs. The mindset necessary to actualize this challenge is an acceptance that *change is the only management constant.* The customer-driven organization of tomorrow must be prepared to constantly improve and redesign the organization in the never-ending search for superior customer service and marketplace leadership.

SUMMARY

Over the past decade, it has become increasingly clear that to remain competitive in the emerging global markets of the new century companies can no longer depend on their own core strengths to drive marketplace leadership but must look to the competencies of their supply chain partners for new avenues of cost reduction and innovation. Six key dynamics are driving this dramatic shift in both corporate governance and worklife at the dawn of the twenty-first century. The first is the growing power of the customer. Instead of a passive player, today's customer is seeking to expand their control over the entire channel fulfillment process, demanding the power to configure the product/service mix to match unique solutions, and flawless, fast flow delivery all at the lowest price. The second dynamic is the explosion in globalization. This dynamic is characterized by the growth of strategic alliances and partnerships on a global scale. The close interlinkage of companies along a supply chain has produced the third dynamic, the establishment of inter-enterprise "virtual" organizations capable of leveraging the skills and resources of a matrix of companies and the ability to utilize Internet technologies to exploit the peer-to-peer networking of channel partners anywhere, at any time on the earth.

These factors have engineered a revolution in the fourth dynamic: logistics management. Instead of a purely operational function concerned with the day-to-day management of fulfillment activities, logistics has become a critical strategic enabler permitting companies to successfully manage complex supply channel networks. As the focus of management has moved from the company to the supply chain sphere, so have the requirements for effective cost control and process improvement. The goal is to architect performance models that optimize channel productive capabilities and activate highly agile, lean, and scalable networks capable of being quickly reconfigured to provide pathways of value to the customer. Finally, the last dynamic, information technology, provides the interoperable infrastructure permitting channel partners to synchronizing information about demand and supply requirements and events across each network node in "real time."

Success in managing collectively these dynamics requires a new view of the supply chain. As is the case with most ideas, *supply chain management* (SCM) has its roots in the ages old struggle of producers and distributors to overcome the barriers of space and time to deliver products and services as close as possible to the desires and needs of the customer. Tracing this evolution of the modern Internet-enabled supply chain can be said to have progressed through five stages. In the first, the role of distribution was simply to execute the day-to-day activities of material management and fulfillment. In this stage logistics functions were decentralized and absorbed into various company departments such as sales and finance. In stage 2, companies began to centralize what became to known as logistics into distinct departments in order to better control the "total cost" of distribution by assigning it a management team and set of performance targets.

By the 1980s executives began to understand that a focus solely on logistics total cost management presented a passive approach to the marketplace. Organizational strategists began to consider a new model that sought to integrate logistics with other business departments in the pursuit of both operational optimization and as a way of enhancing customer value. Stage 3 logistics enabled companies to closely align logistics capabilities and marketing, sales, and operations objectives to provide customers with a unified approach to demand fulfillment. In Stage 4, the concept of *integrated logistics* was significantly enhanced by the growth of the concept of *supply chain management* (SCM). The impact of new marketplace dynamics required businesses to look beyond the four walls of their companies to their trading partners for new sources of competitiveness. Planners began to regard the development of close collaborative relations with their channel partners as critical in mobilizing the agile, scalable, lean organizations necessary to match the speed of global business.

The application of the Internet to SCM provides the foundation for stage 5: e-SCM. This most recent stage can be defined as a

> supply chain operational and strategic management philosophy that utilizes Internet-enabling technologies to effect the continuous regeneration of networks of supply channel partners empowered to execute superlative, unique customer-winning value at the lowest cost through the collaborative, real-time synchronization of product/service transfer, demand priorities, vital marketplace information, and logistics delivery capabilities.

e-SCM consists of four critical components. Enabling the full potential of e-SCM requires strategists to first of all understand the connectivity power of Internet-driven information. e-SCM enables the "real-time" synchronization of information from all quadrants of the supply chain and provides for the instantaneous visibility of events necessary for collaborative decision-making across channel regions. Second, the goal of this interconnectedness of supply chain information is to ensure new ways of providing customer-winning value. "Value chains" continuously seek the generation of channels of unique configurations of trading partners capable of providing solutions to the unique, individualized needs and priorities of customers anywhere, at any time.

While the use of e-information to respond to today's customer is critical, the real challenge is to present it concurrently so that all points in the supply chain can receive it at the same time. The value of such synchronization is obvious: intelligence concerning actual demand and supply dynamics can be broadcast simultaneously to all channel constituents so that effective planning and operations decisions can be made. The final component of e-SCM is a corollary of the preceding three: nothing will work without constant attention among all channel partners to enrich channel collaborative relationships. Collaboration is really about sharing. Synchronization is possessing the channel intelligence to be able to know how the right product and service can be accessed by the customer at any point in the channel network. Such a management philosophy will require more than just acquiring the right connectivity tools: it is demanding that all channel network partners embrace the accompanying cultural and organizational changes as well.

The rise of SCM has expanded the role of logistics. SCM requires logistics functions to shoulder the task of creating competitive value by optimizing operations costs, efficiently utilizing channel assets, and facilitating supply and fulfillment functions. The daily activities of logistics is concerned with the management of five critical operations elements. The first is performing the task of actual network design which involves determining how many of each of the different facilities are needed, where they should be located, and the nature of the tasks to be performed. The second activity is optimizing the performance of the operational functions involved in order management, production and procurement, freight costing and service management, warehouse management, transportation, and load planning. The third activity is to develop effective logistics outsourcing opportunities with service providers willing to engage in collaborative relationships. The fourth activity is to search for and implement computerized technologies that assist in automating non-value-added functions while providing tools to expand critical enablers such as shipment visibility, fulfillment event management, and providing customer with the ability to perform self-service ordering and shipment tracking. Finally, the last activity is determining the cross-channel logistics metrics that will allow effective review of company and channel productivity and service performance through the establishment of performance systems permitting the collection of data from business systems and data warehouses across the channel network.

QUESTIONS FOR REVIEW

1. What is the relationship between SCM and logistics?
2. How can logistics functions influence economic systems?
3. Supply chains can be described as extended enterprises. What does this mean?
4. What has been the impact of the "power of the customer" on the utilization of supply chains?
5. It has been stated that the changes brought about by global competition and the power of the customer have radically changed the business climate. Describe how these and other issues have required companies to rethink their logistics functions.
6. Of the challenges facing today's distribution function, which will be the most significant in the next several years. Why?

7. Whereas cost trade-offs are important in guiding enterprise decisions, they can also have a negative affect on enterprise competitiveness. Discuss.
8. Why is the application of IT tools to SCM so important?
9. What is impact on worklife and organizational behavior of the SCM concept?

REFERENCES

1. These comments have been summarized in part from Ross, David F., *Introduction to e-Supply Chain Management: Engaging Technology to Build Market-Winning Business Partnerships.* Boca Raton, FL: St. Lucie Press, 2003, pp. 2-4; Ross, David F., *Competing Through Supply Chain Management: Creating Market-Winning Strategies Through Supply Chain Partnerships.* Boston, MA: Kluwer Academic Publishers, 1998, pp. ix-xi; and, Coyle, John J., Bardi, Edward J., and Langley, C. John, *The Management of Business Logistics,* 7th ed. New York: West Publishing Co., 2003, pp. 5-11.
2. Coyle, et al., p. 9 and Deloitte & Touche, "The Challenge of Complexity in Global Manufacturing – Trends in Supply Chain Management," 2003.
3. For more detail on the historical evolution of the SCM concept see Ross, *Competing Through Supply Chain Management*, pp. 72-107.
4. For an interesting historical approach to logistics in the late 1960's see the articles in Bowersox, Donald J., LaLonde, Bernard J., and Smykay, Edward W., eds., *Readings in Physical Distribution Management: The Logistics of Marketing.* London: Macmillan, 1969.
5. For a more in-depth analysis of the problems besetting conventional SCM channels see Small, Jeffrey C., "Convergence of Technology: The Supply Chain Meets the Web," *Supply Chain Management Review,* 5, 1, 2001, pp. 52-59 and Harrington, Lisa H., "Adversity Breeds Creativity," *Inbound Logistics,* 22, 12, 2002, pp. 43-46.
6. See the comments in Radjou, Navi, "Exit Supply Chains; Enter Adapative Supply Networks," *Supply Chain e-Business,* (July/August), 2002, pp. 42-43.
7. For a more detailed treatment of this topic see Ross, *Competing Through Supply Chain Management,* pp. 13-33.
8. This definition has been adapted from Ibid, p.18.
9. Reary, Rob and Springer, Alicia, "Return on Relationship: a Different Lens on Business," in *Achieving Supply Chain Excellence Through Technology,* 3, Anderson, David L., ed., Montgomery Research, San Francisco, 2001, 41.
10. See the analysis in Haydock, Michael, "Supply Chain Intelligence," in *Achieving Supply Chain Excellence Through Technology,* 5, Mulani, Narendra, ed., San Francisco, CA: Montgomery Research, Inc., 2003, pp. 15-21 and Aberdeen Group, "Strategic e-Sourcing: A Framework for Negotiating Competitive Advantage," April, 2001.
11. Bovet, David and Martha, Joseph, *Value Nets: Breaking the Supply Chain to Unlock Hidden Profits.* New York: John Wiley, 2000, p. 4.
12. These three principles have been defined in Ibid, pp. 37-53.
13. Ross, *Introduction to e-Supply Chain Management,* p. 53.
14. Treacy, Michael and Dobrin, David, "Make Progress in Small Steps," *Optimize Magazine,* November, 2001, pp. 53-60.
15. Prahalad, C.K. and Ramaswamy, Venkatram, "The Collaboration Continuum," *Optimize Magazine,* November, 2001, pp. 31-39.
16. Delaney, Robert V., "14th Annual 'State of Logistics Report,' The Case for Reconfiguration," ProLogis/Cass Information Systems, June 2, 2003, Figure #7.

17. See Ross, *Introduction to e-Supply Chain Management,* p. 285.
18. Ibid, pp. 280-281.
19. For a greater treatment of these basic measurements consult Bowersox, Donald J. and Closs, David J., *Logistical Management: The Integrated Supply Chain Process.* New York: The McGraw-Hill Companies, Inc., 1996, pp. 41-43.
20. Lambert, Douglas M. and Stock, James R., *Strategic Logistics Management,* 3rd ed., Homewood, IL: Irwin, 1993, pp. 632-633. See also La Londe, Bernard L. and Masters, James M., "Organizational Trends and Career Paths in Distribution," in *The Distribution Management Handbook,* Tompkins, James A. and Harmelink, Dale A., eds., New York: McGraw-Hill, 1994, pp. 7.5-7.11.

2

COMPONENTS OF DISTRIBUTION MANAGEMENT

Although the components of modern materials and physical distribution management are comparatively easy to define, pinpointing exactly which companies are distributors and which are not is a much more difficult task. The definition of what constitutes a distributor encompasses such a wide range of businesses and marketing permutations that the ultimate results cannot help but to be so all encompassing that they can be somewhat ambiguous. Often the student of logistics finds that determining whether or not a company is a distributor is best pursued by identifying the extent to which they perform functions that clearly belong to other types of businesses, such as manufacturing or retailing. Ultimately, it can be maintained that all enterprises that sell products to retailers and other merchants and/or to industrial, institutional, and commercial users but who do not sell in significant amounts to the ultimate customer can be termed *distributors*. In this sense, instead of being confined to a narrow band of businesses, most companies that deal with the disbursement of raw materials and finished products belong in one sense or another to the distribution industry.

Chapter 2 focuses on defining the nature and functions of the distribution industry. The chapter opens with a detailed discussion of the essential characteristics of the distribution industry. Following this introduction, the chapter turns to a full review of the various types of distributor, ranging from wholesalers, brokers and agents, and manufacturers' and retailers' branches and offices, to exporting and importing distributors. Special attention is paid to the rise of new forms of distribution brought about by the Internet. Next, the role of distribution is described. Among the topics covered are understanding the need for distribution, the channel functions performed by the distributor, and the inbound and outbound material flows found within the typical distribution organization. The chapter concludes with a brief overview of the challenges facing the multi-faceted distribution industry at the dawn of the twenty-first century.

DEFINING THE TERM "DISTRIBUTOR"

References in the previous chapter to *distributors* or the *distribution industry* assumed a general knowledge on the part of the reader as to the content of these terms. Although there are some excellent definitions of logistics and distribution, there are no good concise definitions of what constitutes a *distributor*. Webster's Dictionary, for example, defines a distributor as "one that markets a commodity, such as a wholesaler." The *APICS Dictionary* describes a distributor as "A business that does not manufacture its own products but purchases and resells these products. Such a business usually maintains a finished goods inventory [1]."

Despite the relative simplicity of such generalized statements, arriving at a functional definition of just what constitutes a *distributor* is a difficult one. The term, for example, can apply to enterprises ranging from various forms of stock jobbers, importers, cooperative buying associations, and drop shippers to manufacture distributors, brokers, and commission merchants. In addition, the growing power of Internet storefronts and e-marketplaces, giant retailers like Wal-Mart, and alternative forms of distribution, such as warehouse clubs, catalog sales, marketing channel specialists, and mail order, have blurred functional distinctions and rendered traditional definitions tenuous. What is worse, the term distributor often gets confused with definitions relating to *marketing channels*. Bowersox and Cooper [2], for example, define marketing channels as "a system of relationships existing among businesses that participate in the process of buying and selling products and services." It could be easily argued that such a statement provides a functional definition of the essential activities performed by distributors. The truth of the matter is that no matter what definition can be used, some easily hit the mark in some instances, and completely miss the target in others.

SUPPLY CHANNEL COMPONENTS

Some of the vagueness surrounding the term distributor is the result of the way the various players constituting the supply chain network have been defined. As Figure 2.1 illustrates, the primary channel constituents have traditionally been organized into three essential groups that reflect the basic movement of goods through the channel. The first component, *manufacturers*, are focused primarily on the development and production of products. Although it is true that some products, such as wood, coal, and grains, often by-pass manufacturing and move directly into the supply channel, manufacturing's role as a product originator places it at the opening stage of the distribution process. Some manufacturers, such as Ford Motor Company, Sony, and Gateway Computers, assume the responsibility of assembling and managing a distribution channel, whereas others depend on trading partners to perform that role.

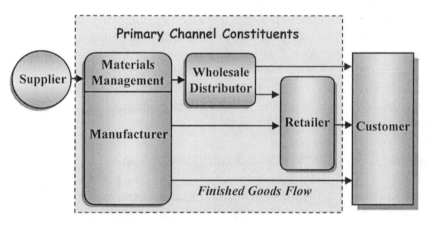

FIGURE 2.1 Supply channel constituents.

If manufacturers can be said to originate the distribution process, then *retailers* can be considered to be at the terminal points in the channel. Whether performed by a manufacturer, a wholesaler, or a retailer, the function of *retailing* is to sell goods and services directly to the customer for their personal, non-business use. In contrast to manufacturers and wholesalers, retailers have a completely different set of business decisions and objectives. Among these concerns are identifying the target market so that retailing operations can be optimally leveraged, meeting customer expectations with the appropriate mix of product assortments, services, and store convenience and ambience, and determining pricing and promotions that will provide competitive differentiation. It would be a gross error to regard retailers purely as passive channel members. Although many retailers are dependent on upstream channel suppliers, others, like Sears, Home Depot, Best Buy, and Wal-Mart, take a very active role in the development and management of the supply channel.

Somewhere in between manufacturers and retailers stands the *wholesale distributor.* Because wholesale distributors are less visible than their two channel partners and can assume a number of different forms, *wholesaling* is more difficult to define. The traditional function of wholesale distributors in the supply channel has been to serve as middlemen, providing retailers with products originating from the manufacturer. Wholesale distributors exist because of their ability to act as a consolidator, assembling and selling merchandise assortments in varying quantities from a number of manufacturers. In addition, wholesale distributors also design and operate channel arrangements between customers and those manufacturers who do not have distribution functions. At the beginning of the twenty-first century, Internet applications and management philosophies, such as *Just-In-Time* (JIT)/Lean Manufacturing and Quick Response, have enabled manufacturers and retailers to expand their role to encompass many of the functions traditionally performed by wholesale distributors. Although it can be expected that supply channel members will continue the search for ways of eliminating pipeline costs and improving customer service, wholesaling, as testified by the strength of such companies as Burgen Brunswig, SYSCO, McKesson, and ACE Hardware, is still an extremely important part of the supply chain.

CHANNEL ORGANIZATIONAL STRUCTURES

Commensurate with their channel roles, manufacturers, wholesalers, and retailers will be organized differently. Manufacturers with distribution functions can be organized according to one of three possible methods. The first and most popular strategy is *processed based.* The object of this model is to manage the entirety of enterprise functions as a single value-added chain. The emphasis is on achieving optimal efficiencies and productivities by managing marketing and sales, product development and manufacturing, logistics, and finance as an integrated system. The second possible organizational strategy pursued by manufacturers is *market based.* This strategy is concerned with managing a limited set of logistics functions across a multidivisional enterprise or across multiple-enterprise units. The object of the model is to execute joint product shipments to customers originating across the enterprise or to facilitate sales and logistical coordination by a single-order invoice. The final manufacturing strategy is *channel based*. In this strategy a manufacturer seeks to manage the distribution process by forming functional alliances with wholesalers and retailers. Enterprises that employ this strategy typically have large amounts of finished goods in the supply channel [3].

The organizational structure of wholesale distributors reflects their position as being the link connecting manufacturers with retailers. Because wholesalers do not produce products, the focal point of operations is centered on two critical functions: sales and the execution of logistics activities. In many cases, wholesalers are much more conscious of marketing and sales issues than manufacturers. Like retailers, the life blood of wholesaling is extremely merchandise and promotion oriented, centered on strong order processing functions and exceptional customer service. In addition to warehousing and delivery, wholesalers today must also be organized to provide value-added services such as ease of product search, EDI, Internet transactions, and value-added processing.

Because they represent the end point in the supply channel, retailers are organized around meeting the needs and expectations of the end customer. Similar to, but to a much greater degree than wholesalers, retailers are organized around promotions, selling, customer service, and inventory and warehousing functions. Typically, retailers stock a very broad assortment of products. A large grocery chain, for example, stocks over 11,000 products; mass merchandisers and department stores stock even more. The supply channels of retailers characteristically are geographically focused, with central supplying warehouses generally located one or two day's delivery distance from a cluster of stores. To facilitate this process, retailers are constantly restructuring and integrating their organizations. For example, the traditional dependence on central warehouses and transportation functions has been giving way in the 2000s to leveraging manufacturing and wholesale channel partners, or even to using a third-party service provider. Finally, today's retailers have accelerated the process of buying direct from the manufacturer. Techniques such as the use of EDI, the Internet, and centralized retail buying offices that facilitate the process of cost-effective shipment consolidation and "milk-run" delivery practices result in lower logistics costs while maintaining a high level of customer service.

In addition to the three structures above, a number of enterprises exhibit hybrid combinations. Of the three possible combinations, that of wholesaler and retailer is the most common. An example of a typical hybrid organization is a large food-service company identified by Bowersox [4].

This company operates a number of regional distribution centers, each serving approximately 5,000 restaurants or other food-service establishments. Products are sold at wholesale prices to these traditional customers. Over the past ten years, this firm has begun to open retail stores which sell wholesale products at discount retail prices directly to consumers. Typically, the firm operates a single retail location in a given city. The image maintained at retail is one of a large, institutional package size store with few conveniences. The appeal is price, unusual products or large sizes, coupled with the feel of shopping at wholesale.

Another example is Wal-Mart's Sam's Wholesale Club which presents customers with a wholesale type of retail environment. Regardless of the mix of enterprise type, hybrid operations pose special organizational challenges. Among the most important is the logistical capability of the company to support supply channel positions occurring on multiple levels.

Because of the great variety of distributors, there can be no optimal organizational structure that fits all channel components. The actual structure of an organization is dependent on a number of factors, such the goals of the business strategy, availability of capital, extent of international involvement, nature of the product, capacities of transportation, capabilities of information technologies, and predilections of the enterprise's management. Often companies occupying similar positions in the supply chain can have radically different organizations. Bowersox, for example, found two large mass merchandisers with different views of the supply channel. One company was heavily committed to maintaining an extensive distribution channel, whereas the other sought to eliminate their channel structure, preferring to pursue direct shipments from the manufacturer/wholesaler to retail outlets [5].

THE MAGNITUDE OF WHOLESALE DISTRIBUTION

Although the wholesaling industry has been losing ground over the past decade to alternate forms of distribution, it still represents a formidable portion of the U.S. total economy. Merchant wholesale distribution sales in 1992 approached $1.9 trillion dollars. This figure can be contrasted against the 1997 sales figures by Special Industry Code (SIC). According to the U.S. Department of Commerce, Bureau of the Census, in 1997 total durable wholesale distribution sales in that year amounted to $2.1 trillion, whereas nondurable wholesaling amounted to $1.9 trillion. Altogether, wholesale distribution sales totaled $4.1 trillion. In addition to these figures, the wholesale distribution industry consisted of approximately 455,000 enterprises. These companies, furthermore, employed 5.8 million people.

CHARACTERISTICS OF THE WHOLESALE DISTRIBUTOR

Although the above descriptions provide a useful way of categorizing the different types of industry constituting the supply channel, it only indirectly sheds light on which businesses can be considered as "distributors." The problem can be resolved by abstracting the essential characteristics of what constitutes the functions of a distributor. Essentially, three fundamental characteristics are apparent: the acquisition of products, the movement of products, and the nature of product transactions.

- *Product acquisition.* Current definitions describe distributors as acquiring products in a finished or semi-finished state from either a manufacturer or through another distributor higher up in the supply channel. These products are then processed to a finished state and/or sold as-is to other levels in the supply chain for resale or to be consumed in the production process. These functions can be performed by independent channel intermediaries or by the distribution facilities of manufacturing companies.

- *Product movement.* The central activity of a distributor is the management of product *delivery*. Delivery encompasses those activities necessary to satisfy the marketing utilities of *time, place*, and *possession* by ensuring that the right product is available to the customer at the right time and place. Often this means that a distributor must maintain a structure of central, branch, and field warehouses that are geographically located to achieve optimum customer service based on marketing analysis. When an internal distribution channel exists, network planners must also ensure the timely movement of product to stocking nodes within the network, as well as externally to the customer. In this sense, any manufacturer or retailer that must expend significant effort on product movement up or down the supply channel is performing the functions of a distributor.

- *Product transaction.* For the most part, distributors can be characterized as selling products in bulk quantities solely for the purpose of resale or business use. Downstream businesses will then sell these products to other distributors, retailers who will sell them directly to the end customer, or manufacturers who will consume the materials/components in the production process. This characteristic can best be seen when contrasted with retailing. Classically, retailers sell products individually to the final customer through a wide variety of outlets, such as department stores (Bloomingdale's), specialty stores (boutiques), supermarkets, superstores, or combination stores (Wal-Mart), discount stores, warehouse stores, and catalog showrooms. Often the division between retailing and distributing becomes unclear when it comes to direct marketing forms of product transaction. Companies who sell through a catalog, perform telemarketing activities, or engage in television marketing and Internet shopping can be selling either to the end customer or for resale. Finally, large franchising and merchandizing conglomerates, such as McDonald's, Nordstrom's, and Gateway, contain complex distribution functions responsible for the transaction and movement of product to independent affiliates or corporate chain stores.

The three functional characteristics describing a distributor come very close to the formal definition of *wholesaling* as formulated by the U.S. Bureau of the Census.

Wholesaling is concerned with the activities of those persons or establishments which sell to retailers and other merchants, and/or to industrial, institutional, and commercial users, but who do not sell in significant amounts to ultimate consumers.

Accepting the ultimate logic of this definition would mean that every sale made by every organization to anyone but the end consumer would be a "wholesale sale." Such an interpretation would apply to merchant wholesalers, all manufacturers (except those who sell to the public from factory outlets), internal supply chain replenishment management, mail-order distributors, Internet sales, and mega-retailers that possess distribution channels. This definition becomes clearer when the idea of a distributor is separated from being attached to a *type* of business and is thought of as a *series of functions*. Although it is true that many manufacturers and retailers have created vertical organizations to eliminate wholesale distributors from their supply channels, they have become, in the process, distributors as well as product producers and retailers. Regardless of the identity of the players within a given supply channel, the three characteristics of a distributor outlined above must be assumed by one or multiple channel members.

This definition of what constitutes a distributor is perhaps the most fundamental principle in this text. By adopting this definition, the scope of this book can be expanded to cover nearly every form of materials management and physical distribution activity performed by channel constituents, except for the processes of manufacturing and retailing. Instead of concentrating just on marketing channels or logistics functions, the text seeks to explore the great diversity of distribution in various business environments. As stated in Chapter 1, this viewpoint has particular relevance in today's business climate. As the opportunities and challenges of global distribution accelerate and companies scramble to find ways of gaining and sustaining competitive advantage, the traditional divisions among producer, wholesale distributor and retailer will become even more tenuous. In addition, the rise of supply chain management requires that all channel network trading partners be increasingly focused on superior customer service through the application of technology and management techniques that seek to integrate product, delivery, and enterprise resources. In this, an understanding of the principles and functions of distribution stand as essential for survival in today's extremely competitive global economy.

TYPES OF WHOLESALE DISTRIBUTORS

In this section the various types of wholesale distributor will be detailed. Distributors can be divided into five general types: merchant wholesalers, brokers and agents, manufacturers' and retailers' branches and offices, exporting and importing distributors, and miscellaneous wholesalers. Each of these areas are described below [6].

Merchant Wholesalers. Merchant wholesalers are independent enterprises that buy finished products from producers and other wholesalers and sell to companies for resale or manufacturing consumption. Although this type of business has been declining over the past decade in response to challenges from powerful retailers, such as Wal-Mart, and alternative channel marketers, such as warehouse clubs and Internet sales, merchant wholesalers account for at least 50 percent in sales volume and number of businesses of all types of wholesale distributor. Merchant wholesalers can be further divided into full-service wholesalers and limited-service wholesalers.

- *Full-Service Wholesalers.* This subtype of distributor provides a wide range of products and services to the customer. Besides stocking inventory and maintaining a sales force, other value-added functions such as sales order management, credit, transportation, EDI, and Web communications are also performed. In this grouping can be found the following types of companies.
  - *Wholesale Merchants.* This type of distributor generally provides products and a full range of value-added services to the retail industry. Wholesale merchants can be categorized further by the robustness of the product lines they offer to the marketplace. *General merchandise wholesalers* will normally stock a targeted range of products within several merchandise lines in an effort to service both multi-line and single-line retailers. In contrast *general-line wholesalers* will carry an extensive assortment of products in one or multiple product lines. Auto parts, drug store, and clothing whole-

salers are possible examples. Finally, *specialty wholesalers* focus on carrying in great depth the products of a single line. Examples include produce, meat and fish, and fashion apparel wholesalers.

– *Industrial Distributors.* This type of distributor is composed of wholesale merchants who sell products exclusively to manufacturers. Similar to retail distributors, they may carry a multitude of products lines (often called a mill supply house), a general line, or a specialty line. Many industrial distributors also may focus their inventories around MRO items (maintenance, repair, and operating supplies), OEM items (original equipment supplies), or industrial equipment (such as machinery).

- *Limited-Service Wholesalers.* Distributors in this type are characterized by the fact that they offer a limited range of services to their suppliers and customers. There are several kinds of distributor in this subgroup.

  – *Cash-and-Carry Wholesalers.* This type of distributor normally stocks a limited line of fast-moving products that are sold to small retailers. Cash-and-carry distributors require the customer to pick up and pay for the goods at the point of transaction. An example would be a small grocer who each morning picks up and pays for vegetables from a produce distributor.

  – *Truck Wholesalers.* Often termed a *truck jobber*, this type of distributor performs primarily a selling and delivery function only. They normally carry a limited line of products (such as milk, bread, and soft drinks) that they sell for cash to supermarkets, small groceries, restaurants, business and institutional cafeterias, and hotels.

  – *Drop Shippers.* This type of distributor operates in industries associated with commodities handled in bulk, such as building materials, coal, lumber, and heavy equipment. Drop shippers normally do not inventory or transport the product. When they receive a customer order, they will locate a suitable supplier who, in turn, delivers the product to the customer. Drop shippers assume title and risk for the inventory from the moment the order is placed with the supplier until the time it is delivered to the customer.

  – *Rack Jobbers.* This type of distributor normally provides highly advertised, brand-name nonfood products and accompanying services to grocery, convenience, and drug stores. Examples of products supplied by rack jobbers are toys, paperback books, greeting cards, hardware items, and health and beauty aids. Rack jobbers are responsible for delivery of the product to the retailer, product setup and display, pricing, item rotation, effectivity dating, and inventory maintenance. Inventories are stocked in consignment: that is the rack jobber retains title to the inventory, billing the retailer only for the goods sold since the last visit.

- *Producers' Cooperatives.* This type of distribution organization is formed by a group of agricultural producers who assemble food products from co-op members for sale in local markets. An important goal of these organizations is the promotion of brand names, such as Sun Maid raisins or Sunkist oranges, and increased product quality. The profits from sales are distributed to the members at year's end.

- *Mail-Order Wholesalers.* This type of distributor depends on the sale of products from a catalog. Customers span the range from industrial to retail and institutional. Products are selected from the catalog, and then delivered by mail, truck, or other means of transportation. Their main customers are located in rural or geographically isolated regions.

Brokers and Agents. This category of distributor differs from merchant wholesalers in two important regards: they do not take ownership of inventory and they offer their customers an extremely limited number of services. For the most part their function is to act as middlemen, who for a commission, facilitate the buying and selling of products between suppliers and customers. Similar to merchant wholesalers, they generally specialize by product line or customer types.

- *Brokers.* The primary role of brokers is to serve as middlemen, bringing seller and buyer together and assisting in price, product, and delivery negotiations. Brokers do not take possession of inventories, assume risk, or provide financing. They are usually paid for their services by the party that contracted them.

- *Agents.* There are several types of buyer and seller agents who represent or are contracted to represent either the producer or act in the role of a buyer.

  - *Manufacturer's Agents.* Also termed *manufacturers' representatives*, these independent agents usually represent two or more manufacturers that produce complimentary product lines. Normally, they enter into a formal written agreement with each manufacturer relating to pricing policies, territories, order handling procedures, delivery service and warranties, and commission rates. Most manufacturers' agents are small firms composed of highly skilled sales people who have an extensive knowledge of the products they represent and the best marketplaces in which to sell them. They are often contracted by small manufacturing firms that cannot afford an extensive sales force, or large manufacturers who wish to explore new marketplaces but which as yet do not generate sufficient revenue to support a full-time sales staff. Manufacturers' agents are used to sell such products as furniture, apparel, and electrical goods.

— *Selling Agents.* In contrast to manufacturers' agents, selling agents are contracted by a manufacturer to sell the firm's entire production output. In most cases, the manufacturer does not wish or is incapable of employing a sales staff. Functioning as the de facto marketing and sales function of the company, they have a significant influence over prices, buying terms, and conditions of sale. This type of agent is found in such industries as textiles, industrial machinery and equipment, coal and coke, chemicals, and metals.

— *Purchasing Agents.* This type of agent is normally a product expert who, besides obtaining for the customer the best goods and prices available, can provide consultative services. Purchasing agents generally have a long-term relationship with their customers, often purchasing, receiving, inspecting, warehousing, and shipping the goods to customers based on agreement with company buyers.

— *Commission Merchants.* Often termed *commission houses,* this type of agent takes possession of goods from the producer and then sells them in the marketplace for the best price. After deducting a fee covering the commission and miscellaneous expenses, the balance is then passed back to the producer. They are most often used in agricultural marketing by farmers who do not wish to sell their own produce or who do not belong to a producers' cooperative.

Manufacturers' and Retailers' Branches and Offices. The third major category of distributor consists of manufacturers and retailers who perform the functions of sales and distribution themselves without the assistance of an independent wholesaler. Organizations in this category operate either as wholly owned and operated divisions of a manufacturing or retailing company or as independent businesses belonging to a large, multicompany corporation. Manufacturer channel formats can be described as follows:

- *Factory Direct.* In this format, product is shipped and serviced directly from the manufacturer's warehouse. Company catalogues, the sales force, or agents are responsible for the sale.

- *Sales Branches and Offices.* In this format can be found manufacturers who distribute their own products through simple or complex matrices of sales offices and channel warehouses. *Sales offices* do not carry inventory but are responsible for regional marketing, pricing, promotion, customer order processing, and customer service. In contrast, *channel warehouses* do stock inventory targeted at satisfying local marketplace delivery and services requirements.

- *Manufacturer-Owned Full-Service Wholesale Distributor.* This format describes an acquired wholesale distribution company serving the parent's markets. Typically, these enterprises form the connecting link between a company's manufacturing and distribution operations. When demand warrants, these companies will also distribute the products of other manufacturers. Examples can be found in the clothing and apparel industries.

- *Manufacturer's Outlets.* These stores are actually retail outlets located in high-density markets. Although they are primarily used to liquidate seconds and excess inventory, such as designer clothing and athletic wear, they, nevertheless, provide easy access to branded consumer products.

- *License.* In this format, a manufacturer contracts with an independent distributor or retailer, granting product and marketing function exclusivity for a specific period of time. This distribution method is often used for products in the development stage of their life cycles.

Retailer channel formats can be described as follows:

- *Franchise.* In this format, product, brand recognition, and marketing expertise are sold to small entrepreneurs who in turn execute the functions of product sales and delivery.

- *Buying Clubs.* Although largely consumer oriented, this format provides manufacturers with the opportunity to penetrate certain niche markets or experiment with product variations. Normally, product selection is limited and products are usually sold in bulk quantities.

- *Mail Order/Catalog.* In this format, product is sold through catalog literature. Normally, a central or regional distribution centers are responsible for warehousing and shipping direct to the customer.

- *Food Retailer.* This type of retailer sells a wide range of foodstuffs, health and beauty aids, and general merchandise bought from manufacturers and wholesalers. Warehouses are used as consolidation points to facilitate receiving and inventory deployment.

- *Department Stores and Mass Merchandisers.* These types of national retailers stock a broad mix of soft goods (clothing, food, and linens) and hard goods (appliance and hardware). Distribution centers act as receivers and consolidators, often with a direct link with the manufacturer.

Exporting and Importing Distributors. The fourth major category of distributor consists of companies that specialize in international distribution. The strategy of some multinational organizations is to develop and maintain their own international supply channels, complete with foreign sales offices and warehouses. Others may choose to engage in global trade by using an international distributor. The various types of international distributor are described below.

- *International Trading Company.* This type of international intermediary performs many functions. Among them are the purchasing and selling of goods, arrangement of logistics services between the exporter and the importer, financing currency conversion and rate fluctuations, assisting with consulting advice, and other marketing and logistics issues.

- *Export Merchants.* Export merchants act as a form of international wholesaler. Similar to merchant wholesalers in the domestic marketplace, they purchase goods from domestic manufacturers and wholesalers and then pack and ship them to distribution points in foreign markets. Although some export merchants may have facilities located in foreign countries close to the target market, they mostly deal with foreign distributors in the country of destination.

- *Resident Buyers.* Large international firms will often locate their own buyers directly in an exporting country. Their responsibility is to locate, purchase, and ship goods back to their home country or to company distribution facilities across the globe.

- *Export Commission House.* This type of international intermediary performs the same functions as a *resident buyer*, except that the buyer is not a company employee but rather a contracted agent empowered to negotiate, buy, and ship products located in foreign markets. In return, the agent is paid a commission by the foreign buyer.

- *Allied Manufacturer.* In this type of arrangement, firms will export and import products by using a foreign business partner. Normally, both companies will negotiate to "piggyback" their products through the international channel. There are a number of advantages. By carrying each others products, both firms can improve market share by presenting foreign markets with extended product lines, or achieving high logistics utilization. The end result is that both companies can enjoy the benefits of a mature foreign distribution system without the investment.

- *Export Management Company.* This type of distributor acts as a product line or foreign market specialist, who represents that export for one or a group of noncompeting manufacturers and/or distributors. Although most act as selling agents for the companies they represent, some of the larger firms will stock inventories for resale.

Miscellaneous Distributors. In addition to the categories detailed above, there also exist specialized distributors found in certain sectors of the economy, such as agricultural assemblers, petroleum bulk plants and terminals, and auction companies.

Durable and Nondurable Goods Distributors. Distributors can also be categorized by the type of goods that they sell. There are two classifications of goods: durable and nondurable. *Durable goods* can be defined as products that are designed to last for an extended period of time without rapid deterioration or obsolescence. Examples of products in this group are motor vehicles and automotive parts and supplies, construction materials, professional and commercial equipment and supplies, metals and minerals, electrical goods, hardware, plumbing and heating equipment and supplies, machinery, equipment, and supplies, and miscellaneous goods such as sports equipment, toys and hobbies, jewelry, and scrap and waste materials. In 1997 total sales for this category totaled $2.2 trillion.

Nondurable goods can be defined as products that are consumed or must be consumed quickly or that deteriorate rapidly. Products in this group consist of paper and paper products, apparel and footwear, groceries and processed foods, raw farm products and materials, chemicals and allied products, distilled beverages, and miscellaneous goods such as printed matter, flowers and nursery stock, tobacco, and paints, varnishes, and supplies. Total sales for nondurable goods totaled $1.9 trillion in 1990.

RISE OF NEW FORMS OF e-BUSINESSES [7]

While the forms of wholesale distribution described above are a permanent feature of today's economic landscape, the rise of new and very different types of Internet-driven e-businesses have required their inclusion as a critical type of distributor. Historically, distributors have existed because of their ability to serve as intermediaries, providing retailers with products originating from the manufacturer or direct sales to the end-customer. Their ability to act as aggregators, assembling and selling merchandise assortments in varying quantities originating from a number of manufacturers fills a critical position in the economy. With the advent of e-business, this traditional role has come under attack. In the high-flying days on the dot-com, it was even suggested that the wholesale distributor would eventually disappear as they were "disintermediated" from the supply chain.

The argument was compelling. By combining the advertising and ordering capabilities of the Web, even the smallest of companies could now by-pass costly channel intermediaries and be able to present its products and process orders from anywhere in the world, at any time. In addition to the growth of direct sales, the Internet also provided the opportunity for the birth of a new type of "electronic marketplace" where buyers and sellers were brought together through auction sites, private exchanges, buyer/seller matching, and other functions. The Internet seemingly had provided all companies with the power to continuously reconfigure their supply networks, eliminating costly channel partners, streamlining the flow of information and products, and enabling the creation of radically different types of customer value.

Although this process of supply channel "disintermediation" has been identified as signifying the coming end of the traditional broker, distributor, and freight-forwarder, such prognostications have proven to be premature. While some are doomed, forward-thinking channel intermediaries have been building new competencies by using the Internet to "re-intermediate" themselves at critical points in their supply channels. According to AMR Research, the traditional linear, sequential supply channel will give way to the evolution of real-time, electronically connected networks composed of the traditional players described above, joined by a number of nontraditional intermediaries. In the past, companies used vertically integrated business models to cut costs from the channel system, speed transaction through-put, and connect directly with the customer. In the "Internet Age" savvy entrepreneurs will utilize the Web to transfer non-value-added functions to channel partners while continuing to cut costs and tightening their connection to the marketplace.

In contrast to traditional supply chains where inventory flows down through the channel network node by node, the new Internet-enabled "cyber-mediaries" may never even own or physically inventory the product. Their role in the supply network is to leverage the Internet to perform matching of products and buyers or coordinate marketing and transaction processes among network trading partners. Take for instance the partnership between Amazon.com and Circuit City. The partnership is designed to provide shoppers with the option of buying electronics from the Amazon Web site and then picking them up at one of 600 Circuit City stores or having them sent directly to consumers' homes. Amazon, who will never touch the product, will be able to increase its consumer electronics inventories by several thousand items and will receive a percentage of the sales originating from the Web site.

According to AMR Research [8] at least four new e-SCM business cyber-mediary models are emerging today:

- *Virtual Manufacturers.* This channel component actually does not physically manufacture any products. Its role is to control product development, marketing, and sales as well as coordinate customer service for its products. An example is Sun Microelectronics which outsources the manufacturer of its electronic boards while retaining control of all product designs.

- *Virtual Distributors.* This channel component neither owns any warehouses nor does it physically distribute any products. Its role is to perform marketing and sales functions while coordinating order management by using contract manufacturers, third-party logistics, and fulfillment service providers.

- *Virtual Retailers.* This channel component does not own any "brick-and-mortar" stores, but rather utilizes the Internet to present to customers products displayed in on-line catalogs and other Web mediums. e-Tailers like Barnes and Noble.com and Grainger control the order management process while relying on their own distribution capabilities, or those of partners, to execute order fulfillment.

- *Virtual Service Providers.* This channel component provides channel services without possessing any physical assets. Examples would include *lead logistics providers* (LLPs) that perform contract logistics functions or *logistics exchanges* (LX) which use Internet exchanges to purchase and monitor logistics functions.

As time moves forward, it can be expected that new e-business models will appear. The goal of all such virtual business models is to leverage the Internet to locate and use channel partners to perform non-core functions while linking supply networks closer together by providing for the sharing of real-time information and decoupling the flow of goods and information from traditional supply chain flows.

ROLE OF THE DISTRIBUTION FUNCTION

Whether carried out by the sales and distribution division of a manufacturing company, a mega-retailer, or by an independent merchant wholesaler, there are a number of critical functions performed by the channel distributor. These functions are described below.

Selling and Promoting. This function is extremely important to manufacturers. Whereas retailers develop complex place and promotion strategies to reach the marketplace, manufacturers have only a limited number of locations and have great difficulty in executing sales, promotions, and fulfillment as customers are located geographically further from the home factory. To counter this deficiency, manufacturers can pursue two strategies. In the first, the manufacturer establishes its own marketing and direct sales staff responsible for channel development and logistics and locates finished goods warehouses close to wholesale and retail customers. The advantages of this strategy are direct control over products, pricing, and marketplace identity. Disadvantages include the people, physical plant, and inventory carrying costs associated with the maintenance of these organizations.

The second strategy involves the use of a wholesale distributor to carry out the responsibilities of product deployment. Wholesalers have direct-selling organizations, are often marketing experts in their industry, and have a detailed knowledge of local customers and their expectations. What is more, because of the scale of operations and specialized skill in channel management, most wholesalers can significantly improve *place, time,* and *possession* utilities by housing inventories close to the target market. The advantages of using a wholesaler are enabling the manufacturer to reach many small, distant customers at a relatively low cost, keeping manufacturing expenditures focused on product development and core production processes, and improving finished goods carrying costs. Disadvantages include loss of price and promotion control, disruption in the direct flow of information concerning marketplace needs, and possible gaps in expectations regarding products and services.

Buying and Building Product Assortments. This function is extremely important to retailers. Unless they are a highly specialized business selling products made by only one or a few manufacturers, most retailers prefer to deal with suppliers that can provide as wide an assortment of products that closely fit their merchandizing strategy as is possible. The reason is simple: the more products that can be sourced from a single supplier, the less the cost involved in purchasing, transportation, and merchandizing. Wholesalers are particularly structured to serve this requirement. By purchasing related product families from multiple manufacturers they have the ability to assemble the right combination of products and quantities to meet the requirements of the retailer and deliver it in a cost-effective manner.

Bulk Breaking. Along with building product assortments, this function is one of the fundamental reasons for the existence of distributors. The term refers to the fact that whereas manufacturers normally produce large quantities of a limited number of products, retailers normally require a small quantity of a large number of diverse products. Take, for instance, a candy manufacturer who must produce large lot quantities of product due to cooking and ingredient requirements. The retailer, however, needs only a portion of this lot, thereby forcing the manufacturer to perform bulk breaking and repackaging activities designed to fit marketplace requirements. Often manufacturers will sell bulk lots to wholesalers who will perform bulk break functions. In addition, by combining confectionery-type products from several manufacturers, the wholesaler can also offer a wider assortment to the retailer in the desired quantities than can a single manufacturer. In today's competitive environment, Lean Manufacturing techniques are continuously seeking ways to reduce lot sizes and produce exactly to customer requirements. These techniques have solved some of the problems associated with bulk breaking, especially with goods produced by assembly line and continuous flow production methods. Manufacturers who use such techniques have been able to eliminate channel middlemen by being able to sell just the right quantity of products as demanded by the retailer.

Value-Added Processing. Distributors today are increasingly involved in transforming finished goods derived from the manufacturer into their final form through the processes of sorting, labeling, blending, kitting, packaging, and light final assembly performed at one or various nodes in the supply channel. The economic justification for *value-added processing* rests on the Principle of Postponement. Postponement seeks to minimize the risk of carrying finished forms of inventory by delaying product differentiation to the latest possible moment before customer purchase. Stocking and transportation cost savings are attained by keeping product at the highest level possible in the pipeline and by moving products through the supply channel in large, generic quantities that can be customized into their final form as close as possible to the actual sale. A large apple juice manufacturer, for example, bottles product in nine different unmarked container sizes. This unlabeled product is then shipped to distribution warehouses across the Midwest. As orders from food retailers and wholesalers are received, the appropriate brand and store labels are fixed on the containers. This practice enables the company to carry a great deal less product in the pipeline, shrink warehousing and handling, and significantly reduce end-product obsolescence.

Transportation. The movement of goods from the manufacturing source to the retailer is one of the most critical functions performed by the distributor. The ability to move goods from one node in the supply channel to another is fundamental in assisting companies achieve time and place utilities. Simply, no matter how sophisticated the marketing and warehousing system, if a product is not available at the time and place wanted by the customer, the result will be a lost sale, faltering customer confidence, and possible increased costs resulting from order expediting. Transportation attempts to solve this problem by ensuring that goods are positioned properly in the channel by moving them as quickly, cost-effectively, and consistently as possible from the point of origin to the point of consumption. The marketing strategies of some manufacturers and retailers require that they maintain their own transport fleets, whereas others can effectively use common and contract carriers. Wholesalers also perform a critical role in product movement. Because of their close proximity to the customer, possession of transport fleets, and expertise, many wholesalers can move product to the customer much quicker than distantly located manufacturers.

Warehousing. The function of warehousing is to ensure that the supply channel possesses sufficient stock to satisfy anticipated customer requirements and to act as a buffer, guarding against uncertainties in supply and demand. Warehousing also exists simply because demand for products are often geographically located far from the place where they are produced. Most manufacturers and retailers perform some form of finished goods warehousing in order to assure the even flow of goods in the supply channel. In addition to maintaining their own facilities and channels of distribution, they can also use a wholesaler. Because of their specialized logistics skills and knowledge of local markets, wholesalers can provide products to a wide range of marketplaces that manufacturers, functioning independently, can not possibly penetrate. By serving as middleman, wholesalers provide retailers with access to a spectrum of products and ease of resupply while simultaneously minimizing inventories.

Sequencing. As finished goods move closer to the customer, distributors also perform product sequencing. Sequencing consists of sorting goods into unique configurations necessary to fit the requirements of specific customers. The goal of sequencing is to reduce customer receiving, sorting, and put-away activities by combining a mix of products into single lots or arranging components in the sequence in which they are to be used by the manufacturer during the production process. For example, Continental Freezers of Illinois sequences mixed lots of frozen foods that allow direct delivery to Jewel Foods grocery stores. By creating small lots of frozen food products, handling and storage in the channel on the part of distributors and Jewel can be eliminated, thereby reducing total costs and leveraging the efficiency of direct manufacturer to retailer distribution. Another important form of sequencing is utilized by Lean Manufacturing. The goal is to have components delivered to the production process in the order in which they are to be used. Manufacturing sequencing is typically provided by channel distributors who will combine components acquired from one or multiple suppliers into kits sequenced to match the assembly schedule. Because of the cost and highly customized nature of delivery sequencing, recent trends have been to contract with distributors who specialize in such services.

Merchandizing. In many cases, product coming out of the manufacturer is not ready to be delivered directly to the retailer without additional handling and modification. Some of this value-added service involves bulk breaking manufactured product into smaller lots that can be easily digested through the supply chain. In other instances, product is placed into special packaging or assembled in a display unit determined by marketing and sales campaigns. One of the most visible forms of merchandizing performed by a distributor is the assembly and maintenance of specialized point-of-sale display units found at the check-out counter of every grocery store. Distributors will work close with retailers to ensure the best mix of product and service displays in response to special promotions. Another example is the promotional pack that is assembled by the distributor to meet the needs of a special sale to be given by the retailer or wholesaler. The pack normally consists of a product family or related products. The promotional pack has the advantage of offering the customer a volume discount while enabling the retailer or wholesaler to transact volume quantities and avoid restricted labeling.

Marketing Information. A severe problem encountered by the manufacturer without a strong supply channel is the quality and timeliness of information arising from the customer base relative to product quality and performance. Manufacturers who sell direct to a geographically dispersed end-user marketplace often must rely on the scant information arising from customer complaints and voluntary product assurance cards. In contrast, manufacturers with a robust supply channel can receive information regarding product, marketplace issues, and competitors' activities in a relatively short time.

UNDERSTANDING THE WHOLESALE DISTRIBUTION INDUSTRY

Wholesale distributors serve as one of the three primary facilitators of the supply channel management process. Fundamentally, wholesale distributors differ from manufacturers in that they are not engaged in the process of production, and differ from retailers who are concerned with selling small quantities of goods to the end user from fixed store locations, catalogs, and showrooms. Unfortunately, because distribution is in the middle of these two fairly recognizable industries, many people have rigidly misidentified the *function* of distributing with the industry. Although it is true that all wholesalers are distributors, it is also true, as has been pointed out, that many manufacturers and retailers perform complex distribution functions. In fact, some manufacturers and retailers engage in more elaborate distribution activities and support a more extensive network of warehouses and transportation consolidation points than do large wholesalers. Finally, the maze of enterprises constituting the distributive trades adds to the confusion.

THE NEED FOR WHOLESALE DISTRIBUTION

Distribution channels are formed to solve three critical distribution problems: *functional performance, reduced complexity,* and *specialization* [6]. The problem of increasing the efficiency of time, place, and delivery utilities is the central focus of channel functional performance. When product availability and delivery is immediate, the functions of exchange and delivery can be performed directly by the producer. As the number of producers and the size and geographical dispersion of the customer base grows, however, so does the need for internal and external intermediaries who can facilitate the flow of products, services, and information through the marketing and distribution process. In fact, by streamlining information, marketing, and product flows in a distribution channel, an intermediary can substantially reduce the number of transactions between producers and customers. For example, say that three producers trade directly with five customers. To calculate the number of trading links, the number of producers would be multiplied by the number of customers. As illustrated in Figure 2.2, this would mean that there would be a maximum of fifteen exchange transactions.

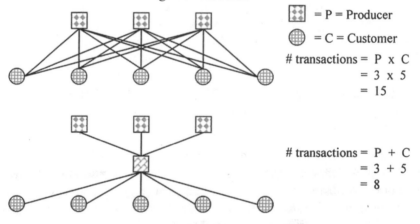

= P = Producer

= C = Customer

transactions = P x C
= 3 x 5
= 15

transactions = P + C
= 3 + 5
= 8

FIGURE 2.2 Role of channel intermediaries.

By positioning a channel intermediary in between producers and customers, the number of transactions in the channel would be dramatically cut. In the illustration, the positioning of an intermediary would reduce the number of possible transactions from fifteen to eight. The role of an intermediary grows in importance in facilitating channel efficiencies as the number of producers and customers expands. If there are just 20 producers and 2000 customers, the number of transactions without an intermediary would be calculated at 40,000. With the presence of a single intermediary, the number of transactions drops to 2020 or over a 95 percent reduction in total channel transactions. Channel efficiencies can be further achieved by the addition of a second tier of intermediaries. Depending on the product and the marketing approach, intermediaries are a key part of the business strategy of many producers. It would be impossible to think of Coca-Cola selling it products directly to the consumer from the bottling plant! Whether a company operated and serviced its own distribution centers or a wholesale distributor performs the channel management tasks, intermediaries reduce the number of transactions and consolidate flows of information and products through the supply network channel.

The creation of distribution arrangements can also decrease overall channel complexity in other areas. Channel intermediaries also assist in the *routinization* of business functions and product *sorting*. Routinization refers to the policies and procedures that provide channel members and new entrants with common goals, channel arrangements, and expectations, and structures channel exchange mechanisms to facilitate transactional efficiencies. Sorting is defined as a group of activities associated with transforming products and product quantities acquired from producers into the assortments and lot sizes demanded by the marketplace. The "sorting" process can be broken down into four primary functions:

1. *Sorting.* The function of physically separating a heterogeneous group of items into homogeneous subgroups. Examples of sorting are grading and then grouping individual items into an inventory lot by quality or eliminating defects from a lot.
2. *Accumulating.* The function of combining homogeneous stocks of products into larger groups of supply. An example is a television distributor who combines the products of different manufacturers into a television product line.
3. *Allocation.* The function of breaking down large lots of products into smaller salable units. Often wholesalers will purchase products in bulk and then break the quantities down into case lots or even down into individual units. A hardware distributor may, for example, purchase fasteners in kegs and then repackage them into a variety of quantities.
4. *Assorting.* The function of mixing similar or functionally related items into assortments to meet customer demand. For example, an automotive distributor may package the components necessary for brake repair into a kit.

Few producers wish to perform the sorting and consolidation functions undertaken by channel intermediaries. In addition, most producers would be extremely reluctant to carry and market similar products produced by competitors alongside their own.

The final reason why distribution channels are formed is to solve the problem of *specialization*. As the supply chain grows more complex, costs and inefficiencies tend to grow in the channel. To overcome this deficiency, many marketing channels contain partners that will specialize in one or more of the elements of distribution, such as exchange or warehousing. The net effect of specialization is to increase the velocity of goods and value-added services through the distribution pipeline by reducing costs associated with selling, transportation, carrying inventory, warehousing, order processing, and credit. Sometimes a dominant channel member, such as the manufacturer, may seek to eliminate a specialist partner by absorbing the function into its own operations. Vertical integration can be beneficial if it seeks to facilitate the flow of product, decrease cycle times, decrease costs, and eliminate redundancies.

One school of thought, on the other hand, feels that not only will companies move away from vertical organization and focus most of their attention on core competencies, but channels will be structured around "virtual" network organizations. According to this model, the distribution channel, supported by the integrative power of the Internet, will be composed of temporary alliances of independent specialists, ranging from suppliers to possible competitors that rapidly coalesce to form an operational unit to satisfy a market need, and then disbands when the need is satisfied. The concept underlying this theory is that the optimization of the core competencies of each partner in the network would provide the best value to both customer and participating channel members. Regardless of the form of the arrangement, the goal is the same: the integration of each of the parties' operations to obtain mutual benefit.

TRANSACTION FUNCTIONS OF THE WHOLESALE DISTRIBUTOR

Perhaps the best way to define a wholesale distributor is to detail the supply channel transaction functions that they perform. To begin with, it is quite true that many manufacturers do market and distribute goods through the supply channel directly to the retailer or end customer. Similarly, some buyers in large retail and industrial firms will bypass the wholesaler altogether and purchase directly from product sources. These *dominant buyers*, so called because of their purchasing power, will purchase from the manufacturer in an effort to achieve quality, lot size, delivery, and price benefits. Wholesalers exist, however, because of certain efficiencies and economies that many manufacturers and retailers either do not or chose not to possess. For the most part, many of these enterprises do not have the financial resources to develop the necessary marketing, sales, and logistics functions to effectively run a distribution channel. The cost of housing inventory, establishing distribution centers, some of which may be thousands of miles away from the manufacturing facility, transportation costs, and heavy capital investment for people and equipment are beyond their reach. Performing such functions would severely dilute their enterprise and product strategies and force them to radically shift their business focus, organization, and the available range of technologies and skills.

Wholesale distributors are used most effectively when performing one or more of the following transaction functions [10]:

- *Logistics Services.* Because of their logistics expertise and channel connections, wholesale distributors have the capacity to store goods in anticipation of customer demand close to the target market. This proximity enables them to respond to the needs of the retail customer much more quickly than can centralized manufacturing facilities.

- *Selling and Promoting.* Wholesale distributors can reach a much larger customer base than most manufacturers. By providing national and localized marketing and sales forces, wholesalers can target specific market segments. Often the wholesaler can leverage their contacts and reputation to sell product that cannot be reached by the distant manufacturer. In addition, because of their knowledge of local and national markets, wholesalers can gain greater market share than the manufacturer by targeted promotion campaigns using special pricing, product offerings, and value-added services such as short delivery cycles, financing, and transportation economies.

- *Ownership.* Merchant wholesalers take possession of and inventory goods. In this sense, they absorb manufacturer and retailer carrying cost. Customers also can reduce their carrying costs by being able to purchase goods in much smaller lots than they could when buying directly from the manufacturer. It would be hard to conceive of the Mars Candy Company selling a single display's worth of *M & M's* to a local retailer.

- *Value-Added Processing.* As detailed above, one of the fundamental functions of a wholesaler is transforming goods as they move through the supply channel through the processes of sorting, bulk breaking, labeling, blending, kitting, packaging, and light assembly. Value-added processing enables the wholesaler to attain economies of scale by purchasing in large, undifferentiated lots which can then be processed into smaller units and product assortments required by the retailer.

- *Risk.* By assuming possession and ownership of goods, wholesalers incur a much greater risk than manufacturers or retailers of financial loss caused by inventory shifts in the marketplace, carrying costs, obsolescence, and spoilage. In addition, many wholesalers will also assume responsibility for product failures, warranties, and price fluctuations. In some cases, they will even guarantee product satisfaction, accepting returns for full credit.

- *Negotiations.* The transfer of ownership of goods from one independent business unit in the channel to another usually involves attaining agreement on price and other sales terms. Negotiation should always be supportive of the overall competitiveness of the distribution system.

- *Ordering Flow.* The actual placement of customer and inventory replenishment orders, as well as information concerning marketing trends, provides critical information for the supply network. This information cascades backward from the end consumer through retailers, distributors, and manufacturers, ending up eventually with the components and raw materials supplier.

- *Payment Flow.* The flow of cash payment proceeds backward through the distribution channel. Often banks and other financial institutions are involved in payment for goods and services.

- *Financing.* Wholesalers must finance the distribution process by purchasing inventories, providing for transportation, managing accounts receivables, and extending credit to their retail customers. When a distributor assumes physical possession of inventory, the distributor is, in effect, financing the manufacturer by exchanging capital for inventory. Often wholesalers will receive assistance in the form of advice and capital from financial institutions, such as commercial banks, brokerage houses, and finance companies.

- *Information Services.* The explosion in information technology and communications has required some manufacturers and retailers to contract with specialist wholesalers who possess the necessary equipment and technical skills. These services exist on several levels. Some wholesalers provide equipment, such as telephones, computers, leased lines, and facsimile machines essential to the maintenance of sales and logistics continuity. In recent years, more complex communications technology and accompanying channel specialists have appeared. Perhaps the most critical has been the growth of *Electronic Data Interchange* (EDI) and Internet Web-services. Many wholesalers offer this service to their channel partners who do not wish or who do not have the technical expertise and equipment.

- *Management Services and Consulting.* In some instances, wholesalers can assist their channel partners to enhance their operations or provide targeted services. Wholesalers can assist retailers by training their point-of-sales staffs, helping with stores and stockroom layout, building and arranging displays, and setting up inventory and accounting systems. Manufacturers can be assisted through staff training, plant layout, equipment usage, and technical services.

- *Marketing Information.* Wholesalers engage in a wide spectrum of sales and marketing activities, such as promotions, customer service, catalog data tracking, and advertising. The information arising from these activities is critical in ensuring that upstream manufacturing plants are making the right products and that the correct inventory in the proper quantities is moving through the supply channel. More sophisticated wholesalers maintain on-line sales, inventory, and purchasing systems that can directly transmit critical marketing information to concerned channel partners.

Channel transaction functions, such as physical possession, ownership, and promotion, are usually characterized as *forward flows*, describing the movement of goods and services from the supplier to the end customer. Inventory, for example, moves "down" through the distribution network until it reaches the consumer. On the other hand, functions such as ordering and payment are *backward flows* from customer to supply source. Finally, marketing information, negotiating, finance, and risk taking move in *both* directions up and down the channel. In addition, negotiation and ordering can be grouped under the term *exchange flows* because they facilitate the buying and selling of goods. Inventory title can alternately be described as a *logistics flow* because the activities of transportation and storage occur with the transfer of the ownership of goods. Finally, financing, risk, and payment flows collectively can be called *facilitating flows* because their performance is necessary to complete financial exchange and logistic transfer [11].

The supply channel should be designed to facilitate and make as efficient as possible each one of these transactional flows. Regardless of the physical structure of the distribution network, each of these functions *must* be performed someplace by one or multiple business units in the distribution network. Channel members can be eliminated or substituted; the above functions, however, cannot be eliminated and must be assumed by remaining business units either upstream or downstream in the distribution pipeline. A manufacturer, for example, may elect to sell direct to the end customer, bypassing the distribution middleman. Such a channel strategy would require the manufacturer to perform a number of forward and backward transactional flows previously provided by channel partners. When a trading partner is eliminated and its function is transferred to one or more channel members due to inefficiencies, redundancies, or cost, it is termed *channel absorption.* Conversely, when functions are transferred to one or more channel members, it is termed *channel functional spin-off.* In the final analysis, the real value of the structure of a particular distribution system is that it provides a form of synergy, permitting individual channel partners to reach objectives they would otherwise be unable to achieve acting individually.

Channel functions can be performed multiples times depending on the number of levels in the distribution system. Marketing channels can be composed of one or multiple levels. Figure 2.3 illustrates several different marketing channels. A *zero-level channel* consists of a manufacturer who sells directly to the end customer from the factory. A manufacturer who sells direct through their own distribution channels also fits within this category. A *one-level channel* consists of one intermediary business unit between the manufacturer and the customer. A *two-level channel* contains two intermediaries, and so on. As the number of levels in the supply channel grow, it becomes more difficult to maintain functional efficiencies and productivity due to lack of timeliness and accuracy of information and the cost incurred to move and store inventory in the pipeline.

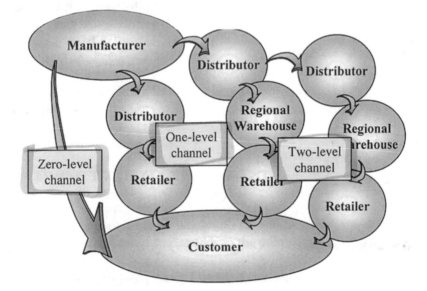

FIGURE 2.3 Types of channel structures.

ELEMENTS OF PHYSICAL DISTRIBUTION FLOW MANAGEMENT

Most enterprises organize the physical flow of goods through the firm into two separate but related phases. The first management cycle is concerned with the flow of products and information *into* the enterprise and is commonly termed *Materials Management.* The second management cycle is concerned with the flow of products and information *out* of the enterprise and is commonly termed *Physical Distribution.* As outlined in Chapter 1, when these two management cycles are combined in a continuous flow, they constitute the *logistics function.* The separation of the two cycles does not imply that they are independent of one other. Functionally, they are interdependent. As customer demand pulls finished goods through the system, physical distribution responds by ensuring that product is at the right node in the distribution structure, and when it is not, triggers a requirement to materials management to either build or purchase more products. The interrelatedness of the two cycles is further accentuated by the similarity of the supply chain functions they perform. Each is concerned with the basic activities of transportation, warehousing, and management. In addition, the system processing activities associated with customer order management are similar to the functions performed in purchasing. A high-level illustration of the relation of these entities can be found in Figure 2.4. A detailed examination of each of these areas is described below.

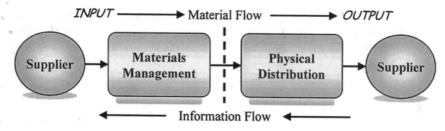

FIGURE 2.4 Supply channel materials flow.

Incoming Materials and Information. This segment of the materials flow cycle encompasses the activities associated with the planning and control of all inbound materials (finished goods, materials, and component parts) into the enterprise. It also extends in many organizations to the management of production inventories for those firms that are manufacturers. The major sub functions involved in incoming materials management are briefly described as follows:

- *Material Planning and Control.* The ability to plan for inventory both in the short- and long-term is absolutely essential to every enterprise. The goals of this function are to effectively translate marketing and sales forecasts into detailed production and finished goods requirements, to project resource requirements associated with capital, manpower, materials, and physical plant, and to perform strategic simulation to validate overall enterprise goals. System tools used by material planners include *Material Requirements Planning* (MRP) for manufacturing inventory planning and statistical inventory replenishment models and *Distribution Requirements Planning* (DRP) for distribution inventory planning. Just-In-Time techniques are applicable to both areas.

- *Purchasing.* Activities associated with the procurement of raw materials, components, finished goods, and MRO inventories is the responsibility of purchasing. The primary functions of purchasing include value analysis, supplier selection, price and delivery negotiation, the generation of purchase orders and the expedition of on-time receipt when necessary, acting as a liaison between the company and the supplier relating to issues of quality, cost, and delivery, and the development of supplier partnerships.

- *Receiving.* The receiving process involves the actual physical receipt of purchased material into the firm. Critical activities occurring in this function are physical shipment verification, receiving inspection of goods, claims, and documentation completion.

- *Warehousing and Storage.* These functions are concerned with the physical management of materials, components, finished goods, and MRO items. Critical activities center on efficiently storing received and inspected materials, issuing and accepting material returns, maintaining the physical accuracy of the inventory, and performing periodic and annual physical inventories.

- *Materials Handling.* This function consists of two activities. The first revolves around analyzing, designing, and improving the processes involved in the efficient physical movement of inventory. The second activity is concerned with the actual physical movement of products to and from storage areas to the points where they will be used.

Outgoing Products and Information. Often termed *distribution,* this function can be defined as the management of the storage and movement of finished goods originating from the supply source, and concluding with delivery to the customer. Often physical distribution activities must also perform transportation functions that link together storage nodes into a distribution network. Objectives of physical distribution can be defined as providing superior customer service, optimizing total distribution costs, minimizing finished goods inventories in the supply channel, minimizing the order processing cycle, and providing cost effective transportation. The major sub-functions of physical distribution consist of the following:

- *Order Processing.* This sub-function is responsible for the timely, accurate, and efficient processing of customer orders into the firm. Order processing can be described as consisting of three interrelated processes: order entry, inventory allocation and picking, and order confirmation and shipping. A critical part of this function is the management of customer service.

- *Warehousing.* The purpose of warehousing is to satisfy the discrepancies that arise between inventory availability and the *time* and *place* requirements of the marketplace. The goal of warehousing is to have inventory available for customer sale at the least possible cost. Although some companies inventory and ship from one warehouse, many organizations have simple to complex channels consisting of various levels of warehouses. *Storage warehouses* are used to house unsold or promotion goods for medium to long periods of time. *Distribution warehouses*, on the other hand, receive products from upstream outside and inside suppliers for the purpose of immediate or short-term sales.

- *Finished Goods Management.* The control of finished goods inventories covers a wide spectrum of activities ranging from managing stocking levels and order picking, to interbranch warehouse transfer and customer order shipment. Perhaps the most critical task involves determining the proper amount of stock to carry in the supply channel to satisfy customer requirements without stockout while minimizing the inventory carrying cost. Optimizing inventories is the responsibility of the firm's inventory planners who can utilize computerized statistical or time-phased methods for item review and ordering.

- *Materials Handling and Packaging.* This function consists of such activities as containerization, vehicle loading, hazardous product handling, and packaging.

- *Shipping.* Although the former is concerned with the management of *incoming orders* and the latter with *outgoing orders*, receiving and shipping have many similarities. Both work with docks and carriers; both utilize the same material handling equipment and often the same personnel; and sometimes both are organized into a single department. The main functions of shipping consist of customer order packing, vehicle loading, order confirmation, and shipment documentation.

- *Transportation.* For many distributors, transportation is one of the most costly parts of the business, sometimes accounting for over 50 percent or more of the cost of goods. Distributors have the option of using five methods of transport: motor carrier, railroads, pipelines, water, and aircraft. The goals of transportation are to provide for the continuous flow of product through the supply channel, optimize vehicle capacities and loading equipment during shipment, provide speedy and timely delivery, and minimize shipment damage and theft.

WHOLESALE DISTRIBUTION INDUSTRY CHALLENGES

The maturing of the U.S. economy, the growing power of alternative forms of distribution, and the expansion of manufacturers and retailers into distribution have created formidable challenges for today's wholesale distributors. Like other sectors of the U.S. economy, wholesalers can expect continued mergers and consolidations, growing demand on the part of channel partners for more complex value-added services at lower prices, shrinking margins, and declining profitability. The most critical issues facing wholesale distributors at mid-point in the first decade of the twenty-first century can be summarized as follows:

- The growing movement for channel disintermediation in order to squeeze every unnecessary cost out of the supply chain can only be expected to intensify. To survive and flourish in this environment wholesale distributors will have to continuously pursue new forms of organization and new types of business if they are to remain competitive. These changes will take the form of consolidation, organizational re-engineering, increased use of information technology, and closer ties with supply channel partners.

- Both manufacturers and retailers will continue to narrow the number of channel partners with whom they do business. Requirements for optimized operational functions, such as quality, delivery and price, as well as increased collaboration among channel partners, spanning everything from product development to information connectivity, will push channel strategists to continually shrink the number of suppliers they deal with.

- Although wholesalers as an industry have improved productivity and the variety of available services, greater leaps of productivity through a more aggressive application of technology tools have become imperative.

- Although the implementation of Lean/JIT and Quick Response has been gaining ground with wholesalers, they still lag behind considerably in these areas as compared to manufacturers and retailers.

- Many wholesalers have not taken the growing power of alternate channel formats seriously, such as warehouse clubs, co-ops, mass merchants, and telemarketing. Often, these new forms of competition are viewed by wholesalers as businesses targeted at narrow market niches. To counter this form of competition, wholesalers' sales mix is expected to change to emphasize more direct mail/catalog, Internet sales, retail sales, as well as increased valued-added processing.

- There is significant excess capacity in the industry. This means that underperformers face a bleak future as compared to their more streamlined and focused competitors. Mergers and acquisitions in the industry can be expected to continue focused not on diversification but rather on how to better penetrate existing markets, eliminate weak competitors, and gain market share.
- Gross margins can no longer be improved by increasing prices for products and value-added services. Prices and margins have been and will continue to be squeezed by the maturing of the economy and competitive pressures.
- Many wholesale distributors have been unwilling to risk or unable to attract the capital investment necessary to retool their information systems, human resources, physical plants, and marketing strategies to tackle these and other issues.

The ability of wholesalers to respond to these challenges is clearly related to their ability to identify and willingness to aggressively seize on the internal and external factors affecting growth in the industry. The development of new value-added services and implementation of technology connectivity enablers followed by quality and productivity improvements and increased product diversification are the factors that will provide the most growth. How these factors will improve competitive positioning is to be seen in the range of possible strategies to be pursued by wholesalers. Perhaps the most critical is using competitive factors, like the Internet, to retain and better penetrate their current customer base. Secondary strategies focus on expanding geographically and decreasing reliance on product/commodity line diversification. This shift from being product oriented to customer oriented is an acknowledgment that the costs involved in gaining new and losing existing customers to competitors is prohibitive. Another key strategy targeted at increased customer base penetration is the addition of new value-added services or improving those basic services the firm already offers. As detailed in Table 2.1, the sum total of these service criteria are to reduce or eliminate costs and channel redundancies and poor quality while enabling distributors to capitalize on marketplace opportunities by possessing recognizably superior products and services.

SUMMARY

As the pace of global competition and demands for flawlessly executed customer service accelerate at the opening of the twenty-first century, the requirements for effective and efficient distribution functions can be expected to grow accordingly. Far from being associated with a narrow segment of in-

TABLE 2.1 **Wholesale Distribution Strategies**

Strategy Objective	Impact on Supply Chain	Examples
Lower cost for value received	Reduced product/service cost	Utilization of Internet sales; growth of warehouse/ wholesale clubs; power buying; manufacturer direct and other channel formats targeted at cost reduction
Improved efficiency	Reduced channel investment	Focus on collaborative relations; Lean/JIT and Quick Response
Improved quality	Reduced cost of errors	Implementation of Total Quality management programs
Channel simplification	Reduced redundant channel functions	Growth in contracted services
Improved information	Increased channel connectivity and collaboration	Implementation of Internet-enabled system connectivity; integration of internal business functions; co-op advertising and marketing programs
Improved value-added services	Increased ease of customer management	Customer empowerment to design products and services; engaging in value-creating relationships; agile and scalable functions; fast flow delivery; focus on e-commerce enablers

dustry, the dynamic nature of today's supply channel requires expanding the definition of what constitutes a distributor by describing it broadly as any organization that sells finished goods to retailers or industrial, institutional, and commercial users but that do not sell in significant amounts to the end consumer. Such an interpretation would apply to wholesalers, all manufacturers (except those who sell factory direct), internal supply chain replenishment management, mail-order distributors, Internet e-marketplaces, and mega-retailers that possess distribution channels

The essence of what constitutes a distributor is perhaps best detailed by abstracting the essential characteristics of distribution. Essentially, three fundamental characteristics are apparent: how products are acquired; how products are moved through the supply channel to the customer; and, finally, how products are transacted. The content of these characteristics make it fairly easy to divide distributors from the other two components in the supply chain

– manufacturers and retailers. From this analysis, five types of distributor emerge: merchant wholesalers, brokers and agents, manufacturers' and retailers' branches and offices, exporting and importing distributors, and miscellaneous wholesalers. In addition, a whole new class of Internet-enabled "cybermediary" has begun to emerge over the last half decade capable of utilizing the Web to generate new forms of business and radically different approaches to managing the supply chain.

Whether carried out by the sales and distribution division of a manufacturing company, a mega-retailer, or by an independent merchant wholesaler, there are a number of critical functions performed by the channel distributor. To begin with, distributors solve three critical supply channel problems: *functional performance, reduced complexity,* and *specialization.* The goal of distribution is to increase the efficiency of time, place, and delivery utilities by acting as intermediaries focused on facilitating and rationalizing the flow of products, services, and information through the marketing and distribution process. In addition, distribution functions facilitate the performance of *forward flows* (physical possession, ownership, and promotion), *backward flows* (marketing information, negotiating, and risk taking), *exchange flows* (buying and selling), *logistics flows* (transportation and storage), and *facilitating flows* (financing and payment).

The tremendous changes brought about by the maturing of today's industrial economies, the growth of alternative forms of distribution, and the expansion of manufacturers and retailers into areas once the preserve of the independent wholesaler have created a new set of formidable challenges to the wholesale distribution industry. Several critical issues come to mind. Increased "disintermediation" of the supply channel, continued industry consolidation, growth of collaborative supply chain strategies, and narrowing of the base of channel partners have forced many distributors to search for ways to leverage technology and new management styles to cut channel cycle times and costs, respond to warehouse clubs, mass merchants, and Internet sales formats, and enable improvements to both fixed and human resources to remain competitive

QUESTIONS FOR REVIEW

1. What are the components of the supply channel and how do they differ from one another?
2. Why is defining the term "distributor" and the distribution industry so difficult?
3. Why would manufacturers and retailers use a wholesaler?
4. Why has the wholesale industry declined during the past 15 years?
5. How can wholesale distributors "re-intermediate" themselves into today's supply chain?
6. Material movement can be essentially divided into two fundamental flow processes. Discuss.
7. Physical distribution has a special relationship to sales and marketing. Why is this relationship so special?

REFERENCES

1. *The APICS Dictionary*, 9th ed. Falls Church, VA: American Production and Inventory Control Society, 1998, p. 27.
2. Bowersox, Donald J. and Cooper, M. Bixby, *Strategic Marketing Channel Management*. New York: McGraw-Hill, 1993, p. 4.
3. Bowersox, Donald J., Daugherty, Patricia J., Droge, Cornelia L., Rogers, Dale S., and Wardlow, Daniel L., *Leading Edge Logistics: Competitive Positioning for the 1990s*. Oak Brook, IL: Council of Logistics Management, 1989, pp. 34-35.
4. Ibid, p. 41.
5. Ibid, pp. 83-84.
6. These classifications have been attained from *The Standard Industry And Classification Manual*. Springfield, VA: National Technical Information Service, 1987, pp. 287-314; Kotler, Philip, *Marketing Management*, 6th ed. Englewood Cliffs, NJ: Prentice Hall, 1988, pp. 571-573; and Bowersox and Cooper, *Strategic Marketing Channel Management*, pp. 40-44.
7. This section has been abstracted from Ross, David F., *Introduction to e-Supply Chain Management: Engaging Technology to Build Market-Winning Business Partnerships*. (Boca Raton, FL: St. Lucie Press, 2003), pp. 62-65.
8. Lapide, Larry, "The Innovators Will Control the e-Supply Chain," in *Achieving Supply Chain Excellence Through Technology*, 3, Anderson, David L., ed., Montgomery Research, San Francisco, 2001, 186.
9. Bowersox and Cooper, *Strategic Marketing Channel Management*, pp. 14-22 and Stern, Louis W. and El-Ansary, Adel, *Marketing Channels*, 3rd ed., Englewood Cliffs, NJ: Prentice-Hall, 1988, pp. 3-10.
10. For further discussion on these points see Kotler, p. 570 and Bowersox and Cooper, *Strategic Marketing Channel Management*, pp. 74-79.
11. These elements are further discussed Bowersox and Cooper, *Strategic Marketing Channel Management*, pp. 15-16.

UNIT 2

TOP MANAGEMENT PLANNING

CHAPTERS:

Unit 1 focused on defining the terms and organizational structures, as well as the challenges and opportunities, constituting SCM and modern logistics. Of primary importance was examining the ways today's global business, marketing, and customer requirements have reshaped traditional perceptions of the function of supply channel management. In the 2000s, distributors can no longer treat distribution as performing a purely operational function: channel management must be viewed as a strategic function that provides individual enterprises and associated trading partners with distinct competitive advantage. As was discussed, fundamental to the activation of new paradigms is the utilization of SCM and Internet technologies. The convergence of these two critical enablers was defined as the networking of the collective productive capacities and resources of cross-channel systems through the application of Web-based technologies in the search for innovative solutions and the synchronization of channel capabilities dedicated to the creation of unique individualized sources of customer value. e-SCM provides today's supply chain with the tools to reshape individual organizations and supply channels flows in the search for global marketplace leadership.

With the basics of modern e-SCM defined, Unit 2 begins the discussion of enterprise planning and control by examining the first step in the planning flow: *top management planning.* Top management planning is concerned with the formulation of the overall goals and strategic objectives of the firm. Top management planning identifies the long-range financial, marketing, sales, and aggregate supply channel requirements necessary to satisfy these corporate objectives. The goal is to ensure that the enterprise possess the capacities and capabilities to achieve the marketplace position and financial targets specified in the business plan. The formulation of effective top management plans will, in turn, drive the operations plans of each business department.

Unit 2 opens with a review of the business planning process. Chapter 3 begins with a description of the contents of the business plan. Of primary importance is the formulation of effective enterprise goals and their translation into the operating strategies that will guide the firm's business functions. Planning on this level consists of four essential activities: goal and mission statement definition, creation of the business forecast, development of current and long-term asset plans, and plan disaggregation. The success of the business plan consists in the ability of top management to develop flexible organizations to meet the needs of an ever-changing marketplace, the implementation of information, communications, and automation technologies designed to network the entire supply chain, and leveraging strategic alliances with channel partners and outside service providers that facilitate operational flexibility and reduce channel costs.

Chapter 4 examines the role of forecasting in the business planning process. Perhaps no other activity has as much immediate and long-range effect on enterprise operations as forecasting. Effective forecasts are required on all business planning levels. Long-range forecasts assist top management analyze the impact of strategic goals on the resource capacities and marketplace position of the firm. Forecasts assist departmental managers match business plan requirements with medium-range functional area capacities. Finally, short-range forecasts assist operations managers and supervisors plan for weekly and everyday requirements. Good forecasting assists companies by eliminating waste in the form of excess inventory, by reducing shortages, missed due dates, lost sales, and expensive expediting, and by providing visibility to control capacity requirements such as plant size, labor, equipment, and transportation.

Unit 2 concludes with a detailed discussion of the demand, operations, and channel planning processes. *Demand planning* determines the sales potential of the marketplace and the products, services, and channel structures required to satisfy the revenue objectives identified in the business plan. *Production planning* determines the finished goods targets, production rates, manufacturing capacities, and performance metrics necessary to ensure that manufacturing functions are responding in a cost effective manner to customer requirements. *Logistics planning* determines the channel inventory plan, availability of aggregate inventory, transportation, warehouse, and labor and equipment resources, the components of the value-added processing plan, and the shipment plan. Finally, the *Supply channel plan* identifies the overall supply channel business mission, the design of the channel, the channel operations plan, and all global channel infrastructure and operations requirements. Each of the three chapters in Unit 2 attempts to provide companies with the essential keys to solving the challenges posed by expanding products and services, intensified competition, requirements for purposeful communications with manufacturers and retailers in the supply channel, and the pace of changing marketplace needs characteristic of business in the twenty-first century.

3

BUSINESS AND
STRATEGIC PLANNING

During the quarter century after the conclusion of the Second World War, U.S. manufacturers and distributors could achieve marketplace, profitability, and performance objectives without serious attention to the strategic planning needs of their individual enterprises or the supply chains in which they participated. The decade of the 1970s, however, brought a series of upheavals fueled by spiraling energy costs, economic inflation and uncertainty, and expanding overseas competition that required companies to move beyond their largely single-minded focus on operations planning and control. No longer could U.S. industry take market dominance for granted. The result was a growing interest in preparing the enterprise for change through a planning process that not only focused on business strategic elements, such as corporate objectives and resources, but also could guide the organization through the shoals of shrinking margins, the synchronization of world economies, increasing labor and materials costs, and the struggle for competitive advantage that characterized the decades that followed. Instead of stagnant, hierarchical, vertical organizations managing massive physical plant and productive assets, the paradigm rapidly shifted to highly agile, flexible organizations, dependent on information technologies and collaborative supply chain relationships centered on continuous cost reduction and optimization of core and channel resources. Today, the rapidly expanding global economy is requiring companies to acknowledge an entirely new set of dynamics based on geopolitical change, the ability of communications technologies to access labor pools from any place on earth, and new concepts of product development, quality, and channels of distribution.

Chapter 3 is concerned with detailing the business and strategic planning processes necessary to harness the forces of change confronting today's distribution industry. The chapter begins with a description of the nature of business planning and strategic plan development. Following this section, attention is given to the elements of the strategic planning process: strategy formulation, developing the business forecast, creating the asset plan, and business unit budget disaggregation. An examination of metrics necessary to monitor an effective business plan follows. Among the performance measurements detailed are the income statement and balance sheet; investment, profit, asset, and capital planning; and supply chain *key performance indicators* (KPIs) that utilize computerized toolsets to gather, analyze, and disseminate supply chain performance.

DEFINING BUSINESS GOALS AND STRATEGIES

The goal of all business enterprises resides in providing products and value-added services that do not merely permit them to compete but that continually win the customer's order. Whether it is a manufacturer of toasters or a travel agency, successful companies develop winning strategies and execute finely-tuned operations plans that assure the customer that the product or service received possesses outstanding and unique value. This dynamic is graphically portrayed in Figure 3.1. As can be seen, firms must approach the marketplace on many levels. The needs and expectations of the customer must be known. The marketing function must identify the proper mix of products and services and what is the composition of the marketplace. Finally, the firm's operational functions (sales and order processing, logistics, manufacturing, and finance) must be poised to satisfy the customer at a level that not just meets, but far exceeds the competition. Enterprises that aspire to marketplace leadership must begin by developing focused business goals and targeted strategies that provide a single consistent and coherent direction guiding and coordinating the company's operational activities. These two elements of top management planning provide the firm with identity and define the objectives and values by which the company will compete.

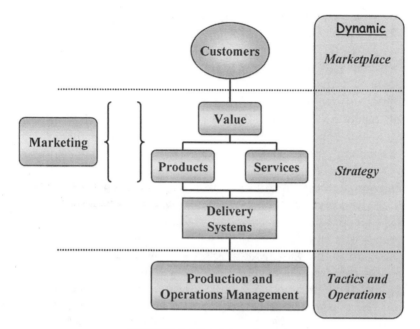

FIGURE 3.1 Marketplace dynamics.

UNDERSTANDING ENTERPRISE GOALS

The business planning process begins with the formulation and articulation of the matrix of values, beliefs, and cultural attitudes that define the internal and external direction of the enterprise. The development and implementation of these organizational *goals* takes place over long periods of time, requires the acceptance of all functions within the company, and are difficult to change once in place. Hayes and Wheelwright [1] term these vague but powerful attitudes and values an enterprise's *business philosophy,* and define it as "the set of guiding principles, driving forces, and ingrained attitudes that help communicate goals, plans, and policies to all employees and that are reinforced through conscious and subconscious behavior at all levels of the organization." An enterprise's business philosophy provides the framework for purposeful action and the grounds upon which competitive, marketplace, governmental, and environmental norms are developed.

An enterprise's business philosophy usually consists of multiple goals. Some are obvious financial goals such as profitability, corporate growth targets, and return on investment. Others focus on providing quality of work life, service commitment, the furthering of community and societal object-tives, the minimization of risks to promote orderly growth, and so on. Such slogans as SAP's "The best-run businesses run SAP" and UPS's "What can brown do for you?" are targeted at communicating basic enterprise values and product and service commitments to the marketplace. Corporate goals serve a multitude of purposes. They help focus corporate, business unit, and functional business area strategies on a common game plan. They provide the basis for operational decisions and establish the boundaries of strategic options available. Finally, corporate goals assist managers in making trade-off decisions among performance measures such as cost, inventory investment, delivery, serviceability, and between short-term and long-term strategies [2].

Business goals are defined by five interwoven elements that give the firm its distinct character. The first element is the company's *history*. Every company has a record of past achievements, traditions, and policies that provide it with a sense of continuity and identity. In redefining business goals, strategists must ensure that new directions sought for the enterprise are a logical extension of the past and supportive of long agreed upon objectives. The second element arises from the *current preferences* of the owners/executives charged with managing the business. A critical role of the firm's leadership is formulating the vision of the business and the direction it would like the company to move. Third, *environmental* and *social factors* can have a dramatic affect on the business. For example, stricter air pollution laws have had an enormous impact on the automotive and petroleum industries. The availability of the enterprise's *financial* and *physical resources* forms the fourth element determining goal definition. A small pharmacy chain, for example, could not hope to compete head to head with Walgreen's or Wal-Mart in terms of price and product availability. Finally, companies structure their approach to the marketplace based on their *distinctive competence*. Maytag uses its strong reputation with washing machines to spearhead their marketing campaigns in the home appliance market [3].

Drafting business goals is an interactive, iterative exercise, culminating in the formulation of concise *mission statements* that are to guide the firm for years and maybe decades to come. These mission statements consist of the vision and direction top management wishes the firm to take, the policies to be followed by the organization relating to customers, products, services, and business partners, the structure of the distribution channel, and the sense of community of purpose and enthusiasm guiding everyone in the organization in their endeavors to realize personal and, by extension, company goals.

FORMULATING ENTERPRISE STRATEGIES

Strategic planning can be described as the process of establishing the courses of action an enterprise must follow if overall corporate goals are to be achieved. Strategies differ from goals in several important ways. To begin with, goals are defined as broad, long-term statements of what the enterprise would like to achieve. Strategies, on the other hand, are more specific directives regarding a defined set of particular actions to be completed necessary to accomplish detailed *objectives*. The firm's top management uses strategies to assist in the realization of its goals. Strategies attempt to answer questions ranging from asking: "What business should the company be in?" to issues revolving around the definition of products and growth targets of the firm for a specified time frame. Collectively, strategies encompass the general plans directing the enterprise, and as such will remain in effect for long periods of time.

In his book on the nature of management control, Anthony [4] feels that companies develop strategies in response to *threats* or to capitalize on *opportunities*. Threats for the most part arise from attacks by competitors on market position. Other examples of threats are product and/or process innovation, information technologies, governmental policies, economic swings, and changes in the public's buying habits. Opportunities, on the other hand, can be found in the enabling capabilities of a new technology, evolution in the wants and needs of the customer, and even improvements in the functioning of the firm's organization. Effectively managing threats and opportunities requires executive planners to respond by developing strategies that will seek to dampen the impact of adverse conditions while leveraging company strengths to take advantage of favorable circumstances.

The strategic planning process is an iterative task that involves the identification of threats and opportunities, problem solving to arrive at the best possible courses of action, evaluation of the consequences of possible solutions, and selection of the direction the firm will take. Kotler defines strategic planning as

> the managerial process of developing and maintaining a viable fit between an organization's *objectives* and *resources*, and its changing *market opportunities*. The aim of strategic planning is to shape and reshape the company's businesses and products so that they continue to produce satisfactory profits and growth [5].

Much in the fashion of a mechanical gear train, strategic planning provides motion or objectives to the major business functions of the organization. These gears, in turn, drive additional departmental gears, which in turn, drive operational execution activities. The focus of the whole process is to answer the central challenge facing the enterprise: how to improve profitability by increasing productivity and optimizing the application of resources to capitalize on the "best" marketplace opportunities.

As illustrated in Figure 3.2, the development of business strategies has four

FIGURE 3.2 Enterprise strategies.

boundaries: *enterprise goals, opportunities, constraints,* and *risks and uncertainties.* In effectively weighing the impact of each of these factors on business strategies, corporate planners need to view the business on three levels as exhibited in Figure 3.3. The first level can be termed *corporate strategy.* Depending on the nature of the business, planning at this level will focuses on five critical strategies as detailed in Table 3.1. Business planning begins with concise definitions of the competitive positioning, profit, ROI, and growth strategies that are to govern enterprise direction. These goals in turn must be supported by product mix and volume, services, channel distribution, and technology enabler strategies that will describe the market potential and products that will mature the revenue plan. The competitive values chosen by the firm will determine how orders are to be won in the marketplace, and will in turn influence process and channel structure choices. For example, if a com-

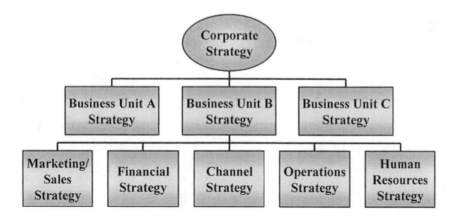

FIGURE 3.3 Three levels of business planning.

pany chooses to compete by offering a commodity-type product centered on minimal product variation, then low price, processes supporting agile make-to-stock, low cost, and Lean/JIT will be the optimal choices. In addition, strategists would select complex channels of distribution, a heavy dependence on channel partners, minimal product postponement, high levels of spatial convenience, and intensive distribution.

TABLE 3.1 Strategic framework.

Corporate Strategy	Marketing Strategy	Competitive Values	Channel Strategy	
			Process Issues	Channel Structure
Competitive differentiation	Marketing plan	Price	Make-to-Stock	Single channel
Profit plan	Product life cycle	Quality	Assemble-to-Order	Complex channel
Asset plan	Product range, mix, volume	Delivery	Make-to-Order	Postponement strategy
Earnings plan	Channel distribution	Image	Outsourcing intensity	Value-added processing strategy
Capital budgets	Service goals	Flexibility	Collaborative intensity	Intensity of channel dependence
	Customization/ configurability	Product Design	Capacity management	Basic service outputs definition
	Use of technology enablers	Service	Lean/JIT/Agility	Level of market exposure
			Cost improvement	Globalization
			Globalization	

The second level of strategic planning is focused on the strategic business units that make up the enterprise. Strategic business units can take a variety of forms and may be described as subsidiaries, divisions, distribution centers, warehouses, or even product lines. Business unit strategies can be viewed from two perspectives. Strategists must first of all ascertain the extent to which each business unit possesses the ability to succeed in the marketplace. Planners must measure the product, market, and channel strength of each business unit and ensure that the strategies formulated are in support of the objectives of the corporation as a whole. Factors associated with business unit strategy development are overall market size, annual growth rate, historical profit margins, technology requirements, competitive intensity, energy requirements, and environmental impact.

Of equal importance in developing effective business unit strategies is understanding the basis by which a competitive advantage will be achieved and maintained. Porter [6] states that competitive advantage can be expressed as three generic types. These types he defines as:

- *Cost Leadership.* In this strategy, the firm seeks to offer goods and services at the lowest cost in the industry. The source of cost advantage may focus on economies of scale, proprietary technology, transportation, geography, and other factors. Wal-Mart, Best Buy, and Home Depot are examples of companies who pursue this strategy.

- *Differentiation.* In this strategy, the firm seeks to offer some product or service that is unique in the industry and is widely valued by the marketplace. Differentiation can be based on products, the delivery systems by which the product is transacted, marketing approach, and other factors. Lexus and Volvo separate themselves from other automobiles by offering superior quality, service, and safety.

- *Focus.* In this strategy, the enterprise focuses on a particular cost or product differentiation advantage in one or a selected number of target market segments. Gucci and St. John's Knits seek to penetrate the specialty clothing market by marketing high-quality goods and services that discount stores do not offer.

Some of the factors associated with understanding business unit competitiveness are market and product growth, product quality, brand reputation, the distribution pipeline, promotional effectiveness, logistics efficiencies, costing, inventory position, and managerial personnel. In this area, business strategies fostering growth are the most important. Growth can take the form of increasing market share through market penetration, market development, and product positioning. Growth can also take place through the acquisition of suppliers at one end of the distribution pipeline, the creation of additional distribution points or the purchase of wholesalers or retailers downstream in the pipeline, or the acquisition of competitors. Finally, a business unit strategy might target growth through diversifying into new products or even new industries.

The final level of strategic planning is concerned with the development of *functional business area strategies.* Once business unit strategies have been formulated, operational and budgetary objectives need to be established that will drive the functional business areas within each business unit. As illustrated in Figure 3.3, functional areas found in most companies, such as marketing, sales, finance, and logistics, must each have operational strategies supporting the overall business unit strategy. For example, decisions concerning the location, size, staffing, inventory capacities, and costs of the distribution network must promote competitive advantages specified in the business unit strategy. Effective strategic planning occurs when the objectives of each strategic planning level are executed in alignment with and in support of one another. Strategic planning is an iterative process in which performance measurements link each level together and assure that overall enterprise goals are being accomplished.

The objective of functional business area strategies is to ensure that the capacities and capabilities of the organization are consistent with the competitive advantages being sought. In translating the business plan, strategists must match business unit objectives with those activities associated with the physical acquisition or production of goods, warehousing, sales, and delivery to the customer as well as after-sales service. Porter [7] identifies five generic categories involved in planning the functional business area environment:

- *Inbound Logistics.* This category is associated with the acquisition and storage of materials and components. External activities in this category are associated with supplier negotiations, order management, supplier scheduling, and delivery. Internal activities are comprised of receiving, quality, material handling, warehousing, inventory control, vehicle scheduling, and supplier returns.
- *Operations.* This category is associated with value-added processing. Activities performed by distributors in this category consist of bulk breaking, kitting, labeling, packaging, light assembly, and facilities operations.
- *Outbound Logistics.* This category is associated with the distribution of goods. External activities in this category focus on wholesale and retail channels, and transportation. Internal activities are concerned with finished goods warehousing, material handling, replenishment planning, delivery vehicle operations, and scheduling.

- *Marketing and Sales.* This category is associated with product sales. Activities include advertising, promotion, sales force management, order management, distribution channel selection, and pricing.
- *Service.* This category is associated with pre-sales and post-sale services. Activities in this category focus on product enhancement or maintenance including installation, repair, training, warranty, and service parts.

Although programs associated with inbound and outbound logistics are of paramount importance, each category described above is critical in executing the business plan. The functional business area planning process must weigh the costs incurred in each category against the expected operational objectives. Selecting and measuring the generic distribution categories necessary to execute the business plan must be accomplished by matching the proposed overall distribution system benefits with the projected logistics cost. The goal is to pursue programs that seek to minimize cost in each category while optimizing existing capacities and resources.

THE STRATEGIC PLANNING PROCESS

The creation of a comprehensive business plan is the responsibility of the firm's president, board of directors, and senior management staff. In a divisional environment, the general managers and their staffs are also included. The goal of the planning process is the drafting of the broad strategic objectives that will serve to drive the corporate mission as well as determine the policies that will be communicated to the firm's business units as they derive their individual operational strategies. The resulting plans should link the enterprise together through commonly determined sales, inventory, profit, and return on investment targets. The resulting enterprise business plan should clearly establish the competitive posture of each node in the channel structure and provide the mechanism for overall performance measurement.

In developing effective business plans and strategies, the top management team must determine answers to such questions as the following:

- What are the long-range goals of the business?
- How best should the enterprise manage its fixed and current assets?
- What return on investment is expected in order to meet profit targets and shareholder expectations?
- What is the climate of the business economy?
- What is the scope of the enterprise's competitive drivers today, and what should they be in the future?
- What markets should the enterprise target, with what products and services?

- What are the organization's competitive strengths and weaknesses?
- What changes will be required to gain and maintain market competitiveness today and in the future?
- How should external and internal changes be measured to ensure that corporate goals are being attained?

In answering these and other questions, corporate planners must seek to align company goals, strategies, and ambitions with economic and market-place realities. To stay competitive, the enterprise must be constantly reposi-tioned to exploit marketplace changes and competitive advantages and to identify shifts in economic conditions, products, and services, customer wants and needs, technology enablers, and laws and government regulations. As is illustrated in Figure 3.4, the business planning process begins with the defini-

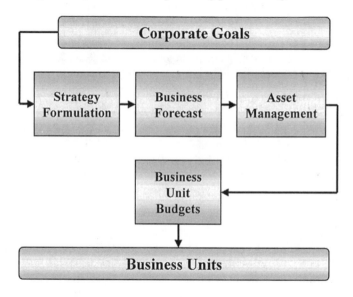

FIGURE 3.4 Business planning process.

tion of enterprise goals. As described earlier, *goals* are broad, long-range ob-jectives and attitudes that guide the efforts of the organization as a whole as well as the individual actions of all of its employees. Defining business goals is an interactive process whereby the management team of the enterprise peri-odically raises fundamental questions concerning the well-being of the enter-prise and redirects the operating strategies of the firm necessary to meet the challenges that emerge. In addition, business goals will define the boundaries and set the parameters against which actual results can be measured, the con-sistency of the plan validated, and necessary changes to the plan executed.

Overall, this step can be described as an attempt to pursue a balance, as illustrated in Figure 3.5, between the corporate objectives focused on growth, profitability, and return on investment and the strategies built on the enterprise's markets, products, and resources.

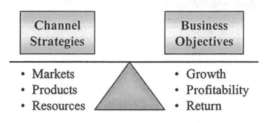

FIGURE 3.5 Business strategy formulation.

The second step in the business planning process is the creation of the business forecast. The business forecast seeks to detail expected enterprise financial growth, return on investment, and total projected net income for a specific time period, usually no less than one year and often for several years into the future. In developing this portion of the business plan, corporate planners must balance expected aggregate revenues arising from sales and other sources with incurred costs and other liabilities, and weigh the impact the revenue plan will have on company resources and stockholder investment. In addition, business planners must review qualitative factors, such as economic, political, social, environmental, technical, and competitive forces in drafting the corporate forecast. This portion of the business plan takes the form of a detailed statement of sales volumes, cost of goods sold, margins, selling and operating expenses, and taxes. Once these estimates have been defined, they will be passed over to the marketing, sales, production, and channel operations functions, who will then translate them into market segment, product and services, and sales and distribution channel strategies.

The third step in the business planning process focuses on the current and long-term assets necessary to support the revenue plans detailed in the business forecast. A typical company's assets can be divided into two general categories: *current assets,* normally described as available cash, open accounts receivable, and merchandise inventory, and *fixed* or *capital assets,* normally consisting of land, buildings, equipment, investment, and other tangible and intangible resources. During this portion of the business planning process, mangers must ascertain whether the enterprise possesses resources sufficient to realize the revenue objectives and, if not, what must be done to acquire those capacities that are currently not available.

The final step in the business planning process is the disaggregation of the profit and liabilities plans down to the enterprise's business units in the form of the operating budget. These business units can take many forms. For example, each business unit could be a separate financial and operating entity possessing its own management, products, customers, competitors, business plans, and performance measurements. On the other hand, the business might consist of a channel of business entities having common products and competitors but which are semi-independent, with different customers, business objectives, and performance measurements. Regardless of business unit role, the goal of the corporate business plan is to ensure that the firm's object-tives can be realized by the existing business units found in the distribution channel structure. In doing so, corporate planners must detail for each business unit the objectives, strategies, and budgets required for that entity to realize its portion of the overall company business plan. Kotler points out that corporate planners will select from the following four strategies in defining the business unit strategy: *build* the business unit to increase its market share, *hold* its current market share and seek to prevent decay, *harvest* its market position by focusing on short-term cash profits regardless of long-term affects, or *divest* it through liquidation or sale [8].

An effective business plan is absolutely necessary to the survival and growth of the enterprise. The business plan provides the following benefits:

- *Strategic Definition.* The primary focus of the business plan is to identify the strategic objectives of the enterprise. These objectives range from defining broadly the firm's markets, products and services, and channel structures, to detailing the revenue, asset, and business unit strategies necessary to achieve overall corporate goals.

- *Plan Integrity.* A well-defined business plan seeks to establish a corporate strategy that is compatible with the capabilities of the enterprise. The result of the planning process is a series of operational directives and metrics providing a method of performance measurement whereby the efforts of the separate business units constituting the distribution channel should add up to the aggregate numbers established in the corporate plan.

- *Communication System.* The business plan enables the top management team to establish, broadcast, and maintain the detailed strategic objectives for all levels within the enterprise and for associated units and partners out in the channel network. The business plan provides the input used by marketing, sales, and procurement management to construct their operating plans. Finally, the business plan provides corporate benchmarks to guide and measure how well the efforts of the entire firm are realizing planned objectives.

DEVELOPING THE BUSINESS PLAN

Before a business plan can be communicated to the operations levels of the enterprise, it must be verified to ensure that total income is sufficient not only to pay cost of sales, operating expenses, and taxes but also enables the business to achieve corporate growth, return on investment, and dividend payout objectives. Ensuring that the business is generating the necessary financial numbers requires effective reporting and analysis relating to progress on the business forecast and how well productive assets are managed. The following documents are normally used in measuring business plan progress.

INCOME STATEMENT AND BALANCE SHEET

Perhaps the most widely used documents in analyzing corporate strength are the *income statement* and the *balance sheet.* These documents provide business strategists with a widow into the business in order to evaluate historical performance, current capabilities, and future opportunities.

The Income Statement. This document describes a firm's aggregate revenues and expenses. The income statement helps to answer such questions as: Did the firm earn a profit or incur losses? Why? At what rate? What contributed to the firm's success, and what impeded planned opportunities from being realized? The income statement is calculated by summarizing total sales and deducting costs, expenses, and taxes to determine net income or loss. Wholesale distributors are particularly sensitive to gross profit. Because of the enormous investment in inventory, even a small change in gross profit can have a disproportionate impact on net income. Consequently, the statement of gross profit is a critical decision variable for wholesale distributors. The statement is compared to the results of one or more previous years to indicate trends in performance. An example of the income statement format for a wholesale distributor appears in Figure 3.6.

The document begins with Sales and subtracts out Cost of Goods, which includes inventory, labor, and overhead, to produce the Gross Margin. From the Gross Margin, other expenses, which include Selling, Operating, and Non-Operating expenses are subtracted to leave the Net Income. Finally, Taxes and Dividends to stockholders are deducted from the Net Income, leaving the Returned Earnings that can then be invested back into the business. The Retained Earnings will end up appearing on the next critical document, the *balance sheet.*

The Balance Sheet. The balance sheet describes a firm's financial position by listing the balances of total assets, liabilities and stockholder's equity. The

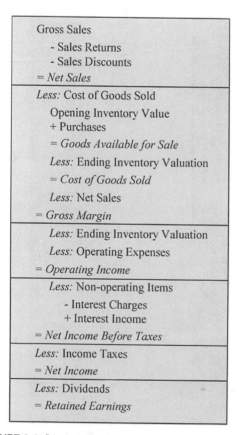

FIGURE 3.6 Income statement for a wholesale/distributor

left side of the balance sheet consists of a statement of company assets. Assets are broken down into current assets, which include cash, accounts receivables, and inventory, and fixed assets, which include land, buildings, and equipment. The other side of the balance sheet is the statement of the firm's liabilities. This section consists of current liabilities, such as accounts payable, salaries and wages, and taxes, and long-term liabilities, such as bonds, notes, and mortgages. Included in the liabilities is a section illustrating stockholder's equity. Total assets must equal total liabilities plus stockholder's equity. Growth in stockholder's equity is critical to the growth of the enterprise and is one of the primary financial goals of the company. An example of the format of the balance sheet appears in Figure 3.7.

ASSETS	LIABILITIES
Current Assets	Current Liabilities
Cash	Accounts Payable
Accounts Receivables	Maturity of Long-Term Debt
Marketable Securities	Salaries and Wages
Merchandise Inventory	Interest
= *Total Current Assets*	Taxes
Fixed Assets	= *Total Current Liabilities*
Land	Long Term Debt
Facilities	Sinking Fund Bonds
Equipment	Promissory Notes
Intangibles	Mortgages
= *Total Fixed Assets*	= *Total Liabilities*
Other Assets	Stockholders' Equity
Investments	Stock
Deferred Charges	Retained Earnings
= *Total Current Assets*	= *Total Stockholders' Equity*
= **Total Assets**	= **Total Liabilities and Shareholders' Equity**

FIGURE 3.7 Balance sheet example.

Return on Investment. The *return on investment* (ROI) is generally considered to be the best barometer of a company's financial performance. ROI can be expressed two ways, depending on fiscal requirements. The first method attempts to measure the *return on assets* (ROA) or *return on total capital.* The technique attempts to separate investment return from the income that has accrued from trading on the equity. ROA is calculated by dividing the net operating income by the average total assets. For example, if company XYZ's *average total assets* equaled $66 million, with total operating income of $9 million, the return on total assets would be 13.6 percent. The second method of expressing ROI is *return on stockholders' equity.* This technique attempts to demonstrate how profitable the company is to its owners. The ratio is calculated by dividing net income by the average total stockholders' equity. If company XYZ's net income is $6 million and the average stockholders' equity is $52 million, then the return on stockholders' equity would be 11.5 percent.

The real value of the ROI analysis can be found in assisting corporate planners target one or more of the components of the ROI calculation for improvement. Growth in total sales can be achieved by developing new products and value-added services, opening new markets, pricing decisions, deeper penetration of the existing customer base, or attacking markets held by competitors. Reductions in the cost of sales by decreasing purchasing costs arising from JIT procedures, contract pricing, and improved inventory productivity will increase gross margins. Operating costs can be lowered by decreasing stockable inventories, implementing information technologies techniques like ERP and the Internet, and by relentlessly pursuing the elimination of waste and improving the productivity of warehousing, transportation, and labor functions. Improvements in net worth can be achieved by increased turnover in asset investment which will reduce total capital investment and provide resources for new development. Finally, liabilities can be reduced by increasing or decreasing debt or equity, thereby increasing net worth.

Economic Value Added (EVA)

Today's hottest financial idea is termed EVA. Developed by consulting firm Stern Stewart & Co, the method help planners ensure a given business unit is adding to stockholder value, while providing investors with signals that a stock is likely to increase in value, by measuring its true profitability.

One of the criticisms of traditional accounting methods is that they tend to favor short-term profits and revenues while neglecting the long-term economic well-being and potential profitability of the enterprise.

To remedy this shortcoming, some financial planners advocate assessing a company's performance based on its return on capital or economic value-add. The EVA model attempts to quantify the value created by taking the after-tax operating profit of a company and subtracting the annual cost of all the capital the firm uses. Companies can also apply the model to measure their value-added contribution to total supply network profit. A defect of the model is that, while useful in assessing earnings above the cost of capital to be included in the executive portion of a balanced scorecard, it is less useful in structuring detailed supply chain metrics.

INVESTMENT, PROFIT, ASSET, AND CAPITAL PLANNING [9]

While the income statement, balance sheet, and ROI/ROA will provide overall scoreboards as to the financial well-being of the enterprise, the business planning process detailed above requires close management of more detailed plans centered on investments, profits, assets, and capital.

Business Forecast Plans. As detailed above, the *business forecast* seeks to detail the expected financial enterprise growth, return on investment, and total projected net income. There are two critical plans found in this planning area. The first, *investment planning*, determines the net earnings necessary to support expected enterprise growth. Net earnings can be used for two purposes: they can be paid out in the form of dividends to shareholders in the expectation of further stock purchase or they can be reinvested into the business. An example of an investment plan is illustrated in Figure 3.8. The plan begins by determining expected company growth by considering new market strategies, historical performance, and current capabilities, and then multiplying the percent of growth by the current Net Worth to arrive at the Estimated Net Worth. Once this value has been calculated, the expected ROI percent is then determined and multiplied against the Estimated Net Worth to arrive at the Net Earnings. The goal is to produce the Net Earnings. A critical decision must at this point be made as to the disposition of the Net Earnings. In the example, it has been decided to grant shareholders 16.6 percent of Net Earnings as a dividend, with the remaining balance returned to the company as seed money to fund the Estimated Growth percentage.

	$000,000
Description	*Target*
Beginning Net Worth	17.5
Estimated Growth	15%
Estimated Net Worth	20.0
ROI Target	15%
Net Earnings	3.0
Dividend Target = 16.6%	.5
Reinvested Earnings	2.5

FIGURE 3.8 Investment plan

Once the investment plan has been determined, the second forecast plan, the *profit plan,* must be created. This plan seeks to determine the After Tax Profit of the business driven by the sales effort. As illustrated in Figure 3.9, the plan begins by taking the Net Earnings from the *investment plan* and determining the percent of profit the Net Earnings represents to the company. Once this percent objective has been set, the Sales Revenue can be calculating. If 5 percent after tax is 3 million, then 100% equals $60 million. The Sales Revenue target can then be passed to sales and marketing planners who will have to determine whether they can realize the revenue goal. In conjunction with manufacturing they must set the expected Cost of Goods to verify if the company can produce, market, and sell the necessary products constituting the revenue plan while meeting the expected Gross Profit. Finally, the Gross Profit is reduced by the tax rate and reconciled to the After Tax Profit target.

Description	Percent	$000,000 Target
After-Tax Profit	5	3
Sales Revenue	100	60
Cost of Goods	90	54.0
Gross Profit	10	6.0
Taxes @ 50%	5	3.0

FIGURE 3.9 Profit plan

Asset Management Plan. As detailed above, the *asset management plan* is concerned with defining the current and long-term assets necessary to support the revenue plans detailed in the business forecast. There are two critical plans found in this planning area. The first, *asset planning*, sets the financial levels of the company's productive assets. As illustrated in Figure 3.10, the core of asset planning is determining the investment in plant and equipment necessary to actualize the sales revenue plan. As such, the planning process begins by calculating the estimated average daily sales achieved by dividing the Sales Revenue plan by the number of company working days. Once this figure is attained, planners can then calculate the necessary current (cash, receivables, and inventory) and fixed (plant and equipment) assets. For example, by first determining the daily cash flow arising from such elements as receivables, payables, interest, and payroll resulting from the revenue plan, it has been determined in Figure 3.10 that 10 days of cash or a total of $1.7 million will be required. Similar judgments will have to be made for the number of days of open receivables and inventory turns. Once the Current Assets have been calculated, attention must be turned to the fixed assets. A simple calculation is to determine the number of dollars needed to make each dollar sold. In the example, it has been determined that it takes one dollar of plant and equipment costs for every four dollars of sales. Dividing $60 million by $4 indicates that fixed asset expenses will total about $15 million. By combining the *Total Current Assets* and the fixed assets the Total Assets necessary to support the revenue plan can be determined.

		$000,000
Description	*Factor*	*Target*
Average Daily Demand = $60 / 360		.166
Cash – Days of Sales on Hand	10	1.7
Receivables – Aged Days of Sales	60	10.0
Inventory – COG / Turns	3	13.3
Total Current Assets		25.0
Plant & Equipment – Sales / Avg. Cost	$4	15.0
Total Current/Fixed Assets		40.0

FIGURE 3.10 Asset plan.

Determining the *asset plan* is one critical management step; figuring out how the current and fixed assets are going to be paid for is the subject of the final plan, *capital planning.* As illustrated in Figure 3.11, the plan begins by

		$000,000
Description	*Factor*	*Target*
Total Assets		40.0
Current Ratio / Liabilities	2.5	10.0
Total Available Capital		30.0
Investor Equity		17.5
Debt		12.5
Allowable Financing	40%	12.0
Debt Positioning + / -		-.5

FIGURE 3.11 Capital plan.

identifying the Total Assets calculated in the *asset plan.* The next step is to subtract the current liabilities from the current assets to provide how much capital will have to be funded. This figure is attained by determining the ratio of liabilities to assets which, in the example, has been set at 2.5 or $10 million in liabilities. This results in a debt of $30 million to be financed.

When investor equity is subtracted from this figure, the company is left with a debt of $12.5 million to meet the asset plan. Management has determined that unfinanced debt should not exceed 40 percent of Total Capital requirements or $12 million. In the example, this figure has been exceeded by $.5 million. Such a shortfall means that the company can not fund the excess debt. Solving this problem will require a revision in the revenue or the asset plans. For example, the shortage could be resolved through better cash management, reduction in open receivables, or an increase in inventory turns.

SUPPLY CHAIN PLANNING

In today's fast-paced environment strategic planners have become aware that depending on metrics that focus solely on company performance are becoming increasingly inadequate in providing a complete perspective on business planning. As discussed in Chapter 1, companies have begun to see themselves, not as individual players in the marketplace, but as components in a supply chain ecosystem focused on total customer value. As such, it has become imperative that executives dedicate a portion of their planning processes to the development of supply chain strategies. Supply chain strategies attempt to answer questions such as:

- Has the supply channel been correctly structured to actualize the corporate goals found in the business plans?
- How is the supply chain enhancing or eroding profitability and shareholder value?
- How much current asset is tied-up in slow moving inventories located in the supply chain?
- What would be the impact on growth initiatives as well as customer service if current assets were reduced across the supply channel?
- Can supply chain trading partners provide targeted productive assets that will free capital investment while simultaneously increase customer value?
- What are the service levels provided to channel customers and how can they be adjusted to increase customer value while reducing costs?
- How is information regarding profits and costs being passed back up the channel to feed executive scoreboards detailing the on-going performance of the business plan?

While recognizing the importance of finding answers to such questions, many business planners have, however, historically neglected to formulate satisfactory supply chain business plans. The reasons are many. To begin with, supply chain business strategies require the creation and tracking of performance metrics that are beyond the core business. Faced with the fact that supply chains are inherently dynamic, consisting of often oscillating coalitions of trading partners (factories, transportation, wholesalers, retailers), developing performance tools to monitor the significant costs that pass through each supply network node can be a complex process. Secondly, trading partners may be reluctant to provide information on performance. Data may be considered proprietary and not open to the eyes of outsiders. In addition, many executives have a traditional view of supply channel functions and do not realize its impact on all areas of financial performance. Supply chain performance is narrowly focused on only one aspect of overall performance: operating costs.

Key Performance Targets. Utilizing the supply chain as a source for total shareholder return and customer value will require reformulation of the traditional place of the supply chain in the business plan. As stated above, the key objective of the business plan is to identify three key performance targets:

- How can the revenue plan be increased for the entire planning horizon?
- What is the net income after deducting operating ex-penses. This is often termed the *operating profit margin*?
- What is the revenue return for each dollar invested in capital (current and fixed assets)?

The goal is for strategists to determine the role of the supply chain in managing these three critical financial performance drivers.

- *Growth:* Supply chains can provide a variety of critical enablers that directly impact profit and growth. Enablers, such as reducing channel-wide stockouts, increasing customer service, facilitating new product development and speed to market, increasing capital utilization, and decreasing asset costs, can directly increase revenues. For example, in Figure 3.12 improvements made by supply channel partners have resulted in a 2 percent increase in revenues. By utilizing the *profit plan* format discussed above, this increase in sales (assuming no increases in Cost of Goods) will result in a 2 percent increase in Gross Profit and a full percent in Revised After-Tax Profits.
- *Profitability.* Profitability is the balance of revenue after paying all operating expenses. Historically, planners have viewed enhancements to the supply channel in terms of operating cost reduction. The management of logistics costs (transportation, inventory, warehousing, administration) can reach nine to ten percent or more of the average company's revenue dollar. The impact on profitability by a five percent reduction in supply channel current assets is illustrated in Figure 3.13. The increase in market value can be used to fund new product development, attract new shareholders, or even acquire another company.

Description	Percent	$000,000 Target
Sales Revenue		60.0
Supply Chain Increase	2%	1.2
Cost of Goods	90%	54.0
Gross Profit	12%	7.2
Taxes @ 50%		3.6
Original After-Tax Profit	5%	3.0
Revised After-Tax Profit	5.9%	3.6

FIGURE 3.12 Impact of SCM on revenue growth

- *Capital Utilization.* This portion of supply chain management measures how efficiently a company utilizes capital to generate revenues.

Description	Factor	$000,000 Target
Average Daily Demand = $60 / 360		.166
Cash – Days of Sales on Hand	10	1.7
Receivables – Aged Days of Sales	60	10.0
Inventory – COG / Turns	3	13.3
Total Current Assets		25.0
Supply Chain Cost Reduction	5%	1.25
Adjusted Total Current Assets		23.8
Plant & Equipment – Sales / Avg. Cost	$4	15.0
Total Current/Fixed Assets		38.75

FIGURE 3.13 Asset plan.

Simplistically, this value is calculated as the revenue generated for every dollar invested in capital. It can also be said that the more capital intensive the investment, the lower the revenue expressed as a ratio to capital. As a whole it can be stated that the faster revenue can be generated, the faster a business can grow, the higher its financial performance, and, ultimately, the greater its returns to shareholders. In Figure 3.14, a decision to increase inventory turns from three to four has resulted in a drop of capital investment of $3.2 million. When combined the new Current Assets is combined with the fixed assets for plant and equipment, the new Total Available Capital and Debt drops $2 million. The overall result is that financial planners are now $1.5 million under the Allowable Financing ceiling. While reducing current capital is inherently good, the real benefit is that the company's stock price or value has grown, permitting the execution of strategic plans to fund another product line or even acquire another company.

		$000,000
Description	*Factor*	*Target*
Total Assets		40.0
Cash – Days of Sales on Hand	10	1.7
Receivables – Aged Days of Sales	60	10.0
Inventory – COG / Turns	4	10.0
Total Current Assets		21.7
New Current Ratio / Liabilities	2.5	8.7
Old Current Ratio / Liabilities	2.5	10.0
New Current Available Capital		13.0
Plant & Equipment		15.0
New Total Available Capital		28.0
Investor Equity		17.5
Debt		10.5
Allowable Financing	40%	12.0
Debt Positioning + / -		+1.5

FIGURE 3.14 Capital utilization plan.

SCM Data Collection and Analysis. Utilizing the cross-channel business reporting described above requires the application of computerized toolsets that enable supply chain partners to pass *key performance indicators* (KPIs) and communicate with each other. While establishing a networked business information exchange complete with analytical tools for assembling operational and strategic information can appear at the outset to be an almost impossible task, software architectures and even standardized packages are available today. These systems utilize the connectivity power of the Internet to create a network model and a common database so that channel members can assemble data and monitor performance. These systems extract data feeds from participating supply chain members, aggregate it, calculate performance targets based on targeted KPIs, and provide a solution to all channel partners. Some systems also provide an event-driven simulation that maps how a given supply chain behaves over time and provides participating companies opportunities to develop response strategies when unplanned events occurring the supply channel. Often the statistics are posted on the network so that all channel partners can view their performance relative to other channel members [10].

Another tool for managing inter-company business planning is to apply the *Balanced Scorecard* to supply chain management. Developed by Kaplan and Norton [11], the concept is designed to provide strategic planners with a performance methodology designed to generate business plans from four perspectives: *financial results* (return on capital employed, asset utilization, profitability, growth), the *customer* (viability of the value proposition), *business processes* (effectiveness of the quality, flexibility, productivity, and costs accumulated by each business process), and *innovation and learning* (core competencies and skills, access to strategic information, organizational learning and growth).

While not directly created for supply network business planning, the method can be easily adapted to a supply chain environment. According to Brewer and Speh [12] implementing a supply chain balanced scorecard requires the following steps:

- *Step 1: Formulate Strategy and Build Consensus*. The first step is for each channel partner to define their supply chain strategic objectives and understand where the strategies of each network participant converge/diverge. This activity will drive the metric-selection process that will permit definition of the parameters detailing optimal performance for each supply chain participant.

- *Step 2: Select Metrics in Alignment with the Supply Chain Strategy*. The performance measurements selected should support the four scorecard perspectives described above. For example, supply chain *financial* targets, such as increased market share, *customer* targets, such as on-time delivery requiring increased channel velocity, *business process* targets, such as facilitating the value chain from design through manufacturing, distribution, and delivery to the end customer, and *innovation and learning*, such as integrating cross-enterprise design functions to ensure the efficient generation of the next generation of products, could be agreed upon by channel network partners.

- *Step 3: Integrate and Communicate the Metrics.* The general statements of desired performance must be disaggregated into detailed, understandable, and actionable metrics that can guide internal and well as cross-channel daily operations.
- *Step 4: Drive the Organization to Maintain and Optimize the Desired Results.* Ensuring that the metrics detailed at the strategic and operational level of the supply chain scorecard are performed, accountability for performance, targets for improvement, action plans, performance progress reviews, and linkage to individual performance and reward must be established and agreed to by all channel managers.

Figure 3.15 illustrates a supply chain balanced scorecard where network

*Supply Chain Objective: **Increased Channel Flexibility***

	Strategic Theme	Strategic Objectives	Strategic Measures
Financial	Increased Supply Chain Flexibility	Channel cost reduction Increased profit margins Revenue growth High return on assets	Increased cash flow Reduced channel inventory Improved fixed asset utilization

Customer	Perception of flexible response to customers	Customers drive product
		  finalization
		Service individualization
		Increased product variety
			Flexibility and agility of
			  the supply channel
			Ability to deliver
			  customized solutions

Business Processes	Postponement and value-added strategies	Increased synchronization
		Increased communication
		Fast flow of inventories
		Multi-purpose facilities
			Channel finished goods
			  reduction
			Increased inventory turns
			Processing efficiencies
			  and utilizations
			Optimize transportation
			Warehouse storage
			  reduction

Innovation And Learning	Increased material handling and processing capabilities	Increasing core competencies Motivating workers Skilling workers	Employee survey Personal balanced scorecard Total supply chain competency available

FIGURE 3.15 SCM balanced scorecard.

partners have selected increased channel *flexibility* as the critical success factor. The *financial* perspective opens the scorecard. The objectives to be pursued are centered on total channel cost reduction and revenue growth by leveraging material and conversion strategies. It has been determined that a more flexible supply channel will cut finished goods inventories, improve product throughput, and increase gross margins. Realizing this goal will require measures that demonstrate how well each channel partner's operating costs and gross margins are progressing.

The purpose of emphasizing flexibility as the critical success factor is to gain *customers* by permitting them to drive finalization of products in real time and receive individualized service. Being able to meet this criteria rests on the capabilities of the *business processes.* Increased postponement and value-added processing will place a burden on channel nodes to increase the variety of products available while simultaneously maintaining or decreasing the time it takes for order configuration support. Realizing this goal will require measures that indicate the productivity of processing operations, total dollar value of finished goods and how well warehousing and transportation costs are being optimized. Finally, the *innovation and learning* perspective can be critical in the execution of the flexibility strategy. Depending on the level of skill of the workforces of each channel partner to perform value-added process functions, effective execution of the strategy could be a difficult one. Core competencies might have to be built or attained from outside the organization. New incentives and motivational programs might have to be enacted.

Architecting a supply chain balanced scorecard provides strategic planners will radically new and different challenges. Successful execution of the methodology requires companies to move beyond simply measuring the progress of the internal business (often an enormous task in itself!) to a perspective that considers channel collaboration, consensus, and total supply chain performance as the cornerstone of success. According to Brewer and Speh [13], there are eight critical hurdles that must be spanned to make supply chain balanced scorecards a reality. They are: *trust* among channel members in sharing data and measuring performance; *understanding* concerning the impact of how multi-organizational measurements might invite individual company negative consequences; lack of *control* over measures that depend on inter-organization efforts; presence of *different goals and objectives* among channel members; incompatible *information systems* that inhibit data transfer and visibility; varying definition of the format, structure, and measurement approach to *performance measurements;* difficulty in *linking measures to customer value*; and, *deciding where to begin.*

While a daunting task, the complexity should not dissuade companies from taking up the challenge: there is just too much to be gained by harnessing the productive power of collaborative supply chains. The first place to start is to form cross-enterprise performance design teams. To begin with, these teams will need to move beyond a concern with local function-based measurements, which tend to splinter the performance development effort and focus on

	Frequently Used Supply Chain Metrics
Cash Management	
Days sales outstanding (DSO) $\dfrac{\text{Accounts receivable x working days}}{\text{Total inventory}}$	High DSO includes too many invoice errors, excessive delivery times, payment delays due to returns and re-invoicing, and customer dissatisfaction
Cash to cycle time Days sales outstanding (DSO) + Inventory days supply - Days Payable outstanding	This metrics is designed to show how fast cash is begin generated from the expenditures made in inventory and production
Receivables turnover $\dfrac{\text{Total Revenue}}{\text{Receivables}}$	Low receivables indicates problems in collections, credit management. Also highlights possible slowing of sales.
Asset Management	
Asset turns $\dfrac{\text{Total revenue}}{\text{Total assets}}$	Low turns indicates high level of fixed assets and inventory used to meet service target. Also, could indicate lack of collaborative relationships with channel partners
ROA – Return on assets $\dfrac{\text{Net income}}{\text{Total assets}}$	Indicates low fixed and current asset return. Indicates lack of collaborative partnerships with channel partners.
Inventory Management	
Inventory turns $\dfrac{\text{Cost of goods sold}}{\text{Total inventory}}$	Large stockpiles necessary to meet service targets. Weaknesses in channel demand/supply communication. Poor forecasting, MPS/MRP planning, purchasing, and fulfillment
Inventory days on hand $\dfrac{\text{Working days}}{\text{Inventory turn ratio}}$	Indicates excessive stockpiles to meet service targets. Poor safety stock targets, planning data, demand forecasting. In ability to meet supply chain demand

cross-functional processes and accompanying metrics that will crystallize objectives designed to increase cross-network channel integration. The goal is not to eliminate function-based measurements, but rather to broaden their effectiveness by integrating them with supply chain level metrics that will reveal how well each network business node is individually working toward goals that will improve not only their own performance but also the overall performance of the entire supply chain. In addition, teams must be strong enough to tackle several other critical problems inherent in determining supply chain metrics. The measures decided upon must be in synchronization with individual company and total supply chain strategies. The tendency to capture too many measurements must also be avoided. Participating companies must be encouraged to provide meaningful information on their performance. And finally, supply chain measurements can be beset by problems in defining basic terminology necessary to ensure common understanding of performance standards.

SUMMARY

The central challenge to distribution management in the twenty-first century can be simply stated as the ability of the enterprise to establish and maintain a competitive advantage through the effective allocation of productive resources to capitalize on marketplace opportunities. The first step required to meet this challenge is the establishment of an effective strategic business plan. In developing plans and strategies, corporate planners must seek to align company goals, strategies, and growth expectations with today's economic and marketplace realities. The development of effective business plans involves four essential activities. The first step in the business planning process is the definition of the company goals and their translation into concise mission statements. The second step is the creation of the business forecast. This step seeks to detail expected enterprise financial growth, return on investment, and total projected net income. In the third step, management focuses on the current and long-term assets necessary to support the revenue plans outlined in the firm's business forecast. Finally, in the last step, corporate plans are disaggregated and passed down to the firm's business units. The goal is to ensure that strategic objectives can be realized by the existing business unit structure. The role of supply chain management planners in all three levels of strategic planning is critical. Their input is not only pivotal in the formulation of marketing, sales, and financial plans but also in allocating the fixed and liquid capital necessary in business plan execution.

Before a business plan can be communicated to the operations levels of the business, it must be verified to ensure that total income is sufficient not only to pay for current and fixed assets, but also to support targeted corporate growth, return on investment, and dividend payout objectives. Several critical performance documents are essential in validating the business plan. The first is the *income statement*. This document describes a firm's aggregate revenues and expenses. It seeks to answers such questions as: Did the firm earn a profit? What contributed to its success or failure? The second document, the *balance sheet*, describes a firm's financial position by listing the balance of total assets, liabilities, and stockholder equity in relation to the company's assets. The final document is *return on investment* (ROI). ROI can be expressed in two ways: *return on assets* (ROA) and *return on stockholders' equity*.

While the above documents will provide overall scorecards as to the financial well-being of the enterprise, the utilization of more detailed plans is necessary. The first set of business performance plans focuses on the *business forecast* and consists of the *investment plan* (which determines the net earnings necessary to support enterprise growth) and the *profit plan* (which determines the after tax profit of the business driven by the sales effort.) The second set of plans is centered on metrics associated with *asset management* and consists of the *asset plan* (which sets the financial levels of the company's productive assets) and the *capital plan* (which details how the current and fixed assets are going to be paid for).

In today's fast-paced environment strategic planners have become aware that depending on metrics that focus solely on company performance are becoming increasingly inadequate in providing a complete perspective on business planning. Increasingly, executive planners have come to view how critical the performance of *growth, profitability,* and *capital utilization* out in the supply chain is to overall business success. Developing and communicating cross-enterprise *key performance factors* (KPIs) has become the foremost frontier in the creation and monitoring of a successful business plan. Tackling this mission provides many challenges to supply chain business planners involving the generation of supply chain partner trust, the creation of common, meaningful metrics, the accurate and timely passage of performance information from across the channel, and the joint implementation of toolsets, like the supply chain balanced scorecard.

QUESTIONS FOR REVIEW

1. Why are effective business strategies essential for competitive success?
2. Properly aligned enterprise strategies are fundamental for effective top management planning. Discuss.
3. Would you describe Wal-Mart as following a competitive strategy based on cost leadership, differentiation, or focus? Explain your answer.
4. How have new management concepts centered on networking, tech-nology, and virtual teams changed traditional strategic planning?
5. What is the role of logistics management in business strategy de-velopment?
6. Detail how the logistics function can be used as a competitive weapon.
7. Firms seeking to improve cash flow and return on assets historically have focused on reducing accounts receivables and investment in in-ventories. What are the consequences of such actions without chang-ing the firm's logistics systems?
8. Based on the data in Table 3.1, calculate the return on assets for a company with the following year-end financial data (in $Millions) if the goal was to reduce accounts receivables by 18% and inventory in-vestment by 25%.

Sales	$50
Net Profit	$3
Current Asset	$25
Acct. Receivable	$11
Inventory	$13

9. Based on the calculation for Question 8, what percentage would an-nual sales have to increase to attain the same return on assets?

REFERENCES

1. Hayes, Robert H. and Wheelwright, Steven C., *Restoring Our Competitive Edge.* New York: John Wiley & Sons, 1984, p. 25.
2. Porter, Michael E., *Competitive Strategy.* New York: The Free Press, 1980, pp. 3-33.
3. These basic principles are elaborated by Kotler, Philip, *Marketing Management,* 6th ed. Englewood Cliffs, NJ: Prentice-Hall, 1988, p. 37.
4. Anthony, Robert N., *The Management Control Function.* Boston, MA: Harvard Business School Press, 1988, pp. 31-34.
5. Kotler, p. 33.
6. Porter, Michael E., *Competitive Advantage.* New York: The Free Press, 1985, pp. 62-163.
7. See the analysis in Porter, *Competitive Advantage,* p. 3.
8. Kotler, p. 42.
9. This section has been adapted from Schultz, Terry R., *BRP: The Journey to Excellence.* Milwaukee, WI: The Forum Ltd, 1986, pp. 23-30.
10. See the commentary in Dilger, Karen Abramic, "Say Good-bye to the Weakest Link with Supply-Chain Metrics," *Global Logistics and Supply Chain Strategies,* 5, 6, 2001, pp. 34-40.
11. Kaplan, Robert S. and Norton, David P., "The Balanced Scorecard: Measures That Drive Performance," *Harvard Business Review,* (January-February, 1992), pp, 71-79; Kaplan, Robert S. and Norton, David P., *The Balanced Scorecard: Translating Strategy into Action.* Boston: Harvard Business School Press, 1996; and, Kaplan, Robert S. and Norton, David P., *The Strategy-Focused Organization: How Balanced Scorecard Companies Thrive in the New Business Environment.* Boston: Harvard Business School Press, 2001.
12. Brewer, Peter C. and Speh, Thomas W., "Adapting the Balanced Scorecard to Supply Chain Management," *Supply Chain Management Review,* 5, 2, 2001, pp 48-56.
13. Ibid.

4

FORECASTING IN THE
SUPPLY CHAIN ENVIRONMENT

Much of the success of enterprise planning and decision-making processes depends on the formulation of accurate forecasts. Although it has often been said that nothing really happens until a company receives a customer order, unless the enterprise has developed sound plans that enable it to purchase the proper inventory, establish the necessary supply channels, and deliver goods on a competitive basis, the business cannot possibly hope to achieve corporate objectives. In addition, forecasting permits firms to establish performance measurements for customer service, plan the level of total inventory investment, choose between alternative operating strategies, and develop assumptions about the ability of the business to respond to the future needs of the marketplace. Effective forecasts can dramatically improve enterprise profitability, productivity, and customer service and ensure competitive advantage. Good forecasting also assists strategic planners to eliminate waste in the form of excess inventory, reduce lost sales and expensive expediting, and control costs involved in maintaining plant size, labor, equipment, and transportation. Finally, the communication of accurate and timely forecasts enables entire supply chains to construct agile and scalable supply networks, architect unique channels of collaborative, value-creating relationships, and continuously align supply network capabilities with the requirements of the customer.

Developing and maintaining accurate forecasts is critical to effective decision making at all levels in the organization. All areas, from top management planning to transportation and warehousing, require some level of forecasting for sound departmental planning and control. As the Internet and global competition accelerate requirements for timely product introduction, supply chain management, and logistics accuracy, forecasting has taken on added importance. In the past, many enterprises could be characterized as having not one but several forecasts, each reflecting the narrow operational objectives of each functional business area. Sometimes the forecasts were out of alignment with each other, projecting different sets of critical performance indicators reflective of departmental goals. Today, supply chain strategists conceive of forecasting as an integrative and iterative process whereby the strategic goals are formulated, integrated with the capabilities of supply chain partners, and then disaggregated down through the organization. As the forecast unfolds through time, data concerning actual activity is utilized for forecast revision and then communicated to channel partners. The objective of the whole process is to ensure that each supply chain node is utilizing the very latest data in the development of manufacturing, supply chain, and logistics plans.

In this chapter, forecasting in today's supply chain environment will be explored. The chapter begins with an overview of forecasting as a tool for enterprise planning. From this vantage point, the discussion will proceed to a review of the forecasting types available: qualitative, quantitative, and causal forecasting. Included will be an in-depth analysis of the short-term forecasting techniques available to distributors. Next, the steps necessary for effective forecast development and management will be detailed as well as a discussion of why forecasts fail. Finally, the chapter concludes with a review of the challenges of forecasting in the age of e-business.

FORECASTING – AN OVERVIEW

The *APICS Dictionary* defines *forecasting* as "the business function that attempts to predict sales and use of products so they can be purchased or manufactured in appropriate quantities in advance" [1]. Implicit in the definition are two critical concepts:

1. A *forecast* is an objective estimate of future demand attained by projecting the pattern of the events of the past into the future. Literally,

the word forecast means to "throw ahead," to continue what has historically been happening.

2. A *prediction* is a subjective estimate of what events will be happening in the future, based on extrapolating or interpreting data that occurred in the past. Prediction or "saying beforehand" is the process whereby management uses subjective judgment to decide whether events will be repeated based on past experience or to anticipate changes arising from new environmental, geographical, political, or demand patterns.

Forecasting is fundamentally a calculative process whereby a sequence of historical numeric values reflected of demand is first attained, to which various statistical techniques are then applied in order to arrive at an estimate of what the next number or the next several numbers in the sequence are most likely going to be. A *prediction,* on the other hand, is a matter of judgment that takes into account not only the quantitative values arising from a forecast calculation but also qualitative data derived from events in the business environment for the purpose of determining the course of future events. If, for example, a strike is anticipated in the plant of a competitor, a firm's management may very well predict that the demand on their products will rise despite what the current forecast has calculated based on past history.

Forecasting is a necessity because the future *is* uncertain. In the physical world where patterns are perfect and relationships are exact, mathematical models can be developed that calculate the outcome of any occurrence. In the business world, however, unless a company has a complete monopoly on an unsaturated market, a similar degree of predictability cannot be achieved. To begin with, instead of mathematically calculable factors, the world of human affairs is marked by randomness and endless variation. Patterns and relationships change, often dramatically. Therefore, instead of a process that will pro-duce exact calculations that can be readily applied in management decision making, forecasters will do well to begin with an understanding of the limitations and uncertainties that reside at the core of forecasting. Strategic planners must realize that forecasts will always be subject to error and that, although there are techniques available to improve forecast accuracy, the amount of effort expended soon reaches a point of diminishing returns. Beyond this point, forecasters should concentrate more on coping with forecast error than on architecting even more complex forecasting models [2].

In developing and deploying forecasting techniques, strategists must be aware of the following general characteristics of forecasting [3]:

1. Forecasts will be wrong.
2. Forecasts are most useful when accompanied by a method for measuring forecast error.
3. Forecasts are more accurate the larger the statistical population used.
4. Forecasts are more accurate for shorter periods of time.

In addition to the basic inability of forecasting to provide exact information for decision making, many supply chain planners have cultures that militate against forecast success. Common complaints range from laments that the forecasting effort has been so splintered that it is meaningless and that no one really understands the statistical mechanics, to problems in the collection of accurate and forecastable data.

Although forecasting for supply chain management is often characterized more as an art and less as a science, there are, nevertheless, principles and statistical approaches that can be utilized to assist the forecaster. Like a physical scientist attempting to understand all the forces acting on an experiment, the forecaster can use known postulates and techniques to abstract general principles from the apparent randomness occurring in the detail. The solution to creating accurate forecasts is to develop a formal forecasting program that uses relevant techniques and consists of an effective system that detects, measures, and provides the mechanics to enable forecasters to react quickly to discovered errors. The goal is to determine predictable data that the business planning process can employ to assist in making good decisions about the best marketplace alternatives available for the enterprise.

In their exhaustive study of forecasting, Makridakis and Wheelwright have identified six characteristics or dimensions that play a critical role in determining the requirements necessary to establishing effective forecasting [4]. A short description of each follows:

1. *Time Horizon*. In formulating business plans strategists must forecast the probable course of events that might occur over varying lengths of time. Forecasting normally occurs on four levels. The critical factor separating each level is the length of the forecast.

    -   The highest level can be described as *long-range* forecasting. This level has a time horizon of at least 1 year and is used in the development of top management planning. Among the decisions associated with this level of forecasting are developing corporate goals and objectives, performing corporate capital budgeting, planning for facilities, equipment and other fixed assets, and structuring channel networks.

    -   The next level, *medium-range* forecasting, has a time horizon of six months to one year and is normally applied to operations planning and control activities. Forecasting decisions on this level impact sales planning, planning warehouse and transportation capacities, business area capital planning, and contracting for public warehousing and transportation services.

    -   *Short-range* forecasting comprises the third level of forecast planning. Business functions required to project operations execution activities one to three months out into the future will use this level of forecasting. Forecasting decisions on this level will impact such activities as manufacturing scheduling, supplier scheduling, inventory procurement plans, transportation planning, material handling equipment utilization, and detailed operating budgets.

- Finally, *immediate-range* forecasting is used for everyday performance of ongoing activities. Examples include transportation scheduling, receiving, stock put away, shop floor and value-added processing scheduling, order filling, and accounts receivables and payables flow through.

Each forecast level possesses its own unique characteristics relative to the most appropriate forecasting method and data required. It would be improper, for example, to employ a forecast method used to calculate product demand on a weekly basis for the purpose of determining yearly aggregate sales income.

2. *Level of Aggregate Detail.* Forecasting in the supply chain planning environment occurs at many levels. Forecasts are used in the development of business, marketing, sales, logistics, and detailed inventory plans. Each forecastable area differs in two regards: the methods employed and the level of detail required. As strategists move from the general to the specific, the level of forecast detail correspondingly moves from a concern with aggregate data to gross detail. In selecting the appropriate forecast for a specific plan, forecasters must be aware of the level of detail required for that forecast if it is to be useful in decision making. Corporate planners, for example, are usually concerned with aggregate estimates of dollars and product groups and would find a forecast of the weekly sales of a given item of little value. Generally, as forecasts become more specific, the size of forecastable data grows exponentially, necessitating the use of a computerized technique, and vice versa.

3. *Size of the Forecastable Database.* The number of elements in a forecastable population will have a direct impact on the forecasting methods employed. In general, as the number of occurrences to be calculated in a forecast grow, the simpler the forecasting method. The reason is that the larger the number of occurrences, the more valid the statistical mean. Conversely, the smaller the size of the data to be used in a forecast, the more complex must be the forecasting technique if variation is to be smoothed and accounted for. For example, a sales manager forecasting the sales by week of an inventory of 1,000 end items would not use the same techniques as another sales manager charged with forecasting 100 product groups for a business quarter.

4. *Forecasting Control.* When forecasting, planners will need to utilize a method that renders accurate and timely feedback to permit management control. The method must indicate when the actual events have moved beyond a predetermined acceptable forecast variance boundary and to allow alteration to adjust for changes in basic patterns or relationships. The objective is to provide forecasters with management controls to ensure that business forecast decisions are being made that are in alignment with actual events. An example would be a forecast of sales established for a new product group. Because the new product group lacks the historical data needed for fore-cast development, planners will have to frequently monitor the forecast to ensure that actual sales supports the forecast, and if not, what pat-terns are emerging that will permit the formulation of a more accurate forecast.

5. *Constancy.* Forecasting events or relationships of events that exhibit great stability over time is quite different from calculating the future of occurrences that demonstrate a wide range of variation. The principle underlying this dimension is simply the more random variation that occurs in the forecast, the more weight recent events and patterns must have in forecast adjustment. In a stable environment, a quantitative fore-cast based on historical data can be adopted and reviewed periodically to confirm its appropriateness. On the other hand, when there is great variation in forecastable data a method that reflects current events, past history, and qualitative information is a better choice.

6. *Existing Planning Procedures.* Forecasting methods should be chosen that support the firm's planning and decision-making processes, as well as enhance and improve upon existing operational norms. Companies often confuse *forecasting* and *planning.* According to Armstrong [5], strategists employ forecasting methods to simulate the outcomes of plans. After possible results are validated, they can then revise plans, obtain new forecasts, and repeat the process until the forecasted outcomes are satisfactory. Once a forecast has been decided upon and as actual events unfold, they can revise plans until the next forecasting period. A common mistake of companies is that if events do not match the expected outcome, they revise their forecasts and not their plans. The supposition is that changing the forecast will change behavior.

There are undoubtedly other dimensions that exist that characterize specific forecasting situations. Once these and other possible dimensions are understood, forecasters can advance to an investigation of the basic types of forecasting.

Table 4.1. FORECASTING CLASSIFICATION

Forecasting Technique	Accuracy Range			Business Area Application					
	Short	Medium	Long	Business Strategy	Marketing	Procurement	Sales	Inventory	Pricing
I. Judgemental									
Individual Judgement	X	X	X	X	X	X	X	X	X
Sales Force Estimates	X	X			X	X	X	X	
Panel Consensus	X	X	X	X	X	X	X		
Market Reserach	X	X			X		X		X
Delphi			X	X	X				X
Visionary Forecast			X	X	X				
II. Quantitative									
Simple Average	X						X	X	
Moving Average	X	X					X	X	X
Exponential Smoothing	X	X			X	X	X	X	X
Decomposition	X	X			X	X	X	X	
Focus Forecasting	X	X			X	X	X	X	X
III. Causal									
Econometric		X		X	X	X	X	X	X
Regression Analysis			X	X	X	X	X	X	X
Historical Analogy	X	X	X	X	X				
Leading Indicator			X	X	X	X	X	X	
Life Cycle Analysis	X	X	X	X	X				X

FORECASTING TYPES

The variety of forecasting methods available can be organized into three basic forecasting types: *qualitative* or *judgmental, quantitative,* and *causal.* Each major type is composed of several techniques as summarized in Table 4.1. The first type uses qualitative data such as expert judgment, intuition, and subjective evaluation and is best used for forecasting marketing, product development, and promotional strategies. The second type employs time-series analysis and projection to search for historical patterns that can be extrapolated into the future. The final forecasting type is the most sophisticated type of forecasting tool. It attempts to express mathematically the relationships between the forecast objective and factors such as technological, political, economic, and socioeconomic forces.

Figure 4.1 is a schematic flow of the forecasting function. Each of the three forecasting types can be seen in their relationship to each other. Of critical importance is the closed-loop nature of the forecasting process. Forecasts can originate using *qualitative, quantitative,* or *causal* methods. As actual events occur, the forecast system must be able to provide forecasters with the ability to respond to forecast error, evaluate variances, and make informed changes to the current forecast.

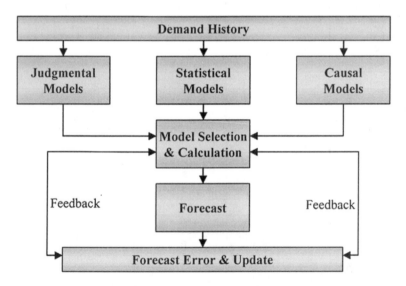

FIGURE 4.1 Forecasting model.

QUALITATIVE TECHNIQUES

Qualitative or *judgmental techniques* are generally used when data are scarce or when developing aggregate sales or inventory forecasts. The objective is to use human judgment based on analysis to convert collected data into a forecast of probable events. In formulating qualitative forecasts historical data may or may not be utilized. Such techniques are frequently used in creating forecasts in technology areas or when a completely new product is being introduced into the market, especially when the relationship to historical data of analogous products is tenuous. A very simple example of qualitative forecasting is illustrated in Figure 4.2. The example demonstrates the development of a forecast of monthly sales based on the projections of a panel composed of three company executives.

$$\text{Monthly Forecast} = \frac{\text{Executive 1 Forecast} + \text{Executive 2 Forecast} + \text{Executive 3 Forecast}}{3}$$

$$\text{Monthly Forecast} = \frac{500 + 600 + 550}{3} = \mathbf{550}$$

FIGURE 4.2 Three-executive panel forecast

The following points detail the standard types of qualitative forecasts in use today.

- *Personal Insight.* The most common technique used is individual judgment based on intuition. In this method an industry expert is used who employs personal knowledge and past experience to produce a forecast based purely on subjective judgment. Advantages of this technique are its relative low cost and speed of formulation. Drawbacks focus around the fact that although the method may render some good forecasts, results are extremely variable. Besides, it has been demonstrated that forecasters who follow a formal fore-casting process will always out-perform forecasts based on subjective opinions.

- *Sales Force Estimates.* This method represents an aggregate approach to the individual judgment technique. The technique consists of the projection of future sales compiled by the firm's sales force based on individual salesperson estimates, management expertise, or surveys of supply chain demand. The advantage of using this technique is that it employs the specialized knowledge of those closest to the marketplace.

- *Panel Consensus.* The panel consensus approach brings together experts from across the supply chain to review and estimate the optimal forecast for a product, product group, or service. Advantages of this technique are that it is quick and easy, requires minimal preparation of statistical data, and pools the collective experience and judgment of experts from across the supply network.
- *Market Research.* This technique attempts to forecast future demand trends and activity levels by surveying a market segment whose past behavior and actions could indicate future buying patterns. The drawback with using this technique is that market surveys are expensive and time-consuming to execute and monitor. In addition, they rely on the accuracy of the randomness of the sample and the conclusions drawn from the analyses.
- *Visionary Forecasting.* Another qualitative type is visionary forecasting. This technique is the most radical and consists of a prophecy of the future based on personal insight, judgment, and, when available, historical analogies that can be extrapolated into possible future forecasts. It is characterized by subjective guesswork and imagination, and, in general, the methods used are nonscientific and non-quantitative.
- *Delphi Method.* One of the most popular qualitative techniques is the Delphi Method. In this approach, a panel of experts, who do not physically meet, is interrogated by a sequence of questionnaires concerning a new product, event, or process. Responses to the questionnaires are passed on to all the panel members for evaluation and rating as to the likelihood of occurrence and are then used to produce the next set of questionnaires. The object is to narrow down a field of opinions that can be used as forecastable data.

Qualitative methods of forecasting have advantages and disadvantages. In general, a critical advantage of this type lies in the ability of strategists to develop forecastable data for products and services that lack initial quantifiable data or when the variations in recorded occurrences are so dramatic that it is impossible to determine stable patterns and relationships. In addition, forecasts using this type can be easily and quickly assembled without complex statistical computation. Disadvantages can be summarized as follows:

1. Lack of supporting evidence for forecasting decisions
2. Overconfidence in the elements used and the results of the chosen forecast
3. Possibility of over conformity of the individual to collective values and attitudes when group qualitative types are used
4. High cost of development and maintenance when used in computerized forecasting systems

Collectively, these limitations tend to create judgmental biases especially when the forecast is dependent on established patterns or relationships of data [7].

QUANTITATIVE TECHNIQUES

Quantitative techniques are best used for forecasting when there exist sizeable historical data and when the relationships and patterns of these data are both clear and relatively stable. The fundamental assumption of quantitative forecasting is that the future can be accurately extrapolated from the occurrences of the past. The operating principle is relatively simple. The forecaster should use the accumulated data on historical performance to attain a reading on the current rate of activity (sales, for example) and how fast this rate is increasing or decreasing. Once this rate is ascertained, various statistical techniques can be employed to calculate the future based on the assumption that existing demand patterns will continue into the future.

Unfortunately, it is very difficult to develop accurate forecasts using raw data because changes in the rates of activity are not directly observable. Cycles, trends, seasonality and other factors can create variations within the data. In addition, patterns can be distorted by management decisions such as a promotion or special pricing that cause abnormal spikes of data to occur during select periods. Therefore, to use historical data effectively, forecasters must massage the raw data by analyzing activity rates and uncovering patterns and applying the proper statistical forecasting technique.

Much has been written concerning actual use of *qualitative* versus *quantitative* types of forecasting. Some surveys reporting on the status of forecasting have found that managers utilize qualitative methods far more than quantitative methods [8]. This fact is particularly true among distributors. In a survey of managers from manufacturing and distribution, it was found that only 69.8 percent of distribution managers versus 81.3 percent for manufacturing managers had a working knowledge of quantitative forecasting methods [9]. This conclusion would seem to be at odds with the fact that quantitative techniques are superior to qualitative techniques in accuracy and timeliness and that they are free of the biases inherent in judgmental forecasting.

Actually, both types of forecasting possess individual advantages and disadvantages. Quantitative forecasts are clearly more advantageous when it comes to objectivity, consistency, repetitively calculating a large-sized task (such as forecasting 10,000 items), and cost of execution. In contrast, qualitative forecasts are superior when historical data are lacking, inside information or knowledge is critical, and ease of evaluation and modification is paramount. In reality, even when established patterns or relationships are constant, forecasters cannot blindly accept statistical output without analyzing the applicability of the data to the current environment and reviewing the accuracy of the technique employed. In fact, both forecasting types are complementary and must be integrated to produce accurate and usable forecasts.

TIME-SERIES ANALYSIS

In analyzing raw historical data, forecasters can utilize a wide range of possible quantitative forecasting models. By understanding the purposes and characteristics of the techniques, planners can better analyze the nature of raw forecastable data and be able to measure the advantages and disadvantages of employing a specific technique to match a specific situation.

For the most part, quantitative forecasting techniques utilize time-series analysis. Collectively, these techniques attempt to use the time-sequenced history of activity as the source data to forecast future activity. Examples of time-series data are portrayed in Figure 4.3. As can be seen, time-series analysis is composed of two elements: the data series and the time periods used. Time-series techniques always assume that patterns of activity recur over time. After establishing the time period to be used as the benchmark for review, data are identified and calculated. The results are then extrapolated, employing observable patterns, into future time periods as the forecast.

I. Weekly Demand for Sump Pump #401-325-01

Date	Jan 7	Jan 14	Jan 21	Jan 28	Feb 4	Feb 11
Demand	21	28	30	26	24	33

II. Monthly Sales Forecast of Submersible Sump Pumps

Month	Jan	Feb	March	April	May	June
Demand	101	118	145	170	200	250

III. Quarterly Forecast of Shipped Dollars

Quarter	1st	2nd	3rd	4th	1st	2nd
Dollars	$235,000	$244,000	$310,000	$375,000	$421,000	$503,000

IV. Yearly Sales of ABC Company

Year	1997	1998	1999	2000	2001	2002
Sales (m)	$145	$148	$151	$156	$162	$165

FIGURE 4.3 Time series examples.

Time-series analysis assists forecasters in isolating patterns that may be occurring in the raw data. Some typical time-series patterns are illustrated in Figure 4.4. Time-series patterns can be summarized into five groups: (1) hor-

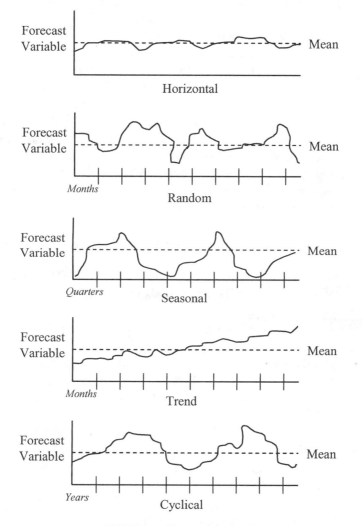

FIGURE 4.4 Types of time series.

izontal, (2) trends, (3) seasonality, (4) cycles, and (5) random. *Horizontal patterns* exhibit relative stability and consistency in actual occurrences in comparison to the forecast. Such patterns are characteristic of products with stable sales patterns or arising from aggregate forecast populations. *Trends* are consistent upward or downward patterns observable in the occurrence of a series of data values continuing for approximately seven or more periods.

Forecasters normally employ weighted moving averages, exponential smoothing, and regression techniques in calculating trends. *Seasonality* is described as a consistent pattern of activity that occurs within a limited time frame year after year. Examples would be demand for snow shovels during the winter months and beach equipment during the summer months. Forecasters utilize time-series decomposition techniques when working with seasonality. *Cyclical* patterns are used by forecasters to track long-range trends in the overall economy that could have an impact on the firm's strategies. Cyclical influences often last for one to five years and then recur. Forecasting cycles is difficult because the data do not reoccur at constant intervals of time and its duration is not uniform. Various qualitative and quantitative techniques are employed to forecast business cycles. *Random* patterns of activities or *outliers* are the most difficult to forecast because they, in fact, exhibit no historical pattern. Forecasters can use weighted moving averages, exponential smoothing, and regression techniques in determining the forecast of elements characterized by this type of pattern [10].

SELECTING QUANTITATIVE FORECASTING TECHNIQUES

When selecting forecast techniques, forecasters must search for the most appropriate method that meets the enterprise's requirements. Forecasters must ask themselves several questions:

- What is the best forecast type - qualitative or quantitative - to use when forecasting a given set of historical data?
- If a quantitative method is selected, what will be the cost and the amount of effort required to develop and execute the forecast?
- What is the level of data accuracy required by the forecast technique selected?
- Which forecasting technique will best match historical issues such as trend, seasonality, and so on?
- Does the firm possess the necessary data processing tools for the desired forecast computation?

In this section, the major quantitative forecasting techniques will be explored. The goal is to equip the reader with a working knowledge of basic quantitative methods to assist in answering the above questions.

Simple Models. The simplest form of forecasting is referred to as *Naive Forecast 1*. The elements necessary for the calculation of are easy to understand and apply. The equation on which the technique is based is

$$F_{t+i} = X_t \qquad (4.1)$$

where F_{t+i} is the forecast for period $t + i$, t is the present period, i is the number of periods ahead to be forecasted, and X_t is the latest actual value (for period t).

This equation uses the most recent actual demand value, disregards the value of the past forecast for the same period, and extrapolates it as the new forecast for the next period(s). For example if the actual demand for period X is 125 that value then becomes the forecast for the next period(s), and so on. This technique could be used to forecast data where turning points indicating error can not be predicted. For forecasts exhibiting seasonality *Naive Forecast 2* can be employed. This variation, which uses the same equation as *Naive Forecast 1*, requires the forecaster to remove seasonality from the original data in order to obtain seasonally adjusted data that in turn can be used as a forecast for the next seasonally adjusted value [11].

Averages. Forecasts can be calculated by the use of several forms of *average*. The first is a *simple average*. In this technique, the actual demand found in the present period is added to the actual demand of the past period, and the average is then calculated. The resulting value is the new forecast. For example, if sales totaled 400 units for the past period and 420 units in the current period, the new forecast would be calculated as $(400 + 420) / 2 = 410$. Another popular form of forecast average is the *year-to-date average*. In this technique, actual demand is recorded as it occurs period by period and added together. The calculated value is then divided by the number of periods used with the resulting value being posted as the forecast for the next period. As an example, say that the sales over a period of the last 3 months equaled 200, 210, and 190. The forecast would be determined as $(200 + 210 + 190) / 3 = 200$. If the sales for month four equaled 220, the forecast would be calculated as $(200 + 210 + 190 + 220) / 4 = 205$. The value of these two forms of forecasting is their simplicity and ease of use. Drawbacks are insensitivity to variation and unavailability of turning points for forecast adjust-ment.

One of the main problems associated with using a simple average is that the equation places equal weight on present and past data; year-to-date average places too much weight on past data, especially as time moves forward. The result is that both techniques are insensitive to trends or outliers. One solution is to use a *moving average*. This technique calculates the sum of historical values for a set number of periods, finds their average, and then uses the result as the forecast for the next period. The average is moving because as time moves forward, the last period is dropped from the calculation and the current period value is added. The number of periods used can range from 2 to 12 or more with 3 to 5 being the most common. The formula for the moving average is

$$D1,2,3 = \frac{D1 + D2 + D3}{3} = F4 \qquad (4.2)$$

$$D2,3,4 = \frac{D2 + D3 + D4}{3} = F5 .$$

Although the moving average technique assists forecasters with solving the problem of period weighting, it does not work very well if the forecast exhibits trend or seasonality. In such cases the moving average will consistently lag behind trends in actual demand [12].

Weighted Average. While the moving average will significantly assist forecasters to smooth past demand to ensure a more accurate forecast, the ability to place a "weight" on instances of past demand will enable planners to determine how much of an influence the relationship of past demand will have in the forecast calculation. Simply put, an "unweighted" time series of two instances of demand assigns a 50 percent weight to each demand value. The *weighted moving average* technique enables forecasters to "weight" each instance of demand in the time series in an effort to determine a forecast that more closely resembles reality. The formula for this calculation utilizes the moving average technique plus the addition of a weighting factor that is multiplied by each instance of demand and then divided by the sum of all weighting factors. The formula for the weighted three period moving average is

$$D1,2,3 = \frac{wD1 + wD2 + wD3}{w1 + w2 + w3} = F4 \qquad (4.3)$$

$$D2,3,4 = \frac{wD2 + wD3 + wD4}{w2 + w3 + w4} = F5 .$$

where D is the demand and w is the weight. For example, if the demand for periods one through three were 200, 220, and 210 respectively and the weights correspondingly assigned at 2, 3, and 4, then the calculation of the new forecast would be as follows:

$$2(200) + 3(220) + 4(240) = 2020 / 9 = 224.44$$

The weighted moving average can only be used when there are sufficient periods of demand data available. The weighting factors applied can be any

values and are determined by the forecaster in relation to the relative importance of instance of past demand. While the weighted moving average will
produce a forecast that is more receptive to changes in demand patterns, it
will still lag behind possible trends. In the example above, the new forecast
is still considerably dampened in what appears to be an upward trend in sales.

Exponential Smoothing. The use of a moving average has at least three important limitations. To begin with, to calculate a moving average necessitates
the storage of an enormous amount of data, especially if the demand history is
significant. Second, as the amount of historical data grows, it becomes more
difficult to flag occurrences exhibiting trends or seasonality. Finally, the
moving average method gives equal weight to old and new observed values.
It can be argued that when preparing a forecast, the most recent events should
be given relatively more or less weight in the calculation than older ones. *Exponential smoothing* is a technique that offers a solution to these problems.
The advantages of exponential smoothing are that it permits forecasters to assign weights to past historical and present period data to reflect demand pattern realities such as trends and seasonality. In addition exponential smoothing requires only minimal computer space to store data.
   The components of the exponential smoothing calculation consist of the
value of the old forecast, the value of the current observed data, and the percentage chosen to weight the equation. While there are several exponential
smoothing techniques, the most commonly used equation is expressed as

$$ESF_t = \alpha\,(D_t) + (1 - \alpha)\,(F_{t-1}) \tag{4.4}$$

where ESF_t is the exponential smoothed new forecast, t is the current period
in which the most recent actual demand is known, D is the current period actual demand, α is the *alpha factor* (forecast weight), and F is the exponential
smoothed forecast of one period past.
   The key to exponential smoothing is the *smoothing constant* expressed as
α. The purpose of the constant is to give relative weights to the actual values
of the last past period and the historical forecasted values. If greater weight
is to be given to the most recent actual values, then a high smoothing constant
is chosen, and *vice versa*. Calculation of α or weight is normally based on
the number of periods the forecaster would use if a moving average was being
employed. The equation for calculating α is

$$\alpha = \frac{2}{(n + 1)} \tag{4.5}$$

Example:

Calculation for a five period moving average: $\dfrac{2}{(5+1)} = .33.$

The exponential smoothing calculation using data for a sales forecast can be seen in Figure 4.5. The calculation uses the value of the previous forecast

		Average	Weighted
Old Weekly Forecast = 500		x 0.5 = 250	x 0.8 = 400
Actual Sales = 450		x 0.5 = 225	x 0.2 = 90
New Weekly Forecast		475	490

FIGURE 4.5 Weighted calculation.

(500) and the actual value that occurred (450). The first calculation illustrates a straight average calculation and the resulting forecast. The second calculation uses an alpha factor that places 80 percent weight on the old forecast and 20 percent weight on the current actual value. The results of the smoothed calculation show greater stability in the new forecast than the straight average and permit forecasters to review the data to detect for trends that might be occurring. When utilizing the formula (Eq. 4.4), the equation for the same calculation would read:

$$\alpha = .20(450) + 1 - \alpha = .80\,(500) = 490$$

The exponential smoothing equation (Eq. 4.4) is termed *first-order smoothing*. Although the equation functions well when demand is steady, the calculated forecast will lag behind actual demand if a significant trend exits. To use exponential smoothing to forecast using a trend a further calculation to account for and smooth the trend must be added to the equation. Equation (4.6) will calculate the *base value* of the previous forecast. The base value is nothing more than the actual demand plus the trend. Notice that this calculation requires the input of the trend.

Base value$_t$ = α(Actual demand) + $(1 - \alpha)$ (Base value$_{t-1}$ + Trend$_{t-1}$) (4.6)

where α is the smoothing factor, t is the current period, Base value $t-1$ is the base value computed one period previously, and Trend$_{t-1}$ is the trend value computed one period previously.

Once the new base value of the current period has been calculated, the new trend can be formulated. This calculation (Eq 4.7) also includes the smoothing of the trend.

$$\text{Trend}_t = \beta \ (\text{Base value}_t - \text{Base value}_{t-1}) + (1 - \beta) \ (\text{Trend}_t) \qquad (4.7)$$

where β is the smoothing factor, Base value$_t$ is the base value computed for the current period, Base value$_{t-1}$ is the base value for the previous period, and Trend$_{t-1}$ is the trend value for the previous period.

Now that new base and trend values have been computed, the new forecast calculation can be made. Notice that this equation can be used to calculate forecasts for multiple future periods:

$$\text{New Forecast}_{t+X} = \text{Base Value}_t + X \ (\text{Trend}_t) \qquad (4.8)$$

where X is the number of future periods, t is the current period, Base value$_t$ is the current exponentially smoothed base value, and Trend$_t$ is the current exponentially smoothed trend.

A sample calculation of exponential smoothing employing a trend follows:

Data: $\alpha = 0.2$; $\beta = 0.1$; Trend$_{t}$ -1 = 50; Base value$_{t}$-1 = 500
Previous base value + trend = 500 + 50 = 550
Actual demand for current period = 560
New base value = 0.2 (560) + (1 - 0.2) (500 + 50) = 552
New trend = 0.1 (552 - 500) + (1 - 0.1) (50) = 50.2
Next period forecast = 552 + (1 period) 50.2 = 602.2
Forecast for three periods from now = 552 + (3) 50.2 = 702.6

The exponential smoothing techniques presented above are the most popular models in use. There are, however, a number of other smoothing techniques of much greater complexity. Linear (Holt's) Exponential Smoothing is used when data exhibits a constant trend. Winter's Linear and Seasonal Exponential Smoothing is useful when the data contains seasonality as well as trend. Damped Trend Exponential Smoothing can be employed when trend in demand does not extend over long forecast periods. When forecasters are considering the use of exponential smoothing models they must be careful to select techniques commiserate with the cost and complexity required [13].

Adaptive Exponential Smoothing. Choosing the correct *smoothing factor* is critical for exponential smoothing to provide the information necessary for effective forecasting. According to DeLurgio and Bhame (14), the following rule of thumb can be applied when selecting a *smoothing factor:*

Use a low *alpha* for a very random series
Use a high *alpha* for a very smooth series

In general, when deciding upon a *smoothing factor* using heuristic methods, the primary issue is deciding upon the number of periods to be used in the computation. When calculating the alpha based on the number of desired periods the following formula can be used:

$$\alpha = 2/(n + 1) \quad \text{or} \quad n = 2/\alpha - 1 \qquad\qquad 4\text{-}9$$

Using this formula, the following chart can be produced:

For *alpha* of **.1**: $n = 2/.1 - 1 = 19$ period average
For *alpha* of **.3**: $n = 2/.3 - 1 = 5.67$ period average
For *alpha* of **.6**: $n = 2/.6 - 1 = 2.33$ period average
For *alpha* of **.9**: $n = 2/.9 - 1 = 1.22$ period average

When choosing an *alpha*, the goal is to select a value that yields the most accurate forecast and that value can best be described as the one that achieves the lowest standard deviation of forecast error. In other words, when choosing an *alpha*, the object is to reduce the standard deviation of the forecast errors to as low as possible. To achieve this objective, simulation calculations can be used to determine the alpha exhibiting the lowest error. This alpha would then be used in the next forecast generation. The goal is to have the *alpha* be *adaptive* to the ratio of the absolute value of two averages: *average error* and *average absolute forecast error.*

The formula for calculating an *alpha* from forecast deviation is as follows:

$$alpha = \left| \frac{\text{Mean Error}}{\text{MAD}} \right| \qquad\qquad 4\text{-}10$$

The *alpha* generated by the calculation is in reality a *tracking signal* that demonstrates forecast error over time. For example, when a series moves rapidly up or down, a high *alpha* is automatically used. In contrast, if the series is consistent and has low forecast error, then a low *alpha* is used. Also, if the model is systematically under or over the forecast then the *alpha* is impacted. The value of the calculated *alpha* can never be greater than **1** or less than **0**. Because it adapts to the magnitude of the errors, the *alpha* is referred to as an *adaptive alpha*. Further discussion on calculating the mean error and the MAD is found later in this chapter.

Seasonality. Many supply chains inventory products that are subject to seasonal demand. A snow shovel will exhibit high sales in late autumn and early winter, peak during the winter months, and decline dramatically in the spring and summer. The key to forecasting seasonal products is using the proper historical data. The most useful way to calculate a forecast exhibiting seasonality is to employ a *seasonal index*. For example, a firm may sell 125 snow shovels a month on average. In reality, during the fall and winter seasons, 200 are sold each month, and an average of 50 is sold during the warmer months of the year. Accordingly, during the peak season the index would be 1.6(200/125), and 0.4(50/125) for the nonseasonal months. This index ratio can then be used to adjust forecasts for seasonal patterns.

A simple calculation is to create a seasonal index based on a percent of sales. In Table 4.2 data on snow shovel sales has been collected by month for a given year. In preparing the index the actual sales are added and then divided by 12 to arrive at a normalized average. For each month the actual sales are then divided by the yearly average to attain the seasonal index. The final step would be to multiply the new forecast by month by the corresponding seasonal index.

TABLE 4.2 Calculating the Seasonal Index for Snow Shovels

Month	Demand	Calculation	Index
January	220	220/132	1.7
February	205	205/132	1.6
March	110	110/132	0.9
April	55	55/132	0.4
May	50	50/132	0.4
June	50	50/132	0.4
July	40	40/132	0.3
August	55	55/132	0.4
September	110	110/132	0.9
October	205	205/132	1.6
November	250	250/132	1.9
December	230	230/132	1.7
Average	1580/12 = 132		

A more complicated calculation would be to use exponential smoothing when forecasting with seasonality. Calculating seasonality utilizing a smoothing technique requires the use of a base value and a seasonal index. The equation (4.11) consists of three parts: calculation of a new base value by smoothing "deseasonalized" demand data, calculation of a smoothed seasonal index, and calculation of the seasonalized forecast for next period [15].

$$\text{Base value}_t = \alpha \left(\frac{\text{Actual demand}_t}{\text{Old index}}\right) + (1 - \alpha)(\text{Base value}_{t-1}), \qquad (4.11)$$

$$\text{New index} = s \left(\frac{\text{Actual demand}_t}{\text{Base value}_t}\right) + (1 - s)(\text{Old index}),$$

$$\text{New seasonal forecast} = \text{New base value} \times \text{New index},$$

where α is the smoothing factor for base value, s is the smoothing factor for seasonal index, and Base value$_{t-1}$ is the previous period base value.

A sample exponentially smoothed seasonal forecast for the snow shovel example during the 6 months of high demand follows:

Data: $\alpha = 0.2$, $s = 0.3$, old index (seasonal months) = 1.24
Base value (November) = 180; actual demand (December) = 210
  1. 0.2 (210/1.24) + (1 - 0.2)(180) = 177.9,
  2. 0.3 (210/177.9) + (1 - 0.3)(1.24) = 1.22,
  3. Forecast for January = 177.9 (1.22) = 217.

Focus Forecasting. All quantitative forecasting systems depend on a statistical concept called the *normal distribution*. Whether variants of the average or exponential smoothing calculations, these techniques focus on forecasting using an average value or mean, and the distribution of errors from the mean. The problem with the use of the normal distribution is that, although it works well when based on large volumes of transactions and long periods of time, it functions poorly when the statistical population is intermittent or is characterized by low volume. In addition, most supply chains experience several kinds of demand patterns, such as trend, seasonality, and so forth that require forecasters to employ several models based on the forecast objective. Finally, following a Pareto distribution, only about 20 percent of a firm's inventory possesses the volumes necessary for effective statistical forecasting. The result is that the vast majority of a distributor's inventory limps along under forecasting models that poorly fit forecasting needs.

In 1978, an entirely new concept of forecasting, termed *focus forecasting*, was introduced by Bernard T. Smith to address these problems. Focus forecasting can be defined as a computerized forecasting system that allows forecasters to simulate the effectiveness of a number of forecast rules and to choose the rule that best fits the historical data. Some forecasts work better for some items than for others; some forecasts work better at certain times of the year than others. The mechanics of focus forecasting allow calculation of the future of an item using all the rules that have been successfully used in the past. All of these rules are then simulated, permitting the forecaster to choose the one that is the best choice for the item today. Some of the rules that can be developed are the following:

1. We will probably have the average historical increase on this item.
2. We will probably sell what we sold last year at this time.
3. We will probably sell what we sold during the last 3 months.
4. We will probably sell half of what we sold during the last 6 months.
5. Whatever we sold last month, we will sell in the next 3 months.

In developing the formula to be fed into the computer, very simple components are used. As an example, "we will probably sell in the second quarter this year is what we sold during the first 3 months last year" would be expressed as *A* (actual demand) *LY* (last year) *1 through 3* (months) = *F* (forecast) *TY* (this year) *4 through 6* (months). An example of the forecast calculation using this formula follows:

Example:

	Jan	Feb	Mar	Apr	May	Jun	Jul	Aug	Sep	Oct	Nov	Dec
Last Year	100	95	90	95	105	110	105	115	120	115	125	130
This Year	105	100	95									

(Last year = 100 + 95 + 90) = Forecast of 285 or 95 per month for April, May, and June

In selecting the proper forecast the computer would need the forecaster to tell the system what actual quarterly data to compare with the results of the two forecast rules. Say the actual demand (found in the above example) of first quarter this year was selected. The demand would be calculated as (105 + 100 + 95) = 300. In the example there are only two rules:

1. We will probably sell in the second quarter this year what we sold in the second quarter last year.

2. We will probably sell in the second quarter this year what we sold in the last quarter of last year.

Steps:
1. $(95 + 105 + 110) = F(310)$
2. $(115 + 125 + 130) = F(370)$
3. Forecast Rule #1 = 310 - 300 (1st Quarter This Year) = +10.
4. Forecast Rule #2 = 370 - 300 = +70.
5. Forecast Rule #1 would be selected because it is closest to comparison quarter.

Focus forecasting provides forecasters with a powerful yet easy way to understand techniques to forecast trends, seasonality, items with sporadic history, and other demand conditions. The forecasting process works whether there are 2 or 20 formulas. Beyond the fact that the software must be purchased, all that forecasters are required to do is to monitor rule effectiveness and add or delete rules that no longer provide adequate data to describe the firm's demand patterns [16].

CAUSAL TYPES

The last forecasting type involves the use of *causal models*. Also known as *explanatory* or *extrinsic forecasting,* these techniques seek to predict the future by using additional related data beyond the time series data recorded for a specific occurrence (say, weekly sales of a given product). The idea behind the method is to leverage other occurrences in the marketplace up and above historical data to attempt to predict more precisely the course of future demand. Quantitative methods merely attempt to detail the mathematical relationships of events occurring in the past. In contrast, causal methods try to *explain* why these events occurred in the pattern in which they did. The information provided by causal forecasts can assist companies to better utilize their quantitative forecasts by illuminating key insights into demand trends.

Another critical difference between quantitative and causal forecasting relates to the size of the planning horizon and data sample. The quantitative methods discussed above are primarily short-range to medium-range techniques used to calculate discrete historical requirements. Causal methods, on the other hand, focus on long-range forecasts that use qualitative and quantitative macro measurements such as political, demographical, new technology, and other forces to predict the future. In addition, they are best employed when making projections of aggregate demand such as the total sales demand of a company, sales of a product group, or sales in a specific geographical region. Examples of possible causal forecasts would be predicting when a new product or process will be available, what the impact of new inventions or discoveries will have on the marketplace, or what effects or changes might emerge as a result of developments in technology. An example would be attempting to forecast the year's sales of sump pumps based on the projected number of housing and commercial building starts. In this causal forecast, building starts are referred to as *predictor* or *independent variables*, and sump pump sales as the *predicted* or *dependent variable.*

The strength of explanatory methods lies in the use of a wide range of forecasts that can be formulated using a field of related variables. Drawbacks to using this type are that it is useful only for aggregate forecasts, the data requirements are larger than what is required for time-series models, it usually takes longer to develop, and it is impacted more by changes in the underlying relationships than would be the case employing a time-series model. In addition, causal methods are more costly to develop than intrinsic (quantitative) methods due to the additional costs stemming from external data collection and the time engaged in analysis. For the most part, causal methods are rarely used in operational forecasting systems [17].

Simple Causal Model. Causal methods can use relatively simple or very complex mathematical calculations. Equation (4.12) portrays a simple three-variable model for calculating sump pump demand.

$$New\ forecast = \text{New period forecast} + 0.2(LMS) + 1(WC) + 0.5(NHS) \quad (4.12)$$
$$= 100\ +\ 0.2(125)\ +\ 1(0.3)\ +\ 0.5(300)\ =\ 275$$

where LMS is the last month's sales, WC is the weather conditions, and NHS is the new housing starts.

Beyond this simple model, there are a number of more complex techniques. *Regression analysis* is a causal technique used for forecasting aggregate or group demands such as company or product-line demands for the medium-range to long-range term. This technique seeks to model past relationships between dependent and independent variables. Another technique is the use of historical analogies that employ comparative analysis in viewing the introduction and growth of products or processes in the past with new entrants that possess similar characteristics. Life-cycle analysis seeks to forecast new product growth rates based on *S curves*. The object is to plot phases of product acceptance by various groups such as innovators, early adapters, early majority, late majority, and laggards that can be used to project the demand cycles of similar products [18].

Regression Analysis. Regression analysis distinguishes between the *depen-dent variable* (commonly denoted by *Y*) and the *independent variable* (or *X*). The formula used to denote regression analysis is as follows:

$$Y = A + \beta X \qquad\qquad (4.13)$$

Where Y is the value of the dependent variable, A is the Y-axis intercept, β is the slope of the regression line, and X is the independent variable.

The mechanics of the technique are as follows:

1. Identify the relationship between the dependent and the independent variable
2. Measure the error in using that relationship to predict values of the dependent variable
3. Measure the degree of association between the two variables

The following example will illustrate how regression analysis attempts to answer these questions.

Acme Pump, Inc. has found that their volume of sales over time is dependent on the number of new housing starts in their city. The following table details sales and new housing starts over the past 5 years.

Yearly Sales Dollars ($000,000), Y variable	Number of Housing Starts (0,000 of housing units), β variable
2.0	1
3.0	3
2.0	2
2.5	3
3.5	4

The first step is to determine the mathematical relationship between yearly sales and the number of housing starts. This can be accomplished by following the least-squares regression approach.

1. Relationship of X and Y

Yearly Sales, Y	Housing Starts, X	X	XY
2.0	1	1	2.0
3.0	4	16	12.0
2.0	3	9	6.0
2.5	3	9	7.5
3.5	4	16	14.0
13.0	15	51	41.5

With these data in hand, the calculation is as follows:

2. Average values of X and Y

$$X = \frac{X}{(n) \text{ number of years}} = \frac{15}{5} = 3,$$

$$Y = \frac{Y}{n} = \frac{13}{5} = 2.6,$$

where n is the number of years.

3. Slope of the regression line

$$B = \frac{XY - nXY}{X - nX} = \frac{41.5 - (5)(3)(2.6)}{51 - (5)(3)} = 0.42.$$

4. Y-axis intercept

$$A = Y - \beta X = 2.6 - (0.42)(3) = 1.34$$

5. The value of the dependent variable (Y)

$$y = 1.34 \text{ (sales)} + .42 \text{ (housing starts)}.$$

6. If next year's anticipated housing starts will be 3000, then the forecasted pump sales will be

$$\text{Sales} = 1.34 + 0.42(3) = 2.6(\$100,000) = \$260,000.$$

Once the relationship between the dependent and independent variables have been established, it is now possible to calculate the degree of forecast error. The forecast of $260,000 is, in reality, the mean or expected value of possible sales. To measure the error, it will be necessary to calculate the *standard error of the estimate* (Sy,x). A useful formula for computing this error is as follows:

$$Sy,x = \sqrt{\frac{(y - yc)2}{n - 2}}$$

4-14

where y is the y-value of each data point, yc is the calculated value of the dependent variable, from the regression equation, and n is the number of data points.

By placing into the equation the data detailed above, the forecast error would be calculated as

$$Sy,x = \sqrt{\frac{35.5 - 1.34(13.0) - 0.42(41.5)}{5 - 2}}$$

When multiplied by $ hundred thousands, the estimate of forecast error would be $46,547.

Multiple Regression Analysis. In the above forecast of pump sales, only one independent variable (housing starts) was used in the calculation. When constructing a regression analysis, forecasters should build in more than one independent variable. As an example, ACME Pump, Inc. might want to include the average annual interest rate in its model. As such, the new equation would be expressed as

$$Y = A + \beta 1 X1 + \beta 2 X2 \ldots \beta n Xn + e \qquad (4.15)$$

where Y is the dependent variable (pump sales), A is the Y-intercept, $X1$ is the independent variable 1 (housing starts), and $\beta 1$ is the independent variable 2 (average annual interest rate). The obvious negative of this technique is the enormous computation involved, which is normally performed by a computer. The benefit is that multiple regression measures the simultaneous influence of several independent variables on the dependent variable to broaden the forecasted value [19].

MANAGING THE FORECAST

In developing forecasts, planners must perform the following steps:

1. Define the purpose of the forecast
2. Select the appropriate forecasting model(s)
3. Prepare the statistical components
4. Ensure the interaction of the firm's functional area managers
5. Execute the forecast
6. Track and maintain the forecast through timely and accurate feedback

Before a forecasting technique can be chosen, forecasters must first determine the purpose of the proposed forecast. In accomplishing this task planners are faced with three critical tasks. To begin with, they must match the proper forecasting method with the stated object-tives of the firm's business units, ranging from long-term to short-term goals. Second, forecasters must also utilize forecasting methods that can be easily integrated together to provide the enterprise with a comprehensive game plan that is supportive of both departmental as well as corporate performance tar-gets. Finally, the forecasts must be capable of being communicated to supply chain partners. Failure to integrate the various forecasts not only through each business unit throughout the firm, but also externally with each trading partner, will result in dysfunctional management decisions where business entities pursue separate objectives and potentially opposing measures of performance.

Once the purpose of the forecast has been defined, forecasters can then proceed to the selection of the techniques necessary to fulfill the forecasting objectives. Choosing the proper technique(s) is perhaps the most critical stage in the forecasting process and consists of the following elements:

1. *System Dynamics.* The first stage in forecast technique selection is to determine the dynamics and components of the business system elements to be forecasted. This can be attained initially by clarifying the relationships of the different elements of the enterprise, such as the marketing and sales system, the procurement system, the distribution system, and so on, and, secondly, by effectively mapping out the supply chain structure. The forecasting system that is constructed should indicate where input is controlled by the company and where input is in the control of external forces. Such an analysis will provide forecasters with the ability to match the technique with the source of input data. The more the firm has control over input, the more *quantitative* the forecast technique; correspondingly, the less control, the more *qualitative* the forecast method.

2. *Technology Elements.* The requirements for computational power, integration with backbone data warehouses, and electronic interoperability with supply chain partners make the selection and application of computerized forecasting systems a must before real forecasting strategies can be developed. Today's ERP, stand-alone applications, and Internet enablers provide a wide-range of software capabilities targeted at facilitating the gathering, analytical compilation, transmission, and receipt of forecasts in real-time from any node in the supply chain. The choice of technologies must closely support the purpose of the forecast as identified in the pervious step.

3. *Time Horizon.* Selection of the proper time horizon is critical in the determination of the length of time to be considered by the forecast. Gen-

erally, qualitative methods are employed to calculate long-range forecasts, and quantitative methods are employed to calculate medium- to short-range forecasts. In addition, the data of the proposed forecast is also affected by the time horizon to be used. By using the requirements of the functional business area as one dimension and the time horizon for planning as the other, characteristics such as size of forecasted period (weekly, monthly, etc.), frequency of review, and unit of measure can be determined. Purchasing, for example, has forecasting requirements that extend through all three time horizons. In the short range, purchase order release, review, cash availability, and performance measurement are the key elements in forecast selection. Medium-range concerns focus on purchasing planning to support the inventory plan. Finally, in the long range purchasers are concerned with supplier partnership management, contracts, and delivery scheduling that requires aggregate business forecasts capable of being shared with upstream supply points.

4. *Data.* In selecting forecasting techniques, strategists must understand the nature of the data required and the availability and accuracy of that data within the organization and outside in the supply chain. Fundamental to the appropriateness of the data is understanding the kinds of patterns found in the existing data. Some data, for example, may exhibit an average (mean) value with fairly limited random variation; on the other hand, other data may contain an historical trend or seasonal demand. Finally, other data may consist of combinations of these patterns. Furthermore, a desired forecasting technique may require data that the firm either does not possess or that has been poorly recorded. In such an instance, forecasters may be required to use qualitative rather than quantitative techniques in forecast creation. In the end, techniques that match the objectives of the forecast with the existence and observed patterns of the data to be employed in the calculations must be carefully chosen.

5. *Cost.* As the utility of any forecast is reflected in the quality of the decisions based on the forecast, ideally, selection of forecasting models should be based on a simple correlation of forecast cost and the value of the forecasted decision. Silver and Peterson suggest a basic formula in which the total cost of using a technique is calculated by adding the cost of operating a procedure to the cost of resulting forecast error [20]. One simple criterion for forecast selection would be to use as low a cost as possible per forecast. As an example, the preparation of a forecast necessary to calculate the future demand on thousands of items on a weekly basis requires a technique that is simple, effective, and low cost. In general, the shorter the range of the forecast, the more low-cost

forecast techniques should be used, with the more costly methods reserved for aggregate long-range forecasts.

6. *Accuracy.* Besides appropriateness, the data used must be accurate if forecast output is to be meaningful. Before a particular technique can be selected, forecasters must understand how the data have been obtained, verified, recorded, and transmitted. To ensure accuracy, forecasters must employ tools that control errors and provide for appropriate adjustment of nonrecurring events. *Forecast alarms,* for example, can assist by focusing attention on occurrences outside a predetermined band of high and low values. In summary, forecasters must examine the collection, calculation, completeness, source, and accuracy of the data before selecting a forecast technique.

7. *Ease of Use and Simplicity.* Many planners make the mistake of overcomplicating their forecasts by trying to use complex mathematical formulas to solve relatively simple business problems. The literature of forecasting is filled with obtuse mathematical approaches. The problem with these techniques is that they are potentially very costly solutions requiring computer disk space, manual coding and file maintenance, and a trained expert to understand them. In reality, forecasters should select techniques that are simplistic, minimize file maintenance, and are easy for the user to understand.

The third step in forecast development is data preparation. It has already been stated that accurate data must be available *before* a forecasting technique is chosen. Data preparation, however, must extend beyond the subject of the forecast (say, historical sales figures) to consider other data that has impacted sales in the past. Looking purely at sales history without related information such as price increases, shortages, sales promotions, new products, the impact of competitors, and other factors will produce a biased view of the data. In addition, the forecaster must determine just what is to be forecasted. For example, consider the forecaster who is attempting to derive product-level forecasts summarized from four distribution centers. One approach would be to forecast demand individually at each distribution center. If this data set is used, forecasts will be affected by the variations experienced at each distribution center. An alternative would be to calculate a product national forecast and to reduce it to the SKU level on the basis of historical percentages. Finally, time must be allotted for actual data preparation. As a rule, the shorter the time frame to be forecast, the quicker the data must be ready. For most forecasting methods, computer programs have been developed that can greatly increase the speed and accuracy in calculation. Urgency and the length of time required for forecast preparation are key elements in forecast technique selection.

Before the forecast can be executed, it must gain the consensus of the firm's management team. A firm that blindly executes the statistical portion of the forecast without soliciting the input of all impacted functional managers, and sometimes channel partners, will get variable results. For example, marketing and sales has decided to run a promotion on a specific product group in an effort to increase market share. It is critical that expected sales projections be communicated to logistics management, who, in turn, must forecast purchasing, warehousing, and transportation requirements in anticipation of the impact increased demand will have on company and supporting channel partner resources. Without the proper communication and alignment of forecasts between these entities, it is doubtful whether the firm will be able to effective respond to the promotion and achieve the targeted revenue and cost objectives. Other forms of marketing and sales intelligence are critical to effective forecasting. Such factors as special pricing, loss of market share, attempts to gain market share, introduction of new products, changes to the supply chain structure, and others need to be communicated to ensure the organization and its trading partners are pursuing a common plan. When developing forecasts, inventory control and marketing should generate a "first-cut" forecast that would then be reviewed by internal managers from sales, purchasing, warehousing, manufacturing, and finance, as well as outside channel partners who can assist in evaluating the appropriateness of the data before the final forecast is calculated.

Execution of the forecast can potentially be a difficult task. Many companies have products exhibiting several different historical demand patterns that must be accounted for in the forecast calculation. For example, a distributor may have demand that is widely varied. Some products have demand that is horizontal: Sales are consistent over time with minimum variation. Older items may exhibit intermittent demand where sales are very irregular. Still other items might exhibit a trend. To ensure the proper forecasting technique is being applied to match demand patterns, forecasters need to employ systems that are flexible enough to satisfy the forecasting requirements of each type of event. Supply chain strategists must always keep referring back to the goals of the proposed forecast in guiding them in the selection and use of forecasting systems.

The final step in forecast development is monitoring forecast feedback. Forecasting should be conceived as a continuous process of measurement, like statistical quality control. As such, monitoring feedback has two separate but connected activities. To begin with, feedback alerts the forecaster when the process is out of control. Second, feedback signals how far the process is out of control and what must be done to regain forecast control. There are several techniques revolving around the concept of a *tracking signal* that can assist forecasters in monitoring feedback. A simple tool is the use of *forecast alarms* whereby significant errors that exceed a predetermined range are flagged for review.

UNDERSTANDING FORECAST ERROR

It can truly be said that every forecast is always correct - it is just that reality is perverse and it is variation rather than constancy that subverts the accuracy of every forecast. In a universe were patterns of occurrences were uniform and predictable, forecasts would be unnecessary. Ensuring the correctness of any forecast can, therefore, be said to be more of an exercise in determining the degree of forecast error than in searching for the optimum forecast. Forecasting can be compared to searching for the philosopher's stone: the solution always seems to be just in reach with the promise of turn-ing dismal computations concerning seemingly disparate atoms of data into gold.

To a surprising extent, the effectiveness of forecasting systems is dependent on how well they handle stochastic demand. Consistent patterns in demand are effectively handled by forecasting methods that model trend, seasonality, and random components of demand. Unusual demands, or outliers, present serious problems unless they are adjusted in the forecast. Detecting when a forecast model is no longer representative of demand is an important component of a good forecasting system. A model can go out of control because of large, one-time abnormal occurrences (outliers) or because several minor events that cause the model to consistently over- or underforecast (i.e. bias). These differences may result from problems in either the forecast or actual demand. Figure 4.6 illustrates the mapping of such occurrences.

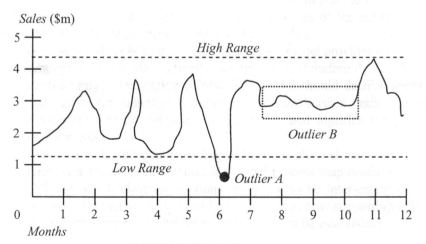

FIGURE 4.6 Viewing forecast error.

Even if large outliers are eliminated, the forecasting process can go out of control. Several techniques are available to assist forecasters to detect such conditions. As mentioned above, simple tracking signals can be employed. A simple tracking signal would be to arrive at a ratio determined by dividing actual sales by the past average forecast over n periods. An instance of demand outside of a range, say 0.8 to 1.2 would be marked for review. Table 4.3 illustrates the computation.

TABLE 4.3 Simple Forecast Error Tracking Signal

	Period			
	1	2	3	4
Forecast Demand	1500	1600	1400	1500
Actual Demand	1600	1500	1300	1400

$$TC = \frac{\text{Last AD} = 1400}{F(150 + 1600 + 1400 + 1500)/n(4) = 1500} = 0.93$$

where

TC = tracking signal
F = forecast
AD = actual demand
n = number of periods

A more complex example would be to compute the tracking signal as the ratio of the running sum of forecast error to the average error. Perhaps the most employed tracking signals are calculating the *mean error* and the *mean absolute deviation* (MAD) by using exponential smoothing. The smoothing constant permits the forecaster to weight forecast error. The larger the α the more heavily weighted will be the value of the most recent forecast error. The formula below illustrates the calculation [21].

1. Smoothed Error = α(Actual Demand$t$ - Forecast$t$) + (1 - α (Smoothed Error$t$ -1)
2. Smoothed MAD = α|Actual Demand$t$ - Forecast$t$| + (1 - α (Smoothed MADt - 1)
3. Tracking Signal = $\dfrac{\text{Smoothed Error}t}{\text{Smoothed MAD}t}$

As an example, take the following data:

Forecast$t$ = 100, Actual Demand$t$ = 90, α(alpha) = .1
Smoothed Error$t$ -1 = -1, Smoothed MADt -1 = 5
1. Smoothed Error = .1(90 - 100) + (1 - .1) (-1) = -1.9
2. Smoothed MAD = .1|90 - 100| + (1 -.1) (5) = 5.5
3. Tracking Signal = -1.9/5.5 = -0.345

The second activity in forecast monitoring is adjusting the forecast to account for error. Forecast revision depends on determining the reason why the error occurred. For a standard product, for example, if actual sales are less than anticipated, forecasters must review past measurements to see if a downward trend is occurring and make adjustments accordingly. On the other hand, a forecast for a new product that shows an upward growth trend may not only require a forecast change, but possibly also a new forecast technique. In any case, changing the forecast requires the participation of key company managers and supply chain partners. Continuous communication between forecasters and users is critical in promoting better understanding, and ensures quick and authoritative response to changing conditions.

WHY FORECASTS FAIL

Developing, maintaining, and using forecasting techniques are critical functions in the successful execution of the various planning processes of the enterprise. The following points attempt to illustrate the reasons why forecasts fail [22].

- *Management Involvement.* Effective forecasting is needed at the top management, operations management, and operations execution levels of the firm. What is more, these forecasts must be in alignment with one another. Perhaps the foremost reason why forecasts fail is because of a lack of participation by functional management both in the development and in the execution of the forecast in process. To be successful, forecasting should be viewed as a team effort and not be entrusted solely to an expert or "black box" approach.
- *Over-sophistication and Cost.* Forecasting systems that are too difficult to understand are doomed to failure. Most organizations rely on simple, yet effective, "rules of thumb" in developing a forecast. Complex statistical techniques that require sophisticated calculations turn forecasting into a "black box" activity that divorces users from the process. In addition, the more complex the forecasting model, the more

forecasters will have to code and maintain system elements. Finally, the more complex the system, the more costly it is to run and maintain.

- *Compatibility.* Forecasts fail when there is a lack of compatibility between the forecasting system and the capabilities of the using organizations. When internal managers and channel partners do not understand the techniques employed nor trust the output produced, there is a strong likelihood that they will not follow the forecast. The result is that managers bypass the formal system in favor of their own informal techniques. The unnecessary proliferation of separate functional forecasts produces a dysfunctional approach where values promoting alignment and team work are replaced by departmentalism and the uncoupling of the business planning process.

- *Data Accuracy.* Although it is obvious that the data used by a forecasting technique must be accurate, errors do arise in the data collection process. Data collection errors can arise in seven areas:

  1. Sampling methods. Although an important tool in qualitative forecasting, sampling can contain errors due to the size of the sample and incorrect application in statistical calculations. In addition, the patterns and relationships of the data on which the sample is based can change over time, also creating error.

  2. Measurement errors. These errors occur in the collection, data entry, and forecast calculation. The more these activities are automated, the less the chance for error.

  3. Hidden information. Sometimes information may be unintentionally left out or deliberately falsified or withheld.

  4. Poorly designed questionnaires. Questionnaires can suffer from a number of errors ranging from respondent misunderstanding to lack of questionnaire comprehensiveness.

  5. Data aggregates. Errors in aggregate data collection can occur as a result of omitting or double-counting data elements.

  6. Classification and definition. Data elements need to be as sharply defined as possible. Lack of definition causes data either to be left out or double counted.

  7. Time factors. It is critical that the time periods and the data collected are in alignment. An example would be inventory transaction data that is not reported in the same time period as accounting information.

- *Unnecessary Items.* Often forecasts are developed for items that should not be forecasted. One example is *dependent demand* item usage. In this category can be found components within a Bill of Material. Forecasters, however, must be careful to create forecasts for dependent demand items that may also be subject to independent demand, such as service parts. Also, forecasts should not be established for final assembled products that are the result of features and options. An example is several models of bicycle that can be assembled from a combination of modular subassembly, common parts, and individual items. Forecasting such products should be done at the feature and option and not at the end product level.

- *Lack of Management Control.* Review and maintenance are critical to forecast effectiveness. By its very nature, every forecast developed is likely to be wrong. Forecasters must be diligent in mon-itoring the forecast to ascertain the degree of error, when the forecast should be altered, and what parameters should be used to guide forecast adjustment.

Ensuring forecast effectiveness is an ongoing process that requires the participation not only of internal managers but also of the entire supply chain. To guard against incorrect and misleading forecasts, planners must be careful to select the proper forecasting techniques that fit the needs of the organization and the supply channel, audit and maintain data accuracy, track closely actual activities against forecasted results, and promptly update forecasts that have exceeded acceptable boundaries.

SUMMARY

Forecasting is a necessary part of the business planning process. Perhaps no other activity has as much immediate and long-range effect on the operations of the supply chain as forecasting. An effective forecast can dramatically improve channel-wide profitability, productivity, and customer service and ensure competitive advantage. Effective forecasting is also fundamental to the well-being of individual enterprises and supply networks. Good forecasting assists companies by eliminating waste in the form of excess inventory, by reducing shortages, missed due dates, lost sales, lost customers, and expensive expediting, and by providing visibility to control capacity requirements such as plant size, labor, equipment, and transportation.

The various forecasting models available can be broken down into three types. The first type employs qualitative models that combine human judgment along with collected data. These techniques are best used when historical data are scarce or when developing aggregate forecasts. The second forecasting type utilizes quantitative models in forecast development. Quantitative techniques are best used when there exists historical data and when the relationships and historical patterns of these data are both clear and relatively stable. The forecasting models in this type depend on statistical tools to extrapolate the probable future from the occurrences of the past. The final forecasting type utilizes causal models focused primarily on developing long-range forecasts that use qualitative and quantitative macro measure-ments such as political, demographical, new technology, and other forces to predict the future. Causal forecasts could be employed to predict the impact a new invention or product or process discoveries would have on the market-place.

The forecast development process is a critical function that is guided by a sequence of steps. To begin with, forecasters must be careful to define the overall purpose and goal of the forecast. Next, forecasters can proceed to the selection of the proper types, techniques, and computerized models necessary to fulfill forecast objectives. The third step in forecast development is data preparation. Critical activities in this step are auditing data accuracy, the speed and accuracy of forecast calculation, and the urgency and length of time required for forecast preparation. The fourth step consists in gaining the consensus of the firm's management team. After these preparation steps have been completed, the forecast can be executed. Forecasters can choose from a variety of forecasting methods such as simple averages, moving averages, exponential smoothing regression, and focus forecasting. The final step in forecast development is monitoring the feedback and performing appropriate action to regain forecast control.

QUESTIONS FOR REVIEW

1. Why is effective forecasting so critical to the survival of the enterprise?
2. Briefly detail the steps used to develop a forecasting system.
3. Forecasting is more of an art than a science. Is this a true statement, and what are the reasons.
4. The dynamics of forecasting method selection and control change as the time horizon shrinks. Why is this the case?
5. The sales staff of a major industrial supplies distributor has developed a product group forecast for the company's entire inventory. How useful is this forecast to the company? How must it be interpreted by the logistics division?
6. Discuss the advantages and disadvantages of using qualitative and quantitative forecasting models.
7. Your company has just purchased a Focus Forecasting system. The sale manager has ready about a new but complex calculation to help in sales planning. What are your actions?
8. It is often said of forecasting, "Forecast only what you must; calculate whatever you can." Discuss this statement.

PROBLEMS

1. Using the moving average forecasting technique to determine the next period forecast for an item with the following data elements.

Number of periods = 8
Previous demand by period = 232, 242, 223, 221, 226, 234, 244, 255, 260, 265

After performing the calculation, how accurate do you think the new forecast will be to the actual, and why?

2. Based on the following data, develop a three-period moving average forecast of demand.

Period	Demand
1	16
2	19
3	15
4	19
5	23
6	18
7	22
8	23
9	19
10	21

3.   Using the same information, develop a four-period moving average.

4.   Assuming the alpha factor was 0.2, calculate the forecast using exponential smoothing. Based on the results of Questions 2 and 3, what would be the best forecast for period 11?

5.   Using trend-adjusted exponential smoothing, what would the new forecast be for the following data:

Period	Demand
1	50
2	110
3	100

Base value smoothing factor: $\alpha = 0.1$
Trend value smoothing factor: $\beta = 0.2$

6.   Wholesale Distributors, a major home appliance distributor, has experienced the following sales (in $Millions) during the past 6 years: $1.2, $1.24, $1.33, $1.31, $1.36, and $1.40. A critical statistic is the credit card interest rate which, correspondingly, has stood at 17.5%, 18.1%, 18.5%, 17.4%, 17.1%, and 16.8%. Based on these data, construct the forecast for year 7. Also, calculate the standard error of the estimate.

7.   Develop a seasonal index for the following pattern of item demand:

Month	Demand	Month	Demand
Jan.	65	July	35
Feb.	60	Aug.	50
Mar.	50	Sep.	60
Apr.	40	Oct.	70
May.	25	Nov.	75
June	30	Dec.	70

8.   Demand for Product XYZ over the past 6 months is shown below.

Period	Sales
June	140
July	170
Aug.	120
Sept.	140
Oct.	160
Nov.	110

(a) Assuming an initial forecast of 140 units, use an alpha factor of 0.2 to calculate the forecasts of each month.

(b) What is the MAD for this product?

(c) Compute the RSFE and tracking signals. Are they within acceptable limits?

REFERENCES

1. *The APICS Dictionary.* 9th ed. Falls Church, VA: American Production and Inventory Control Society, 1998, p. 37.
2. See the comment in Makridakis, Spyros and Wheelwright, Steven, *Forecasting Methods for Management.* New York: John Wiley & Sons, 1989, pp. 12-13; and Brown, Robert G., *Statistical Forecasting for Inventory Control.* New York: McGraw-Hill, 1959, pp. 1-25.
3. Plossl, George *Production and Inventory Control: Principles and Techniques.* 2nd ed. Englewood Cliffs: Prentice-Hall, 1985, pp. 62-68.
4. Makridakis and Wheelwright, pp. 26-28.
5. Armstrong, J. Scott, *Principles of Forecasting: A Handbook for Researchers and Practitioners.* Boston: Kluwer Academic Publishers, 2001, pp. 2-3.
6. Chambers, John C., Mullick, Santinder K., and Smith, Donald D., "How To Choose The Right Forecasting Technique." *Harvard Business Review*, 55-64 (August-July, 1971); and Makridakis and Wheelwright, pp. 14-15.
7. Makridakis and Wheelwright, pp. 240-275; DeLurgio, Stephen A. and Bhame, Carl D., *Forecasting Systems for Inventory Management.* Homewood, IL: Business One Irwin, 1991, pp. 201-204; and Waters, C.D.J., Inventory *Control and Management.* New York: John Wiley & Sons, 1992, pp. 176-179.
8. Dalrymple, D.J., "Sales Forecasting Practices--Results from a United States Survey." *International Journal of Forecasting* 379-381 (Summer 1987); Mentzer, J. and Cox, J., "Familiarity, Application and Performance of Sales Forecasting Techniques." *Journal of Forecasting* 227-236 (Summer 1984); Murdick, R.G., and Georgoff, D.M., "How to Choose the Best Technique--or Combination of Techniques--to Help Solve Your Particular Forecasting Dilemma." *Harvard Business Review* 110-120 (January-February 1986); Sanders, Nada R., "Corporate Forecasting Practices in the Manufacturing Industry." *Production and Inventory Management Journal,* 54-57 (Third Quarter, 1992); and, Wheelwright, Steven C. and Clarke, D.G. "Corporate Forecasting: Promise and Reality," Harvard *Business Review,* 40-42 (November-December, 1976).
9. Sanders, 54-55.
10. Makridakis and Wheelwright, pp. 61-63 and Waters, pp. 179-181.
11. Makridakis and Wheelwright, pp. 49-65; Waters, pp. 194-201; Silver, Edward A. and Petersen, Rein, *Decision Systems for Inventory Management and Production Control.* 2nd ed. New York: John Wiley & Sons, 1985, pp. 103-105.
12. Gill, Lynn E., "Demand Forecasting: A Vital Tool in Logistics Management," in *The Distribution Handbook.* New York: The Free Press, 1985, pp. 455-458; DeLurgio and Bhame, pp. 231-237; Waters, pp. 201-207; and, Silver and Petersen, pp. 105-115.
13. DeLurgio and Bhame, pp. 239-257, 311-351; Makridakis and Wheelwright, pp. 76-91; and, Waters, pp. 207-214.
14. DeLurgio and Bhame, pp. 244-245.

15. Vollmann, Thomas E., Berry, William Lee, and Whybark, D. Clay, *Manufacturing Planning and Control Systems.* 2nd ed. Homewood, IL: Dow-Jones Irwin, 1988, pp. 689-690.
16. Smith, Bernard T., *Focus Forecasting: Computer Techniques for Inventory Control.* Essex Junction, VT: Oliver Wight Publications, 1984, pp. 1-33; and, Smith, Bernard T., *Focus Forecasting and DRP.* New York: Vantage Press, 1991, pp. 17-40.
17. DeLurgio and Bhame, pp. 198-201; Fogarty, Donald W., Blackstone, John H., and Hoffmann, Thomas R., *Production and Inventory Management.* 2nd ed. Cincinnati, OH: South-Western Pub. Co., 1991, pp. 114-115; and, Makridakis and Wheelwright, pp. 52-53.
18. DeLurgio and Bhame, pp. 198-201; and, Makridakis and Wheelwright, pp. 318-336.
19. DeLurgio and Bhame, pp. 261-279; and, Heizer, Jay and Render, Barry, *Production and Operations Management.* 3rd ed. (Boston: Allyn & Bacon, 1993), pp. 142-147.
20. Silver and Peterson, pp. 90-91.
21. *Ibid,* pp. 126-140.
22. Makridakis and Wheelwright, pp. 424-426.

5

DEMAND, OPERATIONS, AND CHANNEL PLANNING

The marketplace is comprised of four interdependent dimensions: the customer, products and services, the capabilities of logistics, and supply chain design. How these dimensions are managed on the strategic level is the result of the planning and execution activities of the enterprise's marketing, sales, production, and logistics functions. As has been pointed out in Chapter 3, the purpose of the business planning process is to define the marketplace objecttives and operational strategies the firm must pursue if it is to achieve enterprise goals and sustain marketplace advantage. The business plan determines how the company will be structured to leverage critical resources and what are its competitive values. Once these enterprise plans have been formulated, it is the responsibility of the marketing, sales, production, and logistics functions to develop supporting strategies detailing customer, product, manufacturing, supply channel, and service objectives. The demand, operations, and channel planning processes attempt to answer such questions as: "Into what markets does the firm plan to sell its products?" "What products and services does it expect to sell?" "What resources are required to meet sales, production, and inventory objectives?" "What should the supply chain look like?"

Chapter 5 will detail how demand, operations, and supply channel planning address these and other long-range planning questions. The chapter begins with a detailed description of the *Demand, Operations, and Channel Planning* (DO&CP) process. The goal of this process is the creation of a set of highly integrated business functional plans that ensure that the five critical plans constituting the core of the executive planning process – the marketing plan, the sales plan, the production plan, the logistics plan, and the supply chain plan – are in balance. Next, each one of these five plans is explored in depth. A four-step planning methodology is suggested for each of these plans and critical topics surrounding plan execution is covered. The chapter concludes with a methodology for aggregating the five plans into a single DO&C plan that can then be used by corporate strategists to measure plan success and isolate areas for adjustment.

DEMAND, OPERATIONS, AND CHANNEL PLANNING - OVERVIEW

Demand, Operations, and Channel Planning (DO&CP) is the culmination of the top management planning process that began with the formulation of the business plan. In the past, functional area managers often received their portion of the business plan and formulated strategies that sought to optimize localized performance, often to the detriment of other business areas. Today, this practice has largely been discredited and replaced with collaborative plan development where functional executives works closely to-gether to produce strategies that provide for a single, integrated demand management, resource, and channel enterprise plan. Together, each functional plan must be feasible, supportive of overall enterprise goals, and in alignment with the objectives of the other area plans. The overall objective is to ensure expected demand and available supply is in balance. The output of these plans then drives the operations management planning processes that defines the firm's medium-range inventory, production, and logistics support strategies.

Planning at the DO&CP level requires strategists to adjust their thinking to focus on utilizing aggregate data in developing business area plans. A key distinction is understanding the difference between *volume* and *mix* planning. Questions of volume center on strategic issues, such as determining the overall rates of product family sales and production, aggregate inventories, supply chain value delivery, and logistic capacities. The planning *time range* extends for a minimum of a year and beyond, the *focus* is on product families, and the *review frequency* is normally monthly. Planning at this level is the reserve of DO&CP. In contrast, questions of product mix are concerned with the execution of daily operations and consist in the identification of the actual finished goods to make, inventory, and ship; the operations of individual channel suppliers, manufacturers, wholesalers, and retailers; and the deployment of transportation and warehouse resources to satisfy product shipments. The planning *time range* extends for six months to a year, the *focus* is on individual finished products, and the *review frequency* is normally weekly. This area is properly the reserve of *master scheduling* and *distribution resource planning*.

When considering volume and mix it is critical that planners first find answers to issues associated with *volume*. The development of effective volume or aggregate plans precede those of mix or operations plans. Simply, if conflicts in demand and supply can be resolved on the aggregate level, planners will find that problems associated with operations (individual products and orders) will be easier to resolve. The DO&CP process supports this objective by reconciling all demand, supply, new product, and channel management plans at the aggregate level and ensures continuity with the business plan. In addition, DO&CP enables operations execution performance measurements and the development of strategic and detail efforts directed at continuous improvement.

In summary, DO&CP can be defined as a strategic planning process dedicated to maintaining the balance between demand and supply up and down the supply chain. By focusing on aggregate volumes, such as product families, the capabilities of the supply chain, and overall logistics resources, DO&CP enables the effective execution of daily operations functions centered on mix issues relating to individual products and orders. DO&CP is a formal process that is performed on a monthly basis and involves the collaborative participation of executives from sales, marketing, product development, operations, logistics, and finance, including the division president or CEO. The goal of DO&CP is to bring together the business and functional area strategic plans into an single integrated plan that, in turn, will drive the operations processes responsible for executing the day-to-day activities of demand management, channel inventories, master scheduling, production scheduling, purchasing, and logistics. A properly formulated DO&C plan will enable entire supply chains to optimize channel inventories, production functions, and channel fulfillment resources that enhance customer value, reduce channel costs, and provide for superior competitive advantage [1].

COMPONENTS OF DO&CP

As illustrated in Figure 5.1, DO&CP consists of five interwoven components

FIGURE 5.1 Components of strategic planning.

linked together by the enterprise business plan. As discussed in the Chapter 3, the *business strategy* provides a comprehensive definition of enterprise goals and performance measurement targets, the asset and investments plans necessary to support the organization, and the projected profit plan. It is the role of the business strategy to provide clear direction and enable the translation of the collective enterprise strategy into detailed mission statements for each of the five supporting business areas. Once overall enterprise goals have been established, it is then possible for the *marketing plan* to begin the process of identifying the structure of the marketplace the firm intends work in, the products and services to be sold, issues relating to price and promotions, and the mechanics of the distribution channel. As the nature of the marketplace begins to emerge, it is the function of the *sales plan* to develop the forecasts of expected product sales, draft the sales campaign, ensure sales capacities, and define sales performance metrics.

For businesses with manufacturing functions, the *production plan* must be established. The production plan determines the production rates and aggregate resources required to satisfy the shipment, inventory, and cost of sales objectives stated in the business and marketing plans. To effectively manage fulfillment, it is then the goal of the *logistics plan* to ensure that inventory storage capacities and transportation resources are sufficient to support planned levels of sales. Finally, an effective DO&C process would be incomplete without a comprehensive *supply chain plan.* This component defines how the supply channel network is designed, how it is operated, and the nature of the level of integration and collaboration existing between supplier, manufacturer, wholesaler, and retailer constituents. Each of these components of strategic planning will be further described below.

DO&CP INPUTS AND OUTPUTS

The mechanics of effective DO&CP planning are driven by several critical inputs and result in a series of accompanying planning outputs. The *inputs* to the DO&CP process consist of the following:

- *Strategic targets.* This input comes from the business plan and establishes the strategic targets to be met by the actual performance of all business functions.
- *Product and service mix.* This input comes from the marketing plan and is composed of the range of products and services the enterprise expects to sell through the supply channel. This driver also should contain intelligence regarding the introduction of new products and product changes that could impact the overall business strategy.
- *Marketing environmental scanning.* This input contains intelligence concerning the nature of external environmental factors occurring in the marketplace that could impact product and service demand. Among the possible elements is found general demand trends, the current state of economic conditions, forecasts by market experts, potential government and regulatory actions, new information technologies, and others.
- *Family level forecasting.* This input is one of the prime responsibilities of sales and consists of the forecasts and forecast performance tools ne-

eded to keep the estimated marketplace demand and supplying capacities in balance. The family forecast is the prime driver of production, inventory, and logistics planning.

- *Capacity and capability management.* Once concise demand plans have been formulated, they can, in turn, be used to calculate and provide for the continuous adjustment of manufacturing capacities and the capability of the supply chain to deliver finished goods as required by customer orders. This driver should also include the introduction of new processes or changes to existing processes for product manufacture or channel inventory distribution.
- *Channel network architecture.* Supply chains are inherently dynamic. The structure and functions of channel partners, availability of channel resources, degree of dependence on channel participants, and the robustness of collaborative relationships are powerful drivers of all DO&C plans.
- *Financial resources.* Besides overall strategic direction, the business plan should provide information regarding the amount of funding available to support the execution of marketing, sales, production, logistics, and supply chains and provide for the development of new initiatives directed at continuing performance optimization.

The *outputs* from the DO&CP process consist of a series of detailed business plans that are used to direct and determine the performance of everyday operations. Among these plans can be found the

- *Marketing plan* consisting of the marketplace, product, and distribution strategy
- *Sales plan* containing the product level forecast and sales campaign strategy
- *Production plan* detailing the product family priority plan
- *Resource capacity plan* containing the calculation of available aggregate capacities to meet the priority plan
- *Backlog plan* determining production response to customer orders in assemble-to-order and make-to-order environments
- *Channel inventory plan* detailing finished goods levels, costs, and channel deployment
- *Supply chain plan* illustrating the structure of the supply network, depth of partner dependence, and level of collaboration
- *Logistics plan* structuring the composition of transportation and warehouse capacities
- *Product and process development plans* describing the nature of the impact of new products and processes on existing plans

- *Financial plan* accounting for how asset, developmental funding, and investment is to be performed and measured
- *Workforce plan* describing how the necessary people resources are to be assembled to meet all DO&C plans

ELEMENTS OF MARKETING PLANNING

The purpose of the marketing planning process is to determine what products and services the firm is to offer its customers, the sales potential of the marketplace, and the mechanics of how the supply chain should operate. A successful marketing plan seeks to reconcile enterprise strategic objectives with the realities of current business trends, shifting marketplace segments, market growth and decline, existing and planned products, the impact of environmental, governmental, and information technology issues, and the scope of channels of distribution. The marketing plan is the central instrument for directing and coordinating the marketing effort. Without effective and closely integrated marketing, sales, supply chain, and operations strategies the enterprise cannot hope to achieve the performance targets set forth in the corporate business forecast.

Marketing planning is the collective responsibility of the marketing management team. With the assistance of sales, supply chain, and operations management, the marketing function must determine answers to questions such as the following:

- Into what markets does the firm plan to sell its products and services?
- What are the market entry and exit strategies?
- What market trends are occurring, and how can they be leveraged to create new business opportunities?
- What products and services does the firm plan to sell?
- What value-added services should be focused on to achieve and maintain competitive advantage?
- At what stages in their life cycles are the company's products and services?
- What kind of delivery and transportation functions will be required?
- What should be the size and location of the supply channel network?
- What manufacturing/value-added processing activities should be performed?
- How do the company's products, services, and marketing channels compare to the competition?

In answering these and other questions, marketers must seek to develop plans that balance corporate strategies with the realities of marketplace demand.

THE MARKETING PLANNING PROCESS

As illustrated in Figure 5.2, the marketing planning process begins with a

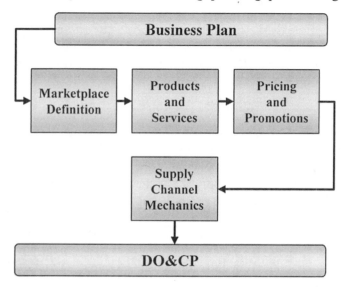

FIGURE 5.2 Marketing planning process.

statement of the firm's marketplace. In this step, marketers must determine whether they are pursuing either a "niched market" or a "mass market" approach, the Internet strategy, what market segments are to be targeted, the size of the customer base, customer buying criteria (quality, price, service), customer industry (manufacturers, retailers, other distributors, or mixed), channel distribution point locations, and delivery requirements. Also, in this step marketers must gain an understanding of customer needs and expectations and how they can build collaborative partnerships by enabling initiatives such as automating the exchange of information, training and sales assistance, integrating the distribution chain closer together, and negotiating capacity scheduling. Finally, marketing planning evaluates the firm's competetive strengths and weaknesses. Competitive advantage is weighed by benchmarking each competitor's market strategies regarding pricing, discounting, delivery, and old and new products, and how they compare to the firm's own sales strategies and product and services offerings. Ultimately, it is marketing's responsibility to develop the product and services strategies that provide customers with superior value that simply cannot be attained when dealing with the competition.

The second step in the marketing planning process is assessing the competitiveness of the company's products and services. A particularly useful management model for ensuring that the firm is not only offering competitive products but is also investing in the right products is to use *product life cycle analysis*. The goal of the analysis is to determine the relative position of products in their sales history. Products characterized by high profit growth and market share should be protected from competitors and promoted with continued investment. Conversely, products demonstrating low growth and declining market share should be divested and the capital re-invested in new or existing growth-oriented products. Product life cycle analysis will be further described below. In addition, marketers must weigh the cost of the value-added services. The scope of services can be a significant competitive advantage, especially when businesses find their inventories stocked with a large proportion of the same or similar products that their competitors are offering to the same marketplace. Value-added services provide a basis for differentiation by offering customers new avenues to meet expectations, reduce costs, increase productivity, and increase sales.

The third step in the marketing planning process focuses on price and promotion decisions. Although companies hope that the products and value-added services they offer will be sufficient to maintain current marketplace leadership or to gain entry into a new market, often special pricing or periodic sales promotions are necessary to stave off competitors or to entice new customers away from competitors. Pricing decisions will have a direct impact on the volume of the profits the company must gain to meet business plan objectives. Marketing programs targeted at increasing profits through pricing decisions can take the form of lowering fixed costs such as inventory, plant size, and equipment while increasing productivity, and service and product quality. In addition, increases in the number of deliveries can actually assist in lowering prices by permitting companies to shrink inventory carrying costs. Another option would be to reduce variable costs such as labor. Finally, firms can increase profits by increasing prices. Promotion decisions also will affect profitability. Trade advertising, sales promotions and deals, and publicity can all be used to open markets and increase sales of targeted products and value-added services.

The final step in the marketing planning process is structuring internal distribution channel operations. Simply having the right mixture of products and services is insufficient to meet targeted sales and profit objectives. Companies must have the delivery mechanisms in place to penetrate the marketplace and increase customer service. Options include building additional warehouses close to the targeted market, renting space in public warehouses, outsourcing logistics functions, and acquiring a competitor or a trading partner positioned in the distribution pipeline. In mapping the channel network, marketing planners must be careful to measure both the estimated costs as well as the benefits. A distribution network must be designed that will provide the firm with sufficient return on investment by offsetting investment in plant, equipment, staff, and inventory with increases in sales and profitability.

PRODUCTS AND SERVICES

Perhaps the prime focus of the marketing planning process is defining the products and services the firm intends to compete with in the marketplace. A product is a matrix of physical characteristics and customer perceptions. As physical entities, products possess weight, volume, shape, functionality, cost, and other attributes. As a customer perception, products possess intangible features such as convenience, status, quality, usability, accessibility, and distinctiveness. In terms of a formal definition a *product* is *a physical good offered to the market for acquisition, use, or consumption that might satisfy a want or need.* Products can be broadly grouped as *durable* goods, products that are designed to last for an extended period of time without rapid deterioration or obsolescence, and *non-durable* goods, products that are consumed or must be consumed quickly or that deteriorate rapidly. Products can range from low-cost, high-volume goods such as Coca-Cola or Bic Pens, to high-cost, low-volume goods such as industrial machinery and automobiles.

Products are best understood when related to other products. One way to view products is to position them in a product hierarchy. Products can be defined in ascending order as belonging to a *product type* (individual items within a product line sharing attributes common to a generic product), a *product line* (individual items grouped together within a product class because of functional, cost, or customer requirements similarities), a *product class* (individual items grouped together within a product family that fit broad functional characteristics), and a *product family* (a general grouping of individual items that satisfy a general need). As an example, a bicycle distributor would consider men's trail bicycles as a product type; all adult-sized trail bikes as a product line; and all trail bikes as a product class which belongs to a product family called adult recreational bicycles. In addition, products are often described as belonging to a *product system.* A product system can be defined as a diverse set of products that are sold together as a set. As an example, hardware stores stock fastener sets that consist of many kinds of bolts, nuts, washers, and nails packed in a variety of drawered cases that can easily be stored on a workbench. Finally, products can be described as a *product mix* or *assortment* of all possible goods a distributor makes available to the marketplace [2].

Products can be further classified into two major categories based on product characteristics [3]. The first category is defined as *industrial goods*. Products in this category can belong to three subcategories.

- *Raw materials and component parts.* In this category is found farm and natural products such as foodstuffs, lumber, petroleum and iron ore, and fabricated or manufactured component materials. For the most part, these products are distributed through source supplier channels and are used by manufacturers who convert them into finished products. Supply channels for servicing this category tend to be limited to one or two levels. Marketing considerations focus on price and service.

- *Capital goods.* In this category can be found fixed and accessory equipment such as generators, computers, automobiles, material handling equipment, and office furniture. Products in this category are considered finished goods and are not normally used to create other finished goods by purchasers. Manufacturers, for the most part, use channel partners to distribute these products. Marketing considerations focus on quality, price, product features, and service.

- *Maintenance, repair, and operating goods.* In this category can be found consumer type goods such as paint, nails, office supplies, small tools, lubricants, and fuels. These products are, for the most part, distributed through a complex matrix of channel intermediaries who provide time and place utilities. Marketing considerations focus on price, service, availability, and delivery.

The second major product category is defined as *consumer goods*. Products in this category can belong to three subcategories.

- *Convenience goods.* In this category can be found products that are usually purchased frequently, immediately, and with the minimum of effort in comparison or buying. Examples include staples such as bread, milk, and toothpaste, impulse goods such as chewing gum, candy, and magazines, and emergency goods such as medical supplies, snow shovels, and cold weather clothing. Distribution channels for such products are very complex, focusing on volume to offset small margins and high distribution costs which can be as high as one-third of cost of sales. Marketing considerations are focused on availability and price.

- *Shopping goods.* In this category can be found products that customers normally will shop for in many locations and compare such elements as price, quality, performance, and suitability before a decision to purchase is made. Examples include such products as fashion clothes, appliances, books, and home furnishings. Because customers are willing to search for goods in this category, the distribution channel is designed to have a limited number of outlets within a given geographical area. In contrast to convenience goods, distribution costs for shopping goods are approximately 15 percent of total sales costs. Marketing considerations focus on quality, brand name considerations, availability, price, and service warranty.

- *Specialty goods.* In this category can be found products that possess unique characteristics and/or brand recognition for which customers are willing to expend a significant effort to acquire them. Examples include such products as art work and furs, and such brands as Mercedes in automobiles and Armani in women's fashions. Distribution channels for such products are normally restricted to specialized consumer markets and are usually characterized by lower service factors such as availability and convenience. Marketing considerations are focused on quality, warranty, and repair.

Although the above breakdown into groups of industrial and consumer goods is a convenient way of organizing products, it has certain limitations when used to aid marketing management. For example, the product categories are somewhat subjective and can be arguable from the stand-point of actual buying behavior and method of distribution. Because the above classifications are subject to interpretation, the following five additional characteristics of products should be observed when making marketing decisions [4]:

1. *Replacement rate.* This characteristic refers to the frequency with which a product is purchased. This factor will have an impact on channel size and distribution costs.
2. *Level of service.* Some products require specific levels of service during the distribution process necessary to meet customer expectations. Such services may take the form of training, warranty, repair, or other factors.
3. *Time to product consumption.* Although closely related to replacement, this characteristic refers to how fast the product will be consumed. A can of paint, for example, may be quickly used but would not be replaced until a future redecorating project.
4. *Search time.* This characteristic refers to the average time the end customer is willing to spend searching for a product.
5. *Gross margin.* Perhaps the fundamental measurement of a product is calculating the difference between the total cost of distributing a product from point of production to point of sale, and the selling price.

6. *Perishability.* Goods with short life cycles require very short distribution channels, the minimum of handling, and quick time to market.
7. *Bulk.* Goods handled in bulk are expensive to transport and store. Products with this characteristic should be delivered directly from the producer to the end customer.
8. *Degree of customization.* Nonstandardized products often require special assistance for installation, training, or other forms of servicing that must be performed by the producer. The level of contact between producer and customer associated with standardized products is much lower.

PRODUCT FAMILIES

The ability to apply the above classifications in the designation of *product families* is critical to the development of DO&CP. Since the focus of DO&CP is aggregate volumes, product families provide all areas of the planning process – marketing, sales, production, logistics, and supply chain management – with common product units permitting easy points of communication, transfer of data, and final plan consolidation. Meaningfully defined product families enable senior managers to focus on the right level of product data for effective decision making. Without a common nomenclature to formulate individual DO&C plans, the effort will be stillborn due to mismatches relating to product family definition, unit of measure, budgeting, and resource and capacity requirements.

For the most part, companies should be able to breakdown their actual products into no more then perhaps a dozen product families. A number greater than twelve begins to thwart the concept of aggregate planning and will complicate the process of plan compilation and communication. While most companies have historically defined their product families, newcomers can begin the process by selecting from the following options [5]:

- Product type (pumps, switches, hardware)
- Product characteristics (cost, performance, grade)
- Product size (large, medium, small)
- Brand (Coca Cola, Pepsi, Royal Crown)
- Market segment (consumer goods, industrial, government)
- Customer

Two other components must be considered. The first is determination of the unit of measure to be applied to the product families. There are many choices: each, case, pounds, kilos, tons, and others. Often the nature of the product families makes it difficult to assign a common unit of measure. In such a case it might be convenient to use a higher level measurement, such as dollars. This might require the use of conversion factors to calculate the common unit of measure from original product group units of measure. Another component to consider is ensuring that the product families match the way the company acquires and presents its products to the marketplace. Ideally, the product families that emerge should reflect either a common manufacturing process or are purchased by family. The goal is to provide aggregation models that can facilitate the planning processes of the five major components of the DO&CP process.

THE PRODUCT LIFE CYCLE

One of the most important elements of product management is understanding the *product life cycle.* The theory behind the product life cycle is that the average product can be divided into distinct sales stages, each characterized by differing marketing, investment, and distribution requirements. Although the universality of the model can be debated, it does provide marketers with a useful framework for linking a product's life cycle stage with marketing strategies focusing on competition, product design, pricing, promotion, distribution, and informational requirements. Kotler [6] feels that there are four underlying assumptions in understanding the product life cycle-concept.

1. Products have a limited life. Changes in taste and technology dictate that no product will remain in demand by customers indefinitely.
2. Products pass through distinct stages. These stages can be described as introductory, rapid growth, maturation, and decline (Figure 5.3).
3. Profits rise and fall at different stages in the product life cycle.
4. A firm's marketing effort, sales volume, distribution channel size, and financial investment is impacted by a product's life-cycle stage.

Table 5.1 suggests how the position a product occupies in its product life cycle will impact supply chain elements such as product availability, product volume in the channel, sales volume, form of distribution structure, enterprise inventory and marketing investment, and nature of competition. In the *introductory stage*, companies are reluctant to stock large volumes of inventory. Because the new product has not yet received market acceptance, sales volume is low. In contrast, research and development costs are high as product bugs are fixed and features solidified. Channel product availability is restricted to a few targeted locations and market areas capable of generating margins high enough to support heavy promotional spending. In addition, logistics management must be integrated early in the process to guarantee effective product rollout. At this stage, the competitive strategy is to offer customers products and features not generally available in the marketplace.

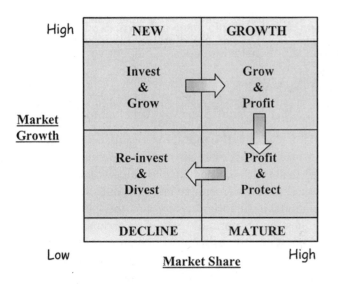

FIGURE 5.3 Product life cycle.

If the product begins to acquire customer acceptance, the growth in sales volumes will require companies to increase inventory investment and product availability. In addition, expanded transportation and storage, promotional expenses, aggressive discounting, and competitive pricing will increase costs.

TABLE 5.1 Stages of supply chain collaboration

Characteristic	Introduction	Growth	Mature	Decline
Product availability	Low	Increase	Level	Low
Product volume	Low	Increase	Level	Low
Sales volume	Low	Increase	Level	Low
Form of distribution structure	Minimum	Increase	Complex	Minimum
Investment	High	High	Level	Low
Form of competition	Product features	Quality, Availability	Price, Dependability	Availability

Decisions regarding the structure of the distribution channel are particularly difficult in this *growth stage*. Although product demand is much greater, it is still too irregular, rendering sales and marketing information often unreliable as a source for channel planning. Judgmental methods in forecasting are mostly employed in this stage in determining the depth and volume of inventory stocked at supply network nodes. Competitive strategies are designed to capitalize on growing market demand by focusing on attributes relating to product quality and availability.

The growth stage can be long or short depending on the extent of the competitive turbulence arising from the marketplace. Success will generate aggressive emulators who will contest for established market niches and customer loyalty through price and distribution counter strategies. During the *maturity stage* that follows, product and sales volume is no longer experiencing the same dramatic percentage increase and can be forecasted and planned using accumulated historical usage. At this point, product demand has reached its highest point, normally requiring companies to maintain high inventory and promotional investment to remain competitive. The distribution structure can be characterized as intensive and extensive, with a strong emphasis on keeping delivery points as fully stocked as possible while trying to minimize inventory investment. Competitive strategies focus on competitor activities, cost and price decisions, maintaining brand and customer loyalty, and product and value-added service dependability.

During the final product life-cycle stage, sales volumes decline as a result of changes in technology, competition, or customer interest. As sales revenues decline, so does investment in inventory and promotional activities. At this point, planners usually begin to scale back general inventory availability throughout the channel, restricting product to centralized warehouses or to targeted locations with enough residual customer demand. Finally, planners must develop effective strategies to discontinue "dead stock" clogging the distribution pipeline, plan for market exit, and redirect resources to more profitable products. Competitive strategies at this point focus on price and availability as competitors also phase out the product and increase prices to cover inventory storage and services costs.

Besides providing a window into product and marketplace dynamics, the product life cycle presents marketers with a tool to assist in making channel support decisions. To begin with, whereas companies need to continually promote existing products, they must also focus on the introduction of new products. Second, the product life cycle indicates that marketers need to create separate strategies for products as they enter differing product life cycles. Finally, the product development life cycle illustrates the importance of planning for new products as they are being introduced. Without effective product planning, estimated and actual long-run profitability and return on investment may vary dramatically. Similarly, the product development life cycle permits marketers to review the profitability of older products. What appears to be a "star" may, after closer analysis, be, in reality, a liability draining away critical resources. The effective management of old products can have as great a financial impact on the enterprise as the introduction of new products with high current profits [7].

UNDERSTANDING SERVICES

Most companies not only market products but they also offer customers services that add value to goods purchased. *Service can be defined as any product-oriented activity or performance provided by a firm that does not involve the transfer of ownership of tangible goods.* For the most, part companies offer tangible goods accompanied by one or more services targeted at enhancing product appeal. These product services can take the form of pre-sales services such as supplier contracts, technical advice, discounting, quality and delivery reliability, sales representative availability, and credit. In addition, businesses often offer after-sales services such as transportation, warranty, repair, technical support, trade-in allowances, product guaranties, and user training.

Services differ from products in several different ways. To begin with, a service is usually an *intangible* exchange of value, in contrast to tangible value as found in a physical product. Second, services are often produced and consumed simultaneously. In this sense, services can be perceived as providing value that extends beyond the product itself. The service value found in product delivery, for instance, is value received with the activity of the delivery process. Third, the services received by a customer are often unique to that customer. For example, the education services provided by a software firm for their customer base will always be adapted to accommodate the particular needs of each customer even though the entire customer base is receiving the same software product. The factor that makes each service unique is found in the fourth characteristic: high customer-service interaction. Service uniqueness arises out of the particular needs communicated by each customer and how the product and standard services offerings are shaped to respond to those needs. The last characteristic of services can be found in their lack of precise definition. While products are rigorously defined as to form and function, services normally consist of a core value around which a variety of different outcomes can occur. A discount, for example, may not only differ between customers, but may also be different with each sale, even for the same customer [8].

The services companies offer their customers have two dimensions. Many of the traditional services can be described as being almost "commodity" in nature because they directly accompany the product. Such services as warranty, packaging, rebates, and training allow customers to receive additional value with the receipt of the tangible product. Such *intrinsic* services have become so commonplace that most customers assume that suppliers will automatically provide them. There are, however, other services that are *extrinsic* to the product. Such services as discounting, improved supply channel efficiency, credit, product assortment, and others add value to products by reducing customer internal costs, facilitating the flow of business information, and improving productivity. In a marketplace in which competitors provide a large proportion of the same products, extrinsic value-added services have become a competitive advantage, differentiating one distributor from another.

Like products, value-added services can also be viewed as possessing a life cycle. In the *development stage,* marketers will experiment with new forms of value-added services that they anticipate will provide a point of differentiation separating their firms from the competition. Costs for development and delivery are high, although the customer perceives the value to be low. During the *growth stage,* planners are still investing in services development, but customers are beginning to see that the new service is providing sufficient value to persuade them to purchase the product. During the *maturity stage,* investment declines as the service becomes standardized, while increasing customer market demand for the product and accompanying service allows cost recovery and profit. As competitors begin to copy the new service in an effort to decrease competitive differentiation, the service enters the *saturation stage.* Customers feel the service is part of the product offering, often requiring that it be offered with little or no charge attached. At this point, the service migrates from a value-add to a requirement if the product is to remain competitive, but in itself offers little or no competitive advantage. In developing product value-added services strategies, marketers need to plot the life cycles of both product and services offerings and forecast to determine the trade-off of cost and potential sales.

DEVELOPING MARKETS

To be successful, marketers must constantly search for ways to recognize the unique requirements of their markets and customers. The value of effectively structured supply channels and focused products and services are accentuated by marketing strategies that competitively meet the specific needs of customers while avoiding the trap of trying to offer all things to all people. The fundamental goal overall of DO&CP is the effective management of a firm's portfolio of organizational, product, and service investments to achieve optimal profit return from the customer base. In pursuing such objectives, marketers must have strategies in place that identify the most attractive market segments available and measure individual customer profitability.

In viewing the marketplace, marketers must perform three activities:
1. *Segment* the potential customer base according to wants, resources, geographical locations, buying attitudes, and practices.
2. *Target* those market segments that manifest the proper size and growth, are attractive in regard to a lack of competitors, match existing products and services, and leverage the business's internal and external strengths and resources.
3. *Position* the company's image, products, and value-added services so that customers within selected market segments understand the firm's competitive value.

Once the market segment has been targeted, and products and services identified, marketers can then develop a strategy to optimize market niche. A *market niche* can be defined as a target market demonstrating a specialized need that is differentiated from the broader market in which a firm can achieve a low-cost and/or a unique capability for servicing that market. Within each market niche are leaders, challengers, and followers. The goal is to create such a strong niche presence that competitors could not justify entry due to the meager returns expected. Rolls Royce, for example, enjoys a global automotive market niche. Timex uses low-priced, quality watches available through mass-merchandizing channels to maintain its market niche. The elements of an effective *niche market* center on customer growth potential, lack of interest by competitors, possession of special skills and resources required by niche customers, and brand recognition or customer loyalty. Niche marketing should provide the firm with a lasting opportunity and is structured around stable demographic, cultural and technological wants and needs.

As illustrated in Figure 5.4, an effective market niche strategy attempts to

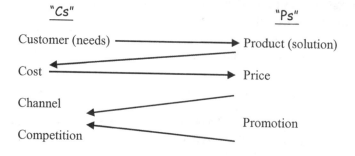

FIGURE 5.4 Factors of marketing strategy.

align the three "Ps" of a successful marketing plan (product, price, and promotion) with the four "Cs" (customer, cost, channels, and competition). Well-defined and articulated customer needs should be satisfied with the proper products and value-added services at a cost that matches or exceeds the value of what the customer expects and will pay for. The strategy will be successful if the cost to distribute and promote the product is less than the revenue generated in the face of the competition.

As the changing markets of the 1990s had forced companies to abandon the mass-marketing approach in favor of market niches, so in the twenty-first century the maturing of the global marketplace and acceleration of the rate of change in technology, product services, and market demand are forcing entire supply chains to work closely with each customer on an individual basis, matching their concerns with a specific set of products and services that respond directly to those concerns. Activated by enabling technologies like the Internet, supply chains are rapidly moving beyond the mass market and market niche models to a *market segment of one* approach. This strategy requires that marketers first have a firm grasp of the product and service strengths that give them a competitive advantage. Once this is done, they must advance to a position that views each customer as if they were a separate market. Such a view requires sales and service functions to know the key strategic issues not for a group of customers, but for each individual customer. This involves a process of continually evaluating supplier and customer performance, quantifying value-added services against cost, and communicating this information back to the customer. In addition, managers of product and service functions must know the requirements of each customer, and each employee, in turn, must understand how their actions are the foundations of "world-class" customer service. A *marketing strategy of one* approach requires that the entire business understands the investment and market potential of each new product and service required by the customer and how to develop strategies to build the business to a critical mass.

In managing customers, marketers must be careful to measure customer profitability. In every customer base are "stars" that provide the bulk of the firm's sales, a broad mass of customers whose revenue contribution varies from good to fair, and a group of "dogs" that are not only a severe drain on resources but also divert effort away from servicing the "stars" and expose them to be lost to competitors. One way to rank customers is to calculate an *operating profit contribution* for each. A first-cut equation follows.

Gross profit (12 months) - [Invoices (12 months) x Avg Cost Per Invoice] = Operating profit contribution.

The average cost per invoice is calculated by taking the entire operating cost of running the business for the year and dividing it by the grand total of invoices for the same period.

The next step would be to rank all of the accounts from high to low by their estimated profit contribution and then to calculate cumulative percentages for customers and profits. A possible breakdown for one company is illustrated as follows:

> Customers in top 10 percent provide 90 percent of the profits
> Customers in top 20 percent provide 130 percent of the profits
> Customers in top 40 percent provide 140 percent of the profits
> Customers in bottom 60 percent provide (- 40 percent) of the profits

This analysis suggests that the top 40 percent of the customer base generates 140 percent of the profits, whereas the bottom 40 percent actually results in a loss of 40 percent. Marketing and sales management should identify and develop strategies to protect the top 20 percent, cultivate the 60 percent in the middle, and individually review and eliminate losers residing at the bottom 20 percent. Another reporting mechanism would be to rank all customers by their ratio of credits issued divided by the number of invoices billed for a twelve month period. Exception ranking for slow-paying customers can also assist in pinpointing losing accounts.

The ability of the marketing and sales force to understand the composition and needs of the customer base is the key to the DO&CP process. As companies are increasingly forced to turn to growing profits and market share by finding new customers in existing markets and better penetrating existing accounts, customer channel relationships are becoming more critical. Fundamental to survival is therefore the ability to understand who the best customers are and what extra steps should be taken to further secure and proactively anticipate their changing needs.

ELEMENTS OF SALES PLANNING

The objective of the sales planning process is to drive the business strategy down through the field sales organization and to reconcile the demands to achieve corporate goals with the company's sales resources. In formulating effective plans, sales management must ensure that sales objectives match the goals of the marketing plan, the capabilities of manufacturing to make the necessary products, and the logistics capacities necessary to execute delivery expectations. Where capacities are insufficient, the business plan must either be changed or the enterprise must explore other avenues in order to gain the required resources. In addition, the effective utilization of the sales force is fundamental not only to a competitive position but also to organizational efficiency. After transportation and inventory, the cost of performing sales functions is the second largest source of expenditure, averaging 25 to 30 percent of gross margin and can range as high as 40 percent for some commodity lines such as paper. Sales planning must find answers to such questions as the following:

- What forecasts are to be used to drive the sales and product procurement effort?
- What are the sales quotas to be set to support the business plan?
- How should the marketplace be segmented to optimize the sales effort?
- What kinds of techniques should be used to find new customers and how can existing accounts be better penetrated?
- What kinds of compensation should be offered to motivate the sales force?
- What kinds of relationships should the sales force develop with the customer base?
- How should customer profitability, account penetration, and sales force productivity be measured?

In answering these and other questions, sales management must develop a comprehensive plan that details sales objectives and goals. As illustrated in Figure 5.5, the sales planning process begins with the translation of the busi-

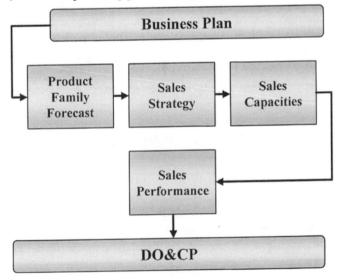

FIGURE 5.5 Sales planning process

ness plan into a forecast of product group sales. Marketing is the intelligence side of sales assisting with market research, product information, pricing, promotions, and deployment of the sales force. Past sales histories should be meticulously "mined" to assist in the conversion of business revenue plans into product group forecasts in units and/or dollars by time period. For the most part, product groups are employed simply because the total number of products may be quantitatively too large to be manage effectively. An aggregate sales plan may be developed for a product group, a distribution center, division, or the whole enterprise, or a geographical area. Disaggregating the sales forecast into item-level forecasts is the responsibility of the supply chain inventory planning process described in Chapter 6. Calculating the expected demand for each product group will result in a statement of aggregate sales demand. This summary figure can then be compared to the total sales plan required to support the revenue objectives detailed in the business plan.

The second step in the sales planning process is determining the sales strategy. There are several elements composing the sales strategy. The first is defining the market segments or territories and aligning them with the sales force and supply channels. Another key element is knowledge of and communication to operations management regarding any upcoming promotions, changes in product pricing, the beginning and end of any special deals, and the introduction or discontinuance of products. A new and increasingly important element is the degree of technology investment necessary to handle order processing and information needs and any training required to retool the sales force. Finally, the sales strategy should define the compensation techniques to be implemented to motivate the sales force. Decisions as to the blend of salary and commission should be made on the basis of the product life cycle and the objectives specified in the sales quota.

Aligning available sales force resources with the sales and revenue campaign takes place in the third step of the sales planning process. Once sales market segmentation and product group forecasts have been developed, sales management must ensure that both the sales force and the existing distribution channel possess the capacity to realize the anticipated aggregate sales demand. Where direct sales capacities are insufficient to meet expected demand, the corporate revenue plans must be revised downward, the sales force expanded, or the contracting of outside agents and representatives explored. Similarly, if the sales plan calls for a supply channel network to meet delivery strategies that exceed current capacities, then either the channel sales plan needs to be changed or the firm must rent additional space, acquire new facilities, or locate new supply channel partners.

The final step in the sales planning process is sales performance. To be effective, sales planning must be compared to actual performance. Sales performance can be measured through the use of a number of reporting techniques. Whereas actual sales compared to forecast is the most obvious, enhanced performance systems must be architected that measure customer potential, customer profitability contribution, account penetration, and sales force productivity. In addition, a mechanism is needed that can not only pinpoint when sales patterns deviate from the forecast but also communicate demand changes through the DO&CP process to other parts of the supply chain in as expeditiously a manner as possible so that supporting resources can be effectively realigned.

DEVELOPING THE SALES FORECAST

One of the most important functions of the sales planning process is the development of the product family forecast. As was stated in Chapter 4, the forecasting process occurs at various levels and time horizons. The goal is to select the proper level that enables forecasting to provide meaningful data to the DO&CP process. Forecasting at the business plan level, for example, is too high a level. Its purpose is to provide a single set of numbers that can be used by the entire company and is not specific enough in terms of products and processes to provide enough detail to permit meaningful sales, operations, and supply chain planning. Conversely, forecasting down on the SKU level, while providing massive detail about individual products, is not aggregate enough to allow for effective management planning. As the principles of forecasting state, the more detailed the level of forecastable elements, the shorter the time horizon, the greater the need for massive data handling and frequent review, and the greater the probability of error.

The solution to forecasting at the sales planning level is to utilize *product families*. As discussed above, effectively constructed product families provide a variety of benefits. To begin with, product families should be organized to match the actual SKUs the supply channel sells to the marketplace as well as how they are processed or purchased. Secondly, since product families should never exceed more than perhaps a dozen, they are easily identifiable by all DO&CP planners. Third, product families permit sales to use detailed financial and demand history data. This data can be "rolled-up" from actual SKUs and summarized into the product families to which they belong. Finally, as actual sales occurs through time and the data is rolled-up into the appropriate product families, sales is provided with a more accurate view of the viability of their forecasts. For example, while the actual mix of SKUs constituting a product family may deviate from the forecast, aggregate sales dollars may show that the product family is on target to meet forecasted sales revenues.

Pyramid Forecasting. When developing the sales forecast, forecasters can derive information for use in forecast development from many sources. Qualitative techniques, such as personal insight, sales force estimates, and market research, can be used. Causal methods that attempt to factor in economic trends, changes in technology, or political forces can also be used. Perhaps the best source, however, is to roll-up the detailed forecasts located at the actual SKU level in both units sold and revenues gained into their respective product families to provide a summarized view. Once the aggregate total has been calculated, forecasters can then utilize qualitative decisions to massage the forecast numbers, and then pass them back down to the SKU level where they will then be input into the demand portion of the Master Schedule.

Monthly Forecast - July 2003
Product Family: **PC-1501**   **PC Computers**

Step 1:	SKU	Forecasted Quantity	Price
	PC-1501-001	3,250	$1,245.00
	PC-1501-002	2,450	$1,255.00
	PC-1501-003	2,750	$1,275.00
	PC-1501-004	3,150	$1,285.00
	Totals:	*11,600* *Avg. price*	*$1,265.09*

Step 2:   Sales Family Forecast Adjustment: 12,500

Step 3:   New SKU Forecast – July 2003

$$\text{Adjustment Factor: } \frac{12,500}{11,600} = \mathbf{1.08} \text{ (rounded)}$$

Step 4:	SKU	Factor		Old Forecast		New Forecast	Price
	PC-1501-001	1.08	x	3,250	=	3,510	$1,245.00
	PC-1501-002	1.08	x	2,450	=	2,646	$1,255.00
	PC-1501-003	1.08	x	2,750	=	2,970	$1,245.00
	PC-1501-001	1.08	x	3,150	=	3,402	$1,245.00
	Totals:			*11,600*		*12,528*	*Avg. $1,247.11*

FIGURE 5.6 Pyramid forecast – by quantity.

Figure 5.6 provides a simplified example of the calculation. In *Step 1,* the four items constituting product group PC-1501 have been forecasted using historical sales data. In *Step 2,* sales and marketing planners have determined that the PC Computer family can be expected to sell 12,500 in total for the next month. In *Step 3* the ratio of forecasted family sales to the sales estimate is determined. Finally, in *Step 4* this ratio is applied to the original base forecast to provide the new forecast. This value is then passed down to the Master Schedule as the total forecasted quantity for each PC-1501 SKU. Often, the sales product forecast is expressed not in units but in revenue dollars. As illustrated in Figure 5.7, this can be easily accomplished by using the basic forecast found in Figure 5.6 and extending unit values by dollars. In the illustration sales has decided to establish the sales forecast for family PC-1500 at $15 million for the month of July. By calculating and applying the ratio between forecasted dollars and the new revenue target, a new per-unit level forecast can be developed and transferred to the Master Schedule.

Monthly Forecast – July 2003
Product Family: **PC-1501**   **PC Computers**

Step 1: SKU	Forecasted Quantity	Price	Cum Price
PC-1501-001	3,250	$1,245.00	$4,046,250
PC-1501-002	2,450	$1,255.00	$3,074,750
PC-1501-003	2,750	$1,275.00	$3,506,250
PC-1501-004	3,150	$1,285.00	$4,047,750
Totals:	11,600	Total Dollars	$14,675,000

Step 2: Sales Family Forecast Adjustment: $15,000,000

Step 3: New SKU Forecast – July 2003

Adjustment Factor: $\frac{\$15,000,000}{\$14,675,000} = $ **1.02** (rounded)

Step 4: SKU	Factor	Old Forecast	New Forecast	Cum Price
PC-1501-001	1.02 x	3,250 =	3,315	$4,127,175
PC-1501-002	1.02 x	2,450 =	2,499	$3,136,245
PC-1501-003	1.02 x	2,750 =	2,805	$3,576,375
PC-1501-001	1.02 x	3,150 =	3,213	$4,128,705
Totals:		11,600	11,832	Total $14,968,500

FIGURE 5.7 Pyramid forecast – by dollars.

SALES FORECAST TRACKING

Once the sales forecast plan has been created, it is critical that the statement of actual sales be tracked against the forecast estimates. Figure 5.8 illustrates a typical time-phased grid portraying visually the interplay of actual sales against planned for each product family. A critical decision to be made by planners is determining the size and number of periods to be used in the grid. This decision is dependent on several factors including the nature of the product, constancy of the marketplace, accuracy of the forecast, the length of the sales campaign, and other factors. In Figure 5.8 the size of the first nine periods are one month long, after which the plan continues on for two additional years consisting of calendar quarters. Finally, the grid displays the forecast to actual sales history of the first four periods of the year.

Product Family: **PC-1501**		**PC Computers**								*(in thousands)*	
Period	Jan	Feb	Mar	Apr	May	Jun	Jul	Aug	Sep	4thQt	1stQt
Sales Plan	13.4	13.2	12.9	12.5	12.1	11.8	11.4	11.1	12.3	38.2	39.6
Actual Sales	12.9	13.4	12.8	12.7							
Variance	-.5	+.2	-.1	+.2							
Cum Var.	-.5	-.3	-.4	-.2							

FIGURE 5.8 Sales plan actual to forecast.

The detail of the sales plan grid contains the following elements:

- *Sales plan.* This row contains the estimated sales forecast developed by applying the pyramid forecasting technique to product family sales history. Each period contains the projected anticipated sales volume for the product family. In the example, the forecast demand has been expressed in units.
- *Actual sales.* This row displays the shipped and booked customer orders occurring during the first three periods of the year. The values expressed are in units and are used to calculate the variance between the expected and the actual sales.
- *Variance.* This row contains the variance between forecasted and actual sales by period. A positive sign indicates that sales exceeded plan, while conversely a negative sign indicates below expected performance.

- *Cum variance.* This final row provides a running total of the variances occurring in each period beginning with January sales. This value will demonstrate such forecasting measurements as out-of-bounds conditions, trending, seasonality, or other forecast biases.

As an example of how the sales plan grid can yield statistics, it is evident that a lack of sales in the first period has dampened slightly the actual sales to the plan over the course of the first four periods. While February and April exhibited less than a two percent growth in sales, March experienced a slight decline. If anything can be said, the sales effort is performing below par. May appears to be a pivotal month to keep sales moving in a positive direction.

ELEMENTS OF PRODUCTION PLANNING

The production plan is a component of the DO&CP process normally developed for companies that have manufacturing functions. Pure distributors would be focused on developing the *procurement plan* for finished goods that will be covered below in the logistics planning process. The objective of the production planning process is to drive the business strategy down through the manufacturing organization and ensure that aggregate product family production rates match the goals of the sales and finished goods plans. A critical component of the production plan is the availability of production resources capable of producing the volume of product family quantities necessary to meet aggregate demand. Where capacities are insufficient, the business plan must either be changed or the enterprise must explore other avenues in order to gain the required resources. Production planning must find answers to such questions as the following:

- What production rates are required to support the business plan?
- How much finished goods should there be at the end of each planning period?
- How are planners to utilize the sales forecast plan?
- Is there sufficient capacity to realize the production plan?
- What will it cost to build the production plan?
- What strategies should production use in managing production rates to meet demand?
- How is the production plan to be integrated into the sales, logistics, and supply chain plans?

Providing answers to these questions requires the formulation of manufacturing plans that enable the pursuit of detailed, measurable objectives and goals. As illustrated in Figure 5.9, the production planning process begins with the development of the finished goods inventory plan. In make-to-stock

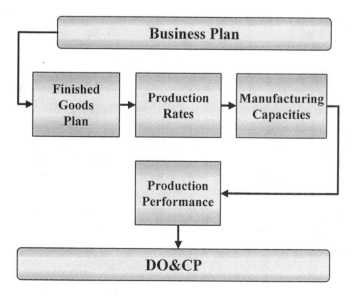

FIGURE 5.9 Production planning process.

environments, management policy will normally specify a targeted product group inventory quantity that should be on-hand at all times to support demand. Calculating this quantity is a function of several variables including the size of the planning period, opening product group inventory balance, family average sales, and a decision as to the targeted inventory balance. The first calculation is to determine the average sales by product family by planning period. For example, for product group PC-1501 the sales over the past twelve periods totaled 157,200. When divided by twelve periods, average sales per period was 13,100. Management has decided it required ten days of inventory available at all times. Since there was a total of 261 working days in the calendar, dividing 13,100 by 261 produced the average daily demand of 50 units (rounded). By multiplying the 50 units per ten days, the ending inventory balance should be placed at 500 units per period.

The second step in the production planning process is to establish the rate of production. Since most manufacturing environments must produce a minimum quantity of products to remain cost positive while also recognizing maximum output levels, a viable production plan must establish production levels that never exceed these boundaries while ensuring product is available to meet demand. In addition, since dramatic changes to the shop floor even within defined low/high boundaries is expensive, an level production rate enables planners to optimize productive resources while minimizing ramp-up and ramp-down costs.

204 TOP MANAGEMENT PLANNING

Once the rates of production have been established, the production planning process shifts to calculating the aggregate capacity necessary to build the production rate. While the production rate satisfies the priority plan necessary to match forecast demand, planners must also convert the production rate into a load plan that can be matched against aggregate capacities. In performing this activity, planners must first determine an aggregate planning work center/resource that is representative of the actual workcenters needed to produce all of the SKUs in the product family. This *resource capacity profile* must be expressed in a common production unit of measure and contain resource characteristics such as the amount of capacity available in a time period (usually a day), number of productive units (people/machines), efficiencies, and utilizations. Next, the product family plan must be converted into the resource capacity unit of measure. This is accomplished through a *resource load profile* which serves as a sort of aggregate process routing. Multiplying the load profile by the production rate will produce a load value that can then be compared to available resource capacity.

The final step in the production planning process is production performance. Production performance can be measured through the use of a number of reporting techniques. Probably the most obvious is the variance between planned and actual production. Besides providing a metric on how well the plan is progressing, the variances can be used to monitor the impact on the sales and inventory plans. Production performance thus provides a critical component in the mechanisms used to communicate changes through the DO&CP process to other parts of the supply chain.

CREATING THE PRODUCTION PLAN

Before planners can begin production plan development, several critical prerequisites must be in place. Among these can be found the following:
- A detailed product and sales plan existing at the product family level
- A statement of aggregate product family on hand balance
- A planning horizon that extends at least one year into the future
- Agreed upon common planning unit of measure
- Detailed load profiles for each product family
- Detailed capacity profiles for each aggregate work center, including desired efficiencies and utilizations
- Defined aggregate production planning objective
- Compatibility with the MPS

Once these elements have been completed, calculating the production plan components is a fairly easy process. The first task is to define the production strategy by choosing from one of the following:

- *Level production rate.* The goal of this strategy is to produce inventory, regardless of changes in actual demand, according to as level a production rate as possible to meet average demand. Excess inventories built during slow demand periods are assumed to cover for periods of excess demand.
- *Demand matching* (Chase strategy). This strategy seeks to produce inventory in exact quantities to meet demand through time. The objective of this strategy is to avoid high inventory costs by varying production rates and employee levels. This strategy requires highly flexible production resources that are capable of being easily idled and restarted.
- *Combination.* Often production management will seek to use a level production rate with the option of switching to a chase strategy based on certain sales volume or production or inventory cost benchmarks. For example, during periods where demand remains fairly consistent a level rate strategy could be used. As variability grows in demand, planners might switch over to a chase strategy to avoid excess costs.

An graphic example of these strategies can be seen in Figure 5.10.

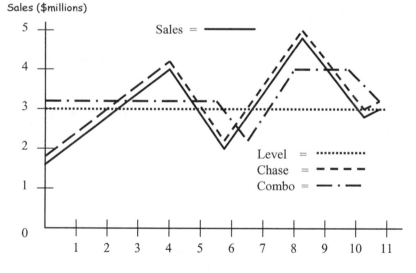

FIGURE 5.10 Types of Production Plan strategies.

Determining the Production Rate. Once the planning strategy has been selected the production plan can be established. The production plan actually consists of two interrelated plans: the *production rate plan* and a *re-*

source requirements plan. The production rate plan is created by performing the following steps:

1. Review the detailed sales product group forecast.
2. Load the product group forecast into a time-phased format by period.
3. The planning horizon should extend out into the future for at least one year.
4. Determine the aggregate beginning on-hand balance for the product family.
5. Determine the target ending inventory.
6. Determine all inventory and/or production changes by volume constraints.
7. Calculate the production plan for each product group by period.

An example of this procedure is illustrated by starting with the sales forecast exhibited in Figure 5.8. The sales forecast is the main driver for the production plan. Two other critical decisions have to be made: the targeted inventory balance and the production rate strategy to be used per product group. In the example, it has been determined that for product group PC-1501 a minimum of 250 SKUs must be on-hand at all times, and that the targeted on-hand is to be 500 SKUs. Also, it has been determined that production planning will follow a level rate strategy and that it will extend for three periods, after which it will be recalculated.

The results of the calculation can be seen in Figure 5.11. In *Plan A,* the sales plan has been loaded by time period. A cumulative on-hand beginning balance of 700 PC-1501 has been identified. The *production plan* has then been computed by following a simple formula expressed as

$$P = \frac{E - B + F}{N}$$

where P is the total inventory to be purchased during the planning period, E is the product group ending inventory, B is the product group starting inventory, F is the sales forecast for the product group by period, and, N is the number of periods in the planning period.

As an example, product group PC-1501 is calculated as follows:

1. Starting inventory is 700 units.
2. Targeted ending inventory at the end of the planning period January, February, and March is 500.
3. Sales forecasts customer demand of 39,300.

Then

$$P = \frac{500 - 700 + 39,300}{3} = 13,100.$$

4. This process is continued through the planning horizon.

Plan A: Original Production Plan

Product Family: **PC-1501**		**PC Computers**							(*in thousands*)	
Period	Jan	Feb	Mar	Apr	May	Jun	Jul	Aug	Sep	4thQt
Sales Plan	13.4	13.2	12.9	12.5	12.1	11.8	11.4	11.1	12.3	38.2
Production Plan	13.1	13.1	13.1	12.13	12.13	12.14	11.6	11.6	11.6	38.2
Inventory Plan .7	.4	.3	.5	.133	.166	.5	.7	1.2	.5	.5

Plan B: Adjusted F

Product Family: **PC-1501**		**PC Computers**							(*in thousands*)	
Period	Jan	Feb	Mar	Apr	May	Jun	Jul	Aug	Sep	4thQt
Sales Plan	13.4	13.2	12.9	12.5	12.1	11.8	11.4	11.1	12.3	38.2
Production Plan	13.1	13.1	13.1	12.25	12.25	12.25	11.48	11.48	11.48	38.2
.7	.4	.3	.5	.25	.4	.85	.933	1.316	.5	.5

FIGURE 5.11 Production and inventory plan.

When the plan has been completed, it must then be viewed for any constraints that emerge. Such a constraint appears in April where the ending period inventory balance falls below the required 250 SKU limit. In this case, a higher production rate for the second quarter must be calculated to account for the shortfall as illustrated in *Plan B* (Figure 5.11). The new rate enables the planner to accomplish two objectives: the minimum balance is preserved and inventory can be efficiently built to cover the ramp-up in sales in September. Often when creating a production plan planners must be careful to validate that the changes in production rate between periods can be accomplished. For example, in each quarter the production rate is dropping by about 6.5 percent. Planners would have to investigate the impact on personnel and plant utilization before actually decreasing the production rates.

Calculating the Resource Requirements Plan. While the production plan sets the aggregate levels of production and inventories over the product family planning horizon, planners must also match the plan against the aggregate capacity needed to manufacture the products. The steps necessary to create the resource capacity plan can be stated as follows:

1. Creation and authorization of a production rate plan for each product family extending at least one year into the future.
2. Determination of the load profile for each product family.
3. Determination of the resource profile for each product family.
4. Calculation of the resource capacity plan by matching load requirements against available capacity.
5. Validation of the resource plan and solve all periods with excess load.

Beyond *Step 1*, the next activity in capacity plan development is determineing the *load profile* for each product family. This "aggregate routing" is the common time required to produce any individual SKU within the product family and is composed of the processing time of all subassemblies and final assembly. Calculating the product family load profile can be performed by determining the historical percentage of sales of each SKU in the product family, multiplying this value by the actual process routing of the SKU, and adding each processing time to attain the average product family processing time as shown in Table 5.2. The average assembly time is then multiplied by

TABLE 5.2 Product Family Load Profile

Product Family: **PC-1501**   **PC Computers**

SKU	Sales Percentage	Standard (hrs) Processing Time	Average Assembly Time
PC-1501-001	35%	1.50	.525
PC-1501-002	43%	1.45	.625
PC-1501-003	13%	1.75	.228
PC-1501-004	9%	1.65	.149

Average Process Time: 1.527

the period production plan (*Production Plan B*, Figure 5.11) to produce the aggregate hours of load for the product family as shown in Figure 5.12.

The next step is to define the resource work centers that are used to build the product family. Normally, resource work centers are used for planning only. Their capacity is calculated used the same elements (daily capacity, efficiency, utilization, number of work units, and shifts) as actual work centers.

Product Family: **PC-1501 PC Computers**				Work Center: **Assembly**		
Period	Jan	Feb	Mar	Apr	May	Jun
Production Plan	13,100	13,100	13,100	12,250	12,250	12,250
Family Load (hrs)	20,003	20,003	20,003	18,706	18,706	18,706
Resource Capacity	19,000	19,000	19,000	19,000	19,000	19,000
Cum Variance	-1,003	-2,006	-3,006	-2,712	-2,418	-2,124

FIGURE 5.12 Capacity plan.

In the example used to create the capacity used in Figure 5.12, work center capacity by period has been calculated by multiplying the daily capacity of 950 hours by the number of days in the week (five days is being used) by four (average number of weeks in a month) to arrive at the aggregate available capacity of 19,000 hours a month or a little under 12,500 a period.

Once these figures have been compiled, it is fairly easy to generate a resource capacity plan (Figure 5.12). *Production Plan B* has been multiplied by the load profile of 1.527 hours a unit (Table 5.2) to arrive at the total hours of load by period found in row *Family Load*. Next, the *Resource Capacity* by period is entered in each period. Finally, the variance between load and capacity is calculated. In the example, the first three periods have excess load that will have to be resolved by the planners if the plan is to succeed. Starting the period in April there is over-capacity that can be used to factor in the response to the early over-load condition of the work center.

PRODUCTION PLAN PERFORMANCE

Once the production plan has been created, it is critical that actual production be tracked against the original estimates. Figure 5.13 presents the time-phased grid illustrating actual production against actual sales for product family PC-1501. In addition, the grid also tracks how closely actual production output is meeting ending inventory requirements. The calculation is simple. The opening *Actual Inventory* of 700 units is added to the *Actual Production* of 12,800 units in the first period and then subtracted from the *Actual Sales* of 12,900. The ending *Actual Inventory* for the first period is calculated at 600 units. This calculation is then performed for all subsequent periods.

As an example of how the production plan grid can yield data for decision making, it is evident that the high sales in the first three periods have significantly driven the production department to produce beyond current demonstrated capacity. While working overtime in the first three periods has enabled finished goods to stay close to the target ending inventory, an increase in sales in April has actually driven the ending inventory target to zero balance. Based on the new demand from actual sales, planners can now adjust production plan rates to be able to handle the short term increase in sales while observing the planned increases in inventories expected in the late summer and autumn periods.

Product Family: **PC-1501**	**PC Computers**								*(in thousands)*	
Period	Jan	Feb	Mar	Apr	May	Jun	Jul	Aug	Sep	4thQt
Actual Sales	12.9	13.4	12.8	12.7						
Production Plan	13.1	13.1	13.1	12.25	12.25	12.25	11.48	11.48	11.48	38.2
Actual Production	12.8	12.9	12.9	12.6						
Variance	-.3	-.2	-.2	.35						
Cum Variance	-.3	-.5	-.7	.35						
Inventory Plan .7	.4	.3	.5	.25	.4	.85	.933	1.316	.5	.5
Actual Inventory .7	.6	.1	.2	.1						
Cum Variance	+.2	0	-.3	-.45						

ELEMENTS OF LOGISTICS PLANNING

Regardless of whether the enterprise manufactures their own products or purchases them from suppliers for resale, it is the responsibility of the logistics function to establish the supply channel inventory levels and determine the logistics capacities necessary to support projected channel network demand. In developing the logistics plan, planners must find solutions to such questions as the following:

- How much channel inventory should be available to support the sales plan?
- What should be the deployment of inventories to supply chain locations?
- What is the monthly channel shipment plan necessary to satisfy business plan revenue targets?
- How much capital will be required to meet inventory replenishment requirements?

- What are the storage requirements necessary to house the inventory?
- What should be the size of the workforce necessary for efficient material handling?
- What type and how much material handling equipment will be required?
- What impact will customer delivery strategies have on the existing transportation structure?

In answering these and other questions, logistics planners must determine what resources need to be in place to support the sales plan and provide the necessary input to drive detail product replenishment, storage, and delivery resources. As is illustrated in Figure 5.14, the logistics planning process be-

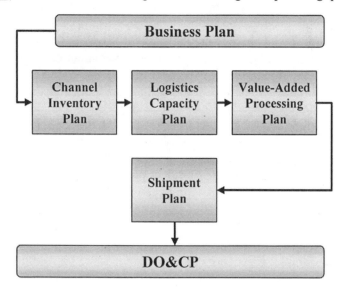

FIGURE 5.14 Logistics planning process.

gins with the translation of the aggregate sales forecast into product family channel stocking requirements. The objective of the inventory channel plan is to provide the firm with an aggregate schedule of product group requirements that can be matched against expected channel level sales and ending inventory targets. Similar to the production plan, the output is generally specified in aggregate units of measure such as dollars or total units. The channel inventory plan should be established at least once a year and reviewed and updated on a periodic basis (at least quarterly and, preferably, monthly). To be effective, it should be consistent with marketing and sales plans, as well as with the company budgets set forth in the business plan. Once the plan has been completed, however, it is the responsibility of logistics management to achieve the plan; that is, having product and transportation capacities available as planned.

The second step in the logistics planning process is determining the total logistics resource requirements plan. Capacity planning at this level is concerned with the aggregate resources required to support sales, shipping, and inventory targets. Resources in the typical enterprise can be categorized into four components: inventory investment, transportation costs, warehouse space capacities, and labor and equipment needs. The mechanics involved in establishing aggregate logistics capacities are to obtain the planned procurement for each product group by period, determine the resource profiles required of the four capacity components, and then to compare calculated resource needs with existing capacities.

In today's fast paced channel networks, the ability of supply nodes to delay product differentiation to the very last moment before actual customer sale is absolutely critical to marketplace success. Known as product *postponement*, the object is to place value-added processing capabilities at various key positions in the supply chain. In many ways today's distribution center is looking more and more like a manufacturing facility. Rather than fulfilling simply a product storage function, the channel warehouse is rapidly evolving into a fast-paced operations center, return goods depot, or fulfillment repository focused on inventory velocity and product process enhancement. Designing the strategy for value-added processing comprises the third step in the logistics planning process.

Finally, the most critical planning performance measurement in logistics planning is developing and monitoring the product-level shipping plan. The contents of the shipping plan are expressed in the same product groups, units of measure, and time periods as the sales plan and are composed of the following elements: the current customer order backlog, current customer backorders, and forecast by product group. This shipment plan is a critical part of the DO&C plan and should be combined with the detailed sales, production, and inventory plans to provide a balanced view of how well the company and the entire supply chain is progressing.

Drafting the formal logistics plan provides channel strategists with a road map detailing the direction of logistics activities and how well they are meeting the needs of the demand and channel supply plans. The plan establishes future objectives and goals outlining performance expectations, technology adoption, workforce attitudes, and enterprise culture. Far from being just a "budget" specifying costs and revenues, the logistics plan is, more importantly, a long-term statement delineating the human, material, and informational resources required of the whole supply chains. Finally, the formal logistics strategic plan links and aligns logistics with the overall business, marketing, sales, and production strategic plans.

LOGISTICS RESOURCE REQUIREMENTS PLANNING

The logistics planning process can be used to calculate the logistic resources required to execute the aggregate channel inventory and shipment plans. The logistics plan should cover a specified planning horizon extending at least one year into the future and should be reviewed and updated at least on a quarterly, but preferably a monthly, basis. The output of the logistics planning process is composed of the aggregate inventories, shipments, and warehouse and transportation capacities necessary to support the marketing and sales plans. It is the responsibility of sales to actualize the demand side of the shipment plan by attaining sales plan objectives; it is the responsibility of logistics management to have sufficient inventories and delivery capacities to meet shipment objectives. The actual shipments and available inventory form the scorecard tracking the overall success of the DO&CP process.

The Inventory Replenishment Plan. Developing the channel inventory plan is an iterative, highly structured process that closely resembles the development of the production rate in manufacturing. The planning process begins by receiving the product family aggregate sales forecast and all company open order demand covering one year or more into the future. In some planning environments this will mean summarizing local forecasts and open orders to achieve a single corporate statement of channel demand. The aggregate demand for each product family should be expressed in total units and then spread over the planning horizon. Planners must be careful to respond to seasonality, sales cycles, or peaks produced by sales promotions. Next, any target increases or decreases in inventory or backlog levels are established. The inventory levels defined are usually determined in the business plan and can be used as benchmarks to measure actual sales and procurement performance. Finally, the opening balance for each product family should be calculated.

Once these steps have been completed, planners can apply simple time phased computer processing logic to generate the actual replenishment plan. Safety stock can be used to indicate an ending balance target. For example, assume the sales forecast for product family PC-1501 (Figure 5.8) represents total expected channel demand. The planning elements are as follows:

1. Starting cum channel inventory is 700 units.
2. Ending cum channel inventory is 500 units.

3. The minimum order quantity is 200 units.
4. Since inventory distribution occurs through interbranch resupply, the lead time is negligent.

The calculation is straightforward (Figure 5.15): in January the forecast of 13,400 units is added to the ending balance of 500. The resulting 13,900 is then reduced by the opening balance of 700 to produce a net requirement of 13,200. Since the requirement is evenly divisible by the minimum order quantity of 200 units, the planned replenishment requirement would be 13,200. This replenishment quantity satisfies the demand plan, while leaving an ending balance of 500 units.

Product Family: **PC-1501**			**PC Computers**						(*in thousands*)	
Period	Jan	Feb	Mar	Apr	May	Jun	Jul	Aug	Sep	4thQt
Demand Plan	13.4	13.2	12.9	12.5	12.1	11.8	11.4	11.1	12.3	38.2
End On-hand Bal .7	.5	.5	.6	.5	.6	.6	.6	.5	.6	.5
Net Requirements	-13.2	-13.2	-12.9	-12.4	-12.1	-11.7	-11.3	-11.0	-12.3	-39.1
Replenishment Ord.	13.2	13.2	13.0	12.4	12.2	11.8	11.4	11.0	12.4	39.2

FIGURE 5.15 Channel inventory replenishment planning.

Once aggregate channel product family replenishment totals have been compiled, the output can be used to calculate other logistics capacity requirements for inventory investment, transportation cost, warehouse space, and labor and equipment needs. In addition, the requirements plan can be easily disaggregated into individual channel warehouse plans. This can be done by assigning a percentage value to each warehouse stocking the product family and dividing by the aggregate replenishment totals. For example if the channel was composed of three warehouses with a split of 60 percent, 25 percent, and 15 percent, the replenishment plan would post 7,920 units to the first warehouse, 3,300 to the second, and 1,980 to the third.

Inventory Investment. If the total logistics plan is to be successfully executed, planners must ensure that the firm possesses sufficient financial resources to support inventory acquisition, storage, and material handling requirements. Historically, companies have used turnover ratios, inventory as a percentage of sales (the inverse of turnover), or some other theoretical macro technique to measure total inventory investment. Obviously, factors such as mid-stream changes in products, markets, customer service policies, the distribution network, and other events could negate the validity of such a measurement standard.

A much more effective method of projecting aggregate inventory costs is to utilize a *Replenishment Input/Output Report*. The report uses planned and actual replenishment, shipment, and inventory balances to calculate projected inventory costs. The planned replenishment and shipment figures are gathered from each product family's DO&C plans. Actual replenishment and shipment figures are accumulated and entered through time. Figure 5.16 illustrates a *Replenishment Input/Output Report* utilizing the sales information from Figure 5.8 and replenishment information from Figure 5.15. The use of such an Input/Output Report not only presents managers with an analysis of the financial position of the inventory of the firm, it also permits visibility to out of bounds situations and provides a mechanism to ensure that the company is effectively executing the sales and replenishment plans necessary to support business objectives.

Product Family: **PC-1501** **PC Computers** (*in thousands*) Avg. Price (per unit): $1,265.00 Avg. Cost (per unit): $1,075.00											
Per.	$ Replenishment			$ Ship			Inventory			Inventory Cost		
	P	A	V	P	A	V	P	A	V	P	A	V
Jan	14,190	14,190	0	16,951	16,319	-632	13.7	13.7	0	14,728	14,728	0
Feb	14,190	13,975	-215	16,698	16,951	+253	13.7	13.5	-.2	14,728	14,513	-215
Mar	13,975	13,868	-107	16,319	16,192	-127	13.6	13.5	-.1	14,620	14,513	-107
Apr	13,330	13,545	+215	15,813	16,066	+253	12.9	13.1	+.2	13,868	14,083	+215
May	13,115			15,307			12.8			13,760		

P = Plan
A = Actual
V = Variance

FIGURE 5.16 Replenishment input-output report.

Transportation. An effective logistics plan provides traffic planners with a window into the transportation requirements necessary to ensure that inventory is available at channel distribution points. Calculating transportation needs is critical. In many companies, the cost for transportation is the largest single logistics cost, accounting in some instances for more than half of the total cost. Although the most obvious benefit of transportation planning is to measure actual costs to budgets, it also provides planners with the ability to negotiate freight rates, make intelligent decisions as to the use of company-owned transportation versus contractors, and view areas for transportation cost savings.

The most effective tool for calculating aggregate transportation requirements is the *Transportation Planning Report*. The report is a combination of the following elements:

1. *Transportation unit factors.* In developing transportation unit factors, planners must first identify the normal units of transportation by which their products are shipped. Possible units may be number of pallets, weight, and storage volume.

2. *Calculation of transportation unit costs.* Once transportation units have been identified, the cost of transporting products can be determined. Costs must be calculated for the shipment of goods from supplying warehouses to each stocking warehouse in the distribution channel. As an example, a company transports PCs from the Chicago distribution center to the Los Angeles field warehouse by rail. Each rail car holds 100,000 pounds of goods and contains 2500 cubic feet of volume. The rail company offers the follows rates:

Car Weight	Avg. Cost per CWT
0 to 1,000 lbs	$10.00/cwt
1,001 to 8,000 lbs	$9.00/cwt
8,001 to 12,000 lbs	$8.00/cwt
12,001 to 15,000 lbs	$6.00/cwt

3. *Product group transportation profiles.* The transportation elements of each product group in the procurement plan must be assigned a val-ue. For example, the standard weight of PC-1501 is six pounds and is stacked 30 boxed units on pallet requiring 64 cubic feet of space.

Once these elements have been determined, it is relatively easy to calculate the aggregate cost of transportation. A sample *Transportation Planning Report* appears in Figure 5.17. The supply channel replenishment quantity for product PC-1501 has been extended first by the product family transportation profile values, and then by the associated transportation costs for shipping an average load of 1,000 units a week from Chicago to Los Angeles by the rail rates detailed above. By adding the totals of each product family and shipping location, planners can review total transportation costs and other shipping elements necessary to execute the shipping plan.

Warehouse Space Requirements. Once inventory and transportation plans have been established, planners can calculate the total warehouse space necessary to house the aggregate inventory plan. As a whole, warehousing activities account for roughly one-fifth of logistics expenditure. Executing the

Product Family: PC-1501		Weight: 6lbs	Cube Space: 64 ft	
Period	Quantity	Weight	Cube	$ Cost
Jan	4,000/1,000 avg.	24,000/6,000 avg.	8,534/2,134 avg.	2,160/540 avg.
Feb	4,400/1,100 avg.	26,400/6,600 avg.	9,387/2,347 avg.	2,376/594 avg.
Mar	4,200/1,050 avg.	25,200/6,300 avg.	8,960/2,240 avg.	2,268/567 avg.
Apr	4,600/1,150 avg.	27,600/6,900 avg.	9,814/2,454 avg.	2,484/621 avg.

FIGURE 5.17 Transportation planning report

aggregate inventory plan without effective warehouse plans can be expensive, resulting in such problems as unnecessary material handling costs, product damage and obsolescence, record keeping redundancies and errors, time wasted in product search, excess transportation costs, and the expense for public warehousing or other extra storage facilities.

Logistics management can plan for aggregate warehouse space requirements in much the same fashion as they plan for transportation requirements. In developing the *Warehouse Space Requirements Report*, the following elements can be used:

1. *Product group storage profiles.* For each product group, an aggregate weight, number of pallets, and volume space requirements are determined. These figures represent the basic storage characteristics of the product family to house the stocking unit of measure. Products can be stored in bins, racks, barrels, pallets, and so on.
2. *Total warehouse space.* The total space in the warehouse must be determined by the storage area unit of measure. Logistics must calculate how many cubic feet of shelf space, pallet racking, floor space, barrels, and so on, are available per warehouse.
3. *Warehouse space calculation.* The aggregate warehouse space requirements are calculated by extending the average stocked quantity during the replenishment lead time plus safety stock for each product family by the storage profiles established for each product family. These aggregate space requirements are then netted against total available warehouse space by storage area to reveal both filled and open space.

An example of a *Warehouse Space Requirements Report* appears in Figure 5.18. The calculations use the same quantities, weight, and cube specified in Figure 5.17. Warehouse planners would need to calculate the space requirements for each product group for each warehouse in the distribution network.

Although actual space requirements for products will vary due to sales growth, shifts in sales patterns, geography, new product introduction, and other factors, aggregate space estimates should be accurate enough in general to support the procurement plan.

Product Family: **PC-1501**		Weight: 6lbs	Cube Space: **64 ft**	
Period	Quantity	Weight	Cube	No. Pallets
Jan	1,250	7,500	2,688	42
Feb	1,350	8,100	2,880	45
Mar	1,500	9,000	3,200	50
Apr	1,400	8,400	3,008	47

FIGURE 5.18 Product family space requirements report.

Labor and Equipment Needs. Effective logistics planning requires that planners be able to determine the aggregate manpower and equipment needs of each warehouse in the distribution channel. Too much or too little manpower can be expensive, as can the fixed asset costs of unused equipment or lost productivity due to equipment shortages. In addition, labor and equipment planning is even more essential for distributors with seasonal peaks and valleys.

Much in the fashion of a manufacturing routing, logistics planners can develop aggregate labor and equipment processing work standards per product group. Routings in a manufacturing environment specify the operations to be performed, the equipment to be used, and the number of hours required to build a specific lot size of a product. By using the same principles, logistics planners can develop product family labor and equipment work standards. These standards should detail labor hours and equipment needs for the two main distribution activities: product receiving and material put-away, and order picking and shipping. The first standard encompasses determining the work requirements needed to load and unload trucks or railcars, and material put-away. The second can be calculated by developing standards for order picking and shipping. Capacity requirements can then be calculated by extending processing times by the aggregate totals found in the inventory and shipping plans. The results of the calculation should yield an aggregate statement of manpower and capacity required to actualize DO&CP objectives.

An example of a Labor and Equipment Capacity Report appears in Figure 5.19. Across the top can be found the standard labor and equipment times to handle a lot size of 500 units of Product Family PC-1501 at the Chicago warehouse. The detail labor and equipment times can be attained by dividing the expected inventory quantity by the lot size and then extending the value by the detail standard for labor and equipment. After each product family capacity requirements are compiled, they can then be summarized to provide the total product family required labor and equipment times for the warehouse in each period.

Routing Detail:

1. Lot Size: 500 units

2. Labor Requirements
   Receiving and Putaway: 20 hrs
   Picking and Shipping: 10 hrs

3. Equipment Requirements
   Fork Lift: 19 hrs
   Picker Vehicle: 12 hrs

Product Family: **PC-1501** PC Computers				Warehouse: Chicago	
		Labor (hrs)		Equipment (hrs)	
Period	Quantity	Rec/Putaway	Pick/Ship	Fork Lift	Picker Vehicle
Jan	1,250	50	25	48	30
Feb	1,350	54	27	52	33
Mar	1,500	60	30	57	36
Apr	1,400	56	28	54	34

FIGURE 5.19 Labor and equipment capacity report.

VALUE-ADDED PROCESSING PLAN

A key element in the logistics plan is determining if stocking points in the supply channel are going to further process received products and materials into final configured finished goods. Historically, distribution channels have been unconcerned with forms of manufacturing. Today, increasing customer demands for perfect orders, increasing speed, decreasing costs, continuous improvement, and greater selection and customization are requiring companies to delay product differentiation (postponement) to the customer-facing node in the supply chain. In fact, the concept of the warehouse as a storage function is being replaced by a new concept that requires the warehouse to be increasingly focused on value-added services such as product configuration, packaging, labeling, cross-docking, pricing, and merchandizing. Designing a strategy to manage collectively these *value-added processing* functions is a critical component in logistics plan development.

Advantages of value-added processing. There are several reasons for this growing interest in value-added processing.

- *Reducing Channel Costs.* Traditionally, as products moved from the manufacturer out into the distribution pipeline, value was often added by channel partners who performed quantity, packaging, or other value-added activities as products passed through the supply chain. The problem with this arrangement is that at each node in the channel network cost was added to the product that was subsequently passed on to the next channel level. In an effort to offer the same product at lower prices, many companies have decided to eliminate costly upstream channel partners and perform the value-added processing themselves. Although they will have to bear additional costs for plant, equipment, and personnel, the expense is more than offset by reductions in channel-wide finished goods inventories and lower transportation costs.

- *Lead-Time Reduction.* By eliminating channel stocking point redundancies, network supply nodes can increase the velocity of product to market. As products no longer have to proceed through costly and time consuming processes as they pass from one channel level to the next, delivery time to the customer from the originating manufacturer can be significantly reduced.

- *Inventory Reduction.* Because the number of stocking points in the network are reduced, so is the total value of stocked inventory in the pipeline. Besides reducing channel carrying costs, reduced inventories enable better control of product obsolescence and spoilage.

- *Customer Response and Flexibility.* Because downstream channel network nodes can now receive products in bulk or in an unassembled state, their ability to respond to customer requests is increased. In the past, distribution points received goods in a finished assembly quantity or prepackaged state. By buying goods, for example, in bulk and packaging them per customer order, response flexibility can be expanded without increasing inventory investment.

- *Material Handling.* Value-added processing targeted at *unitization* can help reduce labor and material handling costs while accelerating product movement. Unitization can be defined as the consolidation of product into units of measure that facilitate warehouse and transportation handling. An example would be palletizing many small units to reduce the number of pieces handled.

Elements of value-added processing. The economic justification for value-added processing rests on the *Principle of Postponement*. The objective of this principle is to explore inventory management strategies that can assist both internal company distribution facilities and channel partners minimize the risk of carrying finished products in downstream channel nodes by delaying product differentiation to the latest possible moment before customer purchase. Stocking and transportation cost savings are attained by keeping base product at the highest level possible in the supply chain and by moving generic goods through the pipeline in large quantities. Obviously, the key to postponement strategies is the ability of supply channel locations to convert undifferentiated goods and bulk quantities quickly and inexpensively into finished product as close as possible to the time and place required by the customer. This process of adding final value to the product is fundamental to understanding and leveraging value-added processing to create a unique competitive advantage.

When developing a value-added processing policy, channel planners are faced with a number of critical questions:

- What is the cost of value-added processing at various stocking points in the distribution network?
- When should value-added processing activities occur?
- At what stocking point should generic products be converted into brands?
- What is the cost advantage of bulk shipment of the product?
- What are the quality risks involved in remote value-added processing?
- Can the product skip one or more points in the channel of distribution?
- What postponement strategies are being pursued by the competition?
- What is the level of customer service attained by the postponement strategy?

Once answers to these and other questions have been made, strategists must decide on the processing methods to be deployed by selecting from the following list of processing alternatives:

- *Sorting.* In this activity, a heterogeneous supply of a particular product is organized into distinct finished goods that are relatively homogeneous. This form of processing is normally identified with certain raw materials and agricultural products, such as grading eggs according to size, and beef as either choice or prime.
- *Bulk breaking* (allocation). Economies in transportation, handling, storage, and other related costs can often be achieved by shipping products through the supply channel network in large quantities and then breaking them down into several smaller *stockkeeping units* (SKUs). For example, a large Midwest manufacturer of hardware products purchases various types of fasteners by the keg from Far Eastern sources. Afterwards, the fasteners are processed into smaller finished goods

packaged sizes, or the contents are mixed with other fasteners manufactured by the company to form end-product assortments sold to retail outlets.

- *Labeling.* This form of value-added processing is used most often in differentiating generic products through a labeling or branding process. As an example, a large Midwestern fruit juice bottler produces various sizes of bottled but unlabeled product. The product is shipped in bulk to the distribution points in the channel and left unlabeled until the receipt of a customer order for a specific brand and container size. Processing steps involve issuing the required common product size from stock, labeling, packaging, and shipping to the customer.

- *Blending.* Petroleum, paint, pharmaceuticals, and other process-manufactured products can be shipped and stored in the distribution channel in an unblended state. Once actual orders are received, the proper blend to match finished goods specifications is processed. Similar to labeling postponement, delaying the commitment of inventories until the actual customer order is received reduces inventory carrying costs and spoilage. An example would be a paint distributor who blends base colors to customer order specification.

- *Kitting* (assorting). This value-added processing activity is used to assemble heterogeneous items and materials linked by functional use into finished products sold as a group. An example would be assembling an automotive brake kit composed of various tools and accessories. The kitting process enables customers to purchase an assembled unit rather than having to choose each of the components separately. Kits can both be preassembled and inventoried, or they can be assembled per customer order.

- *Packaging.* Although all products are packaged in some manner, channel distributors may choose to repackage the products they receive for the following four reasons: (1) protection, (2) containment, (3) information, and (4) utility. Less than adequate packaging can lead to excessive costs due to damage and redundancies in handling. Excessive packaging, on the other hand, can lead to additional costs associated with bulk breaking and storage and equipment requirements. In addition, repackaging may occur to assist in unitization and identification.

- *Light final assembly.* Performing light assembly of products is the closest channel warehouses come to true manufacturing. Light assembly requires such activities as snapping, bolting, gluing, or wiring components together, label stamping or other forms of product identification, and painting. For the most part, light assembly consists of highly labor intensive, but low-skill and low-cost processes. Light assembly requires channel distributors to make significant financial commitments in equipment, level of employee skill, facilities, and information systems.

Contrasts with manufacturing. The use of the term "value-added processing" as opposed to "manufacturing" is meant to communicate an important difference. Although it is true that kitting and light assembly come close to manufacturing, these functions are distinctly different from those performed by manufacturers. One of the key differences relates to the *product positioning strategy*. Distributors basically maintain one type of inventory: finished goods normally purchased from sources outside the enterprise or transferred from upstream manufacturing plants. When value-added processing does occur, it is usually confined to manipulating the unit of measure of a product or grouping it with other products. In contrast, manufacturers normally alter fundamentally the form, fit, and function of item components in the process of manufacturing conversion.

Another contrasting point can be found in the *production process design strategy*. For the most part, distributors have simple value-added processes geared toward manipulating the *quantity* and not the *nature* of the product. The investment in manufacturing assets, therefore, is minimal, the labor force needs only basic skills, and simple, even manual, process control systems are often sufficient to execute build priorities. Manufacturers, on the other hand, design their manufacturing processes to transform materials and components into fundamentally new products. Processes are usually characterized by the use of highly skilled labor, complex machinery, and sophisticated information systems that plan, track, and record performance and costing data.

ELEMENTS OF SUPPLY CHANNEL PLANNING

In Chapter 2 the supply channel was defined from several perspectives. It was compared as a pipeline through which the flow of products and information from the supply source to the point of customer sales was planned and controlled. The supply channel was also conceived as a partnership of suppliers, manufacturers, distributors, retailers, and customers who were linked as integrated nodes in a *distribution system*. Finally, the supply channel was portrayed as the medium by which the activities of ownership, title transfer, promotions, negotiations, ordering, and payment flows were performed. The focus of supply channel management is *delivery*, and can be summarized as *the process of making a product or service available for use or consumption.*

Designing effective channel strategies requires planners to find answers to such questions as the following:

- What is the physical structure of the supply channel?
- What is the optimum channel structure to deliver the necessary value demanded by the customer?
- What marketing and logistics functions are to be performed by the supply channel?
- What are the value-producing attributes (such as speed, reliability, price, best value, service, depth of available products/services, technology tools) that are to guide channel operations?
- What impact will postponement and value-added strategies have upon the supply channel?
- What types of relationship are required to achieve the desired level of channel collaboration?

Providing answers to these questions requires the formulation of channel management plans capable of laying the foundation for tactical activities, such as basic channel and marketing functions, as well as operational and partnership strategies. As illustrated in Figure 5.20, the channel planning

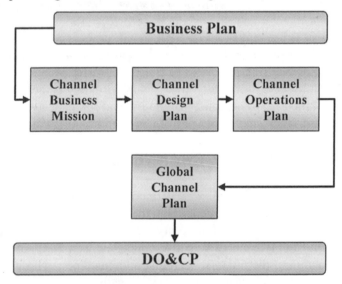

FIGURE 5.20 Channel planning process.

process begins with the development of the channel business mission statement. The objective of this step is to define how the supply chain is going to compete in the marketplace. Although the nature and function of supply channels will vary by industry, they all have a common business mission: to continuously create superlative, customer-winning product and service value at the lowest possible operating and investment cost. An effective mission statement will determine how the five critical elements of the supply channel – the customer, the service strategy, people resources, trading partners, and information technologies – are to be integrated into a seamless, highly competitive value chain.

The second step in the channel planning process is the construction of the supply channel system. Distribution systems provide the medium by which products are moved from the point of origin to the point of consumption. There are two critical elements that must be considered when designing the channel to accomplish this basic objective. The first centers on the *complexity of product delivery*. Several critical question come to mind: How deep and how broad is the targeted market penetration? Does the nature of the product require special transportation, storage, and handling? How extensively does the firm want to control these functions? The second critical element influencing the supply channel structure rests upon the *degree of channel partner dependence*. The more extensive the channel, normally the more dependency grows on trading partners for cooperation and sharing of critical functions and processes.

Once the design of the channel has been determined, channel network participants must define the processes capable of creating unique and unassailable value to the customer. The operational imperatives must realize the following market-winning objectives: superior customer service, continuous reduction of all forms of cycle time, high levels of channel performance, and reduced costs. Besides defining core competitive guidelines, such as completeness and reliability of delivery, high product/service quality, speed and frequency of deliveries, and least total delivered cost, planners should strive to continuously compress cycle times in manufacturing, distribution, and customer delivery. The final topic in this area is tackling total supply network costs. Supply channel operating costs are complex and consist of a matrix of drivers such as labor, facilities operations, inventory investment, transportation, and long-term asset investment.

In many supply channels planners are increasingly have to come to grips with establishing global supply channels. Even mature supply chains must expend significant effort at developing channel structures and product and service mixes that will appeal to a global market. Often new core competencies will have to be built or acquired in foreign countries, new mechanisms for the performance of global trade functions constructed, and new partnerships architected capable of handling the flow of products and services through global trading networks. In addition, less strategic issues such as intermodal transport, government regulations, tariffs, environmental concerns, and local labor force and cultural issues will have to be reviewed. A full treatment of global trading channels is found in Chapter 13.

UNDERSTANDING SUPPLY CHANNELS - OVERVIEW

Few products are sold by their producers directly to the end customer. For the most part, products travel through one or more intermediaries, such as company-owned distribution functions, wholesalers, dealers, brokers, and retailers. The channels that emerge out of these trading relationships are governed by the transfer of ownership and the flow of goods and information as they make their way through the distribution system. The structure of supply channels can be viewed from either an *institutional* or a *functional* approach. Institutionally, supply channels can be described as confederations of aligned companies that participate in a interconnected process of buying and selling products and services. On the other hand, a supply channel could also be a group composed of geographically dispersed warehouses owned by a single corporate parent. Finally, the channel could be a mixture of internal and trading partner inventory storage or distribution points. Channel structures can take a number of forms based on corporate goals, operating paradigms, channel strengths and weaknesses, and customer expectations. Some distributors can have multiple structures based on market segment. Zenith, for example, will sell television sets through large retail outlets like Best Buy, small retail electronic appliance stores, and a network of distributors and dealers.

Supply channels, however, can also be defined by the functions executed by channel partners associated with the movement of product through the distribution pipeline. As illustrated in Figure 5.21, some channels are single level: The manufacturer performs all the functions relating to marketing, products and services, transportation, and warehousing. Other channels are composed of multiple levels of manufacturers, distributors, and retailers, each performing some or all of the marketing and logistics functions and the cost of operations. The level of integration and cooperation depends largely on the nature of the product and market objectives. For example, a fresh vegetable distribution channel requires a tightly knit linkage of channel partners who depend on speedy delivery, communications, title transfer, and financing flows to bring product to market.

In practice, it is almost impossible to separate the institutional from the functional activities performed by the members of a supply channel. Still, it is far more useful to describe channel agents by the activities they perform than by attaching institutional nomenclature, such as "producer," "wholesaler," or "retailer." Such an approach assists channel strategists in focusing on the actual mechanics of the supply channel rather than a strictly organizational view. This factor also recognizes that the institutional structure of a supply channel can remain constant even though responsibility for performing channel functions may shift between channel members.

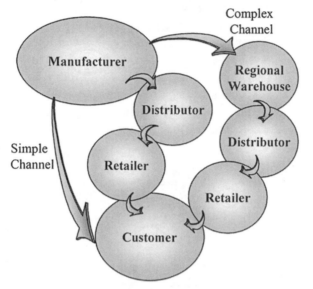

FIGURE 5.21 Types of supply channel structures

DEFINING THE SUPPLY CHANNEL MISSION

The objective of the *channel business mission* is to determine how to arrange internal channel functions and external partners into a highly competitive value chain. Although the structure of supply channels will vary by industry, they can all be said to have a basic business mission: *to continuously create superlative, customer-winning product and service value at the lowest possible operating and investment cost.* The core components of the channel mission statement are revealing. The first component, *continuously create*, implies that productive processes within the channel must be constantly focused and refocused on a ceaseless search for innovation both in the products and services the channel offers and in the way they are delivered to the marketplace. This component describes the strategy by which the channel is going to compete. *Customer value* refers to the mix of products and services to be presented to the marketplace. Defining key attributes, such as quality, price, delivery, product robustness and configurability, and level of service, illuminates performance goals and unifies channel participants and directs them toward a common objective. This component describes who is the target of the channel. Finally, the *operating and in-*

vestment cost of achieving channel objectives provides the financial perform-ance measurements and necessary channel organizational mechanisms guiding operations. This element describes how the channel is going to compete.

A useful framework for developing the channel mission statement is to identify the strategies to manage the five critical dimensions of channel man-agement: the customer, the service strategy, the workforce, channel partners, and technologies systems strategy. These areas are portrayed in Figure 5.22. At the center of the supply channel mission stands the customer. It is customer wants, needs, and expectations that drive channel objectives and define channel structure and marketplace values. Responding to this central channel compon-ent will impact the core channel functions of the following:

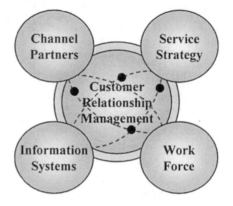

FIGURE 5.22 Channel mission components

- *Marketing.* Identifies the products and services that meets customer wants and needs. Market foresight teams will also be responsible for lo-cating tomorrow's newest and most profitable industries and identifying the skills and competencies required for effective participation.
- *Supplier management.* Integrates with each upstream supply node to en-sure the timely delivery of quality materials and components at the lowest possible cost.
- *Product development.* Develops products and services that possess un-paralleled customer value in the shortest cycle time possible and at the lowest cost.
- *Production operations.* Creates the highest quality products through the use of flexible processes and quick response that enable custom manu-facture while decreasing lot sizes and cost.
- *Demand management.* Provides short order cycle times and responsive service and delivery through the use of computerized information systems and electronic commerce.

- *Channel management.* Integrates products and information to ensure their rapid flow through the supply pipeline to the customer at the shortest possible time and lowest cost.

Clearly identifying the channel's customer service mission forms the foundation for the formulation and implementation of the channel's service strategy. The service strategy consists of an *internal* commitment to service centered on the formal channel mission statement and an *external* commitment to executing those service attributes promised to the customer through the sales cycle.

The collective management of the human resources comprising the channel is the third critical dimension of the channel mission. Human resources provide the central competencies that drive each business and remedying deficiencies is a fundamental role of channel partners. The fact that this area is connected to the service strategy means that there must be a shared vision if service values are to permeate not only each enterprise but the whole supply channel. The link between people resources and service represents the everyday communication that occurs between the channel's work force and the customer.

Perhaps the central pillar of the supply chain management concept is the utilization of business partners to create tightly integrated business channels. This means more than just outsourcing a peripheral channel function: it is about architecting a collaborative community of trading partners collectively driven by a common mission to deliver the highest level of customer service possible. The realization of inter-enterprise structures capable of mutually supporting objectives and synchronous information flows will require the following process and strategic attributes:

1. *A shared inter-enterprise vision.* The goal is not only to establish a mechanism for cross-channel business, but also to use the framework to leverage the product, services, and competencies of the entire channel ecosystem to deliver breakthrough customer value.
2. *Inter-enterprise channel model.* The channel model provides a high-level description of how the network is constructed, including the loca-tion of inter-enterprise integration points. The model should detail mar-keting and customer management goals, product/service mix, product development roles, financial measurements, and logistics management requirements.
3. *Inter-enterprise process modeling.* Once the channel vision and structural model have been detailed, a channel process map needs to created defining which channel functions are going to be inter-enterprise processes, what technologies must be in place, and how supporting internal and external organizational infrastructures are to be established.

The final component of the channel mission is the channel's information systems. The role of information systems is to link the other components of the channel framework. People resources utilize the channel's systems to execute functions, record information, and communicate with each other and with customers. These *systems* are multidimensional and are composed of management systems that determine channel goals, internal and externally devised rules and regulations systems, the mechanical technical systems, and the channel's collective social systems that guide problem solving, teamwork, and service values. The customer must use the systems employed by their suppliers to make their wishes, needs, and expectations known. Finally, information systems can be heavily influenced by the customer-service-centered culture strategy.

CHANNEL DESIGN

Once the channel business mission has been defined, planners must turn their attention to channel design. The output from this planning process is usually defined as the *channel structure design*. The task of keeping the channel focused on competitive goals and objectives is termed *channel leadership*. The combined tasks of designing the channel structure and providing leadership is referred to as *channel management* [9]. In deciding on the structure of the channel network, firms must align products and services with the *time, place,* and *delivery* needs of the marketplace. One method used in defining the marketing channel is to gauge the marketing flow functions in terms of *service outputs*. There are four basic service outputs to be considered:

- *Product Variety.* The depth and breath of a supplier's product assortment reduces the need for buyers to search the marketplace to meet product and service requirements. Robustness of product variety reduces buyer costs associated with order placement, receiving, warehousing, and accounts payable.
- *Waiting Time.* This is the time intervening between order placement and delivery of goods and services. The faster the delivery time, the less customers have to stock safety inventories and extend their planning horizons out into the future.
- *Lot Size.* The size of the required purchase quantity directly affects customer service levels. The smaller the lot size and the faster the delivery, the greater the level of service. Small lot sizes permit customers to reduce payables cash flow, reduce the need for storage, and help contain costs stemming from damage and obsolescence.
- *Spatial Convenience.* This service output refers to the degree of channel decentralization. Time and place utilities are critical to customers.

The closer the outlet to the customer, the more costs associated with supplier search and transportation can be reduced.

How service outputs will be used in channel design depends to a large extent on the degree of market exposure companies seek for their products. Kotler [10] differentiates three levels of market exposure:

1. *Intensive distribution.* In this strategy, producers typically seek to distribute their products through as many distribution points as possible to maximize product availability in the marketplace. Companies distributing low-cost consumer goods, such as candy and soft drinks that require little customer service and whose quality is not associated with the nature of the outlet, will use this method of channel organization.

2. *Exclusive distribution.* Some producers will deliberately limit the number of channel partners handling their products. The most extreme manifestation of this strategy is exclusive distribution, where a limited number of intermediaries are granted exclusive right to distribute certain products. Often producers will also mandate *exclusive dealing*, where dealers cannot stock competitor product lines. Examples of products in this category are new automobiles and some appliances and fashion apparel. The goal of exclusive distribution is to gain more control over the channel in regard to sales, marketing, promotion, price, credit, and other value-added services.

3. *Selective distribution.* Some producers may follow a market exposure strategy that confines the sale of products to a selected group of targeted intermediaries capable of providing a specified level of customer service, marketing, and other service criteria. The objective is to win reputable dealers and retailers through a promise of exclusive product distribution. In return, the producer can gain significant market penetration while achieving more control and reduced cost than what can be obtained through intensive distribution.

The second element of channel design revolves around the degree of the acknowledged dependence of channel participants. The more channel members are dependent on one another, the greater the need for cooperation and sharing of critical information and processes. The less the dependence, the more individual companies must depend on their own competencies and vertically integrated resources to sustain competitive advantage. According to Bowersox and Cooper [11], channel structures are grouped around the following classifications, ranging from least to most open acknowledgment of dependence:

- *Single-transaction channels.* A great many marketing transactions occur in supply channels that are considered onetime and nonrepeatable. Examples of single-transaction arrangements can be found in real estate, construction, international trading, and the purchase of capital equipment. Normally, supply channels in such environments are transitory and founded for the sole purpose of facilitating a unique transaction. Once the requirements originally agreed to by the channel participants have been completed, the basis for the channel ceases to exist.

- *Conventional channels.* This category of channel arrangement is also known as a *free-flow channel*. The main characteristic of this type of channel is the comparatively high degree of independence maintained by channel participants. The reason why they participate in the channel at all is to leverage the different forms of specialization they can offer the marketplace. The motive is purely opportunistic: they seek to attain channel efficiencies without becoming fully committed members of a networked channel system. Despite the benefits, there are certain drawbacks. Free-flow channels will, over time, be more volatile than dependent channel systems, as members move freely between multiple channels in the pursuit of short-term efficiencies and opportunities. Second, relations between members are typically adversarial, as members continuously maneuver for cost and price benefits. Finally, channel arrangements can be terminated abruptly by either party if and when once perceived advantages disappear.

- *Networked supply channel systems.* This type is characterized by the fact that channel members both acknowledge and desire interdependence. As such, these organizations feel that short-term ability to maximize operational efficiencies and marketplace exposure and their long-term capability to maintain competitive advantage depend on their participation and close integration with partner companies in a networked channel system. The basic advantage of this form of channel arrangement is the ability of individual companies to achieve a level of performance and capability for innovation far above what they could achieve acting on their own. Although there is the potential for conflict among channel members, the value of the synergy engendered by the networked channel provides strong inducements for conflict resolution and convergence of objectives.

When considered together the above elements can be used to create a *channel attribute matrix* (Figure 5.23) to guide planners in channel design. Across the top of the matrix is arrayed the various levels of market exposure, starting with a very limited *direct channel* approach on the left and a very robust *intensive distribution* approach on the far right. Down the vertical side of the matrix can be found the various *service outputs*. Across the bottom is found the channel values. Channels that focus on capital (industrial) or specialty (commercial) buying will normally consider distribution flexibility and dependence on quality related differentiators such as image, flexibility, product design, and service.

On the other hand, channels that focus on MRO (industrial) or convenience (commercial) buying will rely on competitive attributes centered on price, delivery, and availability.

	Direct Channel	Internal Channel	Exclusive/Selective Distribution	Intense Distribution
Product Type	Capital/ Specialty	Materials & Components/ Shopping		MRO/ Convenience
Product Variety	High	Medium	Medium	Low
Wait Time	High	High	Medium	Low
Lot Size	Low	Medium	Medium	High
Spatial Convience	Low	Low	Medium	High
Cost	High	High	Medium	Low

⟸ Flexibility/Quality   Standardization/Cost ⟹

FIGURE 5.23 Channel attribute matrix

CHANNEL OPERATIONS [12]

The primary purpose of the integrated supply channel network is to facilitate the fundamental operations activities of manufacturing, distribution, and customer delivery. The objective of these three channel processes is to create unique and unassailable value to the customer that cannot be copied by the competition. In accomplishing this mission, the supply channel must activate the following critical customer-satisfying drivers: superior customer service, decreased channel cycle times, high levels of channel performance, and reduced costs. Today's best supply channels seek to leverage operational excellence, strive for quality and continuous improvement, and foster the creation of new, innovative techniques possessed by their members to achieve superlative, customer-winning processes unmatched by the competition.

Continuously executing value-added operations requires the channel-wide performance of those critical metrics most valued by the customer. Some of these values center on the fulfillment process and consist of such deliverables as completeness and reliability of deliveries, high product/service quality, best value for the price, speed/frequency of deliveries, breadth and depth of available products/services, and use of electronic commerce technologies. To these "basic" elements can be added other values. Among these can be found the appearance the whole channel projects to the customer through such tangibles as new facilities, state-of-the-art technology, commitment to quality, and highly qualified personnel. In addition, other elements such as reliability, responsiveness, and competence project to the customer a sense of dealing with acknowledged and measurable standards of service, a supply partner who can respond quickly and concisely to their needs, and confidence that their product and service issues will be satisfied by a supplier who possesses the necessary skills and knowledge. Finally, other service attributes can be found in the courtesy by which customers are treated, the feeling of credibility and honesty when dealing with the supplier, a sense of security and peace of mind when the transaction is completed, and the degree of communication and ability of the service provider to unearth and respond purposefully to their needs, desires, and expectations.

Perhaps the key to achieving superlative customer service is controlling the total time it takes goods and services to move from the point of manufacture to the point of customer delivery. The effective management of cycle times results in high customer service, greater operational flexibility, lower investments in working capital tied up in inventories, and lower operating costs. Managing the cycle times of the three fundamental supply channel operations processes can briefly be described as follows:

- *Manufacturing process cycle times.* Production processes stand at the gateway to channel cycle time management. The ability of manufacturing to quickly convert raw materials and components into the finished goods the market wants requires the establishment of agile and flexible processes. The goal of supply channel manufacturing cycle time management is to improve planning and scheduling, continuously shrink setup and processing times, produce in lot sizes identical to actual customer demand, achieve the highest possible product quality, and move goods as rapidly as possible to the distribution functions in the supply channel.

- *Distribution process cycle times.* The time it takes products to move through the distribution portion of the supply pipeline is directly related to the geographical size and number of transfer nodes found within the supply network. Three critical elements dominate cycle time management in distribution: the speed of the transportation services used, the capacity of supply point nodes to move goods through their processing operations, and the speed and accuracy of information transfer.

- *Customer delivery cycle times.* Cycle time management in this area revolves around the effective management of the order process. Order management requires the channel to ensure the timely and accurate movement of both *internal* supply channel orders as well as orders that are delivered to the end customer. Besides the timely delivery of product, delivery cycle time management is also concerned with triggering accurate resupply information back through the channel to the source of manufacture.

Another critical area of supply channel operations is the development and monitoring of performance levels. Although each supply channel may focus on a specific performance objective, there are essentially six major performance areas to consider [13]:

- *Customer satisfaction.* In this area can be found metrics associated with customer delivery, such as product availability, ease of order processing, order information, delivery timeliness, delivery completeness, number of customer complaints, and customer rating.

- *Quality.* This area of performance has several attributes. Some refer to product issues such as reliability, conformance to standards, durability, and serviceability. Other metrics focus on service issues such as errors in order contents, incomplete orders, late shipments, and poor inventory replenishment planning.

- *Asset utilization.* This metric attempts to assess the competitive advantage gained for each physical asset possessed by the channel and considers such measurements as inventory turnover, return on assets employed, and working capital employed. Although this measurement focuses primarily on each channel participant's asset utilization, the collective productivity of total channel assets will have a direct impact on such issues as price and operating cost that invariably make their way down the channel pipeline.

- *Operating costs.* This area of performance measurement covers the expense incurred by each member in operating the channel. Among the metrics to be monitored are cost of labor, transportation, maintenance, taxes and insurance, information services, and rentals.

- *Cycle time.* As detailed above, the measurement of the time between operations cycles, such as production processing times, order processing, picking and shipping, and delivery, is critical to the competitive position of the entire channel.

- *Productivity.* This final metric attempts to measure performance against some critical channel benchmark. These metrics are fairly detailed and consist of such goals as orders processed per unit of time, shipments per facility, operating costs per asset and process unit, and network costs per sales unit.

Although it may be difficult to gather the data occurring throughout the supply channel necessary to compile the above metrics, accurate and complete performance measurements can significantly assist channel planners in making the right decisions concerning network design, operation, and investment.

The final area comprising channel operations is understanding total supply network costs. The objectives of the supply channel are straightforward: total customer satisfaction, high profitability, and low operating cost. Achieving these goals requires channel members to make correct trade-off decisions between costs and expected benefits. Supply channel operating and investment costs are complex and can consist of a matrix of possible cost and investment drivers. The critical components of supply channel costs are comprised of several internal fixed and variable cost elements, such as labor, facilities operation, inventory investment, and transportation, and short-term and long-term investment arising from facilities expansion and improvement, information and communications equipment, and other capital outlays. The key is to make decisions that provide not only individual enterprise but also channel-wide competitive advantage.

INTEGRATING DEMAND, OPERATIONS, AND CHANNEL PLANS

The purpose of the DO&CP process is to develop a set of aggregate enterprise plans that can be integrated together to provide corporate decision makers with a medium- to long-range "rough-cut" window into demand and corresponding resources required to meet the overall business plan. How complex the factors used in developing these plans depends on the business environment, the availability of the data, and the objectives of the management planning team. The data elements outlined above are simplistic and probably should be used as a basis to construct more realistic plans.

Once the DO&CP process has been completed, strategists can develop a single integrated top management plan that will illustrate the aggregate estimates of the channel revenues, production requirements, total operations costs, and inventories for the next twelve months or longer. The DO&C plan should be reviewed preferably monthly, to reflect changing marketplace, product, and channel management situations. Figure 5.24 illustrates an integrated top management aggregate plan for a single product group. The plan is stated in monthly periods for the first nine months and in quarterly periods for the remainder of a two year plan. Each product group would have to be calculated and then summed together to provide planners with a total picture of the over supply chain plan.

The purpose of the integrated DO&C plan is to assist the business and channel management teams in making informed decisions as part of the process of aligning the resources of the entire supply chain with the objectives

Product Family: **PC-1501**		**PC Computers**							(*in thousands*)
Period	Jan	Feb	Mar	Apr	May	Jun	Jul	Aug	Sep	4thQt
Sales Plan	13.4	13.2	12.9	12.5	12.1	11.8	11.4	11.1	12.3	38.2
Actual Sales	12.9	13.4	12.8	12.7						
Cum Variance	-.5	-.3	-.4	-.2						
Production Plan	13.1	13.1	13.1	12.25	12.25	12.25	11.48	11.48	11.48	38.2
Actual Production	12.8	12.9	12.9	12.6						
Variance	-.3	-.2	-.2	.35						
Cum Variance	-.3	-.5	-.7	.35						
Inventory Plan .7	.4	.3	.5	.25	.4	.85	.933	1.316	.5	.5
Actual Inventory .7	.6	.1	.2	.1						
Variance	+.2	0	-.3	-.45						
Channel Demand	13.4	13.2	12.9	12.5	12.1	11.8	11.4	11.1	12.3	38.2
Plan Replen Ord.	13.2	13.2	13.0	12.4	12.2	11.8	11.4	11.0	12.4	39.2
Actual Demand	12.9	13.4	12.8	12.7						
Actual Replen Ord.	12.8	12.9	12.9	12.6						
Plan OHB .7	.5	.5	.6	.5	.6	.6	.6	.5	.6	.5
Actual OHB .7	.6	.1	.2	.1						
Cum Variance	.1	-.3	-.7	-1.1						

FIGURE 5.24 DO&C plan - summary.

stated in the Business Plan. The DO&C plan provides a window into supply channel revenue and replenishment costs while assuring sufficient inventory, financial resources, transportation, warehouse space, and labor and equipment necessary to meet aggregate product and value-added services requirements. The plan, furthermore, is critical in providing planners with the data necessary to help solve problems in the aggregate plan due to variation in customer ordering caused by changes in demand patterns, seasonality, new production introduction, or competitive pressures.

For example, the PC-1501 product group indicates that the sales forecast and actual sales are fairly close to plan with a slight negative variance of only

200 units. Most likely it could be said that original promotions, advertising, and price incentives campaigns to stimulate customer sales have been successful to date. At this point there would be nothing to recommend a change in the original sales forecast. The only issue is that sales managers will have to be careful to manage the product line during the slow summer months ahead.

On the supply side, the level production plan strategy has been not been successful even though the inventory plan balances are not showing a shortage during the first four periods. During the first three periods actual production to plan was 700 units short. This caused actual ending inventory balance to slip significantly below that target of 500 units. The result would have been a change in the planned production rate in period four to make up for the failure of the first quarter. Even the increase of 350 in production in April has still left the actual inventory plan some 450 units short of the original ending plan. On the other hand, the product family is moving into its slow sales period and a solid performance over the next several months should provide sufficient stock. Production planners, however, must be careful to start building inventories to meet the increasing sales that begin with the autumn quarter. A careful review of the capacity plan will be critical in ensuring the availability of sufficient resources.

Finally, the performance of the channel demand plan has been dismal. The shortage of inventories caused by the production plan has put a significant squeeze on channel stocks. The unexpectedly high order total of 13,400 in February drained channel inventories far below the desired ending balance level of 500 units, and the lack of production over the subsequent periods has resulted in a cumulative variance of over 1,100 units. While the channel had been lucky to escape stockout over the first quarter, even a slight increase in sales could result in lost sales. While not exhibited, it would be fairly ease to perform the channel plan for each product group by channel warehouse. The goal would be to see the impact of the lack of inventory in each location and the cost of channel inventory balancing as possible demand shortages threaten.

SUMMARY

Demand, Operations, and Channel Planning (DO&CP) is the culmination of the enterprise planning process that began with the formulation of the business plan. The object of the DO&CP process is to develop aggregate plans spanning that span the key business areas of the enterprise. Individually, each of these plans attempts to define the strategies and operations decisions that must occur if the overall business mission is to be achieved. Collectively, these plans should be closely integrated and mutually supportive. In detail, these plans center on strategic operations issues, such as determining the overall rates of product family sales and production, aggregate inventories, supply chain value delivery, and logistics capacities. The planning *time range* extends for a minimum of a year and beyond, the *focus* is on product families, and the *review frequency* is normally monthly. If conflicts in channel demand and supply can be resolved on the aggregate level, planners will find that problems associated with detailed operations will be easier to resolve. The DO&CP process supports this objective by reconciling all demand, supply, new product, and channel management plans at both the detail and aggregate levels and ensures continuity with the business plan. In addition, DO&CP enables operations performance measurement and the development of strategic and detail efforts directed at continuous improvement.

As illustrated in Figure 5.1, the DO&CP process consists of five interwoven components linked together by the enterprise business plan. The *business strategy* provides a comprehensive definition of enterprise goals and performance measurement targets, the asset and investments plans necessary to support the organization, and the projected profit plan. It is the role of the business strategy to provide clear direction and enable the translation of the collective enterprise strategy into detailed mission statements for each of the five supporting business areas. Once overall enterprise goals have been established, it is then possible for the *marketing plan* to begin the process of identifying the structure of the marketplace the firm intends work in, the products and services to be sold, issues relating to price and promotions, and the mechanics of the distribution channel. As the nature of the marketplace begins to emerge, it is the function of the *sales plan* to develop the forecasts of expected product sales, draft the sales campaign, ensure sales capacities, and define sales performance metrics.

For businesses with manufacturing functions, the *production plan* must be established. The production plan determines the production rates and aggregate resources required to satisfy the shipment, inventory, and cost of sales objectives stated in the business and marketing plans. To effectively manage fulfillment, it is then the goal of the *logistics plan* to ensure that inventory storage capacities and transportation resources are sufficient to support planned levels of sales. Finally, effective DO&C planning would be incomplete without a comprehensive *supply chain plan*. This planning component defines how the supply channel network is designed, how it is operated, and the nature of the level of integration and collaboration existing between supplier, manufacturer, wholesaler, and retailer constituents.

Once each of these aggregate plans has been developed, they can be integrated together to provide corporate decision makers with a medium- to long-range "rough-cut" window into how well individual enterprises and whole supply chains are responding to meet the overall business plans. The aggregate DO&C plan will illustrate the aggregate estimates of the channel revenues, production requirements, total operations costs, and inventories for the next twelve months or longer. In addition, the aggregate DO&C plan will assist in charting supply channel requirements for financial resources, transportation, warehouse space, and labor and equipment necessary to meet aggregate product and value-added services requirements.

QUESTIONS FOR REVIEW

1. Best Buy, Circuit City, and Sears all sell personal computers (PCs). Discuss the competitive strategies used by these companies in marketing PCs.

2. Marketing planning has been described as a strategic exercise which determines the tactical direction of sales and logistics planning. Explain.

3. Compare and contrast a "niched market" approach, a "mass market" approach, and a "market segment of one" approach to marketing planning.

4. A distributor's marketing plan calls for an increase in sales of $120,000. The plan will mean that the firm's current investment in inventory will have to increase from $400,000 to $500,000. If the inventory carrying cost is 22% and the gross profit on sales is 20%, is it wise to increase the firm's inventory investment?

5. A national home appliance distributor is contemplating offering a new line of microwave ovens. Develop a product life-cycle analysis for the product line and the likely policies regarding price, quantity, advertising, promotional selling, and channels of distribution.

6. Companies offering high customer service must bear high distribution channel costs in relation to sales. Do you agree, and why?

7. What are the basic outputs guiding the structuring of a marketing channel?

8. Why are the product and services life cycles of critical importance to distributors?

9. Should a distributor treat all customers equally? Defend your reasoning.

10. Describe the various aggregate planning processes found in the text. Why are they so essential for enterprise strategic and operational survival?

REFERENCES

1. This paragraph has been adapted from Wallace, Thomas F., *Sales & Operations Planning*. Cincinnati, Ohio: T.F. Wallace & Co., 2000, p. 7.
2. For additional discussion reference Ballou, Ronald H., *Business Logistics Management: Planning and Control*, 2nd ed. Englewood Cliffs, NJ: Prentice-Hall, 1985, pp. 110-112; and Kotler, Philip, *Marketing Management*. 6th ed., Englewood Cliffs, NJ: Prentice-Hall, 1988, p. 447-448.
3. Additional definitions on product nomenclature can be found in *Marketing Definitions: A Glossary of Marketing Terms*. Chicago: American Marketing Association, 1960; Kotler, pp. 448-451; and Ballou, pp. 111-112.
4. These points have been summarized from McKinnon, Alan C., *Physical Distribution Systems*. New York: Routledge, 1989, pp. 39-41.
5. This list is abstracted from Wallace, p. 70.
6. Philip Kotler, pp. 347-349.
7. For more discussion on these critical elements of product life cycle analysis see Hayes, Robert H., and Wheelwright, Steven C., *Restoring Our Competitive Edge*. New York: John Wiley & Sons, 1984, pp. 199-204; Kotler, pp. 347-368; and, Webster, Frederick, *Industrial Marketing Strategy*. New York: John Wiley & Sons, 1984, pp. 106-109.
8. For more information of the nature of services see Heizer, Jay and Render, Barry, *Production and Operations Management*. 3rd ed., Boston: Allyn and Bacon, 1993, p. 265.
9. These terms can be found in Bowersox and Cooper, p. 17.
10. Kotler, *Marketing Management*, p. 533.
11. Bowersox and Cooper, pp. 102-108.
12. This section is summarized from Ross, David Frederick, *Competing Through Supply Chain Management: Creating Market-Winning Strategies Through Supply Chain Partnerships,* New York: Chapman & Hall, 1998, pp. 162-166.
13. These measurements have been abstracted from Gopal, Christopher and Cypress, Harold, *Integrated Distribution Management*. Homewood, IL: Business One Irwin, 1993, pp. 135-142.

UNIT 3

DISTRIBUTION OPERATIONS PLANNING

CHAPTERS:

6. Managing Supply Chain Inventories
7. Replenishment Inventory Planning
8. Distribution Requirements Planning

Unit 2 explored planning in the enterprise from the *top management* or *strategic* perspective. The focus of the planning process was the formulation of the strategic objectives that are to guide company operations planning and execution. In developing the business plan corporate planners seek to align the company *mission statements* with economic and marketplace realities and with the capacities and capabilities of the firm. Once these objectives have been established, they can then be translated into more detailed plans concerning investment, physical plant, inventory positioning, transportation, and staffing resources to be followed by the firm's associated business units. Effective strategic business planning occurs when the objectives of corporate, business unit, and business functional areas are executed in alignment with and in support of one another.

Unit 3 continues the discussion of enterprise planning by examining the next step in the planning flow: *distribution operations planning*. Operations planning is concerned with the translation of strategic financial, marketing, sales, and aggregate supply channel plans into medium-range inventory procurement and logistics capacity plans. The goal is to ensure that sufficient inventory and logistics capacities are available to support strategic planning objectives. The formulation of effective distribution operations plans will, in turn, drive the detailed short-range *distribution operations execution* activities associated with functions such as customer order processing, product procurement, transportation, and warehousing.

Unit 3 begins with a review of the nature and function of inventory in the distribution environment. Chapter 6 examines the key role that inventory plays in assisting the enterprise gain and maintain competitive advantage. Historically, decisions concerning inventory have been executed in isolation from the strategic objectives of the firm. The requirements of integrated supply chain distribution, however, are forcing planners to reevaluate this traditional decision process. Effective inventory planning in the twenty-first century requires that not just individual companies but the entire supply network optimize the ability to respond rapidly to changes in shorter product life cycles and product proliferation, increased customer service levels and product and service expectations, advances in technology, globalization of the marketplace, and increased competition and pressure on margins. The new imperatives for inventory planning can be summarized as the ceaseless improvement and maintenance of the highest level of customer service, the reduction of overall distribution cycle times, commitment to value-added services, and finally, reduction of total distribution costs.

Chapter 7 is concerned with a detailed review of statistical inventory planning techniques. Because most distribution inventories are exposed to *independent demand*, traditional statistical tools for inventory planning and ordering are widely used by distributors. This chapter details the statistical inventory planning process and explores, in depth, replenishment methods and their application. Among the topics covered are calculating the order point, satisfying customer service levels, understanding the economic order point, and using alternative order quantity methods. The chapter will also discuss inventory decision rules for item *ABC Classes* and working with replenishment planning in single and multiechelon environments.

The availability of computerized *Distribution Requirements Planning* (DRP) has provided distributors with an integrative tool to better plan and control inventories in a multi-echelon environment. By linking logistics operations planning with top management planning DRP presents the distribution enterprise with the ability to integrate the firm's planning, operations, and execution functions, thereby optimizing company resources, channel efficiencies, and customer service requirements. Finally, DRP provides the mechanism for detailed transportation, warehousing, and staffing capacity requirements.

These elements of DRP are examined in depth in Chapter 8. After detailing the logic and functions of DRP, the chapter proceeds to a discussion of the avenues DRP presents distributors for not only efficiently planning inventories but, more importantly, connecting the enterprise with its channel business partners. DRP is seen as an effective mechanism for the close integration of the distribution channel necessary to attain competitive objectives. The chapter concludes with the formulation of the materials acquisition, transportation, warehousing, and staffing plans necessary for logistics execution.

6

MANAGING SUPPLY
CHAIN INVENTORIES

One of the most important challenges facing supply chain managers is the effective control of inventory. Supply chain inventories consist of the raw materials, components, assemblies, and finished goods necessary to support demand throughout the supply channel pipeline. At the core of inventory management resides a fundamental dilemma. When it comes to the timely fulfillment of customer requirements, inventory is necessary and useful; however, too much or the wrong inventory at the wrong place is destructive of corporate well-being. Inventory ties up capital, incurs carrying costs, needs to be transported, requires receiving and material handling, needs to be warehoused, and can become obsolete over time. When it is improperly controlled, inventory can become a significant liability, a huge financial millstone around the neck of the enterprise, reducing profitability and sapping away the vitality of strategic supply chain initiatives targeted at increasing competitive advantage or exploring new markets. On the other hand, the value of a properly managed inventory exceeds its cost. Product availability at the time, location, quantity, quality, and price desired by the customer not only provides immediate profits but also secures long-term customer allegiance and market segment leadership. When it is effectively controlled, inventory management enables the realization of channel marketing, sales, and logistics strategies and provides the lubricant for the smooth flow of product and service value from supplier to the customer.

Chapter 6 describes the role of inventory in the supply chain environment. The chapter begins by defining the nature and function of supply chain inventories. Following these introductory comments, the chapter proceeds to a discussion of the impact of current trends in inventory and supply chain management and how they are revolutionizing past principles of the inventory function. The chapter then continues with a detailed discussion of the inventory planning process. Inventory planning requires the enterprise to establish the inventory management strategy necessary to support the marketing and sales plans not only of individual companies but of the supply chains in which they are entwined. Afterward, attention is shifted to defining inventory costs and how they can be effectively managed. Among the topics reviewed are the elements of inventory cost, costs relating to inventory operations and decisions, and the various methods of valuing inventory. The chapter concludes with a discussion of item classification models and cycle counting, and a review of inventory performance measurements.

ELEMENTS OF SUPPLY CHAIN INVENTORY MANAGEMENT

The proper planning and control of inventories resides at the very core of supply chain management. The prime purpose of inventory is to provide any trading partner in the supply chain network with the ability to satisfy any customer with the desired product at the time and place required. Unfortunately, whereas everyone can agree on the *purpose* of inventories, there has been considerable disagreement in regard to how best it should be managed. The sales department, for example, considers inventory availability as fundamental to customer service and views the ratio between customer orders filled and lost as the prime measurement of enterprise success. Finance, on the other hand, while accounting for inventories on the asset side of the balance sheet, nevertheless considers inventories as a necessary evil that ties up capital and should be eliminated whenever possible. Finally, operations is caught somewhere in between. Inventory management must walk a thin line between two contradictory measurements: They must continually search for ways to reduce inventory costs while at the same time stocking just the right quantity of products to satisfy targeted customer service levels.

In responding to these apparent dichotomies residing at the heart of supply chain inventory management, inventory planners must strike an effective balance between inventory and demand. This balancing requires answers to six major questions [1]:

1. *What is the optimal balance between inventory and customer service?* As a general principle, it can be stated that the higher the stocked inventory and the wider the variety of product selection, the higher the customer service level, and vice versa. Although today's *Enterprise Resource Planning* (ERP) and *Supply Chain Planning* (SCP) systems provide new technologies to better manage inventories in the face of increased demand variability, determining the level of inventory necessary to meet customer service targets constitutes the fundamental decision facing planners across the supply chain.

2. *What is the level of control an enterprise should establish over its channel inventories?* Large corporations tend to favor vertical integration in an effort to remove channel redundancies, leverage economies of scale, and maintain specific performance levels, whereas small companies and niche players require a network of strong supporting players positioned at key points in the supply channel.

3. *Under what circumstances should control over inventories be changed?* Changes in markets, technologies, channel direction, government regulation, and the status of supply network alliances can alter channel equilibrium and cause once profitable channel inventory strategies to loose their value. In addition, trading partners should always be searching for new opportunities to reduce total supply chain inventory costs by either assuming channel inventory management functions or off-loading them to new partners who can perform non-core functions more efficiently and at lower cost.

4. *What is the optimum balance between inventory investment and associated carrying costs?* As inventory grows in response to better customer service, the carrying cost will grow proportionately. Inventory planners must be careful to ensure that costs resulting from decisions calling for incremental increases in inventory levels do not nullify expected sales profits.

5. *What is the optimum balance between inventory investment and replenishment costs?* The size of the replenishment order quantity will

have a direct impact on both inventory and procurement costs. Generally, as the purchasing lot size decreases, the inventory carrying cost decreases. However, as the lot size decreases, purchasers must order more frequently, thereby driving up ordering, receiving, stock put-away and payables costs. Increases in lot sizes will have an opposite effect. While ordering costs will decline, inventory carrying costs will increase.

6. *What is the optimum balance between inventory investment and transportation costs?* As the replenishment lot size decreases, the cost of more frequent deliveries in less than truckload quantities will increase. Because many firms are turning to intermodal methods, supplier scheduling, innovations in transport vehicle designs and capabilities, and computerization, planners must thoroughly research the cost of product transportation decisions when exploring inventory ordering strategies.

Determining the optimal balance between the value of holding inventory and the costs incurred requires supply chain planners to possess a complete understanding of the deployment, function, and expected value of inventories as they appear across the supply channel network.

WHAT IS SUPPLY CHAIN INVENTORY?

Inventory can be found throughout the supply chain in various forms and quantities based on strategic and operational objectives. As illustrated in Figure 6.1, the physical flow of supply chain inventories can be said to progress

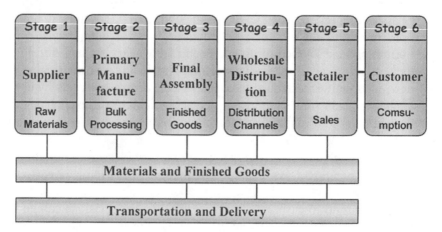

FIGURE 6.1 Supply channel materials flow

through six stages. The origins of the channel pipeline can be said to begin with the extraction and refinement of raw materials. The key inventory management issues during this stage revolve around production processes, supplier selection and qualification, contract partnerships, supplier scheduling, transportation and delivery, and performance measurement.

In stages 2 and 3, raw materials are transformed into semifinished and finished products through the manufacturing process. Stage 2, termed *primary manufacturing*, is focused on the conversion of basic raw materials into components through the process of fabrication. An example would be a manufacturer who converts steel rods into nuts, bolts, and twist drills. In stage 3, raw materials and fabricated components are *final assembled* into finished products for end customers. Production processes at this level can follow a single or mixed mode manufacturing strategy determined by how inventory is to be managed: make-to-stock, assemble-to-order, or make-to-order. The choice of manufacturing strategy is determined by such factors as product characteristics, depth of marketplace demand, strength of the competition, transportation, and warehousing requirements. Critical inventory decisions in these two stages center on volume and variety issues. Products produced in volume tend to be inventoried, whereas products with intermittent demand tend to be produced to order and are rarely stocked in anticipation of sales.

Stage 4 marks the beginning of the physical distribution channel flow. Perhaps the most critical decision to be made in this stage is the determination of the structure of the supply chain. As illustrated in Figure 6.2, there are three possible supply channels that can be constructed. In the first, product is sold directly by the manufacturer to the end customer. The second channel type represents a more complex, multiechelon channel comprised of field warehouses who sell to the customer. The warehouses could be company owned or they could be public warehouses. This type of channel is much more expensive and difficult to control than factory direct distribution. Finally, in the last type, the channel is characterized by extreme complexity and consists of multiple levels of manufacturing plants, field warehouses, and retailers. Critical inventory issues include channel marketing strategies, total logistics costs, the number, location, and size of distribution centers, channel inventory levels, order processsing, postponement strategies, and customer service. Finally, in stages 5 and 6, products are conveyed to the retail portion of the supply channel for eventual delivery to the customer. The exact configuration of the supply chain can vary widely by channel network. In some supply pipelines, the flow is dominated by a single company, such as a Sears or an Abbott Laboratories, who performs most of the functions necessary to move products to the end customer. Wal-Mart, on the other hand, prefers to buy directly from the manufacturer, thereby reducing the number of levels in the supply network.

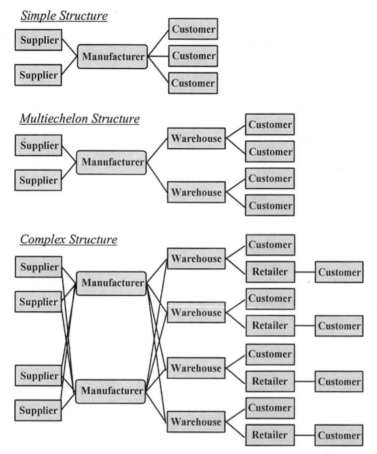

FIGURE 6.2 Channel structures.

THE MAGNITUDE OF INVENTORY

One of the best ways to understand the impact of inventory, not only on a given channel system but on the economy as a whole, is to examine inventory statistics. Today, inventories can represent anywhere from 40 to 80 percent of a typical company's sales dollar. Effectively managing this huge investment is critical to the financial well-being of the entire supply chain. The following figures provide a quick reference to the sheer financial investment in inventory and related logistics costs. In 2002, the average inventory investment by all U.S. businesses, including agriculture, mining, construction, utilities, services, manufacturing, wholesale, and retail trade, was $1.44 trillion. This figure alone was equivalent to 13.7 percent of the entire U.S. GNP. The cost of carrying inventory during 2002 was 20.6 percent, or $298 billion. In addition, U.S. firms spent $612 billion for transportation and administration associated with moving this inventory through the distribution pipeline [2].

NATURE OF INVENTORY

Inventory can come in a variety of forms. A firm that distributes home appliances will purchase, store, and sell inventory in quite a different physical state than a petroleum distributor. In addition, not all companies sell inventory in exactly the same form as they build or acquire it. Product quantities may be broken down into smaller lots, relabeled, repackaged, assembled, or kitted to form new end assemblies. Classically, inventory has been classified as residing in four possible forms.

- *Raw materials.* Products classified as raw materials are normally extracted from nature. Examples include steel, wood, certain chemicals, paper, grains, cloth, and other unfinished commodities. Although these products can be sold as received, normally they are not useful until they have been fabricated into semi-finished or component products.
- *Components.* For the most part, components are finished items that are consumed in a higher final assembly process. Components that are also sold as service parts fall within this category when they are used in manufacturing but are properly classified as finished goods when sold stand-alone.
- *Work-in-process.* Inventory in this category can be classified as raw materials, components, and subassemblies that are in the process of being or are waiting to be transformed through manufacturing into assemblies or finished goods. Although distributors historically stock little or no manufacturing inventory, marketing and cost requirements for economies and value-added services have forced many firms into performing light assembly, repackaging, kitting, labeling, and other postponement techniques to remain competitive.
- *Finished goods.* Products classified as finished goods can be defined as purchased items, assemblies, or service parts whose demand comes from a customer order or sales forecast.

The value of classifying inventory by its processing state is that it allows designation of which products are available for customer order, assists in decision making in production planning and inventory management, and facilitates record keeping and costing.

FUNCTIONS OF INVENTORY

The fundamental function of inventory is to act as a *buffer* that decouples the organization from the discontinuousness of customer demand on the one hand and limitations in supplier delivery capacities on the other. Optimally, businesses would like to carry as little inventory as possible, preferring to move purchase order receipts directly to the shipping dock to be met just-in-time with customer orders. In reality, the firm needs inventory to buffer it from the uncertainties of supply and demand.

Inventory control literature has traditionally identified five general functions for holding inventory: Cycle stock (or lot-size), safety stock, anticipation, transportation, and hedge (or speculative). A review of these functions is as follows:

- *Cycle* (or lot-size) *inventory*. This class of inventory is the result of ordering requirements that force planners to purchase, manufacture, and transport inventory in batches that exceed the original demand quantity. The basic reason why cycle stock inventory exists is because of economies realized by trading-off the cost of ordering or producing and the cost of carrying the inventory. In addition, cost trade-off economies occur for several other reasons. The frequency of item order cycles also may require the stocking of inventory in large lots. As the rate of the receipt of customer orders increases for a given product, planners normally will increase the acquisition lot size versus increase the replenishment order cycle. Finally, those channel nodes that perform manufacturing functions often will produce lot-size inventory due to the cost of setting up a production line and gains in productivity attained by producing larger inventory quantities than required.

- *Safety stocks*. This type of inventory is held on hand to cover unplanned fluctuations in customer demand and the uncertainty of supply. If demand was to remain constant, inventory planners could rely on cycle stock to guarantee that there would always be sufficient stock on hand to meet demand. However, because products subject to *independent demand* can expect random periods of above average demand to occur, cycle stocks function best when there is a safety stock buffer. The amount of safety stock depends on the degree of random variation in demand, the lead time required to replenish stock, and the service reliability policy established at the stocking point. The larger the safety stock, relative to demand variation, the higher the percentage of customer serviceability. Figure 6.3 illustrates the function of safety stock.

- *Anticipation inventory*. Often inventories will be built in advance of demand to enable effective response to seasonal sales, a marketing pro-

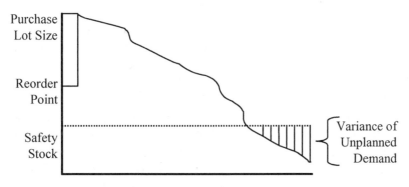

FIGURE 6.3 Safety stock function.

motional campaign, or problems in supplier delivery. A sporting goods distributor, for example, may begin to warehouse winter sports equipment during the summer months to take advantage of sales discounts from manufacturers and to avoid higher prices and potential stockouts as the winter season approaches.

- *Transportation inventory.* Inventory in this category can be defined as products in transit (for example, in ships, railcars, or truck transport) from one node in the channel network to another. Transportation inventory exist because *time* is required to physically move stock through the channel. Supply chain nodes must plan to have additional inventories on hand to cover demand while inventories are in transit. As an example, if delivery of a product takes 3 weeks, and sales average 1000 units a week, normally a total of 3000 units would reside in the channel pipeline. Transportation inventory costs must be carefully examined when structuring a supply channel. The following formula can be used in calculating a critical performance metric: the yearly *transportation inventory cost* (TIC):

$$TIC = C \times D \times UC \times T$$

where C is the transportation carrying cost, D is the demand requirements per period, UC is the item unit cost, and T is the transportation time. For example, in calculating the yearly transportation inventory cost for the 3000 units in transit described above, the unit cost is $20 each and the carrying cost is 15 percent. Then

$$TIC = 15\% \times 1000 \text{ per week} \times \$20 \times 3 \text{ weeks} = \$9,000 \text{ per year}.$$

Management could reduce the transportation inventory cost by changing the mode of transportation or switching to a supplier closer to the plant. If 1 week of transit time was eliminated, the cost savings would amount to $3000 per year. On the other hand, another approach might be to gain economies by reducing the lot size of inventory received. Although this might mean more frequent deliveries and higher transportation costs, the overall decline in inventory carrying costs might justify the approach.

- *Work-in-process* (WIP) is a form of transportation inventory associated with manufacturing. The size of WIP inventory depends on such factors as the length of the process, nature of the product, and volume and variety decisions. In practice, the size of WIP is governed by company policies and decisions regarding the appropriate trade-off between carrying and acquisition costs. MRP, JIT, quality management, and other inventory management practices have directly focused on reducing WIP inventories while increasing throughput and customer service.

- *Hedge inventory.* The final function of inventory is to provide planners with the opportunity to purchase large quantities of raw materials or components to take advantage of temporarily low replenishment prices, the possibility of a strike, or other opportunities. The critical element in purchasing speculation inventory is knowledge of price trends, risk of spoilage or obsolescence, and handling commodity futures. The utility of hedge stocks is measured by the resulting percent of profit or return on investment.

The primary function of inventory is to have products available to meet customer demand as it occurs in the supply channel while minimizing total carrying cost. The existence of pools of inventory located at strategic points in the channel pipeline provide essential buffers protecting network nodes from the occurrence of unplanned variance in demand and supply or enable pursuit of quick-response opportunities to meet unexpected customer demand. On the other hand, inventory buffers inherently contain several serious drawbacks. To begin with, buffer inventories can potentially incur more cost in the form of obsolescence, material handling, and storage than the value they create. Second, they hinder the velocity by which products move through the supply chain. Finally, buffer inventories mask the true nature of channel demand and supply, conceal channel inventory management inefficiencies, and gloss over costly channel inventory and capacity imbalances.

Recently, JIT/Lean Manufacturing techniques have prompted manufacturers and distributors to rethink the role of inventory in their organizations. No matter how it is accounted for, inventories add cost to the firm. Inventory can divert capital badly needed for improvement elsewhere; it creates costs necessary to maintain record accuracy; it must be moved and stored; often it needs to be sorted, packaged, and re-containerized; and staff must be available to expedite, search for, and inspect it. Poorly managed inventories can double or triple the cost of maintenance and destroy profitability. The challenge to both individual firms and the entire supply chain is to develop programs that cut inventories by eliminating "dead stock," improving quality, inventory planning, and ordering practices, and increasing organizational and supply channel flexibility while maintaining customer serviceability levels that exceed the competition.

PRINCIPLES OF SUPPLY CHAIN INVENTORY MANAGEMENT

The overriding objective of inventory management in the twentieth century was the creation of mass-production and mass-distribution infrastructures that served as a conduit for the flow of standardized goods and services from the manufacturer to the mass market. Based on the assumption that the marketplace consisted of a few archetypal customers, whose needs and desires could be determined by marketing analysis, the supply system's role was to push non-customized products utilizing mass-production era advertising, media, and distribution channels out to the consumer. Buyers, in turn, searched available suppliers to locate product and service offerings that came closest to matching their needs or desires. In such a supply system, consumers had little linkage with producers whose channel systems focused on moving large, unsynchronized batches of rigidly defined products serially from supply node to supply node through the channel network. Customized products, where there was participation by the customer in the design and manufacturing process, were considered to be very costly and the reserve of specialized supply channels.

Today, this view of supply channel management has largely been exploded. In the place of "push" systems focused on distributing a narrow range of highly standardized products, supply chain processes today are being restructured to accommodate product proliferation, dramatic declines in product life cycles, high velocity response necessary for high customer service, universal commitment to quality, and ability to customize products at the last stages in the fulfillment cycle characteristic of the marketplace of the twenty-first century. Unlike the passive supplier-customer relationship of the past, today's dynamic supply channels provide for a high level of interaction and partnership between producer and consumer to ensure the production and timely delivery of configured, customized goods based on the unique needs of the customer.

UNDERSTANDING SUPPLY CHAIN INVENTORY VALUE

This dramatic shift in the role of the supply chain is directly attributable to changing views of inventory value. Although JIT/Lean philosophies require trading partners at all points in the supply channel to continuously reduce inventories, stock buffers do exist. Simply stated as a fundamental SCM postulate, the challenge of effective channel inventory management is to identify new planning and control methods by which the ratio of value-added to cost-added elements of channel inventory can be continuously improved. In its most basic form, channel inventory management can then be defined as the cost-effective and purposeful deployment and redistribution of raw materials, component parts, work in process, and finished products across an integrated supply network for the purpose of providing value to the customer.

The actual measure of the performance of channel inventories can, therefore, be determined by understanding the two meanings associated with the concept of "inventory value." For the supplier, inventories are valuable to the extent to which associated costs diminish as their value increases. That value can be simply stated as the level of satisfaction attained by the customer as measured by such attributes as availability, immediacy of delivery, conformance to quality, and acceptability of price. Customers, on the other hand, perceive the value they receive from the goods they purchase as providing them with unique solutions to their immediate needs or desires, or enabling them to pursue new opportunities, the benefits of which exceed the original cost of the purchase. In this light, the question becomes not how much inventory or where inventory buffers are held in the supply pipeline, but what customer-satisfying processes are being used to increase its value while continuously decreasing its cost.

The value principle specified above has become even more important in the increasingly complex supply chains of today. Formerly, planners focused on managing and controlling inventory costs and serviceability solely within their own companies. Now, planners are often involved in managing channel inventories that span both their customers' inventory as well as the inventories of their suppliers and suppliers' suppliers. Supply chain inventories provide value through the following five service elements:

1. *Lowest cost for value received.* The effective management of inventory costs enables supply chains to maintain market leadership by keeping prices low, ensuring depth of product assortment and quality, and expanding on capabilities to mass produce customized products. Some of the techniques used to achieve these service attributes are creating channel and cross-channel partnerships that shrink buffers and accelerate inventory flows, utilizing alternate channel formats like warehouse/wholesale clubs, participating in e-marketplace exchanges, selling manufacturer direct, and pursuing JIT contracts that guarantee fixed prices and service levels.

2. *Improved channel efficiency.* By removing excess channel inventory buffers, reengineering distribution processes, implementing JIT, deploying planning tools that provide for real-time cross-channel information

management, and streamlining inventory flows, supply channels can significantly diminish total pipeline costs while ensuring the right product is in the right place to capitalize on marketplace opportunities. Above all, service efficiencies increase product *access*. Access means the degree of ease by which customers can purchase products or contact sales and service functions. Access can also mean the availability of goods within parameters generally accepted by the industry. Finally, access can mean the speed by which after-sales replacement parts and services can be delivered. Customer convenience and access to goods and services are fundamental to competitive advantage.

3. *Improved quality.* Reducing the occurrence of inventory stock-outs, product defects, order fill inaccuracies, and other related inventory management errors can significantly decrease operating costs while increasing customer service. The focal point is service reliability. Supply chains must continually deliver the promised product dependably and accurately each and every time. Reliability of service permits channel suppliers to "lock in" their customers who will gladly pay premium prices for delivered quality and service.

Inventory Visibility at J.F. Braun & Sons

The ability to gain visibility to the supply chain is critical for J.F. Braun & Sons, an importer of dried fruits and nuts. Braun sells goods on contract that it does not yet have, promising to deliver a specified quantity over a set period of time. According to a Braun executive, "If it is going to take 45 days to get here from Asia and we have a contract for delivery in June, then we need to know at the end of April that those goods are on the water." In the past, the only visibility to shipments was a report run at month-end, which meant that in a business where the transit time was 30 to 45 days, the report left the company already 30 days behind.

The solution was the implementation of a supply chain management system. Now, Braun has up to the minute information. Planners can see on one screen outstanding sales, commitments against the product, inbound inventory and where that is in the process, and what is on hand.

Source: Murphy, Jean V., "Seeing Inventory in Real Time Lets you Have and NOT Hold." *Global Logistics and Supply Chain Strategies*, 6, 5, 2002, 34-40.

---

4. *Supply network simplification.* Removing inventory flow bottlenecks and redundant channel functions simplifies and makes all supply channel activities transparent. Increased visibility expands the capability of chan-

nel suppliers to be more responsive to the demands of the marketplace. Simplification can take the form of intense process reengineering at the enterprise level, the discontinuance of channel functions whose costs exceed their value-enhancing capacities, or the use of third party services for inventory and transportation management and accompanying transaction processing.

5. *Improved channel inventory information.* Accurate and accessible information concerning products, stocking levels, location, and order status constitutes the foundation for inventory service value. Internally, information enables network suppliers to control inventory levels, ensure timely and accurate stock replenishment, and leverage price and delivery economies from upstream sources of supply. Externally, information reduces the occurrence of missed customer activities that have a rippling effect back through the entire supply channel (3)

SUBSTITUTING INFORMATION FOR INVENTORY

One of the fundamental postulates of supply channel management is that as uncertainty concerning the status of demand and supply grows, so does pipeline inventory. The roots of channel uncertainty consist of such conditions as unreliable suppliers, poorly developed and communicated forecasts, ineffective scheduling, poor quality, process variability, long cycle times, inaccurate metrics, and others. These problems cascade through each level of the supply network, adding buffer stocks at each channel node. The solution to breaking this cycle of using inventory as a means to counteract uncertainty is to increase the timeliness and bandwidth of the information about what products are really needed and when. The principle is simple: The more information channel nodes have about total supply network needs the better they are able to produce and stock products to respond to the *pull* of demand requirements in the quantities and at the time they are needed [Figure 6.4]. In this way, timely and accurate supply channel information concerning customer and interchannel demand becomes a substitute for inventory buffers.

For such a supply network to work, several conditions are necessary. To begin with supply nodes must continually search for methods to optimize channel inventories by optimizing the total investment of material and process costs for every product stocked in the supply chain, from raw materials to finished goods. Second, supply chains must pursue increased "real-time" visibility to demand and supply conditions throughout the supply network. In the past, trading partners rarely communicated with each other concerning inventory needs except when a replenishment order was launched. Today, breakthroughs in supply chain planning and event management technologies provide channel partners with Internet tools that activate the potential to share demand and supply information within and across enterprises, along with exception management capabilities.

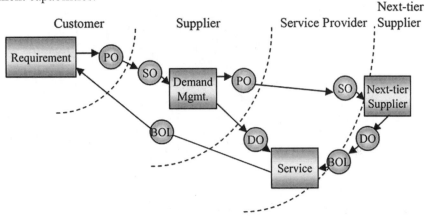

FIGURE 6.4 Order information in the supply channel.

Third, channels must utilize alternative methods of stocking inventories that link suppliers and customers more closely together. For example, various forms of *supplier managed inventory* (SMI) enable suppliers to placed consigned inventories at the customer site where they hold ownership until the moment of sale. Another method is to utilize e-procurement systems that enable customers, through Internet-enabled trading exchanges, to buy and sell on-line. Again, channel partners can station planners and supply storerooms at the customer's site to eliminate the time necessary for the communication of inventory replenishment needs.

Viewing supply chain inventories as if they were a single integrated supply function is the foremost challenge of channel inventory management. Realizing this challenge will require meaningful responses to the following issues:

- *Supply chain integration.* Not just point-of-sale nodes but all channel strategies and processes, beginning with suppliers and manufacturers and progressing through wholesalers and retailers, must be integrated with the needs of the marketplace. Achieving strategic and tactical integration is, by far, the most difficult of the challenges facing channel constituents.

- *Increased flexibility.* The effective management of inventories requires flexible and agile processes that accelerate and add value to materials as they flow through the network. Flexibility goals can be achieved by reducing the size of the pipeline, eliminating channel bottlenecks, shrinking production and distribution lot sizes, building to customer order, and enhancing postponement strategies.

Today's New Supply Chain Inventory Management

Various forms of SMI or VMI are becoming standard for supply chain inventory management. For example:

- Retailers such as Wal-Mart want to sell 100 percent of their products **before** the supplier payment process will begin.
- Some retailers actually rent space and the product is owned by the supplier until it is actually sold.
- Many distributors are carrying the inventories of manufacturers, but are not paying for it until it is actually shipped to the customer.
- In a growing number of manufacturing companies the control and management of inventories is the sole responsibility of the supplier, who is responsible for restocking and physical inventory.
- In JIT point-of-use environments, inventory is controlled by the supplier. The goal is to reduce planning, handling, inspection, paper-

work, and physical storage.

- In the concept of JIT II, the supplier not only is responsible for inventory costs and replenishment, but is expected to physically station employees at their supplier facilities.

These and other forms of inventory management are dramatically reshaping the nature of supply chain inventory management. For customers, the expectations and anticipated results are lower inventories, lower operational costs, and uninterrupted supply. For suppliers, the expectation is single-source supply, new customers, lower production costs, and less competition.

Source: Landis, Gary A., "The Changing Role of Inventory in an Integrated Supply Chain." APICS International Conference Proceedings. Falls Church WV, APICS, 2001.

- *Lower costs.* By considering all channel inventories as functioning as a single supply pipeline, unnecessary buffers that add carrying costs and risk obsolescence can be removed throughout the network. Supply chain planning and event management technologies can assist in matching channel supply to exact demand and reducing finished goods overstocks and distribution point stocking imbalances while increasing product variety.
- *Time-based competition.* Response to today's customer is measured not in weeks, but in days and sometimes hours. Every day that inventories spend in the pipeline adds carrying costs. Every day of lead time required to get the right product in the right place means slower response to customer requirements. As the importance of delivery speed in today's global environment increases, the combination of high costs and lack of responsiveness risks competitive disaster.

- *Telescoping the supply pipeline.* Competitive supply chains are concerned about the length of the supply pipeline. As channel networks grow in length, so inevitably do transit times and buffer inventories. Today's best supply chains seek to continuously shrink pipeline size and shave time and inventory from the channel network through the use of JIT, supplier management, and information technology techniques.
- *Channel performance measurements.* Metrics that document independently the performance of each channel supply node yield little valuable information about the performance of the channel as a whole. Customer service metrics should primarily be based on how productive the entire channel is from raw materials acquisition to customer delivery.

MANAGING INVENTORIES IN AN ERA OF UNCERTAINTY

Much of the changes in supply chain inventory management over the past decade have focused on applying JIT concepts to eliminate inventory redundancies in the supply channel, utilize technology and new management toolsets to provide visibility and collaborative relationships, and accelerate the velocity by which inventory flows through the supply channel. A series of dramatic incidents, including the September 11, 2001 terrorist attacks and the U.S. West coast dock strike in 2002, have, however, exposed the limitations of a total zero-inventories approach. The results have been significant increases in delivery times and potential stockouts due to the growing complexity of security, customs, and inspection activities. Once a universal approach to channel inventory management, JIT concepts are now being tempered by the realities of limitations to the velocity of channel management flows.

While JIT is definitely here to stay, many companies are moving away from a total reliance on a universal low-inventory strategy where product is shipped solely on an as-needed basis. Several new approaches can expect to gain favor as the decade of the 2000s proceeds. According to one expert [4], supply chains will depend more heavily on a game plan that utilizes a limited number of strategically located regional warehouses and distribution centers to hold additional inventories to buffer anticipated future shocks to the supply chain. As a whole, these approaches will expand as companies seek to protect their supply chains from the impact of terrorist attacks, natural disasters, and other economic dislocations by ensuring shipment over relatively short distances at a moment's notice.

In addition, it is expected that companies will be rethinking their approach to supply chain strategies by basing them on mathematical formulas that relate a product's value to its distribution cost. The goal is to determine which products can be economically stocked and which should follow JIT principles and be passed as quickly through the supply chain as possible. As a rule, the higher the value of the goods the more likely they will support direct, long-haul, high speed distribution. Conversely, lower-valued products will be managed by a strategy that seeks to optimize stored inventory and short-haul distribution. Regardless of the actual strategy selected, the ominous beginnings to the twenty-first century have dispelled a blind adherence to pure JIT channel inventory management practices.

THE INVENTORY MANAGEMENT PROCESS

In a perfect supply chain, there would be no need for buffers of inventory. Customers would receive the goods they wanted simply by triggering ordering mechanisms that would design desired finished goods configurations, transmit the exact product specifications to the factory where they would be made, and arrange for delivery as close as possible to the moment of order request. In reality, the existence of channel inventories assist companies to deliver the products customers want as close as possible to when they are wanted. As discussed earlier, inventory buffers exist because of batching or lot-size economies, timing issues such as geographical movement or the duration of the manufacturing process, planned overstocks due to seasonality or speculation, and availability uncertainties due to variances in inventory demand and supply. In any case, inventory constitutes the single largest financial investment to be found in the typical supply channel and its effective management is critical in meeting the needs of customers while reducing costs as much as possible.

Effective inventory management requires supply chain planners to closely define the physical and financial boundaries surrounding channel inventories. The objective of the planning process is the definition of control functions that ensure the accuracy, financial accounting, and timely status reporting of inventory throughout the network pipeline. In addition, the inventory control plan must specify the appropriate ordering techniques and policies necessary for the efficient flow of goods through the supply channel and out to the customer. Ultimately, inventory performance is measured by the ability of each channel trading partner to realize the best return on total inventory investment.

When developing the strategic channel inventory plan, supply chain planners must determine answers to such questions as the following:

- What is the aggregate level of inventory necessary to support expected customer demand?
- What service levels are being achieved by the competition?
- What is the total working capital needed to meet channel inventory deployment targets?

- What are the aggregate operating costs associated with channel service objectives?
- How large should channel supply node buffers be to achieve service-ability targets?
- What is the optimum ratio between channel inventory and transportation costs?
- What information and communications technologies should be implemented that will network channel members closer together and provide for "real-time" information?

The channel inventory planning process, as illustrated in Figure 6.5, begins

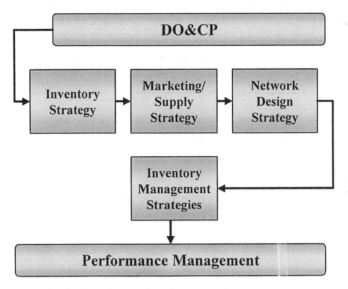

FIGURE 6.5 Supply chain inventory planning process.

with the formulation of the enterprise's inventory strategy. Inventory strategic planning can be defined as

> planning that seeks to optimize customer satisfaction through changes in any or all components of the integrated network, including manufacturing processes, distribution and customer delivery locations, and product flow management processes, rules and policies [5].

Such a strategy involves the identification and implementation of critical capacity changes in any or all components of the supply chain, the physical location of distribution supply nodes, size and location of buffer stocks, transportation capabilities, technologies available for the communication of forecasts and inventory event management focused on mitigating the impact of demand and supply uncertainties, and collaborative sharing of demand information such as promotions, seasonality, and speculation inventories. When designing, concurrently, supply chain inventory goals, each channel partner must be able to respond to the potential dichotomies that exist between each channel level. By exploiting the natural linkages drawing channel businesses together, companies can overcome areas of possible conflict by leveraging information alliances that make transparent an awareness of interconnectedness, facilitate collaborate efforts, multiply efficiencies across the entire pipeline, and synchronize individual competitive goals and capacities.

The second step in the strategic channel inventory planning process consists of two activities: first, assessing the success of existing levels of channel customer satisfaction that have been achieved with current inventory strategies, and second, determining the projected inventories necessary to realize new marketplace strategies. Determining customer satisfaction depends on a matrix of inventory management factors. Some cluster around indicators that measure the success of how the supply channel as a whole has presented and customers accepted product offerings, product pricing, the success of promotions and advertising, and the impact of customer service strategies that govern the sale from pretransactional to posttransactional activities. Other issues center on product delivery and quality. Timely product delivery is the result of having the right product at the right channel location or available through other media such as catalogs, brochures, or e-business marketplaces. The compilation of such metrics must also consider the impact of strategic trade-offs between service levels and inventory investment. While providing critical internal information, such trade-offs must be determined in light of total channel service objectives.

Architecting the most effective physical supply chain network constitutes the third step in the channel inventory planning process. Network design has the potential of having a significant impact on channel inventory planning. Negatively, the number and location of supply channel nodes can be a severe drain on channel costs as excess buffers of inventories build up in the pipeline. In addition, poorly designed supply networks can actually inhibit the creation of customer-winning service value by supporting uncompetitive channel place and timing decisions. Well-designed internal and trading partner supply chains, on the other hand, enable each channel node to stock the proper inventory buffers necessary to support overall network service levels. Effective supply networks also make it easier for planners to determine changes to inventory levels due to the growth or contraction of markets. As the number of channel locations grows to meet rising customer demand, effectively organized supply channels permit planners to determine accurate inventory investment costs.

The fourth step in the strategic channel inventory planning process is establishing the mechanisms to ensure inventory accuracy. This step consists of three basic functions. The first centers on the choice of *inventory accuracy* methods and involves the design of transaction flows, procedures to formalize data input and the necessary output status inquiry and reporting, identification, authorization, and training of appropriate management and line staff in transaction control, and the implementation of inventory accuracy tools such as ABC analysis and cycle counting. Controlling inventory costs constitutes the second function. Decisions concerning costs can be roughly divided into *operational costs,* such as sunk costs, cost of capital, and indirect, direct, and overhead costs, and *inventory decision costs,* such as transportation, warehousing, order processing, obsolescence and damage, lot sizing, and inventory control maintenance. The final function in the planning process is the selection of the inventory *ordering policy.* As demand consumes channel inventories, inventory planners can use one or a combination of the following two techniques: *statistical order point* and *order quantity* or *time-phased MRP/DRP.* A full discussion of the nature, selection, and use of inventory ordering policies takes place in Chapters 7 and 8.

The final step in the channel inventory planning process is the development of adequate performance measurements that ensure that every customer, both external and internal to the pipeline, is consistently receiving the level of service value and quality necessary to meet demand requirements. Channel inventory performance can be measured from two interrelated perspectives: *customer service* and *inventory investment.* Performance metrics oriented around the customer assist in managing uncertainties due to timing and accuracy factors. Timing factors are focused on the interval required for inventory replenishment activities to be completed; accuracy factors are concerned with order contents and quantity, order completeness, and inventory record accuracy. Performance related to inventory investment is concerned with tracking the impact of inventory costs across the channel network. "World-class" channel systems know that high inventory levels translate into increased probabilities of obsolete and damaged stock as well as loss of operating cash committed to pipeline inventories. Effective network performance require that channel members know both the costs in serving their own segment of the channel's market as well as the total inventory costs of the entire supply network.

The development and continuous updating of the supply chain inventory plan is fundamental to the successful execution of the overall financial, marketing, sales, and logistics plans. Without an effective mechanism to control inventory accuracy, accounting and decision trade-off costs, and techniques for inventory replenishment, a supply chain cannot possibly hope to attain its objectives. Resources in most companies are limited. Capital invested needlessly in inventory drains resources necessary for promoting current and new products, facilities, equipment and staff improvement, collaborative channel partner development, and the implementation of information technologies.

INVENTORY COSTS

The cost of inventory has a direct impact on the competitive capabilities of the supply chain. Several critical factors are apparent. To begin with, the cost of inventory often constitutes the largest portion of a typical company's assets. The objective of this investment is to meet or exceed expected customer service levels. The level of inventory that individual companies station at various points in the supply channel determines the level of serviceability offered to its customers. The capability to calculate the trade-off costs between inventory investment and service levels is critical. By preserving cost history, planners can use the financial consequences of past inventory decisions to assist them in determining the *expected cost* results of future actions. Poor control over inventories can affect company profitability in two ways. To begin with, net profit is reduced not only through direct purchase but also for ongoing expenditures associated with a range of inventory carrying costs. Second, the value of the inventory investment must be added to the firm's total assets. As inventory grows, total company asset turnover decreases, resulting in a reduction in return on assets and net worth.

Understanding inventory costs assists supply chain planners answer such questions as:

- What is the appropriate level of inventory and cost to be carried by each supply channel node?
- What are the inventory costs necessary to support customer service, and how can levels be improved while reducing inventory investment?
- Is the selling price too high or too low?
- What will it cost to transport inventory through the supply chain?
- How many supply channel points should there be and what should be their inventory levels?
- What will be the cost of channel postponement and value-added processing strategies?

Finding solutions to these and other questions requires supply chain planners to have a detailed knowledge of inventory cost elements. Accurate inventory cost information is paramount if companies are to exploit new markets, optimize information and communications systems, explore new forms of transportation, and strengthen the integration of the entire supply chain.

ELEMENTS OF INVENTORY COST

The decision to stock inventories requires planners to understand and manage several dimensions of inventory cost. Waters [6] divides inventory costs into the following four basic elements:

- *Unit cost.* Perhaps the most fundamental cost associated with a product is the acquisition cost of the product itself. This cost can be defined as the value charged by the supplier in exchange for ownership of the product, or the material, labor, and overhead costs incurred in producing the product. The unit cost can be determined by reviewing supplier quotations or invoices, or by collecting production cost data. In developing the unit cost, several factors are necessary. To begin with, the costing unit of measure must be known. Establishing the unit of measure can sometimes appear to be a variable, especially if the product is purchased, stocked, and sold in different units of measure. In determining the unit of measure, planners should always use the unit of measure in which a given product is stocked. When a product is manufactured, the unit cost will be the sum not only of the material, but also the processing cost. Take the following cost calculation as an example:

  If:

  Total quantity of an item assembled   = 500 units
  Total manufacturing cost incurred   = $3500

  then

  Unit cost = $3500 / 500 units = $7.00 per unit.

  Unit costs are averages and must be viewed in that light. For example, using the same data for the product calculated above, if the total cost decreased to $5000 when produced in a lot size of 1000 pieces, then the unit cost would drop to $5.00 per unit. In determining the proper lot size for value-added processing or purchasing, planners must make effective inventory cost trade-off decisions [7].
- *Cost of reordering.* Once it is determined that a product needs to be replenished, there are several costs associated with order generation. For purchased items, this cost includes such elements as order preparation (checking, authorization, research, and administration), order entry and verification time, document preparation, communications, receiving, material handling and storage equipment, and stock put-away. Sometimes, receiving incurs additional costs for quality control, interbranch transfer, sorting, and bulk breaking. Finally, when ordering new products, there will be costs associated with sourcing, supplier negotiations, quality assessment, and quotation review. When products are produced by the company, the replenishment cost is composed of elements such as order research and release, shop order documentation, process setup, labor and overhead, WIP maintenance, scrap, and order completion.

- *Carrying cost.* This is the cost of holding product in stock over a period of time. The most obvious carrying cost component is the money tied up in stocks which has either been borrowed or directly spent in exchange for the inventory. Other costs center on insurance, taxes, storage, damage, obsolescence, and shrinkage. The contents of carrying costs will be discussed in detail later in this chapter.

- *Shortage costs.* Of the four cost elements, determining the cost of product shortages is the most difficult to quantify. Everyone can agree that when a sale is lost because of a stockout, it has cost the business direct revenue. The problem involves quantifying exactly what this cost is. Shortages can result in hard to quantify cost such as the loss of customer goodwill and marketplace reputation. In addition, shortages may cause extra costs involved in expediting or using premium suppliers.

In the past, most literature on inventory cost has focused on calculating the trade-off between meeting a certain level of customer service and the inventory it would cost to maintain that level. Although determining what a targeted service level will cost is certainly an important exercise, planners must understand that it is in reality a hypothetical calculation that considers service and the elements of inventory cost as absolutes. Therefore, it has been assumed that as service levels increase, so will costs. However, as JIT and *quick response* (QR) philosophies have demonstrated, the real goal of inventory management has little to do with manipulating stagnant models of cost. In today's supply chain environment, managing inventories is a process by which supply chain planners search for ways to increase service levels while *simultaneously* reducing costs. As the velocity of inventory increases as it moves through the distribution pipeline, performance based on inventory cost in relation to service begins to lose meaning.

OPERATIONAL COSTS

Inventory costs can perhaps best be understood by dividing them into two general classes: *operational costs* and *inventory decision* costs. Operational costs refer to costs incurred to support general inventory acquisition, storage, and fulfillment activities. For the most part, operational costs are confined to *relevant costs* or costs incurred as a direct result of an inventory management decision. Costs the firm has already incurred and are unaffected by future inventory decisions are referred to as *sunk costs.* Capital expenditure for land, plant, equipment, transportation, and personnel are examples of sunk costs.

An important perspective from which to view operational costs relates to how costs arise in relation to inventory activities. *Direct costs* can be directly traced to inventory acquisition. For manufacturing operations direct costs take the form of raw and component materials and labor consumed during product conversion. For purchased inventories, direct costs are traced to such activities as stock receipt, quality review, and inventory putaway. *Indirect costs* also arise from the inventory acquisition process and can be assigned to such functions as plant supervision, tooling, and operating processing equipment. In addition, all companies are subject to *overhead costs*. These costs are the result of expenditures for building maintenance and operations, equipment, management salaries, information processing, transportation, and other activities. A common method of allocating these costs is to apply a percentage burden based on the material or labor content of a product. A more modern tool is the use of *activity based costing* (ABC). This method seeks to utilize the actual source of the overhead cost rather than simply applying an aggregate percentage to a direct cost driver such as purchase or labor cost.

Each cost that occurs needs to be traced back as closely as possible to what activity was performed or what material was consumed during the transaction. Activities such as ordering, receiving, material conversion, material handling, shipping, and customer order processing can be used to determine the level of cost necessary to execute these activities. *Fixed costs* are expenditures that do not vary with the level of activity. As an example, the initial cost expended to acquire material handling equipment does not vary with its use. *Variable costs,* on the other hand, normally vary in proportion to changes in usage volume. Whereas the asset cost of a fork lift is fixed, the costs associated with its use are dependent on its level of activity. Finally, costs may be incurred for inventory that is difficult to quantify or is expressed in values not readily applied to cost categories. Among such *intangible costs* can be found the cost of incomplete information and inefficient operations. One of the most common intangible costs is dealing with customer satisfaction. As mentioned above, quantifying the effect of inventory shortages or poor product quality on customer satisfaction and likelihood of return business is an extremely difficult yet important cost measurement.

INVENTORY DECISION COSTS

The second class of inventory cost arises when making *inventory decisions*. It is clear that supply chains can benefit by having inventory; the cost of maintaining that inventory, however, is not so easily identified. Everyday decisions concerning inventory, can dramatically impact overall enterprise costs and long-term profitability. There are several cost factors that are not part of the traditional aggregate inventory measurement tools employed by management but, nevertheless, need to be considered when making inventory decisions.

The first of these elements is the cost involved in inventory *procurement*. Procurement costs can be divided into two groups: *order preparation* and *order execution costs*. Once it has been determined that a product needs to be ordered, a number of order preparation costs are incurred relative to the processing of the order. These costs include the cost of researching the supplier, reviewing pricing, writing up the order or entering it into a computer, printing and transmission of the order to the supplier, and order follow-up and reporting. Order execution costs include transportation, material handling and processing at the receiving dock, activities such as inspection, bulk breaking, and vendor return, the processing of supplier invoices, and the preparation of accounts payable records and payments. For products requiring manufacture, process order costs will also include the preparation of routing specifications and work center operations setup. In making inventory ordering decisions, planners can use work measurement techniques, such as time study methods, to calculate the labor content of production costs. Another possibility would be to divide the cost of the order processing functions of the firm by the number of orders processed. In any case, cost analysts must be careful to separate the fixed costs of ordering from those costs, such as transportation, processing, and material handling, which vary with order size.

One of the single largest inventory decision cost relates to transportation. Transportation costs are for the most part subject to procurement delivery frequency and volume. In addition, transportation speed will impact cost. The velocity by which goods move through the distribution channel will have a direct impact on the rate charged, the size of the order quantity, and the amount of time goods spend in transit. Finally, transportation costs also grow as the number of nodes in the supply chain expands. A computer can assist in establishing transportation standards and grouping deliveries to minimize freight expense. In addition, reporting can assist in isolating shipping variances and identifying opportunities for transportation cost savings.

The inventory decision cost associated with holding inventory is *inventory carrying cost*. Inventory carrying cost is composed of several expenses. These costs are directly related to the size and value of the inventory and to the length of time the inventory is carried. The value of inventory can range anywhere from 30 to 70 percent of a typical company's current assets and up to 50 percent or more of total assets. In 2003 carrying costs were estimated at around 23 percent. In 1981, for comparison, the carrying cost was almost 35 percent. Literally, if the average annual value of a product was $1000, a carrying cost of 25 percent would mean that the firm spent $250 annually just to hold this single product in stock. In analyzing the carrying cost of inventory, it is useful to divide the cost into four components: capital costs, service costs, risk costs, and storage costs.

Capital Costs. The most significant element in inventory carrying cost is the value of capital tied up in inventory. By committing capital to inventory, the firm forfeits the use of this capital for future investment in the hope of earning a profit when the inventory is sold. Consequently, when planning inventories, executives need to determine return on inventory investment hurdles as they would any other investment venture. For example, a firm might group inventories into high-, medium-, and low-risk categories. High-risk inventories may include new products or goods subject to fashion or seasonality that management targets to receive a 25 percent after-tax return. Products in the medium range normally consist of the company's "bread-and-butter" items that need a 15 percent return. At the bottom is to be found slow-moving items needing only a 10 percent return.

Although the cost of capital can account for as much as 80 percent of the total inventory carrying cost, it is perhaps the most intangible and subjective of all the carrying cost elements. When balancing the cost of capital and the size of the inventory investment, planners must find answers to such questions as "What would be the rate of return if capital was invested in other projects instead of inventory?" "If money needs to be borrowed to attain targeted inventory levels, how much will it cost the firm?" Usually most companies will calculate the cost of capital by referencing the prime rate, the interest rate on short-term securities, or the expected ROI from projects the company is unable to execute because the money has been spent on inventory.

Service Costs. Service costs represent direct cash expenditures necessary to support inventories. An example would be insurance coverage required as a protection against fire, theft, or natural disaster. As inventory is considered an asset, taxes are levied on the physical inventory quantities on hand on the day of assessment. Although insurance and taxes represent only a small fraction of total carrying costs, nevertheless, they represent direct cash flow out of the firm. Like the cost of capital, the cost of insurance and taxes is directly proportional to the level of inventory. Unlike the cost of capital, exact information concerning these two forms of cost is easily obtained for inventory decision making. Expenses for service costs can be calculated as a percentage of that year's inventory value and added to the cost of money component of the total carrying cost. Unless a company undergoes dramatic expansion or downsizing, service costs remain fairly consistent over time.

Risk Costs. Companies always have some form of risk when stocking inventories. All products risk *obsolescence*. Changes in the tastes of the public and in technology are two of the most common reasons why inventory becomes obsolete and can no longer be sold at its original price. Often such inventory is salvaged or sold at a discounted price, the variance showing up in the profit and loss statement as a separate item. The faster inventory turns over, the less a risk for obsolescence.

Damage and *shrinkage* are also elements of inventory risk. Spoilage can happen as a result of natural processes characteristic of products such as foodstuffs and chemicals. Companies also risk inventory loss due to damage. Damage during production, lack of quality and effective training of the company's staff, material handling equipment employed, packaging used, and storage practices are instances of where inventory loss can occur. Incoming inspection is a key element in reducing hidden damage or spoilage. Furthermore, theft is an unfortunate, yet real cost. Pilferage can be reduced through tighter company security measures.

A potentially large area of risk is balancing inventory levels among several channel stocking locations. Relocation costs occur because of poor planning and lack of management visibility into the inventories of the warehouses constituting the distribution network. For the most part, the inventory is relocated in the channel to avoid the possibility of stockout, to reduce channel stocking level imbalances, and to reduce field level replacement purchase orders. Such movement risks further damage and pilferage and cause more cost in the form of interbranch transportation.

Storage Costs. Costs for holding inventory can also be found in warehouse space and material handling costs. Inventory can be stored in four possible types of facilities: company warehouses, public warehouses, rented warehouses, and inventory intransit. The costs associated with company-owned warehouses and the accompanying material handling equipment are primarily fixed in nature and are not part of inventory carrying costs. Any variable costs, however, that change with the level of inventory, such as record keeping, should be considered part of carrying costs. As an example, the annual carrying costs for a given warehouse are the following:

Utilities	$65,000
Personnel	1,400,000
Equipment maintenance	415,000
Plant maintenance	323,000
Security	225,000

Total	$2,428,000

If the average value of the inventory is $18 million, dividing these variable costs by the average inventory will result in the percentage of carrying cost for this cost type or 13.4 percent.

The carrying costs incurred for the use of public, rented, and private warehouses is similarly easy to attain. Only those charges for recurring inventory storage that are explicitly included in the warehouse rates or those costs that are variable with the quantity of inventory held should be considered as carrying cost. As an example, the rate charged by a public warehouse to handle a pallet is $5.00 per month or $60 per year. If 100 pallets are handled during a single month, the charge would be $500.00. The last type of warehouse, inventory intransit, consists of goods that have been shipped from the supplier but have not as yet arrived at the purchasing facility. If the purchaser has accepted ownership at the time of shipment, these goods must be carefully tracked and accounted for until delivery.

Carrying Cost Calculation. Determining the cost of carrying inventory is achieved by combining the relevant expenses specified above for each of the four cost types. The costs for each type are expressed as a percentage of inventory value. Assume the following figures:

Cost of capital (13%)	0.130
Insurance costs (0.7% of value)	0.007
Taxes (3% of value)	0.030
Damage and theft	0.013
Obsolescence	0.020
Storage and handling	0.060

Carrying cost	26%

The calculation of the inventory carrying cost with even the most accurate information is at best an estimate. In reality, the actual costs accumulated are subject to interpretation and management policy. The carrying cost is calculated by multiplying the carrying cost percentage by the average value of the items being stored.

Stockout Costs. A stockout occurs when customer demand for a product exceeds the available inventory. When an item stocks out, two possible conditions may ensue. In the first, the customer order is taken and the stocked-out product is placed on backorder. This means that when the inventory becomes available it will be shipped against the customer order. A backorder condition will remain until the original product on the customer order is completed in full. If the customer chooses not to place the product in a backorder status, the order is lost. The customer may or may not attempt to reorder at a future date. When viewing the cost of a backorder, two issues are present. In the immediate term, the cost of processing a backorder often requires an expedite replenishment order and premium delivery. Such costs may actually exceed the expected sales revenue of the original order. In the long run, however, the cost involved in lost orders is even more damaging to the enterprise. Poor customer service can cost a company dearly in lost future opportunities, customer goodwill, and marketplace reputation.

Although the total impact of stockout costs is difficult to calculate, they are, nevertheless, critical when making inventory decisions. The most frequently used method of calculating stockout cost is to arrive at the carrying cost of inventory necessary to maintain a certain level of customer serviceability. The targeted level of customer service is set by management and can be expressed as the percentage of units available to ship upon the receipt of a customer order, the average length of time to fill complete open backorders, or the percentage of replenishment order cycles in which a backorder occurs. The cost of a stockout can be calculated as follows:

1. The inventory cost of a given product to maintain a targeted customer service level = $350.00.
2. The calculated inventory carrying cost = 26%.
3. The total cost of a stock out = 0.26 x $350 = $91.

This formula can also be used to calculate the inventory investment necessary to support a given customer service level. As is illustrated in Figure 6.6, as

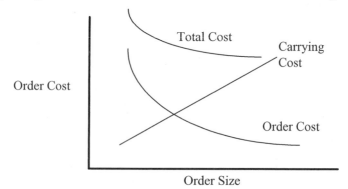

FIGURE 6.6 Inventory and sales trade-off costs.

the cost of inventory grows to support higher customer service levels, the cost of lost sales decreases. However, as customer service increases, the costs of carrying the accompanying inventory increases correspondingly. By calculating stockout costs for several proposed customer service levels, logistics managers will be able to execute informed inventory cost/customer service trade-off decisions.

Incremental Costs. The final cost category involved when making inventory decisions is *incremental cost*. Basically, incremental costs occur when changes in the actual cost, actual expenditure, or a forfeited profit occurs because of an inventory management decision. As an example, if the rise in aggregate inventory unit volume causes relevant costs to increase from $100,000 to $120,000, then $20,000 is the incremental cost of the decision to stock more units. Executives must be careful when determining these costs to separate costs that vary because of increases in unit volume from those that do not. The cost, for example, of maintaining the purchasing staff remains relatively constant regardless of the volume of orders processed through the department. However, paying for over-time, hiring and training more purchasers and supervisors, temporary help, and acquiring additional computer terminals because of an increase in order volume are incremental costs. Measuring the impact of inventory decisions can often be a time-consuming affair, requiring precise definition of relevant costs.

INVENTORY VALUATION

The process of determining the value of supply chain inventories requires a number of critical decisions. Such factors as how inventory is to be recorded, how fixed and variable costs are to be used, and what inventory accounting method is to be applied require serious consideration and need to be in alignment with overall corporate objectives and goals.

Physical Accounting Systems. Before inventory can be valued, the quantity of each product must be known. There are two common methods for determining the size of a company's inventory as a prelude to valuation: the *periodic inventory system* and the *perpetual inventory system.* The use of one or both methods depends on company decisions as to the purpose of inventory transaction data collection. In the periodic inventory system, the size of the inventory is determined by an actual physical count of stocked balances at specific dates, normally no later than year-end. The most significant advantage of this method is ease of record keeping. No daily inventory transactions to balances on hand for receiving, in-transit, scrap, or sales are maintained. The disadvantages are that the firm does not know exact inventory quantities or total value until the physical inventory is performed. In addition, a complete physical is an expensive, time-consuming process. Companies stocking products that are of relatively low value or are slow moving use periodic inventory systems because of the high cost of maintaining detailed records versus the benefit.

Perpetual inventory systems, on the other hand, are characterized by a careful and timely recording of each inventory transaction as it occurs. In this system, each time a purchase order receipt, adjustment, scrap, movement, issue, in-transit, or sales transaction occurs, the value is recorded and the inventory balance on hand is adjusted. The advantages of the perpetual inventory system are that exact information concerning inventory movement and on-hand balances is available at all times. In addition, through the use of an effective cycle count program, the annual physical inventory in most cases can be eliminated. Finally, this method allows financial managers to calculate the value of the inventory at any given time. The disadvantages of the method are that the maintenance cost of the system is very high and it usually requires a computer. Businesses that carry high to medium cost products with constant to high transaction volumes are most likely to use some form of perpetual inventory system to track and value their inventories.

Direct Versus Absorption Costing. Although the term *valuation* is commonly used when discussing inventory, in reality inventory accounting considers the value of inventory as a reflection of cost. As a prelude to the use of inventory valuation methods, firms must determine whether they are using *variable costing* (also known as *direct costing*) to determine the value of inventory or some form of *absorption costing*. Definitions of these two methods are [8]:

- *Variable costing* is a method of inventory costing in which all *direct costs*, such as material or purchase price, and all *variable overhead costs*, such as labor, transportation, direct machine, and setup, are combined to provide inventoriable costs. *Fixed overhead costs*, such as plant and equipment, are excluded and are considered costs of the period in which they are incurred.
- *Absorption costing* is a method of inventory costing in which all *direct, variable overhead,* and *fixed costs* are considered as inventoriable costs. In other words the total cost of a product is attained by "absorbing" all these costs.

The application of absorption versus direct costing is critical in making inventory decisions. Elements involved in fixed costs will not change as a result of inventory policy, whereas variations in direct costs will have an impact on carrying costs and cash flow.

Inventory Valuation Methods. Once accounting management has determined the components of inventory costing, inventory value can then be determined. Inventory valuation is important for several reasons. To begin with, good inventory accountability is necessary to assure correct reporting of interim and yearly profits. Accurate inventory valuation ensures that the difference between booked and physical inventories is as small as possible. Also, proper inventory accountability is a requirement for quarterly submission to the Securities and Exchanges Commission. This reporting is fundamental for assessing the profitability of publicly traded companies. There are five recognized methods by which a company can value its inventory:

1. *Standard cost.* This method of determining inventory value is determined by assigning cost standards to manufactured and purchased products. A *standard* is defined as a good or best level of performance for a process. Inventory standards serve as benchmarks permitting managers to determine what inventory costs should be and to measure actual costs against budgets. The standard is computed by using elements such as the purchased materials cost, direct labor expended in operational activities such as receiving, stock put-away, manufacturing, order picking and packing, and shipping, and overhead costs such as management salaries and carrying costs. Inventory at any point in the year up to creation of a new standard is valued at the given standard regardless of actual costs incurred. One of the advantages of standard costing is that the company needs to revalue inventory usually only once a year. Furthermore, the cost standard permits managers to calculate ongoing cost variances to the standard occurring in material, labor, or overheads. Variance analysis enables managers to investigate root causes of cost change and to take remedial action when necessary. While primarily used by manufacturers, distributors can easily prepare labor and overhead costs as portrayed in Figure 6.7

2. *First-in-first-out* (FIFO). This method of inventory valuation assumes that the cost of items sold in a period consists of the oldest inventory cost just prior to sales. By charging the oldest costs in inventory to the sale, FIFO assumes that inventory at the end of the period consists of the most recent costs incurred. The rationale behind FIFO is that it reflects the fact that companies generally use the oldest items in inventory first so that they can continually turn over stock and prevent deterioration or obsolescence. FIFO is widely used in times of stable pricing. However, in periods of continuous inflation, FIFO tends to result in "inventory profits" stemming from lower fixed inventory cost and increasing sales margins. FIFO methods of inventory are commonly used to inventory perishable goods, such as foods, pharmaceuticals, or other products with short shelf lives. Stockkeeping in a FIFO system requires that the oldest product always be rotated to the front upon the receipt of a new inventory lot.

I. Determination of Direct Labor Standard

Function	U/M	Labor hr Std	$ Labor hr	Std Cost U/M
Receiving	SKU	400 hrs	$16.00	$0.04
Stocking	SKU	400 hrs	$16.00	$0.04
Ordering	SKU	100 hrs	$16.00	$0.16
Picking	SKU	160 hrs	$16.00	$0.10
Shipping	SKU	50 hrs	$16.00	$0.32
			Std Labor Cost per U/M	$0.66

II. Determination of Standard Cost for Product #1-100
  a. Supplier Invoice Cost = $2.35
  b. Overhead Burden   =   25%
  c. Direct Labor Cost   = $0.66

  d. (Labor ($0.66) x Overhead (25%)) + Labor ($0.66) +
     Invoice Cost ($2.35) = $3.175 Std Cost per Unit
  e. Inventory Valuation = 354 (OHB) x $3.175 = $1123.95

FIGURE 6.7 Standard cost calculation.

3. *Last-in-first-out* (LIFO). This method of inventory valuation assumes that the cost most recently incurred in the acquisition of a product is the cost used for sales during that period. By charging current costs to sales, LIFO assumes that inventory at the end of a period reflects the oldest costs incurred to acquire inventory to its current level. A key goal of LIFO is to achieve a better match between costs and revenues. The computation of LIFO can perhaps best be seen when compared to FIFO. Assume that at the beginning of a period a company starts with five SKUs purchased at $100 and sold at $150 per SKU. During the period five units are sold. Finally, assume that the cost of replenishment during the period has increased to $110 per SKU. The result of the selection of FIFO or LIFO is indicated in Figure 6.8. The *Gross Profit* difference of $50 constitutes the FIFO profit. Because LIFO considers the increased cost of $10 per SKU, current costs are matched closer to sales, and therefore inventory profits are not reported.

Under LIFO, inventory levels are carried on the balance sheet at the original LIFO cost until they are decreased. Increases are added at the current cost in the year the inventory is acquired. In the above example, the ending inventory would be priced at $500 (five units at $100) even though the current cost is $550. As long as the inventory level remains above five units, the first five units in the closing inventory would continue to be carried at $100 in succeeding periods.

	LIFO	FIFO
Sales	$750	$750
Cost of Sales	500	550
Gross Profit	250	200
Operating Expense	100	100
Income Before Taxes	150	100
Taxes at Assumed Rate of 5%	75	55
Net Income	75	50

FIGURE 6.8 LIFO versus FIFO valuation.

Any increases in inventory at inventory close would be priced using current costs and "layered" on top of the original cost. For example, if the inventory closed at ten units the cost would be

$$(5 \text{ units} \times \$100) + (5 \text{ units} \times \$110) = \$1050.$$

The advantage or disadvantage of LIFO costing depends on whether the economy is experiencing a period of inflation or deflation. When prices are rising, LIFO will result in lower inventory valuation, high cost of goods sold, and lower profits. When prices are declining, the opposite will be true. In addition, it reduces taxes and increases cash flow. Disadvantages are that after many years of use, inventory amounts in the balance sheet may be much lower than current inventory assets. Also, if inventory levels are reduced, older LIFO costs are matched with current revenues and reported income becomes inflated [9].

- *Average cost.* This method of valuation references the current cost of the existing inventory and the cost of the newest supplier invoice, and then uses some form of average to calculate the new inventory value from these two costs. Usually, firms will use some type of weighted moving average in which inventory invoice cost will be weighted by the quantity of the item received. This form of inventory costing is often used with *periodic inventory systems.* An example of the average cost method using a straight average is illustrated in Figure 6.9.
- *Actual cost.* In this costing method, a specific received quantity and invoiced price for a given product are linked together and differentiated from other stocked quantities of the same item by associating the receipt with a unique identifier, usually a *lot number.* When an inventory transaction for the product occurs, it would be necessary for the lot number to be part of the transaction detail. In this way, the discrete cost associated with the lot can be captured along with the quantity transacted. An example of actual costing using the same detail as Fig-

I. Ending Balance = 354 units

II. Prior Item Receipts

1. 200 at $2.35 = $470.00
2. 245 at $2.48 = $607.60
3. 235 at $2.50 = $587.50

III. *Calculation:*

$$\frac{\$470.00 \, + \, \$607.60 \, + \, \$587.50}{680 \text{ (total quantity received)}} = \$2.4486764 \text{ per unit}$$

IV. Ending Inventory Cost:

Ending Inventory = 354 x $2.4486764 = $866.83

FIGURE 6.9 Weighted average cost calculation.

ure 6.9 appears in Table 6.1. Actual costing is used by firms that experience dramatic fluctuations in the acquisition cost of products. By capturing the actual cost, the firm can calculate the actual cost of sales and the earned margin when a specific lot of an item is shipped.

TABLE 6.1 Actual Cost Inventory Calculation

Recpt/ Ship Qty	Recpt Date/ Ship Date	Invoice $ Per Unit	On Hand/ Lot#	Inventory Value
200	03/01/03	$2.35	200/Lot 123	$470.00
150	03/13/03		50/Lot 123	$117.50
245	04/01/03	$2.48	245/Lot 345	$607.60
176	04/25/03		69/Lot 345	$171.12
235	05/01/03	$2.50	235/Lot 543	$587.50
			50/Lot 123	$117.50
	On Hand inventory – 05/01/03		69/Lot 345	$171.12
			235/Lot 543	$587.50
			Total value	$876.12

If it were possible to continually acquire inventory at the same price, the choice of a costing method would make no difference on either reported income or the balance sheet. However, because costs do change, the choice of an appropriate costing method is critical in effectively managing inventory investment. The choice of the proper inventory valuation method depends on a matrix of factors such as the general economic environment, the velocity of how fast inventory moves through the supply pipeline, and the financial reporting motives of individual companies.

INVENTORY CONTROL

As previously stated, inventory is perhaps the largest single financial investment for most companies. Unless the firm's management undertakes a serious and detailed plan to control the physical movement and costs of inventories, inaccuracies can drain away profitability and inhibit effective performance. Many companies, after the annual physical inventory, experience a large variance between the physical and booked values of their inventories. In addition, manufacturers have found their costs for labor and overhead severely understated or overstated. Such discrepancies usually send a tidal wave of concern through the firm. Accurate inventories are essential to assure correct reporting of profits. Investors and shareholders can become apprehensive about profits that do not appear because of poor inventory management. Executives can be surprisingly disappointed to see that business plan goals are unattainable because of negative inventory variances.

In addition to the impact on financial measurements, poor customer serviceability usually accompanies inaccurate inventories. The litany of performance problems is familiar: declining order volumes and high customer turnover, increasing backorders and order cancellations, increasing inventories and expediting costs, significant inventory inequalities in the supply channel, growing inventory obsolescence, and increases in premium purchase order and freight costs. Ineffective inventory control destroys the confidence of the firm to establish meaningful plans and performance measurements and to respond effectively to the competitive challenges of the marketplace.

Inventory discrepancies happen for a variety of reasons. Loss of inventory through theft is a common, although regrettable, occurrence. Although theft accounts for a small fraction of inventory variance, it represents a true loss to the company. Techniques such as employing a security staff, enclosing inventories within a fenced stockroom, maintaining a perpetual inventory, and documenting inventory transactions will greatly assist in decreasing inventory pilferage. Most firms will closely monitor total inventory shrinkage. A commonly used formula and example to calculate inventory shrinkage is

$$\text{Shrinkage ratio} = \frac{\$4,500,000 \text{ (total physical inventory value)}}{\$4,550,000 \text{ (total inventory investment)}} = 98.9\%,$$

$$\text{Percentage of shrinkage} = 100 - 98.8 = 1.1\%.$$

One of the ways companies can reduce inventory loss and vastly improve accuracies is by clearly defining the transaction control points as inventory flows through the channel. Accurate inventory records must be kept from the moment inventory is received to the moment it is shipped to the customer. Figure 6.10 illustrates the typical control points found in a distribution chan-

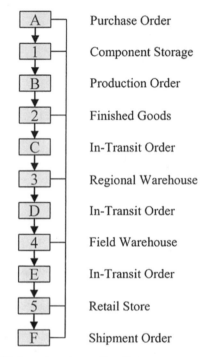

A	Purchase Order
1	Component Storage
B	Production Order
2	Finished Goods
C	In-Transit Order
3	Regional Warehouse
D	In-Transit Order
4	Field Warehouse
E	In-Transit Order
5	Retail Store
F	Shipment Order

FIGURE 6.10 Inventory transaction flow.

nel. In the example, there are **11** inventory control points. Control points 1-5 represent *physical locations*. Inventory in physical locations can be defined as at rest in a stockroom where on-hand balances for raw materials, components, finished assemblies, and finished goods are maintained. Inventory, furthermore, that is in physical locations can be allocated, counted, and shipped. Control points A-F represent *logical locations*. Inventory in logical locations can be described as in motion, yet can be held in discrete repositories such as purchase orders, inspection locations, production orders, in-transit, and shipping orders. Inventory in logical locations cannot be allocated, counted, or shipped to a customer.

The key to clearly identifying inventory control points is to determine those places in the inventory flow where transactions take place. Essentially, there are two types of inventory transaction that can occur: *physical* and *accounting*. Depending on the degree of physical control required by the firm, each time inventory moves from one location to another, an inventory transaction describing the location from, location to, and quantity must be performed. Sometimes the movement of inventory has not only a physical but also a financial effect on inventory value. An example would be a stock *adjustment* where inventory is transacted either to or from a physical location and to or from an inventory adjustment general ledger account number. Effective transaction control must follow inventory through the distribution channel in order to keep the inventory and the accounting systems in alignment with one another. In designing a company's inventory flow transaction system, managers must focus on thoroughness, simplicity, and timeliness.

The final reason why inventory discrepancies occur is improper accounting techniques. Essentially, improper techniques can be grouped into two basic categories: *overstatement of input* and *understatement of relief.* Inaccuracies accompanying the transaction of goods into inventory occur due to poor purchase order receiving practices, incorrect WIP issue reporting, improper handling of customer returns, and improperly designed transactions and valuation. Shortages in inventory often occur because of understatement of inventory relief. Failure to report issues to WIP, scrap, and incorrect Bills of Material are examples. A well-designed inventory transaction system, accompanied by an effective Cycle Count program and a fully-trained and diligent staff, will significantly reduce inventory physical-to-book variances.

ABC ANALYSIS AND CYCLE COUNTING

Two tools commonly employed to ensure inventory accuracy and control are *ABC Analysis* and *Cycle Counting.* Supply chain inventories can consist of thousands, maybe hundreds of thousands, of products. When it comes to procurement and sales, it would be unrealistic to say that each product is reviewed and shipped at the same rate. In fact, the usage rates of a typical company's inventory follows a statistical principle formulated by the 19th-century Italian social scientist, Vilfredo Pareto, termed the "Management Principle of Materiality." Simplistically, the principle states that in any given statistical population, 20 percent of the elements in that population will account for 80 percent of the data occurrences.

When applied to inventory, the principle states that statistically 20 percent of a firm's active products will account for 80 percent of the inventory transactions. The operating principle that can be extended from this statistical law is simple: By dividing the inventory into classes, analysts can focus on those products that account for the bulk of the company's inventory flow. Planning and controlling inventories, even though they can be computerized, still require a great deal of manual effort to input data, check values, update supplier details, confirm orders, make subjective judgments, monitor operations, and other activities. Clearly, the larger an inventory becomes, the less planners will be able to work effectively with the entire inventory. Because the firm possesses limited resources, classifying inventory by transaction value can greatly assist in ascertaining the level of control to be exercised over each product.

For the most part, a typical ABC Classification would seek to break a company's inventory into the following three divisions:

- **A** items would be classified as expensive, high-transaction items needing special attention.
- **B** items would be classified as the bulk of the firm's inventory requiring standard attention.
- **C** items would be classified as relatively inexpensive or low-transaction items requiring minimal attention.

In inventory planning, Class A products would be under close computer control, with balance and reordering decisions made by inventory planners after a thorough review of transaction and planning data. Class B products, on the other hand, would typically be controlled automatically by a computer. Replenishment and data element update would normally be performed automatically by the computer without planner intervention. Finally, Class C products may or may not be included in the computer system. Such items could be satisfactorily controlled through periodic review control systems.

The procedure for developing an ABC analysis begins by determining the content of the classification scheme. Among the most commonly used factors can be found product annual dollar usage, transaction usage, unit cost, lead time, and quality. In developing product classifications, planners must be careful to use more than one of the above criteria. Although the most common method is annual dollar and transaction usage, other criteria can be used depending on inventory characteristics. One technique is to use a two-digit coding system that differentiates between dollar value and actual usage. The first digit determines the class based on descending dollar value. The second code is based on descending usage, serving as an indicator of actual sales usage. For example, an A-1 (with 1 being the highest value) would require close planner review, whereas a C-3 would require minimal review. However, a C-1 would be given much greater attention than an A-3. Planners would use this two-part classification by designating the first digit as the method to control inventory replenishment, and the second, safety stock and forecast management policies. Table 6.2 illustrates an *ABC distribution by value report* calculated by ranking inventory by transaction and by value.

The results of the ABC Classification detailed in Table 6.2 indicate that the first three products represent 74.7 percent of the firm's total sales and have

TABLE 6.2 ABC Distribution by Value Report

Item	Unit Cost	Annual Usage	Cumulative % Usage	Annual Dollar Usage	Cummulate % Dollar Usage	ABC Classification
1-100	$.0074	5,750,000	63.9	$42,550.00	41.3	A
1-500	$.0203	1,265,000	78.0	$25,679.50	66.2	A
2-300	$.0800	110,000	79.2	$8,800.00	74.7	A
1-200	$.0800	105,00	80.4	$8,400.00	82.9	B
2-100	$1.0173	7,500	80.4	$7,629.75	90.3	B
2-600	$.0200	115,000	81.7	$2,300.00	92.5	B
1-300	$1.1438	1,500	81.7	$1,715.70	94.2	B
1-400	$3.1999	500	81.7	$1,599.95	96.8	C
3-100	$.0125	110,000	83.0	$1,375.00	97.1	C
3-200	$.0300	25,300	83.2	$759.00	97.8	C
2-700	$.0200	25,300	83.5	$506.00	98.3	C
4-100	$.0799	500	83.5	$439.95	98.8	C
5-100	$4.5438	70	83.5	$318.06	99.1	C
4-200	$.3000	1,000	83.5	$300.00	99.4	C
3-300	$.0100	25,300	83.8	$253.00	99.6	C
4-300	$.3000	600	83.8	$100.00	99.8	C
6-100	$.0050	25,300	84.1	$126.50	99.9	C
7-100	$.2000	126	84.1	$25.30	99.9	C
6-500	$.0200	1,000	84.1	$20.00	99.9	C
5-500	$.0200	500	84.1	$10.00	99.9	C
4-700	$.0010	525	84.1	$0.52	100	C
5-600	$.0000	0	84.1	$0.00	100	C
2-800	$.0000	0	84.1	$0.00	100	C
4-900	$.0000	0	84.1	$0.00	100	C
5-900	$.0000	0	84.1	$0.00	100	C
6-900	$.0000	1,419,400	99.9	$0.00	100	C
Totals		8,991,491.50		$102,988.23		

been classified as Class A. The next four products represent about 15 percent of total sales and have been assigned to Class B. Finally, the remainder of the inventory accounts for about 5 percent of total sales and have been assigned to Class C. The report also shows four products with no transaction detail at all. These products should be classified as "dead stock" and reviewed for possible removal from active inventory. The last product, #6-900, has a large usage, but because no cost has been applied, the report cannot calculate its dollar usage. This product should be reviewed and action taken accordingly. Figure 6.11 illustrates graphically the *distribution by value* principle used to determine the classification in Table 6.2.

Once determined, an ABC classification can assist planners assign the proper resources to attain the optimum maintenance of the inventory. For example, Class A products may have their inventory status reviewed weekly,

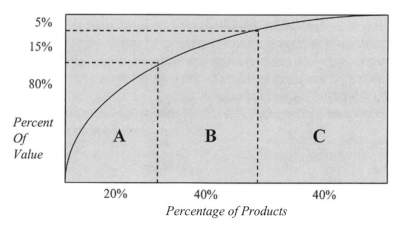

FIGURE 6.11 Distribution by value.

possess tight accuracy tolerances, a 98 percent order fill rate, a high safety stock percentage, and close follow-up and possible expediting of replenishment orders. In contrast, Class B and C products would require less review, safety stock, and expediting. In addition, in a distribution network almost all of the Class C and some of the Class B items would be stocked in central distribution centers only, thereby diminishing the amount of low-value products in the pipeline.

A critical management focus of Class C items should be the elimination of surplus and obsolete inventory. Many companies actually stock about 40 percent more products than they really need. Although periodic sales seem to validate stocking this inventory, in reality the resulting small stream of revenue does not generate enough profit to justify the dollars invested in inventory and is the major reason for low aggregate inventory turnover. Essentially, this inventory falls into the following categories: excess, damaged, recall, rework, outdated, shortdated (will soon become outdated), expired, and dead stock. The elimination of these inventories is critical if supply chains are to improve on inventory investment and turnover rates. An effective excess and dead-stock program consists of the following steps:

1. *Prevention.* In this phase, planners should deploy effective inventory planning tools to eliminate the ordering of excess and dead-stock inventories. Effective prevention also requires a tough attitude toward customers, salesmen, and suppliers.

2. *Identification.* In this phase, the creation of effective inventory transaction/usage reporting is critical. Reporting will assist planners to quickly focus in on products with low to null cost/usage value but have inventory on-hand or zero balances, and a low ratio of cost/usage and available on hand.

3. *Coordination.* In this step, an excess or "dead-stock" project team should be defined to tackle the problem.
4. *Disposal.* Once excess and obsolete inventory has been identified, the project team must develop a program to (1) dispose of the inventory, and (2) maximize the dollars generated from the disposition. Such methods as sell at any price above cost, return to supplier, sell at a certain percentage below cost, sell at any price, sell to a reseller or broker, and scrap can be used to dispose of inventory.

Another method commonly used to control inventory and maintain accurate records is Cycle Counting. The ***APICS Dictionary*** defines cycle counting as "an inventory accuracy audit technique where inventory is counted on a cyclic schedule rather than once a year [10]." Some of the possible techniques used for Cycle Counting are controlled sample, occurrence of purchase order receipt, and product negative balance. By far, the most used technique is *Period ABC*. Fundamental to this cycle count method is the establishment of an effective ABC classification. Because the mechanics of Cycle Counting provide on a predetermined periodic basis a verification of actual-to-book on-hand counts, the technique enables inventory control to review more frequently high-value or fast-moving products while postponing review of low-value or slow-moving products. An example of the Period ABC approach would be to count all Class A products monthly, all Class B's quarterly, and all Class C's twice a year. Often *exception* or *special situation* counts are integrated with the Period ABC method.

Once the parameters of the cycle count technique have been formalized, effective execution will require the counting of a certain number of products every workday with each product counted at a proscribed frequency. Once counting has been completed, the count sheets results need to be verified and variances examined. When variances occur, products can either be recounted or their book inventory values adjusted depending on management policy. Once a week the results of the cycle count program should be reported, and a summary report by ABC class prepared at least monthly.

An effective cycle count program provides a number of significant advantages. To begin with, Cycle Counting assists in the maintenance of a high level of inventory accuracy. When the firm depends on a yearly physical to adjust inventory, variances can go unadjusted for long periods of time. Because the focus of the cycle count program is on those products with the most transactions, repeated review will ensure a high level of accuracy. Additionally, an effective Cycle Counting program enables companies to abolish the expense and operations disruption of the annual physical inventory. Finally, the real benefit of Cycle Counting is the information provided to inventory controllers to investigate and eliminate the root cause of why inventory variances occur at all in the transaction flow. This *Total Quality Management*

(TQM) approach focuses the entire inventory control function on continuous performance excellence.

PERFORMANCE MEASUREMENT

Supply chain inventory performance can be measured from two perspectives: *customer service* and *inventory investment.* Neither of these two measurements can be considered outside of one another. Customer service performance is meaningless without an understanding of its financial affect on inventories; inventory performance measurements are likewise meaningless without reference to the level of customer service they are designed to support. Figure 6.12 illustrates this relation. Inventory investment is shown along the vertical axis, and customer service is shown along the horizontal axis. In describing a single product, the downward slope of the curve indicates that additional inventory will increase the level of customer service. Determination of the effectiveness of inventory/service trade-off strategies is the subject of inventory performance management.

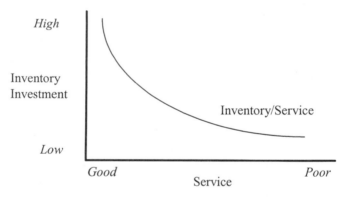

FIGURE 6.12 Inventory customer/service trade-off.

Customer Service. Earlier in this chapter it was stated that the strategic objective of inventory is to provide supply chains with the ability to optimize customer service throughout the entire marketing channel. But while efforts to optimize customer service are the focal point of inventory strategies, choosing the proper measurement criteria to validate objectives is not always easy. For example, a distributor receives the following two orders: four each of product #1-100 at a cost each of $25 and a second line calling for four each of product #2-100 at a cost each of $10 for a total value of $120; and an order for two each product #2-100. There are four each #1-100 on hand, but #2-

100 is stocked out. In determining the customer service measurement for this scenario, there are four possible service measurements:

- 50% piece fill rate
- 71% dollar fill rate
- 33% line fill rate
- 0% order fill rate

The selection of the appropriate performance measurement depends on the marketplace, the nature of the products sold, and the ramifications of the supply channel's inability to completely fill customer orders.

According to Bowersox and Closs [11], the development and implementation of performance measurements utilizes three measurement toolsets. The first seeks to *monitor* performance by tracking and reporting on historical occurrences. Typical monitoring metrics include service level and supply chain cost components. The second measurement tool is *controlling*. Metrics captured can be used to track ongoing performance and ensure channel processes are operating within boundaries or to improve channel processes altogether. For example, if products are continuously delivered damaged, the shipping process might be examined and the root cause of error eliminated. Finally, the third toolset involves *directing* performance measurements. The goal of these metrics is to motivate personnel to achieve higher productivity or quality levels through bonuses or other incentives.

In selecting the most appropriate measurements, managers have the option of selecting from a wide range of activity-based (which focus on the efficiency and effectiveness of specific work tasks) to entirely process-based (which focus on the performance of the whole supply chain) measurements. Activity based metrics revolve around the performance of processes. Among these metrics can be found percentage or value type measurements such as

1. Customer orders shipped on schedule
2. Line items shipped on schedule
3. Total units shipped on schedule
4. Dollar volume shipped on schedule
5. Working days not out of stock
6. Backorders shipped within a specified number of days
7. Order days out of stock
8. Total item days out of stock
9. Average number of days to ship a backorder
10. Backorder aging

Besides the above measurements, which are concerned with customer service and quality performance, business are normally concerned with other metrics that impact inventory management. One of these is the *cost* the company has incurred to meet targeted service goals. Normally, this measurement is used in relation to the budgeting process and is measured in terms of total dollars, as a percent of sales, or as a cost per unit. Another measurement can be found in how well overall supply chain assets are meeting budgetary objectives. In this area can be found aggregated costs for facilities, equipment, personnel, and inventory and how effectively expenditures are meeting ROI objectives. Finally, *quality* must be measured. Quality can refer to the effectiveness of how well processes are being executed to the standard and how much expediting, exception processing, or manual intervention must be performed. Quality measurement can also be applied to the fitness of the product itself and can take the form of recorded defects, failures, and returns.

Inventory Measurements. Measuring inventory is fundamentally a process of determining how quickly inventory cycles through the business and out to the customer. Inventory planners must be careful to ensure that inventory costs are not unduly increased in expectation of future sales revenue. An inventory policy that builds stocks simply to raise customer service levels is usually courting financial disaster. High inventory levels translate into increased probabilities of obsolescence and damage. What is worse, the greater the inventory value, the less operating cash is available to improve channel operations, buy new equipment, train employees, and invest in new products. Maintaining firm controls on inventory investment should, perhaps, be the most important measurement in the company.

The most commonly used inventory measurement technique is to view the aggregate value of inventory investment on a periodic basis. Periodic reviews provide timely data for the analysis and comparison of actual inventory investment to inventory budgets. Resulting variances can then be used to investigate root causes and to effect corrective action. In addition, a periodic review will assist inventory planners in pinpointing inventory out-of-bounds situations caused by seasonal fluctuations and unusual inventory usage trends. Finally, the periodic inventory measurement provides top management planners with an opportunity to realign projected inventory investment with the business's financial capabilities.

Once the firm has an accurate valuation of inventory, there are several measures that can be used to gauge aggregate performance. One of the most popular is *inventory turnover.* Inventory turnover is an expression of how many times per year the aggregate inventory is moved in and out of the warehouse. The formula for this measurement is found in Figure 6.13.

I. Inventory turnover formula:

$$\text{Inventory turnover} = \frac{\text{Cost of inventory sold}}{\text{Inventory investment}}$$

II. *Example*

Annual product sales	$100 M
Margin	50%
Cost of goods sold (CGS)	$50 M
Cost of inventory	$30 M (60% of CGS)
Labor and overhead	$20 M (40% of CGS)
Average annual inventory investment	$8 M

III. *Calculation:*

$$\text{Inventory turnover} = \frac{\$30\ M}{\$8\ M} = \textbf{3.75 turns per year}$$

FIGURE 6.13 Inventory turns calculation.

There is no standard inventory turns formula that is valid for every company. In fact, inventory turnover calculations have little meaning when used as a comparison even for two companies within the same industry. For example, auto assembly plants and oil refiners achieve turnover ratios of fifty or more, whereas department stores and electrical suppliers will generally have stock turnovers below five. What is more, different turn ratio objectives can be developed by inventory class for products within the same inventory. Various other factors can be used in the calculation of the turnover formula. Sales can be expressed as gross sales, net sales, sales at standard cost, sales at actual cost, or annualized forecast cost of sales. In developing an inventory ratio, planners must discern the purpose of the ratio, who will be using it, the accuracy of company accounting data, the profile of the inventory segment to be measured (i.e., product lines, warehouses, classes), and a plan for implementation. Inventory turn measurements must be used with caution. As purely a means of control, they place emphasis on reducing inventories only at the possible expense of customer service.

In addition to inventory sales-based turnover ratios, there are other performance measurements that can be employed under the proper circumstances. These techniques can be described as follows:

- *Inventory to current assets.* Broadly speaking, a firm's *current assets* can be divided into cash, accounts receivable, and inventory. This measurement seeks to calculate the ratio of inventory to total *current assets*. Companies using this technique must be careful to measure the impact of variations in accounting periods or seasonality and economies on total assets.

- *Inventory to total assets.* This method is an extension of the *current assets* ratio. Assets included are all current assets, plus plant and equipment. These asset elements are combined to calculate a *return on assets* ratio by comparing totals to profits.
- *Number of month's supply.* In this method, the total amount of inventory is expressed in terms of the amount of supply necessary to support current inventory sales rates. For example, if inventory turns four times a year, the average amount on hand is 3 months' worth. This ratio is most often used to calculate turns for raw materials and component inventories.
- *Number of days' supply.* This is same concept as above but is calculated in the number of days' worth of inventory. This ratio is most often used with finished goods.
- *Inventory to net working capital.* "Net working capital" is expressed as the difference between current assets and current liabilities. The ratio calculated between inventory investment and net working capital will demonstrate the amount of cash available in the short run. If the value of inventory is equal to or greater than the net working capital, then inventories are probably too high and are squeezing cash flow. The ratio calculated should be less than one, indicating that cash and receivables are available for short-term investment [12].

Similar to other measurement tools, inventory performance ratios can be abused and misapplied to produce the wrong decision based on incorrect assumptions. Nevertheless, the techniques outlined above can provide companies with effective measurement tools if used carefully.

SUMMARY

During the past decade, the role of inventory in the manufacturing, distribution, and retail environments has undergone drastic change. Inventory management is no longer viewed as a narrow discipline centered on calcu-lating lot sizes and economic order quantities, and expediting replenishment and customer orders. Increasingly, academics and practitioners alike have be-gun to see effective inventory management as the key to marketplace leader-ship and to integrate it with strategic and competitive planning. Effective inventory management in the twenty-first century is concerned with *overall* inventory performance and customer service levels as they impact not just individual companies, but the entire supply chain. Decisions concerning inventory cannot be made in isolation from strategic channel network objectives. Instead, inventory must be seen as an aggregate resource that spans and connects all nodes in the supply chain network and directs them to aggregate customer service goals.

Reevaluating the role of inventory requires a thorough understanding of the nature, functions, and costs associated with inventory. Inventory can be stocked as raw materials, components used in the assembly process, and finished goods. The fundamental reason why inventory is held is to serve as a *buffer* that decouples supply nodes from the vagaries of customer demand on the one hand and limitations in the delivery capacities of suppliers on the other. In managing inventory buffers, planners must be diligent in determining and tracking costs arising out of both operations and inventory decisions. Informed inventory cost decisions are necessary if the firm is to be run effectively and efficiently. Control of inventory cost is paramount if supply channels are to exploit new markets, optimize information and communications systems, explore new forms of transportation, and strengthen the integration of the supply chain.

Without effective inventory control, the supply channel network will experience cost discrepancies and poor customer serviceability. Individual companies can vastly improve inventory accuracies with the use of several control tools. Fundamental is the clear definition of transaction control points in the flow of inventory as it moves through the supply channel. Transaction control will not only ensure that material is properly accounted for, but it also serves as a gateway to minimizing inventory shrinkage and the mismatching of material and costs as they flow through the system. ABC Classification and Cycle Counting are additional tools that can be employed by inventory managers. Finally, the true test of channel inventory is how well it measures up to customer service and inventory investment performance objectives. The ability to provide the right product at the time and place desired by the customer at the lowest possible inventory investment is the foremost objective of every node in the channel network. In developing effective customer service performance measurements, companies must be precise in defining the relation of perceived customer wants and the ability of their channel of supply to match those wants. In the final analysis, customer service and inventory performance measurements cannot be considered independently of each other.

QUESTIONS FOR REVIEW

1. Discuss the nature and functions of inventory in today's enterprise.
2. Based on statistical evidence, why have inventory investment costs been steadily declining over the past 5 years?
3. Analyze the elements of inventory carrying cost.
4. Discuss the financial difference between a periodic review system and a perpetual inventory system.
5. What are the five inventory valuation methods. Explain why companies would use one method over another.
6. Why is inventory transaction control absolutely essential to effective inventory management?
7. Explain the uses of ABC Analysis and Cycle Counting.
8. It has been said that customer service and inventory investment are two measurements that cannot be considered outside of one another. Explain.

PROBLEMS

1. M & K distributors stocks about 5000 SKUs in their finished goods inventory. After a recent ABC Classification report was run, it was determined that the firm had 500 A items, 1750 B items, and 2750 C items. If the Cycle Counting program required that A items be counted complete monthly (every 20 working days), B items quarterly (every 60 working days), and C items biannually (every 120 working days), how many items will cycle counters have to count each day?
2. Develop an ABC classification for the following 10 items.

Item	Annual Demand	Cost/Unit
A100-100	4000	$ 50
A200-100	5000	13
A300-200	2000	45
B100-100	7000	9
B300-220	900	22
C350-200	400	525
D250-450	500	1300
E400-300	700	15
F500-200	2200	9
G200-450	3000	4

3. Based on the data below, calculate the inventory turnover ratio at the end of period 3.

Period	Forecast	Demand	Inventory
1	7.3	7.2	9.1
2	7.4	7.3	10.3
3	7.5	7.6	10.9
4	8.5		
5	10.1		
6	11.3		

4. In examining the cost to stock the following three product lines, the following data has been collected. What is the carrying cost for each of the product groups?

	Prod Grp I	Prod Grp II	Prod Grp III
Cost of capital	0.9	0.9	0.9
Insurance	0.4	0.4	0.4
Taxes	1.5	1.5	1.5
Damage and theft	2.5	0.3	1.5
Obsolescence	3.0	0.2	0.8
Storage and handling	6.5	10.5	5.0

5. The accounts payable file for Product A100-125 shows the following four purchase order receipts:

1. 1250 units at $4.55 received 1/23/95
2. 2500 units at $4.65 received 2/27/95
3. 2200 units at $4.45 received 4/13/95
4. 3195 units at $4.35 received 6/10/95

After examining theses past receipts, calculate what the average cost would be. What would the average cost be if receipts were weighted by a 40% ratio?

6. A distributor receives the following two orders. The first order consists of the following line items: 10 each #A100-100 at a price of $22.50, 7 each #B200-220 at a price of $10.50, and 23 each #C100-450 at a price of $15.45. The second order consists of 12 each #A100-100 and 18 each #C100-450. The on-hand balance for these items is as follows: #A100-100 = 11 units, #B200-220 = 25 units and #C100-450 = 12 units. Calculate the following:

1. The piece fill rate
2. The dollar fill rate
3. The line fill rate
4. The order fill rate

REFERENCES

1. See the discussion in Plossl, George, *Production and Inventory Control: Principles and Techniques.* 2nd ed. Englewood Cliffs, NJ: Prentice Hall, 1985, p. 18 and Ross, David Frederick, *Competing Through Supply Chain Management.* Boston: Kluwer, 1998, pp. 197-198.
2. Delaney, Robert V., *14th Annual State of Logistics Report.* St. Louis, MO: Cass ProLogis, June 2003, Fig. 8, The Cost of the Business Logistics System in Relation to Gross Domestic Product.
3. This postulate is expressed in Ross, *Competing Through Supply Chain Management,* pp. 201-204.
4. Editor, "Protecting Inventory During Supply Chain Disruptions," *Inbound Logistics*, 22, 11, 2002, pp. 18-19.
5. Gopal, Christopher and Cypress, Harold, *Integrated Distribution Management.* Homewood, IL: Business One Irwin, 1993, pp. 109-117.
6. Water, C.D.J., *Inventory Control and Management.* New York: John Wiley & Sons, 1992, pp. 18-21.
7. Horngren, Charles T., Foster, George, and Datar, Srikant, *Cost Accounting: A Managerial Emphasis.* 8th ed., Englewood Cliffs NJ: Prentice-Hall, 1994, pp. 33-34.
8. These definitions have been modified from Horngren, *et al.,* pp 388-189.
9. For more information on these methods see Dudick, Thomas, *Cost Accounting Desk Reference Book.* New York: Van Nostrand Reinhold, 1986, pp. 161-194; Coughlan, Joseph D., "Inventories." In *Handbook of Modern Accounting,* 3rd ed. New York: McGraw-Hill, 1983, pp. 16-23 - 16-37, and Horngren, *et al.,* pp. 606-610, 620.
10. *APICS Dictionary,* 9th ed. Falls Church, VA: American Production and Inventory Control Society, 1998, pp. 21-22.
11. Bowersox, Donald J. and Close, David J., *Logistical Management: The Integrated Supply Chain Process.* New York: McGraw-Hill, 1996, pp. 670-672.
12. Bonsack, Robert A., "Inventory Ratios: Reader Beware," In *Inventory Management Reprints.* Falls Church, VA: American Production and Inventory Control Society, 1986, pp. 92-100.

7
REPLENISHMENT INVENTORY PLANNING

The final step in the inventory control planning process outlined in Chapter 6 is the selection of the inventory ordering policies that are to guide in determining what products need to be ordered, when orders should be released, and what should be the order quantity. In selecting the proper ordering method, inventory management has the choice of using two basic techniques: some form of *statistical inventory replenishment* or *time-phased order point* (TPOP). The decision to use one or a combination of these techniques is based on a number of factors, such as the nature of customer demand, mechanics of the inventory control system employed, characteristics of the products to be ordered, existence of a distribution channel, availability and type of enterprise business system possessed by the firm, and how easily information can be transmitted to and from supply chain trading partners. Determining the proper replenishment techniques is one of a company's most important tasks, requiring a firm understanding and application knowledge of both general inventory concepts and detailed mathematical models and formulas.

This chapter details the concepts and elements of statistical inventory replenishment. Inventory planners have a wide spectrum of replenishment techniques available. The first section in the chapter details the contents of these techniques. From simple heuristic methods, such as visual and period review, to sophisticated computerized applications, such as *Distribution Requirements Planning* (DRP) and supply chain optimization, each technique can be used effectively, given the proper inventory environment. Following the general overview, the chapter proceeds to a detailed discussion of statistical inventory replenishment, and an in-depth exploration of order point and order quantity methods. Particular attention is paid to illustrating the relevant mathematical formulas and their proper application. Once the basics of statistical inventory control have been reviewed, the chapter goes on to outline the inventory planning process linking the inventory plan to the purchasing and value-added processing execution functions to be covered in Chapter 10. The chapter concludes with an analysis of inventory planning in a supply chain environment. Topics include deploying inventory in the supply channel, reviewing the mechanics of *push* and *pull* channel inventory management systems, and correcting channel inventory imbalances. This chapter sets the stage for the discussion of DRP and supply chain optimization, planning, and event management computerized techniques found in Chapter 8.

INVENTORY PLANNING TECHNIQUES

Inventory represents perhaps the single largest investment made by the typical company. Effectively managing this huge investment enables firms to pursue targeted customer service levels and corporate profitability objectives and to utilize the capabilities and capacities of the enterprise to attain and sustain competitive advantage. Fundamental to leveraging inventory is determining when procurement orders are to be released and what the order quantity should be. Selecting the proper ordering technique is the primary responsibility of inventory management who must facilitate the actualization of business objectives while executing inventory planning and control functions designed to achieve least total cost and high serviceability for inventory, transportation, warehousing, and staffing.

UNDERSTANDING INVENTORY DEMAND

Before a planning method can be selected, inventory planners must determine the *nature* of item demand. According to Orlicky [1], the nature (or source) of item demand provides the key to inventory ordering technique selection and applicability. The principle guiding inventory management can be found in the concept of *independent* versus *dependent demand.* Demand for a given item is independent when such demand is unrelated to demand for other items. The source of independent item demand comes from direct orders arising from customer and interbranch requirements. For the most part, demand for products in the distribution environment can be described as *independent* demand. Inventory is usually received as a finished product from the manufacturer, warehoused, and then sold directly to the customer. The prime characteristics of independent demand are the following:

- Demand for these items is independent of company inventory decisions
- Demand for these items is subject to a level of random variation
- These items are usually planned and managed without reference to other items
- Planning for these items usually involves the use of forecasting techniques designed to foretell future demand based on past historical usage
- These items are best planned with some form of safety or reserve stock to counterbalance forecast error
- The critical question for inventory availability is one of *quantity* rather than *timing*

Conversely, an item is subject to *dependent demand* when it is directly related to, or derived from, demand for another part. Item dependencies can be described as *vertical*, such as when a component is required to build a subassembly or finished product, or *horizontal*, as in the case of an accessory that must accompany the product. Dependent demand is characteristic of production inventories in a typical manufacturing company. Manufacturers will purchase raw materials, components, or subassemblies that are never sold as received but are stocked and then issued in matched sets to build the finished products the firm does sell. This demand can be conceived as being created internally as a function of scheduling items to be converted into higher-level assemblies and finished products. Dependent items can be described as follows:

- Dependent items are always planned and managed in relation to other items as detailed in the Bills of Material in which they are specified

- Replenishment quantities for production inventories can be precisely determined by referencing the source of the demand
- Future demand for production inventories should never be forecasted
- Management inventory planning decisions directly impact the demand for these items
- Dependent demand items rarely use safety or reserve stocks
- The critical question for inventory availability is one of *timing* rather than *quantity*

In some cases, a given raw material item, component, or subassembly can be subject to *both* independent as well as dependent demand. Dual demand can exist for components sold separately in spare-part service. Figure 7.1 provides a simple example of a Bill of Material structure containing items subject to *both* independent and dependent demand. In such cases, the portion of the demand on the item that is subject to independent demand must be planned by using some form of forecast. This forecasted demand is then added to the item's calculated dependent demand to provide the total demand.

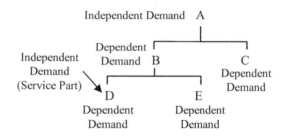

FIGURE 7.1 Independent versus dependent demand.

Determination of item demand status is the first step in selecting the appropriate inventory planning technique. Independent demand items are best planned using ordering methods that utilize forecasts to project demand into future periods. Such techniques plan products based on individual item demand *magnitude* without reference to other items. Dependent demand items, on the other hand, are best planned using time-phased inventory planning techniques (like *Material Requirements Planning* (MRP)) that link items together so that matched sets of components can be ordered together and in the proper quantities as specified in the product structures to which they belong.

INVENTORY ORDERING TECHNIQUES

In a business environment where the demand is constant and goods arrive in small lots just as they are needed to satisfy customer requirements, companies can function with little or almost no stocked inventories. In most environments, however, neither of these two constants are possible. The small quantity of *cycle stock* that would be available could not guarantee that adequate stock would always be on hand to satisfy customer demand. Inventory planners, therefore, must use replenishment techniques that provide sufficient coverage of demand requirements while constantly searching for methods to reduce carrying costs. There are many types of systems for planning and controlling inventories. Some are very simple techniques that utilize rule-of-thumb heuristics. Other systems require complex mathematical and computerized models. Regardless of their sophistication, all ordering techniques attempt to answer the following fundamental questions:

- What is the demand?
- What is currently available?
- What is on order?
- What will need to be ordered?
- When will orders need to be released?
- How much should be ordered?

How a firm seeks to answer these questions is critical in selecting the proper inventory management method. Replenishment decision models for products subject to independent demand can take many forms, but they are all related to one of the following:

Visual Review System. This method consists of a relatively simple inventory control technique in which replenishment is determined by physically reviewing the quantity of inventory on hand. If replenishment is required, a target quantity is ordered that restores balances to a preestablished stocking level. Replenishment levels are determined by such simple decision rules as reorder when the bin is half-full, or when there are two pallets of stock remaining. Visual review systems can be used effectively for very low-volume or low-cost items with short lead times and for controlling floor stocks located near the point of use. The prime advantages of this system are that the cost for record keeping and the training level for employees are minimal. The disadvantages are that there is no way to ensure items are being reviewed on a timely basis, random storage may make it difficult to view all of the stocked inventory on a given item, and reordering rules are rarely updated to reflect changes in current demand, supply, and lead-time patterns resulting in either overstocks or shortages.

Two-Bin System. Classically, this technique is a fixed order system in which inventory is carried in two bins (or some other form of container), one of which is located in the picking area and the other is held in reserve in a non-picking location in the stockroom. Procedurally, when the picking bin is emptied, the reserve bin is brought forward to service demand. The empty bin serves as the trigger for replenishment. The quantity required per bin is calculated as the minimum stock necessary to service demand while waiting for the arrival of the replenishment stock from the supplier. When the purchased quantity arrives, it is placed in the empty bin and stocked in a non-picking location until the picking bin's inventory is depleted. The advantages of a two-bin system are ease of record keeping and physical control. The disadvantages are the system requires procedural training and discipline. In addition, bin quantities are rarely adjusted properly to keep pace with changing demand patterns.

Visual review and two-bin systems are widely used for inventory control. These techniques are easy to understand and implement and cost very little to operate. Because they are so easy to use, however, they can be abused and misapplied. The following points must be taken into consideration when using these two techniques:

- They are best used for very low-cost, bulk or low-volume items whose replenishment lead times are short. Items using these methods for the most part would be classified as C items in an ABC Classification distribution.

- These techniques require carrying relatively high levels of inventory on low-value items. Because stocking levels are not tied directly to customer demand, these two methods will result in needlessly high levels of inventory.

- These techniques are insensitive to changes in demand patterns. Both methods require that a specific order quantity be established. For the most part, the quantity determined is made using demand characteristics of the inventory at the time the decision rule is calculated. Rarely are these quantities adjusted to reflect actual demand through time.

- The advantage of using these techniques is discounted if the time and money saved is not used to establish tighter controls over high-value, high-volume items.

- The use of visual controls is usually associated with loose transaction control, whereas perpetual record keeping is associated with tight controls over inventory. Neither is necessarily true. The key to selecting an inventory ordering technique is to match the level of cost control required with the inventory value of each stock item. As an example, because of its very high usage, a low-cost item, such as a fastener, may be classified as an A item. Using a visual control technique would be the appropriate choice for this item because it would ensure required availability while eliminating needless record-keeping costs.

- For those companies involved in manufacture or value-added processing, the assembly of a finished good item requires the availability of Class C as well as Class A items. Poorly controlled C items will result in item shortages, preventing the completion of manufactured products. The basic rule for managing low-cost items using a two-bin system is to "have plenty on-hand".

Periodic Review. In this ordering system, a *fixed review cycle* is established for each product, and replenishment orders are generated at the conclusion of the review to meet a predetermined max stock level. The review cycle can be established in days, weeks, months, or quarters, whichever best satisfies the demand requirements. This method is also called a *fixed-cycle/variable-order quantity system.* There are several advantages to using this method. It does not require perpetual inventory record keeping and is inexpensive to use. The system, also, can be maintained manually without the use of a computer. Periodic review is best used to control large inventories characterized by many small issues, such as occurs in a grocery store or an automotive small parts service business.

Order Point. In this ordering system, a targeted stocked quantity is determined that is used as the order point. When the inventory position falls below this stocking point, reorder action must be taken to replenish quantities back above the order point. The quantity to order can be manually determined, or some form of *economic order quantity* (EOQ) can be used. This method is also called a *fixed-order quantity/variable-cycle system.* Unlike visual review, two-bin, and periodic review methods, the order point technique requires close perpetual inventory transaction control. As receipts, adjustments, scrap, shipments, transfers, and so on occur, the inventory control function must perform record keeping activities that enable planners to determine whether resulting balances have fallen below the assigned stock trigger levels and warrant replenishment action.

Time Phased Order Point (TPOP). Whereas the replenishment review and action mechanisms of the four methods discussed above are different, conceptually they are all closely related. Each attempts to establish the point *when* a replenishment order needs to be generated to prevent stockout in the face of normal demand and then to suggest an economic or target order quantity to be purchased. In contrast to these systems, TPOP is a computerized management tool that plans inventory needs in a priority-sequenced, time-phased manner to meet customer and forecast demand as it occurs. This technique is at the heart of MRP and DRP systems used for the control of manufacturing and distribution channel inventories. The major advantage of the

TPOP method is that inventory order action is triggered by matching supply with anticipated demand as it occurs in time. At the point where demand exceeds the supply, the system will alert the inventory planner to order the item according to a predetermined lot size and to have it available at the anticipated date on which stockout will occur. In addition, each time the TPOP is generated, the system will resequence demand and supply relationships and suggest a new set of required order actions for the order planner. This method will be reviewed in detail in Chapter 8.

Just-In-Time (JIT). During the past decade, the use of JIT techniques to run supply chain inventories has been growing. Although the technique originated on the manufacturing floor as a way to eliminate waste in the production process, supply chain planners have found that JIT offers them an approach targeted at eliminating waste in such logistics system functions as transportation, warehousing, and quality control. In addition, JIT provides supply channels with new opportunities for inventory control, purchasing management, and buyer-supplier relationships. JIT techniques can be found in the use of such tools as *Kanban* cards to trigger inventory replenishment and the development and execution of purchasing contracts that ensure product quality and delivery.

Supply Chain Optimization. Increasingly, inventory management in the twenty-first century will require planning systems that enable the optimization of inventory, not just within an individual company, but within entire supply chains. As product life cycles continue to shrink and global sourcing, spurred on by the Internet, expands, it will be the ability of whole supply chains to rapidly and efficiently move product through the supply channel network that will determine market leadership. Based on TPOP application logic and JIT principles, a new breed of inventory control system termed *supply chain planning* (SCP) has begun to supplant the primacy of former methods of inventory management that were restricted to the four walls of the enterprise. Utilizing sets of optimization rules and driven by individual company MRP/DRP business applications, these supply management systems encompass a variety of critical functions including demand planning, supply planning, strategic network optimization, fulfillment scheduling, and collaborative forecast and replenishment management. The goal of the whole process is to utilize optimization formulas to determine the best possible distribution of inventories across the supply channel that meets criteria for the lowest total cost while responding to forecasted and actual demand. These advanced SCM toolsets will be reviewed in detail in Chapter 8.

Each of these inventory ordering techniques can be used effectively by supply chain planners for stock replenishment. In fact, all of the techniques address the ordering needs of products that are subject to fairly continuous and *independent demand,* such as finished goods and service parts inventories. With the exception of TPOP and JIT, these techniques are not intended for component and subassembly items where demand is subject to lot sizes and is *dependent* on higher-level assemblies. In choosing one or a combination of these techniques, channel planners need to examine such elements as the level of planning and control desired, item cost, item physical characteristics, resupply lead time, continuousness of demand, dollar-value usage, storage and handling requirements, shipping characteristics, and the availability of data processing systems.

INVENTORY REPLENISHMENT TECHNIQUES – AN OVERVIEW

Before the mechanics of the various forms of statistical inventory replenishment are explored in detail, it is useful is describe the scope and elements common to the available methods.

CONCEPT OF STOCK REPLENISHMENT

Of the inventory planning techniques described above, visual review, two-bin system, periodic review, and order point are defined as belonging broadly to the concept of stock replenishment. The theory behind stock replenishment is that for each item, an optimal stocking and ordering quantity can be determined either statistically or through some form of validated heuristic. *Replenishment* means to become full again; to restore to a state of original fullness. Simplistically, the object of stock replenishment techniques is to ensure that the optimum stocking level for each item is maintained at a targeted service level. Stock replenishment techniques are structured to compensate for the inability of planners to determine the precise timing and quantity of demand in the short-term future. As it is often difficult to calculate exactly when a customer order will arrive, planners using replenishment techniques must project the anticipated demand and always have sufficient on-hand stock to satisfy the customer orders that do materialize. Incorrectly determined inventory levels or failure to resupply on a timely basis risks item stockout.

When viewed from the standpoint of planning, inventory balances can be said to consist of two functions. The first function, termed *cycle* or *working stock,* can be described as inventory that provides the firm with the ability to respond to the average level of customer demand occurring during the period between replenishment order release and receipt. The second function of inventory, termed *safety* or *buffer stock,* is to provide additional inventory that is added to cycle stock in the event of variance in the normal distribution of demand. The critical factor is determining when resupply order action should occur to preserve the integrity of inventory serviceability.

The triggering mechanism that alerts planners to that a stockout is eminent is some form of order point. Whether it is derived using a mathematical model or rule of thumb, the order point provides the planner with a message to order that must be acted on to avoid a stockout. Order points attempt to estimate demand during the replenishment lead time, to which is added a calculated safety stock to compensate for possible fluctuation in demand.

Once the order point has been tripped, an appropriate stock replenishment order needs to be created. The calculation of the exact quantity to order has historically been a hotly debated topic. Whether it be a simple or complex ordering technique, each attempts to strike a balance between the cost of ordering and the cost of stocking inventory. The more an item is ordered, the less the stocking cost but the greater the overall cost of ordering. Conversely, the less an item is ordered, the less the ordering cost, but the greater the stocking cost. Choosing a replenishment technique is, therefore, more than selecting the appropriate models; it is also a strategic decision to choose an inventory planning concept that requires planners to structure customer service and inventory control around how costs are to be accumulated.

Visually, the inventory replenishment concept can be illustrated through the use of a saw tooth chart (Figure 7.2). The chart illustrates for a given

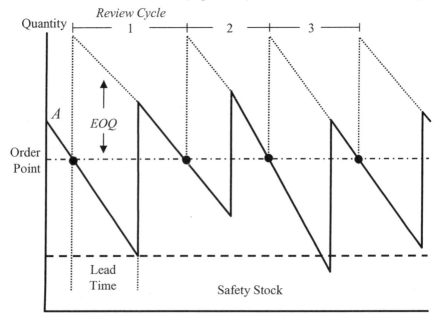

FIGURE 7.2 Basic order point model.

product the relationship of the critical replenishment elements such as safety stock, stocked balance, order point, and order quantity. Mechanically, the model functions as such. At a given moment in time, the quantity of the product in inventory is indicated by A. At this point, the quantity is sufficiently large enough to satisfy the normal anticipated demand through time. As customer orders consume inventory, the stocked quantity is reduced, as shown by the downward-sloping line. When the inventory reaches the predetermined order point, the system alerts the inventory planner to release a replenishment order that will restore the stock level to some point above the order point. The remaining inventory continues to be consumed by customer demand during the replenishment lead time until the supply order is received. Because in real situations it is extremely difficult to calculate with a great degree of precision customer demand, the replenishment technique is best used with some form of reserve or safety stock. Whether or not this inventory is actually consumed depends on random variations in the pattern of demand and supply. In the first two replenishment cycles as shown in Figure 7.2 the safety stock was not impacted by demand. In the third cycle, however, demand drove available inventory below the safety stock level, and safety stock was consumed. Once the replenishment order is received, it is added to the remaining quantity, and the replenishment cycle begins once again.

In using stock replenishment techniques the following principles should be understood:

1. The basic components of the method (order points, replenishment quantities, lead times, and safety stock) are fixed, do not reflect short-term variations, and need to be recalculated and reimplemented to match the changing dynamics of demand and supply.
2. Exactly when an item will trip its order point is unknown until the actual moment it occurs.
3. The size of the replenishment order quantity usually corresponds to some calculation that balances the cost of ordering and the cost of stocking a given item.
4. With the exception of the fixed order review technique, the interval between replenishment ordering is variable. The higher the usage, the shorter the order interval, and vice versa.
5. The reserve or safety stock inventory is considered to be on-hand at all times to guard against demand and supply variation.
6. Statistically, the inventory balance of a given item will be equal to one-half the order point quantity plus the required safety stock [2].

REPLENISHMENT REVIEW INTERVAL

One of the fundamental decisions that must be made when using inventory replenishment techniques is determining when an item's inventory position should be reviewed. The inventory review interval can be viewed from two perspectives. As described above, replenishment models can be described as subject to *continuous* (variable-cycle/fixed-order quantity) or *periodic* (fixed-cycle/variable-order quantity) review. If demand is constant, these two models will produce similar results. Differences occur when demand is uncertain.

Replenishment techniques utilizing a continuous review cycle correspond closely to the example illustrated in Figure 7.2. Order points and variants like min/max are examples of replenishment systems that require continuous review to function properly. When using these techniques, planners continuously record inventory transactions that either add or subtract item quantities from on-hand stock. Each item's quantity level must be examined after each transaction and matched against the item's established order point. Order replenishment action occurs at the unplanned occasion when the order point is tripped. Exactly when the order point will be triggered is, therefore, a variable based on actual demand. Continuous review systems do not necessarily need a computer system to function. Manual perpetual inventory systems such as "Kardex" or "VISI-Record" have, for years, been used successfully to control and replenish inventories (Figure 7.3). The availability of affordable

Part Number: A100-021			Description: ½ hp Sump Pump			
Min Inv: 100		Order Point: 100		Order Quantity: 250		
Unit Price: 10.03		Lead Time: 5 days		Notes: Boxed Unit		
Date	PO Number	Quantity Ordered	Quantity Received	Order Number	Quantity Issued	Balance Quantity
011303						95
011703	12356	250	250			345
012003				4985	35	310
012203				4993	56	254

FIGURE 7.3 Kardex card.

computers and software, however, have all but made manual methods obsolete. Tools such as bar code readers and wireless scanners are pushing inventory accuracy and timeliness of reporting to new dimensions necessary to profitably manage the inventory systems of the twenty-first century.

The mechanics of a periodic review system, on the other hand, are very different from continuous review. There are two critical components of periodic review that need to be established by inventory planners on an item-by-item basis: an *order-up-to* inventory level and a *fixed review interval*. As the review interval date for each item arrives, inventory planners will order for each item under review sufficient quantities to raise the inventory position to the order-up-to point. During the period in between order intervals, inventory stocking level records are not reviewed, resulting in considerable uncertainty as to the actual inventory balance. Sufficient inventories are assumed to have been ordered at the time of the previous review to last until the next interval without stockout.

The use of continuous and periodic review systems pose several distinct advantages and disadvantages as illustrated in Table 7.1. The most obvious

TABLE 7.1: Continuous Versus Period Review Systems

Issue	Continuous	Periodic
Maintenance expense		X
Ordering by item family		X
Lower inventory investment	X	
Replenishment predictability		X
Overall control	X	
Fast moving items	X	
Slow moving items		X
Higher customer service	X	
Computerization	X	
Lower purchasing costs		X

distinction between the two systems is operational expense. Continuous review requires significant manpower and computerized resources to analyze and keep inventory balance records accurate. A periodic review system, on the other hand, does not need ongoing transaction control and requires item review only when the order interval occurs. Whereas continuous review systems permit greater overall inventory and item cost control, periodic systems provide planners with replenishment predictability. Because the review cycle is fixed, inventory management can plan resources and budgets for inventory review at minimum cost. In regard to item control, continuous review is best used to control fast-moving products, whereas periodic review is best used for slow-moving items and for products ordered together in product families. Finally, continuous review systems provide for higher levels of customer serviceability by providing timely on-hand balance status and safety stock protection against random variation in demand. The choice of continuous or period review systems depends on several factors such as customer satisfaction strategies, product cost, storage and transportation, and the availability of information systems and support staffs.

DEFINING THE ORDER POINT

This section is concerned with the anatomy of the order point technique. Order points attempt to answer two key questions:
1. When should the inventory balance of a given product be reviewed for possible replenishment action?
2. When should a stock replenishment order be released?
In answering these two questions, several possible techniques can be used. During the course of the section to follow, the most commonly used methods and their calculation components will be discussed.

DEFINING INVENTORY REPLENISHMENT TERMS

Although Figure 7.2 illustrates the basic mechanics of the inventory replenishment model, it may be useful at this juncture to define in detail each of the components of the model.
- *On-hand inventory.* This is the quantity that the perpetual inventory system shows as being *physically* in stock regardless of open orders and allocations. This value should never be negative. The on-hand inventory is the starting point for the replenishment calculation.
- *Available inventory.* The available inventory value is calculated by subtracting from on-hand inventory all order demand quantities, whether allocated or unallocated. The balance remaining is the quantity available to immediately satisfy new customer demands. This value can be negative if open customer orders exceed on-hand inventory.
- *Inventory position.* This quantity is a *logical* value that is determined for a given item by subtracting the inventory requirements generated by open customer and interbranch transfer orders, allocated (committed), and backorders from the total on-hand stock and expected on-order inventory. Determination of this value is one of the fundamental elements of the inventory replenishment calculation.
- *On-order inventory.* On-order inventory is replenishment stock that has been ordered but has not yet been received. Although the inventory position calculation considers on-order inventory as if it were on-hand,

this stock should not be allocated to open customer orders or existing backorders within the replenishment lead time.

- *Safety stock.* This is a quantity of inventory added to the calculated inventory balance to support unplanned variances in demand during the replenishment cycle. If available inventory was planned to be at zero just as the replenishment order is received, then the safety stock would be set to zero. Safety stock provides a buffer guarding against possible stockout caused by variations in demand and supply. Calculating the size of a safety stock value is normally dependent on the desired level of customer serviceability without incurring a stockout.

REORDER POINT BASICS

The replenishment order point (OP) is classically expressed by the following formula:

$$OP = \text{Anticipated demand during lead time} + \text{Safety stock.}$$

For example, if the average historical usage (sales) for a given item is 100 units a week, the replenishment lead time from the supplier is 2 weeks, and the safety stock is 50,

then:

$$OP = 100 \text{ (usage)} \times 2 \text{ (weeks)} + 50 \text{ (safety stock)} = 250 \text{ units.}$$

In other words, the order point consists of sufficient inventory to satisfy projected customer demand (*usage*) while waiting for stock replenishment orders to arrive (*lead time*), plus a quantity of reserve inventory (*safety stock*) to account for variation in supply and demand. Before proceeding further, it is important to review in detail each of the elements of the order point calculation.

Item Usage. Of the elements of the order point formula, calculation of usage is perhaps the most important. *Usage* can be defined as the quantity consumed by demand for a designated period of time. Demand originates from a number of sources. It can come from actual customer orders, interbranch resupply requirements originating from satellite warehouses in the distribution network, production processing, and internal company needs. In calculating order point usage, planners must first be certain that all demand transactions are posted. Inventory history is recorded for all types of transactions from receipts and adjustments to transfers and scrap. In compiling historical usage used in the order point calculation, only valid demand should be considered. Customer orders, for example, are always considered as historical usage.

On the other hand, transactions created by interplant transfers and inventory expended for internal use, such as assembly, kits, and so on, need to be closely examined before being counted as order point usage. Normally, transactions generated by interplant transfers from the manufacturing plant or the central ordering warehouse to satellite warehouses should be considered as valid order point usage. In this case, the satellite warehouse should be considered as an *internal customer* whose requirements are as important as the supplying warehouse's external customers. When, however, a satellite warehouse transfers goods to another satellite warehouse, the transactions should *not* be considered as order point usage. The reason for this is simple. When the collective demand for both warehouses is calculated and orders placed on the supplying warehouse, the demand will be overstated by the satellite-to-satellite warehouse transfers. Replenishment inventory planning in a supply chain environment will be further discussed later in this chapter. Finally, all forms of internal usage, that is, for components consumed in the production pro-cess, should *never* be included as part of order point usage. Such items, in fact, are really subject to dependent demand and are best planned through the use of *Material Requirements Planning* (MRP).

Accurately estimating usage is a critical part of the replenishment system. According to Graham [3], calculating usage has three requirements:

1. Usage must be developed for each inventory product independently.
2. Usage must be expressed as a specific number of units.
3. Usage must be related to a defined time period.

All three of these requirements rest on a simple assumption: *The actual demand for inventory that occurred in the immediate past will most likely be repeated in the immediate future.* In other words, if sales for the past 6 months of a given product averaged 225 a month, then it can be safely assumed that sales for the next month will also average the same amount.

Obviously, even though this assumption must be used with caution. When demand for a given product during replenishment lead time is, indeed, *level* or *deterministic*, inventory planners can safely assume that future demand will be similar to the past. In reality, planners can rarely count on products having such predictable and constant demand. As a result, order points are best planned by determining the past demand usage combined with either historical or forecasted estimates of the fluctuations around that expected usage. Adding additional inventory to meet the expected deviation from a product's historical demand will permit planners to avoid possible stockout.

Often inventory planners will observe upward or downward trends in demand for a given product through time. Although the calculation of a new usage average, say on a monthly basis, will adjust the current usage to accommodate trend variations in the past usage average, the new value will lag behind actual demand. A simple calculation that adjusts expected usage during lead time for trend is expressed as:

New order point usage = (Expected usage demand) x (Lead time).

Calculating a *trend percentage* to be factored against the current usage is the key to the formula. Determining the *expected usage demand* involves a three-step process. In the first step, the current trend must be computed as exhibited by

Current trend = New usage average - Old average.

In order to eliminate random variations in the demand, the current trend needs to be smoothed by using

New trend = α (current trend) + (1 - α) (old trend).

Once the correction for trend lag has been determined, the new expected order point usage can be computed as

$$\text{New order point usage} = \text{New average} + \frac{1 - a}{a} \text{(new trend)}.$$

The result of these calculations will permit the planner to determine expected usage based on actual versus estimated trends occurring through time. Periodically, the usage for all products would have to be updated so that valid order points could be recalculated.

In addition to products exhibiting trend usage, inventory planners are often required to calculate usage for items exhibiting random demand patterns. Random demand means that values of demand examined at selected points through time exhibit little or no correlation with past values. The best way to calculate random demand usage is to use as much historical data as possible to arrive at the new expected usage. The formula is

New average = α (current demand) + (1 - α) (old average).

Finally, many companies have inventory subject to cyclical or seasonality patterns. As time passes, demand usage for such products rises and declines according to regularly expected cycles. Planning such products involves two calculations. The first seeks to arrive at a ratio of the current month's demand and the previous period demand, and then computing the new order point by comparing the ratio with the demand in a corresponding period the previous year or several previous years. This ratio is expressed as

$$\text{Demand ratio} = \frac{\text{Demand in the current month}}{\text{Value of the base series for the previous month}}$$

For example, if the demand at the end of February of a given year was 100 and the base series for January was 95, the demand ratio would be 1.05. If a given item had a three month lead time, determining the new order point at the beginning of March this year would be calculated based on the base series of the demand from the same 3 months (March, April, and May) occurring last year. If the base series for these months were respectively 110, 125, and 130, the expected demand during the lead time would be

$$110 + 125 + 130 = 365,$$
$$\text{Demand during lead time} = 365\,(1.05) = 383.25.$$

The variations in demand usage detailed above all represent various methods of calculating maximum reasonable demand during replenishment lead time. Selecting the appropriate formula for each stocked product is a time-consuming affair that must bear the proof of correlation to actual demand through time. The most appropriate test is to simulate each before one is finally selected. Usually, the choice comes down to either a technique that focuses on inventory cost or on customer service. In the final analysis, the choice depends on the strategic inventory objectives of the firm [4].

Lead Time. While not as complex a concept as demand usage, the identification of lead-time values necessary for the order point calculation can be a slippery affair. Lead time can be defined as:

> the total amount of time that spans the period beginning from the date an inventory replenishment order is identified until the date the stock is received, located, recorded in the inventory control system, and available for sale.

As is emphasized above, valid lead times provide the buyer with the *total* time it will take to identify, order, and have inventory ready for sale. The elements of distribution lead time are the following:

- *Replenishment order action identification.* The time it takes for the inventory planner to review and select products for replenishment order action. Time elements at this stage are composed of such activities as visually reviewing stock levels or analyzing an order point status report.

- *Order preparation.* Once products to be ordered have been identified, time must be allocated for such order preparation actions as purchase order entry or grouping product lines to meet supplier discount requirements. Another important element at this stage is the time it takes to search and select the proper supplier, as well as any pricing or transportation negotiation that must transpire.
- *Order transmission.* Purchase orders need to be printed, verified and transmitted to the appropriate supplier. Technology tools, such as EDI and the Internet, have significantly reduced the time required for order transmission almost to a matter of moments.
- *Supplier processing time.* This is the total time required for the supplier to process the order, pick and pack it, and transport it to the customer.
- *Receiving.* Once the replenishment order arrives, time is spent in such activities as receiving and checking, quality control, and staging.
- *Item restocking.* This final element of lead time is composed of receipt movement, put-away, and any final information recording. Once the receipt quantity has been recorded as being available for customer shipment, the product's lead-time cycle can be considered as being completed.

Lead times are notorious for being approximations or estimates rather than a precise value that inventory planners can consider as fixed constants. When determining lead times exhibiting variability, several techniques can be used. In one method, planners could designate a lead time for a product long enough to include all reasonable resupply timing occurrences. Another technique is to average the actual recorded lead times and use that value, or a smoothed value, as the valid lead time for the next order. In today's fast past environments, approximations and rule-of-thumb techniques are falling into disfavor. Customer service strategies are not only demanding firm lead times but also process improvement programs aimed at continuously shortening every step in the fulfillment process.

Safety Stock. If a company had a totally captive marketplace where customer demand was deterministic, historical usage during lead time could be calculated accurately with a great deal of certainty. In such an environment, safety stock would be unnecessary. Supply orders would arrive just in time to replenish stock to meet new demand. In reality, demand usage is subject to uncertainties. A wide variety of factors, such as prevailing economic conditions, cycles in popular taste, government regulation, technology, and changes in customer buying habits, transit times, order processing times, and production schedules, can cause wide variances in demand. In addition, uncertainties caused by variations in supplier lead times and delivery quantity and quality can expose the firm to potential stockout. Of these elements, variances in demand and lead time have the most unfavorable impact on statistical planning models.

Table 7.2 provides an example of the average weekly demand for a product for a 10 week time period. Lead time is 1 week, and demand has normally averaged around 1000 units per week. The order point calculation would place the order point for this product at 1000 units (1 week lead time x 1000 average usage = 1000 units). Actual customer orders for the item during the past 10 weeks, however, have ranged from as small as 550 units to as large as 1425 units a week. Whereas it is true the 1000 unit order point satisfies the average demand, there were occasions when actual orders exceeded the available inventory and the item was stocked out. In fact, 4 out of the 10 weeks experienced demand that exceeded the average inventory. In order to protect against stockout, the order point could be augmented with an additional safety stock quantity of 425 units. Historically this inventory buffer should then prevent a future stockout from occurring. However, by stocking the max quantity the firm would incur excess inventory carrying costs during the 6 weeks when demand was either at or below the weekly average.

TABLE 7.2 Instance of Item Demand

Week	Quantity	Average	Deviation
1	550	1000	450
2	1350	1000	-350
3	1175	1000	-175
4	1000	1000	---
5	750	1000	250
6	1425	1000	-425
7	675	1000	325
8	1000	1000	---
9	1300	1000	-300
10	875	1000	125
		Absolute deviation	2400

In calculating safety stocks, inventory planners must decide on just how much of an inventory buffer is to be kept on-hand. A firm, obviously, could not possibly carry inventory to cover all probable levels of demand for all the products stocked. If demand is lower than the expected demand, the firm can expect high customer service levels but accompanying high inventory stocking costs. Conversely, if demand is higher than expected, inventory carrying costs will drop, but so will customer service.

There are several methods of determining just how much safety stock should be kept. Traditionally, inventory planners have used a number of rules of thumb for determining safety stock quantities. One method is to keep a month's supply as reserve. Graham recommends that 50 percent of the usage times the lead time be used as safety stock [5]. Another popular method is to determine safety stock based on safety days or a safety percent. The formula for the first is expressed as: number of safety stock days times the daily average demand. The second formula is stated as: safety stock percent times lead time times the daily average demand. Regardless of the technique, determination of the safety days or percent variable is based on a management decision. A negative to these approaches is that while the management policy variable may be set high enough to give acceptable service to products with a high standard deviation, unfortunately there will also be considerable wasted safety stock on products whose usage patterns permit the application of more precise forecasts.

More sophisticated models of safety stock calculation attempt to determine safety stock by utilizing the standard deviation of forecast errors. Basically, the calculation utilizes a management policy regarding a desired serviceability percent that is matched to a table of standard deviations of forecast error (usually between zero and three) times the square root of replenishment lead time. The first step in calculating safety stock is computing the *normal distribution* of demand. Statistically, the instances of demand tend to cluster around the average demand and are measured by the deviation from the mean. The assumption of *normality* makes it possible to establish a direct relationship between the extent to which demand deviates from the mean and the probability of a stockout occurring. Figure 7.4 illustrates this concept using the

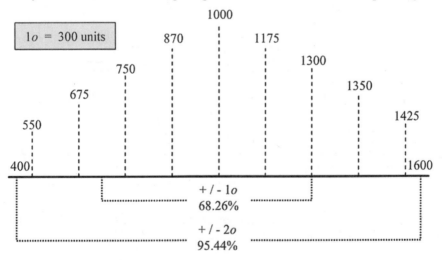

Figure 7.4. The normal distribution.

demand history for the product described above. The key mathematical component in working with normal distribution is the application of the *standard
deviation* (σ, or sigma) from the mean. Statistically, one standard deviation
(or 1σ) accounts for +/- 34.13 percent of the deviation from the mean. A
standard deviation of 2σ would add an additional +/- 13.59 percent, and 3σ
would add +/- 2.15 percent to the mean. Calculation of the actual standard
deviation from the average for the product appearing in Table 7.2 is computed by dividing the absolute deviation by the number of periods to attain the
mean absolute deviation and then multiplying this figure by the *mean absolute deviation safety factor* comparable to the standard deviation as found in
Table 7.3. The calculation using the data from Table 7.2 is as follows:

TABLE 7.3. Table of Safety Factors

Service Level (w/o stockout	Standard Deviation	Mean Absolute Deviation
50%	0.00	0.00
75%	0.67	0.84
80%	0.84	1.05
84.13%	1.00	1.25
85%	1.04	1.30
89.44%	1.25	1.56
90%	1.28	1.60
93.32%	1.50	1.88
94%	1.56	1.95
95%	1.65	2.06
96%	1.75	2.19
97%	1.88	2.35
98%	2.05	2.56
99%	2.33	2.91
99.5%	2.57	3.20
99.6%	2.65	3.31
99.7%	2.75	3.44
99.8%	2.88	3.60
99.9%	3.09	3.85
99.93%	3.20	4.00
99.99%	4.00	5.00

1. Mean absolute deviation (MAD) = Absolute deviation (2400)/10
   weeks = 240.
2. Standard deviation = MAD x 1.25 = 240 x 1.25 = 300.

In other words, 1σ for the part number as illustrated in Figure 7.4 equals +/-
300 units from the mean of 1000.

Once the safety standard deviation has been calculated, it is fairly easy to adjust the order point to attain a targeted service level. When computing the safety stock, planners obviously focus on those periods when demand *exceeded* the order point. According to Figure 7.4, a given product subject to probabilistic demand without safety stock can be expected to provide a 50 percent customer service level over the long run. If the planner calculates a safety stock quantity based on one standard deviation, sufficient inventory will be stocked to cover an additional 34.13 percent or a total of approximately 84 percent of demand during replenishment lead time. For the product detailed in Table 7.2, one standard deviation equals 300 units. When combined with the current average usage of 1000, the new order point would equal 1300 units. If two standard deviations were used in the calculation, the new order point would be around 1600 units, providing a serviceability level of approximately 98 percent. This relation is illustrated in Figure 7.5. In using the MAD safety stock calculation, inventory planners must be careful to ensure that the actual average demand and the historical usage are equal. For example, if the item's demand was consistently above the forecast, the average historical usage element in the order point should be recalculated. The resulting new order point would reduce the amount of deviation during replenishment lead time and, therefore, reduce the amount of safety stock required.

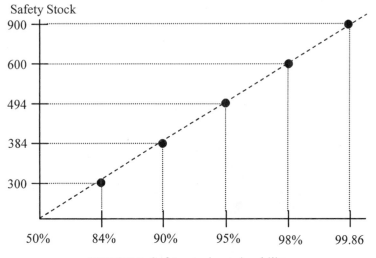

FIGURE 7.5 Safety stock serviceability

Another method of computing safety stocks is possible when the cost of a stockout is known. The objective of the exercise is to find a safety stock that minimizes the total cost of carrying inventory above the order point, as well as the cost of incurring a stockout on an annual basis. The cost of calculating the holding cost is straightforward. If the annual carrying cost of a unit is

$2.50 per year and a safety stock of 20 units was determined, the annual carrying cost of the safety stock quantity would be $50. To compute the cost of a stockout, the expected number of shortages for a given safety stock level is multiplied by the stockout cost by the number of times per year the stockout can occur. Finally, the stockout cost for each safety stock level is combined.

As an example, assume the following for a given product: The order point (demand x lead time) is 100 units, the carrying cost per unit is $2.50, and the stockout cost is $50. The product is ordered monthly. In addition, the product has been experiencing the following demand patterns:

	Number of Units	Probability of Stockout
	80	,2
	90	.2
Order Point	100	.3
	110	.2
	120	.1
		1

Following the above formula, the choice of the proper safety stock would be calculated as such:

Safety Stock	Additional Holding Cost	Stockout Cost	Total Cost
20	(20 units)($2.50) = $50	$0	$100
10	(10 units)($2.50) = $25	(10)(.1)($50)(12) = $600	$625
0	$0	(10)(.1)($50)(12) + (10)(.1)($50)(12) = $1800	$1800

When analyzing the safety stock calculation, planners would choose the safety stock with the lowest total cost. In the above computation, a safety stock of 20 would be chosen. The new order point for the item would therefore be 100 + 20 = 120 units.

The objective of the safety stock computation is to ensure that targeted customer service levels can be achieved. Brown [6] feels that customer service can be measured several different ways. The first is to determine stocking levels in terms of the expected value of demand (usually in dollars) that will be filled from available stock. Another metric is the expected number of occasions when orders must be backordered due to shortages. Finally, still another measurement seeks to establish the expected cost of expediting resupply orders to respond to emergency demand using stock from the best location. Basically, service level is determined as the proportion of occurrences of customer demand satisfied from stock. This measurement can be performed several ways, including the following:
- Percentage of orders completely satisfied from stock
- Percentage of units required filled from stock

- Percentage of units required delivered on time
- Percentage of item stockout
- Percentage of stock cycles without shortages
- Percentage of item-months without stockout

Each of these measurements is calculated against a desired percent of service. Obviously, such a percentage could be used effectively in calculating an order point that would minimize stockouts, assist in the control of inventories, and contribute to overall profitability. A commonly used formula for calculating safety stock based on the extent to which demand varies about the mean and the desired level of safety stock is expressed in the following formula:

$$SS = k\sigma \sqrt{LT}$$

where k is the number of standard deviations above mean demand corresponding to the desired service level, σ is the standard deviation of the level of demand, and LT is the item lead time.

To compute the new order point when safety stock is required the following formula can be used:

$$OP = ULT + k\sigma \sqrt{LT}$$

where U is the usage.

Inventory planners must be careful when calculating safety stocks for a single site versus a multiechelon channel environment. When calculating safety stock for a satellite warehouse in a distribution network, the formula would be based on the standard deviation of the variances in demand occurring in its own usage history. By centralizing safety stock and servicing the channel from a single location, individual satellite warehouse inventory variances in demand can be aggregated. Because the standard deviation does not increase in direct proportion to the aggregated demand, less safety stock would be carried. In a centralized environment, safety stock would grow equivalent to the square root of the number of satellite warehouse in the channel network. The ratio of safety stock in a centralized versus a decentralized channel system can be expressed as

$$SSd / SSc = \sqrt{n}$$

where SSd is the level of safety stock in the decentralized system, SSc is the level of safety stock in the centralized system, and n is the number of warehouses in the decentralized system. The reduction in safety stock resulting from centralization can be calculated by formula:

$$SS = SSd \, [1 - (1 / \sqrt{n})]$$

Because the number of warehouses in the channel is greater than one, a centralized system will always result in less safety stock being carried than in a decentralized system. Mathematically, the amount of safety stock carried in a distribution channel would decline by 68 percent by centralizing the combined safety stock inventories from 10 satellite warehouses into just one national supplying warehouse.

ORDER POINT METHODS

Once the components of statistical replenishment have been determined for each product, inventory planners have the option of selecting from four basic order point techniques. These methods can be divided into two types based on the point when items are reviewed for possible replenishment. Two of the techniques (order point and min/max) are dependent on a *continuous review cycle,* whereas the remaining two (period order quantity and line point) are considered as *periodic review* ordering systems. Later in this chapter, the order quantity techniques used by these order point systems will be discussed.

Statistical Order Point. As detailed above, the order point under conditions of demand uncertainty is determined through the following calculation:

OP = Anticipated demand during lead time + Safety stock.

Visually, the order point system is illustrated in Figure 7.6. When the inventory position for a given item drops below the order point, a fixed replenishment quantity is ordered. Because of the condition of uncertainty of demand, the actual point that the order point is tripped is determined by actual demand occurring through time rather than a fixed cycle as it would be if the demand were certain. Note that the inventory position rather than the net stock is used as the triggering mechanism. The inventory position is the correct quantity because it includes the available inventory plus all on-order inventory. If available inventory only was used, replenishment orders could be placed for stock already ordered, thereby overstating supply.

Statistical order point is best used with independent demand items exhibiting little usage variability. The basis of the method focuses on the simple assumption that future customer demand will closely resemble past demand. The technique requires that inventory planners continually review both historical usage and lead times so that changes in demand caused by trends, seasonality, sales promotions, and general economic conditions can be reflected in the elements of the order point calculation.

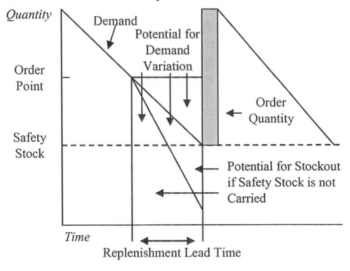

FIGURE 7.6 Order point system.

Minimum/Maximum. This ordering technique requires continuous review and identification of a replenishment order whenever the inventory position drops below the defined minimum order point. In contrast to the fixed order quantity found in the statistical order point, the order quantity in this technique is a variable, sufficient to raise the inventory level to a predetermined maximum quantity. The technique is called a *min/max* system because the inventory position should always be a quantity located between the minimum and maximum stocking values. The minimum quantity can be calculated using the standard order point formula.

Determining the maximum inventory quantity is a function of demand and the optimum replenishment order cost. The max quantity can be calculated for a given item as the order point (minimum) plus the quantity required during the replenishment lead time. When the minimum's quantity is triggered, the order quantity used in the calculation is always a variable because it represents the minimum quantity plus the quantity below the targeted maximum quantity.

Planners often misuse the min/max technique and confuse it with the statistical order point. Min/max should never be used to order from an outside supplier. Statistical order points are equipped to handle the problems caused by variations found in historical usage, lead times, and order quantity unit-cost issues. Min/max, on the other hand, should be used only by satellite warehouses that receive their inventories from a supplying distribution center. Interbranch resupply is not subject to the same variations as supply from a supplier. First of all, the lead time between supply nodes in an internal supply chain network is usually very short with little or no variation. In addition, because lead times are short, the satellite warehouse does not have to order as large a lot as would be necessary if inventory was ordered from a supplier. The calculations for min/max are designed to assist satellite warehouse planners keep inventories within restricted stocking space, avoid stockouts, and maximize inventory turns by setting appropriate upper and lower control limits.

Joint Replenishment. Often inventory planners are faced with the problem of buying products that are sold only in a product group (such as an assortment) in order to take advantage of economies arising from reductions in unit purchase and transportation costs. Literally, when a given product is required, the supplier will only sell it as part of group of related products and the planner will have to purchase the entire family consisting of some products that are not yet ready to be reordered. Joint replenishment poses a unique challenge to the reorder point method. Normally, an individual product is flagged for replenishment when the order point is tripped. But, because all products using statistical replenishment are independent of one another, their order points are usually triggered at different times, making it impossible to group products together for purchasing purposes. In addition, items within product families usually experience very different demand usages, making it even more difficult to link fast-moving items that need to be ordered and slow movers that do not. Often planners will purchase product families regardless of the actual replenishment needs of individual items. The result is that inventory becomes imbalanced, as fast movers stockout waiting for slow movers, and slow movers become overstocked as they are prematurely purchased to prevent stockout of fast-moving items.

The solution to the product line buying problem is the use of an upper control limit above the normal order point. Joint replenishment ordering involves determining a common inventory review time for a given product line and then finding the maximum order point level for each item dictated by its costs and customer service level. Graham [7] feels that a simple set of calculations will solve the line buying problem. The concept behind the *line point* technique is that the upper control limit for the product line can be statistically calculated from demand usage during the review cycle and combined with each associated item's normal order point. The formula for the *line point* is

Line point = Order point + Usage during the review cycle.

At this point, it may be worthwhile to investigate the contents of this formula.

Because of the diverse usage patterns of items within a given product line, they are usually purchased together in fairly regular "cycles." For the most part, inventory planners have developed a *total-order purchasing product line target*, usually expressed in dollars that they use to guide replenishment. This target could be determined by quantity discounts, shipping minimums, order dollar minimums, or other criteria. Once the ordering target has been defined, it is easy to calculate the review cycle by dividing the last 12 months' total dollars purchase for the product line by the purchase target. The following is an example for a product line:

> Last 12 months purchase = $3600
> Dollar value required for vendor discount = $150
> 3600 / $150 = 24 purchases a year (order cycle).

Nonstock items can also be placed in the calculation to assist in qualifying the purchase. For items subject to seasonality, only periods in season are used for the computation and are calculated by using demand data from the same cycle the previous year.

Once the review cycle has been determined, the line point can be calculated for each item within the product line. The formula is a two-part computation where an item's order point is first determined and then combined with the usage quantity during the product line review cycle. An example of the full line point calculation for a given item is as follows:

1. Usage During Review Cycle Quantity:
   a. Average monthly usage = 100 units
   b. Review cycle = 0.5 month
   c. Usage During Review Cycle Quantity =
      100 (monthly usage) / 0.5 month (review cycle) = 50 units.

2. Line point calculation:
   a. Factors: Usage rate =   100 units per month
                Lead time =   1 month
                Safety stock =   50 units
                Review cycle quantity: =   50 units
   b. Order point calculation:
      (100 usage x 1 month) + Safety stock = 150 Units.
   c. Line point calculation:
      150 (OP) + 50 (review cycle quantity) = 200 units.

When the fixed review cycle occurs, all items whose inventory positions are below both their order points and their line points will be ordered. Items above the line point will be excluded. Because replenishment orders are only triggered when they exceed their review cycles, buyers are always assured of the most economic purchase. Obviously, inventory planners must use the line point technique with a great deal of caution. The data elements of the formula must be continually updated at least monthly to prevent time and demand drift. In addition, product lines that have review cycles longer than a month need to be closely examined to prevent excess inventory buildup.

Periodic Review. Often supply chain planners are faced with replenishing products that do not lend themselves to *continuous review* techniques. Usually, these products are characterized by the following conditions:

1. It is difficult to record withdrawals and additions to and from stock on a continuous basis. Process-type products, such as liquids or bulk materials, fall within this category.
2. Items are ordered in product families where economies of scale in order preparation and supplier discounting make it economical to combine items in one order. Fasteners, small tools, and office supplies are products that fit this category.
3. Items that have a limited shelf life. Farm produce, chemicals, and food products are in this class.
4. Significant economies can be gained by ordering full carloads [8].

Such products are managed best by a *periodic review* system. Products utilizing this method are reviewed periodically and replenishment orders are launched for each product at each review. The order quantity contains sufficient stock to bring the inventory position up to a predetermined quantity level.

The periodic review system has often been called the *fixed-cycle technique*. Figure 7.7 presents a visual representation of the mechanics of the technique. Mathematically, the periodic review technique is governed by two formulas: one to determine the optimal order review cycle and the other to determine the target inventory level. The review period can be easily calculated by dividing a product's annually units sold by the EOQ. For example, if the annual usage was 1000 units and the EOQ was 100, then the optimum review period would be 36.5 days [365 / (1,000/100)]. The formula for calculating the inventory target level would be expressed as

$$TI = D(RP + LT) + SS$$
$$\text{and}$$
$$OQ = TI - I,$$

where TI is the target inventory level, LT is the item lead time, D is the demand rate, RP is the review period, SS is the safety stock, and OQ is the order

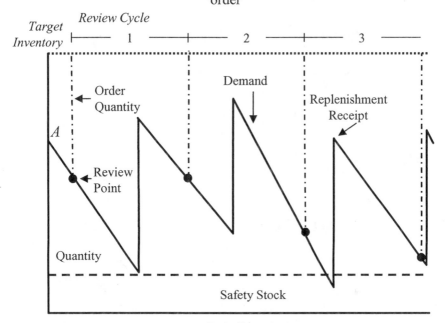

FIGURE 7.7 Periodic review system.

quantity, and I is the inventory position. For example, the normal weekly usage is 1000 units, the review period is every four weeks, the lead time from the supplier is two weeks, and the safety stock is 500 units. Currently, the inventory position stands at 2250 units. Using the above formula, the target inventory level and the order quantity would be calculated as follows:

$$\text{TI} = D(\text{RP} + \text{LT}) + \text{SS}$$
$$1000 \ (4 + 2) + 500 = 6500$$

and

$$\text{OQ} = \text{TI} - I$$
$$6500 - 2250 = 4250 \text{ units.}$$

The inventory planner would release a replenishment order for 4250 units.

Combining Techniques. On occasion, supply chain planners may combine aspects of continuous and periodic review systems to resolve distinct inventory control problems. As an example, for expensive products that experience excessive lead-time variation, planners can use a mixture of order point and periodic review techniques. Procedurally, as inventory is deducted and the order point is tripped, planners will buy up to the maximum quantity. If the order point is not triggered, the planner has the option of replenishing stock up to the target inventory level at cycle review time. The only requirement for the effective use of such a hybrid system is an inventory control mechanism that provides for perpetual inventory control.

Another combination is to use the inverse of the above. An order point and a maximum target inventory level are established, and a perpetual inventory record is kept of each transaction. If the inventory quantity trips the order point *before* the review cycle is reached, a replenishment order is generated restoring the item balance back to the inventory target. If, on the other hand, the quantity is *greater* than the order point at review cycle time, no replenishment order is created even though the inventory position is less than the target maximum.

ORDER QUANTITY TECHNIQUES

The objective of the order point is to provide inventory planners with answers to such questions as "When should the inventory position of a given product be determined?" and "When should a replenishment order be released?" The key question the order point does not answer is, "What quantity should be ordered once the order point has been triggered?" Although it is true that such techniques as periodic review and min/max provide for the replenishment order quantity based on calculating the variance of the inventory position from the target inventory level, companies stock many products that require other methods if inventory is to be replenished effectively and economically. Products subject to lumpy, deterministic, and erratic demand are best controlled by fixed order quantity systems. Those products, however, that have constant but varying demand are best replenished through ordering techniques that seek to balance ordering and stocking costs while maintaining targeted serviceability levels.

In making inventory replenishment ordering decisions, the fundamental responsibility of planners is to constantly seek ways to reduce *relevant costs*. Costs in ordering are, indeed, relevant costs because the size of the replenishment quantity will directly impact the firm's operational costs. There are two critical costs involved in inventory replenishment. The first relates to *purchase order costs*. There are several costs related to the frequency inventory replenishment orders are placed. Some of the costs incurred include the maintenance of the firm's perpetual inventory system and salaries for planners. Other costs are incurred with purchasing activities such as supplier negotiations, purchase order preparation, order transmission, order status tracking, receiving, inspection, and stock put-away.

The second cost area consists of *inventory carrying costs*. The decision to stock inventory commits the firm to costs arising from the size, value, and length of time that inventory is stocked. Capital invested in inventory, taxes, insurance, obsolescence, facilities, and handling are all forms of cost that mount as the level of inventory rises. Other costing issues revolve around *shortage* or *stockout costs* and *incremental costs*. The latter results from decisions to increase inventory quantities that will require the firm to incur costs above normal overhead costs. For example, a decision to increase inventories may require hiring a new purchaser, improving existing inventory control systems, or buying additional material handling equipment.

THE ECONOMIC ORDER QUANTITY

The affect of inventory decisions on costs can be demonstrated by the following example. The annual usage of a given product is 24,000 units. If the standard cost is $0.25 per unit then the annual purchase cost equals $6000. The purchasing manager of the firm has calculated that the cost of researching and launching a purchase order is $20. Finally, the accounting department has established that the cost of carrying inventory is 24%. Based on these data elements, several possible replenishment quantities could be used when a purchase order is created. The problem facing the planner is what should be the optimum quantity used in the order. The *optimum quantity* is defined as the quantity that provides sufficient inventory to satisfy projected demand while minimizing ordering and carrying costs. As illustrated in Table 7.4, if, for example, the item was ordered 12 times a year, the annual cost

TABLE 7.4 EOQ Calculation

Order Quantity	Orders Per Year	Carrying Cost	Reorder Cost	Total Cost
2,000	12	$60	$240	$300
4,000	6	$120	$120	$240
8,000	3	$240	$60	$300
12,000	2	$360	$40	$400
24,000	1	$720	$20	$740

of carrying the resultant inventory would be $60 and the annual cost of ordering the item would be $240, for a total annual cost of $300. The cost of carrying inventory is calculated by multiplying the proposed order quantity, annual carrying cost percent, and the item cost, and then computing the average. The cost of ordering is determined by multiplying the cost of order preparation by the annual usage, divided by the proposed order quantity. The equations are

$$\text{Carrying cost} = (QkUC)/2$$
$$\text{Ordering cost} = (OCR)/Q,$$

where Q is the order quantity, k is the inventory carrying cost percent, UC is the item unit cost, OC is the cost of ordering, and R is the item annual usage. Figure 7.8 attempts to illustrate graphically the calculations found in Table 7.4. In the example above, ordering the item six times a year would provide the optimum replenishment quantity.

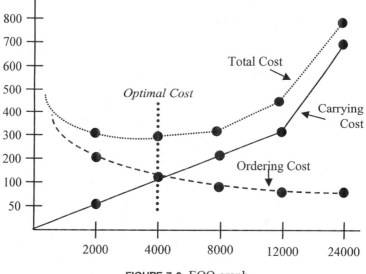

FIGURE 7.8 EOQ graph.

Obviously, to calculate and graph the *economic order quantity* (EOQ) in this manner for a typical firm's inventory is clearly impossible. Fortunately, there is a square root formula that will significantly speed up the process [9]. Using the data elements in Table 7.4, the EOQ calculation can be performed as follows:

$$\text{EOQ} = \sqrt{\frac{2 \times \text{Cost of ordering (OC)} \times \text{Usage (R)}}{\text{Carrying cost }(k) \times \text{Unit cost (UC)}}}$$

When applying the EOQ calculation to the item detailed above, the results would be as follows

$$EOQ = \sqrt{\frac{2 \times \$20 \times 24{,}000 \text{ units}}{24\% \times \$.25}} = 4000 \text{ units}$$

The EOQ formula expressed above uses the average usage history for a whole year. Graham [10] feels that too much variation can occur by using a year's worth of history and recommends applying a rolling monthly average of the past contiguous 12 months. In calculating the EOQ with a rolling monthly usage, a *constant* of 24 instead of 2 would be used. The *usage* then would reflect the average rolling monthly usage for a year rather than simply averaging the usage for a calendar year. The EOQ formula can also provide information relating to optimal order interval, associated variable cost, and total annual cost. The optimal order interval (OI) would be calculated using the above values as follows:

$$OI = \sqrt{\frac{2 \times OC}{R(k \times UC)}}$$

$$= \sqrt{\frac{2 \times \$20}{24{,}000(24\% \times \$.25)}} = 0.173 \text{ years} = 2 \text{ months}$$

The associated variable cost (VC) is:

$$VC = \sqrt{2 \times OC \times (kUC)R}$$

$$= \sqrt{2 \times 20(24\% \times \$.25)24{,}000} = \$240 \text{ a year}$$

By inserting the variable cost into the following equation, the total yearly cost (TC) can be attained:

$$TC = UC \times R + VC = \$.25 \times 24{,}000 + \$240 = \$6240 \text{ a year.}$$

Quantity Discounts. Often planners are required to calculate a replenishment order quantity where the supplier offers discounts based on quantity or transportation factors. In determining discounted order quantities, trade-offs between ordering and item costs must be weighed against increases in inventory carrying cost when the replenishment quantity is increased and vice versa. As an example, for the product detailed above, the vendor has quoted a $0.05 reduction per piece when a quantity of 6000 units is purchased. The problem facing planners is that the computed EOQ for the product is 4000 units. Although the unit cost has dropped to $0.20 per piece, a decision must be made as to whether or not the firm should take advantage of the discount.

The determination of a replenishment quantity involving discounting requires several calculations and ultimately rests on a management decision. Magee and Boodman [11] suggest a five-step process:

1. Calculate the EOQ using the discounted quantity and unit cost. If the quantity is within range of the EOQ order minimum, it should be accepted. The calculation for the item and quantity discount detailed above would be

$$\text{EOQ} = \sqrt{2(24,000)\ (\$20)\ /\ (24\%)\ \$0.20} = 4472 \text{ units}$$

2. As the quantity computed is *less* than the supplier's required quantity of 6000 units, the next step would be to calculate the total annual cost for the discounted quantity. If there were multiple price breaks each would be calculated.

$$\text{Total annual cost} = \$0.20 \times 24,000 + \$20(24,000/6000) + 24\% \times \$0.20(6000/2) = \$5024$$

3. Calculate the EOQ for each $0.25 unit price.

$$\text{EOQ} = \sqrt{2(24,000)\ (\$20)\ /\ (24\%)\ \$0.25} = 4000 \text{ units}$$

4. Calculate the total annual cost for each EOQ determined in step 3.

$$\text{Total annual cost} = \$0.25 \times 24,0000 + \$20 \times (24,000/4000) + 24\% \times \$0.25 \times (4000/2) = \$6240.$$

5. Select the lowest cost from either step 2 or step 4. The minimum cost order quantity is 6000 units.

EOQ Assumptions. The effective utilization of the EOQ technique rests on certain assumptions concerning item usage and costs. In the example in Table 7.4, the calculated EOQ results in an inventory turnover of about six times per year (24,000/4000). If the annual usage and the unit cost of the item dropped to 1200 units and $0.10, respectively, the EOQ would provide far different results. The EOQ would be as follows:

$$\text{EOQ} = \sqrt{2(12,000)\ (\$20)\ /\ (24\%)\ \$0.10} = 1414 \text{ units}$$

Such a replenishment quantity means that the inventory would turn over once every 14 months. Although the total cost of the replenishment quantity is only $141.42, multiplying excess inventory cost by thousands of items is clearly a negative feature of the EOQ under certain circumstances.

The following are the basic assumptions underlying the effective use of the EOQ technique:

- The cost of the product does not depend on the replenishment quantity. This means that the cost quoted by the supplier is not impacted by the purchase quantity or the unit transportation cost.
- There are no minimum or maximum restrictions on the replenishment quantity.
- Items considered are totally independent of other items. This means that the items are not subject to dependent demand, nor do they enjoy any benefits from joint replenishment.
- Lead time is zero (delivery is received as soon as the order is placed).
- No shortages are permitted, and the *entire* order quantity is delivered at the same time.
- The minimum purchase quantity from the supplier is not three or four times the calculated EOQ.
- Purchase order preparation and carrying costs are known and are constant.
- Very high or very low product usage needs to be reviewed in relation to unit costs before applying the EOQ technique [12].

Many of the finished goods inventory carried in the typical supply channel, maybe as high as 30 percent, has difficulty using the EOQ when determining the replenishment quantity. In addition, the natures of other products make the application of EOQ difficult. Products manufactured in a process environment, such as petroleum and chemicals and items with short shelf life, are examples.

REPLENISHMENT BY ITEM CLASS

Another approach in ascertaining the replenishment quantity is to use the output from item ABC Classification. In Chapter 6, it was stated that products in a given inventory could be separated into classes based on transaction, cost, or other factors. Statistically, the fast-selling products would constitute about 20 percent of the total products and would account for about 80 percent of total sales. Products in this category would form the Class A items. The next 20 percent of the items would fall within Class B, and about 50 percent would fall within Class C. The remainder of the products, for the most part, is composed of dead and obsolete stock that should be reviewed for possible removal.

The steps in using the ABC Classification for replenishment are as follows:

1. Divide the inventory into classes based on usage/dollar value or other targets.
2. For each inventory class, assign a target turnover value.
3. Determine the level below which only dead and obsolete products reside. Eliminate this class from the procedure.
4. Establish the replenishment quantity for each class by dividing the turnover value by 12. If an item turned 12 times a year, the inventory system should recommend that the planner purchase 1 month's worth of stock whenever the order point is tripped.
5. Recalculate the inventory classification scheme for all items at least once a month, depending on the expected inventory turnover [13].

As an example, Graham [14] suggests the following classification (Table 7.5).

TABLE 7.5. Usage Class Replenishment

ABC Class	% of Total Items	Expected Turns	Quantity to Purchase
1	7.5	12	1 month
2	7.5	6	2 months
3	10	4	3 months
4	10	3	4 months
5	8	2.4	5 months
6	8	2	6 months
7	8	1.7	7 months
8	8	1.5	8 months
9	8	1.3	9 months
10	8	1.2	10 months
11	8	1.1	11 months
12	9	1	12 months

An alternate method would be to determine the order interval through a derivation of the EOQ formula. The calculation is as follows:

$$OI = \sqrt{2 \times OC / R (kUC)}$$

$$OI = \sqrt{2 \times \$20 / 24{,}000(24\% \times \$0.25)} = 0.173 \text{ years} = 2 \text{ months}$$

$$\frac{\text{Annual usage}}{\text{Order interval}} = \text{Order quantity} = 24{,}000/6 = 4000 \text{ units}$$

The advantages of using the ABC Classification as an order quantity technique are readily apparent. To begin with, the method is easy to understand and manipulate. Furthermore, although not as exact as the EOQ, it does provide for effective replenishment based on past usage. When it is considered that the first four classes statistically account for about 90 percent of a firm's active stocked items, the ABC Classification technique can significantly assist planners in focusing their energies on the firm's critical products.

JUST-IN-TIME

Originally *Just-In-Time* (JIT) was developed as an operations planning and control *philosophy* focused on assisting manufacturers attain continuous improvements in product quality and process productivity. Terms such as *zero inventories* and *stockless production* are usually employed when discussing JIT. In a broader context, JIT has been identified with company programs focused on eliminating waste throughout the organization: waste from overproduction, waiting time, transportation, processing, inventory, motion, and product defects. In practice, JIT is the name given to a set of principles that collectively define a comprehensive approach to business management. Although an important element in JIT, inventory is but one facet of a total management philosophy. JIT philosophy encompasses the following paradigms:

- *Operations excellence.* In its broadest context, this principle requires the enterprise to be dedicated to continuous product and process improvement at all levels, focused on total customer service.
- *Value-added processes.* This principle requires companies to critically examine and eliminate all business functions and activities that do not add value to the product or the customer. Such non-value-added processes simply add cost to the enterprise and erode company and supply chain competitive advantage.
- *Continuous improvement.* Increases in productivity and decreases in cost are considered to be continuous. This means that every aspect of manufacturing, logistics support, and supply chain throughput must be dedicated to incremental improvement in ways great and small.
- *JIT/TQM.* This abbreviation suggests a combination of JIT techniques focused on productivity, total quality management (TQM), and people empowerment. The abbreviation encapsulates the need for enterprise dedication to customer service, elimination of wastes, simplification, flexibility in responding to customer and channel demands, and enterprise centered performance measurements.

JIT in Supply Chain Management

Although JIT was originally developed for manufacturing, JIT can easily be used to govern inventory flow through any supply chain pipeline. According to Hall (15), inventory in the supply chain should be related to its rate of flow, using the smallest time intervals possible. If channel inventories are moving across the supply network in perfect flow, then

$$Throughput\ time\ =\ Supply\ chain\ stock\ \times\ Cycle\ time\ of\ use$$

In reality, channel pipelines are often marked by discontinuous flows and can be expressed by the equation,

$$Period\ of\ stock\ on\ hand\ =\ Balance\ on\ hand\ \times\ (1\ /\ Expected\ usage\ during\ period)$$

For example, if the balance on hand was 100 and the weekly usage was 50, there would be 2 weeks of inventory in the supply pipeline.

Being able, however, to describe the supply chain flow in an equation and actually controlling the velocity of product flow are two different things. Supply channel planners are very cognizant that achieving the optimal flow of product to the end customer requires the timely and detailed synchronization of each distribution, manufacturing, and materials supply node throughout the channel pipeline. In the past each network trading partner was responsible for their own performance as demand information serially moved up and corresponding product quantities moved down the supply channel. However, as the velocity of channel inventory increases, it correspondingly becomes more difficult for each node in the supply network to act independently of the channel as a whole. JIT attempts to solve this problem by providing an approach to inventory management that not only shrinks wastes in the form of excess lead times, channel stocks, and related distribution costs, but also provides for the establishment of increasingly agile and flexible supply chains capable of achieving dramatically higher levels of customer service than the competition.

The critical factor in JIT supply chain management is to regard the volume of inventory as a measurement of how much waste is in the channel delivery system. Rather than an asset buffering functions from variation in demand, the size of channel inventories are directly correlated to such problems as poor product quality, poor production processes, disconnected demand planning, and inefficient logistics systems that require trading partners everywhere in the supply channel to hold costly safety stocks. As JIT continuous improvement solves these problems on the company and supply chain levels, the need for inventory buffers will grow less and less, thereby speeding up the velocity of channel throughput time as expressed in the above equation. This phenomenon can be seen in the following illustration (Figure 7.9). Before removing the obstacles preventing the smooth and rapid flow of water (inventory) through the channel, pools (safety buffers) accumulate around the obstructions. Once the obstacles are removed, not only is there less water (inventory), but the speed of the flow is equally fast at all points even though the total volume of the input remains constant.

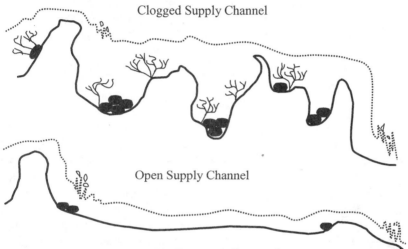

Clogged Supply Channel

Open Supply Channel

FIGURE 7.9 Inventory flow analogy

JIT MECHANICS

JIT operates in a manner very similar to the two bin system described earlier in the chapter. The technique begins with the recognition of demand at some supply point in the distribution channel. As inventory is pulled for order fulfillment, a trigger, in the form of a replenishment signal, will eventually be tripped, alerting planners that replenishment from suppliers is necessary to avoid future stockout. An order is then placed utilizing some form of authorization such as a simple replenishment card or even empty containers that are picked up by the supplier, filled to specification, and returned. The assumption is that the entire channel inventory system works the same way from customer to supplier to manufacturer, and, eventually, raw materials acquisition. Instead of elaborate computer systems or complicated EOQs that create safety buffers to guard against unplanned demand, the replenishment signal determines when order action should occur. In addition, since product must be consumed in order to release a replenishment signal, the system responds to real-world changes and is self-regulating.

JIT Pipeline Management

A distributor carried a steel casting that was purchased from a single supplier and sold to a narrow market segment. Over the past year demand on the item averaged around 1600 SKUs a month, or about 80 a day. Due to stocking and transportation economies the casting was received in containers carrying 16 SKUs. Due to a requirement to move to a JIT replenishment system arising from the company's largest customer, the distributor decided to enact a JIT pull-system both for internal stocking and replenishment from the foundry. Inventory planners determined that the container itself would act as a perfect pull signal. The challenge was to determine how the containers should be stocked.

Planners solved the problem by applying the JIT signal formula.

The following data was identified:
Demand (D) = 80 castings a day.
Castings per container (Q) = 16.
Deliveries per day (Tp) = 1.
Transit delay (Td) = 2 days.
Safety stock (S) = 2 percent.

Using the formula would reveal the answer:

$$\frac{80\,(2+2)\,(1+.2)}{1 \times 16} = \frac{384}{16} = 24$$

The answer shows that a total of 24 containers (384 SKUs) should be in the system to service the daily demand. If a quality improvement program was put in place that eliminated the safety percent, the number of containers in the system would drop to 20, and would result in a drop of 64 SKUs in total carrying costs.

To make a JIT supply channel system function, planners must determine just how much inventory should be stocked and what devices are going to be used to alert supply nodes that replenishment is required. To calculate channel inventory levels, supply chain planners can utilize a simple formula, with a few modifications, to determine JIT production and withdrawal signals. The number of signals, whether cards or some other device, is directly related to the total number of containers of a defined quantity of a single product that are in the system. The number of these signals can be expressed by the following formula (16).

$$\text{\# Signals} = \frac{D\,(2+Td)\,(1+S)}{Tp \times Q}$$

where D is the average customer daily demand, 2 is the minimum number of scheduled trips (one to pick up the replenishment signal and one to return with the product), Td is the transit delay or the number of additional scheduled trips between the one when the replenishment signal (move card or empty container) is picked up and the product is delivered, S is the safety stock, Tp is the deliveries per day currently scheduled, and Q is the container quantity.

Using JIT to manage inventories in a supply chain requires that demand and supply be synchronized at each stage of the supply pipeline. The key is to regard the entire supply network as a single customer satisfying entity. Instead of each supply node planning and executing demand plans in isolation, each channel entity pulls inventories from their supplying partners driven by the drum beat of the pull of actual demand beginning with the customer and ending with materials suppliers. Safety or signal inventories (such as kanban containers) and manufacturing buffer capacities are found at each supply node to absorb possible variability in the system (Figure 7.10). The key to the synchronized supply chain is *communication* of demand and replenishment requirements as close to real-time as possible. In addition, the pursuit of continuous improvement objectives dedicated to removing wastes and maximizing the velocity of channel product flow would tame the bull-whip effect and ever more closely link the entire supply chain to the end customer.

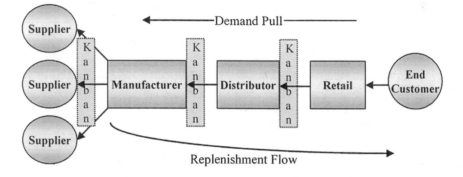

FIGURE 7.10 JIT synchronized supply chain.

The advantages of such a control system are obvious. Beyond its apparent simplicity, however, reside a number of critical assumptions. To begin with, the system demands 100 percent quality. Without large inventory buffers at every channel node, defective products will quickly result in stockout. Second, a very close collaborative relationship must exist between channel partners. This element requires consensus on a range of issues such as standardization of processes and equipment and agreed upon levels of service and flexibility, to a mutual sharing of benefits and risks. Finally, JIT requires channel partners to jointly undertake programs designed at the continuous improvement of the system. While JIT does resemble a two bin system, the differences between the two are dramatic. Two bin techniques seek to arrive at a stable system that mechanically services demand. JIT continuous improvement, on the other hand, seeks to disrupt the stasis of a control system, identify the problem areas that arise, determine a solution, and evolve to a new stasis. Once this occurs, however, it is time to upset the system and begin the improvement process all over again with the eventual objective of minimizing or eliminating channel inventories altogether. In the sidebar example, destabilizing the system would occur simply by the removal of a few containers and then responding in a problem-solving mode to the constraints that emerge.

THE FUTURE OF SUPPLY CHAIN JIT

During the 1990s, companies were increasingly faced with the requirement not only to deliver but also to purchase using JIT methods. As JIT began to evolve into what is now termed *Lean Manufacturing* practices, all supply channel nodes found themselves under increasing pressure to architect agile, responsive organizations capable of meeting specific customer schedules, supplying exact quantities, supplying quality products, adjusting quickly to changes in pipeline deliveries and inventories, and performing all of these activities with a minimum of paperwork. JIT practices were seen as the best way to eliminate waste in the form of excess inventory buffers and product movement that simply clogged the channel pipeline, delayed customer service, and unnecessarily increased supply chain costs.

As the new century began, however, the JIT/Lean philosophy received several "shocks" that have dampened down a once unbridled, almost doctrinaire enthusiasm. With the September 11, 2001 terrorist attacks, fractious labor-management relations at U.S. West Coast ports, and international troubles in Iraq, Korea, and Venezuela, whole supply chains suddenly found once free-flowing JIT supply pipelines clogged by security requirements, strikes, spiraling fuel costs, and increased red tape. To meet the increased, and seemingly permanent, growth of supply channel uncertainty, companies have begun to boost inventories and depend more heavily on regional warehouses and distribution centers. While JIT/Lean concepts are far from dead, the uncertainties in the business climate of the early twenty-first century have caused supply chains to temper their impulse toward JIT.

INVENTORY REPLENISHMENT PLANNING PROCESS

Now that the concepts and elements of inventory replenishment have been explored, it is possible to define the planning process to be used by material control. In general, the object of the process is to ensure that the firm has sufficient inventories to meet customer service targets, is minimizing costs as much as possible, and is communicating effectively with supply chain partners. In developing effective inventory replenishment plans, the firm's materials management function must answer such questions as the following:

- What is the current status of each stocked item?
- Are inventory records being updated correctly and with the minimum of delay?
- Is the current on-hand balance sufficient to cover anticipated customer demand?
- Have the order points, order quantities, target inventory levels, and periodic review cycles been calculated correctly.
- Have safety stocks been calculated correctly?
- How is actual demand to be monitored and used to recalculate replenishment data elements?

In answering these and other questions, planners must first begin with an accurate determination of the firm's inventory balances. This requirement forms the first step in the replenishment planning process (Figure 7.11). For

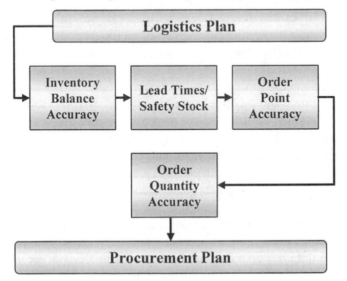

FIGURE 7.11 Replenishment inventory planning process.

products subject to continuous review systems, inventory control must ensure that the on-hand and on-order quantities (the elements constituting the inventory position) are accurate and up to date. Tools like ABC Analysis, Cycle Counting, and effective inventory control procedures will significantly assist in ensuring perpetual inventory accuracy. For products subject to periodic review systems, it is critical that a thorough physical be conducted on a periodic basis so that ordering techniques can begin regularly with accurate on-hand inventory quantities. Fundamental to good inventory accuracy is the execution of the three *P's* (people, places and procedures) of inventory control. Of the three, *people* is the most important. Has the staff who works with the inventory been fully trained and have the regions of responsibility and authority been fully established? Next, have warehouses and stocking areas been defined along with the necessary controlled access requirements? Finally, have well-documented *procedures* been put into place that facilitate and explain inventory transaction control?

The second step in the replenishment planning process is ensuring that replenishment lead times and safety stock calculations reflect accurate information. *Lead time* is basically the offset time that separates the point from when a replenishment requirement is identified to the moment the ordered quantity is in the stocking position ready for the next customer order. *Safety stock*, in general, is a reserve quantity of stock designed to protect against fluctuations in demand and supply. It has already been stated how difficult it is to control in detail these two elements. Planners must constantly be examining lead times and safety stocks with an eye not only toward accuracy but also how these two critical elements can be reduced. Planners must resist the temptation to buffer products from potential stockout by adding extra lead time or safety stock.

After replenishment timing safety factors have been verified, planners must review the accuracy and timeliness of order points. Several factors need to be considered. To begin with, inventory control should be aware of the mechanics of the various order point techniques available and when to apply them so that the various item classes and types can be ordered to attain the optimum balance between ordering and carrying costs. For products controlled by continuous review, planners need to continually update the order point calculation to reflect changes in demand usage and supplier lead times. Finally, for inventory using periodic review techniques, maximum inventory targets and review cycles need to be recalculated regularly. It is recommended that all the order points in a given inventory be updated at least every 90 days, and preferably every 30 days. Computerized planning systems that calculate order points dynamically will significantly assist in ensuring that proper stocking levels are being maintained to support customer demand.

The final step in the inventory replenishment process is reviewing and re-setting order quantities. Most business computer systems have the ability to calculate and update EOQs dynamically. The problem with the technique is not the calculation but the elements of the EOQ formula. Other than the period constant, the other four elements (the cost of ordering, demand usage, the carrying cost, and the unit cost) are all variables. This means that the EOQ calculation must be continually examined and adjusted to prevent significant drift in order quantities that could result in overstock or shortage conditions. Finally, the EOQ assumes discrete linear usage. In reality, every planner knows that stocked quantities are often consumed in large discontinuous lot sizes caused by lumpy demand or joint replenishment requirements. As with the order point, all order quantities need to be updated and reviewed at least once a month.

Effective inventory management is the culmination of a dedicated program designed to provide the highest level of customer service possible while continually reducing ordering and carrying costs. Excessive inventories cover up the real problems facing supply chain planners--lack of management controls, long lead times, inaccurate order points and order quantities, inadequate warehousing, poor employee training, poor quality, and low productivity. Effective inventory planning seeks to eliminate such obstacles to performance in the stockroom, in the inventory control tools, and in the entire distribution network.

INVENTORY OPERATIONS IN THE SUPPLY CHAIN ENVIRONMENT

Up to this point, the discussion of statistical inventory replenishment has assumed that stock is warehoused at a single location. Many firms, however, must contend with the planning and deployment of products in a supply chain environment. Perhaps the critical characteristics of supply channel planning is the fact that products are stocked at more than one location and that many are *dependent* on one or more supplying locations in the channel for replenishment. Distribution network structures can be expressed in much the same manner as manufacturing Bills of Material. Warehouse dependencies are shown as being linked by level to their respective parent supplying warehouses that, in turn, may be dependent on still higher levels of warehouses for resupply. The highest level in the structure is the supplier or product manufacturer. Figure 7.12 illustrates a three-echelon supply channel network. The central warehouse (third echelon) acts as a supply center for inventory replenishment for the branch warehouses (second echelon), which, in turn, act as the supply source for the retail outlets (first echelon).

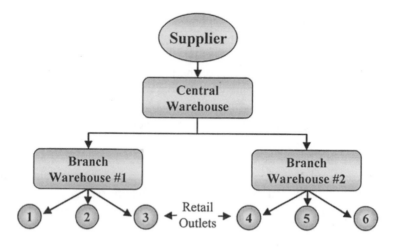

FIGURE 7.12 Supply chain structure.

CONCEPT OF "PUSH" AND "PULL"

Resupply in a supply chain network can be described as being determined by either a "push" or a "pull" system. In channel networks characterized by an *independent deployment* ("pull") *system,* inventory planning is decentralized. Each stocking location maintains its own inventory management system and determines its own replenishment requirements. When the planning system indicates that inventory is below order point, a resupply order is placed on the supplying location. On the other hand, in a *coupled deployment* ("push") *system,* all channel resupply activities are conducted by the central supplying location. Based on the demand patterns of satellite locations or the total network aggregate demand, replenishment planning and execution is centralized with actual inventory disbursement made to each satellite location targeted at meeting corporate turnover targets. Finally, aspects of the two systems can be combined to respond to unique network needs. Factors influencing the choice of an independent deployment system are the existence of value-added processing, short lead times between the satellite and the supplying warehouse, and stocks composed of moderate- to slow-moving items. Factors favoring a coupled system are long procurement lead times, fast-moving items, and significant economies in procurement and transportation [17].

Independent Deployment ("Pull") Systems. Under an *independent deployment system,* each location in the supply channel is responsible for determineing its own ordering techniques, cost factors, service objectives, and resupply lead times. The mechanics of the system are quite simple. Each location calculates its own replenishment requirements and then draws inventory through the network by requisition or actual purchase order from the supplying location, often a regional or central distribution center. The branch location determines order timing, which products are to be ordered, and what are to be the resupply order quantities and delivery requirements. The distribution centers, in turn, will receive a sequence of resupply orders from their branches and attempt to fill and ship them according to some priority rule, usually *first-come first-serve.* Finally, the distribution centers acquire their resupply inventory directly from the manufacturer or the supplier. The "pull" system is illustrated in Figure 7.13. The advantages of a "pull" system are the following:

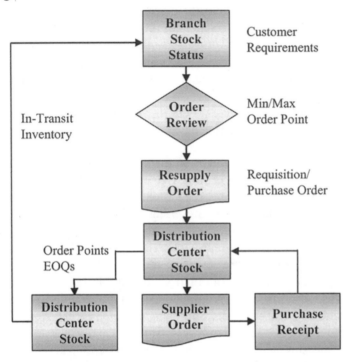

FIGURE 7.13 "Pull" system.

1. *Planning simplicity.* "Pull" systems are easy to operate. Because each supply node is responsible for inventory planning, central functions do not have to perform laborious channel demand analysis. They only have to plan for the total requirements placed on them by the locations in the channel they resupply.
2. *Turnover.* Because the central location is responsible for product acquisition, channel supply, and deployment, satellite locations can draw exactly the necessary resupply quantities. Branches, therefore, can operate with lower stock levels, turning inventory faster than would be possible if inventory had to be ordered directly from the supplier or manufacturer.

3. *Overhead cost reduction.* Branch locations in a "pull" system can leverage the economies of scale resulting from lower inventory acquisition and material distribution costs incurred by central functions in planning for the entire supply channel while receiving the benefits of short delivery, storage, and procurement discounting.

4. *Use of replenishment and DRP ordering techniques.* Standard re-order point and DRP computer system logic provide excellent tools to operate pull systems. Both techniques enable local warehouses to de-termine the exact timing and quantities of replenishment orders. Once these requirements have been calculated, the computer system can then pass the orders through the *bill of distribution* (BOD) directly to the supplying warehouse or manufacturing facilities so that resupply can then be passed back down the channel to respond to the pull of the demand source.

The disadvantages of a "pull" system, for the most part, center on overall inventory carrying costs and deficiencies in information flows, particularly in a supply chain driven by statistical replenishment techniques. Although it is true that branch inventory turns will be high and overhead costs low, the exact opposite can be said of the profitability of the central supplying facilities who must shoulder the cost. Channel systems using a "pull" system must be sure that aggregate costs incurred are offset by higher inventory turns in the branch locations. Furthermore, because each location in the network is responsible for their own service levels, there is a tendency to unnecessarily duplicate safety stock at multiple levels in the channel. In addition, because each location pulls inventory from their supplying location, information concerning downstream inventory requirements is not available to regional and national locations in the network. Supplying warehouses are usually unaware of branch requirements until the order arrives. Finally, the objectives and performance measurements inherent in a "pull" system may actually militate against overall corporate profitability by inflating channel inventories in an effort to improve branch sales levels. As will be discussed in Chapter 8, many of these drawbacks are negated with the use of DRP systems.

To counterbalance "pull" system deficiencies, a number of techniques may be employed. Inventory planning can be governed by implementing a channelwide *periodic review* system. Operationally, branch warehouse inventories would be reviewed periodically and resupply orders generated with sufficient quantities necessary to restore channelwide stock to a targeted level. Another technique would be to utilize a *double order point.* Each branch's inventory would have its order point set by calculating the normal order point *plus* the average demand during the central warehouse's procurement, transportation, and manufacturing lead time. Theoretically, this technique would enable the central supplying location to review its inventory levels relative to anticipated branch orders and plan acquisition and transportation accordingly.

Another method, the *base stock system*, requires each location in the channel to maintain a base level of inventory determined as the facility's statistically computed demand *plus* stock at all upstream warehouses. The inventory position at each level is indicated by

$$IP = ES + RO,$$

where IP is the echelon inventory position, ES is the echelon stock, and RO is the replenishment order. For example, branch facility A is resupplied from warehouse 1. For a given product, branch facility A stocks 100 units and warehouse 1 stocks 300 units. There are also 50 units intransit to branch facility A, and warehouse 1 has an unfilled replenishment order from the supplier for 100 units. Finally, branch facility A has a customer order backlog of 125 units. Then, warehouse 1's inventory position would be

$$IP = (100 + 300 + 50 - 125) + 100 = 425 \text{ units.}$$

Either on a periodic basis or after each transaction, the branch location compares the inventory position to the order point (usually a minimum), and when the order point is tripped, inventory is ordered to raise the inventory position to the base stock level. On the part of the supplying warehouse, total demand from all satellite warehouses can be planned and economical shipping quantities accumulated for transfer to meet channel requirements.

Coupled Deployment ("Push") Systems. The basic mechanism driving the independent deployment system is each location in the distribution channel *pulling* (ordering) stock from the next higher echelon. In contrast, inventory resupply in a coupled deployment system is *pushed* through the channel. Where, in a "pull" system, branch locations have the authority to determine the timing and quantity of replenishment, in a "push" system the supplying location possesses resupply authority. In addition, they also have the ability to adjust the actual replenishment sequence to improve overall channel service or reduce costs. The key to successfully executing a "push" system is effective central inventory planning. Inventory managers must have accurate and timely information as to the stock status of all satellite locations. Whether gathered on a transaction-by-transaction basis or periodically, channel inventory requirements provide the data necessary for aggregate planning and efficient resupply allocation. Functionally, whether using min/max rules, order point, or other techniques, each satellite warehouse's inventory is controlled by a combination of cycle stock used to cover customer demand during replenishment lead time and a safety stock level to provide for usage error.

The role of central deployment locations is to calculate and resupply inventory requirements for the whole channel in accordance with the company's customer satisfaction policies. The "push" system is illustrated in Figure 7.14. The advantages of a "push" system can be described as follows:

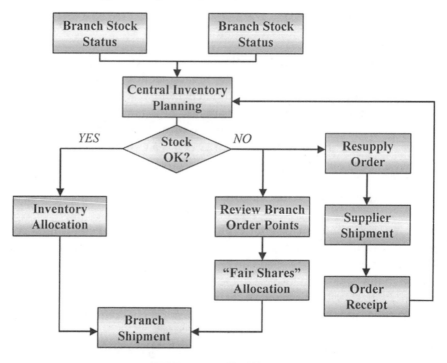

FIGURE 7.14 "Push" system.

1. *Performance measurement.* The "push" system enables corporate planners to leverage the total inventory in the channel to attain global customer service and return on investment goals. Performance is measured not just on the success of discrete stocking points but on how well the whole channel is meeting corporate sales and asset management targets.

2. *Central planning.* By centralizing all inventory planning and resupply allocation, channel planners can create a *single* inventory plan for the ongoing ordering and deployment of total inventory. Central planning enables planners to evaluate globally channel inventories and to remove the normal supply point stock redundancies caused by inaccuracies in local replenishment decision making. In addition, by strategically deploying inventory resources through the channel, stocking inequalities

among branches can be reduced, further cutting costs arising from interbranch transfer and lost customer sales.

3. *Cost reductions.* By centralizing inventory planning and deployment, companies can reduce the total working capital necessary to stock the channel. In addition, operating costs can be reduced by economies attained in transportation and purchasing. Instead of ordering products to satisfy individual branch demand, central purchasing can combine requirements from all branches, thereby reducing transportation and acquisition costs while gaining possible quantity price break discounts.

4. *Safety stock control.* Whereas safety stock is a permanent feature of inventories subject to independent demand, a "push" system enables planners to centralize safety stocks at the branch having the highest usage of the particular product. Centralization assists in eliminating unnecessary safety stock carried by each channel location characteristic of "pull" systems, thereby reducing inventory costs while providing for high channel serviceability.

Disadvantages of a "push" system center on organizational issues. An effective "push" system requires a professionally trained central planning staff that can work with aggregate data and demand forecasting techniques. In addition, inventory accuracy and timely transaction record posting normally require a computer system that can combine the inventory planning data information of each location in the channel. Finally, the introduction of a "push" system requires changes in operational roles. As central planning is now responsible for resupply planning and execution, branch management's role will migrate from focusing on replenishment triggering to ensuring transmission of accurate stock status and sales usage information to the channel's central planning functions.

STOCKING MULTIECHELON WAREHOUSES

Once the number and size of the channel's distribution points have been established, the next problem facing planners is determining which products should be stocked at each warehouse and in what quantities. Obviously, not every product the firm offers can be stored at the same inventory level at every location in the network. By using a technique known as *selective stocking,* planners can maximize available warehouse space in the channel by determining which products are to be stocked at what echelon level based on item ABC Classification. As an example, Class A products might be carried by all locations in the channel. Class B products, on the other hand, might reside at strategically positioned regional distribution centers. Finally, Class C products might only be stocked at the firm's national distribution center. In determining stocking levels, planners must be careful not to inadvertently increase other logistics costs in an attempt to keep stocking costs low. Savings realized by centralizing certain classes of product might be lost to increased transportation costs.

Calculating inventory channel trade-off costs can be computed by using the *square root rule*. This technique seeks to determine the optimal level of inventory to be stocked at a consolidated location based on the inventory value and existing number of distribution points. The formula can be expressed as

$$CI = SI \sqrt{n}$$

where CI is the inventory value if the entire network stock was to be centralized at one stocking location, SI is the amount of a class of inventory stocked at each distribution location, and n is the number of stocking points in the channel. If, for example, each of the 25 locations in a distribution network carrying an annual average of $200,000 Class C products were to be consolidated into a single supply center, the annual savings to the company would be calculated as

$$CI = \$200,000 \sqrt{25 \text{ locations}} = \$1,000,000$$

When it is considered that the total annual cost to stock Class C products at each location totals $5,000,000, consolidation might appear a sensible choice. But before the decision is made, planners need to weigh the potential savings against the added cost of transportation and delivery. If centralization meant that transportation costs to supply the channel with Class C products increased by $93,000 annually and the use of added air freight to maintain the current delivery time equaled $110,000 annually, the inventory/transportation trade-off would be calculated as follows:

Distribution channel inventory reduction	$4,000,000
Inventory carrying cost	x 22%
Annual cost of carrying inventory reduction	$880,000
Increase in annual transportation cost	- $93,000
	$787,000
Cost to maintain current service level	- $110,000
Net annual savings	**$677,000**

Clearly, a total annual savings of $677,000 would warrant serious review of the possible centralization of Class C items at a national distribution center.

Adjusting Channel Imbalances.   From time to time, available inventory in
the channel network will get out of balance. Because of variances in demand
and supply over time, some locations will have excess quantities of a product
while other warehouses may be out of stock. Normally, there is a group of
corporate planners whose job it is to monitor channelwide stocking imbalances and then generate interbranch transfers to redistribute inventory excesses in the channel rather than purchasing or manufacturing more inventory. This function requires the existence of inventory control systems that
permit visibility into both aggregate inventory levels and the detail plans of
each channel location. Currently, there are a number of computerized applications available that not only provide for the timely update of local inventory records but also present corporate planners with the timely and accurate
information necessary to keep channel inventories in balance.

One method of countering channel inventory imbalances is called *least-
cost redistribution.* Assume that a distribution channel consists of a central
warehouse in Chicago and satellite warehouses in New York, Dallas, Denver,
and Los Angeles. For a given product, also assume that the Dallas and Los
Angeles warehouses are stocked out and have open customer backorders for
200 and 300 units, respectively. In contrast, the Chicago distribution center
(DC) has 225 units extra, New York 220, and Denver 190. To summarize,
the channel has open customer orders totaling 500 units that cannot be filled
from the current warehouses, but an excess of 635 units in other warehouses
in the channel. The goal of the exercise is to redistribute the inventory imbalance in as cost-effective a manner as possible.

A common technique used to address this problem is to set up a sequence
of default interbranch transfer relationships. For example, Denver would
always attempt to replenish shortages by first ordering from the Los Angeles
warehouse, then from Dallas, Chicago, and lastly from New York. The resupply sequence is determined by comparing the normal transportation cost
from the source to the destination, the cheapest being the first in the sequence
and so on. The problem with the technique is that when more than one channel warehouse requires inventory and excesses exist in several other warehouses, it becomes difficult to determine the least-cost interbranch transfer.

A more effective method is to develop a simple linear program or even a
spread sheet that will calculate the least-cost redistribution of product.
Visually, the method can be illustrated through the use of a channel transportation cost matrix. A sample matrix with the cost of transporting product
by pound from and to each warehouse in the above distribution channel is illustrated (Table 7.6). The cost is computed in dollars per pound.

The object of the procedure is to redistribute excess inventories among
channel warehouses in such a way as to minimize total transportation costs.

TABLE 7.6 Price/Delivery Matrix

On-Hand	Warehouse	Chicago	New York	Dallas	Denver	Los Angles
225	Chicago	$0.00	$1.35	$1.63	$1.70	$2.10
220	New York	1.45	0.00	1.82	1.80	2.40
-300	Dallas	1.65	1.85	0.00	1.70	2.00
190	Denver	1.75	1.95	1.65	0.00	1.10
-200	Los Angles	2.05	2.25	2.03	1.25	0.00

Assuming that the product that is in imbalance in the channel is one pound per unit, the results of the calculation would be as follows (Table 7.7).

TABLE 7.7 Delivery/Cost Solution

On-Hand	Warehouse	Chicago	New York	Dallas	Denver	Los Angles
225	Chicago					
220	New York					
-300	Dallas	$371.25	$407.00		$323.00	
190	Denver					
-200	Los Angles	$410.00	$450.00		$235.00	

The results of the computation would indicate that the Dallas warehouse requirement would most economically be satisfied by shipping all of the 225 units from Chicago and 75 units from New York for a total shipment cost of $510. The Los Angeles shortage would best be filled with a shipment of all of the Denver warehouse excess, plus 10 units from Chicago for a total delivery cost of $258. In is important to note that interbranch shipments designed to remedy channel inventory imbalances should not be posted as *demand* in the computation of sales usage used in developing warehouse level forecasts. Although it is true that the stock will be deducted from the supplying warehouse's inventory balance, the interbranch inventory transaction must be coded so as not to post such shipments in those demand files used to compute forecasts [18].

"Fair Shares" Techniques. Despite the added control offered by centralized channel planning, there are often occasions when distribution centers possess in-sufficient stock to fill the inventory needs of the entire distribution network. Such an event could occur because of the normal lag time in channel information and material flows or because of unplanned demand or vendor stockout. In responding to such a problem, inventory managers often will use a technique called "fair shares." The basis of this technique is to provide branch locations with equal runout replenishment resupply that should be sufficient to prevent stock out during lead time until supplier receipts arrive at the deployment warehouses.

An example of "fair shares" is illustrated as follows. Say, for example, that the deployment location has 200 units of Product A and the resupply order is not expected for another 10 days. Current on-hand and projected weekly requirements for the three branch locations in the channel are as follows:

Location	On-Hand	Weekly Requirements						Daily Usage
Branch A	30	40	40	40	40	40	40	8
Branch B	37	50	50	50	50	50	50	10
Branch C	33	60	60	60	60	60	60	12
	100	150	150	150	150	150	150	30

Altogether the channel contains 300 units, 200 at the central warehouse and 100 cumulatively in the branches. Because the branches sell an average of 30 units each day, there is a 10-day supply of inventory in the channel. The "fair shares" deployment calculation computed for each branch is

$$Q = d_iCS - I_i,$$

where Q is the runout quantity, d_i is the daily demand for branch location i, CS is the total daily channel supply, and I_i is the on-hand inventory at branch location i.

Using this allocation method, each branch location would receive the follow stock allotment of Product A:

Branch location A	50 units
Branch location B	63 units
Branch location C	87 units

The inventory shipped to each branch location hopefully will cover demand during replenishment lead time. Branch location C, for example, should have sufficient stock on Product A to last for 10 days ([33 + 87] / 12) [19].

SUMMARY

Solving the crucial problems surrounding inventory replenishment is one of the most important tasks of supply chain management. Answering effectively the critical inventory planning questions of *what* products to review for re-supply, the precise timing of *when* resupply order release should take place before stock out occurs, and *how much* inventory should be ordered when replenishment is triggered is essential if each channel partner is to leverage the resources of the entire supply channel to gain and sustain competitive advantage. The responsibility for effective inventory planning and execution resides with inventory management who must facilitate the attainment of customer service targets while simultaneously achieving least total cost for inventory, transportation, warehousing, and staffing.

At the core of all statistical replenishment systems resides a very simple principle: For each product, there is an optimal stocking and ordering quantity in which the total cost of carrying inventory is balanced against the cost of ordering. By calculating optimal order point and order quantities through a variety of statistical replenishment techniques, planners are provided with a triggering mechanism alerting them on a product-by-product basis when order action needs to occur and what the resultant order quantities should be. The effective use of statistical inventory replenishment methods involves a thorough understanding of the elements necessary to calculate order points and order quantities. A firsthand knowledge of such components as demand *usage, lead time*, and *safety stock* are critical for the effective use of such ordering techniques as statistical order point, min/max, joint replenishment, and periodic review. Equally important is a knowledge of the components of various *order quantity* techniques. Computing the *Economic Order Quantity* (EOQ), determining order size when there are quantity discounts, and replenishing by ABC Classification are examples.

Often planners are faced with planning inventories in a multiechelon environment. Resupply in a supply chain network can be described as being dominated by either a "push" or a "pull" system. In a "push" system, all inventory planning is centralized. Corporate planners determine resupply order size and timing based on channel stocking balances and demand usage requirements. In contrast, in a "pull" system, each branch location is responsible for determining resupply order quantities and delivery timing. When replenishment conditions are identified, branches pull inventory from supplying locations that, in turn, attempt to fill branch requests as they are received. There are advantages and disadvantages to both methods. The choice of a system ultimately depends on such factors as product characteristics, carrying cost, transportation, stocking capacities, location, and the availability of information processing tools.

QUESTIONS FOR REVIEW

1. Discuss the two forms of inventory demand. Why are they so important to inventory planners?
2. Explain the concept of stock replenishment. Why is it fundamental to statistical replenishment techniques of inventory management?
3. Explain the mechanics of the periodic review method of inventory control.
4. Why is the EOQ such a valuable tool for calculating order quantities?
5. What are the assumptions of the EOQ model?
6. What is the purpose of carrying safety stock?
7. Why is the EOQ such a valuable tool for calculating order quantities?
8. Explain the concepts of "push" and "pull" in a multiechelon supply channel environment.
9. Describe the difference between a fixed-quantity and a fixed-period inventory planning system.

PROBLEMS

1. A purchased product stocked by ABC Distribution, Inc. has a constant annual demand of 25,000 units. The product costs $1.25. It costs $10.00 to order the item, and inventory carrying costs are estimated to be at 22%.
   1. How many times a year would a replenishment order be placed for this product?
   2. What are the total annual inventory costs?
   3. What should be the economic order quantity?
2. A purchased product has a demand of 14,000 units per year. The distributor has 200 working days a year. If the lead time to acquire the product is 4 days, what would be the order point?
3. A supplier offers the following pricing on a given inventory item: $50/unit on orders less than 2000 units and $43.50 for orders of 2001 or greater. If the annual usage of the item is 4000, the carrying cost is 20%, and the cost of ordering is $50, then what is the total annual cost of the minimum cost order quantity?
4. A given product has a demand of 5000 units per year. The item costs $6.40 each, the carrying cost is 25 percent, and the cost of ordering is $25. If a new supplier offers to sell you the same product for $6.00 per unit if you purchase at least 2500 units per order, should you go with the new supplier or not?
5. A purchased product stocked by a retail outlet has average sales of 200 units a day with an average deviation of 110 units per day. A 1 week's supply of the item is usually ordered at a time. Lead time is 1 day. There is currently 210 units on hand.
   (a) If the store is open 5 days a week, what should be the item's order quantity.

356 DISTRIBUTION OPERATIONS PLANNING

(b)   How much safety stock would be required to provide a 98% serviceability level?

6. Based on the following data, compute the new order point (reference Table 7.3 above).

Weekly forecast usage	250 units
Lead time	2 weeks
MAD	100 units
Targeted service level	98%
Order quantity	200 units

7. A product has an order point without safety stock of 200 units. The inventory carrying cost for the item is $50 per unit and the cost of a stockout is $50 per year. The item is order four times a year. Based on the following demand occurring during the reorder period, what would be the new order point?

	Demand Instances	Probability
	50	.1
	100	.2
Order Point	200	.3
	250	.2
	300	.1
	350	.1
		1.0

REFERENCES

1. Orlicky, Joseph, *Material Requirements Planning*. New York: McGraw-Hill, 1975, pp. 22-25.
2. Orlicky, pp. 5-10; Plossl, George W., *Production and Inventory Control: Principles and Techniques*, 2nd ed. Englewood Cliffs, NJ: Prentice Hall, 1985, pp. 98-100; and, Waters, C.D.J., *Inventory Control and Management*. New York: John Wiley & Sons, 1992, pp. 4-26.
3. Graham, Gordon, *Distribution Inventory Management for the 1990s*. Richardson, TX: Inventory Management Press, 1987, p. 67.
4. Brown, Robert G., *Statistical Forecasting For Inventory Control*. New York: McGraw Hill, 1959, pp. 136-147.
5. Graham, p. 67.
6. Brown, Robert G., *Advanced Service Parts Inventory Control*. Norwich, VT: Materials Management Systems, Inc., 1982, p. 344.
7. Graham, pp. 129-142.
8. Fogarty, Donald W., Blackstone, John H., and Hoffmann, Thomas R., *Production and Inventory Management*, 2nd ed. Cincinnati, OH: South-Western Publishing Co., 1991, p. 228.
9. See in the discussion in Brown, Robert G., *Decision Rules For Inventory Management*. New York: Holt, Rinehart & Winston, 1967, pp. 5-17; Waters, pp. 37-48, Fredendall, Lawrence D. and Hill, Ed, *Basics of Supply Chain Management*. Boca Raton: FL, St. Lucie Press, 2001, pp. 189-193, and, Coyle, John J., Bardi, Edward J., and Langley, John C., *The Management of Business Logistics*, 7th ed. Mason, Ohio: South-Western, 2003, pp. 227-234, 270-281.
10. Graham, p. 147.
11. See the discussion in Magee, John F. and Boodman, D.M., *Production Planning and Inventory Control*. 2nd ed., New York: McGraw-Hill, 1967, p. 210; Vollmann, Thomas E., Berry, William L., and Whybark, D. Clay, *Manufacturing Planning and Control Systems*. 2nd ed. Homewood IL: Dow Jones Irwin, 1988, pp. 728-730; and, Waters, pp. 77-84.
12. See the discussion in Waters, pp. 33-34; Silver, Edward A. and Peterson, Rein, *Decision Systems for Inventory Management And Production Control*. 2nd ed. New York: John Wiley & Sons, 1985, p. 174; Graham, p. 149-151; Fogarty, Blackstone and Hoffmann, p. 208.
13. See the discussion in Silver and Peterson, pp. 173-214; and, Vollmann, Berry, and Whybark, pp. 723-730.
14. Graham, pp. 152-155.
15. Hall, Robert W., *Zero Inventories*. Homewood, IL: Business One Irwin, 1983, p. 232.
16. This formula has been modified from Hall, pp. 235-241 and Wantuck, Kenneth, *Just In Time For America: A Common Sense Production Strategy*. Milwaukee, WI: The Forum, 1989, pp. 275-280.

17. See Magee, John F., Copacino, William C., and Rosenfield, Donald B., *Modern Logistics Management*. New York: John Wiley & Sons, 1985, pp. 98-100; Pyke, David F. and Cohen, Morris A., "Push and Pull in Manufacturing and Distribution Systems." *Journal of Operations Management*, 9 (1), 24-43 (1990); and, Silver and Peterson, pp. 483-487.
18. Brown, *Materials Management Systems*, pp. 340-345.
19. See Silver and Peterson, pp. 483-487; Fogarty, Blackstone and Hoffmann, pp. 313-315; and, Brown, *Materials Management Systems*, pp. 351-356.

8

DISTRIBUTION REQUIREMENTS PLANNING

In the previous chapter, it was stated that inventory planners had their choice of two basic inventory ordering techniques: *statistical replenishment* and *Distribution Requirements Planning* (DRP). Chapter 7 focused on the various methods, elements, and application of statistical tools for inventory ordering, such as order point and economic order quantity (EOQ). In this chapter, the system logic, application, and benefits of using DRP to plan inventory resupply will be examined. Unlike replenishment methods that utilize statistical calculations to determine when orders should be released and what order quantities should be, DRP determines resupply by *time-phasing* supply to meet demand for each product at each warehouse in the distribution channel. Utilizing the same computerized logic as *Material Requirements Planning* (MRP), DRP performs a *gross-to-net requirements* calculation of demand and supply in each time period. When demand exceeds supply, the system generates a *planned resupply order* and alerts the planner that replenishment action is required if stockout is to be avoided. What is more, through the *Bill of Distribution* (BOD), DRP implodes the time-phased requirements up through the distribution network, thereby revealing and linking together the replenishment needs of both supplying and satellite warehouses. The choice of using DRP or combining it with statistical replenishment techniques for product replenishment is a management decision requiring an understanding of the nature of customer demand, the dynamics of the distribution channel, inventory and supplier characteristics, and the application of the necessary computerized tools.

The chapter begins with a review of the limitations associated with the use of statistical inventory replenishment methods and their impact on inventory planning. Following this general overview, the chapter then proceeds to a discussion of the theory and processing logic of DRP. After detailing the data elements and format of DRP, the mechanics of the DRP computer logic are reviewed. Particular attention is paid to analyzing how DRP uses *time-phased* demand and supply input to generate output information that can be used by the inventory planner to guide resupply order action. Now that the concepts and processing logic of DRP have been explored, the focus shifts to outlining the DRP inventory planning process. The chapter concludes with a brief review of the application of *supply chain planning* (SCP) and *supply chain event management* (SCEM) technologies to supply chain management. Based on the inventory planning tools found in DRP, the purpose and content of SCP and SCEM are detailed as prime drivers of today's advanced virtual supply chains.

PROBLEMS WITH STATISTICAL TECHNIQUES

Statistical methods of planning for inventory replenishment have been in use for over a century. In the days before computers and the ability to process large amounts of transaction data on a timely basis, using mathematical calculations and formulas based on statistical averages were the only tools available to inventory planners. Although statistical replenishment models remain a valid technique for controlling inventories subject to *independent demand*, inventory control professionals, nevertheless, have long been aware of severe limitations lurking beneath the "scientific" image the techniques evoke. As Orlicky [1] has pointed out, statistical methods have never really provided the timely and accurate information necessary for effective inventory management. In fact, the seemingly inescapable logic of the mathematical calculations are, in reality, little more than crutches supplying summary, approximated information often based on unpractical assumptions, sometimes force-fitting replenishment patterns so as to validate the use of a technique. As a result, practitioners continue to be plagued by the planning, functional integration, and performance measurements deficiencies that have long accompanied the use of statistical inventory control methods.

Problems associated with the use of statistical methods of inventory replenishment can be divided into two major categories. The first has to deal with inherent shortcomings found at the core of the technique; the second category relates to resulting organizational difficulties caused by the use of replenishment models. The salient points relating to the former can be outlined as follows:

Decisions Based on Statistical Calculations. All inventory replenishment techniques based on statistics seek to arrive at the most *probable* course of future demand usage by determining patterns in the stream of historical data. Statistical models work best when inventory transactions recur consistently with minimal variation; they are less useful when demand and supply information is characterized by random variation in timing and order quantities. Obviously, the vulnerability of statistical approaches resides in the assumption that reality will conform to the elements used in the mathematical model. For example, the order point assumes that inventory demand during the replenishment lead time will match the average past usage. Experience demonstrates, however, that actual usage variation can and does occur despite the most sophisticated mathematical models, resulting in either overstock or stockout. In the final analysis, all statistical replenishment techniques are purely ordering systems. As such, they provide no window into the future and lag behind changing customer, product, delivery, and supplier realities.

Difficult to Use. One of the most important issues associated with the use of statistical models is the difficulty planners and, especially, other members of the enterprise have in understanding the mechanics of the various techniques. For the most part, company members involved with statistical models require formal training to effectively select and apply reorder and order quantity methods. As computerized distribution systems become increasingly automated, even to the point where the software actually performs automatic purchase order release, companies must be on guard against surrendering control and isolating individuals from understanding how the system works.

Safety Stock. Because even the best statistical technique cannot predict with certainty *when* existing stocks will run out, order points are best used with a targeted quantity of safety stock. The problem with safety stock is that, theoretically, if the order point is accurate, safety stock becomes merely an unused buffer forcing companies to carry inventory that is never intended to be sold. What is more, as the level of customer serviceability increases, the required level of safety stock and accompanying inventory cost increases exponentially with no assurance that unexpected demand will still not drive inventory to stockout.

The Order Point Revisited. The formula for calculating the order point is

$$OP = (\text{Item usage} \times \text{Lead time}) + \text{Safety stock}$$

Although a time-proven technique, each of the elements of the order point is subject to variation. To begin with, *item usage*, no matter how it is computed, is always an *average* calculated by dividing demand over a specific number of past periods. In reality, actual usage for an item in any future period may be below or above the average demand, forcing planners to carry stock in some periods that does not sell, while stocking out in others. Although modern computer systems can dynamically update item usage, it, nevertheless, is still an average.

Lead times are notorious for being inaccurate. A myriad of factors can alter lead time: using an alternate supplier, rush orders, changes in lot size, alternate forms of transportation, time-saving computer automation, supplier relocation, and others. Inaccurate lead time data can have a significant impact on inventories. Say, for example, that the average usage for a given item was 1000 units a month, the standard cost $2.35, and the lead time from the supplier 15 days. The order point would be calculated as 1000 x 0.5 = 500 pieces at a stocking cost of $1175. If the supplier cut the lead time in half, the new order point would drop from 500 pieces to _250_ (1000 x .25 = 250). If the inventory planners did not update the item record, the firm would be stocking $587.50 of needless inventory. When multiplied by possibly thousands of items, enormous savings in inventory costs could be gained simply by the continuous reduction and updating of lead times [2].

The EOQ Revisited. The classic formula for calculating the EOQ is expressed as

$$\text{EOQ} = \sqrt{\frac{\text{Period constant x Order cost x Item usage}}{\text{Carrying cost x Unit cost}}}$$

As is the case with the order point formula, each of the elements of the EOQ calculation is subject to variation. To begin with, *unit cost* must be constantly updated to reflect all cost changes. Next, Woolsey [3] argues that the *carrying cost*, usually expressed as a percentage of item unit cost per unit time, is subject to significant variance and has been severely understated in the traditional calculation. Normally, firms compute the carrying cost as the cost of money at prime rate plus points. This calculation results in a flattening out of the total cost in the area of the optimal order quantity. In practice, few firms will run their business with the objective of returning only the prime rate of interest. The real cost of carrying inventory is lower bound by the rate of return earned by the best selling items characterized by high markup and high market demand. If the best mover in the product line had a markup of 65 percent, the total cost of carrying inventory would be significantly higher, with a much smaller band of error surrounding the optimum cost point.

The validity of *historical usage* has already been discussed earlier. If usage is determined by a sales forecast, its chance of accuracy is even less. As was pointed out in Chapter 4, the two things known for sure about a forecast is that it will be *wrong* and that it will *change*. Finally, the period *constant* assumes that demand is continuous and incremental. In reality, demand, no matter how marketing attempts to channel and position it, can exhibit significant variance in any given period.

In addition to potential inaccuracies within the formula, the EOQ is founded on a number of tenuous assumptions. Silver and Peterson [4] point out the following assumptions integral to the EOQ technique:

- Customer demand is constant and deterministic
- The order quantity is neither restricted by a lot size or minimums or maximums on order quantity size
- The item unit variable cost does not depend on the order quantity, and there are no discounts
- Item unit variable cost remains fairly constant over time.
- Benefits attained from joint replenishment are negligible.
- The *entire* order quantity is delivered at the same time.

These assumptions point to the fact that the statistical calculations required for the EOQ perform best when the coefficients are static and not susceptible to variation.

The Problem of Lumpy Demand. Besides randomness in customer buying habits, actual inventory demand is often driven radically upward and downward by lumpiness in actual order quantities. Lumpy demand can be broken down into two categories. The first is lumpiness caused by quantity-driven factors, such as lot-size requirements resulting from purchasing, manufacturing, packaging, shipping, selling, and stocking. In addition, batch order picking, the number of stocking locations, and company inventory stocking policies can also produce lumpy demand. Lumpiness is also caused by time-driven factors, such as seasonality, promotions and deals, price changes, product and packaging changes, and lead times for order processing, purchase order receipt, and shipping. Although promotions and seasonality cause the most nervousness, both quantity- and time-related factors will have an effect that can ripple up and down the distribution network.

Effects on the Distribution Channel. Order point systems provide supplying warehouses in the channel with little visibility into satellite warehouse inventory requirements. In fact, statistical techniques trigger replenishment orders and place them on supplying warehouses with no advanced warning, independent of supply point inventory availability or the needs of other satellite warehouses in the network. In addition, the random arrival of resupply orders makes it difficult for supplying warehouses to plan for cost-effective picking and shipping.

Beyond these core problems at the heart of statistical inventory control techniques can be found even more serious deficiencies that significantly impact negatively the entire supply channel. Supply chain inventory management in the twenty-first century requires real-time, responsive inventory planning systems capable of aligning the changing needs of the customer with the inventory resources of the entire distribution channel network. Statistical methods of running the business result in the application of static operational tools to solve the problems of today's dynamic distribution environment. Some of the major obstacles associated with statistical inventory techniques affecting the achievement of more agile and real-time supply chains are as follows:

Lack of Integration. Because the successful supply chains of the twenty-first century will be those that can rapidly deploy inventory to meet customer service targets, it is imperative that channel inventory planning systems be supportive and closely integrated with the core business functions of the enterprise. Unfortunately, although statistical approaches to inventory control provide satisfactory *tactical* tools, they lack the capacity to provide the necessary *strategic* linkages to draw together and keep in alignment the enterprise's long-range business plans with everyday order processing and inventory procurement activities. Statistical inventory methods determine inventory action based on summary demand information, provide limited simulation capabilities for charting alternative courses of action, are insensitive to capacity issues such as cost, warehouse space, and transportation, calculate inventory replenishment action in isolation from business, marketing, and sales realities, and provide little information that can be utilized to determine the performance of individual companies and the supply chain as a whole. In addition, statistical inventory control techniques lack the mechanism to effectively couple business functions and channel partners together. The lack of *internal* and *external* integration draws the firm's energies away from purposeful planning to be focused on reflex reactions to the problems caused by the decoupling of strategic objec-tives, operations plans, and operations execution functions.

Response to Change. If a single word can be used to describe distribution in today's business climate, it is *change*. However, statistical approaches to business management are, by their very natures, *reactive* rather than *proactive* to change. By depending on the occurrences of the past to predict the course of the future, statistical methods cannot hope to provide distribution managers with the timely information necessary to integrate the resources of their businesses with the demands of their marketing channels.

Channel Management. Inventories in a distribution channel determined by statistical methods are normally managed in a vacuum. Each stocking point calculates its own resupply requirements *independent* of the aggregate flow of information and material as it moves through the channel from supplier to customer. In such an environment, the ability of planners to integrate supply point forecasts with the corporate forecast is seriously diminished. The absence of effective *external* integration renders the distribution enterprise powerless to respond to the constant changes occurring in marketplace demand and supply patterns.

Supplier Negotiations. Because statistical replenishment systems fail to provide a window into future demand requirements, purchasers using such techniques have had a great deal of trouble negotiating long-term contracts with suppliers. For the most part, purchasing methods driven by order points and order quantities consider the purchase order as a unique, one-time contract for specific goods at a determined delivery date. When long-term supplier agreements have occurred, they have traditionally been based on aggregate inventory models determined by historical usage. What is really needed for effective supplier negotiating and contracting is not faster purchase order generation but a way to schedule supplier capacity out through time. In reality, customer demand changes frequently, forcing planners to rely on quick response on the part of their suppliers. Traditional purchasing is concerned with price; world-class purchasing is concerned with *quality* and *timely delivery*.

Excess Inventory. Statistical methods of inventory replenishment force companies to carry excess inventory. As was stated in Chapter 7, the objective of stock replenishment techniques is to restore inventory quantities to a predetermined level sufficient to respond to anticipated demand. The optimal level of stocked inventory is necessary to compensate for the inability of planners to determine the precise timing and quantity of customer demand in the immediate future. Line points and safety stocks provide order points with even higher inventory thresholds before order action is triggered. On the other hand, academics, consultants, and practitioners alike are firm in the belief that zero inventories and the elimination of all lead times constitutes the ideal inventory planning environment. In contrast, statistical replenishment techniques require stocked inventory because they suffer from false assumptions about the demand environment, tend to misinterpret observed demand behavior, and lack the ability to determine the specific timing of future demand [5].

Performance Measurement. Traditionally, in statistical replenishment the inventory size, cost, turnover, and service levels of each stocking point are measured separately and in isolation from the performance of the channel as a whole. However, uncoupled inventory and customer service plans, no matter how successful at the branch level, may actually foster a decline in channel-wide effectiveness. Statistical methods cause higher but avoidable inventory costs, slow down the flow of products to the customer, and conceal operational efficiencies and unbalanced capacities among channel partners. These results are squarely at odds with today's SCM inventory management objectives that require the distribution function to be able to leverage and rapidly deploy the totality of its inventory and working capital to achieve and maintain the competitiveness not only of individual companies, but of the entire supply chain matrix.

HISTORICAL VIEW

Up until the advent of the computer, planners had no choice but to use the traditional statistical methods for inventory planning and control. The size and scope of a firm's daily transactions made detail analysis of inventory demand usage and supply requirements virtually impossible. The development of perpetual inventory systems and the advent of the computer permitted inventory planners to move to a new dimension.

PERPETUAL INVENTORY CONTROL

The use of statistical ordering techniques was provided with a new dimension around 1950 with the introduction of the concept of *perpetual inventory control*. Through the use of inventory management systems like "Kardex" and advances in office automation, such as punch-card data processing tools, inventory planners were presented with the opportunity to move beyond planning inventory levels through the use of summary data and review the impact of inventory transactions in detail as they occurred in time. Perpetual inventory control seemed to offer the answer to the problems facing statistical replenishment. Inventory status information could be vastly expanded by programming computers to continuously calculate the difference between customer demand and on-hand stock plus open purchase order quantities and then suggest new replenishment orders when necessary. The inventory status equation is expressed as

$$OH + OO - QR = QA,$$

where *OH* is the quantity on-hand, *OO* is the quantity on order, *QR* is the quantity required, and *QA* is the quantity available. This equation seemed to work well with statistical replenishment elements. A positive quantity available indicates that a given item had sufficient inventory; a negative indicates that the planner should release a resupply order in the form of the order quantity.

Although the perpetual inventory record did provide planners with better information that answered the questions of what item needed to be order and in what quantities, it was incapable of answering the simple question of *when* will customer demand exceed available and planned supply? No matter how sophisticated the technique, the statistical order point cannot provide information determining what will be the projected inventory balance of a given item a quarter, a month, even a week from now. The system simply alerts the planner that the quantity necessary to satisfy the demand during the replenishment lead time has fallen below the order point and that resupply order action must occur if a stockout is to be prevented. In addition, because order point techniques are basically *due date insensitive,* the planner may be given erroneous data. Say, for example, that the *inventory position* is calculated from the following data elements:

Order point	75 units
Current on-hand	+ 100 units
Open purchase order	+ 200 units
Open customer order	- 200 units
Inventory position	100 units

Because the *inventory position* at the end of the calculation is 25 units above the order point, the planner would not be prompted to order additional stock. Once, however, due dates for the sales and purchase orders are entered into the equation as illustrated below, the situation radically changes.

Current date	August 28
Current on-hand	100 units
Open purchase order	200 units due September 15
Open customer order	200 units due September 1

Although the *inventory position* is above the order point, the actual dates the orders are due indicates that the customer order will be short 100 units and will actually have to wait an additional 15 days until the purchase order is received. Everyone knows what will happen in the above situation: The customer's order will be short at shipment time and the buyer/planner will have to call the supplier and expedite the open purchase order to arrive as soon as possible.

Equally as bad is the reverse of the above timing conditions. Using the data from the same equation, but with different order dates, different results will occur.

Current on-hand	100 units
Open purchase order	200 units due September 1
Open customer orders	100 units due September 1
	100 units due October 10

Without calculating the timing of order due dates, what appears to be a satisfactory situation will actually result in needlessly stocking a whole month's worth of inventory. In both instances, the stock coverage is adequate in terms of quantity, but the timing is out of synchronization with actual customer demand. In reality, the order action messages to the planner should have been in the first example to "expedite the purchase order in 15 days," and for the latter, "reschedule the purchased quantity of 100 out to October 10."

The above examples illustrate the fundamental weaknesses that reside at the core of statistical replenishment techniques. Essentially, there are three critical areas: (1) information on demand and supply timing is missing, (2) the data on customer and purchase orders represent summaries, and (3) the calculation does not provide for planned (future) requirements. The order point and order quantity formulas are concerned solely with manipulating *inventory quantities*. In reality, what inventory planners are concerned about is managing *time*. When will stock need to be on hand to cover customer orders and anticipated forecast demand? If the firm is planning a promotion, when will additional inventory quantities be needed to prevent stockout? When must open purchase orders be received to satisfy changing customer demand. When should new purchase orders be planned? By focusing on the issue of *time* rather than on *quantity*, the basis of inventory planning shifts from a concern with arithmetical calculations to forecast, sales, and purchase order priority management.

ORIGINS OF DRP

When computers became commercially available, businesses naturally sought to utilize the significant increase in data processing speed and accuracy to solve the host of problems inherent in the statistical techniques. It was reasoned that if information concerning inventory balances, lead times, safety stocks, costs, and customer demand could be processed faster, the persistent problems found in replenishment methods could be eliminated. Inventory planners soon discovered, however, that simply calculating mathematical formulas faster only made more evident the planning, supply channel integration, and performance measurement deficiencies that had long characterized statistical methods. What planners really needed were computerized tools that changed significantly not only the *quantitative* but also the *qualitative* na-ture of the information used to guide the inventory planning process. Statistical replenishment models provided tools for the *tactical* control of inventories. It soon became evident that planners needed information tools that enabled them to leverage inventory planning and control as a *strategic* resource, integrated with top management planning and, in turn, driving the supply channel's execution functions. The breakthrough occurred with the extension of the *time-phase order point* as found in MRP logic to channel inventory management.

The ability to *time-phase* the interplay of supply and demand is the very foundation of DRP - *Distribution Requirements Planning*. According to Andre Martin, the application of DRP to the distribution environment was first implemented in 1975 at Abbott Laboratories, Montreal, Canada [6]. During the years following, the basic concept of DRP was expanded to embrace not only inventory planning and control but also logistics functions. By the early 1980s, DRP, renamed *Distribution Resource Planning*, was being championed by consultants as the standard approach to be used for planning and controlling the matrix of distribution logistics activities. Since that time, the concept has been expanded to embrace not just inventory and logistics but also the business functions of the whole supply channel. Termed DRP II, the basic mechanics of DRP form the core of a business philosophy for "planning the utilization of the totality of a distribution enterprise's resources, while providing for the execution and performance measurement of material procurement, distribution and financial accounting [7]."

Basics of DRP

Adding the element of *time* to the basic perpetual inventory equation requires that the inventory planning system be able to record and store the specific due dates and quantities of forecasts and open customer and supply orders. In addition, the system must be able to time-phase by due date on-hand, demand requirements and resupply stock on order, and calculate the inventory equation each time an order due date appears. This means that the system must be able to subtract the supply from the demand, or add on-order quantities to on-hand quantities, as the due dates of each are referenced through time. If sufficient inventory remains after each calculation, then there is no resupply action to perform. If, on the other hand, the result is a negative, the system should alert the planner that a potential stockout will occur at that point in time so that a counterbalancing planned order quantity can be placed in anticipation of a future shortage. Although, in reality, DRP reviews by due date each occasion of item demand and the corresponding availability of supply stock, a visual format, as portrayed in Figure 8.1, can significantly assist in

On-Hand = 1000 units
Lead Time = 2 Periods
Order Quantity = 500

Periods	1	2	3	4	5	6	7	8
Demand	300	300	300	300	300	300	300	300
Supply	700	400	100	300	0	200	400	100
Net Reqs				200		300	100	
Plan Ord Recpts				500		500	500	
Plan Ord Rel		500		500	500			

FIGURE 8.1. Time-phased format.

making the computation. The contents of the format can be described as the following:

1. *Time Periods.* The time-phased inventory equation is associated with specific time periods or *buckets*. A period can be as short as a minute or day, or as long as a week, a month, or even longer. The exact size of the period and the placement of inventory data within it are governed by several system conventions. Period size is usually determined by the user and can consist of an array of buckets all with the same size, or a mixture of sizes (Figure 8.2). Once the size of the period has been

	Week				Month				Quarter			
	1	2	3	4	2	3	4	5	2	3	4	5
Reqs	5	5	5	5	20	20	20	20	60	60	60	60

FIGURE 8.2 Time bucket variation.

determined, the next decision is to determine exactly *when* an order requirement is due within the period. If the period is of 1 day in duration, this is not an issue. For periods of longer duration, however, it must be determined whether customer and supply orders are due on the first day of the period, midpoint in the period, on the last day of the period, or anytime during the period but no later than the last day. For the most part, the convention is to use the first day of the period. Finally, when the DRP generates a *planned supply order* in response to an impending shortage, the system must place both the planned order's due date and release date in the appropriate time buckets. The difference between the due date and the release date is the item's lead time (Figure 8.3). The point where the planned order falls due within the bucket is not an optional decision but must always follow the same convention as used for positioning customer and interbranch supply orders.

Periods	1	2	3	4	5	6	7	8
Plan Ord Recpts			20			40		
Plan Ord Rel	20			40				

FIGURE 8.3 Two week lead time offset

2. *Gross Requirements.* This term defines the quantity of an item that will have to be issued from inventory to support demand. Demand on an

item originates essentially from three sources: the backlog of open customer orders, forecasts, and interbranch resupply orders. Each form of gross requirement must contain the following data elements for the DRP to function properly: a discrete item number, the required quantity, and the date each requirement is due. Time-phasing summarizes the required quantity of each of these sources of demand by due date and then places the total in the appropriate time bucket. The content of the gross requirements is normally determined by the type of distribution activity. For a retail distributor, forecasts form the gross requirements. A regional distribution center's gross requirements, on the other hand, may consist solely of interbranch resupply orders from satellite warehouses. Finally, a regional distribution center that also services customers may have all three types of gross requirements.

3. *Scheduled Receipts.* This term defines the total quantity of open replenishment orders for an item. Replenishment orders in the distribution environment can take three forms: supplier purchase, value-added processing, and interbranch resupply orders. Purchase orders specify products and inventory quantities that must be purchased from the firm's suppliers. If a distributor has value-added processing functions, inventory could be restocked by bulk breaking, sorting, kitting, light assembly, and other processing activities. Finally, for companies with distribution channels, branch warehouses will draw needed inventory from their parent warehouses through the use of a resupply order. In addition, inventory in-transit from one warehouse to another is also considered as a form of resupply order. Each of the forms of replenishment order must contain the following elements for DRP to function: a discrete order number, the products to be resupplied, the quantities required, and the date the order is due. Once orders have been released, they represent *firm* commitments on the part of the supply source to deliver the orders complete on the date required. As such, DRP considers on-order quantities as available inventory in the calculation of projected on-hand quantities in that time period.

4. *On-Hand Balance.* Unlike the statistical replenishment calculation, which is a straight arithmetical computation, DRP provides the planner visibility to *projected on-hand* quantities by time period after supply has been subtracted from the demand. The assumption is that forecasts and future open customer and supply orders are firm and will occur when their due dates are reached. The logic of the on-hand computation can be expressed as

Balance on hand at the end of the current period
plus   The total of scheduled receipts due in the succeeding period
minus The total of gross requirements of the succeeding period
equals The projected on-hand balance at the end of the succeeding period

If no inventory activity occurs in a period, the projected on-hand balance from the previous period is carried forward to the next. The projected on-hand balance calculation is illustrated in Figure 8.4.

On-Hand = 1300 units

Periods	1	2	3	4	5	6	7	8
Gross Reqs	300	300	300	300	300	300	300	300
Sch Recpts					200			
POH	1000	700	400	100		-300	-600	-900
Net Reqs						300	300	300

FIGURE 8.4 Projected on-hand balance.

5. *Planned Order Receipt.* When demand exceeds supply forcing the on-hand quantities in a particular time period to go negative, the system records the negative amount as a *net requirement.* In a DRP system, all *net requirements* are covered by system generated *planned orders.* A planned order is an *unreleased* supply order. The generation of a planned order is governed by the following elements:
    1.   The date when the net requirement is recorded.
    2.   The order policy rule which determines the lot-size quantity necessary to satisfy the net requirement.
The replenishment lot-size quantity must equal or exceed the net requirement in the first period in which a projected negative on-hand is found. The due date of the planned order is the required date of the source of the demand that triggered the net requirement. The planned order should provide sufficient inventory to cover all actual customer orders and unconsumed forecast in the period starting with the due date of the first demand and ending at the date of the last day of the period. Because of the quantity of the lot size, it may be large enough to cover the net requirements of one or more subsequent time periods.
6. *Planned Order Release.* Once a planned order has been generated, the DRP system will seek to determine the release date of the order. The date a planned order is to be released is calculated by subtracting the

value of the product's *replenishment lead time* from the planned order receipt date. As an example,

Planned order receipt date	Week 7
Lead time (weeks)	- 2
Planned order release date	Week 5

After the release date has been determined for the product, the DRP system will reference the item's order policy code. This code will tell the system how the actual replenishment quantity will be calculated. Once these data elements have been generated, the planner will be alerted to transform the planned order into an actual resupply order.

The DRP time-phased format outlined above is designed to assist the inventory planner in visually understanding the interaction of supply and demand. The computer system will populate each time bucket with the appropriate customer and purchase orders by due date and then calculate the required planned orders. The planner, in turn, must be able to interpret the data and respond with the recommended resupply order action.

DRP PROCESSING

The advantage of DRP over order point techniques resides in the ability of the inventory planner to see the relationship of supply and demand, not just as it occurs in the current planning period, but also as it is projected out through time. The time-phasing technique permits the user to be proactive to potential inventory shortages before they occur to ensure the highest service level at the least inventory cost.

DATA ELEMENTS

Before the DRP system can effectively process demand and supply data, several other key pieces of additional item-level information must be added to the equation. In the standard DRP system, these data would be input into each product's planning data master file.

Order Policies. When resupply order action is triggered for an item, the system must know the replenishment lot-size quantity associated with the product. The most common order policies used in DRP systems are the following:

1. *Discrete* (lot-for-lot). This order policy will recommend a resupply quantity that matches exactly each item's net requirements by due date.

This technique must be used with caution. It will generate a planned order pegged to each requirement.

2. *Fixed period requirements.* In this technique, the system will calculate the replenishment quantity based on a simple rule of ordering *n* period's supply. A field in the item record is input with a value representing the number of forward periods the DRP looks when processing begins. All the net requirements spanning the periods defined are then summed, and a discrete planned order quantity matching this sum is placed in the Planned Order Release row in the first of the defined set of periods.

3. *Discrete above the standard lot size.* Often an item is to be resupplied in quantities of a certain lot size because of discounting or shipping purposes. This order policy requires the user to set the required lot-size quantity in the product master record. In the first period in which the product has a net requirement the system will recommend purchase of at least the lot size *plus* additional quantity sufficient to cover exactly the remaining net requirement. If the net requirement is less than the lot size, then only the lot size is purchased.

4. *Incremental above the standard lot size.* This order policy is based on two values entered in the product master record: the lot size and an incremental quantity that is to be added to the lot size when the net requirement is greater than the lot size. For example, if the lot size is 100 units and the incremental quantity is 25 units, a net requirement for 130 units will result in the system calculating a planned order quantity of 150 units.

5. *Multiples of a standard lot size.* When using this order policy, the system will attempt to satisfy the net requirement with the product's replenishment lot size. If the requirement is greater than the lot size, the system will counter with multiples of the lot size until the planned order quantity covers the net requirement. For example, if the lot size is 100 units, a net requirement for 130 units will result in the generation of a planned order for 200 units.

6. *EOQ models.* The use of an order quantity derived from the standard EOQ calculation discussed in Chapter 7 can also be used to determine order quantities. Although never intended for a time phased requirements planning environment, an EOQ can be easily incorporated into the DRP logic. The steps would be first to determine the EOQ for each product. Then, when the DRP performs the gross-to-net calculation, the planned order quantities that would be generated in response to a net requirement would be expressed in lot sizes of the EOQ. Use of an EOQ in a DRP system can only be justified when the demand for stocked products is both continuous and governed by a steady rate. The

more a company's demand is discontinuous and nonuniform, the less applicable an EOQ order policy will be.

7. *Lot costing models.* The final order policy model is to use some form of lot size that, like the EOQ, seeks to minimize the sum of inventory carrying costs. *Least unit cost, least total cost,* and various forms of mathematical or computerized lot sizing techniques, such as the *Wagner-Whitin algorithm,* fall with this model.

Lead Time. Lead time enables the DRP system to *backschedule* order release based on the planned receipt date. The content of a product's lead time is composed of several elements, including planning time, supplier search and order generation, supplier picking, preparation, and transportation activities, and receiving and stock put-away. Although critical to the effective functioning of DRP, absolute lead-time accuracy is not crucial. In the final analysis, empirically derived lead-time values are sufficient for the ef-fective functioning of DRP. As will be pointed out in Chapter 10, purchasers would be far better off concentrating their energies on building collaborative partnerships and negotiating supplier scheduling than chasing lead-time accuracy.

Forecast Demand Type. For those distribution points that utilize forecasting, the DRP system should provide the user with the option of choosing how the system is to use the relationship between forecasts and booked customer orders when determining an item's gross requirements. There are four possible options.

1. *Customer orders consume forecast.* This option is the most widely used of the four. In this technique, the computer is programmed to reduce the period product forecast by the total quantity of customer orders due in that same period. For example, if the original forecast for a product in a given period was 100 units and the customer orders booked in that period totaled 80 units, the system would recalculate the new forecast as 20 units. If the quantity of booked customer orders for a time bucket exceeded the product forecast, then the order total would be used as the period's total demand requirement. In addition, provision must be made for forecast that is unrealized and falls past due. Should unsold forecast be simply forgotten, or should it be added to the forecast of the current period in anticipation of late customer orders that should have matured in the previous period.

2. *Forecast only.* When this option is chosen, only the forecast is used to determine a product's gross requirements. Although customer orders are tracked, they do not influence gross requirement quantities. This option, for instance, would be used by distributors who want to drive resupply from a buy plan.

3. *Customer orders only.* This is the inverse of the above option. It would be chosen by distributors who have very short replenishment lead times and the ability to respond quickly to customer orders.
4. *Customer orders plus forecast.* This option would provide an extremely conservative approach to managing inventories. The gross requirements for products using this technique would be calculated by *adding* customer order quantities to the forecast as they occur in each period. Distributors inventorying products with very long replenishment lead times might employ this option.

Safety Stock. The use of safety stock is critical when statistical replenishment techniques are used in an environment of probabilistic demand. DRP can also use safety stock to provide a buffer against uncertainty in customer demand. When the DRP processes, it will seek to preserve the integrity of the safety quantity so that it is always on hand (Figure 8.5). As safety stock creates in essence "dead stock" that is never intended to be used, it should be kept to the absolute minimum.

On-Hand = 1300 units
Safety Stock = 125

Periods	1	2	3	4	5	6	7	8
Gross Reqs	300	300	300	300	300	300	300	300
Sch Recpts				200				
POH	1000	700	400	300		-300	-600	-900
Net Reqs					125	300	300	300

FIGURE 8.5 Safety stock calculation.

Planning Horizon. For purposes of inventory replenishment, the length of the planning horizon should at least equal the longest resupply product lead time. If the horizon is too short, the DRP system will not be able to respond in time to prevent product stockout. In addition, too short a planning horizon diminishes the visibility necessary for planning logistics capacity requirements. For the sake of transparency, planners can alter the size of DRP time periods, starting with weeks, then months, then quarters or even years.

THE DRP CALCULATION

The generation of *planned orders* to cover all future product net requirements is the cornerstone of the DRP planning process. For each product with a net requirement, DRP develops a schedule of planned replenishment orders necessary to cover all net requirements out through the planning horizon. Finally, the DRP schedules inventory resupply action that will have to be taken in the future if stockout is to be avoided.

The DRP process is derived from input from the following sources:

- Product forecasts by due date
- Forecast demand code
- Open customer orders by product by due date
- Beginning on-hand quantities by product
- Open purchase, interbranch, and value-added processing orders by product by due date
- Replenishment lead times by product
- Safety stock by product
- Order policy codes by product
- Size of the planning buckets

Once these data elements have been collected by the DRP processor, the system will begin to populate the contents of each planning bucket by referencing forecast, customer, and resupply order due dates and then performing the gross-to-net requirements calculation. When the first net requirement appears, the system will generate a matching planned order with a quantity determined by the product's order policy code. An example of the full DRP processing logic appears in Figure 8.6.

On-Hand = 1000 units
Lead Time = 2 Periods
Safety Stock = 125
Order Quantity = 500

Periods	1	2	3	4	5	6	7	8
Gross Reqs	300	300	300	300	300	300	300	300
Sch Recpts			500					
POH	700	400	600	300	0	-100		
Net Reqs					125			
Plan Ord Recpts					500			
Plan Ord Rel			500					

FIGURE 8.6 Full DRP calculation.

When the DRP calculation is complete, the inventory planner will be provided with output information that can be used to guide resupply order action. The outputs from the DRP calculation are the following:

1. *Exception reporting.* Current commercial DRP systems provide the user with the ability to see the results of the entire DRP run or to print only those products that require order action. An *exception report* will greatly assist planners in focusing in on critical inventory problems and will provide the basis for constructive supplier scheduling. Many DRP systems have sophisticated workbench maintenance screens on which planners can review, change resupply recommendations, and generate purchase orders automatically.

2. *Planned orders.* The DRP generation will provide the planner with a window into the schedule of product planned order release. At a minimum, the planner ***must*** release planned orders into actual resupply orders for all products that have a value greater than zero in their current period planned order release bucket. If order action is not taken, the product will slip inside its replenishment lead time, causing expediting and possible premium purchase costs. This first period is called the *action bucket period.* Planned orders are the essence of the DRP system, illuminating future product requirements and forming the basis for such projections as on-hand inventory, supplier scheduling, and logistic capacity planning.

3. *Action messages.* As an aid to the planner in interpreting the exception report and performing order maintenance, most commercial DRP systems provide planning *action messages.* The following are core action messages.

   a *Release planned order.* The planned order has reached the replenishment lead time and must be converted into a purchase order.

   b *Lead-time violation.* The planned order has slipped inside the replenishment lead time. Immediate order action should be taken and the order expedited.

   c *Expedite in scheduled receipt.* The due date of an open resupply order should be scheduled in to cover a new net requirement. *De-expedite a scheduled receipt.* The due date of an open resupply order should be moved back because of changes in net requirements.

   d *Cancel.* An open supply order should be canceled due to changes in net requirements.

4. *Pegged requirements.* The pegging of requirements provides the planner with the ability to trace product gross requirements to their sources. Because the value in the gross requirements bucket is a summary figure, this feature will pinpoint the actual sources of demand.

Bucketless DRP. Although DRP permits the planner to define system output time periods (buckets), in reality the system records net requirements by due date. Time buckets are merely a convenient way to aggregate demand and supply data for viewing purposes. Most commercial DRP systems provide a bucketless display, permitting the planner to see the projected on-hand balance based on the daily relationship of demand and supply. Table 8.1 provides an example of a bucketless display. Note that released and planned supply orders are included in the on-hand balance calculation. The bucketless format provides a more efficient display of product status in that it provides full visibility to net requirements when they actually occur. A little more skill is required to use this format than the bucketed approach, but it provides the planner with the ability to exercise more detail control over product planning.

TABLE 8.1 Bucketless DRP Display

Product #: 1425-100		1/2hp Sump Pump		SS = 125	
Lead Time = 2 weeks		OHB = 1300		OQ = 1000	
Date	Gross Reqs	Ref #	Scheduled Receipts	Ref #	OHB
01/15/03	300	FOR			1000
01/17/03	300	FOR			700
01/20/03	200	FOR			500
	100	CO123			400
01/23/03			200	PO467	600
	300	FOR			300
01/27/03			1000	PlnOrder	1300
	300	FOR			700
01/30/03	300	FOR			400

DRP Regeneration Frequency. The frequency of DRP regeneration is a critical element in system use and needs to be set as a policy standard by each planning organization. Each DRP regeneration represents a complete repositioning of requirements and supply orders and the deletion and recalculation of all planned orders. Although some DRP systems can recalculate product statuses, such as open order and on-hand balances, dynamically in between regenerations, planned order creation is reserved for the actual DRP processor. As a general rule, the more dynamic the planning environment, the more frequently the DRP will have to be regenerated to keep product demand and supply in balance. As a rule of thumb, the DRP processor should *never* be rerun until all *actions messages* generated from the previous run are reviewed and cleaned-up. Failure to satisfy all action messages will result in a persistent demand/supply imbalance. Normally, most firms using DRP generate the system weekly. In addition, DRP is essentially a *continuous* rather than a *cyclical* planning tool. The DRP planning information is in reality a snapshot of current product availability. However, because product status accuracy begins to deteriorate immediately after generation, frequent regeneration will constantly realign product priorities necessary for timely order action.

DRP Compared to Statistical Order Point. Probably the best way to understand the advantages planner enjoy when using DRP is to contrast the technique with conventional statistical replenishment methods. For example, a product has the following planning factors:

Lead time	2 weeks
Safety stock	125 units
Product usage forecast	300 units per week
Order quantity	1000 units
On-hand	1300 units

The order point for this item would be calculated as follows:

$$OP = (300 \times 2) + 125 = 725 \text{ units.}$$

When the existing on-hand balance for this product falls below 725 units, the system would prompt the planner to purchase an order quantity of 1000 units.

The same planning data is portrayed in a DRP weekly time-phased format in Figure 8.7. The forecasted usage of 300 units has been projected over the

Periods	1	2	3	4	5	6	7	8
Gross Reqs	300	300	300	300	300	300	300	300
Sch Recpts								
POH	1000	700	400	1100	800	500	200	900
Net Reqs				25				225
Plan Ord Recpts				1000				1000
Plan Ord Rel		1000				1000		

FIGURE 8.7 DRP calculation.

length of the planning horizon and is the only source of the product's gross requirements. The gross-to-net requirements calculation indicates that the current on-hand quantities will drop below the safety stock of 125 units in period 4. Accordingly, a planned order receipt for 1000 units is planned to arrive at that time to prevent a shortage. Offsetting for the lead time of 2 weeks, the system has posted a planned order release in period 2. In period 8, the projected quantity will again be less than the safety stock, and a planned order release for 1000 units will be scheduled for period 6.

In the example, the results of using DRP and the statistical order point are identical. The reorder point of 725 units is tripped in period 2, at which time the order quantity of 1000 units would have been generated. DRP, however, does a great deal more than the order point to assist the planner. To begin with, the DRP format develops an entire schedule of planned replenishment orders for the planner. Statistical order point, on the other hand, only alerts the planner to release one order at a time. Second, the point in time when forecast demand is expected to drive the inventory below safety stock is transparent to the planner in DRP. Under statistical replenishment, the planner never knows when the order point will be tripped until it actually happens. Third, the DRP format is easy to understand and manipulate. There are no complicated formulas to memorize. Fourth, although there are no open orders in Figure 8.7, DRP will assist in keeping open supply order due dates valid. Unlike statistical replenishment, DRP will continually reschedule open orders to align them with projected requirements and keep their relative priorities valid. Fifth, DRP can effectively respond to the problems associated with lumpy demand. As irregular demand arising from lot sizes, promotions, as so forth occurs, the gross-to-net requirements calculation provides the planner with the ability to respond quickly with targeted order action to avoid stockout while keeping inventory levels in line with future demand. Finally, as will be illustrated later in this chapter, DRP provides planners with a window into detailed logistics capacities.

In addition, DRP has the ability to overcome forecasting and lead-time inaccuracies, two critical problems that plague traditional statistical replenishment. No matter how erroneous the forecast, DRP can replan quickly, accurately, automatically. Regardless of whether poor forecasts or a variance between forecast and actual demand caused the error, DRP can replan with equal ease. In fact, the self-adjusting nature of DRP renders absolute forecast accuracy unimportant. For example, using the data in Figure 8.7, actual demand in period 1 turns out to be *zero* instead of 300. In such an event, on-hand quantities in period 2 would then be 1300 rather than 1000. In this case, the system would simply schedule the planned order release from period 2 to period 3 to meet the new expected demand projected to occur in period 5. Inversely, if actual demand in period 1 turned out to be 600 units instead of 300, the system would reschedule the planned order release from period 2 to period 1 and give the planner a message to release the order. No matter how large the forecast error, DRP provides the mechanism for automatic adjustment of demand and supply and timely resupply order action.

Finally, DRP is also able to work with inaccurate lead times. Statistical ordering techniques are totally dependent on accurate forecast usages and lead times for their validity and accuracy. The problem is that both of these values are volatile by nature. In contrast, DRP uses lead times as a reference point. When actual purchase order receipt occurs, DRP can quickly adjust and plan for the new net requirements that are calculated. In this sense, DRP techniques enable the inventory planner to adjust quickly to what is actually happening, rather than what was planned to happen.

DRP IN A SUPPLY CHAIN ENVIRONMENT

Up to this point, the discussion of DRP has focused around inventory planning in a single facility environment. Although it is clear that DRP possesses several advantages over statistical replenishment models, the real power of the technique can be seen when planning inventories for a supply channel. The problems associated with statistical inventory control noted above are heightened when warehouse dependencies exist. Martin [8] has explored this point extensively.

DRP Versus Statistical Order Point

Assume that Company XYZ possesses a distribution channel structure as follows: From a central corporate warehouse in Chicago, three regional warehouses located in New York, Kansas City, and Los Angeles, who distribute directly to the customer, are supplied with identical products. Using conventional statistical replenishment techniques, the inventory planning data for a given item inventories throughout the distribution channel is portrayed in Figure 8.8.

When the inventory status of the Chicago warehouse is reviewed, say on the first Monday of the month, the planner would not be prompted to take any action. The order point quantity of 2260 units is below the on-hand quantity of 2300. On the same day, the inventory status of the distribution channel is reviewed. From the data, it is evident that both the New York and Los Angeles warehouses require replenishment orders to be placed, whereas Kansas City appears to have sufficient stock. The New York and Los Angeles resupply orders totaling 2100 units are transmitted to Chicago where they are received, picked, packed, and shipped by the end of Thursday that same week. On Friday morning, the planner in Chicago reviews the inventory and finds a remaining balance of 200 units on hand. Accordingly, a resupply order for 4000 units is placed with the supplier to arrive in three weeks. On the following Monday, the Kansas City warehouse, which appeared to have sufficient inventory the week before but had experienced sales in excess of its normal average usage, has tripped its order point and now sends a replenishment order request to Chicago for 400 units. Even though the planner in Chicago had taken the necessary order action the week before, the unexpected demand on the Kansas City warehouse has not only consumed the remaining 200 units but has resulted in a backorder for the remaining 200 units. Most likely the 200 units will be shipped and the supply order for 4000 units will have to be expedited.

<u>Supply Warehouse</u>

Chicago Warehouse

On-Hand Balance =	2300
Order Point =	2260
Order Quantity =	4000
Supplier Lead Time =	3 weeks
Safety Stock =	565

<u>Satellite Warehouses</u>

	New York	Kansas City	Los Angles
On-Hand Balance	550	275	750
Forecast Usage	210/week	80/week	275/week
Order Point	630	240	825
Order Quantity	1100	400	1000
Interbranch Lead Time	2 weeks	2 weeks	2 weeks
Safety Stock	210	80	275

FIGURE 8.8 Order point channel supply model.

The above scenario is commonplace in most distribution channel environments. The problem is not poor planning or a lack of effort on the part of the planners but the normal variation that products subject to *independent demand* experience. Order point techniques simply are not flexible enough to respond to the constant changes in demand and supply. The real culprit is the assumption that lead times and product usage during the replenishment lead time are fixed and constant. To counter random variation, most companies carry safety stock. But safety stock, no matter how sophisticated the calculation, is not the answer to the problem; indeed, it is actually part of the order point calculation! As Martin points out [9], order points fail to solve everyday problems because they are essentially designed as *ordering systems,* not *scheduling systems* like DRP. Statistical replenishment techniques simply cannot reschedule replenishment quantities as everyday supply and demand conditions change.

BILL OF DISTRIBUTION

Before the application of DRP to the multiechelon environment can be explored, it is essential to begin the discussion by detailing one of the fundamental requirements of the technique--the *Bill of Distribution* (BOD). Utilizing the structure and mechanics of the manufacturing *Bill of Material* (BOM), the BOD links supplying and satellite warehouses together similar to the way the BOM links component items to their assembly parents (Figure 8.9). The difference between the two is subtle but critical. When demand is

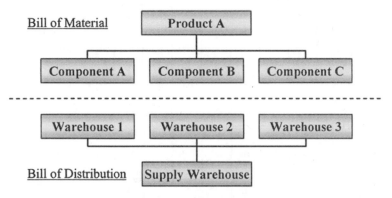

FIGURE 8.9 BOMs and BODs

posted on a parent assembly item, the MRP processor references the assembly's BOM and "explodes" the requirement through the product structure, placing demand on the component parts. The structure of the BOD, on the other hand, has been designed to facilitate the transfer of requirements from the components (the dependent supply warehouses) to the parent (the supplying warehouse). This structure, often called an *inverted BOM,* performs an *implosion* where requirements are passed up the structure rather than down. The exact structure of a BOD can be configured to match a variety of channel inventory flows. For example, not all items may be stocked in every warehouse. Again, a mixture of products might be sold to the customer from the central warehouse or from several regional or even local distribution points. In any case, for the DRP implosion to work effectively, the proper BODs must be structured detailing the flow of each and every product in the distribution channel [10].

The benefits of using the BOD can be summarized as follows:

- A comprehensive distribution channel can be structured, that can guide the computerized implosion process and provide planners with full visibility of supply and demand relationships up and down the channel

- Supplying and satellite warehouse dependencies are clearly established
- The DRP processor can begin its low level coding by beginning with the last warehouse(s) in the channel and progressing up through each level to the appropriate supplying warehouse
- The BOD establishes the framework for total logistics control from the distributor, up the network, and out to the supplier

SS = 210
LT = 2 weeks
OQ = 1100

New York Warehouse

	PD	1	2	3	4	5	6	7	8
Gross Reqs		210	210	210	210	210	210	210	210
Sch Recpts									
POH	550	340	1230	1020	810	600	390	1280	1070
Pln Ord Recpts			1100					1100	
Plan Ord Rel	1100					1100			

SS = 80
LT = 2 weeks
OQ = 400

Kansas City Warehouse

	PD	1	2	3	4	5	6	7	8
Gross Reqs		80	80	80	80	80	80	80	80
Sch Recpts									
POH	275	195	115	435	355	275	195	115	435
Pln Ord Recpts			400						400
Plan Ord Rel		400				400			

SS = 275
LT = 2 weeks
OQ = 1000

Los Angles Warehouse

	PD	1	2	3	4	5	6	7	8
Gross Reqs		275	275	275	275	275	275	275	275
Sch Recpts									
POH	750	475	1200	925	650	375	1100	825	550
Pln Ord Recpts			1000				1000		
Plan Ord Rel	1000				1000				

Supply Chain Requirements Summary

	PD	1	2	3	4	5	6	7	8
Gross Reqs	2100	400			1000	1100	400		

FIGURE 8.10 Branch DRP calculations.

Supply Chain DRP

The functioning of DRP in a supply chain environment can be clearly demonstrated by driving the same demand and supply conditions detailed in Figure 8.8 through the DRP process. After the dependent supply warehouses in New York, Kansas City, and Los Angeles have been linked through the BOD to the central supplying warehouse in Chicago, DRP logic will start time-phasing supply and demand by going to the warehouse at the lowest level in the BOD structure and performing the gross-to-net requirements calculation. As the process at each level in the structure is completed, the net requirements in the form of planned resupply orders are input by due date into the gross requirements buckets of the supplying warehouse, and the process begins again on that level. The DRP processor is completed when all levels in the BOD structure have been reviewed.

The results of the DRP process for the BOD detailed above are illustrated in Figure 8.10. As can be seen, the New York and Los Angles warehouses each have Planned Order Release quantities that have fallen past due. In normal circumstances, the planner would have reacted to both requirements when they had reached the *action bucket* period and would not be past due. In contrast, when the order point system is used, the fact that the order action requirement is within the vendor lead time is not shown. The problem with order points becomes even more visible in resupplying the Kansas City warehouse. The order point indicates that the warehouse possesses sufficient inventory and requires no order action. The DRP calculation, on the other hand, indicates that a replenishment order for 400 units is in the *action bucket* period and needs to be released.

SS = 565 LT = 3 weeks OQ = 4000		**Chicago Central Warehouse**							
	PD	1	2	3	4	5	6	7	8
Gross Reqs	2100	400			1000	1100	400		
Sch Recpts									
POH 2300	200	-200	-200	3800	2800	1700	1300	1300	1300
Pln Ord Recpts				4000					
Plan Ord Rel	4000								

FIGURE 8.11 Supply warehouse summary.

Although the advantages of using DRP in planning the inventory requirements for each warehouse is significant, the real impact of the technique is evident when planning information is driven up to the channel's supplying warehouse. As can be seen in Figure 8.11, the system would have alerted the planner *4 weeks earlier* that the projected demand from the channel would drive on-hand quantities below safety stock. The use of order points shows that before the order from the Kansas City warehouse arrived, the planner at the supplying warehouse would not have been prompted to reorder. What is worse, once the order point was tripped, the planner would have been inside the 3-week lead time and would have had to expedite the replenishment order.

The ability of DRP to provide the inventory planner with effective order action information can be seen more clearly by rolling back the calendar used in the above illustrations. Table 8.2 details the sales history for the same dis-

TABLE 8.2 Channel Sales History

Warehouse	Weekly Forecast	Actual Sales Past 4 Weeks	Current On-Hand	Adjusted On-Hand
New York	210	705	550	1255
Kansas City	80	305	275	580
Los Angles	285	1105	705	1855

tribution channel as it would have occurred 4 weeks previously. Based on the BOD, the planned order requirements for each of the three dependent supply warehouses (Figure 8.12) have been passed up to the Chicago warehouse, and the DRP gross-to-net requirements calculation performed (Figure 8.13). As can be seen, DRP would have alerted the corporate planner at the Chicago distribution center that projected channel demand had created a net requirement in period 4. By backscheduling the Planned Order Receipt by the supplier lead time of 3 weeks, the DRP system has placed a Planned Order Release in the first period. By releasing a purchase order for 4000 units with the supplier, the Chicago distribution center would have had sufficient inventories to meet total channel demand as it occurred.

DRP is a superior tool in comparison to statistical order point for the management of inventory in a distribution channel because it makes the changing requirements of channel demand and supply visible. Regardless of variances in customer and resupply orders, DRP monitors *future* requirements to assist planners in maintaining schedule priorities and preserving lead times to ensure product delivery. The order point technique simply could not project the timing of future demand and supply relationships, and when the order point was tripped, the planner had to expedite an already serious out-of-stock situation.

SS = 210
LT = 2 weeks
OQ = 1100

New York Warehouse

	PD	1	2	3	4	5	6	7	8
Gross Reqs		210	210	210	210	210	210	210	210
Sch Recpts									
POH	1255	1045	835	625	415	1305	1095	885	675
Pln Ord Recpts						1100			
Plan Ord Rel				1100					

SS = 80
LT = 2 weeks
OQ = 400

Kansas City Warehouse

	PD	1	2	3	4	5	6	7	8
Gross Reqs		80	80	80	80	80	80	80	80
Sch Recpts									
POH	580	500	420	340	260	180	100	420	340
Pln Ord Recpts								400	
Plan Ord Rel						400			

SS = 275
LT = 2 weeks
OQ = 1000

Los Angles Warehouse

	PD	1	2	3	4	5	6	7	8
Gross Reqs		275	275	275	275	275	275	275	275
Sch Recpts									
POH	1855	1580	1305	1030	755	480	1205	930	655
Pln Ord Recpts							1000		
Plan Ord Rel					1000				

Supply Chain Requirements Summary

	PD	1	2	3	4	5	6	7	8
Gross Reqs				1100	1000	400			

FIGURE 8.12 Channel revised summary.

DRP PLANNING PROCESS

Now that the concepts and processing logic of DRP have been described, it is possible to explore the management process to be used by inventory planners. In general, the objectives of DRP are the same as statistical replenishment: the creation of an efficient inventory procurement plan that optimizes tar-

SS = 565 LT = 3 weeks OQ = 4000	Chicago Central Warehouse								
	PD	1	2	3	4	5	6	7	8
Gross Reqs				1100	1000	400			
Sch Recpts									
POH	2300	2300	2300	1200	4200	3800	3800	3800	3800
Pln Ord Recpts					4000				
Plan Ord Rel		4000							

FIGURE 8.13 Revised supply warehouse summary.

geted customer service levels while minimizing inventory cost. In developing the DRP plan, inventory planners must answer questions such as the following:

- Is the planning data for each DRP planned product accurate and up to date?
- Have BODs been created that accurately reflect the structure of the distribution channel?
- Are on-hand balances being updated accurately and on a timely basis?
- Are open customer and purchase order due dates and quantities accurate?
- Have replenishment order policies been accurately defined?
- Do product replenishment lead times reflect current delivery realities?
- Have safety stocks been calculated correctly?
- Have DRP regeneration and planning procedures been formalized?

The development of the channel replenishment plan begins by summarizing the total demand for each stocked product. This calculation forms the first step in the DRP planning process (Figure 8.14). To be effective it is necessary for all sources of product demand to be available for the DRP gross requirements computation. Demand can consist of actual customer orders and or forecast. Each requirement must be pegged to a demand source and have a defined due date and quantity. For firms with distribution channels, the system will also record planned interbranch order requirements as gross requirements in the demand records of supplying warehouses at each level of the BOD.

The second step in the DRP planning process focuses on executing the DRP processor and reviewing of the resulting *net requirements* and generated planned orders. This step is the core of DRP and should be closely monitored by inventory planners. Net requirements occur in a given period when the anticipated gross requirements for a product exceed projected available supply. Each time a net requirement occurs and there are no or insufficient open replenishment orders in the planning horizon, DRP will generate a planned or-

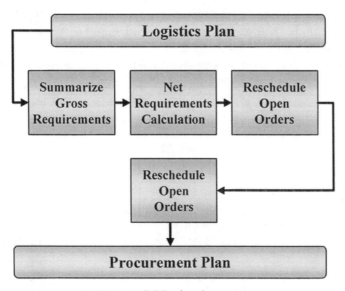

FIGURE 8.14 DRP planning process

der dictated by replenishment order policies and align the order by due date with demand. In addition, the order's release date will be determined by backdating the product's resupply lead time from the due date. The schedule of *Planned Order Releases* defines the scope of replenishment order action to be performed by the planner. Most commercial DRP systems provide on-line workbenches and output reports advising planners of required order release and reschedule activities (Figure 8.15). The generation of net requirements has often been compared to using a shortage list. The critical difference is that products appear on a shortage list when there are customer orders and no available stock. DRP, on the other hand, provides a window into *projected* shortages before they occur.

Once net requirements have been identified, DRP will reference each product's *Scheduled Receipts* to ensure that the replenishment order due dates are correctly scheduled to demand. If a particular order's due date does not correspond to a planning period's gross requirements, the order needs to be rescheduled in or out. For example, if a new customer order caused a net requirement to occur in a period *before* a previously released resupply order, DRP would prompt the planner to *expedite* the order to meet the new statement of demand. If the scheduled order quantity was insufficient to cover the new demand, the system would generate a planned order quantity determined by the replenishment order policy to cover the balance of the requirement. Likewise, if a demand was canceled or moved back, DRP would respond by prompting the planner to *deexpedite* the order to a future period or even to cancel it if not needed. DRP's ability to provide the planner with timely order action information necessary for effective open supply orders rescheduling is one of the technique's most powerful features that is lacking in statistical replenishment planning.

Product #	Order #	Order Quantity	Summary Release	Due	Revised Due	Action Message
1425	Plan	5000	01/01/03	01/14/03		Release
1551	Plan	5000	01/07/03	01/14/03		No Action
2300	1234	345		01/24/03	01/07/03	Expedite
4110	Plan	4500	01/07/03	01/14/03		Release
3320	1267	1234		01/23/03		De-Exped
3345	1275	4567		01/25/03		Cancel

FIGURE 8.15 DRP order action report

The final step in the DRP planning process is the calculation and review of the detailed logistics capacities necessary to meet the schedule of *Planned Orders*. Logistics capacities are composed of four elements: inventory investment, transportation, warehouse space, and labor and equipment. If the priority plan of inventory requirements established by the DRP process is to be executed successfully, it is essential that planners ensure that logistics functions have the required capacities. By extending the schedule of *Planned Orders* by the planning factors found in each capacity area, planners can review the viability of the inventory plan. If insufficient capacities are found in any of the four areas, either the inventory plan must be changed or additional resources must be acquired to supplement the shortfall. Once the priority and the capacity plans are in place, planners can confidently begin the process of inventory procurement.

DRP offers the distribution enterprise a new horizon for attaining the highest levels of customer service while maintaining low inventory costs. By illuminating the relationship of supply and demand through the planning horizon, the DRP planning process provides inventory planners at all levels in the distribution network with a detailed window into the status of inventory in the channel. By effectively linking together marketing and sales planning with inventory investment, warehouse size, labor and equipment, and existing transportation capacities, DRP offers distribution functions an effective method of integrating the resources of the entire channel with the requirements of the marketplace.

DETAILED LOGISTICS CAPACITY PLANNING

The capability to maintain effective inventory control is only half of the benefit a DRP system offers supply chain planners. Just as important as maintaining the critical balance between supply and demand is the balance that must be maintained between demand requirements and supply chain *capacities*. A distribution channel that blindly pursues a policy of demand management without critical attention to enterprise capacities is courting disaster. The following scenario is all too familiar: Marketing and sales embarks on an ambitious campaign that calls for significant growth in inventories. Unfortunately, no one explores the effect this strategy will have on logistics capacities. The result is that existing warehouses are unable to store the new inventory quantities, resulting in the rental of costly alternative warehousing and extra overhead costs. In addition, the existing company-owned transportation fleet cannot keep up with the demand, and other, more costly carriers have to be contracted. What profits the new sales strategy initially intended to realize are soon consumed in added logistics costs.

While the effective management of inventory is fundamental in assuring channel responsiveness, the ability to also effectively manage supply chain *constraints* is absolutely critical for a competitive supply chain network. Today, manufacturers have computerized tools, such as *Capacity Requirements Planning* (CRP), *Advanced Planning Systems* (APS), *Theory of Constraints* (TOC), and *Constraint Programming* (CP) technologies, to assist in managing production bottlenecks. Distribution planners have similar toolsets to assist in removing capacity constraints in channel product deployment by providing visibility to possible constraints in capital, the work force, equipment, and space availability. Being able to *optimize* the supply chain means that distribution points anywhere in the channel network are agile enough to overcome current and future constraints that threaten to impede the flow of goods through the distribution pipeline. Achieving these goals requires that supply chain planners possess information systems that provide a *schedule* of priority requirements that can be translated quickly and accurately into detailed capacity planning elements. DRP provides planners with such a window into required logistics capacities (11).

FINANCIAL ESTIMATING

The fundamental responsibility of inventory management is to ensure that inventory is on hand to respond to customer demand. But in planning for inventory it is also important that companies possess sufficient capital to fund the replenishment plan. Although inventory is considered a *current asset* on the financial statement, it is not cash, and poor inventory planning can drive a company to financial ruin. In the past, businesses utilizing statistical replenishment techniques have had difficulty estimating the investment necessary to support marketing and sales plans. For the most part, estimates were made using spread-sheet simulators based on aggregate product usage histories.

With the use of DRP, on the other hand, inventory planners now have the ability to view as part of the DRP process output the projected financial investment necessary to support the inventory stocking plan. This process could be performed by individual warehouse as well as for the whole distribution channel. The steps in developing a DRP inventory asset plan are relatively simple. To begin with, the size of the DRP *planning horizon* needs to be defined. The length should correspond to the financial time period desired, for example 6 months or 1 year. Second, expected forecasts should be developed for each product matching the length of the planning horizon. Finally, the cost of each product determined by the firm's costing method should be calculated. Once these elements have been defined, the DRP processor can then be run.

The results of the DRP generation can be easily turned into a projected cost report by multiplying each product's generated planned order quantity by the cost. Figure 8.16 illustrates a projected inventory cost report. Notice that the report lists the cost of each product by product family, a cost summary by product family, and, finally, a summary cost by warehouse.

The advantages of using DRP in developing inventory asset planning are the following:
1. *Ease of planning.* Instead of laborious data calculation and spread-sheet development, DRP provides planners with the ability to view projected costs in detail and in the aggregate with relatively little effort. The system, in fact, will calculate the necessary data elements as part of the normal DRP generation. Planners merely have to format the required output reporting.
2. *Accuracy.* DRP provides planners with an extremely accurate calculation of projected inventory costs. By extending each product's planned orders by the cost, DRP can provide a window into the financial assets necessary to respond to each product's schedule of *net require-*

ments. The more accurate the forecast, obviously the more accurate the financial projection.

Warehouse: Chicago		Date From: 01/01/03	Date To: 12/31/03	
Product #	On Hand	Planned Orders	Cost	Projected $
1425	100	15,000	$2.25	$33,975.00
1551	200	22,000	$1.35	$29,970.00
2300	125	19,000	$1.45	$22,731.25
4110	50	12,000	$2.57	$30,969.50
3320	25	900	$3.10	$2,867.50
			Family $$ Total	120,513.25
			Warehouse $$ Total	$22,235,125.00

FIGURE 8.16 Costed DRP inventory report

3. *Simulation.* By inputting alternate forecasts into the system, DRP provides planners with the ability to simulate product level, individual warehouse, and aggregate channel costs. By analyzing each iteration, the proper forecast that fits both the inventory plan and the firm's asset budget can be selected.
4. *Productivity.* The choice of the right inventory plan is critical for the success of the enterprise. DRP permits planners to make the right inventory decisions so that targeted customer service levels can be met while reducing inventory costs.

TRANSPORTATION PLANNING

Perhaps the single most important factor inhibiting transportation planners from effectively controlling transportation costs is lack of visibility into future shipping requirements. Often firms are faced with the problem of having to ship products in quantities that do not take full advantage of rate structures. For example, transportation is forced to ship partial truckloads because the total of current shippable demand is less than a full truck. What transportation planners really need is to be able to view not only current but also the anticipated shipping requirements of future periods when developing a cost-effective shipping plan. Instead of just shipping those products that happen to be available at the time, by having visibility into the schedule of demand for the next couple of days or weeks, future requirements could be moved in and combined with current requirements so that full truckloads can be shipped.

Because of its ability to *time-phase* supply and demand, DRP provides transportation planners with a window into both current and future shipping requirements. By referencing individual product master information relating to weight, volume, and number of pallets, DRP can easily convert each product's schedule of planned orders into transportation planning data elements. Figure 8.17 provides an example of a shipping schedule by weight, volume, and number of pallets derived from combining planned orders to be shipped from a distribution center to its satellite warehouses.

Warehouse: Chicago	Date From: 01/01/03		
Period	Total Weight (lbs)	Volume	Number of Pallets
1	500,000	31,000	2935
2	615,000	36,500	3554
3	550,000	33,300	3256
4	470,000	28,200	2805
5	525,000	31,500	3103

FIGURE 8.17 Transportation report.

The above shipping schedule could be used by transportation planners in the following manner. Say that the distribution center ships products by truck. The standard trailer has the following capacity: maximum weight is 25,000 pounds, with a volume of 1500 cubic feet, and a max of 15 pallets. The goal is to develop a shipping schedule that optimizes truck capacities. In period 1, the shipping schedule indicates that, by weight, 20 trucks will be necessary (500,000/25,000). In addition, by rounding the necessary volume and number of pallets, 20 trucks appears to be the optimal shipping schedule. In the second period, however, the schedule indicates that by weight 24.6 trucks will be required, by volume 24.3, and by pallet 23.6. Once these computations have been done, it would be quite easy for the transportation planner to go to the third period and expedite-in the necessary orders to bring the shipment up to 25 full truck loads. By examining the contents of period three through a detail shipping schedule (Figure 8.18), the planner could select those products to be combined with period 2 orders to maximize on transportation capacities.

The advantages provided by DRP in assisting the firm plan and control transportation capacities are significant. There are four key areas to review [12]:

Warehouse: Chicago		Date From: 01/01/03		Date To: 02/28/03		
Week	Product #	Quantity	Order Type	Weight	Volume Cube	Pallets
1	1425	5000	PLN	128,000	8500	45
	1551	12,000	PLN	125,000	7300	61
	2300	1800	PLN	85,000	6500	75
	4110	1340	PLN	75,000	5200	79
	3320	3260	PLN	87,000	3500	33
				500,000	31,000	293

Weekly Totals

Week	Product #	Quantity	Order Type	Weight	Volume Cube	Pallets
2	1425	7200	PLN	111,000	7200	55
	1551	8,200	PLN	89,000	8200	43

FIGURE 8.18 Detailed shipping schedule.

- The transportation planner has the critical information necessary to schedule effective transportation and loading. DRP provides a window into future requirements, permitting planners vision to develop transportation plans that extend beyond current shipping requirements.
- Through the use of simulation, planners would have the ability to see the impact of different forecast plans and provide essential input into selecting the optimal forecast to the firm's transportation management. For example, planners may total the shipping requirements for the entire year and then contrast them against available capacity. This would be particularly important if the firm possessed its own carrier fleet.
- The aggregate shipping schedule could also assist in planning other critical logistics elements. It could be used to develop transportation freight budgets, negotiate freight rates, and justify the acquisition of additional equipment such as trucks, trailers, and rail cars.
- Because the schedule of planned orders generated by DRP is truly a schedule of what is going to happen, the shipping plan represents what the firm is going to ship and when it must be shipped. This information can be used by other business functions, such as accounting and sales, in their planning processes.

WAREHOUSE SPACE PLANNING

Calculating warehouse capacities is one of the most neglected of the four areas of logistics capacity planning. The failure to effectively plan warehouse space can have an enormous financial impact on the whole distribution channel. Ballou [13] estimates that warehousing activities account for roughly one-fifth of a typical distributor's logistics expenditure. Poor warehouse planning can result is such problems as unnecessary material handling costs, product damage and obsolescence, record-keeping redundancies and errors, time wasted in product search, excess transportation costs, and the cost of public warehousing or other extra storage facilities.

Generating warehouse capacities from DRP output involves the addition of a few data elements to the system. The elements consist of the following:

1. *Product level storage profile.* The starting point of the capacity calculation is defining the weight, volume, and number of pallets required to store the stocking unit of measure for each product in the distribution channel. Most commercial DRP systems provide these data elements as part of the computerized item master record. Planners must make sure that the data are loaded correctly and that there is an audit program in place to keep storage values up to date.

2. *Warehouse storage capacities.* Each storage type in the warehouse must be defined in the DRP system's location master record. Shelf racks, bins, bin boxes, barrels, floor space, and pallets are possible examples of storage types. Next, each of these storage types must be assigned a *stocking volume* based on space dimensions and allowable weight capacities. Finally, each stocked item would be assigned a storage-type code based on its size and projected stocked quantities. The result of the process would be a list of total available locations in the warehouse broken down by type, weight, and volume (Figure 8.19).

3. *Warehouse space calculation.* Computing storage space requirements from DRP output consists of two calculations. In the first, the capacity requirements for each product would be calculated by extending the schedule of planned orders by the product's storage profile. Next, the storage requirements would be computed by dividing each product's capacity requirements by time period by the storage type. For example, a given product's storage volume requirements total 192 cubic feet. The product is stored in an area in the warehouse composed of 4 feet x 8 feet x 4 feet shelf racks. By dividing the requirement by the storage type, the product would require 1.5, 4 x 8 shelf racks.

By reviewing warehouse space capacities each time the DRP is generated, logistics planners can plan for both long- and short-term capacity require-

Warehouse: Chicago			Date From: 01/01/03		Date To: 12/31/03
Storage Type	Location	Code	Weight	Dimension (ft)	Volume (ft3)
Shelf	7010101	SR4	1500	4x8x4	128
Shelf	7010102	SR4	1500	4x8x4	128
Shelf	7010103	SR2	1500	2x8x4	64
				Total	425,000
Bin	6210101	B.5	450	.5x3x3	4.5
Bin	6210102	B.5	450	.5x3x3	4.5
Bin	6210103	B1	450	1x3x3	9
				Total	123,000

FIGURE 8.19 Warehouse capacity report by type.

ments. As the schedule of planned orders changes, DRP will assist planners in viewing the ability of existing warehouses to meet storage requirements, and to reveal serious undercapacity and overcapacity conditions. Effective capacity reporting will assist planners in controlling storage costs and improving overall operating efficiency and profitability.

LABOR AND EQUIPMENT CAPACITY

Effective logistics planning requires that planners be able to predict manpower and equipment capacities. Too much or too little manpower can be expensive, as can the cost of unused equipment or poor customer service due to equipment shortage. DRP can significantly assist logistics managers keep their labor and equipment needs in balance with demand requirements. The schedule of *planned orders* will provide managers with a statement of *which* and *when* products will have to be ordered, received, put-away, picked, and shipped. Warehouse managers, in turn, will have to develop material handling standards for these critical warehouse functions. As an example, after a time study was performed, one distributor set the order picking standard in their bin warehouse to be 60 lines per operator-hour, and the stock put-away in the same area to 30 receipts per operator-hour. By matching the schedule of planned order requirements by time period to standard labor and equipment capacities, warehouse managers can readily ascertain each warehouse's total daily, weekly, and period capacities, identify capacity constraints and excesses, and plan accordingly.

MANUFACTURING SYSTEM INTERFACE

DRP provides supply chain companies with a set of computerized applications that easily integrates with enterprise business systems like ERP. As portrayed in Figure 8.20, most ERP-type systems contain a DRP module that

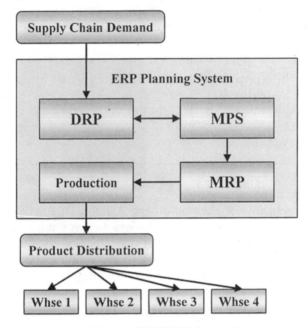

FIGURE 8.20 DRP/MRP integration.

is part of the standard MPS/MRP applications. The functioning of a DRP system is relatively simple. Forecast, interbranch, and customer demands are reviewed by the DRP processor at each channel warehouse when the time-phased net requirements implosion occurs. The net requirements, in turn, filter down through the BOD until they arrive at the manufacturing warehouse. The final statement of product requirements originating from the supply channel is then communicated to the *master production schedule* (MPS) of the manufacturing warehouse in the form of scheduled interbranch resupply orders and placed within the appropriate gross requirements buckets. When the MPS processor is executed, the production master scheduler is provided with a window into the collective channel demand placed on each MPS finished product. After review, the authorized MPS provides the input of finished goods requirements used to generate *Material Requirements Planning* (MRP). Finally, the MRP drives the schedule for all raw material and component part procurement and shop order release and is used to calculate manufacturing capacities. As demand and supply elements change, the MPS has the ability to preserve or recalculate order priorities to keep the entire enterprise on track.

The DRP display and the MPS display work in the same fashion. Because both use the same period calendar, DRP *planned orders* can easily be placed within the correct MPS *gross requirements* planning buckets. As DRP, MPS, and MRP perform their processing activities, planners in purchasing, manufacturing, and logistics are provided with integrated information relating to demand and supply requirements within the entire enterprise. The logic and terminology for all three are identical and many of the computerized reports and screen displays are identical or very similar. In a way that statistical replenishment techniques cannot possibly hope to achieve, the integration of DRP and MRP provides for the implementation of a common system that can be used across the entire enterprise. Such visibility promotes the organizational objectives of the successful supply chain supplier of the first decade of 2000: collaboration, a common solution to problem solving, and a unified focus on customer service and logistics costs.

DRP AND SUPPLY CHAIN MANAGEMENT SYSTEMS

When DRP was first introduced, it was directed at assisting companies to more effectively control their *internal* distribution channels. As companies began to realize that the real benefits of applying DRP occurred when the technique was applied *outside* channel boundaries to the suppliers and customers that constituted their extended supply chain universes, several critical obstacles began to appear. Perhaps the most glaring issue resided around how information and inventory data found in local planning systems scattered throughout the supply network could be integrated and optimized to respond to customer service goals at all points in the channel. Achieving such an objective is indeed a daunting one. Today, companies faced with the task of linking internal planning systems with outside supply chain partners often encounter the following realities.

- *Different business objectives.* Businesses often are faced with managing supply chain activities that span many different types of enterprise. A typical channel may contain manufacturers, distributors, third parties, and retailers. These trading partners may have their own set of corporate objectives and supply chain strategies that can conflict with each other and require channel planners to develop not one, but multiple approaches to the task of integrating information and inventories.
- *Different business environments.* The heterogeneous composition of the supply chain also means that there can be wide disconnects stemming

from industry specific business practices, productive processes, and cultural attitudes. What may be critical to one channel node occupying one point in the supply chain may be actually antithetical to the objectives of another node located somewhere else in the channel.

- *The problem of interoperability.* As the number of trading partners grows in the supply chain the capability of channel information to be easily communicated begins to diminish exponentially. Information architectures can run the gamut from highly sophisticated e-business solutions encapsulated within an advanced ERP system on the one end to manual information management on the other. Even among companies with sophisticated enterprise solutions, issues arising from hardware, software, and connectivity mechanisms can retard the timely flow of the planning and execution decisions originating in DRP systems anywhere along the supply chain continuum.

The above points have historically inhibited the development of plans that synchronize the capabilities of chains of trading partners and guide them to collaborative relationships. However, the rise of new information technologies over the past several years have provided supply chains with radically new avenues to effect the kind of real-time integration that is necessary to shrink cost and lead times from the supply channel and accelerate the flow of goods and services to the customer. Today, these SCM systems, capable of tapping into Internet technologies, have been expanding to include a variety of supply chain functions such as demand and forecast management, supply planning, network optimization, fulfillment scheduling, transportation planning, and transaction event management that enables entire supply chains to move beyond their internal boarders and generate the type of collaborative value chains that are required to compete in today's global market place (Figure 8.21). In the discussion below, two of today's most cutting-edge SCM applications, supply *chain planning* (SCP) and *supply chain event management* (SCEM) will be explored.

SUPPLY CHAIN PLANNING TECHNOLOGIES

While DRP has for decades provided companies with the tools to effectively transmit and time-phase the interplay of channel supply and demand, *supply chain planning* (SCP) systems have recently been deployed to enhance supply chain interoperability and collaboration. SCP can be described as the application of *advanced planning and scheduling* (APS) concepts to supply chain management. Developed during the 1990's, the mission of APS systems is to assist manufacturing planners to more effectively shrink production costs and respond to market demand by applying *theory of constraints* (TOC) planning and optimization techniques to the management of manufacturing resources. Functionally, an APS system seeks to utilize information regarding the planned orders and productive resources necessary to calculate a simulation of the actual delivery capabilities and possible plant constraints of a planned schedule of production. In isolation, APS systems were never designed to provide continuously synchronized plans outside an individual plant and presented a purely asynchronous approach to supply chain planning.

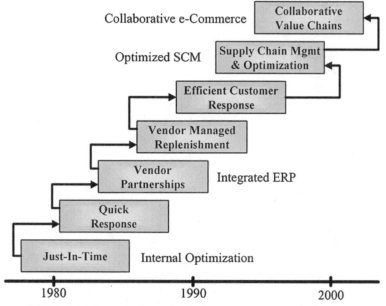

FIGURE 8.21 Stages of supply chain management techniques.

By 2000 the APS concept had been significantly expanded to embrace the need to apply optimization techniques to incorporate supply chain trading partners and synergize the operations of the entire channel network. Today, these SCP systems have tapped into the interoperable power of the Internet in order to create virtual supply chains networks enabling seamless collaboration on all requirements affecting the supply channel. Collaborative demand management has enabled planners to architect supply chain planning and execution cycles fully consistent with customer demand and total channel productive resources. Daily transactional events can be monitored and used to trigger changes in operational plans. According to AMR Research, over $14.9 billion of SCP software has been sold over the period 1999 to 2001, and the market is expected to grow by 20 percent in 2002 to around $7 billion. Similarly, in a survey by industry analysts, 48 percent of companies sampled said that in 2003 they planned to deploy advanced demand/

forecasting, optimization, and supply chain network design computerized technologies (14).

Drivers of SCP/SCEM Adoption

The rise of the SCM concept has driven the growth of new computerized toolsets. Originating as basic APS techniques for production scheduling, these SCM applications have grown to encompass several supply chain functions, including demand planning, supply planning, strategic network optimization, fulfillment scheduling, and CPFR. The integration of these channel functions enables planners to structure an optimized synergy across the entire supply network that permits trading partners to better plan their production plants and distribution facilities and to reduce total channel inventory and transportation costs.

The critical drivers of this movement to SCM systems can be detailed as follows:

1. *Visibility and Collaboration.* The ability to collaboratively plan demand and optimize productive functions and inventories with channel trading partners has become the critical concern of today's executive.

2. *End-to-End Solutions.* SCM visibility requires the implementation of information systems that integrate and synchronize planning and control data from all levels of the supply chain.

3. *Business system integration.* SCP/SCEM applications are today fully integrated with backbone ERP, CRM, PRM, e-business, and data warehouse software suites.

4. *Broadening of SCM scope.* Companies beyond initial manufacturing and distribution have begun to realize the benefits of effective supply chain planning and execution and are looking to integrate SCP/SCEM into their suite of information tools.

5. *Cost Competitive.* Aggressive pricing by software suppliers has made SCM planning tools available to the small to medium company.

6. *Global Viewpoint.* SCM suites assist in entry to international markets by providing global visibility, multi-modal transportation management, and regulatory compliance data.

7. *Internet Interoperability.* The use of Internet and *application service provider* (ASP) technologies has provided companies with a cost-effective approach to integrating channel partner databases and real-time event management.

Source: Jill Jenkins, "Supply-Chain Planning Build on Its Success," *Supply Chain e-Business,* 2, 7, (2001), 26-28

The objective of SCP systems is to provide supply chain planners with optimization capabilities that positions manufacturers and distributors across the channel network to achieve the following objectives:

- Provide answers to such critical questions as what should be the design of the supply channel? How many manufacturing plants and distribution facilities are required? Where should they be located? What products should be made and what are the inventory levels?
- Enable the construction of supply chain communities in order to manage channel complexities through the engineering of enhanced planning and decision-making capabilities, starting with internal ERP systems and extending connectivity to Internet-linked channel trading partners.
- Ensure that channel network costs are minimized and that they are, as much as possible, the most competitive across supply chains.
- Identify the most profitable customers at all locations in the supply chain by creating more compelling, value-based relationships than competing supply channel networks.
- Secure access to the most value-added suppliers on a global basis by establishing collaborative, interoperable supply chains that offer B2B technology and trading partner relationships.
- Engineer flexible, agile organizations and supply channels that can leverage an array of connectivity technologies, ranging from collaborative product commerce to multichannel e-information visibility, to capitalize on opportunities engendered by customer demand changes and shifts in supply-side dynamics.

Overall, an effective SCP system should meet the needs of the following supply chain functions.

- *Collaborative forecast/demand planning.* The SCP architecture should provide for the integration of individual company forecasts, promotions, planned demand schedules, and customer order requirements resident on their enterprise backbone systems (ERP) with the SCP system. This information provides the raw data for the SCP optimization engines. In turn, the optimized plan can then be communicated and updated interactively through tools, such as the Internet, in order to achieve consensus on a shared demand plan. As demand events impact the plan, changes to data can be checked simultaneously and out-of-bound notification provided to channel network planners (Figure 8.22).
- *Collaborative supply and distribution planning.* Besides demand, an SCP system should contain tools to assist supply chain planners concurrently plan for procurement, manufacturing, and transportation requirements. *Supply planning* attempts to reconcile the demand for components and raw materials arising from the MRP generation occur-

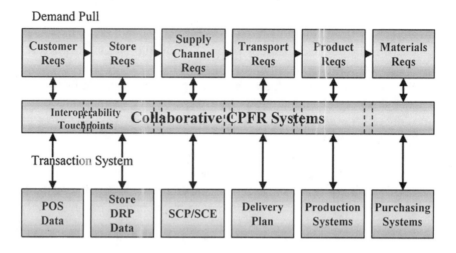

FIGURE 8.22 Supply chain integrated planning and execution.

ring within each network node with the total capabilities of upstream supply partners. The SCP system must employ optimization heuristics that utilize such constraints as quota agreements, lead times, calendars, and lot-sizing rules, to make visible to supply nodes calculations of requirements, sourcing decisions, supply chain capability to promise, and purchasing schedules for production inventories. *Distribution planning* attempts to reconcile the transportation requirements to satisfy channel inventory deployment and transport capacities. The goal is to utilize load algorithms to optimize volume, weight, and number of pallet capacities in order to minimize transportation costs across the channel.

- *Collaborative sales planning*. Normally, each channel trading partner will develop their own sales plan. The sales plan is usually constructed using the firm's internal enterprise business system and will consist of critical initiatives such as sales promotions, special pricing, Internet sales strategies, and critical sales targets by time period. These and other elements of the sales plan are in turn used in the construction of collaborative demand, supply, and distribution plans communicated to the entire supply channel. The goal is to provide data input into supply chain optimizers that can simulate a variety of possible scenarios based on trading partners' basic sales plans and on-going monitoring of alerts and key performance indicators as actual sales cascade through the supply chain network.

While SCP systems provide supply chains with radically new collaborative toolsets to manage the complex and changing flow of supply channel information, establishing a SCP environment across a channel network requires enormous effort involving both operational reengineering and technology acquisition. Regardless of the actual SCP solution eventually implemented, today's SCP architecture must contain the following components (15).

Database Management. The most important requirement of a SCP solution is that it provides for the seamless, inter-active communication of demand and supply information across the supply network. Timely and accurate information is required to ensure the SCP optimization engines are calculating meaningful outputs. In addition, a technology architecture must be assembled, such as the Internet, which provides for database interoperability among all channel partners' enterprise business systems. Among the most important data are to be found the following:

- *Supply chain configuration.* The composition of the actual supply chain must be available to all trading partners. Exactly who is in the supply network, what is their role in the channel, and what are their collaborative capabilities is critical. Answers to such questions determine the effectiveness by which supply chain information, such as demand patters, forecasts, replenishment, and transportation, can be utilized for simulation and transfer back-out to the supply network.

- *Product data.* This data area contains information relating to individual product records and includes such information as product lead times and structures, MRP/DRP generated demand for forecasts, inventory fulfillment, production, warehouse space, and transportation requirements.

- *Supply chain capability-to-promise.* Channel SCP demand and replenishment data will be used to drive the capability of the entire supply chain. The following metrics can be utilized to determine capacity requirements: for *purchasing,* capacity is measured in the number of item units that can be supplied per planning bucket; *transport* is measured in weight or volume units per planning bucket; *production* is based on capacity plans measured in hours per planning bucket; *receiving* is measured in weight or volume units; *dispatch* are the resources that represent equipment/personnel for shipping measured in weight or volume; and *stock area* is the volume or weight for each stock area resource

- *Costs.* The data used for demand and supply must contain sufficient costing information to provide supply chain planners with a basis to determine costs for purchasing, transportation, production, and inventory during simulation.

- *Penalties.* The timely replenishment and delivery of inventory often is ensured by the imposition of penalties for poor performance on the part of individual channel partners. Penalties can consist of two types: missed delivery penalties and bucket production penalties (failure to achieve production optimization by grouping production into fewer periods to produce larger quantities.)

- *Forecasts for end products.* Estimates of future demand can be communicated to the supply chain in the form of either a SCP simulated demand schedule or sales forecasts for markets and customers and must be capable of being transferred directly into the ERP/Server systems of each channel partner on a real-time basis.

- *Feedback to enterprise business systems* (ERP). The simulated schedules and information status data that is generated and communicated through the supply channel network must be capable of being input in real-time into the planning systems of each channel business node.

Planning Timeframe. SCP enables planning on three levels:

- *Strategic* – this level is concerned with corporate decisions relating to where company distribution centers should be located or what capacities are need from the supply channel.

- *Tactical* – this level involves optimizing the flow of goods through a given supply chain configuration over a time horizon and executing sourcing, production, resource deployment, and distribution plans.

- *Operational* – this level is largely involved with detailed scheduling, rescheduling, and execution of production and is usually equated with internal APS planning tools.

Planning Model. Channel planners have the choice of several models that can be used depending on the desired planning timeframe. For example, supply chain planning can proceed from the sources of demand originating with product forecasts and open orders and then progressing up the supply channel through retail, distribution, logistics, and production trading partners, ending with suppliers of raw materials and components at the beginning of the supply network. At each step the demand is driven through optimization planning models and concludes with an synchronized schedule of manufacture and distribution. Another possible model reverses the direction of planning, beginning with MRP/DRP generation at each supply chain node, progressing to detail scheduling, and, finally, to aggregate supply chain planning.

Optimization Techniques. A critical objective of SCP is to provide optimized simulations that can guide planners in achieving the best balance between high throughput, minimum inventories, and low operations costs when making supply chain decisions. Basically, SCP systems utilize one or all of the following optimization techniques:

- *Mathematical models.* These techniques attempt to describe the supply chain environment mathematically and consist of a range of linear and mixed integer programming models. This alternative is best suited to stable, repetitive supply chain demand and supply relationships.
- *Heuristic models.* Models in this group are best deployed by supply chains characterized by complex trading environments where the lack or non-linearity of data negate the use of mathematical techniques. Examples of these models include *theory of constraints* (TOC) and process network-based systems that attempt to connect customer demand with the supply capabilities of pipeline trading partners.
- *Simulation.* This model is characteristic of the earliest types of APS/ SCP systems. Founded upon queuing theory, simulation attempts to optimize total supply chain capabilities by driving customer demand up through the supply network in an effort to uncover constraints and provide possible alternatives to ensure the best solution. This method is the one selected when performing strategic planning scenarios.

Supply Chain Schedule Management. The objective of the SCP planning process is the generation of a supply chain plan that can be communicated to collaborative channel partners. The interoperability of the SCP solutions employed will permit trans-channel planners to import demand schedules and supply capacities from across the network and then to manipulate through optimization and simulation techniques the optimal channel response to the customer. If the best case scenario still contains bottlenecks, the prioritization algorithms in the optimization technique can assist planners to determine which demands are to be satisfied first. In the process, the channel schedule respects all capacity constraints and the supply chain network structure. The overall goal of the entire process is to architect and communicate to each supply network node a cost-optimized, fully synchronized supply chain schedule capable of meeting any customer demand before the competition.

Supply Chain Event Management

Despite the best constructed supply chain plans, unplanned occurrences in demand and supply are a costly reality of supply network management. Bridging this gap between planning and execution is a new set of applications termed *supply chain event management* (SCEM). The mission of SCEM is to provide supply chain planners with advanced warnings of impending network constraints by providing a real-time window into key events occurring across the supply chain. The software utilizes series of increasingly urgent alarms that automatically inform affected trading partners that a threshold event has occurred or a target has been missed. Customized response rules can be attached to the event that automatically suggest or initiate corrective action to prevent a channel bottleneck from occurring. SCEM provides planners visibility to supply chain event exceptions while trusting that normal events are proceeding as planned.

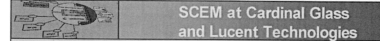

SCEM at Cardinal Glass and Lucent Technologies

SCEM systems are applicable to manufacturers, distributors – anyone involved in the supply chain, particularly if they are interested in collaborating with channel partners and developing the kind of collaboration necessary in today's fast-paced world.

Cardinal Glass supplies glass to Andersen Windows on a just-in-time basis. In the past Cardinal had trouble balancing production scheduling with incoming orders and still be able to respond to Andersen's short lead times. After implementing a SCM system with SCEM capabilities, when Andersen places an order, the event management system checks that there is inventory available to make the items ordered. If not, an e-mail response immediately is sent to Andersen warning that there is a chance Cardinal will not be able to meet the order request. If the missing inventory is already scheduled to be received or produced and there is an estimated time of arrival, Andersen receives that estimated data. If the item is still unavailable when the order is actually picked, Andersen receives an alert that the item will not be part of the shipment.

Such timely information provides Andersen time to recover and potentially modify their synchronized manufacturing process.

Lucent Technologies utilizes their event-management software to aggregate purchasing information and provide complete visibility to open orders. When Lucent receives an order from a company like AT&T or Verizon it can consist of more than 200 lines that will be sourced from various suppliers within Lucent's network. When the order arrives, it is broken apart into multiple POs placed with key and occasionally small specialized suppliers. The SCEM system is used to track these various orders as they move through the picking process, shipment, bill of lading, carton content list, etc., until it reaches a merge-in-transit center operated by a 3PL. The 3PL collects these different orders and delivers them together to an installer at the job site.

Source: Kurt C. Hoffman, "Hate Surprises? SCEM Tech Helps You Deal With Them," *Global Logistics & Supply Chain Strategies,* 6, 2, (2002), 58.62.

SCEM can be described as an application integration layer that standardizes and integrates supply chain information between channel trading partners. SCEM is normally integrated with individual ERP and SCP systems and has the potential to be linked to e-market trading exchanges. Today's SCEM system provides channel planners with the following toolsets:

- *Monitoring.* Capability for order and shipment tracking, workflow management, alert messaging/notification, personalized information portals, and channel event escalation processes.
- *Performance.* Feedback to measure, compare, and report on supply channel performance over time against specific metrics and performance objectives.
- *Planning.* Ability to monitor channel events in real-time, from the point of customer order and demand flow into the supply network to inventory allocation and eventual fulfillment.
- *Controlling.* Use of real-time, computer generated signals that proactively notify channel planners, through Internet technologies, that an action might have to be taken in response to a transaction occurring at some point in the supply channel.
- *Simulating.* Capability to utilize simulation models for issue resolution based on current or expected events occurring in the supply chain.
- *Strategic management.* Enable channel planners at all nodes in the supply network to collectively control the entire supply chain through timely decision making before costly bottlenecks appear.

How does SCEM work? Basically, the system is engaged when an unplanned event occurs in the supply network requiring planner intervention. Depending on the potential severity of the event, the system will trigger a signal, often using Boolean-type logic, to alert planners through a generic workflow process that an occurrence in the fulfillment pipeline has violated predetermined event boundaries. However, while SCEM provides visibility into current events and permits planners to execute operational corrections, the system's real value is to be found on the strategic level where pre-defined KPIs, performance scorecards, and executive dashboards can detail long-term costs and potential bottlenecks in production, inventories, and transportation capabilities anywhere in the channel.

When combined with effective internal systems like ERP, SCP, and CPFR, SCEM can provide supply chain planners with critical tools to assist in the development of new methods to reduce costs, increase efficiencies, reinvent channel models, engineer collaborative relationships, and span supply chain functional, cultural, and personal boundaries. SCP optimization applications enable planners to concentrate on evaluating and making the best channel decisions, while the optimizer does the complex and detailed number crunching.

The "best" solution is the one with the lowest total cost for meeting forecasted demand and the one that follows the selected optimization strategy. The result of an effective SCP system is a feasible and optimized plan that can be communicated to channel partners. SCEM provides planners with an automatic alert to impending channel constraints and the ability to utilize system rules that ensure the smooth and least cost transfer of inventory through the supply chain and out to the customer. Together SCP, CPFR, and SCEM enable today's supply chain manager to dramatically shrink the gap between planning and execution and to drive individual companies and entire supply chains to new levels of productivity and competitiveness.

SUMMARY

As the competition for the global marketplace intensifies, companies and their supply chains are increasingly faced with the dilemma of how to respond even more quickly to ever increasing levels of customer service while decreasing supply channel costs. Effective planning and control of inventory is fundamental if supply chain managers are to achieve these two seemingly opposing goals simultaneously. Traditionally, distributors have focused on the utilization of statistical planning techniques to control inventories. But, although statistical inventory replenishment techniques provide valid methods for controlling inventories subject to independent demand, they, nevertheless, contain inherent flaws. Problems associated with the use of statistical methods can be divided into two major categories: dependence on statistically derived summaries to drive inventory reorder action and the adverse affect these techniques have on organizational optimization. The first set of problems reside in the fact that statistical techniques depend on mathematical averages to arrive at the most *probable* course of customer demand. Furthermore, techniques such as order point and EOQs rest on assumptions concerning demand, lead time, costs, and safety stock that are tenuous. Second, the use of statistical methods of running the business result in the application of static operational tools to solve the problem of today's dynamic supply chain environment. Although providing satisfactory *tactical* tools for inventory control, statistical methods lack the necessary *strategic* linkages to integrate and keep in alignment long-range supply chain business plans with everyday order processing and inventory execution activities.

In the past, inventory planners had but little choice other than to use statistical approaches when planning and controlling inventories. The breakthrough came with the ability of the computer to *time-phase* supply and demand. The logic of time-phasing is at the very foundation of *Distribution Requirements Planning* (DRP). Through the use of a computer system, DRP retrieves key input from such data source files as forecast, open customer order, open replenishment order, on-hand balance, supplier lead times, order policy codes, and safety stock. Once these data elements have been collected, the DRP processor will begin the process of populating the contents of each time period in the planning horizon by referencing forecast, customer, and replenishment order due dates. The system then performs a gross-to-net requirements calculation, time period by time period. When the first net requirement appears, the system will generate a *planned order* with a quantity sufficient to cover the demand based on the item's order policy code. Finally, once the schedule of *planned orders* for all items has been compiled, DRP provides action messages to guide the inventory planner in making effective replenishment order decisions.

The advantages of DRP over statistical replenishment methods are obvious. Statistical techniques are actually little more than order launching systems. In contrast, DRP is, first and foremost, an inventory scheduling system designed to align the firm's resources with customer demands. As marketplace patterns change, DRP provides planners with the ability to be proactive in handling potential stockouts as well as excessive inventories before they occur. Furthermore, by generating a schedule of supply, DRP can facilitate product delivery. The results are increased supplier communications and teamwork and reductions in costs, paperwork, expediting, and lead times. In addition, DRP is particularly effective in a multiechelon environment. Not only does DRP illuminate the inventory requirements at each level in the distribution channel, it also drives these resupply needs up through the network based on warehouse dependencies established in the *Bill of Distribution* (BOD). In this sense, the mechanics of DRP permit planners to have inventory available to respond effectively to customer needs while minimizing inventory costs throughout the entire distribution channel.

While originally designed to plan *internal* channel resupply, DRP stands as the foundation for today's advanced *supply chain planning* (SCP) and *supply chain event management* (SCEM) systems. The goal of these systems is to effect the collaborative linkage of each trading partner in the supply chain to achieve a single, real-time approach to planning and fulfillment execution that results in an extremely agile supply network capable of optimizing and synchronizing individual plant and supply channel network resources to effectively manage channel constraints, search for optimal costs, secure access to the most value-added suppliers, and assemble flexible, agile networks that can meet the challenge of changing customer requirements. Utilizing interoperable tools like the Internet, channel partners can pass interactively the planning information necessary to solve the twin problems of forecast inaccuracy and the capability to utilize exception messaging to notify channel members of impending con-straints in supply and demand.

QUESTIONS FOR REVIEW

1. Although statistical inventory planning is a valid technique for planning products subject to independent demand, they present certain problems to the inventory planner. Discuss these problems.
2. What advantages did the application of perpetual inventory systems offer planners?
3. Describe the elements of the DRP time-phased format.
4. Detail the mechanics of the DRP calculation.
5. Why is DRP a superior tool in contrast to statistical inventory techniques for planning inventories in a multiechelon environment?
6. What is the function of the Bill of Distribution?
7. Describe how DRP can assist planners effectively manage the capacity requirements of the enterprise.
8. Describe how DRP and MRP II systems work together.
9. How can retailers apply DRP to their businesses?
10. In what ways can event-driven concepts be applied to the distribution environment?

PROBLEMS

1. Reference the inventory and inventory planning data for the warehouse supply channel described below. Calculate the requirements on the central warehouse if warehouse A was to received an order for 55 units and warehouse C was to receive an order for 15 units.

	Warehouse			
	A	B	C	D
On hand	272	150	370	1145
Forecast per week	100	50	125	275
Order point	240	120	360	1100
Order quantity	550	225	750	2000
Lead time (days)	5	7	10	15

2. Calculate the Projected On Hand, Planned Order Receipt and Planned Order Release for the item illustrated below. Safety stock = 20 units, order quantity = 20 units, and the lead time = 2 periods.

	1	2	3	4	5	6	7
Gross requirements	20	20	20	20	30	30	30
Scheduled receipts		60					
Projected on-hand 45							
Planned order receipt							
Planned order release							

3. A warehouse channel consists of two satellite warehouses and a central warehouse. Product #A1-100 is stocked in each warehouse. After a DRP generation, warehouse A has planned order releases of 20 units of product #A1-100 in periods 1, 3, and 5. Warehouse B has planned order releases of 40 each in periods 3, 5, and 7. Based on these requirements, complete the DRP calculation for the supplying warehouse as detailed below. Safety stock = 50 units, order quantity = 75 units, and the lead time = two periods.

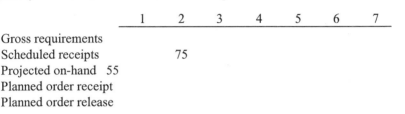

	1	2	3	4	5	6	7
Gross requirements							
Scheduled receipts		75					
Projected on-hand 55							
Planned order receipt							
Planned order release							

4. Calculate the effect on the results of the above exercise if the demand coming from warehouse A in period 3 increased to 95 units and a new demand for 63 units appeared from warehouse B in period 4.
5. Referencing the results in Problem 3, what would be the results if the supplier only shipped 50 units of the scheduled receipt of 75 units due in period 1?
6. The unit cost of Product #A1-100 used in Problem 3 has a unit cost of $125. Construct a graph illustrating the anticipated total channel cost by period of Product #A1-100.

REFERENCES

1. Orlicky, Joseph, *Material Requirements Planning.* New York: McGraw-Hill, 1975, p. 4.
2. Woolsey, Gene "The Never-Fail Spare-Parts Reduction Method: An Editorial," *Production and Inventory Management Journal* (Fourth Quarter, 1988), pp. 64-66.
3. Woolsey, Gene, "A Requiem For The EOQ: An Editorial." *Production and Inventory Management Journal* (Third Quarter, 1988), pp. 68-72.
4. Silver, Edward A. and Peterson, Rein *Decision Systems For Inventory Management and Production Planning,* 2nd ed., New York: John Wiley & Sons, 1985, p. 174.
5. Orlicky, pp. 5-10; Schaeffer, Randall, "A New View Of Inventory Management," *APICS: The Performance Advantage,* 3, 1, 1993, pp. 21-24.
6. Andre Martin, "Distribution Resource Planning," in *Production and Inventory Control Handbook* (James H. Green, ed.) New York: McGraw-Hill, 1987, p. 22.1.
7. Ross, David F., "DRP II: Connecting the Distribution Enterprise." *APICS: The Performance Advantage,* 3, 3, 1993, p. 61.
8. Martin, Andre J., *DRP: Distribution Resource Planning.* Essex Junction, VT: Oliver Wight Publications, 1990, pp. 62-77; Martin, "Distribution Resource Planning," p. 22.3-22.11; Martin, Andre J., "DRP - A Profitable New Corporate Planning Tool," *Canadian Transportation and Distribution Management,* (November 1980), pp. 45-53.
9. Martin, *DRP: Distribution Resource Planning,* p. 44.
10. Martin, "Distribution Resource Planning," pp. 22.22-22.3.
11. Martin, Andre J., "Capacity Planning: The Antidote to Supply Chain Constraints," *Supply Chain Management Review,* 6, 5, 2001, pp. 62-67.
12. Martin, *DRP: Distribution Resource Planning,* p. 226.
13. Ballou, Ronald J., *Business Logistics Management: Planning and Control,* 2nd ed. Englewood Cliffs, NJ: Prentice-Hall, 1985, pp. 495-498.
14. See O'Brien, David and McNerney, Gerald, *Supply Chain Software Yields ROI-But It Takes Time,* AMR Research, January 2002, and Jill Rose, ed., *Supply Chain Management Report 2002,* Fall, 2002, p. 14.
15. These points have been summarized from David F. Ross, *Introduction to e-Supply Chain Management,* Boca Raton, FL: St. Lucie Press, 2003, p. 230.

UNIT 4

DISTRIBUTION OPERATIONS EXECUTION

CHAPTERS:

Unit 3 was concerned with exploring the components of *distribution operations planning*. The goal of the planning process reviewed was to translate overall business objectives and strategies into medium-range inventory replenishment and logistics capacity plans. Of utmost importance was ensuring that sufficient inventory and logistics capacities were available to support the firm's *Demand, Operations, and Channel Planning* strategies. The resulting distribution operations plans act, in turn, as a driver to guide sales, inventory management, warehousing, and traffic management functions as they respond to the every-day flow of customer and supplier orders.

Unit 4 continues the discussion of distribution management by examining the next step in the channel network process: *logistics operations execution*. Distribution operations execution focuses on the short- to immediate-range activities associated with servicing the customer, acquiring and warehousing inventory in the supply channel network, and transportation. The goal of the execution processes is to ensure that the entire supply channel network is capable of realizing revenue, cost, and total customer service objectives.

Unit 4 begins with a detailed analysis of the critical role played by *Customer Relationship Management* (CRM) functions (Chapter 9). Today's marketplace leaders have found that to be successful, the enterprise must be committed to quality and productivity techniques that enable the entire supply chain to respond quickly to ongoing changes in customer product and service needs. Such a philosophy means that the entire enterprise must be diligent in measuring customer perceptions of service quality, identifying shortfalls, and responding decisively to service gaps. Fundamental to the achievement of these goals is superior order processing functions that provide for the speedy and accurate transference of goods, services, and order information through the supply channel network. The chapter concludes with a discussion of how breakthroughs in Internet technologies are changing forever the processes of customer order and service management, performance measurement, and sales force automation.

The functions of *Supplier Relationship Management* (SRM) are the focus of Chapter 10. The chapter begins by exploring the essential activities performed by purchasing, such as the inventory planning interface, supplier selection, purchase order generation, and receiving. After a detailed discussion on the development of effective procurement strategies, the chapter proceeds to outline the purchase order management process. Next, the role of effective purchasing performance measurements is detailed. The chapter concludes with an in-depth analysis of the impact of e-business tools on purchasing.

Chapter 11 is concerned with warehousing. Warehousing is an integral part of every distribution system. Warehousing enables channel systems to fulfill the time and place utilities necessary to satisfy customer delivery and product availability expectations. The chapter begins with a review of the nature and types of warehousing, and then progresses to a discussion of the development of effective warehouse strategies, facility location, and design. The chapter concludes with a review of warehouse operations, equipment, and warehouse productivity measurements.

Transportation plays one of the key roles in distribution. Without efficient transportation functions, time and place utilities cannot be realized. In Chapter 12, the elements of transportation are discussed. The chapter begins with a discussion of the principles, scope of operations, and interaction of transportation with other enterprise functions. Next, the various legal forms, performance characteristics, and modes of transportation are discussed. Of critical importance is the transportation management process, beginning with the establishment of internal and public carrier cost and price standards, and concluding with the development of effective performance measurement standards. The chapter concludes with a review of the impact of logistics service providers (LSP) and transportation management systems on contemporary transportation.

9
CUSTOMER RELATIONSHIP MANAGEMENT

The relentless search for new ways of providing value to the customer has become the dominant objective for firms seeking to utilize the supply chain to sustain leadership in their markets and industries. Historically, the strategies used to manage customer service centered on expanding productive capacities, gaining market share, penetrating new markets, and offering new products. Although critical, companies in the twenty-first century have found that these objectives constitute the bare minimum of competitiveness. With their expectations set by radically new and exciting buying experiences led by world class companies like Wal-Mart, Dell Computer, and Amazon.com, today's customers are demanding to be treated as unique individuals and requiring their supply chains to consistently provide high-quality, configurable combinations of products, services, and information available through ever-more responsive, interactive marketing, order management, and customer service technologies. Companies today are under no illusion that unless they can structure the agile infrastructures and interoperable supply chains necessary to guarantee personalized, quick-response delivery and the ability to provide unique sources of marketplace value even their best customers will not hesitate to search the Internet for a global supplier who will provide the service value they desire.

The immense growth in the power of the customer to determine the shape and mechanics of the marketplace is being accelerated and amplified by the Internet revolution. The ubiquitous presence of the Web implies that whole supply chains are expected to provide all around 7x24x365 service and fulfillment value. Customers now assume that they can click on Internet-enabled product and service sites, or peer through portals, and view marketing materials, catalogs, and price lists, and place orders as well as comparison shop, execute aggregate buys, participate in on-line auctions, receive a variety of information from product specifications to training, review delivery status, and check on invoicing and payment information. Responding to the immediacy of these customer-driven requirements has forced companies to re-examine the place and importance of their supply chains and explore radically new ways to reach and understand their customers. This movement has necessitated the complete overhaul of the past science of customer management and spawned an entirely new and more comprehensive approach termed *customer relationship management* (CRM) while simultaneously transforming and posing radically new challenges to how supply chains should be structured to execute the functions of marketing, sales, and service.

Chapter 9 explores the components of CRM in the age of the Internet. The chapter begins by defining the prominent characteristics and primary mission of CRM. Achieving the goals of CRM requires that all companies along the supply chain network focus on the development of true *customer-centric* organizations and develop detailed solutions to demand management. Following this review of CRM, the chapter turns to an analysis of order and fulfillment management. In contrast to traditional treatments of the subject, order management is seen as the avenue to align the resources of the entire supply channel in the pursuit of total service value. Next, the chapter discusses the elements of effective customer care management. The discussion focuses on the organizational requirements necessary for "world-class" service leadership, defining performance gaps, determining cost trade-offs, developing the service strategy, utilization of Web-based tools, and establishing performance benchmarks. The chapter concludes with an overview of the application of today's technologies to customer management. Among the technologies covered are Internet sales, sales force automation, customer service, partnership relationship management, electronic billing and payment, and marketing and demand analytics.

DEFINING CUSTOMER RELATIONSHIP MANAGEMENT

Until recently, the benchmark used to determine whether a company and its supply chain partners were providing competitive value was measured by how well they were delivering the right product to the right place at the right time at the right price. At the dawn of the twenty-first century, while these fundamental marketing utilities have lost none of their importance, what constitutes the "right way" to respond to the customer has dramatically changed. In the past companies competed by optimizing economies of scale and scope, pushing standardized, mass-distributed products into the marketplace regardless of actual customer wants and needs. Today, instead of constructing rigid supply chains focused solely on volume and throughput, responsiveness to the customer has become the fundamental criteria of channel design. In place of acceptable levels of product and service value, supply chains have had to reinvent themselves around capabilities such as flexibility, scalability, collaboration, fast flow, and Internet-enabled interoperability that provide customers with unique opportunities for total service.

Meeting the requirements of today's marketplace requires companies and their supply channel partners to continuously develop more responsive supply chain models that bring them closer to the customer by enabling the right mechanisms to attract and build sustainable customer loyalty. Effective customer management means finding answers to such questions as

- Who are the supply chain's current and potential customers?
- What level of product and service value can customers currently expect, and what would they like to have?
- How much will it cost to increase supply chain quality and service levels?
- What will be the acceptable trade-offs in price, quality, and service?
- What is the level of quality and service value being offered by the competition?

- What levels of value must the supply chain achieve to maintain competitive advantage?
- How can the entire supply channel be committed to an operating philosophy of continuous improvement in product quality and customer service value?

The development of a winning customer service strategy designed to answer these questions will have a direct impact on how the *goals* of the value chain business strategy are to be attained, what will be the impact on product and sales positioning, how the supply channel will be constructed, what commitments will be required from channel resources, and, finally, how the entire supply chain will gain and maintain competitive advantage.

DEFINING TODAY'S CUSTOMER MANAGEMENT DYNAMICS

There can be little doubt that a new model of customer management is emerging. The power of the customer to drive the marketplace has become the overriding reality for producers and suppliers of goods and services. Over the past half decade a group of new buzzwords has become the rubric for the generation of service value. Businesses must be able to position products and services that meet customers' demands, such as configurability, personalization, super service, convenience in ordering, solutions orientation, and fast flow fulfillment. Increasingly customers are also requiring that service models use digital information to move products rapidly, bypassing costly distribution layers. Finally, customers are also demanding the ability to use interactive tools, like the Internet, to configure their own orders, perform self-service inquires regarding order maintenance and status review, and supervise the delivery process without hassles or mistakes.

The increasing power of the customer can be distilled down two critical points. First, today's customer is *value driven*. While tools such as Internet-enabled trading exchanges and auctions provide radically new and powerful avenues to search globally for suppliers that can meet cost, product and service solution, and delivery requirements, it does not mean that customers will become increasing fickle and move away from business partnerships. It does mean, however, that opportunities for service value provided by the Internet will be factoring in new alternatives in the search to match available options with requirements for individual value. Today's supply chain must move beyond just knowing and responding to past customer profiles and buying patterns to the engineering of service models that continuously create new opportunities to reinvent what constitutes value for each customer.

Second, despite the growing capability to change suppliers based on price and delivery criteria, today's customer is more than ever searching to build strong *partnerships* with their supply chains. In the past, product and service branding drove customer purchases and cemented loyalties. Today, customers are looking beyond just products, prices, and delivery to the capability of their suppliers to provide participative product development, collaborate on sales and demand forecasting, integrate channel resources and competencies to synchronize competitive strengths, and enable the creation of supply chains sensitive enough to be able to respond to changes occurring any place, at any time in the supply network. Ultimately, the goal is to create the opportunity for linked competitive visioning, whereby collaborative partners will pursue joint marketplace development, shared resources, and trust driven by a common strategic vision.

Supply chains can not afford to ignore these growing customer expectations for value and collaborative relationships. In today's Internet-enabled environment customer are very aware of the matrix of product, service, price, and delivery values that they have received and what is available elsewhere in the marketplace. A single unfavorable experience provides customers with every reason to search for new partners. Unsatisfied customers can be a significant negative force in today's Internet-empowered environment, destroying time-tested relationships and scrambling formerly successful supply channels. The opposite is also true. Companies that consistently succeed in meeting the individual needs of their customers are communicating their willingness to generate new forms of service value and new collaborative possibilities. Such a strategy is fundamental in building the partnerships capable of withstanding the centripetal forces of an uncertain economy and the encroachment of global competitors [1].

CRM Definitions

Effectively responding to the dynamics of today's marketplace has required supply chains to radically rethink their approach to managing the customer. In the past, customer management was primarily concerned with managing the transaction. Concepts of *brand* and *mass marketing* meant standardization of products and services, as well as pricing, and assumed uniformity of customer wants and needs. The principles of customer management were considered to consist of five critical concepts [2]:

1. The *production concept* held that customers were always predisposed to products that are always available, delivered when needed, and are low in cost.
2. The *product concept* held that customers would always choose products that possessed the most quality, performance, and features.

3. The *selling concept* held that customers were primarily passive and that if left alone would not buy enough of a company's products and services. As a result businesses needed to continually devise effective sales, promotions, and advertising campaigns that presented their product/service value story to the marketplace.

4. The *marketing concept* held that the strategic goal of the business consisted in determining the needs and wants of target markets and delivering the desired satisfactions more effectively and efficiently than the competition.

5. The *societal marketing concept* held that the organization's task was to determine customer wants and needs in a way that preserved or enhanced the well-being of the customer or of society.

While the core elements of these five pillars of customer management are still valid, today's dynamic marketplace has witnessed a redefinition of the customer from a passive recipient of standardized goods and services to an active participator in product/service sourcing, configuration and design, pricing, and the establishment of interactive, one-to-one relationships focused on attaining customized solutions tailored to their personal interests and needs. Past concepts of customer service focused narrowly on formulas for front-end functions such as forecasting, promotions, and marketing. Customer management in the twenty-first century requires companies to continually create, enhance, and manage customer equity, or the value of customers to the enterprise, by establishing collaborative partnerships available through such touch points as traditional marketing campaigns, direct sales, the Internet, and e-mail.

In defining *customer relationship management* (CRM) it can be said that customer management can be viewed from three critical perspectives [3].

- *Customer management as an activity.* In this perspective customer management is considered purely as a transactional function. Among the activities are quotations management, pricing, order processing, proof of delivery, billing and invoicing, and product returns and claims processing. Basic customer services functions, such as handling complaints, training, and documentation are also included.

- *Customer performance measurement.* The second perspective considers customer management from the viewpoint of performance measurement. In this area can be found the development of service metrics such as "percent of orders delivered to the customer within ten days of order receipt" or "percent of orders received and processed in 48 hours with no back orders." The goal is to provide benchmarks on how well the supply chain system is responding to the customer. While critical, this perspective is insufficient for effective customer management.

- *Customer management as a philosophy.* The final perspective attempts to position customer management as an element within the overall *corporate strategy* of the enterprise. While considering transactional and performance management as essential pillars, this perspective seeks to converge marketing, sales, production, distribution, and supply chain partners into a real-time, synchronized customer satisfaction system that enables the development of close participative relationships through personal marketing.

An effective definition of CRM must contain all three of the above perspectives. Because it encapsulates such a wide spectrum of customer management functions, there is wide divergence between practitioners, analysts, and consultant as to a precise definition of the full meaning of CRM. Some feel that it is a business strategy. Others think it is a methodology focused on a set of Internet-enabled processes. Still others consider it an integrated extension of the ERP philosophy.

Perhaps the best way to understand CRM would be to view some of the leading definitions. According to Greenberg [4],

> CRM is a complete system that (1) provides a means and method to enhance the experience of the individual customers so that they will remain customers for life, (2) provides both technological and functional means of identifying, capturing, and retaining customers, and (3) provides a unified view of the customer across an enterprise.

Dyche feels that CRM can be defined as "The infrastructure that enables delineation of and increase in customer value, and the correct means by which to motivate valuable customers to remain loyal – indeed to buy again [5]." The final definition comes from Renner, Accenture's global CRM practice managing partner, who sees CRM as encompassing "all of the activities that go into identifying, attracting, and retaining customers, and focuses on aligning the whole organization to building profitable, lasting relationships with customers [6]."

Another way to approach to defining CRM is to break it into its constituent parts. CRM can be characterized as follows [7]:

- *CRM is supportive of the firm's strategic mission.* Much of today's thinking perceives CRM as a technology toolset that utilizes Internet-enabled functions to facilitate the order and service function. In reality CRM is a supply chain philosophy focused on the architecting of value-generating productivities of whole supply channel networks in the search to build profitable, sustainable relationships with customers.
- *CRM is focused on facilitating the customer management process.* Being more responsive to the customer requires sales and service func-

tions to make effective customer management decisions based on their capability to identify what brings value to the customer. Often success requires the availability of metrics and analytical tools that provide a comprehensive, cohesive, and centralized portrait of the customer that in turn can drive customer acquisition and retention programs.

- *CRM is focused on optimizing the customer's experience.* CRM is concerned with the goal of "owning the customer experience." CRM initiatives that continually win the customer can span objectives from providing a level of personalized service and customized products to utilizing advertising, ease in ordering a product, or ensuring a service call-back that will positively influence a customer's perception of the buying experience. The end result is to make customers feel good and personally connected to their supplier.

- *CRM opens a window into the customer.* The goal of a CRM system is to provide everyone in the supply chain who can influence the customer experience with a comprehensive marketing profile that includes detailing what service values the customer considers the most important and how they can ensure the customer has a positive buying experience. Access to customer-winning attributes, such as buying habits, pricing and promotions, channel preferences, and historical contact information, must be all-pervasive, integrated, and insightful.

- *CRM assists suppliers to measure customer profitability.* An effective CRM system enables customer management functions to determine which customers are profitable and which are not, what values drive profitability for each customer, and how the entire supply chain can architect sales and marketing processes that consistently deliver to each customer the values they desire the most.

- *CRM is about partnership management.* While utilizing technology tools such as the Internet to facilitate and provide new avenues for customer service management is certainly important, the real value of CRM is ascertaining and satisfying the needs, values, and visions of each customer. CRM is about nurturing mutually beneficial, long-term relationships intimate enough to provide on-going improvement opportunities and tailored solutions to meet mutual needs beyond physical product and service delivery.

- *CRM is a major facilitator of supply chain collaboration.* No individual customer transaction can be executed in a vacuum. Customer product and service delivery must be considered as actually a single occurrence in what is often a complex set of actions that ripple up and down the supply chain. Businesses capable of architecting integrated, synchronized supply chain processes that can provide a seamless appearance to the customer will be the ones that will have sustainable competitive advantage.

The goal of CRM is to provide a 360 degree perspective of the customer. CRM is a radically enhanced view of traditional customer management that seeks to employ today's Internet-enabled technology toolsets to create an infrastructure that spans supply chain boundaries in the search to identify, capture, and retain customers. Besides creating channel processes that accurately determine customers' behaviors, preferences, and sales history, CRM also understands customers to be value chain collaborators who regard their suppliers as the primary contact node in an extended, integrated supply chain assembled to provide the highest level of service and value.

CREATING THE CRM-CENTRIC ORGANIZATION

The emergence of CRM has required a redefinition of the organizational and supply chain structures formerly used to manage the customer. In the past the "supply chain" was narrowly conceived as a pipeline where products and information flowed sequentially from source to customer. The traditional supply chain manufactured standardized, relatively undifferentiated products that in turn were "pushed" through distribution channels whose missions were to provide cost efficiency and acceptable service. Supply chain management was regarded as a tactical activity termed logistics management, a back-office function concerned purely with transportation rate management and order chasing. The ability to manage the customer was dramatically impacted by these constraints. Products moved slowly and serially through each channel node, with buffer inventories massed as a safeguard against poorly understood demand in downstream nodes and uncertain supply from suppliers located at the source. Finally, information regarding changes to supply and demand was inaccurate and erratic, causing further chaos in the supply chain.

The dynamics of managing today's customer has obsoleted this archaic view of the supply chain. In place of static, rigid supply channels, meeting the demands of customers in the twenty-first century requires fast, flexible, agile supply networks capable of providing technologies that enable customer self-service, the configuration of customized product/service wraps that realize individualized value-solutions, and fulfillment functions responsive to the demand pull of the marketplace. Actualizing such value-attributes requires re-drafting of the basic structure and purpose of the supply chain. CRM requires the architecting of supply chains possessed of the following business and organizational values [8]:

- *Strategic advantage.* Supply chains provide *strategic* as well as tactical value. In the "Internet Age" value is driven by the interoperability of all levels of business processes across supply network partners. Leveraging channel value requires elevating supply chain management to the prime position in the development of business strategy.

- *Customer-centric.* Today's supply chains are no longer simply pipelines of product and information populated by passive customers, but should be conceived as dynamic, high-performance networks responsive to the demand pull of the marketplace. In place of a one-size-fits-all strategy, the goal is to produce and deliver products at the time and in the quantity desired by the customer without costly inventory buffers.

- *Collaboration.* Competing in today's business environment requires supply chain partners to engage in the generation of networks capable of unique value-creating partnerships. The goal is to seek out and develop channel competencies capable of performing specialized functions that will facilitate over-all supply chain processes.

- *Agile and scalable.* The ability to effectively respond to customer-driven changes in product/service mix, channel design, and fulfillment constitutes the foundation of CRM-responsive supply chains. Being agile in this context means being able to respond as quickly as possible to demand through the establishment of flexible production, distribution, and information flow processes. Service attributes in this area refer to the capability of organizations to reduce or eliminate physical plant, processing times, unnecessary vertical integration, large R&D investment, and high technology investment hurdles. As the nature of demand changes, supply chains must be able to quickly scale internal and external resources to solve particular volume and variety imperatives.

- *Fast flow.* The basis of demand management today is the rapid fulfillment of individualized customer solutions anywhere, any time on the globe. The ability of customers to access competing suppliers through the Internet has placed a premium on compressing and accelerating supply chain throughput, reliable and convenient ordering and delivery, and availability of supporting services. Fast flow espouses the attributes of *Lean Thinking*, requiring the elimination of all forms of channel waste, optimizing the value stream, increase of the transparency between channel network nodes, dramatic reduction in batch production and inventory buffers, and ability to design, schedule, build, and deliver to exact customer demand.

- *Migration to e-Commerce.* The universal access to and interoperability of information through digital tools like the Internet resides at the heart of today's revolution in customer relationship management. The goal is to leverage the continuing explosion in integrative computerized toolsets to provide the pathways linking and coordinating the demand and supply activities of channel network trading partners. Contemporary supply chain systems seek to integrate ERP backbones, forecasting, order management, and supply chain event-driven applications to enable real-time linkages to critical databases as well as impending channel constraints threatening the alignment of information and material flows and customer service needs and fulfillment priorities.

Today, many organizations have invested heavily in computerized tools, such as *enterprise resource planning* (ERP), *supply chain planning* (SCP), and CRM in the search to become more customer oriented. While these application toolsets have significantly assisted companies to rationalize and systematize enterprise operations, their true value can only be realized when organizational structures are truly demand-driven. Customer-centric organizations can be seen as developing through four distinct stages [9]. In the first stage, *company-focused* enterprises utilize *Lean Thinking* techniques to execute service improvements that seek to eliminate internal wastes and barriers that inhibit the pursuit of customer-focused operational processes, technologies, and fulfillment. Once companies have become inwardly customer-focused, they can then proceed to become *supply chain focused.* In this stage, companies seek out existing supply chain partners to establish collaborative initiatives on such inter-company processes as forecasting, planning, fulfillment, product development, marketing, and logistics. In stage three, *virtual organization focused*, channel trading partners seek to synchronize and integrate productive functions, such as marketing, sales, product development, finance, and manufacturing, based on joint channel demand-driven decisions. In the final stage, *market focused*, all channel decision-making and productive processes both within and in the supply chain are reconstructed to provide a single, seamless response to the marketplace. In this stage, channel constituents continually structure supply chain models providing for the interactive, proactive, real-time deployment of strategic, tactical, and operational resources capable of meeting any customer opportunity before the competition.

DEMAND MANAGEMENT

In today's highly competitive environment the effective management of the customer has progressed beyond narrow attempts to influence marketplace demand by focusing solely on marketing techniques such as promotions, advertising, and the annual sales campaign. Market-winning CRM requires a new perspective that has coalesced around the concept of *demand management.* While forecasting and traditional marketing remain central, demand management denotes a much broader set of activities that seek to integrate and optimize the totality of supply and demand satisfying functions, including replenishment, sales and operations planning, marketing, and order and customer management. Instead of belonging only to the marketing and sales function, demand management is also the responsibility of multiple disciplines and departments, including production, logistics, supply chain, planning, and finance. Although the concept is, in fact, still evolving, it can be said that the objective of demand management is to enable the "demand chain," beginning with product manufacture and concluding with customer delivery, to develop closely synchronized, collaborative strategies and processes that dramatically increase the velocity of inventory, services, information, and capital through the supply chain and out to the customer. Figure 9.1 attempts to visually display the components of demand management.

FIGURE 9.1 Components of demand management.

DEMAND MANAGEMENT STRATEGIES

The nature, intensity, and distribution of marketplace demand will directly influence the scope, objectives, and resource requirements of any supply chain. Traditionally, companies have sought to leverage the science of marketing to uncover as well as influence patterns of customer demand. Businesses usually begin with a value proposition surrounded by strategic decisions associated with such factors as the type of market to be pursued, its geographical scope, the mix of products and services offered, and the capabilities of resources to be deployed. Once the demand strategy has been assembled, the marketplace, in turn, reacts over time to the value proposition, transmitting transactions, information, and behavioral patterns as to the effectiveness of the original product/service value wrap. As demand feedback returns to each supply chain constituent, strategic planners can then re-evaluate the original value proposition and supply chain capabilities and execute necessary changes.

The strategic response to demand management input can be grouped into four areas [10].

- *Growth strategies* are focused around determining how companies can develop competencies and synergies through merger or acquisition. Demand management assists corporate strategists to build value proposition models that enable it to leverage new resources to drive as well as capitalize on marketplace statements regarding product/service mixes, pricing and promotions, delivery chain structures, and technology enablers.

- *Portfolio strategies* are concerned with the type, scope, nature, and life cycles of the range of product/services offerings constituting the value proposition. Based on demand feedback, portfolio management is concerned with four critical criteria. *Design* focuses around the capability of product offerings to meet existing standards for quality, usability, life cycle positioning, and opportunity to wrap intelligent services and activate logistics functions to speed supply chain fulfillment. *Cost* requires planners not only to pursue opportunities for process improvement and cost reduction, but also to continuously squeeze the time it takes from product idea conception to sales. *Services* provide new tools to deliver product-enhancing values such as self-service, real-time pricing, credit management, documentation, even classroom and e-learning opportunities. Finally, *quality* enables supply chains to be more responsive not just to base expectations of performance, reliability, conformance, etc., but also to the ability to assist customers in selecting the right combination of product/service wrap, and then configuring the solution to meet *individual* requirements. Effectively managing these dimensions will ensure strategic diversification of the product portfolio to match demand expectations.

- *Positioning strategies* seek to continuously architect the supply chain structure necessary to effectively determine product/service placement within the various supply channel networks based on demand and operating economics. Among the most important activities can be found determining the optimal placement of the highest value-producing products in the most strategic channels, determination of postponement strategies, utilization of geographical deployment, and enhancement of logistics capabilities.

- *Investment strategies* are concerned with the creation of a flexible portfolio of assets that provide strategic planners with the capability to
  managing capital, research and development budgets, marketing expenditures, and human and physical plant resources that optimize the demand forecast of potential product/service wraps and delivery functions. Based on demand feedback, this area would be critical in determining which products, services, channel structures, network partnerships, and human and physical assets should be invested in to support
  overall competitive advantage.

Demand management has dramatically changed from being a narrow, tactical tool that estimates, coordinates, and oversees the efficient flow of goods
and services through the supply chain to a dynamic, strategic function capable of continuously determining and optimizing the relationship between a
company's value proposition, its product/service wrap portfolio, and its
ability to continuously respond to the nature, intensity, and distribution of the
marketplace's demand for increased value.

FORECASTING DEMAND

Once supply chains have architected a comprehensive demand management
strategy, businesses must turn their attention to the process of converting customer, product, marketing channel, and sales positioning into estimates of demand that can be used to plan operations, execute decisions, and serve as a
source of performance measurement. The basics, techniques, and scope of
traditional forecasting were covered in detail in Chapter 4. Historically, the
approaches and methods described have provided companies with inexpensive and relatively effective processes to generate forecasts that can be used
to guide demand and supply planning and decision making. Whether simple
or complex, forecasting application tools seek to automate the tasks of providing visibility to past patterns and demand relationships, thereby assisting
strategists to better understanding the future.

While traditional forecasting methods provide the foundation for modern
demand management, it has become increasingly clear that they are becoming
unresponsive to today's demand management requirements. Forecasts work
well when demand patterns are stable and can be easily manipulated by statistical techniques, there is a large repository of historical data available, and organizations possess significant continuity in regards to product, processes,
and approaches to the marketplace. These forecasting tools work best with
relatively long-lived products and stable demand environments where standardized products are "pushed" repetitively through the marketplace.

In contrast the demand for highly flexible, agile product design and fulfill-ment structures capable of more frequent new product introduction, shorter lifecycles, and individualized configurability has rendered past "passive" ap-proaches to forecasting of decreasing value and engendered a number of de-mand management alternatives [11]. Today's marketplace requires demand forecasting tools that can provide for the development of a consensus forecast in which multiple supply chain partners share and reconcile forecasts to create a single supply chain plan. Demand-planning toolsets utilize algo-rithms to incorporate expected demand data, such as promotions, incentives, or even climate projections, to create a plan that can be utilized by each chan-nel constituent to respond to local demand by brand or sales territory. Such dynamic planning tools facilitate the activation of demand and supply balan-cing strategies by tracking the impact of pricing and promotions, providing visibility to supply in real time, enabling response to unexpected demand sig-nals, and seamlessly integrating channel enterprise business systems.

Among the more "dynamic models" for demand management can be found *supply chain engineering* (SCE). This radical method ignores the traditional statistical forecasting elements altogether and seeks to determine demand by removing channel barriers to the real-time flow of customer information. By focusing on making the supply chain more flexible and agile, channel part-ners have the ability to capture demand as it is actually occurring, thereby linking fulfillment functions directly with customer requirements as they occur. Instead of forecasting tools that calculate abstract patterns of expected demand, SCE attempts to compress the time it takes to identify and fulfill de-mand by concentrating supply capabilities directly on the customer demand pull.

The *demand smoothing* (DS) approach is founded on the assumption that smooth demand patterns can be forecasted with greater accuracy than patterns subject to wide variation. The objective of forecasters employing this model is to actively pursue channel management techniques that smooth demand, rather than depend on traditional passive forecasting tools that accept demand patterns as given. Under the DS approach, planners are constantly reviewing and making changes to existing standardized practices in sales, marketing, promotions, distribution, and transportation that cause forecast variation. Ex-amples would be requirements that product be manufactured and shipped in large lot sizes or the use of specific pricing models that encourage end-of-month sales cycles.

A third alternative to traditional statistical forecasting is *customer col-laboration* (CC). This model seeks to leverage the synergy and synchroni-zation between buyer and seller achievable only through close demand and fulfillment collaboration. By utilizing interoperable technologies and integra-tive practices, this model seeks to establish an open, real-time sharing of demand-related information. In utilizing this method forecasters must recognize that achieving results can be difficult and expensive. Normally this method would be used only when a single customer dominates demand and they can provide a very stable forecast. Also, while very desirable, collaborative alliances are time consuming, and the value of its pursuit must be borne out by the value of the forecast management it provides.

By far, the most talked about alternative to traditional forecasting is *collaborative planning, forecasting, and replenishment* (CPFR). Historically, forecasters have tried to apply a variety of channel management philosophies and technologies to provide more active methods of linking directly with customer demand. Beginning in mid-1980 with *electronic data interchange* (EDI), companies sought in turn to deploy integration initiatives such as *quick response* (QR), *vendor-managed inventories* (VMI), *continuous-replenishment planning* (CPR), and *efficient consumer response* (ECR) to scale the barriers inhibiting channel information and inventory integration. Unfortunately, while achieving inventory reductions, none of these techniques really addressed the critical issue: *how could channel trading partners achieve the level of continuous, systematic collaboration necessary to link total channel demand and supply*. Over the past decade CPFR has been deployed to respond to this gap in channel demand management.

What is CPFR? CPFR can be defined as the implementation of data and information transfer tools that facilitate the timely, interactive communication of demand forecasts and inventory statuses among a chain of trading partners. The objective of CPFR is to enable channel retailers, distributors, transportation providers, and manufacturers with the capability to synchronize total supply with total network demand from one end of the channel to the other. In the past, supply chains were burdened by forecast, planning, and inventory systems that were disconnected from each other, lacked accurate and timely demand information, and clouded visibility beyond immediate trading partners. CPFR simplifies and connects overall channel demand planning by providing a single, real-time plan of forecast and supply.

CPFR is reported to have begun in the consumer goods industry in the mid-1990s as an integrative toolset to increase forecast accuracy and synchronize product inventories with demand requirements. Since that time CPFR has emerged as a strategic initiative assisting today's leading corporations in the quest for lower costs and higher customer service. In 1996 the CPFR concept was institutionalized with the formation of the Voluntary Inter-Industry Commerce Standards Association (VICS) which was invested with the task of defining CPFR supply chain business process, organizational, and technology standards. While primarily targeted at the consumer goods industry, CPFR concepts have come to form the foundation for the communication of forecasting and channel inventories for all industry sectors.

How does CPFR work? The overriding objective of CPFR is to directly link the consumer with the entire supply chain. While management toolsets such as CRP, VMI, and QR were employed to remove excess inventory from the supply channel and smooth out demand variances, they were incapable of solving the twin problems residing at the core of channel management: the timely communication of forecast inaccuracies and the capability to utilize exception messaging that alerted channel partners of impeding bumps in network supply and demand. A CPFR initiative begins with the establishment of a collaborative partnership between two or more members of a supply chain (retailers, transport planners, distributors, and manufacturers) with the intent of creating the technical and operations management architectures necessary to address the existing gaps impeding the synchronization of critical supply chain information. Next, CPFR partners agree to share critical demand information detailing what products are going to be marketed, how they are going to be promoted and merchandized, and when sales cycles are to begin. Using DRP-like software, a unified channel forecast by *stock keeping unit* (SKU) by time period and quantity is communicated to the supply network.

Finally, each partner agrees to implement techniques that provide for the real-time sharing of channel inventory levels, *point of sales* (POS) transactions, and internal supply chain constraints. In addition, each trading partner is responsible for ensuring continuous forecast and inventory accuracy as well as database update. When these requirements have been fulfilled, the illumination of unnecessary inventory buffers and hidden bottlenecks in the network flow should be revealed and initiatives put in place to eliminate them. Furthermore, by establishing interoperable technology toolsets that promote the timely communication of total channel supply and demand, CPFR makes visible all plans and ongoing planning variances, thereby assisting companies to improve forecasting and replenishment decisions that yield optimal results.

Demand forecasting in the twenty-first century is really composed of three interrelated elements: the forecast, inventory management, and revenue management. More and more, companies have come to realize that demand forecasting is really a continuous process whereby the sales plan is integrally linked with channel inventory management and how sales issues like pricing and promotions are going to impact revenues. For example, a change in pricing or unplanned demand can cause an unforeseen inventory excess regardless of the original accuracy of the forecast. Today's solutions providers are responding to this need by developing Web-based applications, termed *Adaptive Logistics Management*, that attempt to track in real-time supply chain variables, such as forecasting, product movement, inventories, service levels, revenue streams, and other supply chain components, so supply channel nodes can adapt and optimize fulfillment strategies as the actually occur.

CPFR in Consumer Goods

In the late 1990's, Henkel KGaA, a German-based maker of household cleaners, toiletries and other home care products watched profitability dramatically fall due to serious flaws in its forecasting and execution methods. Inventory levels were high and so were stockouts, delivery errors and invoicing complaints; transportation was inefficient and costly. Forecasts were not synchronized with production at one end of the company and customer demand at the other end.

Part of the solution came with the implementation of a demand planning system and a wholesale re-engineering of Henkel's internal business processes. However, while shipments increased, lead times and costs decreased, and production capacity, product availability, and replenishment functions became better managed, Henkel became aware that their real problems stemmed from a lack of effective connectivity with their supply chain. Visibility to channel demand, pipeline inventory positions, efficient logistics, promotional activity, and supply channel structure began to surface as critical requirements for competitiveness.

To solve this problem Henkel began a process of implementing CPFR, a set of collaborative processes that would enable the company to more effectively communicate its requirements and synchronize its organiza-tion with trading partners out in the supply chain.

By 2000 Henkel had enlisted its first CPFR partner, Grupo Eroski, the Spanish grocery chain. Eroski was a natural candidate with a range of distribution functions from large warehouses to thousands of mini-markets. The partners began exchanging information once a day on outgoing stock, inventories and orders; once a week on order forecasts; every 15 days on sales forecasts, and every four months on the promotional events calendar. Using the Internet, the companies developed common business and promotional plans, compared sales forecasts and channel exceptions, and exchanged information on changes in promotions and product availability. They also established a series of key measurements to ensure performance.

After two years, the results of the CPFR project were dramatic: a 98 percent increase in customer service levels, 2 percent stockout rate, excess of 85 percent forecast reliability, 98 percent truck fill rate, and an increase in new product introduction success ratios.

Source: Robert J. Bowman, "European Grocery Supplier Shows How CPFR Really Works," *Global Logistics & Supply Chain Strategies,* 6, 12, (2002), 24-28

ORDER MANAGEMENT AND FULFILLMENT

Perhaps the most pivotal set of CRM functions can be found in the capability of the supply chain to execute order management and fulfillment process in a manner that meets the expectations of the customer. The order processing function is the primary contact between customer and the supply chain. Its purpose is to serve as the gateway into which orders are placed, priced, allocated, and tracked, and from which goods and services are delivered to the customer. Customer demand can be regarded as the prime mover that sets the whole logistics process into motion. As such, the quality, speed, and accuracy of the order processing function will have a fundamental impact on the cost and efficiency of all supply channel elements. Order processing functions that provide for the speedy and accurate transference of goods, services, and order information will facilitate the customer service function and act as the foundation for competitive advantage. Ineffective, inaccurate, and unresponsive order processing functions add cost to the customer, build excess inventories in the distribution channel, result in higher transportation and storage costs, and mask poor quality and performance measurements.

Researchers have identified several fundamental dimensions commonly associated with world-class order management. These dimensions are detailed below [12]:

- *Cycle time.* Perhaps one of the most critical features of effective order fulfillment is the management of order cycle times. Cycle time can be defined as the total elapsed time from the moment the customer identifies a product or service need to the moment stock is placed into the customer's inventory or the service is rendered. Normally order cycle time is divided into the following subprocesses: *order transmission* is concerned with the time it takes for a customer to transmit an order to a supplier; *order entry* is the time required for the supplier to enter an order into their business system; *order allocation and picking* is the time required to verify product availability and to perform picking functions; *order packing* is the time it takes to package the order; *order delivery* is the time required to perform logistics functions such as carrier selection, documentation, transport, and delivery; and, *order invoicing and payment* is the time necessary to generate payment documentation, billing transmission, and actual payment.

    Continuously reducing these cycle times is critical to effective *customer service management* (CSM). Cycle times can be attacked from two angles: the application of JIT methods and the implementation of information technology tools. JIT programs targeted at the elimination of waste in each of the order processing steps are an inexpensive yet powerful method for cycle time reduction. By eliminating redundancies in the order flow, useless paperwork, procedures, red tape, inaccuracies in information, costly order handling, checking and rechecking, and a host of other snags that add time to order processing, cycle times can be reduced. Also, computer tools such as Web-based order entry, EDI, bar coding, carton labeling, and others can eliminate cycle time by facilitating speedy and accurate information flows.

- *Availability.* This order management dimension refers to the capacity of the supply chain to have the products or services available when desired by the customer. Several inventory strategies can be followed depending on competitive marketplace cycle times and logistics objectives. One method is to stock products in anticipation of customer orders. This model requires decisions regarding the size and value of inventory and the number, location, and stocking policies of channel warehouses. Another model, followed by many manufacturers, is assemble-to-order or make-to-order based on actual order configuration. Such a decision dramatically cuts inventory and warehousing costs. A negative is that it can add considerably to order lead times and to processing complexity.

- *Dependability.* Effective order management requires supply chains to match actual cycle times, inventory availability, and operational performance with published service standards. In many cases, customers may consider dependability as their most sought after service value. The timely receipt of replenishment orders enables customers to continuously reduce their dependence on internal buffer inventories, and shrink order processing and planning, and receiving and plant costs. In addition, increased supply reliability enables channel customers to better service their own customers by reducing the chance of stockout.

- *Convenience.* In the customer-centric business environment of today, easy of order entry has become a critical value. In the past, customers had to search through pre-printed documentation to find the suppliers and products they needed. In addition, once located, they had to utilize cumbersome and time consuming methods, such as ordering by phone, fax, or EDI, to place orders. Often they had to wait for validation of requested product configurations, quantities, delivery dates, associated support services, and delivery options. Today's Internet-based solutions have dramatically changed the customers' expectations regarding ease of ordering. Web browsers enable customers to see on-line information about supplier products and services, work with on-line catalogs, perform research and comparison shopping, configure and enter orders directly on line, determine delivery options, and perform self-service order tracking.

- *Performance.* This final dimension of order management refers to the ability of suppliers to perform within published and competitive order management standards. There are four specific areas to consider. The first refers to the speed of *cycle times* necessary to meet customer expectations. Generally the shorter the order fulfillment cycle, the greater the competitive edge. The second refers to the *consistency* with which suppliers' order management and logistics functions execute accurate orders and deliver products on time. The third performance standard measures how *agile and flexible* are fulfillment functions to respond to customer requirements, manage new product introduction as well as product phase-out, customize logistics capabilities, and accommodate reverse logistics requirements. Finally, CSM performance is concerned with the ability of suppliers to handle *out-of-bounds* situations such as massive logistics or system failures, quality problems, new technology introduction, and contract changes.

THE ORDER MANAGEMENT PLANNING PROCESS

While the above critical attributes describe the environment for sound customer management, the order management cycle is the place where these attributes are activated. Order management is traditionally the responsibility of Marketing or Sales whose job it is to maintain customer master records, promise inventory to fulfill enterprise inventory demands, and release orders for picking and shipping. It is also the responsibility of this function to maintain valid order due date priorities and quantities. The schedule of demand that arises from the order processing function serves as the driver for the calculation of product sales usage that is used in MRP/ROP/DRP inventory resupply computations. In planning and controlling the order management process, the order processing department must determine answers to such questions as the following:

- Are customer master records accurate?
- Have the proper prices for products been determined?
- Are there any promotions or special prices in effect?
- Is there sufficient inventory to meet order requirements?
- When should inventory be allocated to open orders?
- What are the policies governing returns and backorders?
- How is customer credit being reviewed?
- Are current open order due dates accurate?

- How are order processing performance measurements to be determined?

The order management planning process as illustrated in Figure 9.2 begins with the accurate maintenance of database elements necessary for timely and accurate order processing. Among these databases is found the customer master, price master, and the product available-to-promise files, as well as variable database files such as customer quotations, open sales orders, and sales history. The next step in the sales order management process is executing the order processing cycle. The processing of customer orders can be viewed as belonging to three distinct cycles. These cycles can be described respectively as order receipt and entry, inventory allocation and picking, and order shipment and invoicing. Two external activities performed by the customer also accompany this process: order preparation and transmittal at the beginning of the process, and order receipt and stock disposition at the end.

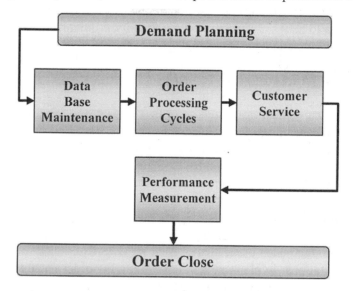

FIGURE 9.2 Order management planning process.

The third step in the order management process is monitoring order status. Once orders have been entered into the open order file, customer service can view order ship dates, backorders, and inventory quantities so that order priorities are maintained. Once the order has been shipped, order history reports can assist in tracking order delivery and quality related data. Order status reports show the order due date, quantity required, and quantity shipped for each open order. Timely and accurate customer order reporting is essential for good customer service. Besides providing a window into current order status, effective reporting enables customer service personnel to closely monitor not only order priorities but the entire replenishment system and keep it up to date.

The final step in the order management process is defining and monitoring performance measurements. For the most part, order management performance is concerned with process measurements. Among these metrics can be found the number of lines and orders filled complete, shipment by customer due date, percentage of stockouts, total order cycle time, billing adjustments, administrative errors, and profit margins. While providing information on the order process itself, performance measurements also provide data on how well the entire supply channel is responding to customer requirements. The ongoing benefits of a "world-class" order processing system are the following:

- *Continuous decline in average order cycle lead times.* This is the span of time from the moment an order arrives until it reaches the customer.
- *Improved customer relations.* Effective systems provide customer service with the critical information necessary to service the customer in as expeditious a manner as possible.
- *Increased order accuracy.* On-line data validation and system record defaults not only improve accuracy but also speed up the order processing cycle.
- *Decrease in operating costs.* With the ability to process data quickly and accurately, integrated order processing systems can eliminate internal costs associated with order review and expediting. What is more, linking the entire distribution channel systems can eliminate costs associated with order processing redundancies, excess inventories, and unprofitable transportation.
- *Timelier invoicing and accounting.* Effective order processing systems accelerate the transfer of accounts receivable data resulting from order shipment. Improvements in order shipments decrease the occurrences of invoice inaccuracies and improve on receivables collection.

THE ORDER MANAGEMENT CYCLE

The order management cycle is the key to effective customer service and deserves more attention. In a classic study by LaLonde and Zinszer [13], the order management cycle was conceived of as consisting of three phases: *pretransaction, transaction,* and *posttransaction.* The argument is that each phase usually requires the presence of specific customer quality and service elements if the sale is to be successfully executed.

Pretransaction Elements. The service dimensions in this phase of the sales cycle are, for the most part, focused on setting customer expectations and formalizing the sales and support structures of the firm. The specific elements consist of the following.

- *Written customer service policy.* A clear and concise definition of customer service objectives provides a formalized approach that can guide all service activities and be communicated to the customer. The contents of the policy statement should consist at a minimum of a statement of the service mission, detailed service standards, and a list of quantifiable performance measurements. The goal of the policy statement is to clearly delineate customer expectations and serve as a benchmarking tool to measure ongoing service performance.

- *Service policy communication.* Once a detailed service policy has been devised, it must be communicated to the customer. A formal service policy will assist customers to formulate proper expectations as to the level of performance they can expect as well as detail the proper channels to communicate with product/service providers if specific performance standards are not being met.

- *Organization structure.* Each channel partner must architect a service organization capable of executing the mission statement and service performance objectives. The goal of the organization is to facilitate communication and cooperation between the customer and the firm's product, sales, logistics, and financial functions. The identity of the management and staff of the service organization must be communicated to the customer base, as well as the means by which they can be contacted.

- *System flexibility.* The design of the service organization must be flexible enough to enable response to customer requirements regardless of environmental factors.

- *Management services.* The final *pretransaction* element of customer service is the availability from the supplier of training and printed materials to assist customers in performing their own problem-solving diagnostics. Education courses, training seminars, and training manuals are key components of management services. Functions in this area have been greatly expanded by the use of Internet marketing and service sites.

Transaction Elements. The service dimensions in this phase of the sales cycle are focused on sales order execution. The specific elements consist of the following:

- *Stockout level.* The availability of products in the right quantity and at the right place is fundamental to effective order management. Customer serviceability levels are the key performance measurement for this element. Serviceability is defined as the percentage of times customers' product requirements were met without a stockout. Once a stockout does occur, actions, such as offering a suitable substitute or expediting, are also part of this service element.
- *Order information.* This service element focuses on the ability of order management to respond quickly and accurately to customer inquiries during order placement. Order information consists of such data elements as inventory status, credit, pricing, shipping and handling costs, delivery, and open order and backorder status.
- *Elements of order cycle time.* The order cycle can be defined as the time that transpires between the moment a order is placed until the date it is delivered. In reality, there are three distinct subcycles that must be completed during the full order cycle: order entry, order allocation and picking, and order shipment and delivery. The contents of these cycles will be explored later in this chapter. Fast and accurate order cycle processing is fundamental to competitive advantage.
- *Expedite shipments.* Expedited shipments fall into two categories. The first is concerned with expediting through the order processing cycle those customer orders that are to receive special handling. For the most part, customers usually pay premium prices for expedited orders. When suppliers absorb expediting costs, it is absolutely essential that management not only review who is to receive this service but how further expediting can be eliminated for future orders. The second category of expediting occurs when a customer backorder occurs. Expediting in this instance encompasses swift resupply order action, receipt, and premium delivery to the customer. Service management should be constantly vigilant in ways to eliminate expediting. Expediting incurs costs that directly impact corporate profitability and are symptomatic of deficiencies in inventory ordering and control, sales, and delivery functions.
- *Transshipments.* This service element refers to the transfer of inventory between stocking points in the distribution channel necessary to meet customer demand. While inventory inequalities will occur over time in the supply chain network, planning tools like DRP should be used to eliminate this often costly alternative to stockout.
- *System accuracy.* Order processing inaccuracies, such as incorrect items, prices, quantities, shipping information, due dates, and billing, are costly to both the supply chain and the customer. Instances of order

cycle inaccuracy should be recorded and used as data in performance measurement calculations.

- *Order convenience.* This element refers to the degree of ease by which customers can place orders and have access to open order information. The Internet has dramatically changed this area. Service attributes such as 24x7x365 service, real-time information, on-line customer support, instantaneous availability of documentation, self-service, and Web-page personalization enable today's Web-savvy customers to receive a truly unique, interactive buying experience.

- *Product substitution.* The ability of the supplier to offer and the customer to accept product substitutes can have a dramatic impact on total inventory investment as well as the level of attained customer service. For example, by offering two substitutes for a given item, a company found that a previous customer service level of 70 percent increased dramatically to 97 percent with no additional inventory investment.

Posttransaction Elements. The service dimensions in the final area of the sales cycle are concerned with after-sale product support. Specific elements consist of the following:

- *Installation, warranty, alterations, repairs, and service parts.* These postsales elements are value-added to the product and are part of the reason why customers will choose to purchase from a specific firm. A company offering these services must have the following functions in place: assurance that the product will function as documented, demonstrated availability of service parts and support staff for advise or installation, full product documentation that explains product functioning, troubleshooting tips, and parts lists, and a product and services warranty administrative function that serves as a point of customer contact and contract tracking.

- *Product tracing.* Many products such as food, pharmaceuticals, medical supplies, and large-ticket items require maintenance of lot and/or serial number tracing. The availability of such information enables companies to recall products due to defect, spoilage, or obsolescence, or to record historical information used in marketing and future product design.

- *Customer claims, complaints, and returns.* Factors concerning customer claims, complaints, and returns should have been clearly defined in the written customer service policy detailed above. In the after-sale environment, policies regarding these and other customer issues must be rigorously followed if the firm's reliability, responsiveness, and credibility is to be maintained. Information arising from this element provides valuable data that can be used for product redesign, marketing programs, shipment and delivery, and other channel functions.

- *Product replacement.* In some cases, products that are required but are not in stock or that must be repaired require the firm to offer a temporary replacement. Costs borne by the supplier are considered part of the warranty or of the presales arrangement.

FULFILLMENT

Regardless of the type of demand order management used, whether traditional, EDI, or Internet-based, today's customer is not only demanding an integrated fulfillment approach that seeks to optimize the right warehousing, transport, and service solutions, but also the deployment of new types of networked relationships supported by new technologies and services. Historically, fulfillment was considered a "backoffice" function concerned with such activities as telemarketing operations, customer service, warehousing and shipping, procurement, inventory management, postponement processing, and disposition of returns. It was the role of fulfillment to navigate often poorly synchronized, inflexible supply chains and deliver products to the marketplace that met acceptable lead times and costs. Because fulfillment often lacked visibility to the movement of goods and information across the supply chain, lead times tended to elongate and inventory to accumulate to buffer against random events impacting channel process flowthrough. Such discontinuities resulted in supply chains that lacked the integration and interoperability necessary to provide the level of operations efficiency and velocity required for the short delivery cycles, customized fulfillment capabilities, and personalization demanded by customers increasingly acclimated to the online, real-time capabilities of Internet trade.

Today's fulfillment systems must be designed to provide transparency of supply chain data and events simultaneously to all regions of the channel network, solving the critical issues of connectivity and visibility that have traditionally blocked effective fulfillment. Re-architecting the supply chain around demand management principles and technology enablers provides individual channel partners with the capability to

- Leverage information from beyond the "four walls" of the enterprise to generate truly integrated fulfillment capabilities that dismantle the barriers set by past information bottlenecks, redundant processes, and excess channel buffers
- Improve inbound and outbound inventory visibility, thereby reducing excess inventory costs, potential obsolescence, and cycle times

- Expand outsourcing capabilities while enhancing the focus on internal core competencies
- Gain a better view on performance within the business and through the fulfillment network
- Engineer more fluid business relationships and accelerating information and product flows
- Achieve high-velocity, tightly synchronized business processes agile enough to adapt to changing business conditions and objectives
- Develop personalized service capabilities for customers [14].

Achieving such a radical redefinition of fulfillment management requires whole supply chains to respond to three critical challenges [15]. To begin with, fulfillment in the Internet Age requires the development of new types of relationships to meet the needs of today's increasingly Web-enabled customer. Critical attributes include more collaboration between network suppliers and customers, the effective utilization of outsourced functions to ensure "best-of-breed" response centered on the unique service competencies of channel partners, and the establishment of "win-win" commercial arrangements that enhance the relationship between customers and fulfillment service providers. Competitive leadership will go to those supply chains capable of rapid deployment to meet change, creating new kinds of relationships, and implementing radically new fulfillment solutions.

The second challenge is focused on an unbending dedication on the part of all supply chain constituents to continuous operations excellence. While technology interoperability and enablement has occupied much of the limelight in recent fulfillment literature, it has become clear that a "back-to-basics" approach that emphasizes the development of new fulfillment networks and make/buy strategies and the implementation of agile and flexible channel facilities and processes is critical to engineering supply chains capable of responding effectively to today's fast paced environment. Only those supply networks capable of quickly customizing the logistics network, integrating demand and supply planning, integrating product, information, and financial flows, sourcing strategically, leveraging postponement strategies, and establishing pan-supply chain performance metrics will be able to seize and sustain competitive fulfillment leadership in their markets.

Finally, competitive fulfillment in the twenty-first century depends on the deployment of new technologies and services. In the past, supply chains consisted of individualized one dimensional service functions such as inbound/outbound freight, carrier management, total cost control, operations outsourcing decisions, load planning, routing and scheduling, and execution of administrative services. Today, emerging supply chain networks, utilization of outsourcing strategies, and the continuous shortening of all cycle times have generated the need for new types of services, while technologies have enabled the exploration of new means of delivery. For example, many companies are exploring the use of Web-based services, such as fulfillment exchanges, auctions, and reverse auctions, for such functions as freight and parcel carrier selection. Another area is the use of *infomediaries* who utilize Internet technologies to facilitate the flow of fulfillment information such as shipment track-and-trace, real-time alert messaging, supply channel modeling, "what-if" simulation, and performance measurement tracking. Finally, in another area can be found channel providers offering *flow management solutions* that enable Web-based control of such fulfillment functions as transaction management across multi-partner networks, expediting, and channel event management.

CUSTOMER CARE MANAGEMENT

Over the past twenty-five years the purpose, scope, and mission of *customer service management* (CSM) has changed dramatically. In the beginning, customer service consisted in receiving and answering personally correspondence with customers who had questions or problems with products or services. Next came the *help desk* where, instead of writing, customers could talk directly to a service rep about their issues. By the 1990's the purpose and function of CSM had evolved beyond just an 800 telephone number to encompass a wide field of customer care objectives and activities. Known as *contact centers* or *customer interaction centers* (CIC), service functions sought to deploy a range of multimedia tools to not only relate order and account status, but also to manage every component affecting the customer from product information to maintenance, warranties, and upgrades.

Today, the capabilities of CICs have been expanding into new dimensions with the advent of exciting new toolsets, such as the Internet, wireless communications, speech recognition, and video, to join older technologies such as phone, caller-ID, fax, e-mail, and EDI. Such applications provide customers with even more opportunities for control of service dimensions while enabling companies to integrate all avenues of customer interaction on a central platform. Self-service opens a new dimension of customer service at less cost while service databases improve knowledge of customer behavior that enable the delivery of customized sales and service one customer at a time [16].

DEFINING CUSTOMER SERVICE MANAGEMENT

Although it can be said that CSM is perhaps the central activity of the every business, few would be able to exactly define what it is or what it actually does. CSM is commonly described by the use of two expressions: *easy to do business with* and *sensitive to customer needs*. While these concepts are easy to understand, they lack, however, detailed content. There are several valuable definitions available. LaLonde and Zinser [17] state that CSM can be best understood when seen from three perspectives: as an *activity* consisting of functions such as order processing, proof of delivery, invoicing accuracy, timeliness of delivery, and others; as a set of *performance* related criteria focused on service and satisfaction metrics; and, finally, as a *corporate philosophy* concerned with imbedding CSM within the long-term strategies of the enterprise.

Another definition describes customer service as a process that results in

> A value added to the product or service exchanged. This value added in the exchange process might be short term as in a single transaction or long term as in a contractual relationship. The value added is also shared, in that each of the parties to the transaction or contract are better off at the completion of the transaction than they were before the transaction took place. Thus, in a process view: Customer service is a process for providing significant value-added benefits to the supply chain in a cost effective way [18].

In a similar vein, Band [19] defines CSM as "the state in which customer needs, wants, and expectations, through the transaction cycle, are met or exceeded, resulting in repurchase and continuing loyalty." In other words, if customer satisfaction could be expressed as a ratio it would look as follows:

$$\text{Customer Satisfaction} = \frac{\text{Perceived quality}}{\text{Needs, wants, and expectations}}$$

Another perspective on the meaning of CSM can be found by viewing its fundamental elements. Perhaps the most concise list of service elements has been formulated by Zeithaml, *et al.* [20]. These elements are:

- *Tangibles.* This element refers to the *appearance* a firm's service functions project to the customer. Often the image of quality a company wishes to communicate to the marketplace includes such tangibles as new facilities, state-of-the-art technology, highly qualified personnel, and the latest equipment. Tangibles are designed to give the customer a sense of confidence and assurance that the services they are receiving are truly "world class."

- *Reliability.* Once a company publishes their commitment to a specific level of customer service, their ability to live up to that standard is the measurement of their reliability. Service leaders must continually perform the promised service dependably and accurately each and every time. Reliability of service permits supply chains to "lock-in" their customers who will gladly pay premium prices for delivered quality.

- *Responsiveness.* The ability of a supply chain to respond to customer needs quickly and concisely lets customers know that their time and costs are important. Whether it is in rendering prompt presales service or a willingness to assist with product quality issues, a helpful attitude and timely service will always leave the customer with the sense of dealing with a winner.

- *Competence.* When customers purchase goods and services, they need to feel assured that the supplier possesses the required skills and knowledge to assist them when product or support issues arise. Firms that back up their products with cost-effective and competent services will always be leaders in their marketplace.

- *Courtesy.* Many a sale is won or lost based on the way the customer is treated in the presales and postsales cycles. Companies who do not respond to their customers with politeness, respect, consideration, and professionalism are destined to lose them to competitors who do.

- *Credibility.* Service leaders base their success on high standards of honesty, trustworthiness, and believability. Customers purchase products from firms that live up to claims of the best quality possible at the lowest price.

- *Security.* The delivery of products and services must be accompanied by a sense of security on the part of the purchaser. Issues range from Internet transaction security to confidence about the safety and value of purchased products and services. Security frees customers from doubts and provides "peace of mind" for the products and accompanying services they purchase.

- *Access.* This element of customer service has several facets. Foremost, access means the degree of ease by which customers can purchase products or contact sales and service functions. Access can mean the availability of goods and services within a time limit generally accepted by the industry. Access can also mean the speed by which after-sales replacement parts and services can be delivered to the customer. Customer convenience and access to goods and services are fundamental to competitive advantage.

- *Communication.* The availability of sales and services staff to respond quickly and intelligently to customer questions concerning products, services, account status, and the status of open orders is the primary tier of a firm's customer communication function. Other communication forms such as printed literature, manuals, product and service newsletter updates, and advertising form the second tier. Effective customer communication stands as a fundamental cornerstone for service leadership.

- *Understanding the Customer.* Unearthing and responding to the needs, desires, and expectations of the customer is the first element in effective sales and service. Firms that provide the products and services customers really want will always enjoy an edge over their competitors.

The above list of service dimensions is applicable to all types of businesses. Even though specific targets of service quality may vary from industry to industry, the ten dimensions represent benchmarks by which supply chains can measure themselves.

MANAGING CUSTOMER SERVICE

Problems in any one of the dimensions of customer service can have an enormous impact on customer satisfaction. Product quality, for example, is usually singled out as the touchstone of customer satisfaction. Effective communications, such as advertising, promotions, and in-store ambience also play a key role in setting expectations. For other products, after-sales support, warranties, training, and service part availability affect service satisfaction. Although individually important, none of the service dimensions by themselves can completely determine the boundaries of customer satisfaction. In reality, effective customer service must be managed. The expectations and needs of each customer must, first of all, be discovered and defined, and then weighed against channel service offerings, understanding which are essential standards of service and which are secondary. A useful framework for managing customer service divides the service dimensions into four distinct areas: the customer, the service strategy, people resources, and information systems [Figure 9.3].

At the center of the service framework stands the *customer*. It is customer wants, needs, and expectations that drive the service function. As has been pointed out, these aspects often change as the customer moves through the sales cycle. Clearly identifying the service characteristics of the customer forms the foundation for the formulation and implementation of the firm's service strategy. The *service strategy* consists of two parts: an internal commitment to service centered on the formal corporate service mission statement and an external commitment to executing those service attributes promised to the customer through the sales cycle. Positioned in the third area of the customer service framework are the *people*, the management and staff of the organization. The fact that this area is connected to the service strategy means that there must be a shared vision of service values that permeates the whole company. In addition, the line connecting people resources to the customer represents the everyday communication that occurs between the firm's employees and the customer.

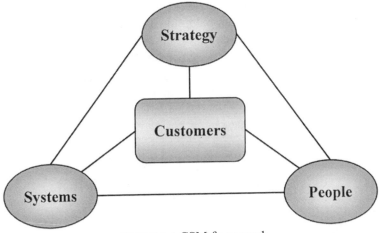

FIGURE 9.3 CSM framework

The final area of the customer service framework is the enterprise's *information systems*. As the diagram illustrates, information systems link the other elements of the service framework. People resources utilize the company's systems to execute functions, record information, and communicate with customers. These technologies are multidimensional and are composed of management systems that determine enterprise goals, internal and externally devised rules and regulations systems, the mechanical technical systems, and the company's social systems that guide problem solving, teamwork, and service values. The customer must use the systems employed by their suppliers to make their wishes, needs, and expectations known. Finally, the information systems can be heavily influenced by the service strategy. Strategic objectives shape the firm's matrix of systems as they seek to engineer a customer service-centered culture.

ELEMENTS OF EFFECTIVE SERVICE MANAGEMENT

According to Gopal and Cahill [21], there are nine critical steps in effective CSM (Figure 9.4). The first step is to establish and nurture a culture of continuous improvement through the supply chain. Customer service leaders of the twenty-first century will be those supply channel networks that espouse the concept of continuous incremental improvement at all levels in the organization. The ongoing ability to create value and deliver it to the customer can only be achieved by responsive "world-class" performers who are tireless in their examination of every aspect of channel operations in search of untapped sources of quality and customer satisfaction. Band [22] feels that value creation is strategic, systemic, and continuous. It is *strategic* because delivering quality to customers is at the very heart of supply chain strategy. It is *systemic* because the information, planning, and execution systems utilized by the organization must be continually refocused in the pursuit of customer value. Finally, it is *continuous* because the challenge of gaining and keeping customers in today's marketplace requires an unrelenting dedication to achieving continuous improvement in all levels of performance.

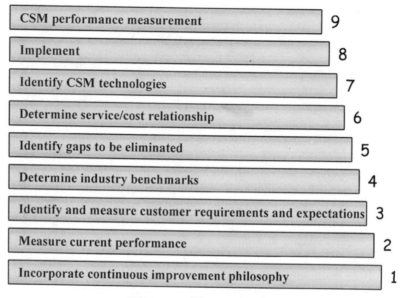

CSM performance measurement	9
Implement	8
Identify CSM technologies	7
Determine service/cost relationship	6
Identify gaps to be eliminated	5
Determine industry benchmarks	4
Identify and measure customer requirements and expectations	3
Measure current performance	2
Incorporate continuous improvement philosophy	1

FIGURE 9.4 Elements of CSM.

Following such a philosophy means managing the supply chain by continuously aligning and realigning operations with corporate objectives and goals, the institutionalization of shared values providing for quality, customer orientation, and the on-going improvement of functional processes, problem solving at all levels, cross-functional operations, people empowerment, and two-way continuous communications. In addition, a dedication to increasing service quality and value means enabling a continuous process for measuring customer perceptions of service quality, identifying service shortfalls, and responding to quality gaps with appropriate action to improve service metrics. Without this management cornerstone in place, supply chains operating in the 2000s will find it difficult to achieve customer service excellence. The elements of creating value for customers are portrayed in Figure 9.5.

Once a strategy of process improvement is in place, supply chain constituents can begin detailing existing performance levels. Not only does this on-going exercise provide management with a window to current service prob-

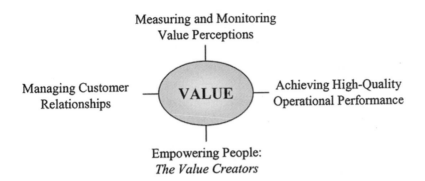

FIGURE 9.5 Elements necessary for creating customer value.

lems, it also clearly marks the path on the way to competitive service leadership. Measuring supply chain service effectiveness consists of two elements: determining customer expectations and needs, and quantifying current service practices and measuring the variance between existing levels and marketplace expectations.

Measuring external service performance consists, first, in performing a thorough marketing study of those elements perceived by the customer as a requirement before and after the purchase, and, second, executing a benchmarking analysis designed to determine customer perceptions of service offered by competitors. The starting point is to identify and rank the relevant customer service attributes. A possible method would be to create a survey of service factors divided into three major areas: marketing (price, sales support, product mix, terms of sale, etc.), service (delivery performance, order turn around, fill rates, accuracy, etc.), and product (quality, reliability, availability, documentation, etc.). In addition, most individual firms could engage a corporate marketing staff, a marketing consulting firm, or even a local university to extend the depth and breadth of the study through the use of several different forms of customer interview, such as telephone, intercept, opportunity, on site, and focus group. This discovery process should provide answers to the following questions:

1. Who are the firm's customers?
2. What service attributes are pivotal in meeting their needs?
3. What service activities are currently being performed to meet these needs?

Once the supply chain *external* services position has been detailed, an *internal* audit of actual service practices needs to be executed. The purpose of the internal audit is to identify actual services and measurement systems. The audit should provide answers to such questions as the following:

- What is the prevailing corporate culture regarding customer service excellence?

- How do business units (Marketing, Sales, Finance, and Logistics) perceive their role in providing customer service?
- How is customer service measured within each business unit?
- What are the performance standards and service objectives?
- What are the internal customer service performance measuring systems, and how are they integrated to provide a corporate viewpoint?
- What are the current performance metrics?
- How are these metrics used to increase service performance?

Answers to these questions can arise by conducting an analysis of existing service performance data and through departmental interviews. Performance metrics can be attained from internal data relating to marketing, product, and service attributes. Interviews conducted with managers, supervisors, and key staff members of each department can also assist in the internal audit. Elements such as organizational structure, performance measurement systems, problem-solving techniques, perception of customer needs, level of direct customer contact, and plans for service improvements will detail current service paradigms and interfaces with other functional departments.

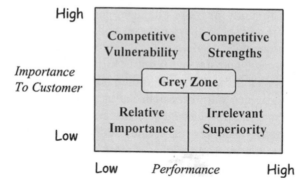

FIGURE 9.6 CSM attribute matrix.

The results of the external and internal services audits can be used to develop a *services attribute matrix*. The model of the matrix appears in Figure 9.6 [23]. The matrix permits the reviewer to rank each attribute by its relative importance to the customer. The same method can be used for competitive benchmarking by ranking the position of the competition contrasted to the firm's performance. The matrix has five zones. The service rank for each attribute is measured by determining the relative importance of the attribute to the customer (or the strength of the competitor) to the actual performance of the firm. By intersecting the lines, service managers can see the strengths or weaknesses relative to customer expectations and the position of competitors. Once each service attribute has been applied to the matrix, service management can begin the task of ranking each by level of importance. Attributes that illustrate a competitive vulnerability require high priority in the service strategy. Attributes, on the other hand, that indicate irrelevant superiority are probably causing unnecessary service costs and should be eliminated. Metrics that indicate that customer expectations (or competitive positioning), and the firm's corresponding performance intersect somewhere in the middle range, means that the service attribute is located in the grey zone. This zone indicates that the level of importance and performance are not of significant strategic importance.

IDENTIFYING PERFORMANCE GAPS

Metrics illustrating performance *gaps* provide a clear understanding of the level of current performance as opposed to both customer perceptions and expectations and to advantages enjoyed by industry leaders. Once these gaps have been quantified, CSM can begin to redesign organizational and value structures, refocusing them on continuous incremental improvements in processes and operational performance. Zeithaml, et al. [24] have formulated a service quality model that highlights the gaps between customer expectations and actual service performance. The model, shown in Figure 9.7, identifies

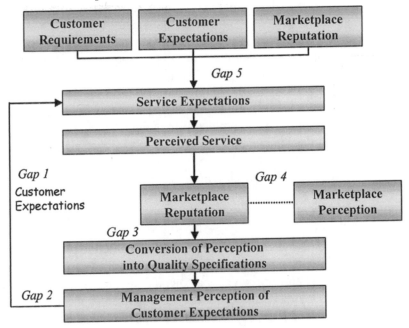

FIGURE 9.7 Service quality model.

five gaps inhibiting "world-class" service delivery. Gaps 1 through 4 are shortfalls that occur within the services organization; Gap 5 is a service-quality shortfall as perceived by the customer. The gaps are described as follows:

- *Gap 1: Customer expectations and management perception.* Perhaps the most fundamental service gap can be found in the variance that exists between what customers expect from products and services and what management perceives as customer requirements. Normally, there is wide congruence between expectations and perceptions. However, management might not always be completely aware of which service attributes constitute high priorities for customers. In addition, even when key attributes are identified, it might be difficult to quantify what exactly is the expected level of service. The external audit should provide service managers with a way of narrowing this gap by revealing accurate information about customer's expectations. As an illustration, a company may feel their customers buy because of low price, when, in reality, it is product delivery that is driving expectations.

- *Gap 2: Management perception and service-quality specification.* Although service managers might formulate correct perceptions of customer expectations, a gap can occur when a firm experiences difficulty translating those expectations into service-quality specifications. These difficulties usual result in the adoption of superficial specifications or ones that are ill-defined. Sometimes managers believe, because of the nature of the product and support, that it is simply impossible to set service levels that will match customer expectations. Again, others feel that the resources necessary are clearly beyond the company's competence. Finally, the most frustrating form of service-quality gap occurs when there are clear specifications, but management is not committed to enforcing them. For example, a firm pledges timely field support for a product but does not hire sufficient staff to meet presales pledges, and then does nothing to remedy the service deficiency.

- *Gap 3: Service quality specifications and service delivery.* Even when firms develop detailed quality-service standards and programs for creating a *customer-centric* organization, service leadership is not a certainty. A gap may exist and continue to widen based on such elements as poorly trained customer-contact personnel, ineffective service-support systems, insufficient capacity, and contradictory performance measurements. When service delivery quality falls short of the standard, the result has a direct impact on what customer can expect (Gap 5).

- *Gap 4: Service delivery and external communications.* A fundamental element shaping customer expectations are service quality standards detailed in advertising media, promised by the sales force, and found in other communications. Take, for instance, a distributor that publishes a 24-hour order turnaround time but lacks the information systems for effective inventory accuracy and picklist generation to meet that objective. When the customer is told and expects next-day delivery of an order and does not get it, the gap begins to widen between what sales tells the customer and what logistics can deliver.

- *Gap 5: Perceived and expected service.* The discrepancy that arises between the expected and the perceived service(s) is detailed in Gap 5. The content of this gap is gathered from the cumulative shortfalls found in each of the four enterprise gaps. Determining this discrepancy is more than just totaling the metrics of Gaps 1 through 4; often the cumulative affect on customer perceptions of service delivery are greater than the sum of the parts. The source of customer service expectations can be found in word-of-mouth communications, past experiences, and customer requirements.

Metrics illuminating performance gaps provide the supply chain with a clear understanding of the level of current performance as opposed to "world-class" leaders. Once these gaps have been quantified, management can then develop an effective services strategy that focuses the organization on continuous incremental improvements in processes and operational performance.

ANALYZING TOTAL COST-SERVICE LEVEL TRADE-OFFS

Defining service gaps and performing competitive benchmarking will assist companies in determining customer service levels. Before, however, effective service strategies and measurement systems can be implemented, not only the current actual cost of selling and servicing the product but also the incremental cost of reaching the next level of service must be calculated. Customer services costs for a typical distributor arise from the following business functions:

- *Transportation.* This is the cost incurred to transport products through the distribution channel and out to the customer. Transportation by far constitutes the largest portion of physical distribution costs.
- *Inventory carrying costs.* The ability to service customer demand requires the distributor to purchase and warehouse inventory. The costs for warehouse facilities, material handling equipment, and personnel, as well as the traditional elements such as the cost of capital, taxes, insurance, obsolescence, and deterioration must accompany all stocking decisions.
- *Production and Purchasing.* The cost of manufacturing and purchasing inventory.

- *Product development.* The costs associated with product development design, prototyping, tooling, and conversion to production.
- *Marketing and Sales.* The cost of marketing research, sales, promotions, and advertising.
- *Order processing and Information Systems.* The cost of processing orders, order status inquiry and reporting, and computer system maintenance.
- *Customer Service.* The cost of maintaining customer satisfaction arising from after-sales service and support.
- *Indirect costs.* Costs incurred for indirect support functions that assist in the execution of logistics and service activities.

Obviously, attaining high levels of customer services cannot be achieved without corresponding growths in performance in other parts of the organization. In the past, it was assumed that as the service level increased so did the costs. As Figure 9.8 illustrates, companies often attempted to chart expected sales revenues and the cost of services and to calculate the optimum service level. Once the increased level of service-logistics costs had been justified, service management could then begin the process of cost-service trade-off analysis. Such cost trade-offs took place in one or several areas within the distribution pipeline: increased stocks and inventory deployment, inbound, interbranch and outbound transportation, procurement and manufacturing processes, intra-organizational and extra-organizational communications facilities, information systems implementation, people empowerment, and customer service systems [25].

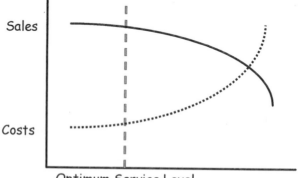

FIGURE 9.8 Charting the optimum service level.

Although a time honored management method, when performing service-cost trade-off analyses channel management must strive not to fall into the fatal attitude of "we win, the customer loses." Regrettably, many a service program devised from cost trade-offs has resulted in a justification for low expectations and performance. For example, it is often said that "quality has its price, and at some point the cost of quality will exceed its benefit." As the quality revolution of the last decade has shown, however, quality pays for itself many times over. The same can be said for SCM initiatives that most companies assume require increases in inventory, people, and expenditures. In reality, management philosophies such as JIT increase the velocity and flexibility of customer services while slashing excess inventories and reducing the need for staff whose work revolves around delay management. The goal of service-cost trade-offs analysis, therefore, is not to look for ways to optimize customer satisfaction versus the anticipated costs but rather to rank and prioritize competitive service elements, and to refocus supply chain resources to continuously improve each service element. Service leaders seek continuous improvement in cost, quality, response time, and flexibility simultaneously.

IDENTIFYING CSM TECHNOLOGIES

Over the past few years, CSM has evolved from banks of service reps connected to the customer by phone and fax to highly automated service centers. The goal is to leverage technologies to activate open dialogues with the customer that are *personalized*, in that they are capable of responding to individual customer concerns; *self-activating,* in that they provide applications for customers to self-service their questions; with *immediacy*, in that critical information can be conveyed in real time; and *intimate,* in that the customer truly feels the supplier is concerned about their problems. When developing the technology element of the CSM strategy, today's service departments can utilize the following toolsets [26]:

- *Automatic call distribution* (ACD). This technology provides for the automatic routing of incoming customer calls to the proper service resources based on call content. ACD seeks to minimize service call wait and queues by automatically switching a call to an open resource, matching call content with service rep expertise, and even prioritizing the call by level of severity or service contract.
- *Interactive voice response* (IVR). This toolsets enables 24x7x365 service access by typing the appropriate keys on a telephone. The goal is to provide access to service information or to qualify and route a call without human interaction. More advanced applications provide automated speech recognition whereby customers can verbally communicate their questions without cumbersome typing of keypad digits.

- *Internet call management.* The use of Web-based self-service has enabled customers to escape from the tedious entry of data characteristic of IVR systems. The advantage of Web-activated service is that customers can enjoy a significant level of self-driven interaction with the service system. Also customers can access proactively a wide range of services ranging from order status tracking to new product introduction to on-line forums.

- *Service cyberagents, bots, and avatars.* While mostly futuristic, the use of intelligent agents capable of performing automated service tasks is expected to expand dramatically. The goal is to equip these tools with specific expertise, instructability, simplified reasoning, and the capability to work with other cyberagents in solving service questions.

- *Call center analytics.* Effective CSM requires a holistic view of the customer. While CRM analytics focus on tracking the marketing side of the customer, the capability to record and analyze the vast amount of service-related data from each customer will be essential for CSM leadership. Analytical data will assist in the selection of the appropriate CSM technologies, the overall corporate service strategy, and the level and type of individualized service provided to each customer.

The power of the customer and enhancements in technologies have transformed the traditional scope and mission of customer service. Until just recently, customer service was considered as purely a cost center and a drain on profitability. In contrast, today's customer service function is seen as absolutely critical in cementing customer loyalties and assuring maximum customer value.

DEVELOPING AND IMPLEMENTING THE SERVICES STRATEGY

In order to achieve superior customer service performance, the firm must do more than establish service goals, understand the gaps in customer service and competitive benchmarks, implement technologies, and set in motion an action plan that will provide for continuous improvement in service levels and corresponding decreases in costs. Service leadership in the Internet Age means that whole supply chains must be concerned with the success of the total business process and not just solely with the satisfaction of the customer. In managing the total business process, service strategies must be architected that are in alignment not only with internal business goals and objectives but also with the goals of the entire supply chain. Perhaps the most effective customer service strategy is one that integrates and facilitates the four major groups (Figure 9.9) impacting the external and internal functions of the enterprise. These groups can be called the customer, the firm's shareholders, the employee, and the supplier channel.

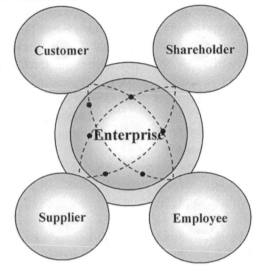

FIGURE 9.9 Enterprise service groups.

The *customer* has by far the greatest impact on service strategy development. Servicing their wants and needs is why the supply chain exists; revenues from their purchases are the central growth variable; their feedback is the only true voice guiding product and service direction. The customer side of implementing an effective service strategy must be focused around the following key elements and accompanying questions:

- *Customer/channel relationship.* What are the current levels of communications and expectations between the customer and the supply chain? Have customer product and service requirements been clearly communicated, and what mechanisms are in place to ensure effective and timely feedback? Has the supply chain established a product and services value proposition that is fully compatible with network capabilities, limitations, and customer expectations?

- *Product strategy.* What is the product unit-cost strategy? Are channel partners to concentrate on low-margin or high full-stream cost or a mixed strategy? Is the product unique or is it highly interchangeable? Is the supply chain offering standard or customized products or a combination of both? What kind of packaging is to be used?

- *Services strategy.* What services are to accompany the product in the presales and postsales cycles? What are the response and mean time to resolution performance targets? What are the return, warranty, and field service policies?

- *Merchandising strategy.* How are products to be marketed to the customer? Is the focus to be on a direct sales force, catalogs, and so on, and how are marketing tools such as promotions, deals, and special pricing to be communicated to the customer? Does demand have seasonality or trends, or is it stable for a given period of time? What are the parameters of the order processing function? Are computerized methods such as the Internet, EDI, direct contact, telemarketing, or other forms to be used, and what are the service performance standards? What are the expected sales volumes per year, and is the supply chain focusing predominantly on long-term customer relationships or is it purely transaction based?

- *Delivery and order requirements.* What are the standards for order response times (hours, days, weeks)? What is the cost of a stockout? What are the limits on order quantities, and how are transportation systems to be used for delivery?

- *Material handling.* What are the handling and storage requirements of the product? Is the product a discrete unit, liquid, or handled in bulk?

- *Stocking requirements.* What should be the scope and structure of the distribution channel? Are products and services to be delivered from a central facility, clustered in specific geographical areas, or scattered to leverage logistics economies?

Right behind the customer, the firm's *shareholders* are also important in the formulation of the service strategy. In a very real sense, this group influences the vision and mission statement of each channel partner. The shareholder objectives must be in alignment with and supportive of the objectives set forth in the services strategy. For the most part, shareholders acknowledge their secondary role in the enterprise behind the customer. Conflict arises when this group begins to pursue goals antipodal to marketplace requirements. The solution is to respond to shareholders as if they were also customers. Instead of goods and services, the shareholder requires sufficient return on investment, evidence of continued progress and growth, and definition of marketplace expectations. In return, the enterprise can expect continued support for products and programs. The same operational strategies calling for continued incremental improvements in product and service quality need to be applied as well to the supplier-shareholder relationship.

Contemporary literature addressing the components of "world-class" CSM also views the *employee* as a customer. In the traditional organization, divided by departmental budgets, narrow job descriptions, procedures, and performance measurements, the vision of the employee as a customer is lost. Not only are such organizations chronically out of alignment with the customer, but they ignore both the creative abilities and needs of the firm's *inter-*

nal customer. To begin with, employee satisfaction should be seen as an objective as important as customer satisfaction. This satisfaction is attained by streamlining work-flows and mandating internal performance measurements that support the firm's dedication to continuous improvement. Second, employee potential is enabled when management provides ongoing training and an atmosphere designed to promote self-empowerment. The company-employee relationship that emerges is defined on one side by management commitment and a clear enunciation of expectations and performance objectives; in turn, employees must be prepared to exercise and expand their skills and contribute to superior service quality through continuous learning. As work centered on narrow tasks and command and compliance management styles give way to multidimensional focused teams responsible for performing whole processes, the nature of work will become more value-added, self-directing, and satisfying. In such an environment, success is measured by the extent to which the entire organization meets the needs and expectations of their internal as well as external customers.

The final component of the overall service strategy involves the level of service found between the firm and its *supplier chain*. At the gateway in the process of acquiring raw materials, components, and finished goods stands the firm's suppliers. As such, the quality of products and services received from the supplier has a direct impact on a company's ability to respond to the needs and expectations of its customers. If supplier product quality, on-time delivery, replenishment order accuracy, financial transference, and service support contain unacceptable performance gaps, the firm cannot help but respond to its customers by passing on the excess costs, lack of quality, and poor service. On the other hand, a superior supplier will enable the firm to jump-start and sustain continuous improvement initiatives that can then be communicated to the customer. When viewed as a customer, companies should provide suppliers with a clear statement of product and service expectations, search to remove redundancies in material movement, delivery, and paperwork, and implement ongoing improvements designed to eliminate costs. On their part suppliers should provide preview of new product development, participation in design, and a window into new market opportunities and trends. Effective supplier partnerships provides a synergy in which both parties can enjoy a level of quality, performance, and continuous improvement unattainable by each working independently.

PERFORMANCE MEASUREMENTS

The last step in managing customer service is structuring a mechanism that will provide ongoing service performance measurement. Just reviewing the opinions and expectations of the customer once a year will hardly provide the kind of metrics necessary for effective service management; there must be flexible measurement tools in place that provide detailed information on an ongoing basis and that change as marketplace expectations change. Once the means to gauge service performance have been formalized, the results can be measured against the standard and corrective action taken to eliminate the variance.

Effective performance measurement of customer service involves implementing programs that measure *both* internal and external metrics. Three general areas of measurement can be used: process measurements, product measurements, and satisfaction measurements. *Process measurements* are the most common measurements employed. These measurements, such as customer complaint statistics, billing adjustments, profit margins, productivity-to-cost ratios, order cycle time, and others, provide metrics that assist in the control of the process by which a product or service is created. *Product measurements* are concerned with how well a product or service conforms to specifications and standards, or the performance after purchase. Such elements as failure rate, service frequency, design, packaging, ease of use, and attractiveness provide the core metrics for this set of measurements. *Satisfaction measurements* utilize data directly from feedback that can be used to assess customers' perceptions of product quality and service. Analysis of complaints, periodic focus groups, toll-free telephone lines, customer comment cards, and management visits are all geared toward gathering metrics relating to performance satisfaction. Effective performance measurement entails using all three of the above techniques. The goal is to ensure that the objectives embodied in the firm's customer value-creation strategies do, indeed, match the expectations of the customer base.

Perhaps the best place to begin developing effective performance measurements is to identify those *key service attributes* desired the most by the customer and are being offered by the competition. The *service attribute matrix* can be used to prioritize these attributes so that management attention can be focused on the critical strengths and weaknesses in services offerings. Although important, formal service metrics are not the sole source of measuring service performance. Informal feedback, face-to-face communications, and on-the-spot data collection all provide sources of customer opinion. Additionally, the information attained from customer complaints is an important source of service-quality measurement. In studies carried out by the United States Office of Consumer Affairs, it has been proven that the average business never hears from 96 percent of those customers dissatisfied with the quality of the products and services they received. In addition, out of those customers who are unhappy, 90 percent will simply stop buying from particular suppliers, never telling them the source of dissatisfaction. Such a high statistic means that the CSM function must not just wait for the customer to complain but take active steps from site visits to ongoing questionnaires to ascertain the level of customer satisfaction.

Finally, the enterprise's performance must also be measured by the satisfaction of the *internal* customer. Such metrics as vendor on-time delivery and quality, the speed by which information and data moves through internal systems, the on-time completion of internal due dates, the elimination of useless procedural red tape, the level of employee proficiency for problem solving, and others must be constantly monitored and steps taken to eliminate variance. A comprehensive service strategy creates a total quality service attitude that enables the entire supply chain to sell better their products and services, deliver them faster and cheaper, respond quicker to serious service-quality gaps, develop service systems that are responsive to customer needs and provide timely performance metrics, and attract and keep service-oriented professionals who are dedicated to excellence and ongoing improvement.

THE INTERNET-ENABLED CRM ENVIRONMENT

While CRM practices have been used to management customers for many years, the rise of Internet technologies have obsoleted many of the conventional techniques and operating philosophies of service management. Today's Web-enabled applications are providing customer management functions with radically new approaches to generate customer value and collaboration, facilitate the sales process, enhance the customer service capabilities, and architect highly integrated, customer-centric infrastructures. In fact, over the past half-decade, CRM application suites have been perhaps the hottest segment of the software marketplace with revenues projected to exceeding 6 billion in 2003. By way of illustration, Figure 9.10 details the possible components of Internet-based or e-CRM software suites.

CRM AND INTERNET SALES

Internet-based selling and service management has opened the door to new and exciting possibilities. Although the dot-com fizzle and the economic slow down of the early 2000s have caused a deep decline in the development of Internet technologies for buying and selling, there can be no denying its potential to radically reshape the landscape of business. For customers, e-CRM provides radically simple, self-directed methods for browsing and locating suppliers and their products, as well as simplified order entry and open-order inquiry. Web-enabled communication tools have made it easy for customers and suppliers to engage in bidirectional communication, a feature

FIGURE 9.10 CRM technology sphere.

that increases one-to-one personalization of the transaction experience. Attributes such as 24x7x365 service, real-time information, on-line customer support, instantaneous availability of documentation, self-service, and Web-page personalization offer customers new ways of realizing value propositions that meet their individual needs.

For suppliers, Web-applications enable companies to sell directly to the end-customer thereby by-passing costly channel intermediaries. Further, because the demand is placed in the system in real time, suppliers have enhanced visibility to improve the effectiveness and better utilize resources. Finally, according to Sawhney and Zabin [27], "technology-enabled selling will be used increasingly to synchronize and integrate all selling channels used by the enterprise, including telesales, the Net, resellers, and the direct sales force, through the use of a common customer relationship repository, a common applications infrastructure, and a shared business process."

e-CRM databases can significantly assist suppliers to deliver tailored responses to their customers by effectively sorting good customers (profitable/valuable) from the bad (unprofitable/non-valuable). According to Poirier and Bauer [28], customer ratings should be based on the following criteria: *volume of a customer's purchases, strategic value of the customer,* and *profitability of the customer.* Based on the ratings, customers then should be arranged into a hierarchy, starting with the small number of super customers located at the top who account for the majority of the business and ending with "suspects" at the bottom who represent a very small proportion of annual sales. Once stratification of the customer base is completed, suppliers can then architect an individualized response commensurate with the expected level of customer profitability potential.

On the invoicing and payment side of sales management, companies have recently begun utilizing the Internet to facilitate payment processes. While currently less than twenty percent of bill payment is handled electronically, this percentage is expected to climb dramatically as increasingly more companies combine it with their CRM toolsets. In general, e-billing utilizes the Web to receive bills, authorize payments, match payments to purchase orders, and download data into ERP and accounting systems in a digital format. The obvious speed, easy of use, and accuracy gained by e-billing will enable companies to offer greater *convenience* to their customers in their abilities to access their accounts and view financial data and greater *personalization* for the biller to customize financial transactions and draw the customer to the Web site. In addition, e-billing provides another avenue for Internet marketing and cross-selling and will significantly assist CSM functions to handle bill and statement information. Finally, e- billing provides customers with further avenues for real-time self-service in the management and analysis of financial data.

SALES FORCE AUTOMATION

Originating in the early 1990's, *sales force automation* (SFA) was conceived as an electronic method to collect and analyze customer information from marketing and contact center organizations that in turn could be used to advance opportunities for customer retention and acquisition as well as enhance marketplace relationships and revenues. In addition, SFA equipped field sales with automation tools to more effectively manage existing accounts, prospect for new customers, track the impact of pricing, promotions, campaigns, forecasts, and other sales efforts on their pipelines, generate meaningful analysis and statistics from their sales database, become more mobile, organize their contact lists, and have real-time customer information in an easily accessed presentation. According to Dyche [29], the mission of SFA "was to put account information directly in the hands of field sales staff, making them responsible for it, and ultimately rendering them (and the rest of the company) more profitable."

Today's SFA systems are driven by technologies capable of synchronizing data from unconnected sources, such as laptops, mobile devices, and desktops, and utilizing flexible and scaleable databases, such as Microsoft SQL or Oracle, and memory-resident PC applications equipped with scoreboards and reporting functionality that can exploit powerful engines such as HTML and

Java to drive real-time information sharing. While the SFA marketplace contains a number of software vendors and competing products, they all posses to some degree or another the following functionality: *contact management* tools that contain customer databases and automated workflows capable of assigning and routing appointments; *account management* tools used to track account and sales data activity; *sales process/activity management* tools that predefine the procedures to be followed by the sales force during the sales cycle, *opportunity management* tools providing for the automated distribution of leads and assistance in lead conversion to sales; *quotation management* applications that enable entry, follow-up and conversion of quotes into orders; and *knowledge management* software concerned with standardizing and automating sales processes by capturing information found in sales handbooks, presentation materials, and forms and templates.

e-CRM MARKETING

Up until fairly recently, marketing was concerned with the promotion of mass produced products and services and assumed uniformity of customer wants and needs. With the advent of Internet buying and selling, companies could escape from the mass marketing approaches of the past and refocus on *personal marketing* – or one-to-one buyer-seller contact. This approach can be defined as the capability of companies to present their goods and services customized to fit the distinct personal interests and needs of the customer. According to Fingar, Kumar, and Sharma [30],

> *Customization* is the byword of the 21st century marketing revolution. By interacting with customers electronically, their buying behavior can be evaluated and responses to their needs can be tailored. Customization provides value to customers by allowing them to find solutions that better fit their needs and saves them time in searching for their solutions. . . . Not only can a solution be pinpointed for a customer, but also as the relationship grows, the more a business knows about individual buying behavior. As a result of the growing relationship, cross-selling opportunities will abound. With the Net, the savvy marketer can sense and respond to customer needs in real-time, one-to-one. . . . In the world of electronic consumer markets the success factor mantra is: relationship, relationship, and relationship.

Leveraging the Internet for marketing requires the use of software applications that enable suppliers to compile, search, and utilize customer databases to define who the customer is and then generate targeted marketing campaigns via e-mail, e-fax, the Web, the telephone, or other technology tools to reach the marketplace. The suite of toolsets available include customer intelligence and data extraction, campaign definition, detailed campaign planning and program launch, scheduling of activities and continuous performance measurement, and response management. While many of the activities appear similar to traditional marketing campaign processes, the major difference is the use of the Internet to capture, extract, and analyze campaign inputs. By tracking campaign results over time, marketers are then better equipped to construct future campaigns that can enhance one-to-one marketing relationships.

Today's CRM applications also contain analytical tools for data analysis. CRM analytics provide suppliers with statistical, modeling, and optimization toolsets that enable marketing organizations to analyze, combine, and stratify data to better understand the status of overall marketing strategies and the status and sales profiles of their customers. In more detail, CRM analytics could be used to determine customer value measurement, risk scoring, campaign measurement, channel analysis, churn analysis and prediction, personalization and collaborative filtering, and revenue analysis. Finally, marketers can also utilize CRM data to drive the development of programs designed to pinpoint individual customer touch points. For example, interactive analytics enable marketers to abstract and combine data to carry-out what-if scenarios that could be used to create a promotions campaign.

PARTNERSHIP RELATIONSHIP MANAGEMENT

One of the cardinal advantages of supply chain management is the ability to leverage the core competencies of channel partners to provide a level of service unavailable by individual companies acting on their own. This *reintermediation* of the supply channel through the application of new management methods and Web-enabled connectivity has coalesced around a subset of CRM termed PRM. PRM can be defined

> as a business strategy and a set of application tools designed to increase the long-term value of a firm's channel network by assisting companies to select the right partners, supporting them by offering timely and accurate information and knowledge management resources to deal successfully with channel customers, collectively searching for ways to improve sales, productivity, and competitiveness, and ensuring that each trading partner contributes to customer satisfaction [31].

PRM began as a means to facilitate channel sales and gather metrics based on the marketing and sales efforts of supply chain partners. Until the advent of Web-based connectivities, communication and assembly of sales capabilities and statistics from all regions of the supply chain was extremely difficult.

Today, the Internet has enabled the growth of several PRM functions. Perhaps the most critical – *partner recruitment, development, and profiling* – is concerned with assembling and qualifying potential channel partners. PRM tools can assist in establishing a partner profile database, ranking partner capabilities, ensuring certification, and determining risks and rewards. Another critical function is *marketing and sales management* whereby companies can use the Internet to network-in partners to sales campaigns and promotions and to be able to measure results. A final function is to grow *PRM Collaboration* to facilitate channel-wide codevelopment of market programs, joint business plans, and the sharing of sales metrics, forecasts, and general customer feedback.

SUMMARY

The changes brought about by the globalization of the marketplace, the spread of Internet technology, and requirements for quality products and value-added services have forced supply chains to reexamine their traditional attitudes toward customer service. In the past, market share was gained by expanding business capacities, introducing new products, and decreasing product delivery lead times. In the twenty-first century, the search for competitive advantage entails a broadening of this strategy to include a philosophy of continuous improvement dedicated to increasing quality and productivity and the adoption of information tools that enable the firm to respond quickly to ongoing changes in customer product and service needs. "World-class" performers are tireless in their examination of every aspect of their firm's operations in search of untapped sources of quality and customer satisfaction. Activating such a vision means that the enterprise must constantly measure customer perceptions of service quality, identify service shortfalls, and respond to service gaps. · Once these gaps have been quantified, management can begin to redesign organizational and value structures, refocusing them on continuous incremental improvements in process and informational performance. Service leaders see quality as one of the fundamental building blocks of market dominance, set levels of service that exceed their customer's expectations and surpass the standards set by the competition, have an action-oriented attitude focused on teamwork and commitment to excellence, and are ceaseless in their endeavor to satisfy the customer at all costs.

Superior customer service also requires order promising functions that provide for the speedy and accurate transference of goods, services, and order information. Order processing is the primary contact between customers and suppliers. It serves as the gateway into which orders are placed, priced, inventory allocated and tracked, and from which goods and services are delivered to the customer. It can also be argued that the requirements of high velocity response driven by the Internet necessitate that the scope of order management be expanded to encompass not only the demand on individual enterprises, but also how that demand impacts the customer service capabilities of the entire supply chain.

The customer order management process begins with the maintenance of the database elements necessary for timely and accurate order processing. Accurate customer master, pricing, and inventory files are absolutely critical for the second step in the order management process: executing the sales order processing cycle. This cycle consists of three separate but integrated activities: order receipt and entry, inventory allocation and picking, and order shipment and invoicing. The third step in the customer order management is monitoring order status. The open order file provides customer service with a window into order ship dates, backorders, and inventory quantities so that order priorities can be maintained. Once the order has been shipped, order history reporting can assist customer service in tracking order delivery and quality-related issues. Finally, the last step in the order management process is defining and maintaining performance measurements.

The rise of Internet commerce has recently provided fresh challenges to customer service management. Today's Web-enabled applications offer companies radically new approaches to generate customer value and collaboration, facilitate the sales process, enhance customer service capabilities, and architect highly integrated, customer-centric infrastructures. For customers, e-CRM provides radically simple, self-directed tools for browsing and locating suppliers and their products, as well as simplified order entry and open-order inquiry. For suppliers, Web applications enable direct sales to the end-customer, thereby by-passing costly channel intermediaries. Further, because demand is placed in the system in real-time, suppliers have enhanced visibility to improve the effectiveness and better use of resources. In the suite of e-CRM applications can be found sales force automation tools, new forms of Internet-based marketing capabilities, and communications tools that deepen customer partnership management.

QUESTIONS FOR REVIEW

1. Define the meaning of CRM and how it impacts customer management.
2. Discuss the ten elements of customer service.
3. What are the three phases of sales cycle, and how can effective services facilitate the successful completion of each cycle?
4. What the foundations for a successful customer service strategy?
5. Determining and measuring service gaps have been established as fundamental in the development of an effective services strategy. Detail the mechanics of determining service gaps.
6. Discuss the effective use of total cost-service level trade-offs.
7. Contemporary literature addressing the components of "world-class" services views the employee also as a customer. Why is this point so important?
8. Why are performance measurements so important in constructing an effective services strategy?
9. Why has the order management process grown in importance for distributors?
10. Discuss why supply chain order management is so critical to overall customer service performance.
11. Detail the computerized tools available for the effective use of CRM.

REFERENCES

1. See the summary in Ross, David F., *Introduction to e-Supply Chain Management: Engaging Technology to Build Market-Winning Business Partnerships.* Coca Ratton: St Lucie Press, 2003, pp. 171-173.
2. For a complete review of the principles of modern marketing see Kotler, Philip, *Marketing Management: Analysis, Planning, Implementation, and Control.* 6th ed. Englewood Cliffs, NJ: Prentice Hall, 1988, pp. 13-31.
3. This definition was first formulated by LaLonde, Bernard and Zinszer, Paul H. *Customer Service: Meaning and Measurement.* Chicago: National Council of Physical Distribution Management, 1976, pp. 203-217, and has been used by many of today's texts on modern distribution and marketing.
4. Greenberg, Paul, *CRM at the Speed of Light: Capturing and Keeping Customers in Internet Real Time.* McGraw-Hill, Berkley, CA, 2001, p. xviii. Greenberg also devotes 33 pages of his first chapter to detailing a variety of comprehensive definitions coming from a number of CEOs and COOs from companies such as PeopleSoft and Onyx Software.
5. Dyche, Jill, *The CRM Handbook: A Business Guide to Customer Relationship Management.* Addison-Wesley, Boston, MA, 2002, p. 4.
6. Renner, Dale H., "Closer to the Customer: Customer Relationship Management and the Supply Chain," in *Achieving Supply Chain Excellence Through*

Technology. 1, Anderson, David L., ed., Montgomery Research, San Francisco, 1999, p. 108.

7. This section is summarized from Ross, *Introduction to e-Supply Chain Management,* pp. 167-168.

8. Some of these points have been adopted from Bovet, David and Martha, Joseph, *Value Nets: Breaking the Supply Chain to Unlock Hidden Profits.* New York: John Wiley & Sons, 2000, p. 1-17.

9. These points have been taken from Feldman, Bart, "Collaborative Demand Management: A Solution for Changing Business Realities." *Global Logistics & Supply Chain Strategies,* 5, 10, 74-76.

10. These points can be found in Langabeer, James R., "Aligning Demand Management with Business Strategy." *Supply Chain Management Review,* 4, 2, 2000, 68.

11. Some of these forecasting models can be found in Gilliland, Michael, "Forecasting the Unforecastable: Dealing with Volatile Demand." 2001 International Conference Proceedings sponsored by APICS, October, 2001; Falls Church, W.V.: APICS, 2001.

12. For more detail on this discussion see Bowersox, Donald J. and Closs, David J., *Logistical Management: The Integrated Supply Chain Process.* New York: McGraw-Hill, 1996, pp. 67-75 and Coyle, John J., Bardi, Edward J., and Langley, C. John, *The Management of Business Logistics: A Supply Chain Perspective.* Mason, Ohio: South-Western, 2003, pp. 97-101.

13. LaLonde, Bernard and Zinszer, Paul H., *Customer Service: Meaning and Measurement.* Chicago: National Council of Physical Distribution Management, 1976, pp. 272-282.

14. These points have been borrowed from Enslow, Beth, "Internet Fulfillment: the Next Supply Chain Frontier," in *Achieving Supply Chain Excellence Through Technology*, I, Anderson, David L., ed., San Francisco, CA: Montgomery Research, 1999, 251-257.

15. See the comments found in Hintlian, James T. and Churchan, Phil, "Integrated Fulfillment: Bringing Together the Vision and Reality." *Supply Chain Management Review Global Supplement*, 5, 1 (2001), pp. 16-20; and, Hintlian, James T., Mann, Robert E., and Churchman, Phil, "E-Fulfillment Challenge – The Holy Grail of B2C and B2B E-Commerce," in *Achieving Supply Chain Excellence Through Technology*, 3, Anderson, David L., ed., San Francisco, CA: Montgomery Research, 2001, 270-274.

16. Ross, *Introduction to e-Supply Chain Management*, p. 186.

17. See note 3 above.

18. LaLonde, Bernard, Cooper, Martha C., and Noordewier, Thomas G., *Customer Service: A Management Perspective.* Chicago: Council of Logistics Management, 1988, p. 5.

19. Band, William A., *Creating Value For Customers.* New York: John Wiley & Sons, Inc, 1991, p. 80.

20. Zeithaml, Valerie A., Parasuraman, A. and Berry, Leonard L. *Delivering Quality Service.* New York: The Free Press, 1990, pp. 20-23; Zeithaml, Valarie A., Parasuraman, A. and Berry, Leonard L. "A Conceptual Model of Service

Quality and Its Implications for Future Research." *Journal of Marketing,* 41-50 (Fall, 1985).

21. Gopal, Christopher and Cahill, Gerard, *Logistics in Manufacturing.* Homewood, IL: Business One Irwin, 1992, pp. 127-162.

22. Band, William A., *Creating Value For Customers.* New York: John Wiley & Sons, Inc, 1991, p. 21.

23. This matrix can be found in Albrecht, Karl and Bradford, Lawrence J, *The Service Advantage.* Homewood, IL: Dow Jones-Irwin, 1990, p. 175.

24. Zeithaml, et al., p. 9-13.

25. See the discussion in Lambert, Douglas M. and Stock, James R., *Strategic Logistics Management.* 3rd ed. Homewood, IL: Irwin, 1993, p. 124.

26. This section has been abstracted from Ross, *Introduction to e-Supply Chain Management,* pp. 187-188.

27. Sawhney, Mohan and Zabin, Jeff, *The Seven Steps to Nirvana: Strategic Insights into e-Business Transformation.* New York: McGraw-Hill, 2001, p. 181.

28. Poirier, Charles C. and Bauer, Michael J., *E-Supply Chain: Using the Internet to Revolutionize Your Supply Chain.* San Francisco: Berrett-Koehler Publishers, Inc., 2000, pp. 176-177.

29. Dyche, p. 80.

30. Fingar, Peter, Kumar, Harsha, and Sharma, Tarun, *Enterprise E-Commerce: The Software Component Breakthrough for Business-to-Business Commerce,* Tampa, FL: Meghan-Kiffer Press, 2000, pp. 89-90.

31. Ross, *Introduction to e-Supply Chain Management,* p.189.

10

SUPPLIER RELATIONSHIP MANAGEMENT

The management of the processes for the acquisition of raw materials, component parts, and finished goods to service the needs of the customer resides at the very core of competitive supply chain management. Effectively designed and executed procurement processes provide several direct advantages. To begin with, procurement plays a fundamental role in actualizing business and operations planning objectives concerning supply chain delivery, flexibility, quality, and costs. Secondly, the sheer size of procurement directly affects the financial stability and profitability of virtually every trading partner in the channel. Depending on the nature of the product offering, procurement costs alone can range from forty to over seventy percent of each sales dollar. Thirdly, the efficiency and quality of procurement has a direct influence on the capability of the entire supply chain to respond effectively to marketplace demand. Because of its significant impact on revenues, costs, and operational efficiencies, procurement has become a key enabler of supply chain strategy.

Finally, effective procurement requires the structuring of strong partnerships. With the rise of Internet-driven tools opening dramatically new vistas for sourcing, cost management, concurrent product development, quality, and delivery, the need for close, highly integrated relationships between buyers and suppliers has expanded concomitantly. In fact, the confluence of these trends has revolutionized past concepts of purchasing and transformed it into a new science: *supplier relationship management* (SRM). In today's fast past environments, academics, consultants, and practitioners have come to understand that while high quality and low cost are critical, it is the relationship that exists between buyer and seller that determines the real value-added component of procurement. The closer the demands and capabilities of customer and supplier are synchronized, the more total costs decline, the more agile suppliers become to meet complex demands, and the faster inventory moves through the channel pipeline. In addition, the more integrated the supply chain, the more channel partners can truly fashion collaborative relationships where core competencies can be merged to generate a common competitive vision.

This chapter focuses on the procurement and supplier management functions found in today's supply chain environment. The chapter begins by defining the role of the purchasing function, purchasing responsibilities, organizational structure, ongoing operational objectives, and requirements for effective *supplier relationship management* (SRM). After a detailed discussion of the steps necessary to architect dynamic procurement and SRM strategies, the chapter proceeds to outline the purchase order management process. The elements of the procurement process – assuring database accuracy, understanding the purchase order processing cycle, transportation decisions, receiving and order closeout, and status reporting activities - are then reviewed in detail. Next, the role of performance measurement in charting the effectiveness and efficiency of the purchasing function is discussed. The chapter concludes with an in depth analysis of the impact of e-business tools on purchasing. e-Sourcing, e-procurement, value-added services, and e-marketplace exchanges are in turn examined.

DEFINING PURCHASING

The acquisition of materials, components, finished goods, and support services is a fundamental activity found in all manufacturing, distribution, and retailing companies. Procurement is concerned with acquiring the necessary resources to satisfy customer, manufacturing, and supply chain demand as determined by the inventory planning process. This process begins with the translation and disaggregation of the enterprise business plan through marketing and sales, manufacturing and distribution, logistics, and detail statistical and MRP/DRP inventory management. In this section the procurement function will be closely defined with a consideration of supplier management to appear later in the chapter.

DEFINING THE PURCHASING FUNCTION

According to *The Purchasing Handbook*, purchasing can be defined as

> the body of integrated activities that focuses on the purchasing of materials, supplies, and services needed to reach organizational goals. In a narrow sense, purchasing describes the process of buying; in a broader context, purchasing involves determining the need; selecting the supplier; arriving at the appropriate price, terms and conditions; issuing the contract or order; and following up to ensure delivery. [1]

The APICS Dictionary defines purchasing in a much wider sense as

> The integration and focusing of the business functions of procurement planning, purchasing, inventory control, traffic, receiving, incoming inspection, and salvage operations on inventory acquisition, receiving, material disposition, and financial accounting. [2]

The purchasing function is normally responsible for the acquisition of all products and services required by the organization. Broadly speaking, there are three types of purchasing: purchasing for consumption or conversion, purchasing for resale, and purchasing for goods and services consumed in maintenance, repair, and operations functions. Purchasing for *conversion or consumption* is the concern of industrial buyers and covers a wide spectrum of activities beginning with a determination of what products the firm should produce or outsource, progressing to raw materials and component sourcing, negotiation, purchase order generation and status monitoring, and concluding with materials receipt. Goods purchased for *resale* are the concern of distribution and retail buyers. In this area buyers determine what goods their customers want, search and buy these goods based on targeted levels of quality, delivery, quantity, and price, and sell them competitively based on price, quality, availability, and service. The final type of purchasing, *maintenance, repair, and operating* (MRO) inventories, is concerned with the acquisition of expensed items and services necessary for the efficient functioning of the business.

The range of products purchased can be seen in the following categories:

- *Finished goods, component inventories, and raw materials.* For the most part, the purchasing organization focuses on the acquisition of products that will be sold directly to the customer or used in production processes to create finished goods which, in turn, will be sold to the customer. This category has by far the largest impact on enterprise customer service, inventory costs, storage requirements, cash flow, and materials conversion processes.

- *Maintenance, Repair, and Operating* (MRO) *inventories and services.* Another important activity of purchasing is the acquisition of standard operating supply items and services. In this category can be found office and general supplies such as copy paper, pens, paper towels, and light bulbs. In addition, normal services such as equipment maintenance, cleaning services, and facilities repair are also included. Once satisfactory suppliers have been located, MRO purchasing is normally an ongoing clerical responsibility, interrupted only by periodic review of supplier performance and pricing changes.

- *Custom equipment and services.* Finally, the purchasing department is also responsible for the acquisition of specialty items and services. In this category can be found products that must be specially designed or fabricated to meet specific needs. Unique machinery, storage and material handling equipment, and computerized information systems are some of the products in this category. Special services such as training, advertising, market research, and consulting services are also included. Because of the uniqueness and cost of these products and services, purchasing usually begins with a requirements definition, request for quote (RFQ), and proposed budget that must be approved by company management before purchasing activities begin. Once approved, it is purchasing's responsibility to support and oversee project development, serve as the intermediary between technical personnel and suppliers, and execute the actual purchase order process.

PURCHASING RESPONSIBILITIES AND PROCESSES

The management, planning, and execution of purchasing activities are normally the responsibility of the purchasing department. It is the job of this function to communicate effectively the purchase requirements of the firm to the right suppliers and to maintain open replenishment order status information that can be used by other enterprise operations. The functions of purchasing encompass a multitude of activities. These functions have been arranged below, starting with activities of strategic importance then progressing to those performed on a daily basis:

- *Sourcing.* This high value-added activity is concerned with matching purchasing requirements with sources of supply, ensuring continuity of supply, exploring alternative sources of supply, and validating the supplier compliance necessary to meet or exceed buyer criteria for quality, delivery, quantity, and price. For the past decade a critical component of sourcing has been reducing needless redundancies in the supplier base and increasing supplier collaborative partnering.

- *Value analysis.* This set of functions is concerned with increasing the value-added elements of the purchasing process. Value analysis can consist of such components as price for quality received, financing, and delivery. An example would be identifying less expensive goods and services that could be used as substitutes at comparable quality and value.

- *Supplier development.* In today's environment, increasing collaboration with suppliers has become a requirement for doing business. Pursuing capabilities that promote supplier partnering require buyers to be knowledgeable of supplier capacities, resources, product lines, and delivery and information system capabilities. A key component in the strengthening of this partnership is the development of pricing, technology, and information-sharing agreements that link supplier and buyer together and provide for a continuous "win-win" environment.

- *Internal integration.* Purchasing needs to be closely integrated with other enterprise business areas such as marketing, sales, inventory planning, transportation, and quality management. By providing key information and streamlining the acquisition process, the purchasing function can assist the enterprise to synchronize replenishment requirements with the overall capacities of the supply network. Buyers should also be members of product market, research, and engineering development teams if the proper inventory at the best quality, delivery, and cost is to be purchased.

- *Supplier scheduling.* One of the keys to effective purchasing is the development of a valid schedule of inventory replenishment. By sharing the schedule of demand from MRP/ROP/DRP techniques, firms can provide detailed visibility to future requirements to supply chain partners, who, in turn, can plan the necessary material and capacity resources to support the schedule. In addition, the increased use of purchasing portals and B2B marketplaces have dramatically expanded buyers' ability to search anywhere in the world for sources to meet product and service replenishment needs.

- *Contracting.* Critical functions in this area consist of the development and analysis of *request for quotation* (RFQ), negotiation when pricing, volume, length of contract time, or specific designs or specifications are significant issues, and supplier selection and monitoring of performance measurements.

- *Cost management.* A critical function of purchasing is the continuous search for ways to reduce administrative costs, purchase prices, and inventory carrying costs while increasing value. The principle activities utilized to accomplish these objectives are purchase cost reduction programs, price change management programs, volume and "stockless" purchasing contracts, cash-flow forecasting, and strategic planning.

- *Purchasing and Receiving.* Activities in this component include order preparation, order entry, order transmission, status reporting, order receiving, quantity checking and stock put-away, invoice and discount review, and order closeout.

- *Performance measurement.* Monitoring the quality and delivery performance of suppliers over time is an integral part of supplier "benchmarking." The ability to measure performance is critical when evaluating the capabilities of competing suppliers and ensuring that costs, delivery, and collaborative targets are being attained [3].

THE PURCHASING ORGANIZATION

The ability to execute the functions of purchasing requires the establishment of an effective purchasing organization. The structure of the purchasing function is determined by how it is utilized by the rest of the organization. Companies that consider purchasing of fundamental importance to the success of the business view purchasing as a strategic advantage and provide it with high-level decision-making power. Conversely, in those companies that perceive purchasing as purely a tactical activity, it is treated as an administrative function without much of a strategic impact on the business. The relative position of purchasing in an organization is also revealed by its level of interaction with other business functions. Purchasing management normally has close communication with Inventory Management, Transportation, Sales, Product Design, Marketing, and Finance and should be an integral part of the strategic planning processes of each of these business areas.

Dobler, *et al* [4] divide the functions found in the traditional purchasing department into five distinct classifications, each of which encompasses a wide range of activities. An effectively structured purchasing organization must be able to execute these activities in as efficient and cost-effective a manner as possible. The five classifications can be detailed as follows:

1. *Management.* Managing the purchasing function involves a matrix of tasks and responsibilities. Foremost among these activities are developing and defining the content of operating procedures, developing the necessary planning and execution controls, and engineering the mechanics for coordinating purchasing operations with other business functions.

2. *Buying.* The process of acquiring goods from suppliers involves such activities as defining procurement requirements, reviewing product specifications, supplier sourcing, performing value analysis, analyzing bids, negotiating, supplier selection, and purchase order release.

3. *Status Reporting and Expediting.* Follow-up of open orders is a fundamental function of purchasing. This involves activities such as supplier liaison, open order status tracking, supplier visits, and expediting late or emergency purchase orders.

4. *Research.* Often purchasing is required to investigate new avenues of supply or to buy products for special projects. Research activities encompass such tasks as value analysis, economic and market studies, special cost analysis, sourcing, and systems research.

5. *Clerical.* Every purchasing department must perform a number of clerical activities. These range from paperwork completion, filing, and data maintenance to purchase order release and price and receipt quality tracking.

The keynote in designing an effective purchasing organization is to focus on those activities that add value to the process while eliminating those that merely add cost. For example, roles concerned with sourcing products and supplier development are value-added; expediting and clerical administrative activities, on the other hand, do not add value to the company and should be kept to the bare minimum, if not eliminated altogether. Ideally, the structure of the purchasing function should consist of four levels. As illustrated in Figure 10.1, on the first level can be found the *Purchasing Manager*. It is the responsibility of this individual to align the goals of the department with the business plan, act as liaison to the other business departments in the firm, formulate and review performance measurements, develop the purchasing staff,

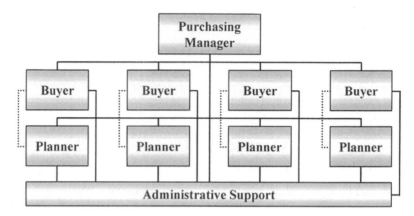

FIGURE 10.1 Standard purchasing organization.

and perform all required administrative functions. The *buyer's role* consists of a number of tasks centered on the value-added work of purchasing. These tasks consist of such activities as product sourcing, supplier development, negotiating, value analysis, and contracting. *Purchasing planners* can be found at the third level. It is the responsibility of this group to communicate the replenishment purchasing schedule to the supplier, launch and expedite orders, reduce order and transportation costs, manage inventory purchase investment, and communicate problems to the buyer and the inventory planning functions. At the fourth level of the purchasing function structure can be found clerical support. The support staff assists the first three levels perform administrative activities such as record keeping, paperwork, statistics, expediting, and data entry and maintenance.

The purchasing organization can be structured around three general approaches: commodity or function, project or product, and matrix. The *commodity* approach is the structure most commonly used by companies. In this organization, the purchasing function is divided into spheres of buying responsibility such as production inventories, maintenance, repair, and operating (MRO) inventory and services, and capital and construction equipment. In addition, other non-buying areas, such as acquisition research, administrative support, and technical liaison, can be integrated into the model. The buyer within each commodity group is responsible for all sourcing, negotiating, and purchase order releasing activities for that commodity area. The advantage of this method of organization is that focused members of the purchasing team are able to acquire specialized knowledge about products and suppliers, serve as the communication point for purchase order requisition, and execute acquisition activities while minimizing product and administrative costs.

For those firms whose products and services are focused on long-term projects, the purchasing function can be organized around specific projects or programs. The goal of the purchasing group in such organizations is the acquisition of the required materials and services necessary to meet project requirements. The advantage of this form of organization is that certain buyers can be linked to specific project segments, thereby ensuring that purchasing requirements are kept within budget targets and scheduled time frames are met. A *matrix* organization is a variation of the purchasing function organized around projects or products. In this structure, buyers are organized into project teams charged with the responsibility of meeting the acquisition needs of the entire project. In essence, these buyer-teams are part of each project or project segment. Such an organizational structure streamlines the purchasing process and eliminates possible redundancies.

Companies with multi-facilities are further faced with the decision of whether to organize their purchasing functions around a *centralized* or *decentralized* structure. In considering a centralized option, a number of critical questions immediately come to mind: "How is the buying function to coordinate the acquisition of products and services?" "Where in the organization are buying decisions to be made?" "How are purchasing decisions and activities to be split between corporate and local facilities?" The decision as to the degree of centralization is weighed by several advantages and disadvantages. The arguments favoring centralization center on buyer "clout" and economies of scale. Centralized functions can often obtain large discounts, better coordinate purchasing requirements through the creation of a single supplier order, more efficiently utilize scarce resources among competing facility units, and develop a specialized professional staff. In contrast, arguments favoring a decentralized purchasing option center on linking acquisition authority with those company branches responsible for inventory availability, coupling specific product and services needs with the requisitioning facility, providing supplier visibility to special product features, services, or transportation needs, and being able to purchase from a local source. In the final analysis, the decision to structure the purchasing function either one way or another is often not clear-cut, with some commodities, such as bulk items and widely used products being purchased by a centralized group, and specialized products and services acquired locally [5].

PURCHASING OBJECTIVES

The most conventional response that is given to the question "What is the objective of purchasing?" is obtaining the right products or services, at the right time, in the right quantities, delivered to the right place, at the right price with perfect quality. As can be imagined from such an answer, the buyer is faced with the task of pursuing not just one but a multitude of objectives, some of which are contradictory. Buyers are continually faced with the dichotomies arising from the often conflicting objectives of pursuing simultaneously optimal quality, service, and price. Rarely will all three elements be obtainable from a single supplier. Often a buyer must select a supplier based on balancing all three of these cost elements or *total cost.*

Although total cost management is perhaps the most fundamental ongoing activity of purchasing, there are several other key objectives. They are as follows:

- *Providing an uninterrupted flow of materials and services.* One of the most common sources of lost productivity and customer dissatis-faction is the result of shortages in materials and service resources. Shortages cause production downtime, interrupt the flow of product and cash through the channel, impair communications between pur-chasing and suppliers, and strain relations with customers on one end of the pipeline and suppliers on the other. The foremost goal of the pur-chasing function is to ensure that the company is not hindered by in-ventory and service capacity shortages. Just buying inventory and other resources, however, is not enough. In addition, purchasers must continually search for methods of increasing the velocity of the flow of goods and services through the distribution channel without accom-panying increases in carrying costs.

- *Purchasing products competitively.* This objective requires purchasers to continuously search for supplier relationships that will provide the best combination of quality, price, and service relative to the enter-prise's needs. Pursuing this objective means that buyers must be infor-med about market forces of demand and supply that regulate prices and product availability. In addition, this objective requires purchasers to understand the cost dynamics of their suppliers, and then to negotiate quality, price, and service arrangements that achieve optimum value.

- *Keeping inventory investment to a minimum.* Although the first pri-ority of the supply chain is to have products available to meet any cus-tomer requirement, the cost of maintaining large inventories can negate sales profits. Effective inventory management requires that purchasing does its part in achieving a reasonable balance between stocking levels and the cost of carrying inventory. In addition, purchasing can signifi-cantly assist the firm in reducing inventory loss due to spoilage, obso-lescence, deterioration, and theft.

- *Developing the supplier base.* Reliable, quality-oriented suppliers are important company resources. Purchasers must continually search for ways to enhance supplier relationships by developing mutually bene-ficial value-added service, quality, and training programs that promote supplier partnerships. In addition, buyers must continually search for and evaluate new suppliers. Performance measurements and periodic evaluations will ensure that suppliers are maintaining quality and response objectives.

- *Provide consistent, quality purchased materials and services.* Purchasing in the 2000s requires buyers to explore all possible avenues to ensure product and service quality. In the past, purchasers spent their time calculating the trade-off costs between a desired quality level and the cost of acquiring it. The result was often low prices with accompanying poor quality that caused expensive customer returns, product rework, and lost customer confidence. Today, purchasers must bargain for nothing short of total product quality while searching for methods to reduce costs. Quality can be maintained by such activities as the communication and continuous review with suppliers of specifications and materials used for production, and close conformance to delivery standards. Again, many customers require their suppliers to pass and maintain specific quality certifications. "World-class" procurement requires both the enterprise and the entire supply channel to follow JIT tools for the elimination of material and operational wastes and to increase the flexibility of material acquisition and service response, while reducing inventories and non-value-added functions and staff.

- *Developing people resources and information tools for productivity optimization.* As the structure of the purchasing organization grows ever leaner, the need for team-based management styles grows proportionately. The continuous development and training of personnel at all levels in the purchasing function results in the creation of a professional staff prepared to shoulder the responsibilities of decentralized decision making, continuous search for improvement, and the acquisition of the technical knowledge required of "world-class" purchasing. In addition, the implementation of information systems that automate clerical functions and provide timely inventory, order, and cost status can also greatly assist in improving productivity and reducing costs [6].

One purchasing objective that is growing in importance is expanding the scope of supplier *value-added services.* The goal of these functions is to reduce wastes in ordering and delivery, and facilitating the flow of goods and information through the supply channel. Three critical flows can be identified:

- *Product flow.* Accelerating the physical movement of goods from the supply source to the point of consumption.
- *Information flow.* Reducing redundancy in the transmission of critical information up and down the channel, such as demand schedules, mar-

ket data, inventory supply levels, warranty and product information, product specifications and application information, and postsales support.

- *Service flow.* Increasing value-added services that improve productivity and eliminate costs such as Internet order placement, advanced shipping notices, order status tracking, electronic transfer of payables and receivables, bar coding, packaging, and delivery.

The continuous development of value-added services is one of the most important objectives of the purchasing function in the 2000s.

DEFINING SUPPLIER RELATIONSHIP MANAGEMENT

The growing power of the customer and the ever-present necessity of continually reducing procurement costs has recently accentuated the importance of the role of the supplier and spawned a new subset of supply chain management: *supplier relationship management* (SRM). Historically, relations with suppliers have been marked by suspicion and focus on short-term partnership. While recently the use of *sales and operations planning* (S&OP) and CFPR toolsets have been increasing, often the only collaboration shared with suppliers has consisted of RFQs and purchase orders. Similar to *customer relationship management* (CRM), the growth of the SRM concept is today directly challenging this lack of cooperation, partnership, and communications. As pressures for cost effective product and service procurement and channel flow velocities accelerate, the need for collaborative supplier partnering has migrated from an option to a strategic requirement for competitive advantage. Enhanced by Internet technologies, SRM is providing trading partners with dramatic breakthroughs in cost savings, collaborative product development, new forms of sourcing, and real-time order management applications that have generated new categories of strategic and operational supply chain value. Whatever the formal arrangement, SRM can be described as the creation of cooperative alliances formed to exponentially expand the capabilities involved in materials requisition, procurement procedures and efficiencies, and product information exchange.

The increasing importance of synchronized, collaborative supplier relationships is the product of several marketplace dynamics. As is illustrated in Table 10.1, supplier relationship management has undergone dramatic modification and is accented by today's requirement for ever-closer working business alliances. The overall goal is to transform suppliers from adversaries into upstream channel partners where they act more like an arm of the procurement organization rather than an outside entity. In such a view SRM is about structuring win-win relationships, mutual commitment to sharing information and resources to achieve common objectives, and engagement in a long-term strategy for mutual competitive advantage. Finally, SRM often means deconstructing traditional attitudes and practices concerning quality and reliability, delivery, price, responsiveness, trust, the sharing of research and development plans, and financial and business stability.

TABLE 10.1 **Traditional Purchasing vs. SRM**

Traditional Approach	SRM Partnerships
Adversarial relationships	Collaborative partnerships
Many competing suppliers	Small core of supply partners
Contracts focused on price	Contracts focused on long term quality, mutual benefits
Proprietary product information	Collaborative sharing of information
Evaluation by bid	Evaluation by commitment to partnership
Supplier excluded from design process	Real-time communication of designs and specifications
Process improvements intermittent and unilateral	Close computer linkages for design and replenishment planning
Quality defects reside with the supplier	Mutual responsibility for total quality management
Clear boundaries of responsibility	"Virtual" organizations

COMPONENTS OF SRM

The mission of today's procurement function is to activate the real-time synchronization of inventory and service requirements with the capabilities of supply chain partners in order to support customers' demand for customized, high quality products while pursuing reductions in procurement costs and sustainable improvements in supply performance. Reaching these objectives requires the realization of several critical supplier management components as illustrated in Figure 10.2. The first component can be described as the *SRM value discovery*. This process is concerned with the drafting of a statement detailing the value proposition to be gained by the establishment of effective supplier partnerships. The results of the analysis should consist of immediate economic benefits as well as long-range strategic advantages. Among the critical benchmarks should be found expected *cost savings* through more effective procurement economies, enhanced *process efficien-*

cies attained through across the board reductions in replenishment cycle times, *inventory optimization* achieved through a closer matching of demand requirements with channel inventory stocks, and increased *process optimization* as a result of closer orchestration of collaboration on product design, increase in visibility to demand requirements, and closer matching of capacities to total channel demands.

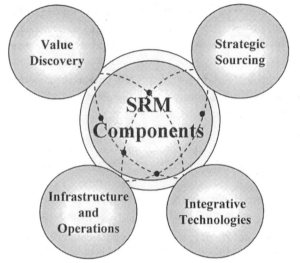

FIGURE 10.2 SRM Components.

Once the value of a SRM initiative has been defined, strategists can pursue the next SRM component: implementing a *strategic sourcing* program. In today's high-velocity environments, the role of supplier management has taken on additional importance beyond the everyday purchase of goods and services and is termed *strategic sourcing.* Traditional sourcing was often focused on haphazard make-or-buy decisions based on price and expediency. Today, sourcing must be supportive of the strategic goals of the organization, efforts to remove cycle time and performance barriers, programs to determine real costs, and collaborative requirements to integrate design, quality management, and immediate and long-term strategic goals. According to Hirsch and Barbalho [7], strategic sourcing is a comprehensive supply management process that involves

> identifying the business requirements that cause you to purchase a good or service in the first place, conducting market analysis to determine typical cost for goods/services within a particular supply system, determining the universe of suppliers that best meet your requirements, determining an overall strategy to procure items in that category, and then selecting the strategic supplier(s).

Depending on the category or type of purchasing to be sourced, other factors, such as the depth of supplier competencies, availability of required services, level of desired product quality, capacity for innovative thinking, and willingness to collaborate, can also be considered key strategic components.

Pursuing strategic sourcing requires the development of cross-channel procurement teams consisting of business and financial management, product and process designers, marketing experts, and purchasing personnel responsible for establishing procurement strategies as well as outsourcing decision making. The activities of strategic sourcing are composed of several critical steps. The first task is to determine the correct level or unit of analysis. This means focusing the sourcing effort not on individual components in isolation but rather on the systems, assemblies, and subassemblies located at the top of product structures. The goal is to determine the competitive value of component(s). Once classification of components into strategic and non-strategic has been completed, the second task is to devise outsourcing programs to buy the non-strategic components. Perhaps the most critical step will involve supplier selection and the desired level of collaborative technical and commercial cooperation. The third task involves attention to details regarding cost, communication of documentation and specifications, creating the outsourcing budget, performance expectations, communication of requirements, and logistics functions. Finally the last task involves the establishment of processes and benchmarks for continuous improvement in areas such as cost reduction, delivery, and product quality.

The scope and depth of SRM initiatives are directly dependent on the third component: the application of *integrative technologies*. Throughout history, the ability of procurement functions to interact with suppliers has been directly driven by technology tools. The first major technology was the telephone. This device made it possible for purchasing to transcend the limits to time and space imposed by the cumbersome processes of person-to-person contact and mail correspondence. The arrival of the fax machine significantly accelerated the possibilities of communications. The use of the fax permitted the quick and easy performance of processes such as negotiating contracts, sending specifications and orders, and verifying delivery status. *Electronic data interchange* (EDI) further enabled trading partners to interface internal planning systems so that demand, order and shipment transmission, and electronic bill payment could be performed in a paperless environment. Today, with the application of the Internet to SRM, purchasers have been able to leverage new forms of procurement functions, such as on-line catalogs, interactive auction sites, radically new opportunities for sourcing and supplier management, and Web-based toolsets that provide for the real-time, simultaneous synchronization of demand and supply from anywhere, anytime in the supply chain network.

The application of e-business to the evolving SRM concept can be said to have spawned a new form of procurement management: *e-SRM*. While still in its infancy, *business-to-business* (B2B) purchasing transactions continue to grow and are offering firms sustainable and meaningful procurement improvement opportunities from shorter sourcing and negotiation cycles, to reduced costs in ordering and more effective ways to ensure quality and delivery. As will be discussed later in this chapter, the concept of e-SRM has come to coalesce around two Internet-driven functions: *e-procurement*, the utilization of Web-toolsets to automate the activities association with purchase order generation, order management, and procurement statistics, and *e-sourcing*, the utilization of the Web to develop long-term supplier relationships that will assist in the growth of collaborative approaches to joint product development, negotiation, contract management, and CPFR. e-SRM can truly be said to have enabled a whole new dimension to supplier management by providing a radically new communication architecture for structuring supply chain relationships focused on facilitating the mechanisms of today's dynamic value-chains [8].

Impact of e-SRM Procurement

While e-business has generally been perceived as part of the dot-com mania, there can be little doubt that today's savvy businesses see it as critical to their SRM strategies. According to a 2003 survey from the *National Association of Manufacturers* and *Ernst & Young LLP,* the use of e-commerce by American manufacturers is on the rise. Nearly 25 percent of about 500 manufacturers surveyed say they are selling six percent or more of their goods via the Internet, a four-fold increase over the previous year. The survey broke e-business use down into the following categories:

General communications	88%
Product catalogues	53%
RFQs/RFPs	51%
Order status	38%
Help/tech support	26%

Despite the reported increased use of e-business, companies remain pessimistic about expected returns. Today's difficult economic environment has made cost and productivity the number one priority, rendering e-business investment of low priority. Once times change, a renewed interest in the benefits of e-commerce are sure to follow.

Source: Editors, "Recession, What Recession?," *Supply Chain Technology News,* March, 2003, p. 1.

The fourth and final component is architecting *SRM driven infrastructures and operations.* Effective supplier management in the twenty-first century requires the establishment of agile procurement functions capable of being rapidly deconstructed and rebuilt to match changing customer requirements and cost and continuous improvement imperatives. Requirements for ever more flexible procurement environments capable of quickly integrating with complimentary supplier organizations, technologies, and processes are essential if customer performance is to be optimized up and down the supply channel.

One of the most critical impacts on the purchasing organization caused by accelerating cost and competitive pressures has been the increased use of *outsourcing*. Companies have long turned to supply chain partners to leverage their core competencies to perform work more economically, provide more technical expertise, free internal resources, and reduce overhead costs. Tackling these expanding responsibilities requires the procurement organization to expand significantly their strategies, operations, and supplier relationships. Effective outsourcing requires a variety of decisions.

- *Cost management.* In this area, purchasers must thoroughly understand their own internal cost structures before outsourcing products and services. This means determining both the trade-off value of making the product in house versus outsourced and the impact on the internal assets that will go unused in an outsourcing effort.

- *Risk factor management.* The use of supply partners requires that trust and risk sharing must be factored into the outsourcing strategy. As the cost of operations and innovation expand, partnership agreements that provide for the equal sharing of risk grow in importance.

- *Supplier selection.* The choice of an outsourcing partner requires due diligence in the review of available quantitative and qualitative performance factors. The goal is to devise a detailed supplier scorecard that enables tracking of historical performance indicators. With such performance factors, procurement professionals and suppliers can collaboratively evaluate which processes can be effectively outsourced and to which suppliers, which are to remain in-house, and how to initiate corrective action and enhance overall performance. This step should conclude with the outsourcing contract.

- *Performance expectations.* Once the scope of outsourcing contract is completed, a clear statement of expected performance expectations and measurements needs to be drafted. These measurements should focus on such things as expected cost reduction percentages, quality, and delivery performance.

Finally, procurement organizations must be able to operate in today's emerging Internet-enabled supply chain environment. Purchasing professionals must learn how to integrate radically new procurement technologies such as *private trading exchanges* (PTXs) and consortiums into their procurement strategies. In addition, they have to learn how to work with new *external* trading entities. For example, procurement functions have had to expand internal processes to accommodate working with third party organizations that run e-marketplaces. Instead of directly providing goods and services, these e-marketplaces act as brokers connecting buyers with multiple suppliers and take responsibility for functions such as payment, credit, and delivery.

ANATOMY OF PURCHASING STRATEGY

In recent years, the need to develop an effective enterprise procurement strategy has arisen in recognition of the impact purchasing has on competitive positioning. Companies that do not develop a comprehensive purchasing strategy risk interruption in the stream of supply due to poorly executed product and supplier planning and sourcing, misunderstood environmental or regulatory constraints, and uncertainty in price and delivery. The exact content of a purchasing strategy can take many forms. From the outset, however, it can be said that the best purchasing strategy is not necessarily the one that promises to optimize efficiency or least total cost but the one that supports the competitive objectives of the supply chain. Factors influencing purchasing strategy development are sophistication of the corporate planning process, degree of dependence of the enterprise on purchased products and services, top management's perception of the purchasing function, the availability of technology enablers, and state of the evolution of the purchasing function from being *tactically* based to being *strategically* based. A possible model to guide overall purchasing strategic development is illustrated in Figure 10.3.

STEP 1: ENVIRONMENTAL SCANNING

Once the corporate strategy has been defined, purchasing management must align it with actual purchasing capabilities and functional objectives. The first step in the process is to match the strategy with the dynamics found in the *internal* company and the *external* marketplace environments. Internal factors include such elements as the stage of enterprise technological development and the nature of corporate culture and values, perception of supplier partnering, outsourcing initiatives, and purchasing organizational structure. External factors include mapping international sources of supply, technological communications capabilities, political and social issues, and government and environmental regulations. The objective of this step is to provide purchasing management with a complete understanding of how they are to support the business's and, by extension, the supply chain's competitive strategy.

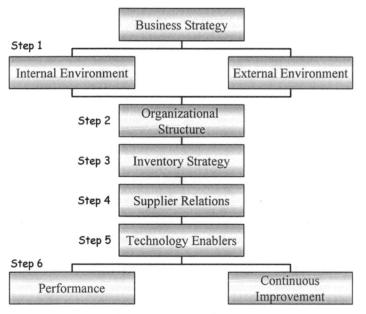

FIGURE 10.3 Purchasing strategy

STEP 2: ORGANIZATIONAL STRUCTURE

The second step in the strategic purchasing model involves identifying the capabilities of the purchasing organization to meet strategic objectives. Several dimensions are present. To begin with, purchasers must review the *organizational structure*. This step will detail the degree to which purchasing is centralized, the geography of the organizational matrix in which task responsibility is assigned and actions are performed, how authority is delegated, the level of strategic influence purchasing has in the business, and the structure of communication flows both within the purchasing organization and between purchasing and other business functions. In addition, *employee capabilities*, determining the qualification of purchasing professionals to execute the purchasing strategy, should also be apparent. *Current purchasing practices* should also be identified. This dimension will detail such work elements as the sophistication of existing purchasing control tools used in order management, capability to perform strategic sourcing, use of technology tools such as e-business and EDI, use of P-cards and supplier contracts, and use of statistics to record and analyze supplier performance.

STEP 3: INVENTORY STRATEGY

Once the organization dynamics have been defined, strategists can move to step three: the *purchasing inventory strategy.* Perhaps the first action will be to conduct a *spend analysis.* The purpose of this activity is to conduct a thorough analysis of all goods and services purchased across the enterprise in an effort to determine the actual spend levels and the degree of supplier fragmentation. The analysis should document how much is being spent on individual products as well as product families. Finally, the analysis should identify how much is being purchased, by category, of goods and type of service from each supplier. The objective of the spend analysis is to unearth answers to questions such as what is being purchased, from whom, from where, and from what location.

A critical part of the purchasing strategy is mapping the *make/buy decision.* This area relates to decisions regarding how extensive is the backward vertical integration strategy. What is to be purchased and what made in house is influenced by a number of factors such as delivery cycle time, current supplier performance, cost advantages, process/technical capabilities, patents and trade secrets, existing supplier contracts, and supplier manufacturing superiority. Conditions impacting make/buy decisions can be detailed as such:

- *Degree of operational change.* If the firm decides to produce in-house, does it currently possess the equipment, personnel, and process-sing experience, so that only a small capital outlay for equipment and personnel is necessary? Would, on the other hand, a decision to produce the product line require the expenditure of significant capital to acquire the equipment, facilities, and know-how?
- *Cost.* The following cost elements must be thoroughly investigated.
  1. Cost of purchasing component parts versus buying the finished products.
  2. Receiving and inspection costs.
  3. Direct labor required to handle components and to perform manufacturing processing.
  4. Cost of purchasing production equipment.
  5. Size of incremental increases in warehouse overhead, managerial, inventory carrying, purchasing, and capital costs.
- *Production processing control.* There are several key elements associated with this factor. What technologies will be required to plan for component requirements? How is order release and WIP maintenance to be performed? What is to be the level of management control over operations, and does that expertise exist within the firm or must it be acquired from the outside?

- *Quality.* How is quality to be measured during and after production processing? What tools should be used and does the firm currently have such expertise?
- *Risk management.* This is a strategic factor that must be resolved by management. Typically risk is low when the enterprise currently possesses the expertise and facilities necessary to produce the desired goods, and conversely high when the firm is venturing out into new managerial, organizational, and operational environments.

Another issue relating to procurement inventory strategy is ranking materials and services to be acquired by their importance to the organization. This principle recognizes that purchasing is not subject to a one-size-fits all approach when it comes to procurement strategies, tactics, use of technologies, and application of resources. Purchasers actually need to develop a strategy centered on two critical factors. The first, *value*, relates to the level of importance the product/service has in ultimately servicing the customer. The greater the value, the more detailed the procurement strategy and the closer the control of the product/service. The other factor, *risk*, relates to the potential damage to competitive positioning caused by product stockout or quality failure. Simply put, as a product/service grows in importance in satisfying a customer, purchasers must exercise greater control to ensure availability and reliability. As illustrated in Figure 10.4, an effective way to ensure high value and low risk is to divide purchased products into the following four distinct quadrants [9]:

	Distinctives	Criticals
Risk	• High risk • Low value • Difficult to attain • Critical for operations	• High risk • High value • Unique items • Critical to final product
	Generics	Commodities
	• Low risk • Low value • Non-production • MRO products	• Low risk • High value • Production item • Not unique • Volume purchasing

Value

FIGURE 10.4 Item purchasing classification matrix

- *Generics.* Purchased items in this quadrant are characterized as of low strategic value and low cost to the organization. *Maintenance, repair, and operation* (MRO) products can be placed in this area. For the most part, products necessary for sales or production are never found in this quadrant. Administratively, the goal is to pursue very low cost methods of sourcing and ordering these items. Recently, the application of e-trading exchanges has been applied to this area to take advantage of low cost procurement, auctions, and even barter.

- *Commodities.* Products in this quadrant can be classified as possessing low acquisition cost, but are often important to production and sales. Because commodities are usually generic and can be acquired from a wide variety of sources, they pose a low risk to organization strategies. These products are also increasingly being sourced through the Internet to attain low cost while ensuring timely delivery. Fasteners, packaging material, paints and lubricants, and transportation services that add direct value to finished goods are examples of commodities.

- *Distinctives.* Products in this quadrant are normally of high risk to competitive strategy, but are low in the value they provide to finished goods. While these products are not outwardly of critical importance in the form, fit, or function of the end item, they may be difficult to source, are subject to long lead times, or are low cost substitutes for very expensive components. Stockout of these items can stop production and require time-consuming rescheduling of the manufacturing floor. Sourcing and ordering distinctives are under the watchful eyes of buyers and planners and normally maintained by MRP planning.

- *Criticals.* In this quadrant can be found products that are of high risk and high value. When used in manufacturing, these components often provide competitive distinctiveness to the finished product and can not be easily substituted for or omitted from the final product configureation. Buyers and planners are very involved in the management of these often unique purchased components, where such values as build to exact specification, value analysis, high quality, cost management, collaborative design, and the building of very close supplier partnerships is absolutely critical.

STEP 4: SUPPLIER RELATIONS

Alongside the formalization of the inventory strategy, supply chain planners must be engaged in developing meaningful supplier partnerships. The goal of collaborative SRM is to architect systems that enable the operations of supply chain partners to be so closely merged that they appear as a single, seamless supply engine. Instead of a relationship based solely on buyer-customer service rep interaction, SRM collaboration requires a broadening of customer-supplier relationships where, for instance, customers' planners work directly with suppliers' planners to optimize product flows; supplier quality departments can also work closely with customers' design teams to improve product and process quality. Achieving such a relationship requires procurement managers to work closely with suppliers in cultivating partnerships that foster the pursuit of common goals and reside on trust and mutual advantage.

Supplier partnership programs normally consist of several critical components. To begin with, businesses must work with the supplier to identify shared goals for tactical purchase order and receiving performance as well as strategic issues such as linkage of supplier manufacturing processes and purchasing requirements, identification of out-of-bounds situations, development of continuous improvement programs, and the application of technology. Once common ground has been documented, purchasers must achieve some level of control over their supplier relationships. For the most part, this control can be lumped under the general category of *quality management.* This category can consist of transaction performance issues such as on-time receipt, quantity completeness, and quality inspection. Another area may involve product and transportation cost control.

Once the basic ground rules for over all objectives and detailed operations processing have been defined, suppliers can use other devices to communicate purchasing expectations and enhance supplier partnerships. The use of evaluation and certification programs, for instance, enables companies to enforce the creation of product quality databases and assurance methods that provide documentation of quality levels. Another tool is the use of supplier rating systems based on actual supplier performance. Activities in this area center on evaluating and ranking suppliers by different award levels based on detailed criteria relating to on-going quality and delivery performance. Any problems must be formally stated and must include a follow-up process to document corrective action taken by the supplier. Finally, suppliers must agree to submit their quality management systems to customer audit. The goal of the audit is to verify supplier conformance of productive process and output to meet the specifications and delivery needs of the purchaser. The output of the audit is a certification that processes are conforming to documented standards while permitting the purchasing audit team to recommend and oversee the necessary adjustments to guarantee future compliance. Audit standards such as ISO9000 or the Malcolm Baldridge Quality Award can be used as models for the audit [10].

Actualizing an effective supplier management program requires multiple levels of collaborative communication: business review meetings, supplier collaboration, and supplier scheduling [11].

- The goal of *business review meetings* is to integrate the long-range business plans and supply chain requirements of customer and supplier.

Topics of discussion are concerned with functions such as supply process optimization, handling of new product introduction, short- and mid-term demand and capacity planning, flow of materials and information, expected standards of quality and delivery, inventory levels, and cash flow between partners. Discussion results should enable the building of strategic consensus and joint ownership of channel processes and flows.

- *Supplier collaboration* meetings are mid-range planning events that should occur at least monthly. In these meeting, demand planners and buyers should work directly with supplier counterparts to address issues such as production levels, required resources, capability-to-promise, inventory levels, obsolescence, concurrent quality/engineering projects, and the capabilities of the existing supply chain. In addition, the meetings should review methods to improve supply chain capabilities relating to ongoing performance metrics, special projects, plant upgrades/shutdowns, and future product/service projects.

- On-going, detailed *supplier scheduling* involves the every-day interaction between buyers, planners, and service reps. The goal of this process is to communicate actual requirements and capacities to guide the sequencing of production and product delivery. The level of interoperability of channel ERP and supply chain management systems can be of dramatic importance in sharing of up-to-the-minute statuses of priorities, production, and process issues and the confirmation of actual order release and delivery and quality schedules.

A partnership communications structure that includes all three of the above levels ensures that all purchasers and suppliers achieve the necessary flow of information. Together, purchasers and suppliers can determine the participants, frequency, the data to be shared, and the output formats to be used at each level. Once these structures are in place, the proper technologies that will enable and enhance the process should be undertaken.

STEP 5: TECHNOLOGY ENABLERS

Over the past several decades purchasers have turned to information technology tools to assist in the development and realization of their procurement strategies. Tools like the telephone, Fax, EDI, linkages between ERP systems, and recently, the Internet, have all been applied to bridge gaps in buyer-supplier relationships. Essentially, technologies have historically been applied to solve several critical procurement requirements. The first, *supplier search*, is concerned with how easily and effectively buyers can locate the best suppliers. Critical dynamics here refer to the ease and comprehensiveness of supplier and product/service search, availability of procurement information and documentation, quality assurance, and capability to buy at competitive prices. The second, *order management access*, refers to how easily buyers can gain access to order management functions to acquire the goods and services they want or need. The third requirement, *service management availability*, refers to how buyers can ensure they are receiving or have access to necessary support capabilities such as communications, help line, documentation, and training. Finally, proper technologies must be deployed that support *strategic purchasing* functions such as outsourcing, services acquisition, and collaborative management.

e-Procurement Strategy at HP

The decision to deploy e-procurement technologies often starts with a desire to reduce indirect materials purchase cost, but then quickly spreads to production inventories.

Keychain, Hewlett-Packard's private e-procurement exchange went live in August 2000. In the first year of operations HP achieved savings of $33 million by aggregating internal materials purchases companywide and reducing by 30% the time employees spent in order management. Those savings alone more than paid for the acquisition and implementation cost of the software solution.

HP also invested in the converge Global Trading Exchange, an industry exchange through which it auctions excess inventory and purchases some production components on the spot market.

HP plans to expand its strategy for the use of e-procurement tools across all its operations, including those that have been acquired through its merger with Compaq. HP management feels that they have received a great deal of value from their e-procurement strategy and they plan to use further Internet-driven procurement tools to make HP as efficient a possible in the future.

Source: Konicki, Steve, "Procurement Power: Companies Slash Order Times and Costs with Online Initiatives," *Information Week*, August 5, 2002, p.48.

The goal of SRM technologies is simple: how to gain connectivity to suppliers. In the past this objective was achieved by deploying manual or person-to-person communication. Recently companies have attempted to use computerized tools like EDI to transmit critical procurement data. Today, purchasing functions are deploying Internet-based applications. The most basic form is the use of a self-service supplier portal where the supplier provides access to buyers to information it wants to share. More sophisticated connectivity can be achieved with a form of private trading network or even direct links to the buyer. These connectivity technologies are available in a wide spectrum of options to support a range of supplier technology capabilities. Once connected, suppliers must be able to offer several electronic enablers for such activities as Request for Information and RFQ, order entry and self-service management, planning functions. These application toolsets permit review of supplier capability-to-promise, channel inventory positions, manufacturing schedules, and availability of real-time analytics and performance scoreboards that empower planners to make rapid decisions on bids, spot sourcing, and pricing and view performance statistics regarding contract compliance and quality targets.

The SRM technology strategy should be formulated to support internal buyer value producing processes and designed to assist procurement managers consolidate and leverage their purchasing power. Exactly which and how sophisticated the level of technology deployed is directly dependent on how closely it is aligned with the over-all company strategy. Failure to implement the proper toolsets will result in a visibility and control gap and will cause the procurement function to fail to extract full value from their existing supplier contracts and explore the depth of the supplier relationship. A comprehensive analysis of today's Internet-based procurement environment appears at the end of this chapter.

STEP 6: PERFORMANCE AND CONTINUOUS IMPROVEMENT

The final phase in the development of a comprehensive purchasing strategy is establishing procurement performance standards and engineering an environment dedicated to continuous improvement. Fundamental to this phase is focusing the purchasing organization's attention on cultivating a "winning" attitude. This can be accomplished by, first, communicating the value of continuous improvement initiatives and stimulating individual and team contribution. Clear performance benchmarks must be accompanied by a review mechanism designed to track progress and ensure that recognition is given for achieved performance. Next, purchasing management must be able to sustain enthusiasm by engineering new operational definitions as circum-stances change. To respond to new challenges, the organization must be pro-vided with necessary skills such as training in statistical quality techniques, problem solving, value analysis, and team building. Finally, a dedication to continuous improvement means being able to effectively and consistently guide resource allocation to respond to new business opportunities and challenges.

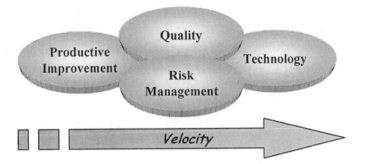

FIGURE 10.5 Purchasing's strategic goals.

The goal of the whole purchasing strategy development process is to assist the enterprise pursue and sustain competitive advantage. As illustrated in Figure 10.5, this objective can be realized by the following:

1. Purchasing and producing defect free products and materials: *Quality*
2. Managing the inherent risks in the external material environment: *Risk Management*
3. Reducing product, process, and channel costs: *Productive Improvement*
4. Achieving and maintaining technological superiority: *Technology*
5. Exploiting *time* to competitive advantage: *Velocity*

An effective purchasing strategy aligns the goals and objectives of the purchasing function with the firm's overall competitive strategy. By implementing value-added philosophies that seek to remove redundancies and activate core capabilities, a comprehensive purchasing strategy can make a direct contribution to the marketplace effectiveness of the firm.

PURCHASE ORDER MANAGEMENT PROCESS

Once the purchasing strategy has been defined, purchasing functions must focus on tactical execution. For the most, part the *purchase order management process* is composed of a series of activities that begin with the identification of a replenishment requirement and end with receiving, put-away, and purchase order closeout. In planning and controlling the purchase order process, the purchasing must determine answers to such questions as follows:

- Are the vendor master records accurate and up to date?
- Have the appropriate purchase order requisitions and requests for quotation been properly completed?
- Have the best suppliers been selected and contacted in preparation for purchase order release?
- Are the quoted prices acceptable?

- What will be the cost of freight and other miscellaneous charges?
- Have open purchase order due dates been properly maintained?
- What are the policies governing rejects, returns, and backorders?
- How are supplier performance measurements to be determined?

Answering these and other questions is the purpose of the purchase order management process illustrated in Figure 10.6.

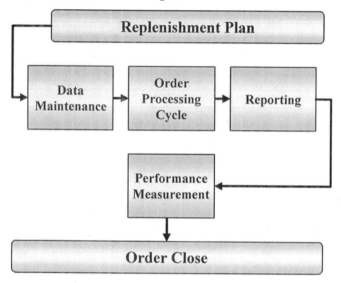

FIGURE 10.6 Purchase order management process.

ASSURING DATABASE ACCURACY

The purchase order management process begins with the maintenance of database elements necessary for effective and accurate purchase order release and control. There are several key files that must be continuously maintained. The first is the *item master file*. This file not only contains a list of the valid items in the stockable inventory, it is also where key planning elements such as supplier lead times, buyer codes, inventory planning codes, default suppliers, and costs are stored. Another key file is the *supplier master record*. This file provides purchasing with essential supplier data such as the supplier's name, ship-from and remittance addresses, contact personnel, phone number, credit information, and payment terms codes. In addition, this file also contains informational data such as ship-via codes, SIC codes, commodity codes, default buyers, default order types, and others.

Another important master file is the *price master*. In this file is kept the current supplier prices for products, price breaks and discounting, promotions, price effectivities, and price histories. The establishment of the base purchase price is often a dynamic and can be achieved through a variety of methods. The price may have been attained through a commodity market price, competitive bid, a cost-plus contract, a specified percentage of the cost, from a published price list, or a negotiated price. Each of these prices stems from particular conditions and is used to purchase specific goods and services. For example, commodity prices, applied to materials such as paper, grains, oil, and natural products like wood and minerals, are determined by market forces of global demand and supply. In contrast, prices stated in suppliers' catalogs are normally standardized for a set period of time, but may be subject to discounting. RFQs are often used to stimulate competitive bidding by possible suppliers. Negotiated prices are used to establish a purchasing contract, whereby the buyer agrees to purchase a defined quantity of product over a specific time period as well as render any necessary assistance while the supplier agrees to freeze the price and guarantee pre-determined quality specifications and delivery targets as their part of the contract.

While one of the cardinal objectives of procurement is the purchase of goods and services at the lowest competitive price, the decision to select a supplier will often result in additional cost elements that will impact the total price. Among the elements of price that must be considered are the following [12]:

- *Base price.* This price is the base charged by the supplier for the acquisition of products and services. Whether from a catalog, a bid, or a negotiation, this price serves as the base line on top of which are applied other possible costs to the buyer.

- *Direct transaction costs.* These costs are incurred with the performance of such activities as inventory review, requisitioning, purchase order entry and transmission, shipping documentation, order monitoring and tracing, receiving and put-away, order close-out, and AP invoicing and payment. The use of electronic functions, such as EDI and the Internet, can dramatically reduce costs in this area.

- *Supplier partnership costs.* Creating and nurturing supplier relationships require a certain amount of cost. Supplier relationship programs normally involve activities such as supplier visits, education and training, and technology linkages facilitating procurement planning, transportation, engineering and product development, and supplier certification. Sometimes buyers will assist suppliers in the acquisition of specialized production or communications assets.

- *Transportation costs.* The cost of transporting goods from supplier to buyer must be added to the overall cost of the product. Costs incurred for specialized value-added processing, packaging, and safety are included in this category. While there a multitude of options, such as private carrier, supplier-selected carrier, or buyer-selected carrier, the choice of transportation should seek to minimize direct and indirect costs while satisfying pre-determined levels of service.

- *Cost of quality.* In today's business environment it is expected that products and services will possess 100% quality. Very high levels of conformance to specification might require some quality expense, but this should be off-set in declines in product scrap and rejects.

- *Operations costs.* In this final category of total purchase cost are grouped expenses incurred for operational activities such as receiving, sorting or grading, packaging, inspection, product staging, and product put-away. Lot-sizing costs may also drive-up expenses for space requirements, handling, and cash flow requirements.

In managing these costs companies normally employ two methods of allocating/absorbing these additional sources of total cost. One method is to accumulate the total costs for each of these areas each financial posting period and then post them to the general ledger as a mass entry. A more sophisticated method is to employ ABC costing methods that "drive" the actual costs at the exact time the product is individually transacted.

In addition to these *static* database files can be found *variable* database files such as the open requisition, the open purchase order, and purchasing history. In the *requisition file* can be found those company requirements for resupply that have not as yet been reviewed and generated into purchase orders. The *open purchase order file* contains a record of each released but not yet received purchase order. Each purchase order consists of two separate but related sections. The first section contains the order header where such data values as the purchase order number, order status, supplier information, and costs are maintained. The second section contains the line item detail and consists of such data values as the purchased item number(s), item descriptions, unit of measure, quantity, price, date required, and receiving information. The final purchasing file, *purchase history*, contains the receiving information for closed purchase orders.

THE PURCHASE ORDER PROCESSING CYCLE

The second step in the *purchase order management process* [Fig. 10.6] is executing the order processing cycle. Essentially, there are five distinct components required for successful purchase order processing. These segments can be respectively described as *order preparation, order entry, transportation, receiving,* and *order closeout.* The purchase order processing cycle is illustrated in Figure 10.7. This cycle can be complicated and requires considerable inventory management, supplier research, and negotiating skills. Two types of purchasing must be planned for during this stage. The first focuses on the acquisition of general *maintenance, repair, and operating* (MRO) inventories. Requirements for MRO products arise out of the everyday use of supporting products and services. In most organizations, the purchase order process commences with the completion by the requestor of a manual or computerized *requisition order*. Once received by purchasing, requisitions must pass through several processes, beginning with supplier sourcing, negotiation, pricing, and authorization, and concluding with purchase order generation.

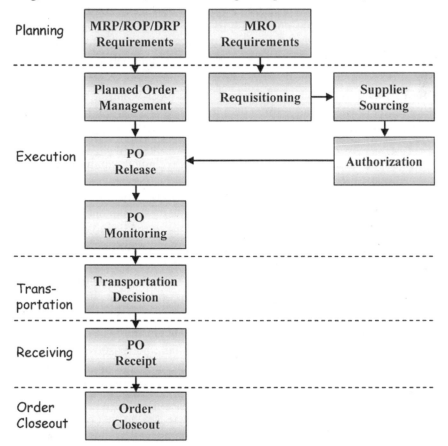

FIGURE 10.7 Purchase order flow.

An important part of the requisition process is the task of selecting the best supplier from among the pool available to the firm. In some environments, this process is very complex, requiring a needs assessment, searching for suppliers, negotiating price and usage criteria, developing contracts, buying, evaluating, and other activities. In other organizations, many of these steps have already been resolved because of long-standing customer-supplier partnerships or single-sourcing purchasing contracts. In evaluating suppliers, purchasers will often use variables such as lead time, past record of on-time delivery, ability to expedite, convenience in ordering/communication, quality, technical and training services available, range of presales and postsales value-added services, competitiveness of price reputation and past experience with the supplier, and availability of technology tools such as EDI and Web-based ordering.

Successful purchasing in the twenty-first century mandates that customers and suppliers think of themselves as *business partners*. As the requirements for e-business, globalization, collaborative product development, and outsourcing accelerate, *partnering* is now no longer an optional but rather a mandatory strategy. Like any partnership, the relationship between buyer and seller must be open and honest; there must be commitment to using available resources to achieve common objectives; there must be an equal share in the risks and the rewards; and it must be a long-term proposition meant to weather the bad as well as the good times. Finally, SRM means redefining the usual ways channel partners think about product quality and reliability, delivery, price, responsiveness, lead time, location, technical capabilities, research and development investment plans, and financial and business stability.

Practically speaking, SRM involves a conscious effort on the part of both purchaser and supplier that begins first with the establishment of a consistent flow of internal communications and progresses to the use of techniques that promote closer external communications and new opportunities for competitive advantage. The process begins on the buyer's part by implementing a formal inventory planning system that aligns business, marketing, and sales needs with the firm's capabilities. Following, a working interface between the scheduling system and the purchasing function must be established. Once these steps have been completed, buyers can begin the task of reducing the supplier base to essential partners. A smaller supplier base will shrink communications and facilitate performance measurement and alignment with enterprise goals. Once these internal tasks have been completed, purchasers will have the opportunity to institute supplier scheduling and capacity planning mechanisms. These techniques will increase the velocity of requirements transmission between buyer and supplier, as well as ensure supplier capacity to respond to these needs. Finally, these activities provide the grounds for the establishment of a continuous search for new techniques, such as supplier certification, Internet trade, and collaborative participation in product design that will enhance the partnership.

Once the supplier has been selected, the next activity involves negotiating the terms of purchase. Often the word "negotiate" is associated with "price chiseling" and haggling and is seen as an adversarial affair where one side wins and the other loses. In reality, purchasing negotiation should be a process of planning, reviewing, and analyzing in which buyer and seller reach acceptable and mutually beneficial agreement. Although the art and strategy of negotiating is a science in itself, Dobler *et al* [13] have broken negotiating down into five common objectives:

1. Obtaining an equitable and reasonable price for the quantity and quality of the goods required
2. Ensuring that the supplier fulfills the terms of the purchase contract
3. Exerting some level of control over the manner in which the contract is performed
4. Persuading the supplier to give maximum cooperation to the buyer's company
5. Developing a continuous and mutually beneficial partnership with the supplier base

The result of the negotiating process is the creation of a contract to buy. Basically, a purchasing contract should not only detail what is to be purchased but should also include the nature of the relationship between buyer and seller, product/service quality, delivery timing, and current and future pricing.

Developing the plan for the purchase of production components and raw materials and finished goods follows a different route than MRO procurement. For the most part, the process begins with the identification of those items to be resupplied based on data arising from the inventory planning system. As detailed in Chapters 7 and 8, replenishment requirements are normally identified by the firm's MRP, statistical inventory planning, and/or DRP systems. For the most part, issues relating to sourcing and pricing have already been determined, leaving the focus on selecting the necessary items, quantities, and required dates. Generally, buyers can utilize two possible methods in developing the procurement plan: buying to requirements or forward buying. The first method seeks to purchase materials based strictly on the detailed schedule of requirements. Forward buying, on the other hand, uses the requirements as a starting point and then seeks to volume purchase based on speculation as to the state of future marketplace pricing and product availability.

Another distinctive feature of this type of buying is that it is normally conducted by the purchase planners rather than the buyers. It is the responsibility of the inventory planners to review the planning system exception messaging, develop the purchasing schedule, firm the order with the supplier, and authorize delivery. Once orders have been released, the planner is responsible for maintaining the accuracy of system planning and open order data. If demand changes, the planning system will alert the planner to contact the supplier and alter quantities and due dates to keep priorities in balance. The buyer's role, on the other hand, shifts from a concern with paperwork and expediting to activating a range of value-add functions supportive of the supplier relationship. The buyer must assure the timely supply of quality goods and services achieved through close supplier selection, negotiation, pricing agreements, value analysis, quality improvement, and alternate sourcing [Table 10.2]. The mechanics of the whole operation are determined by the requirements output from the planning systems supported by the *supplier agreement* fleshed out in advance by the buyer and the supplier's sales force.

TABLE 10.2 Buyer – Planner Roles

Buyer's Role	Planner's Role
Negotiates supplier agreements	Reviews planning system output
Executes changes to supplier agreements	Acts of system exception reporting messages
Explores alternative sourcing	Communicates requirements schedule
Performs value analysis	Manages inventory investment
Negotiates quality agreements	Analyzes excess and obsolete inventory
Develops long-term partnerships	
Performs supplier selection	Reviews receiving quality rejects
Negotiates lead time reduction	Plans new product introductions
Involved on an exception basis with day-to-day buying	Reduces order and transportation costs
	Executes day-to-day buying
Both	
Organized by commodity/supplier	Administration duties
Problem solving	Forecasts and plans inventories
Integrates supplier into the business	Reports problem issues

PURCHASE ORDER ENTRY

Once order preparation activities have been completed, the purchasing flow can move to *purchase order entry*. There are a number of different forms the purchase order can take, depending on the nature of the goods and how they are to be transferred. The most common form is the *discrete purchase order*. This type of order is a one-time contract whereby the supplier promises to deliver specific products or services at a specified quantity, date, and price. Discrete purchase orders are best used for limited MRO needs, special products or components with a specific quantity, and projects of limited duration.

They are not appropriate for the purchase of high-volume, high-usage products, service contracts, or capital equipment. Another form of purchase order is the *blanket order*. This type of purchase order contains a fixed quantity of units for specific items or total dollars that extends over a period of time. When the quantity or dollar amount specified on the order is reached, the order expires. Blanket orders are best used when the quantity required and delivery timing is known by the customer. They can assist buyers attain price break quantity discounts, while ensuring delivery that matches the firm's projected inventory requirements.

A third type of purchase order is the *requirements contract*. In this type of purchase order, the buyer commits to the supplier to purchase a fixed percentage of the company's requirements in exchange for quality, price, availability, and delivery considerations. Instead of a discrete quantity, the buyer normally will furnish the supplier a short-range rolling forecast of requirements, as well as authorizing the supplier to buy and build inventory for a specified number of forecasted periods. *Systems contracting* is another form of purchase order that resembles the *requirements contract*. It has often been called *stockless purchasing*. This type of order is normally used as a method for automating the purchasing cycles of low-value, continuous usage products and materials. Systems contracts are designed to facilitate the movement of inventory and to reduce costs by eliminating formal requirements schedules, paperwork flows, consolidating billings, delivering to the point of use, and realization of the best possible price for the products required. A final form of purchase order is the *service contract*. This type of order is used to purchase nonproduct services or skills in response to a company requirement.

Finally, the use of *direct-ship purchase orders* is today becoming an important strategy by leveraging outsourcing advantages. Often, customers wish to order products the business does not carry due to historically low usage. Instead of turning the order away, the products are ordered from a supplier, who, in turn, ships directly to the customer, bypassing normal in-house receiving, material handling, and shipping. Direct-ship purchasing only works if agreed to by the customer, and the supplier can be quickly notified of the order and can ship within a very short time frame.

Whatever the form selected, the focus of activities in this area is actual purchase order release. For MRO purchases, most computer systems provide functionality for easily converting the requisition into a PO. Similarly, most of today's MRP/DRP systems provide sophisticated "workbench" applications that facilitate planned order release directly into POs. In addition, these interactive computer screens provide buyers with the opportunity to examine the contents of the proposed order before actual release. The buyer/planner can analyze such elements as supplier lead times, proposed order quantity, available discounts, and shipping costs. These steps are particularly important for products to be replenished through a *discrete purchase order*. For repetitively purchased items the system-generated requisitions provide the buyer/planner with a window into future requirements that can be negotiated into *systems contracts*. Once the purchase order type has been determined, the order is entered into the system and transmitted to the supplier.

Recently, the transmission of the purchase order has moved from the delivery of a hard-copy document to computerized transmission. In the early days of computerization, requirements orders were created within customers' business systems, printed, and then sent to the supplier, who, in turn, entered the order into their computer system. Such redundancies are now being eliminated with the rise of EDI and Web-based transmission. Considering the vast amount of purely administrative work involved, streamlining processing activities can significantly add to purchasing efficiency and effectiveness. Emmelhainz [14] points out five major benefits computerization can bring to the purchasing function.

1. Computerization reduces the amount of clerical effort required and decreases errors in order processing
2. Computerization allows for quick access to better, more accurate information resulting in better negotiations in terms of reduced prices, and improved quality
3. Value-added functions of purchasing personnel are increased by eliminating administrative, repetitive tasks
4. Computerized purchasing leads to better supplier relationships by reducing order and documentation errors, providing better information to assist in vendor scheduling, and reducing cycle times
5. The use of the computer also assists in integrating purchasing with other enterprise functions such as logistics, accounting, and marketing.

TRANSPORTATION DECISION

The management of inbound freight for purchased goods has migrated today from the purchase of a generic commodity to a complex decision involving a landscape of price and service options. As a result of deregulation legislation during the mid-1980s, companies today have recognized the need for closer integration of purchasing and transportation departments if they are to attain lower freight costs. In fact, some firms have combined the two functions into a single department. Regardless of the organizational structure, all companies have become acutely aware that many of the techniques used by SRM should also be applied to the selection of transportation partners. Careful evaluation and selection, price analysis, aggressive negotiation, scope of value-added services offered, and a continuous search for cost reduction performed by knowledgeable personnel can effect substantial savings and improved services in the management of inbound freight. Purchasers can no longer simply specify "best way," "ship soon as possible," or leave it up to the supplier. Competitive purchasing requires buyers to work closely with their traffic management departments or utilize *third party service* (3PLs) providers.

One of the critical elements in inbound transportation is selection of the most appropriate mode and carrier. Transportation modes consist of the following types of freight: rail, motor, air, and water. There are essentially four categories of transportation operating in the United States: (1) *Private*--the purchaser owns the transportation; (2) *Common Carriers*--for-hire transportation that cannot discriminate in selecting shippers or receivers; (3) *Contract Carriers*--for-hire transportation that moves freight under contract for certain shippers or receivers; and, (4) *Exempt Carriers*--for-hire carriers that are free from Interstate Commerce Commission (ICC) regulations such as rates, routes, and services. In making in-bound transportation decisions, purchasers must be careful to pick the mode and carrier type that best meets the needs of the organization. Transportation purchasing decisions are influenced by modal factors such as delivery due date, cost, reliability, size, transit, and product type; carrier selection is influenced by on-time delivery, rates, coverage, transit, care and handling, and tracing. By far most purchasers focus on the ability of carriers to deliver on time.

Another critical factor in transportation purchasing is determining the point at which title to the merchandize is transferred. The time and place of title transfer is critical because it defines the boundaries of owner responsibility and risk. The transfer of ownership from a supplier to a purchaser is termed F.O.B. (free on board). If the goods are shipped *F.O.B seller's location*, the buyer automatically acquires title at the moment the shipment is delivered to the carrier. On the other hand, if the goods are shipped *F.O.B. buyer's location*, title is transferred when the carrier delivers the goods to the buyer. Obviously, purchasers must be cognizant of the ramifications of each method because of legal complications over such things as damage, loss, or breach of contract. There are several variations of the terms of sale as listed below [15]:

- *F.O.B. Origin, Freight Collect.* Title passes to purchaser at the seller's facility. Purchaser owns the goods while in transit, pays freight charges, and files any necessary claims.
- *F.O.B. Origin, Freight Prepaid.* Title passes to purchaser at the seller's facility. Freight charges are paid by the seller, but the purchaser owns the goods while in transit and files any necessary claims.
- *F.O.B. Origin, Freight Prepaid and Charged Back.* Same as above, except that seller collects freight charges from buyer by adding the amount to the invoice.

- *F.O.B. Destination, Freight Collect.* Title passes to purchaser upon delivery to the purchaser's facility. The purchaser pays the freight charge, but the seller owns the goods while in transit and files any necessary claims.
- *F.O.B. Destination, Freight Prepaid.* Seller pays the freight charges, owns the goods while in transit, and files any necessary claims. Title passes to purchaser upon delivery.
- *F.O.B. Destination, Freight Collected and Allowed.* Sellers owns the goods while in transit and files any necessary claims. Buyer pays the freight charges but bills them back to the seller by deducting the amount from the invoice.

When making a selection of the above terms of sale, purchasers must be careful to weight such elements as the trade custom, nature of the merchandize, dollar amount of the order, and the possible savings gained by having the supplier handle transportation administration.

RECEIVING AND ORDER CLOSEOUT

The culmination of the purchase order process is *receiving* and *order closeout.* The overall responsibilities of the receiving function are to receive, identify, perform general material inspection, and confirm that the products received from the supplier are what the planner ordered. As such, effective receiving can have a significant impact on costs and operational efficiencies. When allowed to filter down through the organization, receiving errors will result in increased costs, inefficiencies in other business functions, and widening gaps in customer confidence. Typical receiving activities can be described as follows:

- *Unloading.* The first step in receiving is the actual unloading of the material from the carrier. Efficient unloading often requires developing balanced delivery schedules by working with carriers to maximize dock capacities and minimizing manning requirements. Although most unloading is performed by manual handling, receivers can utilize material handling equipment, conveyors, or unitized loads that permit mechanization of the unloading process.
- *Shipment verification.* After unloading, receivers must verify the receipt by referencing the freight bill and the original purchase order. In addition, an important check performed by receiving is verifying the scheduled receipt date as indicated on the purchase order. If the receipt is deemed too early, the material should be returned back to the supplier, depending on company policy and the supplier contract. This

practice can significantly assist companies eliminate unnecessary inventory carrying costs and stores congestion.

- *Unpacking and damage inspection.* The receiver is responsible for three verifications. To begin with, the material received is verified against both the supplier's packing list and the company's purchase order. Second, the quantity is checked in the same fashion. Finally, a general inspection is performed to determine if any external damage was sustained during delivery. If more detailed inspection is required, the receipt would be moved to the inspection department. While in inspection, products should not be allocatable to open orders until final disposition.

- *Unitize materials.* All received materials should be unitized to reduce internal material handling. For example, loose cartons may be palletized on the receiving dock to enable the efficient use of fork lifts and other equipment.

- *Hot list review.* Often newly received products are urgently needed for internal production or to fill backorder conditions. Sometimes the receipt is the result of an expedite order that has been purchased at premium cost to the company. By checking each receipt against a "hot list" personnel can speed the flow of materials through the receiving process.

- *Prepare receiving report.* Most companies utilize standard multicopy receiving forms, computer entry, or bar code readers to record material receipts as well as quality, delivery, and other performance issues. The resulting documentation is provided for accounting, who uses the information when verifying payables invoicing, inventory control for materials disposition, purchasing for supplier performance evaluation, and incoming inspection who will be inspecting the receipt.

- *Delivery of materials.* Often receiving is responsible for transporting materials to the proper stores location or, in the case of nonstock items, directly to the requestor. Upon delivery of the materials, the recipient signs off on the *receiving traveler*, thereby assuming full responsibility for the inventory.

Once receipt has been completed, the original order must be reviewed for possible closeout. All lines received complete or with open balances should be so indicated on the order. Receivers and buyer/planners must be careful to review any unreceived lines and make judgments as to line and overall order status. Any open line balances, no matter how trivial, will remain as open replenishment orders in the supply system and will have to be manually rescheduled to ensure they do not fall past due. Effective receiving procedures will significantly reduce the acceptance of unordered inventories, inaccurate quantities, and costly misidentification of materials.

STATUS REPORTING

The third step in the *purchase order management process* [Fig 10.6] is the generation and interpretation of open order status tracking and internal performance reporting. At any time in the purchase order life cycle purchasing must be able to determine the status of every order and whether it is currently open, received, or closed. The requisition and open purchase order file can be used to create a variety of priority and status reports such as PO priority by supplier and due date, or PO status by product or order number. Regardless of the sort criteria, these reports should show critical information such as purchase order number, scheduled due date, items and quantities ordered, current receiving information, and balance open. Priority reports can be used by buyer/planners as a follow-up tool. In essence, they serve the function of an advanced shortage list that can assist planners in ensuring replenishment orders are received on time without incurring costly expediting or possible material shortages. In addition, a report of open purchase orders can be used as a verification list for communicating with the supplier. Such a practice will ensure that the supplier's list of commitments matches the open purchase order list.

Effective reporting can also assist buyer/planners in maintaining the schedule of open order priorities. The key element is ensuring that scheduled receipt dates are met. The problem occurs when demand and supply circumstances change after the purchase order has been released. The cancellation or postponement of a large customer order will require that the buyer/planner review the status of open purchase orders and perform required order action. There are four basic order actions that can occur due to changes in demand and supply:

- *Generate a new purchase order.* The planner should launch a new purchase order to cover new anticipated requirements.
- *Expedite an existing order.* The planner must communicate with the supplier to see if an open purchase order can be expedited ahead of its original scheduled receipt date.
- *Deexpedite an existing order.* Due to a date change in demand requirements, the original scheduled due date of an order should be pushed back to a later date.
- *Cancel.* Open purchase order(s) should be canceled with the supplier due to a reduction in demand quantities. When performing such an action, planners must be careful to review the cost of order cancellation against possible inventory carrying costs and future requirements.

The ability to alter open purchase orders is critical to the cost-effective and timely control of inventory. Without a MRP/ROP/DRP planning system, which will actually provide these order action messages, buyer/planners can have a difficult time keeping open order due date priorities current.

Finally, effective purchasing reporting is essential in providing the detailed data necessary for enterprise purchasing planning and control. Management reporting should take two forms. The first should provide a monthly or bi-monthly window on purchasing's impact on enterprise operations controls and future planning activities. The content of this report should consist of a summary of the general business climate, a list of specific price increases or decreases for major product lines or commodities, analysis of current lead times for major materials and suppliers, and, finally, a list of possible material shortages and purchasing's strategy to handle each shortage. The second type of management report should provide a monthly or quarterly summary of the state of the purchasing function and efforts to increase the company's profitability and competitive advantage. This report should consist of the following: a summary of quality, reliability, supplier, and cost improvements; operational statistics such as number of employees, operating cost, dollar commitments against budget, and number of purchase orders issued during the period; a brief description of departmental efforts at continuous quality improvements and elimination of wastes; and, a statement of future procurement projects and administrative activities.

PERFORMANCE MEASUREMENT

The final step in the *purchase order management process* is performance measurement. Detailed performance metrics provide the enterprise with the data necessary to chart the effectiveness and efficiency of the purchasing organization and highlight areas for improvement. There are two dimensions to purchasing performance measurement: supplier performance and internal departmental performance. Supplier performance measurement is concerned with ensuring that the goals, expectations, and agreements contracted between the buyer and the supplier are being fulfilled. Regular evaluation of the purchasing function is needed to ensure that departmental activities are being optimized in the pursuit of value-added objectives. Permeating both areas is a commitment to continuous improvement. Successful companies consider continuous improvement as a way of life for suppliers, customers, and employees alike. Integrating purchasing performance measurement programs and continuous improvement objectives are fundamental building blocks of competitive advantage.

Supplier Performance Measurement

The first step in defining supplier performance measurements is to establish, with the supplier's participation, reasonable performance goals and then to implement a realistic time table for reaching them. The focus of this exercise is not to set up absolute metrics to be used as a punishment/reward tool; rather, the objectives outlined represent an opportunity for buyer and supplier to establish common ground and develop a better understanding of each others needs.

Although quality, service (delivery), and price are normally the three performance criteria used by most measurement systems, several others may be used. Selecting the proper measurements is a critical process and should be based on such elements as company objectives, product characteristics, delivery requirements, and others. The following are the most commonly used.

1. *Quality.* By far, quality is normally considered the most important. There are several avenues customers can take with their suppliers to ensure quality. Quality requirements can be stated directly on the purchase order or defined on a separate document negotiated between buyer and seller. Another excellent technique is for buyers to educate and provide those tools to the supplier necessary to attain the desired standards. Often this involves training suppliers on the use of specific *Statistical Process Control* (SPC) techniques that enforce conformance to quality specification, narrowing of process and product variation, and identification of out-of-control processes. The following are examples of possible quality measurements:

   QL = number of lots rejected / number of lots received
   QL = dollar value of rejected items / total dollar value of shipments
   QL = number of parts received / number of parts rejected
   QL = parts per million defective

2. *Delivery.* As a company's inventory planning systems become increasingly focused on scheduled due dates, the requirements for on-time delivery increase. Industry leaders today permit the supplier to ship up to 2 days early, *no days late*. Furthermore, some firms actually require their supply channel to respond at a specific *time* of day, not just the day required. Possible delivery performance measurements can be described as

   DL = Purchase order request date versus actual ship date
   DL = Supplier promise date versus actual ship date
   DL = Supplier promise date versus actual receipt date

DL = Sum of actual delivery points earned / sum of possible delivery points where points equal brackets of days late tied to specific points

3. *Price.* In the past, buying products at the best price was the key criteria in measuring purchasing performance. Today, it does little good for inventory to be purchased in economical lots only to add carrying costs and experience lost sales due to poor quality and delivery. Some buyers measure the cost of buying products against some form of benchmark cost. The problem with this approach is establishing the validity of the standard and interpreting the meaning of price changes that are beyond the purchaser's control. Most companies measure actual price performance against a weighted price index of performance. This measurement is computed first by establishing for each item the price index as illustrated below:

Price at the start of the year	$10.00
Price at the end of the year	$11.00
Price variance	$1.00
Annual usage	5,000 units
Summed price at $10.00	$50,000.00
Summed price at $11.00	$55,000.00

Price index = $55,000 / $50,000 = 1.1

The *price index* is calculated for each item purchased from a given supplier and a summed index derived. Competing suppliers can then be analyzed by comparing their price indexes or by calculating in other performance criteria, such as delivery and quality.

4. *Lead times.* There are two possible measurements regarding lead times. The first is the percentage of times a supplier's delivery matched expected lead times. Although a useful metric that ensures arrival of products to sustain sales, this measurement is neutral. A far more important measurement is the percentage of lead time *reduction* for a given supplier. The use of this metric supports the philosophy of continuous improvement.

5. *Quantity received.* Suppliers may deliver on time but deliver in quantities more or less than specified on the purchase order. The best measurement for analyzing quantity receipt performance is to develop a range of tolerances (+/-) associated with rating points. For example, a 100% delivered quantity rates 100 points; a +/- 5% deviation rates 95 points, and so on. Using this method, the performance percentage would be calculated by dividing the sum of points earned by the sum of possible points.

Other possible measurements are order accuracy, purchase order cycle time, inventory investment, cost reduction/value analysis, inbound freight cost reduction, flexibility, and technical competence [16].

PURCHASING ORGANIZATION PERFORMANCE MEASUREMENTS

Besides charting supplier performance, it is critical that managers be able to document the efficiency and effectiveness of the purchase organization. In measuring and evaluating purchasing performance, managers must review the level of departmental compliance to stated purchasing objectives, professionalism, development and updating of performance standards, control and reporting systems, results evaluation, and parameters governing the corrective action to be taken to adjust deficiencies. Ackerman [17] states that the key reasons for evaluating internal purchasing performance are the following:

1. To direct attention to main purchasing performance areas and objectives so that performance continually improves while objectives are being met.
2. To improve purchasing department organizational structure, policies, and procedures.
3. To identify those areas where additional training and educational efforts may be required.
4. To provide data so that corrective action can be taken where necessary
5. To improve interrelations within purchasing, between purchasing and other business functions, and between purchasing and the firm's suppliers.
6. To evaluate departmental staffing requirements.

As a whole, the evaluation process must focus on the two critical elements of management planning and control: *problem detection,* which illuminates organizational and process deficiencies and *problem prevention,* which seeks to build fail-safe mechanisms into the policies and procedures before the action occurs.

Before performance measurements can be developed, however, it is critical that managers understand that even the most precise quantitative methods may not provide the level of performance measurement their mathematical character would seem to indicate. Say, for example, that a manager wants to evaluate the pricing decisions of a buyer. Is the measurement to be calibrated versus a departmental or industry standard, and how valid is that standard? Does it reflect that products of lower quality and lower price are available? Does it reflect the potential cost reduction if the buyer had negotiated a detailed cost analysis negotiation with the supplier? Does it reflect economies of scale if the product had been purchased in a lot size? When establishing performance metrics it is critical that managers separate performance that can be managed directly, such as departmental administrative efficiencies, from those procurement measurements that are dependent on ratios, cost levels versus current market levels, adherence to budgets, and others. Furthermore, it can be argued that the true meaning of purchasing measurements are not found in individual or departmental achievement, but rather how purchasing contributes to the enterprise's overall competitive advantage.

Purchasing literature perceives internal performance measurement as occurring on three levels: *departmental functional review, purchasing policy and procedural audits,* and *ongoing purchasing efficiency.* The first measurement consists of a broad appraisal of the purchasing function including its policies, procedures, personnel, and interdepartmental relations. Because of its subjectivity, usually the review is performed by someone outside of the purchasing department, such as a private consulting firm or internal staff auditors. Effective reviews attempt to provide answers to such basic questions as "How effective is the purchasing function?" "Has the department been structured to support enterprise objectives?" "What are the future goals of purchasing?" In pursuing answers to these questions, reviewers must follow these general areas of inquiry:

- What is the scope of the purchasing function? How important is it to the enterprise and how well is it integrated into the competitive strategy?
- Has the organizational structure, job descriptions, and lines of communication, responsibility, and authority been clearly defined?
- What is the competency level of purchasing management? Are they qualified administrators, do they have sufficient company and industry experience, and are they knowledgeable about the markets and suppliers with which they deal?
- What is the operational and industry competency of purchasing personnel? What opportunities are there for training? Are there adequate compensation plans, and is the employee turnover rate reasonable?
- Are there formal operating policies outlining purchasing responsebilities and authority and detailing sourcing research procedures, speculative purchasing guidelines, supplier relations, and quality issues?
- Are there formal operating procedures detailing purchase order execution, integration with other business functions, searching for, developing and selecting suppliers, expediting, and performing receiving and material disposition?
- Are purchasing records being maintained in a accurate and timely fashion? What reports are necessary and how are they being presented to management?

In performing the *functional review*, the actual results are collected and compared with expected performance standards. Variances that emerge form the basis for the recommendations considered necessary to close the performance gaps [18].

The second level of internal purchasing performance measurement, *purchasing policy and procedure audits*, is targeted at measuring the level of success purchasing has had in achieving targeted objectives. Performed at least monthly, the goal is to ascertain how well the purchasing function matches predetermined operational standards, and then to provide a basis for corrective action to redirect purchasing activities that exhibit a wide variance from allowable performance tolerances. Dobler *et al* [19] describe the possible criteria for evaluation at this level as follows:

- *Timing.* This measurement focuses on how well purchasing is supporting line operations. It includes metrics such as percentage of overdue orders and stockouts caused by late delivery, number of production stoppages caused by late delivery, actual versus budgeted expediting expense, and premium transportation costs paid.
- *Quantity and inventory investment.* In this category can be found the percentage of stockouts and production stoppages caused by underbuying, actual supply service level compared to the performance target, actual inventory versus targeted inventory levels, value of dead stock, and a list of negotiated supplier stocking arrangements and estimated inventory savings.
- *Purchase price.* Key factors in this measurement are actual price performance charted against a standard, actual expenditure against a budget, price indexes compared to national commodity prices indexes such as the Producer Price Index, cost savings due to negotiation, cost analysis, volume buying, long-term contracting, supplier changes, and transportation cost reduction, and gains and losses from forward-buying activities.
- *Material quality.* Quality measurements can consist of the percentage or number of orders receiving quality rejects, number of vendors who have achieved "certified supplier" status, cost savings generated by SPC, and other value analysis techniques achieved through joint ventures with suppliers.
- *Source reliability.* This category focuses on metrics relating to percentages of late delivery, rejected material, incorrect material, and split shipments. In addition, transportation measurements such as transit times, percentage of damaged shipments, quality, and cost improvements are part of this category.

- *Supplier relations.* Although this area is often difficult to quantify, surveys targeted at compiling data relating to supplier friendliness, helpful attitude, knowledge of company's product and service needs, ability to expedite, ethical standards, and others will provide important measurements.
- *Internal coordination.* The ability to interact with other functional departments is critical to purchasing success. Measurements in this area deal with the degree of success characteristic of joint ventures such as development of material standards with accounting, value analysis reviews with marketing and sales, and order quantities with material control.

In selecting these and other performance audit techniques, management must be careful to accentuate those that seek to uncover operational deficiencies and redundancies based on the nature of the business and the materials purchased.

The last level found in internal purchasing performance measurement consists of a series of metrics designed to reveal the magnitude of purchasing *efficiency*. Effective measurement on this level requires weekly or at least monthly evaluation of day-to-day purchasing procedures and performance results. Although the following list is by no means exhaustive, it does provide the techniques used by must organizations [20].

- *Workload management.* This category contains a number of measurements associated with the ability of the purchasing function to handle by period such activities as timely purchase order issue, number of new long-term contracts executed, average number of dollars expended per purchase order, number of rush orders, and the number of changed orders.
- *Departmental operating costs.* In this category can be found metrics such as departmental actual operating costs against budget per period, number of employees, and turnover ratio. It is important to note that these metrics by themselves mean very little. They are best used in conjunction with trends arising from other efficiency and effectiveness statistics that can assist managers in charting the relationship of departmental costs to other business factors such as business volume, product quality requirements, and total materials costs.
- *Personnel.* Measurements in this area are designed to detail the performance efficiency of purchasing personnel. Metrics employed focus around performance standards for clerical, repetitive work, and time utilization studies designed to pinpoint non-value-added effort. There are a number of models available to assist managers in evaluating employees. The National Association of Purchasing Management, for ex-

ample, has developed a technique called PHASE. The goal of the evaluation method is to detail the strengths and weaknesses of each individual through (1) job analysis, (2) diagnostic evaluation of employee's knowledge of duties, goals, and functions, and (3) employee involvement in training.

The implementation of concise performance measurements is critical to the control of the purchasing process. No matter how well purchasing planning and procurement activities have been executed, much of the results will largely be ineffectual without good performance controls. In developing performance metrics, managers must understand that there is no comprehensive formula, but rather each firm must develop measurements that, first, target those activities deemed necessary for ongoing organization efficiency and effectiveness and second, are adaptive to changing circumstances. In addition, the cost of performance measurement should be weighed against the benefits. Finally, even the best set of performance measurements are no substitute for good management. Managers must effectively communicate the purpose of each measurement and use the entire program as a source to motivate and direct behavior and never to punish individuals.

IMPACT OF e-BUSINESS ON SRM

Up until just a few years ago the purchasing management process was executed through time-honored techniques. Requirements were identified, suppliers contacted, prices negotiated, and orders transmitted the old fashioned way through personal meetings, phone calls, faxes, and mail delivery. While some companies had access to EDI linkages that permitted the passing of purchasing data between ERP systems, the automation of these back-end functions were inward-facing and did little to enhance the integration and collaborative relationships necessary to speed up the front-end processes that were outside resident in the supply chain. With the application of the Internet to SRM functionality, this gap in the automation of procurement as well as full integration with supply chain partners is rapidly disappearing. Similar to what e-CRM has done for customer management, e-SRM is permitting today's cutting edge companies to assemble for the first time a complete picture of their supply relationships, apply Web technologies to dramatically cut cost and time out of sourcing and negotiating, and utilize real-time data to communicate requirements and make effective choices that result in real competitive breakthroughs.

Although the business climate of the post-dot-com era is very cautious about adopting what has come to be known as *business-to-business* (B2B) commerce, the use of Internet-enabled SRM has been growing steadily. At the beginning of 2002 Forrester Research reported, for example, that nearly 73% of the organizations surveyed used the Internet for indirect purchasing and 54% for the purchase of production materials. Others report that e-SRM initiatives have reduced the price of goods and services by five to ten percent as compared to traditional methods. When all the figures are compiled, it is clear that companies consider e-SRM to expand throughout the decade of the 2000s and provide the following benefits [21]:

- *Increased market supply and demand visibility.* B2B e-marketplaces provide customers with an ever-widening range of choices, an exchange point that enables the efficient matching of buyers and product/service mixes, and a larger market for suppliers.

- *Price benefits from increased competition.* Online buying and use of auctions can be employed to increase price competition, thereby resulting in dramatically lower prices.

- *Increased operational efficiencies.* B2B applications have the capability to increase the automation and efficiency of procurement processes through decreased cycle times for supplier sourcing, order processing and management, and buying functions.

- *Enhanced customer management.* e-Marketplaces assist marketers to accumulate and utilize analytical tools that more sharply define customer segmentation and develop new product/service value packages that deepen and make more visible customer sales campaigns.

- *Improved supply chain collaboration.* Today's B2B toolsets enable buyers and sellers to structure enhanced avenues for collaboration for product life cycle management, marketing campaigns, cross-channel demand and supply planning, and logistics support.

- *Synchronized supply chain networks.* The ability of e-markets to drive the real-time interoperability of functions anywhere in the supply network focused on merging information and providing for the execution of optimal choices provides supply partners with the capability to realize strategic and operations objectives. Among these can be included shorter cycle times for new product development and delivery, increased inventory turnover, lower WIP inventories, low-cost logistics, and others.

Figure 10.8 is an attempt to visualize the array of today's Web-enabled SRM functions. The first component, *e-sourcing*, consists of Web-driven activities necessary to develop long-term supplier relationships that will assist channel partners in architecting collaborative approaches to joint product development, negotiation, contract management, and CPFR. The second component, *e-procurement*, is comprised of a group of Internet-enabled toolsets for automating the activities associated with purchase order generation, order

FIGURE 10.8 SRM Internet technology components.

management, and procurement statistics. The third component, *value-added services,* utilizes the Internet to provide services that enhance e-SRM functions such as financials and billing. The final component, *e-marketplace exchanges,* refers to the structure, players, and activities to be found in today's Internet-enabled B2B marketplace.

e-SOURCING FUNCTIONS

The Internet provides procurement functions with radically new toolsets to facilitate the processes preceding purchase order release. In the past, buyers had to perform time-consuming searches through supplier registers and catalogs for sources of products and services. In contrast, today's Web-based browsers can significantly streamline this process. Among the capabilities can be found:

- *Supplier search.* Historically, the search for suppliers was often a fragmented and adversarial affair, marked by a laborious process of locating suppliers, opening up RFQs, pricing, quality, and delivery negotiations, and eventual contract agreement. e-Business tools, on the other hand, provide for dramatic acceleration of these processes. Internet search engines and buying exchanges can provide easy interactive access between buyer and supplier. The real-time capabilities of B2B can significantly cut the time for RFQ and negotiations. In addition, buyers can explore dynamically new purchasing models such as on-line auctions, for sourcing and spot buying.

- *Product search.* Instead of cumbersome hard copy catalogs and price sheets, the Internet provides buyers with real-time 24/7/365 access to products. B2B marketplaces host electronic product searches for all types of goods and services, including MRO, production, administrative, and capital goods. According to Hoque [22], search functionality "can range from a simple keyword search to complex product category classification, parametric search functionality, automatic comparison product offerings, bid-boards for collaborative buying, message boards for posting buyer testimonials, real-time chat for negotiating flexible pricing, and even bidding and auctioning." Effective Web-based applications should enable e-marketplaces to centralize product and service content offerings, permit suppliers to host content on their own sites, and enable buyers to develop customized catalogs.

- *Pre-purchasing services.* The goal of e-SRM is to expand the capability of buyers to automate and optimize purchasing functions while at the same time more fully integrating sourcing decisions with *supply chain planning* (SCP) and ERP transaction engines. These applications can be divided into two categories. The first, *decision support tools,* include applications such as *spend analysis* to track spend by category, supplier, and organizational unit; *item rationalization* to standardize and eliminate redundant items; *contract management* to assist in RFQ, bid analysis, negotiation, and contracting that result in lower opportunity, input, and quality costs and shorter product introduction time; and *supplier monitoring and improvement* capabilities that enable real-time measurement of supplier transaction, quality, and collaborative performance. The second category provides *negotiation automation tools* that streamline *supplier databases* for easy accessibility to supplier capabilities and performance levels to cut the supplier RFQ search effort; *e-RFP* providing Web-applications for electronic request for proposals that link with bid analysis tools; and, *e-Auctions* that utilize Web-based tools to facilitate and fully document auction events.

e-PROCUREMENT FUNCTIONS

The use of Internet tools for procurement processing represents a revolution in the way order management has traditionally been carried out. The application of e-procurement tools can be said to have a simple objective: the streamlining and automation of purchasing tasks. From the beginning, it was realized that the Web offered purchasers tremendous advantages in the acquisition of products characterized by high standardization, high-volume purchase, price as the prime decision point, minimal negotiation, and frequent spot purchase. For suppliers, the process was fairly simple, often amounting to little more than creating an on-line catalog capable of being accessed by the Internet and equipped with order entry and payment instruments. For buyers, all that was needed to gain easy access to a world of goods and services was a good Web browser and a credit card.

Understandably, the first e-procurement efforts focused around the acquisition of MRO and indirect materials that fit perfectly the original B2B model. Recently, this model has increasingly been applied to the acquisition of production inventories as well, but with a modification. Using the Web to search and buy standardized products is one things; acquiring often unique and proprietary components and raw materials from specialized vertical industry suppliers is another. What is more, procurement of this class of inventory is often preceded by complex negotiations regarding quality, delivery, and price and a desire to sustain and develop the supplier relationship. As will be discussed below, companies have turned to the development of private B2B exchanges to solve these problems. This type of exchange permits companies to create private communities of trading partners who can utilize the Internet to facilitate such activities as RFQ, competitive bidding, and order placement.

The key toolsets enabled e-procurement can be detailed as follows:

- *Catalog management.* The center piece of B2B is effective presentation of goods and services to Internet buyers through easily accessible and intelligible catalogs of products and services. Often called a "virtual storefront," the goal is to provide Web buyers with "dynamic content" that always possesses the most current pricing, product information, and ordering techniques. Such catalogs not only provide instant access to the supplier's store, but they also enable buyers to comparison shop for lowest price, highest quality, and desired delivery.

- *Requisitioning.* Advanced e-SRM applications have the capability to facilitate the requisitioning process by integrating Internet product/service catalogs into a single "virtual" catalog. These tools also provide buyers with decision metrics about suppliers, such as comparative pricing, quality performance history, commitment to collaboration, and overall customer care rating. Finally, effective requisition tools will contain other components, such as on-line documentation, chat rooms, RFQ status review, and access to current supplier pricing, productive capacity, and inventory availability.

- *Bid management.* The use of the Internet can dramatically shrink the time and cost found in the RFQ process. By opening up the bid to a form of real-time auction, buyers can easily gain access to a global community and increase marketplace competition. As bidding begins, the Web provides for easy communication of product and contracting information, and once a bid has been chosen, the RFQ can be quickly passed to the PO-generation stage.

- *Shopping tools.* While still in their infancy, purchasers can also utilize automated shopping robots to perform many of the cumbersome and time consuming tasks of Internet browsing. In the future these buying "bots" will have the capability of interacting with other "bots" to locate products and services on the Web, review availability, negotiate price and delivery, and enter orders with a minimum of human intervention.
- *Auctioning.* One of the most widely used applications of e-business is the Web auction. This technique is used primarily as a means to buy and sell products whose value is difficult to determine or are commodity in nature. While there are a variety of different types of auctions, such as classical, reverse, Dutch, and stock market model, based on the type of product offered, they all are focused on providing on-line access to products and services dictated by the market price.
- *PO generation and logistics.* Once the work of the RFQ or bidding is completed, the PO can be generated. POs can be created in the customer's ERP system and then communicated through the Internet or placed directly in the Web site. Once entered, the Web site then acts as a self-service tool for customer order tracking and follow-up. In addition, customers can also utilize an e-Logistics company. These *logistics service providers* (LSP) can offer a wide variety of supporting Web-based services such as inventory tracking, carrier selection, supplier management, shipment management, and freight bill management.

VALUE-ADDED SERVICES

While significantly accelerating procurement search and order entry functions, e-SRM also is leveraging the Internet to activate a wide range of supporting value-added functions. Among these services can be found [23]:

- Financial and billing services, such as the use of *payment cards,* or P-cards, credit approval, corporate check payment, clearinghouse functions, and direct electronic billing
- Comparison shopping functions
- Collaborative design and configuration management functions for complex, make-to-order production
- Advertising, promotions, and dynamic pricing models based on market demand and availability
- Transportation and logistics support to facilitate product fulfillment

- Synchronized supply chain procurement planning
- Establishment of marketplace performance benchmarks and key indicators

For the most part, these value-added services are normally focused on the pursuit of short-term requirements for cost and inventory reduction and synchronization of channel inventory plans. They also provide a new dimension to e-SCM by providing the foundation for the collaboration of supply chain competencies and network partner strategic visions that enable them to evolve into true e-marketplaces communities.

e-MARKETPLACE EXCHANGES

The virtual explosion of the Internet as a method for the buying and selling of products and services has generated a number of strategies and business models as Web technical capabilities have matured. In fact, today's B2B toolsets can be said to have emerged over three distinct periods [24]. In the first, *Web foundations*, the basic components of B2B were established. In this era, e-business was confined to the use of independent portals to offer products and services through techniques such as aggregation, buyer-seller matching, and hosting auctions centered on online catalog search, facilitating the RFQ process, and providing real-time order transaction and management. Overall, despite the immediate advantages, stage one B2B procurement represented little more than moving catalog operations online and did not offer the marketplace a new business model.

In the second period, termed *collaborative commerce,* e-marketplaces became much more concerned with expanding the functions necessary to conduct collaborative procurement and address the issue of direct production materials. This period was short-lived as the field of trading exchanges became dramatically overpopulated and buyers began to look beyond *independent* to *private* and *consortium exchanges* where they had direct control over the membership, security, and content of what was actually a private trading community.

The third period, *networked exchanges*, represents the most advanced stage of B2B and is currently at its opening stages. Perhaps it's central characteristic is the transformation of private, independent, and consortia marketplaces into fully *networked* exchanges featuring robust functions such as single-data models and joint order management, procurement, financial services, logistics, and network planning that facilitate multibuyer/multiseller interaction and collaboration.

Today's e-marketplace can be divided into the following three models [25]:

- *Buyer-driven e-marketplaces:* This simple B2B model is designed to enable companies to optimize internal procurement by linking through Internet tools divisions, partners, or companies. These toolsets usually seek to facilitate RFQ and procurement functions by providing aggregate catalogues either on their own systems or the Web-sites of service providers that can be used in turn by network trading partners.

- *Vertical e-marketplaces:* In this category are found marketplaces that act as hubs servicing a single industry. These marketplaces are employed by industries marked by severe discontinuities or by fragmentation due to the lack of dominant suppliers or buyers. These suppliers use the Internet as a medium to automate sourcing and procurement processes and act as a clearinghouse for information regarding everything from inventory to CPFR to logistics sourcing and contracting.

- *Horizontal e-marketplaces:* B2B marketplaces in this area range from simple portals to sophisticated collaboration hubs. The central function of these marketplaces is to enable multi-buyer/multi-supplier interaction and collaboration. By providing a sort of virtual trading "hub" where buyers and suppliers can be matched and conduct transactions, these Web sites enable manufacturers, distributors, buying groups, and service providers to develop shared marketplaces that deliver real-time, interactive commerce services through the Internet. Finally, because of their role as a medium, these marketplaces enable trading communities to facilitate the exchange of common information and knowledge.

In summary, the use of e-SRM applications is expected to increase with time as supply chains search for solutions that go far beyond simply automating PO functions. While e-SRM began as a Web-based tool for facilitating the search for and purchase of commodities, requirements for quick product cycle times and close partnerships have pushed today's e-SRM functions to evolve to new levels supporting the formation of collaborative marketplace communities. e-SRM tools must be capable of not only supporting the ever-increasing suite of Web-based procurement applications, but it must also enable true customer-supplier collaboration across the supply chain.

SUMMARY

Effective procurement and supplier relationship management are fundamental building blocks for supply chain success in the twenty-first century. The management, planning, and execution of purchasing activities are the responsibility of the firm's purchasing department. It is the job of this function to communicate effectively the company's inventory requirements to the right suppliers, execute efficient item and supplier sourcing, scheduling, contracting, negotiating, and partnership activities, as well as run the day-to-day functions of launching purchase orders, performing receiving functions, and assuring procurement performance measurement. In performing these functions, the purchasing organization must be structured to leverage simultaneously continuous improvements in processes aimed at cost reduction and high customer service. Integral to an effective purchasing function is the existence of a comprehensive purchasing strategy. Companies that do not develop a detailed purchasing strategy risk interruption in the stream of supply due to poorly executed product and supplier sourcing, misunderstood environmental or regulatory constraints, and uncertainty in price and delivery. The purchasing strategy that emerges is not necessarily one that promises to optimize efficiency or least total cost but one that supports the needs of the enterprise and the competitive advantage sought by the entire supply chain.

Managing the purchasing process revolves around the effective planning and control of the three cycles of purchase order management. The first cycle, order preparation, involves developing a buying plan that meets the needs of the firm, timely supplier selection, and negotiating the terms of purchase. The second cycle, order entry, entails choosing the appropriate purchase order type, order generation, and timely transmission of the order to the supplier. The final cycle focuses on product receiving and final order closeout. Both during and after purchase order receipt, the purchasing function is responsible for open order status tracking and internal performance. The final step in the purchase order management process is performance measurement. There are two dimensions to effective purchasing performance measurement: supplier performance and internal departmental performance. In measuring and evaluating purchasing performance, managers must review compliance to stated purchasing objectives, departmental professionalism, control and reporting systems, and commitments to continuous improvement. Integrating supplier and departmental performance objectives is a fundamental building block of competitive advantage.

With the advent of the Internet, the procurement function and the need for close supplier relationships has grown dramatically. Similar to what e-CRM has done for customer management, e-SRM is permitting today's cutting edge purchasing departments to assemble a complete picture of their supply channel relationships, apply Web-based applications to cut cycle times and costs for sourcing and negotiating, and utilize real-time data to communicate requirements and make effective choices that offer real competitive advantage. Internet tools have enabled purchasers to develop revolutionary methods to drive sourcing, procurement, and value–added services that provide enhanced supplier collaboration and supply chain synchronization. In addition, the emergence of e-marketplace exchanges have provided a number of radically new models for the buying and selling of products and services.

QUESTIONS FOR REVIEW

1. Detail the responsibilities of the purchasing department.
2. Discuss the variety of ways a purchasing organization can be structured.
3. Why is the development of an effective purchasing strategy so important?
4. Detail the activities required during the purchase order preparation cycle.
5. How can EDI significantly assist the execution of purchasing functions?
6. What is the central performance measurements needed for effective purchasing?
7. What are the characteristics of JIT purchasing?
8. How would forming close supplier partnerships result in higher-quality, lower-cost products?
9. Explain the mechanics of vendor scheduling. Why is this role superior to the organizational model of buyer and planner?
10. Why is the role of the supplier scheduler superior to older forms of purchasing organization?
11. How can QR tools significantly facilitate the purchasing process.
12. Define the difference between manufacturing and value-added processing.

PROBLEMS

1. The Ajax Distribution Company is currently earning a $10 million profit arising from sales of $50 million. The total cost of purchasing to support sales is $25 million. If the company wants to increase profits by 10%, how much must the purchasing department reduce the cost of purchasing?

2. After a DRP generation, the planner report specified the following planned order by week for three items ordered from the same supplier. If the supplier requires payment within 2 weeks of receipt, what would be the time-phased cash commitment?

Planned Orders

Cost	Item	1	2	3	4	5	6	7	8	9
$15	A	25	25	25	25	25	25	25	25	25
$24	B	0	23	35	45	23	16	3	0	0
$11	C	12	67	75	34	21	11	0	9	7

3. Part A100-100 has been purchased from two vendors. The annual usage is 7500 units of which 4230 were purchased from vendor A and the balance from vendor B. If vendor A's price at the beginning of the year was $11.24 and the last price was $11.75, and vendor B's was $11.45 at the beginning of the year and the last

price was 11.41, which vendor would be chosen if the firm decided to execute a single-source contract based solely on price?

4. A value-added processing order needs to be released. The item has the following data: monthly demand is 225 units; the cost to set up the production area and prepare the order is $22.50; and the calculated cost of carrying inventory on the part is $4.46. What would be the order quantity? How many times a year will an order have to be placed?

5. Reference Problem 4, what would be the cost of a decision to build a month's worth at a time?

REFERENCES

1. Williams, Alvin J. and Dukes, Kathleen A., "The Purchasing Function," in *The Purchasing Handbook*. 5th ed. New York: McGraw-Hill, 1993, p. 5.
2. *APICS Dictionary*, 9th ed. Falls Church, VA: American Production and Inventory Control Society, 1998.
3. See Monczka, Robert M., "Managing the Purchasing Function," in *The Distribution Handbook*. New York: Free Press, 1985, pp. 471-483 and Williams and Dukes, pp. 7-8.
4. Dobler, Donald W., Burt, David N., and Lee, Lamar, *Purchasing and Materials Management*. 5th ed. New York: McGraw-Hill, 1990, pp. 97-98. See also Beckert, Norman C., Riley, L. Wayne, and Pratt, Keith, "Purchasing Organization," in *The Purchasing Handbook*. 5th ed. New York: McGraw-Hill, 1993, pp. 29-66.
5. For further discussion see Monczka, "Managing the Purchasing Function," p. 484; Vollmann, Thomas E., Berry, William L., and Whybark, D. Clay, *Manufacturing Planning and Control Systems*. 2nd ed. Homewood, Il: Dow Jones-Irwin, 1988, pp. 227-228; and, Heinritz, Stuart, Farrell, Paul V., Giunipero, Larry C., and Kolchin, Michael G., *Purchasing: Principles and Applications*. 8th ed. Englewood Cliffs, NJ: Prentice Hall, 1991, pp. 104-126.
6. For further discussion see Leenders, Michael, Fearon, Harold E., and England, Wilbur B., *Purchasing and Inventory Management*. 9th ed. Homewood, IL: Richard D. Irwin, 1989, pp. 24-27; Magad, Eugene L. and Amos, John M., *Total Materials Management*. New York: Van Nostrand Reinhold, 1989, pp. 225-230; Heinritz *et al.*, pp. 10-25; and, Dobler *et al.*, pp. 28-32.
7. Hirsch, Chet and Barbalho, Marcos, "Toward World-Class Procurement," *Supply Chain Management Review*, 6, 5, 2001, 74-80.
8. For further discussion see Ross, David F., *Introduction to e-Supply Chain Management: Engaging Technology to Build Market-Winning Business Partnerships*. Boca Raton: St. Lucie Press, 2003, pp. 243-244.
9. These points have been adapted from Cavinato, Joseph, "Quadrant Technique: Key to Effective Acquisition and Access," ARDC Spectrum, Report #11, Acquisition Research and Development Center, State College, PA.
10. For further information on supplier performance functions see Fredendall, Lawrence D. and Hill, Ed, *Basics of Supply Chain Management*. Boca Raton: St. Lucie Press, 2001, pp. 147-155.
11. A deeper analysis of this approach to SRM collaboration can be found in Wadovick, John D. and Basar, Steven G., "Using Collaboration to Improve Supplier Relationships," APICS, 2002 International Conference Proceedings.
12. This section has been summarized from Coyle, John, J., Bardi, Edward J., and Langley, C. John Jr., *The Management of Business Logistics: A Supply Chain Perspective*. 7th ed., Mason, OH: South-Western, 2003, pp. 129-132.
13. Dobler *et al.*, pp. 297-317.
14. Emmelhainz, Margaret, "Computers in Purchasing/EDI," in *The Purchasing Handbook*. New York: McGraw-Hill, 1993, pp. 107-108.
15. These terms can be found in Heintz, *et al.*, pp. 315-317.

16. See the discussion in Schorr, John E., *Purchasing in the 21st Century.* Essex Junction, VT: Oliver Wight Publications, 1992, pp. 155-172; and, Fogarty, Donald W., Blackstone, John H., and Hoffmann, Thomas R., *Production and Inventory Management.* 2nd ed. Cincinnati, OH: South-Western Publishing Co., 1991, pp. 502-504.

17. Ackerman, Robert B., "Evaluating Purchasing Performance," in *The Purchasing Handbook.* New York: McGraw-Hill, 1993, pp. 316-317.

18. See the discussion in Ackerman, pp. 324-325 and, Dobler, *et al.,* pp. 604-606.

19. Dobler, *et al.,* pp. 606-613.

20. These points have been summarized from Ackerman, pp. 328-354 and, Dobler, *et al.,* pp. 613-617.

21. These benefits have been summarized from Ross, *Introduction to e-Supply Chain Management,* pp. 249-250.

22. Hoque, Faisal, *e-Enterprise: Business Models, Architecture, and Components.* Cambridge University Press, 2000, p. 97.

23. Ross, *Introduction to e-Supply Chain Management,* pp. 255.

24. The phases of B2B can be found in Hajibashi, Mohammed, "E-Marketplaces: The Shape of the New Economy," in *Achieving Supply Chain Excellence Through Technology.* 3, Anderson, David, L., ed. San Francisco: Montgomery Research, 2001, 162-166; and, Temkin, Bruce, "Preparing for the Coming Shake-Out in Online Markets," in *Achieving Supply Chain Excellence Through Technology.* 3, Anderson, David, L., ed., San Francisco: Montgomery Research, 2001, 102-107.

25. This section has been adapted from Ross, *Introduction to e-Supply Chain Management,* pp. 263-265.

11

WAREHOUSING

The key to understanding warehousing in the twenty-first century is to perceive it as a component of several logistics functions that are integrated together to provide the supply chain with unique competitive advantage. In the past, warehousing was looked upon as a tactical function concerned with the long-term storage of raw materials and finished goods. Someone once defined a warehouse as "inventory at zero velocity." The role of warehousing was to ensure that individual companies possessed sufficient stock not only to respond to anticipated customer requirements but also to act as a buffer guarding against the "bullwhip effect" produced by uncertainties in supply and demand characteristic of linear supply chains. As such, the operating philosophy was to search for the appropriate trade-offs between storage, purchasing, and transportation costs on the one hand, and customer serviceability targets on the other.

In today's "Lean" and highly interoperable supply chains, this static perception of warehousing has become obsolete and is being replaced by the term *distribution center*. While, like all terms, the distinction between "warehouse" and "distribution center" has become one of semantics whose meanings have changed as their functions evolve through time, the differences between warehousing as the static storage of inventory and today's high-velocity customer service centers is dramatic. When it is considered that warehousing and logistics services now represent core value-added services, the need to reposition warehouse functions as fundamental strategic sources of competitive differentiation and marketplace leadership has grown. Instead of a lumbering giant accounting for the bulk of the firm's costs and manpower requirements, computerization, automation, and JIT philosophies accentuating information flows and promoting quality and the elimination of wastes have drawn the warehouse function within the sphere of competitive strategy. Effective warehousing in the 2000s requires the enterprise to take an integrative perspective focused on Internet-driven connectivity tools and increased value-added services while simultaneously reducing costs and impediments to service leadership.

The objective of this chapter is to detail the strategies and operational activities associated with warehousing at the beginning of the twenty-first century. The chapter begins by defining warehousing and the many roles performed by warehousing in the logistics system. The chapter then proceeds to a discussion of the basic types and specialized services offered by warehousing. Of critical importance is how globalization of the marketplace, evolution of information technology, new views of customer service and the role of inventory, and closer integration and partnering of the business units constituting the supply chain are impacting traditional views of warehousing objectives and operations. Next, the chapter moves to a review of the warehouse management process, which includes defining warehousing process standards, establishing receiving and shipping functions, detailing the order picking function, and establishing the necessary performance measurements to guide quality and continuous improvement management. Following this theme, the chapter then proceeds to examine the formulation of strategies targeted at leveraging and continually refocusing the warehouse resources that will assist in the realization of business unit and corporate objectives. At this point, the chapter moves to a consideration of the trends impacting modern warehouse management. Among the topics discussed are examining the nature of warehousing in the post 9/11 and Internet environments, technology applications, and growth of the concept of channel partnership management. The chapter concludes with a detailed and comprehensive look at designing the warehouse network, structuring the warehouse, physical layout, and equipment and information technology selection.

DEFINING WAREHOUSING

The effective performance of warehousing activities is integral to the success of supply chain functions. In many industries, product and market characteristics, such as the discontinuity of demand and seasonal peaks and valleys, make it almost impossible to fully synchronize the acquisition of goods with actual demand, forcing companies to stockpile inventory buffers. While many companies consider warehousing to be a negative function, which stops or interrupts the flow of products through the supply chain continuum, others consider the advantage to their marketplace value proposition that inventory availability offers to be more advantageous than the cost. As a result, for companies such as grocery stores, catalog distributors, wholesalers, and large and small retailers from the corner drug store to Wal-Mart, the storage of inventory and the ability to deliver it to the customer at the time, quantity, and place desired provides value-added differentiation and defines marketplace leadership.

In economic terms, the price of warehousing can be enormous and must always be properly balanced with necessary trade-offs in customer service and competitive advantage. In terms of sheer size, warehouse space in the U.S. total some 3.4 billion square feet in 2002. In 2001, the total cost of warehousing in the U.S. for all businesses amounted to over $78 billion. This figure represented a little over eight percent of total logistics costs [1]. According to an estimate by the Boyd Company, a site-location consulting firm, the cost of a typical 75,000 square foot supply chain facility employing 200 hourly workers can run as high as $15.3 million in San Jose, California, and as low as $7.4 million in New Brunswick, Canada [2]. Warehousing can be defined as

> that segment of an enterprise's logistics function responsible for the storage and handling of inventories beginning with supplier receipt and ending at the point of consumption. The management of this process includes the maintenance of accurate and timely information relating to inventory status, location, condition, and disbursement.

WAREHOUSING FUNCTIONS

Warehousing performs many roles in the typical distribution organization. Warehousing can be said to perform the following four basic functions: material handling, storage, order management, and information management. *Material handling* consists of the following elements:

- *Receiving.* This function is the gateway activity in the warehouse management process. The major operations performed by this function are inbound carrier scheduling, order acceptance, material unloading, order audit, inspection, and staging. Critical performance factors in receiving are ensuring labor productivity, equipment utilization, product quality, and unloading efficiency.

- *Sorting.* In some stocking environments, warehousing must sort received merchandise or unitize it as a prelude to stock put-away. Often sorting will require activities such as grading, testing, and grouping. This process will reduce stock handling and the chance of location or picking error.

- *Value-Added Processing.* Often warehouses are responsible for postponement, or final product differentiation, through light assembly or manufacturing. The activities associated with this functions are component picking and staging, labor and machine allocation, processing, labeling, and packaging. Value-added processing provides two essential values. In the first, finished good flexibility can be increased by postponing the decision to produce the final product configuration until actual demand requirements have been determined. A critical advantage is that the chance of stockout is reduced, while the amount of base inventory remains constant. Second, risk and total inventory investment can be reduced by keeping the product as base stock with actual product differentiation not made until the sale is made. Disadvantages are that expenses for production operators and equipment must be incurred, and, second, customers are willing to absorb the extra lead time to complete final assembly processing.

The second basic function of warehousing is *product storage*. Companies possess warehouse storage space for several reasons. To begin with, the decision to store inventories may be the result of economies achieved by trading-off the cost of transportation against the cost of carrying inventories. This is particularly true of products that permit purchasers to leverage quantity discounts by buying in bulk quantities. Another reason why companies use storage is to assist the enterprise in balancing supply and demand over time. Take, for instance, a company that distributes products subject to seasonality and uncertain demand. Planned stocked inventories will smooth acquisition costs and ensure that customer orders are met without the excessive costs normally involved with expediting and lost sales. Again, for companies who purchase speculation inventories, like commodities, storage will enable price economies that more than offset the cost of warehousing the extra inventory. A third reason for warehouse storage is to assist in the production process. Food products such as wine, cheese, and liquors often need to be aged before sale. In addition, inventories stocked in warehouses can be secured or "bonded." This technique allows distributors to defer paying tax on the goods until actual sale. Finally, storage can provide value to marketing by ensuring that inventory is available to satisfy place and delivery strategies.

Warehouse storage consists of the following functions:

- *Storing/Put-Away.* These cardinal functions of warehousing consist of housing received inventory in the proper storage locations in preparation for order allocation and picking.

- *Stockpiling.* Another important storage function is to provide for the access to, protection, accuracy, and orderly stocking of products and materials. Stockpiling can result from production overflows due to seasonality and demand variability, or as a result of sales promotions or deals. The span of time inventory is to be held often determines the configuration and operations of the storage facility. Warehouses can range from long-term, specialized storage (aging liquors, for example) to general-purpose merchandise storage (products subject to seasonality) to temporary storage (as in a consolidation terminal). In the last case, products are stored until economic transportation quantities are assembled.

- *Product rotation.* Some companies stock products that are subject to limited shelf life. A critical responsibility of warehousing is to ensure that first-in-first-out rotation of products, such as foodstuffs, pharmaceuticals, and chemicals, is properly managed to avoid spoilage and obsolescence.

- *Consolidation.* Often companies must acquire products that are shipped *less-than-truckload* (LTL). A method of economically converting many small shipment into full carloads is to have products shipped to a local or regional consolidation center. At the consolidation warehouse, product can be broken down, repackaged, or simply combined with other products that can be transported in full truckloads to the deployment warehouse. Obviously, the savings achieved from more cost-effective shipping must be large enough to justify the consolidation warehouse.

- *Bulk breaking.* This storage function is the direct opposite of product consolidation. Often companies must purchase goods in bulk quantities for pricing or transportation cost purposes. These shipments are received into the warehouse where they are repackaged into smaller quantities necessary to meet customer requirements. Bulk breaking is used most often when inbound transportation rates per unit exceed the customer delivery rates per unit, when distributors sell products in LTL quantities to meet customer demands, and when there is considerable transit distance between manufacturer and distributor. Bulk breaking is a common activity found in terminal or deployment warehouses. The use of consolidation and bulk break is illustrated in Figure 11.1.

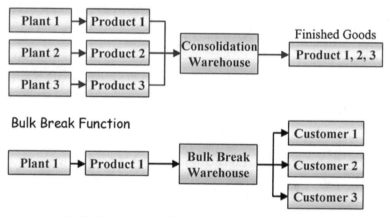

FIGURE 11.1 Consolidation and bulk break functions.

- *Product mixing.* This storage function is used by companies who produce or acquire a wide variety of products and convert them into stocked assortments. When customers order these products they will often request various goods from a product line. Because these products are made or purchased from different acquisition locations, establishing a local product mixing point where these lots can be loaded in full car loads may produce both inbound and outbound transportation economies [Figure 11.2].

- *Cross docking.* This function is similar to product mixing in that a *mixing warehouse* is used to consolidate deliveries (through sorting, assembly, or packaging) from multiple sources into salable or useable assortments. The major difference is that instead of locating these assortments into a stockroom, they are literally moved directed to the shipping dock and out to the customer, by-passing any form of storage. The benefits of this function can be seen in reduced storage and material handling costs, more effective use of the docking facilities, shorter order fulfillment cycle times, and full truck load delivery.

Product Mixing Function

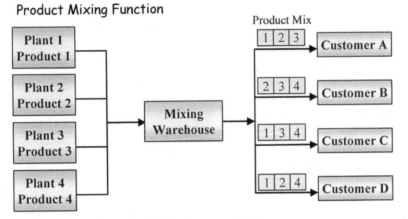

FIGURE 11.2 Product assembly functions.

- *Spot stock.* This function is most employed by distributors faced with stocking finished goods subject to seasonality or limited product lines. The mechanics of the technique are characterized by the "spot" acquisition and storage of products to fulfill customer requirements during a particular marketing season or promotional period. For example, a bathing suit distributor may "spot" inventories in warehouses close to critical retail markets during the spring and early summer, and then, once the season is over, pull inventories back to a regional warehouse.

- *Production support.* In a manufacturing environment warehousing takes on a dual role. It must not only perform finished goods warehousing to support customer sales, it must also provide raw material, component, and subassembly inventories consumed during the production process. Although Lean and flow production initiatives seek to remove a dependence on stores by having production inventories delivered directly to the processing line, long lead times and product lot sizes often will force manufacturers to maintain production warehouse.

The objective of warehouse storage is to maximize on customer service by improving product and location positioning. Success or failure is gauged by weighing the trade-off costs between storage and transportation.

The third function of warehousing is to facilitate order management processes. Among activities can be found the following:

- *Order picking.* Order picking is the physical selection of products from storage required to meet an order request. For the most part, order picking is controlled through a *pick list* generated from the order detail. The major elements of a pick list are the order number, the required date, the items and quantities to be picked, and the picking location. The pick list serves the purpose of an inventory control turnaround document as well as an authorization to pick products for shipping. Because of the quality and accuracy required to satisfy customer expectations and the labor cost involved in handling small volumes of orders, order picking is a critical material handling function.

- *Production order picking.* Companies that both manufacture and distribute their products normally use the warehousing function not only as a storage point for finished goods but also as a storage point for components and raw materials to be consumed by the manufacturing unit of the firm. In such environments it is the responsibility of warehousing to receive, store, pick, and stage these items and deliver them to production for fabrication or manufacture.

- *Traffic management.* Warehousing should be responsible for selecting the carriers to be used for product shipment, subject to review from accounting and auditing. If the firm possesses a traffic management department, warehousing should work closely with it and be responsive to its recommendations. Over the past decade, warehousing and traffic management have been working closely with their carriers to reduce transportation costs. Most of the major freight traffic in the U.S. is covered by master contracts negotiated with fine-tuned precision.

- *Shipping.* Shipping functions are often performed by the warehouse staff. Shipping activities can be divided into two components. The first, *shipment preparation*, is concerned with the performance of any necessary value–added processing and product staging at the outbound dock. Once completed, the second function, *shipping*, can be performed. This functions contains activities such as carrier scheduling, rate determination, loading transportation vehicles, and completing documentation such as bill of lading, packing lists, and record maintenance.

The fourth and final function of warehousing is *information transfer*. Whenever products are received, moved from place to place, or shipped, detailed information relating to the transaction must be captured. In addition to inventory status, the warehouse also provides the firm with information relating to throughput levels, space utilization, equipment and manpower availability, and transportation capacities. For most companies, the administrative/clerical activities associated with information transfer are considerable. Successful warehouses of the twenty-first century will be those that learn how to leverage computerized techniques and Lean methods to automate and eliminate needless manual labor that must be performed in conjunction with tracking warehouse activity. Without timely and accurate information, the enterprise cannot possibly hope to achieve targeted marketing, sales, and customer service objectives.

TYPES OF WAREHOUSING

There are several types of warehousing alternatives that companies can pursue. Choosing the appropriate type of warehouse consists of a matrix of financial, organizational, and legal decisions. The object is to select a type that provides the ability to achieve the least total cost necessary to efficiently and effectively execute logistics functions while facilitating attainment of enterprise strategic performance targets. The optimal warehouse decision should permit the firm to leverage inventory levels and transportation modes that effectively support marketing, sales, order processing, and inventory planning in the quest for competitive advantage. Factors influencing warehouse decisions include the type of industry, supply chain goals, financial capacities, product characteristics such as perishability, size, seasonality, intrinsic value, quantity, potential for obsolescence, strength of the competition, and state of the general economy.

There are four basic forms of warehousing: private, public, contract, and in-transit. *Private* warehousing is differentiated from the other three forms by the fact that the property, facility, and accompanying storage and material handling equipment are owned and operated by the firm. This form of warehouse may be as small as a rack or a stockroom or as large as a network of complex warehouses separated by continents and consisting of hundreds of thousands of square feet of storage. The advantages of private warehousing consist in the following:

1. Private warehousing enables the firm to exercise a high level of direct control over warehouse operations. A high level of control is desirable when dealing with special types of products, such as pharmaceuticals or high-ticket goods, or when special handling or packaging is required. The ability to directly control warehouse operations is also critical when pursuing high levels of efficiency and performance.

2. Private ownership can be less expensive than the alternate types of warehousing. This is particularly true when business operations are characterized by high storage area utilization and volumes that are large and continuous.

3. Real estate and fixed asset ownership may also provide the firm with certain tax advantages or assist in projecting to the community and customer base a sense of commitment and permanence.

4. Private warehouses simplify communication. Critical information relating to such logistics elements as inventory stock status, receiving, and shipping are available directly to the firm's management.

5. Unutilized space may be converted to other uses, such as support function expansion or even value-added processing. In addition, space

may be rented out to other businesses or used to realize public storage opportunities.

Perhaps the most important disadvantage to privately owned warehousing is loss of flexibility. Because of its fixed size and cost, a private warehouse cannot expand and contract to meet changing marketplace needs, nor can it take advantage of possible strategic location options. In addition, when employing private warehousing, companies must carry the burden of fixed costs, risk of damage by fire or natural disaster, and exposure to labor disputes. Finally, private warehousing requires the presence of a skilled management team to ensure optimal operational performance.

Public warehousing is a permanent feature in the physical distribution strategies of many companies. In 2002 the public warehousing industry and associated terminal services represented about 35 percent of total warehousing costs. The growing importance of public warehousing can be traced to the changing nature of the marketplace. By offering a full range of storage, material handling, clerical, and value-added services, public warehouses can provide short- and long-term functions targeted at supporting the supply chain requirements of their customers. The key characteristic of public warehousing is that the facility, labor, and material handling equipment are owned by the warehouse company, which, in turn, contracts warehousing services for a month-to-month fee. In addition to providing rented storage space, public warehousing firms may also perform operational activities, such as receiving, material handling, value-added processing, shipping, and loading operations on a unit-charge basis. Public warehouses normally specialize in handling certain types of products lines, such as hazardous materials, foodstuffs, and bulk storage. Public warehouses also target certain types of customers. Grocery stores, for example, require special warehousing services that facilitate product turnaround to minimize spoilage. Some public warehouses will also provide clerical functions including EDI and Web-based order processing, product inspection, marking, tagging and inspection, and transportation dispatching, traffic accounting, and prepayment of freight charges. The advantages of public warehousing consist of the following:

1. *Capital investment.* Perhaps the major advantage of public warehousing is that it requires no *fixed* capital investment. When using a public warehouse, all costs are *variable* in that they are directly proportional to the extent services are used. This factor may be highly advantageous to a firm attempting to conserve capital expenditure rather than having to invest in private plant and equipment to solve a short-term, nonrepetitive stocking and material handling problem.

2. *Facility obsolescence.* Public warehousing reduces the risk of plant facility and material handling technology obsolescence. When it is considered that the normal operations plan for a warehouse extends out

for 20-40 years, the use of public warehousing can assist planners manage and chart the course of marketplace trends and volumes before investing capital to expand their private warehouses.

3. *Marketplace flexibility.* Public warehouses can provide companies with the flexibility to respond quickly to short-term marketplace requirements without a corresponding rise in expenditure for fixed storage. Whether a small company or a large international enterprise, businesses in an expanding market are wise to utilize public warehousing while measuring whether the expansion is significant enough to justify the acquisition of proprietary facilities. In addition, the services offered by public warehousing enable smaller firms to target a national market and provide the same level of customer service available to much larger firms.

4. *Transportation economies.* The use of public warehousing to perform shipping and transportation activities can provide significant cost savings. Many companies can bear consolidated freight rates but not the costs required to ship small quantities at premium rates. Often the savings in freight alone is sufficient to offset the total public warehousing cost. On their part, the public warehouse makes a profit from the charge for warehousing and consolidation services and, again, from the revenue generated by warehouse-owned transportation vehicles.

5. *Access to special features.* Public warehouses can often provide a number of specialized material handling, storage, and shipping services more economically than a company-owned warehouse. The following are examples of such special services:

   - Material handling equipment such as cranes, lift trucks, conveyor systems, rail sidings, dedicated dock areas, docking facilities, and manpower
   - Special storage requirements such as sterilized and ultraclean rooms, barge and ship facilities, temperature controlled storage, and special bulk storage
   - Broken-case order filling
   - Office space rental for depositor's sales, customer service, marketing, accounting, and other business functional staffs
   - Repackaging of products for shipment
   - Bulk breaking
   - Freight consolidation
   - Invoicing for depositors

6. *Computerization.* Many companies do not have the capital or expertise to respond to the computerized requirements of their customers. Many public warehouses provide computerized tools such as EDI, Internet

access, bar coding, and business system interface that can expand a firm's service functions without actually acquiring the equipment.

7. *Overflow warehousing.* Companies often need storage space to accommodate abnormally large product quantities. Such quantities can arise from a number of sources, such as an opportunity purchase, an impending promotional sale, an unusual surge in customer sales, and seasonality. Public warehousing is an appropriate alternative in such situations, especially when the cost to acquire additional facilities, manpower, and equipment would be more than the cost of temporary storage. It also eliminates the costly practice of personnel hiring and layoff as the volume of business fluctuates.

8. *Tax breaks.* The use of public warehousing enables enterprises to avoid local taxes arising from property ownership. In addition, certain states do not charge taxes on inventories stored in public warehouses.

9. *Inventory backup.* Businesses will often use public warehouses to store products against possible interruptions in supply caused by labor strikes, weather, or international or marketplace conditions. To be most effective, the backup inventory should be stored in a location far from the main warehouse or stored in a manner that will neutralize the threat to the main warehouse.

There are a number of disadvantages to public warehousing. To begin with, lack of timely and accurate communication between the private and the public warehouse may hinder information transfer and create excess inventory and administrative costs. Second, the specialized services required by a company may not always be available from a given public warehouse. This is particularly true of distributors who require regional or national services. Finally, firms may not always have access to public warehouse space and services. Availability and limitations in capacities do periodically occur, adversely affecting enterprise logistics and marketing strategies.

Contract warehousing is a form of public warehousing. The key difference between the two types is the nature of the commitment made to the public warehouse. For the most part, the public warehousing contract is executed for a short-term period with renewal on a month-to-month basis. In contrast, contract warehousing focuses on the creation of a long-term agreement that ties both parties together for a period of time at least as long as is necessary to amortize mutual investment. The goal of the contract is to establish a form of guarantee on the part of the enterprise that the level of business will remain constant over the life of the contract, and on the part of the public warehouse that the level of contracted services will be available throughout the contracted period. In addition to the normal benefits, contract warehousing provides both parties with the opportunity to explore new avenues for cost-cutting and continuous improvement in communications and services. For example, contract warehousing provides a gateway for improvements in warehouse planning, increased accuracy of receiving and shipping functions, development of specialized material handling, storage and transportation equipment, and the elimination of redundancies in transport, information, and administrative services.

In addition to long-term contracts, there are also a number of variations. Among these more limited contracts can be found the following:

- *Leased space.* This contract option provides the distributor with some of the benefits of both private and public warehousing. In this arrangement, the public warehouse guarantees either dedicated storage space in the facility isolated from other storage by fences or other types of barriers, or a guarantee of general space, but not dedicated, except as is specified by the lessee. The advantage to the lessee is that the contract space should cost less than comparable private space or, by guaranteeing a long-term contract, the expense of the lease would be less than the cost of renting space. The public warehouse, on the other hand, will benefit by being able to schedule space, equipment, and manpower, thereby optimizing the full capacity of the warehouse.

- *Leased equipment and manpower.* Normally used in conjunction with leased or dedicated space, businesses can also contract equipment and manpower based on fixed rates per hour. Normally, the rate charges will be higher, often three to five times higher, than comparable private costs. The reason for this premium price is the high overhead and indirect costs that must be borne by the contract warehouse in having these services ready and available. The best contract for equipment and manpower is the one that provides mutual benefit to both parties.

- *Leased administrative services.* Many public warehouses offer clerical support for such activities as transaction recording, inventory management, and customer service.

The final form of warehouse storage is *storage in transit.* This is a special kind of warehousing in which products are stored in the mode of transportation. For example, a company may elect to store product in the truck trailer or railcar in which it was delivered. The firm will rent the storage container from the shipper. Inventory will remain in this temporary warehouse until it is finally unloaded and received into normal storage. Again, depending on transit times, businesses may select a mode that may substantially reduce the need to have space for stocked inventories by having them in transit. This alternative is particularly attractive to distributors dealing with commodity products that must be shipped over long distances.

VARIOUS SPECIALIZED WAREHOUSE SERVICES

Cutting across the four forms of warehousing are various warehouse storage types. For the most part, these types of storage are determined by product characteristics. Selecting the most appropriate type of warehouse is the responsibility of a warehouse professional supported by planners from product management, engineering, accounting, sales, production, and traffic management. Among the possible types of warehouse can be found the following:

- *Cold Storage Warehouse.* Often products must be kept at certain low temperatures to preserve freshness or prevent spoilage. This is particularly true of foodstuffs that must be refrigerated or kept frozen. Obviously, the cost of building, maintaining, and operating a cold storage warehouse is substantially higher than other forms of storage. These costs are a result of higher building material costs, equipment, energy, premium pay for workers, insurance, and refrigerated transportation.

- *Temperature-Controlled Warehouse.* There are some products, such as fresh vegetables, fruit, liquids, and chemicals, that must be stored in warehouses whose temperature is somewhere in between cold storage and "dry" or ambient outside temperature. The temperature of such facilities range from 50 to 68 degrees, and usually include some form of humidity controls. Such warehouses regulate the temperature through air conditioners, heaters, and humidity control equipment. As the facility, equipment, overhead, and labor cost is usually less, this type of warehousing is not as expensive as cold storage to operate.

- *Bonded Warehouse.* Companies often will use a special type of warehouse that will enable them to produce, transfer, and store products without having to pay excise taxes and duties. The regulations determining a bonded warehouse have been defined by government agencies such as the Public Utilities Commission, the Alcohol and Beverage Control Commission, the Customs Services, and others. The most well-known form of bonding is associated with wines and spirits. By keeping these products in a bonded warehouse, a distributor may avoid paying the tax until products are transferred out of bond. The term "bonded" is often used loosely by public warehouses. Normally public warehouses do not insure their customer's inventories. Companies should insure inventories that are stored in public warehouses as if they were stored in private facilities. The extent of legal protection should always be stated by contract.

- *Records Warehouse.* As the cost of office space spirals, firms are increasingly using the more economical alternative of utilizing excess or dedicated warehouse space and personnel for the pickup, filing, storing, retrieving, and delivery of company records. Some public warehouses specialize in record storage, offering on-site pickup, retrieval, and delivery of documents to and from their customers. The requirements for effective record storage are environmental (absence of dust, humidity, and excess heat), confidentiality and security, and the availability of technical equipment such as computerized storage, microfilming, reproduction, FAX, and Internet.

- *General Merchandise Warehouse.* This type of warehouse accounts for, by far, the largest percentage of all warehousing activities. For lack of a better description, it can be defined as the storage of all goods except specialized or commodity products. This type of warehouse can be described as private or public, bonded or unbonded, and may or may not have customs and free-trade-zone privileges. In reality, merchandise warehouses tend to specialize in certain classes of goods driven by storage and material handing factors. An example would be grocery warehouses that must employ certain types of transportation and storage facilities.

- *Commodity Warehouse.* This type of storage specializes in commodity or bulk products such as wood, agricultural goods, cloth, building materials, cotton, and so on. Commodity warehouses can be either public or private. Normally, commodity warehouses are located close to the source of production or extraction or are at the distribution end of the pipeline where they can be close to the consumer. The central advantage of a commodity warehouse is the availability of specialized material handling equipment such as conveyors, heavy lift trucks, containerization, highly trained personnel, and other warehousing features that enable them to achieve significant performance efficiencies. On the other hand, a negative characteristic of commodity warehousing, particularly in the agricultural industry, is their involvement with products dominated by seasonality which produces recurring cycles of boom and bust.

- *Foreign Free-Trade-Zone Warehouse.* This type of warehouse would be used by enterprises engaged in international trade. These storage facilities legally reside outside of U.S. customs territory where they are exempt or have reduced customs duty liability. If the goods are re-exported, no customs duties are owed. In addition, free-trade-zone warehouses permit companies to buy and store goods in excess of permissible import quotas for resale in the next period. Besides the possible avoidance of duties altogether, this type of warehouse will improve cash flow by delaying taxes and duties until the goods are actually sold and shipped. Free-trade-zone warehouses can be either private or public.

- *Miniwarehouse.* This type of warehouse is usually characterized by limitations in total space and the complete absence of warehousing services. They are simply intended as extra storage space, ranging from 20 to 200 square feet. They are normally administered by an on-site caretaker, and they often have a limited assortment of material handling equipment for rent. Besides their relative lack of expense, the prime advantage of miniwarehouses is their close proximity and convenience for renters. Distributors with overcapacity may get into the business of turning their excess space into miniwarehouses.

DEVELOPING WAREHOUSE STRATEGIES

As the waves of change described above wash through the business environment of the 2000s, companies must develop comprehensive strategies that will leverage and continually refocus the resources of their warehousing functions to support the realization of both individual business and supply chain objectives. Although most executive strategies are focused on marketing, sales, and logistics, the sheer size of the asset and operational investment necessary to run warehousing functions requires firms to closely define as well the strategic role of warehousing in the organization. One warehousing expert characterizes the warehousing function as "a business within a business." Warehousing has its own distinct labor force, staff, accounting, management, and information system requirements that are unique from other functional departments.

Normally, warehousing is structured as a service provider to sales and production management and, in effect, "charges" the enterprise for the costs incurred. Obviously, warehouse strategic planning involves more than just building a warehouse, setting up storage racks, purchasing some material handling equipment, and hiring staff. Nor, as has been pointed out, is it a static, one-time activity. Instead, similar to other critical areas of the enterprise, warehouse strategic planning and control is a continuous activity that must be in alignment with overall organizational and customer service objectives.

STRATEGIC OVERVIEW

Before the warehouse planning process can begin, strategists must understand the objectives of other enterprise functions. Planning decisions concerning such elements as product, delivery, price, promotion, asset investment, and costs made by marketing, sales, manufacturing, procurement, and finance will have a direct impact on the formulation of warehousing strategies. For example, if a new marketing strategy is to offer customers a guaranteed 24-hour order delivery cycle, warehouse management will need to explore the capability of the warehousing function to respond to this goal. If enterprise strategies are to be effectively executed, it is imperative that warehouse management be included as a full partner in the strategic planning process and that the warehousing plan be closely integrated with the enterprise's other functional business plans.

In addition to understanding their role in the company's strategic plan, warehouse planners must also be apprised of the anticipated direction of the marketplace and the supplier base. This function is directly the responsibility of the marketing function that can deploy a variety of different techniques from formal marketing surveys consisting of questionnaires, phone surveys, to on-site interviews. Some of the questions posed to customer and suppliers that will directly impact warehouse decisions are as follows:

- What should be the strategy for using a combination of private, public, and contract warehouses?
- What should be the targeted warehouse utilizations?
- How many warehouses should there be and what should be their type?
- Should warehouse decisions be based on customer or product or both?
- What new operational or marketing strategies have been formulated that will require changes in current warehousing practices?
- What new product lines are expected to be introduced and how will they affect warehousing and delivery?
- What changes to warehousing delivery and storage mechanisms, such as equipment and information technologies, are being planned?
- Are there any plans to open or close warehouses, and if so, in what locations?
- What plans are in place that will streamline the existing supply chain warehousing configuration?

By conducting a comprehensive survey of those customers and suppliers that account for the bulk of sales and procurement activities, warehouse planners can develop a reasonably accurate profile of the directions being pursued generally by both groups. The patterns and objectives that emerge will significantly assist in constructing warehousing strategies that aggressively address marketplace trends while maintaining support for the overall objectives of the enterprise [3].

Once a comprehensive understanding of the requirements arising from marketing and supplier management is identified, a detailed strategy can be defined describing the objectives of the three critical resource components of the warehouse: storage space, material handling capacities, and personnel. An effective *storage space* strategy consists of several facets. To begin with, it entails calculating the resource capabilities of existing plant and highlights possible requirements for leased or contracted space. Second, the storage strategy must be based on a clear financial footing that details the cost of maintaining and operating the storage space. Typically, warehouse carrying cost can amount to anywhere from between $0.20 to $0.60 per cubic foot, and can be even higher depending on location. A company not efficiently using warehouse space could be incurring needless costs and decreasing overall productivity.

Once warehouse storage resources have been defined, a strategy must also be devised for the effective utilization or acquisition of *material handling equipment*. Warehousing equipment can range anywhere from forklifts and pickers, to automated conveyors and vehicles, dock facilities, and a variety of computerized information workstations. When combined, these fixed assets can account for a significant portion of the company's capital investment. In addition to equipment, a comprehensive warehouse strategy cannot be complete without planning for *labor resources*. Pickers, stockkeepers, packers, shippers, management and other support personnel can amount to an enormous current cost, accounting for over 50% of the company's entire warehousing cost. Fashioning an effective labor strategy involves more than just determining the necessary staffing levels: it also requires activating an attitude of continuous operational improvement and total quality among the warehouse staff targeted at the elimination of wastes found anywhere in operations and the establishment of practices resulting in greater productivity, mutually beneficial labor relations, and increased employee satisfaction. Tompkins [4] succinctly summarizes the objectives pursued by a successful warehouse strategy as follows:

- Maximizing the effective use of space
- Maximizing the efficient use of warehouse equipment
- Maximizing the efficient use of labor
- Maximizing the accessibility of all stock inventories
- Maximizing the protection of all items from damage, spoilage, and obsolescence.

DEVELOPING THE WAREHOUSE STRATEGIC PLAN

The warehouse strategic plan is directed at accomplishing two overall objectives. The first is to align the resources of the warehouse with the enterprise's long-term supply chain goals. A warehouse strategy cannot be developed in a vacuum but can only have meaning in relation to and support of the strategies of the firm's other business functions. Examples of warehouse strategies would be consolidating a national channel of satellite warehouses into a regional distribution center, building new storage facilities or acquiring new material handling equipment, and determining the percentage of warehousing that should be owned and how much should be contracted from third parties. Second, an effective strategy must forecast future company warehouse requirements so that resources can be acquired in time to meet these requirements. Without such plans, the warehouse will be periodically subjected to executing costly ad hoc solutions that are always detrimental to the overall health of the enterprise. A critical part of the strategy is the development of realistic contingency plans. Contingency planning attempts to provide solutions for possible circumstances beyond the control and estimates of strategic planners. Without a comprehensive contingency plan, the warehouse strategy risks being subjected to unanticipated problems for which there is no solution and which will eventually render the warehouse strategy ineffectual.

Similar to other business areas, the warehouse strategy should be expressed as a formal document detailing what goals are to be accomplished and how they are to be attained over a given planning period. Each of the stated goals should consist of: (1) statement of business requirements, (2) an inventory of existing warehousing assets, (3) business justification for the acquisition of any new warehousing equipment, (4) detailed description of new buildings, material handling equipment, information technologies, and operations, including diagrams or blue prints, (5) required support resources, (6) narrative of organizational changes/impacts, (7) detailed implementation plan, and (8) project capitalization and expected ROI. If possible, each goal should have a detailed implementation plan. Besides establishing project timelines and budgets, the plan should specify each activity, activity dependencies, and responsible roles. The plan should also include clear performance measurements that can provide feedback to management indicating the relative success or failure of the warehouse organization in attaining stated objectives. Finally, an effective warehouse strategy should be bounded by a defined planning horizon. Most strategic plans are typically formulated in years, with a minimum of a quarterly review. A strategic due date gives meaning to detailed activities and provides the whole organization with a recognizable goal to target their efforts.

Tompkins [5] feels that an effective methodology for developing a warehouse strategy consists of the following seven steps:

1. *Document existing warehouse operations.* This step consists of two separate elements. The first is concerned with documenting existing warehouse facilities, cataloging warehouse equipment and capacities, and establishing labor resources by department. The objective is to confirm the nature of these resources and an accurate assessment of

their estimated capacities. The second part of this step involves performing an operations diagnostic, first on each resource and then on the general information and material flows in the entire warehouse. A complete business diagnostics will reveal areas where actual practice deviates from the established standard procedure.

2. *Determine and document the warehouse storage and throughput requirements over the specified planning horizon.* This step requires planners to forecast which products and in what volumes is anticipated to be stocked in the warehouse over the planning horizon. In developing the estimate, planners must be specific as to the impact on existing material handling equipment and available storage space. Ideally, the product forecast should be in terms of unit weight and/or cube to assist in warehouse analysis.

3. *Identify and document deficiencies in existing warehouse operations.* One of the outputs from the operations diagnostics described in *Step 1* is documentation of areas of waste and redundancy that inhibit productivity. Once these processes have been identified, a project can be initiated to eliminate them. However, operations diagnostics might also reveal that critical activities are being performed inefficiently due to a lack of equipment or labor resources. Once documented, warehouse management can use the findings as a basis for the acquisition of the necessary capacity.

4. *Identify and document alternative warehouse plans.* Once deficiencies in storage space, equipment, or labor have been identified in *Step 3*, management must develop a plan that satisfies requirements by determining possible alternatives. One solution might be to expand capacities by acquiring additional resources. Another might be to explore the possibility of using rented equipment, temporary help, or public storage facilities.

5. *Evaluate alternative warehouse plans.* Once alternative warehouse plans have been formulated, each must undergo rigorous financial analysis. Among the financial measurement used are capitalization, cost/benefit justification, after-tax current asset evaluation, and return on investment. In addition to an economic analysis, the proposed plans must also be modeled against business, product, and marketplace objectives detailed in the business plan.

6. *Select the recommended solution.* Based on the results of the financial and business evaluation, the desired plan will be selected. These plans will, in turn, be mapped according to the five elements of the strategic planning process described above. Plans will consist of detailed descriptions of proposed warehouse storage, equipment, personnel, and operating standards objectives for the forthcoming planning horizon.

7. *Update the warehouse strategic plan.* Like all other corporate and business function strategies, the warehouse strategy is not a static, but rather a dynamic document that will change as the circumstances of the marketplace and the competition change. Because it is founded on aggregate forecasts of the future, the warehouse strategy will always require updating as more accurate information about products, customers, and competitors is revealed. As such, warehouse planners must meet at least yearly, preferably quarterly, to review the viability of the strategic plan and to weigh the impact of future requirements.

THE PRIVATE, PUBLIC, AND CONTRACT WAREHOUSE DECISION

One of the most critical components of the warehouse strategy is determining what the mix should be between private, public, and contract warehousing. In may ways this decision is reminiscent of the make-buy conundrum. Should the company spend the capital resources to have its own warehousing facilities and all the synergies and conveniences ownership provides, or should the firm outsource the function to public and contract warehouses? And again, how much control over such a critical logistics area do companies want to surrender to third parties? Whether private or public, either decision involves certain definite risks in handling a wide-range of issues from the financial well-being to how customers grappling with the realities of satisfying customer demand.

While there are some industry sectors, particularly in the e-business environment, that are "virtual" companies and exclusively use public warehousing, most manufacturers and distributors maintain to some extent their own warehouses. The objective of these facilities is to ensure that the company has the capacity to provide inventories for normal production and customer demand. For the most part, full utilization of the typical private warehouse throughout the year is a remote possibility. According to Bowersox and Close [6], most warehouses will in fact be fully utilized only between 75 and 85 percent of the time. Thus 25 percent of the time or less, the capacities of most private warehouses should be sufficient to handle inventory handling requirements.

The problem occurs, however, when certain peak periods require warehousing functions that exceed available private warehouse capacities. Such oc-casions could be driven by events such as product seasonality, new product introduction, promotions, temporary regional demand requirements, or planned plant shut-down. In solving this problem warehouse planners will have to devise a strategy that seeks to utilize a combination of private, public, and contract facilities. For example, it may be decided that temporary warehousing should be contracted to provide coverage during a peak season. Or again, the strategy may be to utilize private warehouses as distribution hubs, with public or contract warehouses used to service regional requirements. A final example may find the use of private warehousing to be more cost effective when the distribution volume is great enough, but will use public and contract services in other markets if they are the least-cost option.

With the rise of the Internet economy and the dramatic shrinkages in product and delivery life cycles, companies have over the past decade been turning to the use of public warehousing to provide a level of service value unreachable through the exclusive use of private warehousing. Two critical warehousing attributes come to mind: *flexibility* and *synergies*. Requirements for the quick delivery of often short-cycle products have placed a premium on the flexibility of companies to bring goods to the marketplace as quickly as possible. Outsourcing permits companies to quickly adjust the number and location of channel warehouses to meet all forms of demand. In addition, public facilities may offer rapid access to material handling or information management tools required at short notice. Public warehousing also provides companies with the opportunity to leverage synergy benefits. By contracting with public facilities that service a wide industry, such as grocery or consumer goods, companies can utilize their expertise to decrease transportation and material handling costs while leveraging a high level of flexibility and responsiveness.

COMPONENTS OF THE COMPLETED WAREHOUSE STRATEGY

The goal of the warehouse strategy is to communicate in clear and unequivocal terms the objectives to be pursued by the warehouse. Often the warehouse function is treated as if it were an outside resource that can be optimized to meet with a minimum of planning the ever-changing requirements of supply chain sales and service. Such a viewpoint results in managers considering a company's warehousing capabilities as if they were a variable resource that instantly expands or contracts to meet variances occurring as a result of changes in the marketplace or product supply. In such an environment, warehouse managers, whose goals are not well defined, are condemned to an endless and non-productive game of attempting to please everyone in the enterprise with the result that they please no one.

An effective warehouse strategy needs to be accompanied by a *warehouse charter* that has arisen out of the strategic planning process and defines in detail the content of the often opposing poles of warehouse operating efficiency and customer service. The warehouse charter should contain the following elements:

1. Clear statement of organizational and reporting structures
2. Performance metrics detailing targeted operating objectives
3. Authority to acquire capital equipment
4. Ability of management to hire, fire, and develop staff
5. Valid operating standards for all warehouse activities
6. Valid space utilization standards and performance measurements for products and storage facilities
7. Clear service standards and performance measurements for all warehouse functions

The warehouse charter is the document that ensures that warehouse objectives are in alignment with both detailed strategies for marketing, sales, procurement, traffic, and accounting and well as general supply chain objectives. The warehousing function is a unique part of the company, charged with the task of managing a complex set of inventory and delivery management activities all of which will determine the degree of success of the plans formulated by upstream departments. The more the warehouse can be managed to the targets established in the warehouse strategy, the more dependable and efficient the warehouse will be. Conversely, as poor enterprise planning and communication increase knee-jerk reactions on the part of the warehouse, the less performance targets and efficiencies will be achieved [7].

THE WAREHOUSE MANAGEMENT PROCESS

The development of effective warehousing strategies enables supply chain planners to successfully execute warehouse management activities. For most companies, warehousing involves a number of functions ranging from product receipt to order shipment. In responding to these activities, warehouse managers must find answers to such questions as follows:

- What size should the warehouse be to respond to desired customer service levels?
- How many warehouses should there be in the channel to handle expected demand?
- What is the cost of running each warehouse in the channel?
- How many employees are required to efficiently run each warehouse?
- What capacities are required of equipment to handle expected demand volumes?
- What should stock receiving, put-away and picking rates be?
- Are packing and docking capacities sufficient to achieve shipment targets?
- Are current information systems capable of providing each warehouse with the necessary data on a timely and accurate basis?

- What should be the performance measurements to ensure each warehouse is achieving optimal efficiency and productivity?

Responding effectively to these and other questions is the objective of the warehouse management process. As illustrated in Figure 11.3, this process consists of four major activities that must be clearly defined if the warehouse is to work effectively and efficiently.

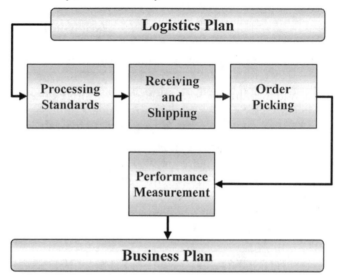

FIGURE 11.3 Warehouse management process.

The first activity in the warehouse management process is determining the process standards for labor, equipment, and storage performance. Operational standards are the pillars of warehouse management and they enable the enterprise to chart in detail overall warehouse processing performance and productivity. Historically, operations standards have been broken down into three broad categories, the sum of which constitutes the statement of warehouse capacity. *Efficiency* measures how well actual activities were performed against the standard times and costs assigned to perform them. For example, a picking standard can be defined as the actual number of lines picked in an hour's time against how many lines should have been picked (Figure 11.4). *Utilization* attempts to measure how much of a warehouse resource was actually used to perform a task against the standard capacity that is available. Comparing the number of hours in a day a picking team actually has available against the number of attendance hours provides an example (Figure 11.5). The standard capacity of an operation can be calculated by combining the number of operators, number of shifts, standard available working hours, the utilization and the efficiency (Figure 11.6).

I. Standard Hours per Bin Picker (6 person crew)

Standard available hours = 6 Pickers x 7 hrs = 42 hrs per day
Standard lines picked per hour per picker = 60 lines
Standard lines picked (per day) = 42 x 60 = 2,520.

II. Demonstrated Picking (per day)

2,520 Lines picked in 39 hours

III. Picking Efficiency Calculation (Picking Crew)

$$Eff = \frac{\text{Std hrs per day}}{\text{Demonstrated hrs}} = \frac{42}{39} = \underline{\textbf{108\%}}$$

FIGURE 11.4 Efficiency calculation.

Warehouse standards can be defined using a number of methods. The first, *historical standards*, is a technique whereby a firm will calculate an average time to perform activities by compiling actual time past work records for a designated period. The disadvantage of using this technique is that standards

I. Capacity Available for Picking Team

Capacity = # Pickers x Daily Hours Available
Capacity = 6 x 7 hrs/per picker = **42** hours

II. Demonstrated Daily Hours Used

Total Hours Used = **40** hours

III. Utilization Calculation

$$U = \frac{\text{Demonstrated Hours}}{\text{Available Hours}} = \frac{40}{42} = \underline{\textbf{95\%}}$$

FIGURE 11.5 Utilization calculation.

are compiled from actual times recorded to perform activities as opposed to the time it should have taken. If the warehouse has poor work habits, these subpar practices will become the standard. Another method is to use *pre-determined standards* published by professional organizations like the U.S. Department of Defense or WERC. These measurements suffer from the same deficiencies as historical standards. A third method consists in a firm performing its own time and work study analysis and determining standards based on the results. By observing and recording the time and motion required to perform tasks, a series of detailed performance standards can be determined. The final method that can be used to develop warehouse standards is through the use of *multiple regression analysis*. This technique seeks to calculate a

I. Data Elements (Picking Team of 6)

Shifts = 2
Picking Team = 6 pickers
Hours Available = 7 hrs
Efficiency = 108%
Utilization = 95%

II. Picking Team Calculation

Cap = 2 x 6 x 7 x 95% x 108% = **86** hrs available per day

FIGURE 11.6 Picking team capacity calculation.

work standard by combining actual work content with the associated values impacting the activity. For example, the time required to pick a given quantity of a given item is not a straight equation but one that utilizes a weighing factor such as the item weight, number of cases, transport capacities and other issues. A simple example is provided in Figure 11.7.

Standard = 60 lines in 1 hour

If weight is greater than 200 lbs	x .10 hr
If cube is greater than 50 ft	x .05 hr
If picking area exceeds 250 ft	x .25 hr
If material is manually picked	x .15 hr
Utilization = 95%	

FIGURE 11.7 Simple multiple regression technique.

Operational and resource capacity standards are necessary for the smooth and efficient functioning of the warehouse. Effective standards enable the warehouse to execute the following critical functions:

1. *Resource availability.* Warehouse standards provide managers with metrics detailing the capacities of labor, equipment, and facilities. These capacity standards form the basis for all subsequent warehouse planning.
2. *Scheduling.* The ability to schedule warehouse resources is critical to actualizing performance targets. Effective scheduling begins by establishing the standard capacity resource profiles of the various operational and storage elements in the warehouse. Next, the resource requirements necessary to accomplish activities such as receiving, stock put-away, picking, packing, and shipping need to be determined. Once these elements are known, warehouse management can then develop an everyday schedule designed to match resources with warehouse requirements. For example, if an order filler can pick sixty lines an hour and the projected load of lines to be picked for a seven hour day equals 4200, the production manager must schedule ten pickers to be avail-

able. Schedules can also assist warehouse managers plan for work backlog. By calculating the resources necessary to satisfy a backlog condition, a plan can be formulated to increase capacities by scheduling overtime, using part-time workers, or outsourcing alternatives. Comparable steps would be taken to handle capacity constraints caused by seasonality.

3. *Problem identification.* The availability of detailed standards can significantly assist warehouse managers improve productivity. Standards will pinpoint efficiency and utilization problems in the warehouse and permit managers to redistribute resources to meet requirements. The real focus of problem identification is to seek out the source of why the problem is occurring in the first place, and then to eliminate it.

4. *Continuous improvement.* Standards also form the basis for all quality programs targeted at continuous improvement. The goal is to remove all forms of waste in the process. Once standards have been defined, management can decrease the standard by a given percentage and see where the bottleneck develops. The object then is to solve the bottleneck, revise the standard, and begin the process all over again. Continuous improvement is the most effective way to reduce warehouse costs while maintaining the same level of service.

5. *Costing.* The selling price of a product can be generally defined as cost plus a percent margin over the cost. The cost, in turn, can be broken down into the cost of product acquisition, direct labor associated with material movement, and fixed and variable overheads associated with a wide range of support operations and other burdened costs. When deter-mining selling prices, it is absolutely necessary that the firm know the exact content of operations cost. When the exact cost is uncertain, companies run the risk of retaining less profit than planned or missing opportunities to achieve price leadership opportunities in the marketplace.

RECEIVING AND SHIPPING FUNCTIONS

The receipt and shipment of products define the input and output boundaries of warehouse activities. Warehousing's accountability for product storage and record accuracy begins when products are received; this accountability ends when those products are shipped to the customer. Understanding each of these functions can perhaps best be achieved by defining and examining the operational activities of each. *Receiving* has been defined as that activity concerned with the orderly receipt of all materials coming into the warehouse, the necessary activities to ensure that the quantity and quality of such materials are as ordered, and the disbursement of the materials to the organizational functions requiring them.

The primary objectives of the receiving function can be described as follows:
- Safe and efficient unloading of carriers
- Prompt and accurate processing of receipts
- Maintenance of accurate records detailing receiving activities
- Timely disbursement of receipts to stocking locations in preparation for picking and shipping [8].

In order to ensure receiving accuracy and the timely processing of necessary documentation, it is imperative that the receiving process be formalized. A conventional receiving flow is illustrated in Figure 11.8. Even before the

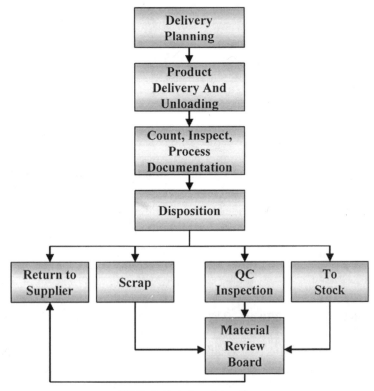

FIGURE 11.8 Receiving flow.

shipment has left the supplier, it is receiving's responsibility, with purchasing's assistance, to plan for the delivery by determining the arrival date and time, the type and quantity of material to be received, the availability of docking and material handling capacities, and preparation of staging areas.

After the carrier arrives and is unloaded, receiving's next step is to unpack, identify, sort, inspect, count, and verify receipts against purchase order and receiving documentation. Following this step, receiving should then post the receipt. For most companies, this is done through a computer terminal which automatically marks the purchase order as completed, posts the inventory to stock, records quality control inspection data and supplier performance statistics, and provides, if necessary, for the scrap or return to supplier of the receipt. Often bar code reading equipment is utilized that significantly assists in item and quantity identification. Included is the completion of documentation noting shortages, overages, and damaged goods. Finally, product is then disbursed to the appropriate stocking or holding area.

In contrast to receiving, *shipping* can be defined as

> those activities performed to ensure the accurate and damage free packaging, marking, weighing and loading of finished goods, raw materials, and components in response to customer order requirements in as cost effective and as expeditious a manner as possible.

The primary objectives of shipping are as follows:
- Efficient receipt and handling of picked orders
- Prompt and accurate checking of order quantities and ship-to information
- Efficient packaging/packing of orders in a manner that will prevent damage, reduce handling costs, and facilitate delivery
- Selection of a carrier that will best deliver the order at the minimum cost
- Development of an effective schedule of docking and loading facilities that eliminates outbound shipment bottlenecks and optimizes labor and equipment availabilities
- Maintenance of shipping documentation that expedites order delivery and permits performance measurement

As illustrated in Figure 11.9, the first step is the selection and scheduling of the common and private carriers to be used to transport products to the customer. There are a multitude of types of carriers, ranging from couriers and taxicabs to barges, the U.S. Postal Service, and United Parcel Service (UPS). In selecting carriers, key attributes such as speed of delivery, scheduling flexibility, service consistency, security, reliability, electronic tracing, and cooperation should be considered. The second step is to design an efficient picked goods staging area. Such an area should facilitate the storage of picked orders and promote the timely and accurate selection of orders for packaging/packing. Once the order has been packed, another staging area is needed to store orders for loading. Included in this step is the final quality check of the order, processing of the shipment record, and the preparation of the necessary packing lists, bills of lading, and documents specifying any special marking (bar codes and hazardous materials labels), loading, and delivery information. The next step involves the physical loading of orders on to the carrier, acknowledgment by the driver of accountability, and sometimes the sealing of the storage vehicle. Finally, shipping documentation is disbursed or entered into the computer for delivery follow-up and performance measurement.

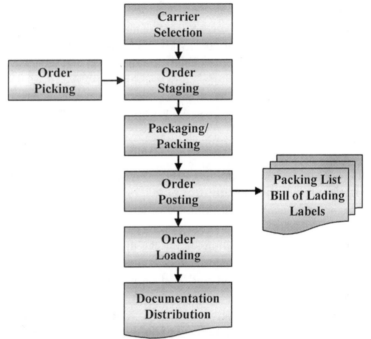

FIGURE 11.9 Shipping flow.

During the past several years, receiving and shipping functions have been profoundly impacted by changes in equipment and management philosophies. The first of these changes has occurred with the development of longer, wider trailers. Due to changes in federal regulations, permissible trailer width capacity has increased from 96 to 102 inches and length from 45 to 48 feet. These new dimensions might require some warehouses to increase their delivery areas and storage yards. The growing use of JIT and cross-docking has also reoriented warehousing away from a traditional concern with picking and storage and toward increased attention to facilitating receiving and shipping activities to achieve maximum product flow through. A third area can be found in the implementation of computers, bar code scanners, radio frequency (RF), wireless technologies, and vehicle tracking networks. These technology tools have allowed for improvements in document preparation, product identification, and work (labor and equipment) scheduling. The final trend changing receiving and shipping is the application of new unloading and loading equipment, such as dock levers, automatic unloading systems, mobile warehouse equipment, and conveyor equipment. Equipment changes have resulted in increasing the flexibility of receiving and shipping departments to handle a wide variety of transportation loads and improving safety, product flow, and warehouse labor productivity.

ORDER PICKING

The third step in the warehouse management process is order picking and management. The picking of inventory to fill customer and manufacturing order requirements is perhaps the most important function of warehousing. The enterprise stocks finished goods to be able to respond to marketplace demand and components and raw materials to ensure manufacturing always has the necessary inventory to build products. It is the responsibility of the warehouse to fill customer and manufacturing orders within the smallest cycle time possible with perfect accuracy. For the most part, order picking is the most labor-intensive and expensive of all warehouse functions. Although automation has greatly assisted in shrinking direct labor content, order picking largely remains a manual activity, requiring significant planning, supervising, quality review, computerized support tools, and management direction. The failure to effectively pick orders can have a dramatic effect on the whole enterprise. For example, it has been estimated that the cost of an inaccurately filled customer order is $10 to $60 not to mention the potential of losing customers due to poor service. In addition, order processing and delivery that is not competitive places the firm at risk of losing business to more efficiently organized rivals.

Actual order picking can be described as taking three forms. In the first, *manual picking*, the picking operation is performed by teams that either walk or operate from a vehicle and pick inventory as determined by paper picking lists or computerized visual displays. The second type of picking, *automated picking*, utilizes computer-controlled systems to retrieve inventory from each picking location, in the quantity and at the time specified to meet order demand. The third type of picking consists of a *combination of manual and automated picking* driven by the nature of demand, the product, and the availability of picking equipment. In addition, there are two order picking routing patterns. The first, *nonsequential,* is characterized by the fact that picking routes are completely random and determined by the random arrangement of the order lines. This method is not recommended. The second, *sequential*, is characterized by the use of several sequencing methods that seek to increase picker productivity, reduce picking time, and reduce picker fatigue by routing the picker level by level down a storage aisle, improve picking location density, and ensure fast-moving products are up front and close to shipping. Some sequential routing techniques are loop, horseshoe, Z, block, stitch, vertical or horizontal, and zone.

Regardless of the automation and the picking technique, most order-picking operations are governed by the three methods detailed below.

- *Unit Load.* In this method, the nature of the product permits the picker to fill the order requirement by pulling a full pallet/container load from stock. An example would be a refrigerator distributor who stocks each product one-per-pallet. This method of picking lends itself best to automated forms of picking.
- *Case Lot.* Often products are pulled to fill orders in full cases only. Case-lot quantities can be stored on a shelf or on a pallet, depending on the order point and replenishment quantities. Although this method can be automated, for the most part it requires manual picking.
- *Broken Case.* This method is used by companies that allow picking quantities in less than full case-lot quantities. Again, this method of picking can be done from a shelf, pallet, or other form of storage unit. This method is very difficult to automate and is almost exclusively a manual operation.

Due to the variances in packaging, product characteristics, required quantities, space availability, and on-hand quantities, warehouses often use a hybrid of these methods.

In addition to the method, the way the picking order is controlled will have an impact on warehouse operations. When *discrete order picking* is used, pickers must fill all the open lines of an order before the next order is begun. Often this means that the filler must pass through multiple storage zones to complete the order. The advantage of discrete order picking is that it maintains order integrity throughout the picking process, works well when the number of items to be picked is small, is simple to execute and easy to control, eliminates excess handling, provides fast customer service, and facilitates quality auditing and establishes direct fill responsibility. Disadvantages include the time required for the picker to traverse the entirety of the warehouse, increasing inefficiency as order size grows, and requirements for a large order filling staff. In contrast, when *batch picking* is used, order requirements are aggregated by product, the summary quantity of the product withdrawn, and the pick located at a consolidation area. In the final step, the discrete identity of the order is reassembled in the consolidation area and then shipped to the customer or moved to the production line. The advantages to batch picking are that it reduces travel and fill times to pick individual products, permits volume picking from bulk storage, and improves supervision by concentrating order completion at the consolidation point. Disadvantages include double handling and sorting in the consolidation area, the allocation of space and labor for the consolidation area, loss of order integrity until consolidation occurs, and difficulty in tracing primary accountability for order line items picked.

A variation on the above methods is the use of *zone picking*. In this technique, picking is oriented around families of products inventoried in specific storage zones. Basically, order pickers are printed at the zone where order fillers pick the zone complete. Three possible zone configurations can be utilized:

- *Serial Zones.* In a fixed-zone picking route, order pickers must follow a prescribed zone sequence. As an order is completed in one zone it is conveyed to the successor zone by use of a cart or conveyor system.
- *Parallel Zones.* In a variable-zone picking route, the filler picks from independent zones, located, for example, on either side of the picking aisle. The picker subsequently can choose to fill orders in a sequence of zones. Finally, the a consolidation point can be used to reassemble the order for shipment for movement to the manufacturing line.
- *Serial/Parallel Zones.* This arrangement permits the existence of number of serial zones arranged in a parallel configuration.

The advantages of using zone picking techniques are that they establish good work standards, increase picking accuracy and productivity, reduce damage and errors, and increase shipping container utilization due to close picker familiarity with zone specific products. Disadvantages are that the techniques require high-volume picking, increase the requirement for management control, and interzone queues slow down other pickers. Zone picking is especially useful for distributors who normally pick products in family groups. It is particularly applicable to storage areas utilizing flow racks.

Often post-order-picking activities involve picking location replenishment. This function is used when products are stored in fixed forward locations with floating reserves. Normally, each product in a forward location has some form of minimum quantity that, once triggered, alerts the planning system. Modern computer systems not only keep track of inventory levels but also generate a picker that can be used by stock personnel to retrieve reserve product and move it to the assigned forward location. Replenishment activities include picking the required quantity of material from the reserve location on schedule, transporting it to the proper forward location, and positioning it in the pick location.

In designing an effective picking system, warehouse management must take into consideration a number of key factors. One of the most important is how the stock location system has been defined. Is the warehouse arranged by fixed location, random storage, fixed forward locations resupplied by a reserve stored in bulk locations, or a combination of methods? Another key factor is fitting the picking system to meet customer-quoted lead times. Besides these factors, another surrounds the acquisition of picking equipment. New types of storage racks or bins, construction of mezzanines, picker vehicles, carrousels, conveyors, computer-controlled stacker cranes, and a host of other equipment can impact picking system design. Before embarking on a new picking system, warehouse managers must thoroughly research its impact on the organization, costs of equipment and labor, and a detailed implementation program. In any case, a new picking system must always be focused on cutting wastes in the process while improving picking accuracies.

PERFORMANCE MEASUREMENT

The final step in the warehouse management process is establishing detailed performance measurements. Warehouse performance metrics have three objectives:
1. They enable management to formulate a clear, quantitative statement of the performance standards to be achieved by the warehouse. These standards can then be used as a benchmark guiding daily activity execution and continuous improvement.
2. They enable managers to chart how effectively warehouse activities are being performed to standard. Because the rest of the organization depends on the warehouse to execute receiving, storing, picking, and shipping functions up to stated efficiency targets, performance measures demonstrate the degree to which the warehouse is responding to enterprise operational needs.
3. They assist managers and associates in pinpointing problems that inhibit productivity so that constructive steps can be taken to eliminate the problem from reoccurring.

Performance measurements provide companies with a means to plan and control the significant variances experienced by the warehouse. The randomness of customer demand, customer service commitments, rush shipments, special marking or packaging, equipment capacities, the environment, and a host of other factors can disrupt normal throughput and require detailed planning and control if the warehouse is to remain productive.

Performance measurement programs work best when designed as a closed-loop system. Actual work is reported against the performance method, and the input and output is analyzed. The results can then be used to enable an improvement initiative, which then communicates directly into work planning and scheduling. Whether a change in the standard has occurred or not, this standard needs to be communicated to warehouse employees as a guide to subsequent work activity. For a performance measurements system to function properly, it must be valid, accurate, complete, cost-effective, and timely. Without these components, the measurements system will generate misleading data and cause managers to formulate false conclusions and execute invalid corrective actions.

There are essentially five warehouse performance measurements. The first, *throughput*, refers to the volume of product storage and retrieval transactions that can be accomplished in a given unit of time. A particular performance measurement might be the percentage of received pallets that can be put away in a day's time. If the standard was set at 98%, then performance metrics could be calculated by dividing the number of actual pallets put away against the standard. Other possible throughput measurements are deliveries unloaded, receipts checked in, orders picked, orders packed, and orders loaded. The next two metrics, *order filling* and *shipping accuracy* are determined by calculating the ratio of actual work outputs to standards. Order filling can be based on a number of criteria such as lines filled without error, orders filled without error, and orders filled on time. Shipping accuracy can be determined by comparing lines packed accurately, total orders packed completely, orders packed and shipped on time, and incidence of packing damage.

As opposed to the previous measurements, the third critical warehouse metric, *inventory record accuracy,* is more difficult to measure. Because of the sheer number of products to control and the size of the warehouse, ensuring inventory accuracy is a full-time role in many firms. The traditional approach is to take a year-end physical inventory. Except for the compilation of accounting measurements, however, this method has no value, and should be replaced by *cycle counting*. As detailed in Chapter 5, cycle counting methods not only are essential for maintaining record accuracy, but of more importance, they provide managers with a means of isolating errors and devising the appropriate action to be taken to eliminate the error from reoccurring. In determining record accuracy, the following formula should be used:

$$\text{Inventory accuracy} = \frac{\text{Physical count} - \text{Record balance}}{\text{Physical count}} \times 100.$$

Another possible method would be to compile inventory accuracy based on a predetermined accuracy target. The formula for this method would be

$$\text{Inventory accuracy} = \frac{\text{\# of items at or exceeding target}}{\text{Total number of items}} \times 100.$$

The final warehouse performance area focuses on *storage utilization*. Many companies neglect to analyze storage space, assuming that plant and equipment are fixed assets and, therefore, the responsibility of accounting. However, as Jenkins points out [9], the burdened cost of one warehouse employee is roughly equivalent to the cost of leasing 10,000 square feet of storage. As such, metrics that assist managers to effectively utilize and evaluate storage is a critical part of overall warehouse performance. The first step in defining storage utilization is to define storage standards. This can be done easily by noting the various types of storage in the warehouse, and then calculating the total capacity available by type and in total. A commonly used measurement unit is cubic feet. As an example, one storage type consists of shelf racks four feet high, four feet deep and eight feet long. The available cube of this space would be 128 cubic feet (4x4x8). The next step would be to determine the storage requirements of every product in the stockable inventory by calculating the cubic space required for the stocking unit of measure multiplied by the total inventory storage requirement. By matching aggregate storage requirements to capacities, planners can determine the percentage of warehouse utilization. In addition, storage metrics can assist managers to review existing procedures, material handling, and storage types with an eye toward optimizing the warehouse by developing new storage techniques as well as rearranging current designs.

The success of warehouse performance measurements depends on the same principles that characterize measurements in other enterprise functions. Effective warehouse measurements include the following principles:

1. *Simplicity.* Because performance metrics are really targeted at warehouse employees, they should be clear and easy to understand. Everyone should know why the measurements exist, how the measurements are calculated, what the results indicate, and what their role in achieving performance targets is.

2. *Goal oriented.* Performance measurements should not only chart the performance of each individual warehouse department and the warehouse as a whole, but they should also clearly illustrate the goals and progress toward goals. This principle provides visual evidence for everyone in the warehouse on how well performance standards are being met. Figure 11.10 provides an example of a graph illustrating on-time delivery.

3. *Standards consistency.* Constant changes in measurements destroy standards integrity and render performance goals meaningless. When too many modifications are made, warehouse associates may feel they are trying to hit a moving target that changes as the whims of management change. Such distrust will negate the purpose for performance measurement.

Category	Month (Apr.) Avg.	12 Month Avg.	Year-to-Date
Orders Shipped	1,985	1,992	1,981
Avg. Lines per Order	3	4	4
Total Items per Order	5,955	7,968	7,924
Orders Shipped on Time	1,883	1,880	1,795
Performance	95%	94%	90.5%

FIGURE 11.10 Warehouse reporting.

4. *Punishment.* Performance measurements should *never* be used as a basis to discipline employees. Effective measurements depend on employee cooperation. When measurements are used as a source of punishment, operators will always find ways to report data that portrays the information as favorable when, in reality, the metrics are unfavorable.

5. *Continuous improvement.* The best performance measurements will provide warehouse managers and associates with quantifiable information to assist in the development of plant, procedures, processes, and policies that will lead to continuous elimination of wastes and impedements to productivity.

TRENDS IN MODERN WAREHOUSING

Similar to other aspects of manufacturing and distributing at the dawn of the twenty-first century, the science and practice of warehousing has undergone fundamental change. The ongoing economic recession, anti-terrorist legislation and fears about security, continued globalization, and the enabling power of the Internet have blurred long-standing principles and changed the purpose of the warehousing function. In the past, warehousing's prime role was to serve as a buffer between supply and demand. Through intricate structures of producers, wholesalers, and retailers, goods were stockpiled at various points in the channel network to service customers and provide buffer supplies against seasonality, promotions, lot-size production, transportation efficiencies, and variances in marketplace demand. The goal of the warehouse channel structure was to have product available to the customer at the right place and time, and at an appropriate trade-off cost to channel partners.

Today's challenges are now requiring fundamental revision of these long-standing perceptions of the role and function of warehousing. In responding to these new operational realities, a whole new set of questions must be answered by logistics management:

- Has the firm developed a comprehensive warehousing strategy?
- Has this strategy been integrated with the goals of the supply chain systems and technologies in which they participate?
- Should the number of warehouses in the channel be expanded or reduced?
- What should be the mix of public and private warehouses?
- How are supplier relations impacting warehouse requirements?
- What opportunities are available for international warehousing?
- What opportunities for customer service and cost reduction are being offered by new information technologies like the Internet and automatic identification?
- How is the level of inventory in the pipeline to be continually decreased while customer service is continually increased?

Enterprises capable of finding answers to these questions and integrating them with effective warehousing strategies will be those that will maintain and expand competitive advantage. In order to better understand warehousing in the 2000s, it will perhaps be helpful to divide them into three groups: nature of warehousing, technology applications, and channel alliances and partnerships.

NATURE OF MODERN WAREHOUSING

A preoccupation with operational and current asset costs is expected to remain as the critical focal point of warehousing in the twenty-first century. During the mid-1990s it was projected that the implementation of Lean concepts, the subsequent streamlining of operational procedures, and the application of new technologies would result in a decrease in warehouse cost. Overall, however, the changes brought about by technologies and management practices designed to cut warehousing costs have been generally offset by requirements of dealing with demand and supply in the Internet Age. Warehouse costs have remained fairly constant over the past nine years and reflect approximately the same percentage of total logistics costs. For example, the total cost of warehousing in 1993 was set at $60 billion and constituted about 9 percent of total logistics costs for that year. In 1996, the figures stood at $67 billion and reflected an 8.4% of total logistics costs. In 2001, the figures stood at $78 billion and accounted for 8 percent of total logistics costs [10].

While it is true that companies of all types believe that large inventories are not only unnecessary but are actually detrimental to the health of the enterprise, market and geopolictal forces have been requiring companies to stock more inventory and not less. At the end of the 1990s managers, analysts and consultant alike strove hard to pursue Lean inventory strategies and consolidate distribution centers in an effort to cut costs and accelerate channel throughput. In reality, warehouse space stands at an all time high and, according to the Colography Group "there's more square footage of warehouse space than at any point in U.S history." This sentiment is corroborated by public warehouse provider ProLogis that showed in a study that warehouse space increased to 3.4 billion square feet in 2002, up from some 3.1 billion in 2000 [11].

Warehousing Strategies at Best Buy

Best Buy, the U.S. largest consumer electronics retailer, has gone to great lengths to minimize response time when a need is identified in a store. Although it is a national retailer, it relies heavily on a regional distribution strategy. It has strategically positioned six general merchandize distribution centers around the country, with a seventh to open in the first half of 2003, to provide direct service to its chain of 538 stores, as well as retail outlets Sam Goody, Suncoast, and Media Play.

The company also distributes media such as CDs and DVDs from a dedicated entertainment facility in the Midwest. In addition, it operates several other DCs dedicated to large-ticket items such as appliances and big-screen TVs where deliveries are cross-docked, and sent to stores or directly to the customer.

To guarantee delivery, Best Buy uses a dedicated fleet through a long-term agreement with a truckload (TL) carrier that picks up product from suppliers and delivers to stores on a twice-weekly basis. It will also use contract carriers as needed or to service a select market.

Source: Jedd, Marcia, "The regional Difference," *DC Velocity*, 1, 1, (2003), pp. 62-65.

Several reasons can be shown for this slightly upward trend in warehouse space and cost. One is the threat to inventory supplies caused by such factors as the possibility of terrorist attacks on supply lines and the resulting significant increase in lead times due to the growing complexity of security, customs, and inspection requirements. Other events such as the U.S. West coast dock strike in 2002 and the outbreaks of SARS have shown the fragility of JIT/Lean practices. Both factors have forced logistics managers to replace a strategy dependent on large consolidation warehouses with the deployment of a greater number of much smaller regional distribution centers that are much closer to the customer. Another factor is the growing popularity of distribution "pull" philosophies whereby stock replenishment is triggered by field demand, rather than "pushed" from consolidation warehouses in response to promotions. This view requires warehouses be much closer to the actual point of sale. All in all, warehousing in the immediate future will be characterized by a growing trend that seeks to optimize strategically located supply points supported by short-haul distribution.

TECHNOLOGY APPLICATIONS

Whereas the type and location criteria of the warehouse of the future are expected to change, so is the level of automation and use of information technologies. The reason for this projected growth is attributed to several factors, the foremost of which are the following:

- Declining costs of warehouse automation
- Increased cost of labor and associated overheads
- Much closer demand for supply chain integration and collaboration
- Value-added philosophies stressing continuous elimination of operational wastes and redundancies
- Requirements for shorter purchasing and customer service cycle times.

The different forms of warehouse automation are illustrated in Figure 11.11. While each area is expressed equally, the biggest impact of technology growth is expected not so much in the installation of material handling equipment but in computerized tools that increase workstation capabilities or automate material movement information. These results are in concert with current thinking about the warehouse, emphasizing the prioritization of the enterprise's knowledge base over material handling mechanization. Indeed, the over-all goal of automation seems not so much to be on moving product in the warehouse but rather in how to engineer sales, marketing, and supply chain objectives so that the need for physical handling becomes obsolete and storage gives way to direct delivery from producer to consumer.

One particular method that significantly facilitates the movement of goods through the distribution pipeline is *cross-docking*. Cross-docking can be defined as a method of moving products from the receiving dock to shipping without putting it into storage. Typically, arriving merchandize is broken down into case or pallet loads, then quickly moved across the warehouse to the shipping dock where they are then loaded onto trucks bound for the next level in the distribution pipeline. Technology tools such as computers, bar codes, radio frequency (RF), and EDI have facilitated the case and pallet

FIGURE 11.11 Forms of warehouse automation.

shuffling required to make cross-docking feasible. There are two fundamental goals driving distributors' interest in cross-docking. The first centers on ways to eliminate handling, storage costs, shrinkage, damage, and product obsolescence. The second is to reduce cycle time and get the product to the end user as quickly as possible.

The goal of these changes in the nature of warehouse operations is to keep warehouse size, equipment, personnel, and transportation in line with enterprise demands. Tompkins [12] calls this the deployment of *modular distribution assets*. When planning warehouse facilities, this means that managers must have access to mechanisms that allow them to expand or contract warehouse services to meet the targeted level of customer service. To manage short-term problems, the expanded use of public warehousing may be more viable, where possibly a more long-term approach would be the expansion of company-owned facilities. The same could be said of transportation: the use of public carriers, the purchase of equipment, leasing equipment, and the viability of long-term contracts would have to be examined in light of short- and long-term fluctuations in traffic requirements.

CHANNEL PARTNERSHIPS

The tremendous pressures for the rapid deployment of inventories across the supply chain can only expect to accelerate as the 2000s progress. Meeting these challenges requires a strong foundation based on collaboration and partnership among all elements of the supply chain: customers, suppliers, distributors, third parties service providers, and transportation. Probably one the most important trends in this area is the changing role of distributors as they move from being stock keepers and order fillers to single point-of-contact suppliers, providing both products and value-added services. With the growth of Internet fulfillment requirements and more integrated supply chains, the warehouse of the twenty-first century must be able to execute many of the functions traditionally performed in the past by predecessor channel suppliers. In fact, today's customers are continually searching to outsource upstream to their suppliers functions considered beyond their core business competencies. These functions include such activities as consolidating, kitting, and shipment of product to customers in a JIT mode, value-added processing, direct management of customers' on-site inventories and production floor stocks, ability to respond immediately to customers' and suppliers' pick-up and delivery requirements, and inspection and quality control.

The availability of information technology tools and systems are also integrating channel members into close alliances. Instead of a series of independent warehouses and accompanying operational functions, technology is removing the barriers of time and place by linking upstream and downstream channel systems and processes in ways that enable the establishment of the virtual supply chain. Internet tools provide direct entry of orders into customer systems and permit, in some cases, visibility to the exact location and status of shipments anywhere in the supply chain. Armed with accurate and up-to-the-minute data, DC managers can monitor transactions and shipments, respond to late or inaccurate shipments, and perform all the tasks normally associated with real-time management of the supply chain. This growing interdependence has even been extended to soliciting the input of channel partners in warehouse design, organizational development, and selection of information systems. Finally, many distributors will, in the future, seek to extend the accumulated experience of employees through the implementation of expert systems. By making available through technology decision-making expertise related to operational functions, enterprise professionals can be freed from administrative and expediting activities to devote their time to more value-added projects. Among the areas where expert systems can be applied are inventory deployment, order processing, carrier management and selection, and customer service cost trade-off analysis.

Another area requiring closer partnership is the growth of third-party warehousing, full-service logistics carriers, and freight forwarders. As distributors look for ways to eliminate cost and improve throughput by outsourcing functions traditionally performed in-house, third-party warehousing can free firms from investing in plant and capacity outside their normal core competencies or can provide resources, a local presence, or transportation economies that actually permit quicker and more reliable delivery at less cost than can be performed through the use of enterprise-owned facilities. Other advantages can be found in sharing the risks associated with delivery, higher control and flexibility of operations, increased responsiveness to market demand, and often at a lower operating cost. Perhaps the most radical development is the growth of service providers who utilize the Internet to enlist third-party firms that provide complete logistics services encompassing warehousing, order processing, delivery, freight rating, and audit to meet a level of customer specification unattainable by distributors acting on their own.

In summary, today's warehousing function is increasingly expected to be more organizationally focused and more closely integrated into the supply channel. As the twenty-first century progresses, distribution functions are expected to divest themselves of unprofitable megalithic channels that are too costly and unresponsive to the Internet-enabled, customer focused, and value-added service driven requirements of tomorrow's global marketplace. In such a climate, the traditional, static perception of the warehouse will be replaced by alliances of customers and suppliers operating as a single supply chain network, sharing the same competitive goals, functional activities, expertise, and costs all linked through interoperable information systems.

DESIGNING THE WAREHOUSE NETWORK

Whether distribution is performed from a single warehouse or a channel network of warehouses, warehouse location and size is a fundamental issue that must be resolved. In determining the location of a warehouse or designing a warehouse channel, planners must reconcile the firm's strategic objectives with product and competitive strategies, network assets (facilities and equipment), working capital, operating budgets, and marketplace strengths in delivery, price, information technology, value-added processing, and business skills. An effective warehouse location or channel strategy must address such questions as follows:

- How many echelons should be in the distribution channel network?
- Where should individual warehouses be located?
- What is the total cost of operating the channel?
- What level of customer service should be attained?
- What are the mix, cost, and quantity of inventories at each facility necessary to support targeted service levels?
- What is the trade-off between customer service and inventory levels throughout the logistic channel?
- What is the trade-off between transportation and channel asset costs?
- How much inventory should be in the pipeline?

- What kind of information system(s) will be necessary to integrate the distribution channel, and what will be the cost in personnel and equipment?

These and other questions require logistics planners to develop answers as to the size, number, and location of warehouses, and how each may be designed to optimize efficiency and productivity. Ultimately, the mission, structure, and operation of the distribution network is guided by the need to satisfy the customer and to ensure an acceptable return on investment for the assets expended in establishing and operating the distribution channel. Finally, each warehouse in the logistics network must be viewed as an integrated node in a single value-added customer supply chain.

OPENING ISSUES

The construction of a warehouse or a channel of warehouses is a critical decision that will have an enormous impact on the enterprise and possibly on the supply chains the business works within. The choice of a warehouse will affect every aspect of a firm's financial well-being: fixed assets, costs of labor, materials and services, size of the marketplace available, customer service and pricing, transportation requirements, supply chain efficiencies, and customers' perception of the company. Besides economic considerations, the choice of a warehouse site may be influenced by other quality of life factors such as climate, a desirable community or cultural life, access to schools, and others that might contribute to employee satisfaction and the ability of the company to attract and retain quality employees. In any event, the final choice involves weighing a matrix of priorities, a determination of which elements are critical, and a process of elimination. Every location has benefits and drawbacks; good decisions are based on intelligent choices that match closely the needs of the enterprise.

Companies seek to establish warehouses for a number of reasons. The following are six common reasons:

- *Relocation.* Often, shifts in product offerings, markets, population, transportation access, industries, technologies, availability of raw materials and energies, growth of competitors, environmental or governmental regulations, general operational expenses, and others will force a company to consider relocating. These and other factors, for example, can be found at the core of the shift of industry from its former stronghold in the Northeast U.S. to the South and Southwest.
- *Flexibility and scalability.* In today's environment, supply networks have increasingly been subjected to an almost perpetual flux as they respond to shifts in customer demand, product innovation, new forms of

technology, and corporate mergers. The result is that supply chains need to be just as flexible to be able to expand, contract, relocate, and outsource to channel partners.

- *Expansion.* There are two possible conditions driving expansion. In the first, it has become apparent that existing facilities are insufficient to serve current or potential customers. "Insufficient" can be defined as limited plant capacity or the existence of obsolete warehouse technology. The second reason driving expansion is a desire to move closer to new markets. Because of the growth in products and/or market share, the firm may wish to expand its reach into new markets currently on the peripheral of its warehouse channel system. Expansion could also include the establishment of new state-of-the-art facilities not possible with the current plant.

- *Product diversification.* When a company diversifies a product line, it might prove advantageous to locate it in a new facility close to product suppliers, raw materials, or markets. Diversification through product acquisition often requires the firm to assume the plant, equipment, and personnel of the former supplier. In any case, the objective is to pursue the best alternatives that will optimize logistics expenses while establishing customer service leadership.

- *Rationalization.* The quickest method to improve ROI and cash flow is to reduce the amount of capital needed to operate large assets such as plants and warehouses. By employing the latest optimization tools and real estate expertise, companies can reduce channel costs by consolidating assets and eliminating unnecessary facilities.

- *Decentralization.* Often, a distributor will seek to establish additional warehouses as a result of a decision to decentralize stocking of various product lines. The reasons for such a decision could be optimization of logistics costs, decline in labor availability, inadequacies in utilities, community zoning restrictions, government or environmental restricttions, and greater specialization of activity, simplified administration, lower overhead costs, and concentrated development of skills.

There can be little doubt that the demands of an increasing globalized, Internet-enabled marketplace will place even more pressure on logistics functions to provide the most efficient platform for supply-chain activities.

SIZE AND NUMBER OF WAREHOUSES

The process of determining the structure of a distribution channel network is concerned with two fundamental issues: what should be the size and location of each facility. As a norm, these two issues have an inverse relationship to each other: that is, as the number of warehouses in the channel grows, the size of each warehouse will decline, and vice versa. The reason is that as the service market is segmented into spheres supplied from regional warehouses, the inventory carried in each, and hence the required size, will decline. However, as the number of warehouses increase in the channel, so does the total channel aggregate inventory level. This occurs not only because each location needs to have sufficient inventory available to service customers, but each must also carry reserve stock to prevent shortages due to variances in interbranch resupply and excessive unplanned customer demand. Simply stated, the more unpredictable the demand, the larger the warehouse necessary to house cycle and reserve stocks.

There are a number of critical factors influencing warehouse size. Some of these are influenced by marketplace consideration such as the desired customer service level, size of the market(s) to be served, number of products to be marketed, demand patterns, and strength of the competition. Other factors focus on storage elements such the size of products, availability and type of material handling systems, labor, stocking layout, and geographical access. Finally, other factors are concerned with productivity metrics such as facility throughput rate and exploitation of economies of scale. Normally, warehouse planners will use not just one, but a matrix of these and other factors in warehouse design. As a rule, larger warehouses are necessary when the size of the product is large (refrigerators, washing machines, furniture, etc.), a large number of SKUs are stocked, there is a high rate of warehouse throughput, the material handling equipment is large or complex (forklifts, cranes, automated put-away and retrieval systems), and the building contains a large office area.

Perhaps the key factor in determining warehouse size is understanding the inventory and throughput requirements necessary to service the marketplace in which the proposed warehouse is to be located. Arriving at warehouse size is a complicated mathematical problem, involving knowledge of product requirements, the space/cube of each product, sales trends, building storage capacity, and costs. Simplistically, warehouse size is calculated by determining estimated sales by month, combining them, and then compiling space requirements by converting units of inventory into required square feet of floor space. Many firms will also plan the use of public warehousing into the equation. When storage requirements fluctuate or cannot be known with precision, building a warehouse to meet maximum requirements usually results in underutilization of the warehouse during nonpeak periods. The most cost-effective plan would be to use a combination of private warehousing to respond to normal demand and public warehousing or leased space during peak periods. Finally, the warehouse sizing exercise cannot be complete without figuring in the space requirements for receiving and shipping, dock requirements, buffer and staging areas, and necessary vehicle maneuvering allowances inside the stocking areas.

In determining the location of warehouses in the channel, planners must seek to balance the fixed and current costs (plant and inventory) with the cost of transportation and overall sales. If these three elements were portrayed graphically, they would resemble the curves found in Figure 11.12. As the

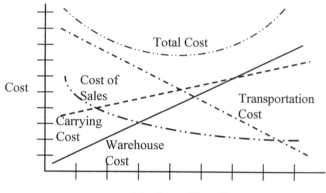

FIGURE 11.12 Determining the number of warehouses by cost.

number of warehouses grows, inventory and facilities costs increase while relative transportation and sales costs would decline due to economies of scale. However, as the number of channel supply points continues to increase, eventually transportation and sales costs would also begin to slope upward as the costs associated not only with interbranch transfer but also customer delivery increase. Simply, as the number of warehouses grow, the ability of the channel to ship on a full truckload (TL) basis declines, requiring the firm to pay a higher transportation rate. Overall, the goal of the location strategy is to maximize the perceived benefits arising from the optimal positioning of each distribution point geographically in the channel.

In addition to calculating optimum transportation and assets cost trade-offs, determining the number of warehouses in the channel must also be guided by targeted customer service levels and, in particular, the speed with which product can be delivered. In theory, the more centralized the pipeline inventories, the greater the average distance between supply points and the customer, and the longer the delivery lead time. This means that if customer service levels are related to the speed of delivery, it is likely that sales will decline as inventory is concentrated, and vice versa. When added to the curves in Figure 11.12, the sales revenue curve would appear to increase as the number of stocking points increase. In a very crude sense, the distance between sales revenue and total network costs is the measure of channel profitability. This means that the optimum number of stocking points can be seen as that point where the gap between the two curves is at its widest. This analysis, however, is based on two assumptions: reducing delivery times generates additional sales and decentralizing channel inventories reduces delivery times. Because neither of these assumptions are necessarily true, planners must be careful to employ analysis methods (such as cost analysis, grid and graphic techniques, and simulation and optimization modeling) that thoroughly explore long-term distribution patterns encompassing customer, plant, product and transportation costs, and opportunities, and to develop effective strategies for deploying goods to be held at various supply point levels in the channel.

DETERMINING WAREHOUSE LOCATION

One of the most heavily explored and a refined area in logistics management is determining warehouse location. During the past 50 years, considerable effort has been expended into developing complex economic and channel analysis techniques, supplemented by computerized simulation models. In the late 1940s, Hoover [13] developed a macro approach that attempted to leverage three types of location strategies: market positioned, product positioned, and intermediately positioned. In the first, warehouses are located nearest to the end customer, the second in close proximity to the sources of supply, and the last somewhere in between customer and supplier. Schmenner [14], on the other hand, employed another macro approach whereby warehouses are located either by a *product strategy* in which a single product or product group is sold from a given warehouse, a *marketing strategy* in which warehouses stocking all the firm's products are positioned in specific market territories, or a *general purpose strategy* in which a full-service warehouse serves a general market region. Greenhut [15] attempted to determine warehouse location by calculating an optimum cost based on transportation costs, proximity to suppliers and final customers, and profitability. Finally, Harmon [16] felt that distributors can quickly determine where warehouses should be located by (1) establishing the geographic dispersion of customers and/or sales volume, (2) locating warehouses near the largest production plant to facilitate communications, (3) locating warehouses in order to serve an established base of customers better or to penetrate a new market region, and (4) increasing stocking point exposure to protect existing market share. An effective macro selection process should include a thorough analysis of transportation costs, census information, local government and business development agency positions, professional associations and other businesses in the area, labor availability and cost, and real estate issues.

In contrast to the macro approach, *micro* methods have been developed to assist in location selection. Jenkins [17] identifies the following twelve critical micro factors that must be considered during the warehouse selection process:

1. *Determine overall warehouse objectives.* Defining the objectives to be served by the warehouse or channel structure is a critical part of the process of site selection. For instance, objectives, such as providing higher levels of customer service or reducing delivery lead time, should form the core elements guiding location selection.

2. *Transportation costs.* This factor is normally considered the most important in warehouse location studies. Easy accessibility to transportation involves the availability of trucking services and specialized water, rail, and air carriers. The cost involved in supply chain replenishment, transit times, possibility of damage and theft, service reliability, and other related factors require planners to search for transportation optimizations that permit effective trade-offs while preserving the overall objectives of the facility.

3. *Personnel considerations.* When either relocating or constructing a new warehouse, consideration must be given to the effect such decisions will have on existing employees, the availability of new labor, and legal and social issues relating to equal opportunity employment.

4. *Real estate considerations.* Both the warehouse and the property it rests on have a fixed asset value that transcends the purpose for which they are to be acquired. When selecting sites planners have the option of building in a nationally known distribution hub, such as Chicago, New York, Los Angeles, Houston, Seattle, Dallas, and others, or opting for a less expensive area. The choice must be guided by warehouse objectives, real estate costs, and possibility of property appreciation.

5. *Tax considerations.* The taxes levied on property, inventory, and payroll by local governments are an important determination in warehouse selection. Depending on the state, these taxes can be minimal to high to prohibitive. In addition, some locales may provide incentives to build warehouses in their communities, whereas others might discourage construction through exceptionally high tax assessments.

6. *Communications.* A critical element in site selection is the existence of adequate telephone and other communication infrastructures. A warehouse that has insufficient communications will soon become inoperative or incur intolerably high costs.

7. *Proximity to customers.* A critical factor determining warehouse selection is the delivery time to customers. Aspects of this factor include meeting the requirements specified in the warehouse objectives, the availability and cost of transportation, travel distance to the customer, and actual travel time for the customer.

8. *Proximity to other warehouses.* The distance between warehouses in the channel network is a critical factor in measuring trade-off costs between customer service and transportation, communications, inventory carrying costs, and facilities. Normally, the more warehouses in the channel, the better the customer service and the lower the freight costs. On the other hand, proliferation of warehouses usually means an increase in total inventory and operating costs.

9. *Facility cost and value.* The asset costs of the facility constitute a prime factor in warehouse selection. Direct components of cost associated with the physical plant are the price of the land, facilities construction, engineering, fees and permits, and financing. More variable sources of cost include the cost of leasing facilities and/or properties, the costs involved in the acquisition of equipment and hiring employees, and determination of the capitalized value of the facility.

10. *Operating costs.* These costs consist of those elements necessary to run the facility such as heat, electricity, and fuel sources. Perhaps the single most important element is the cost of labor and management.

11. *Company image.* The impression the warehouse facilities make on customers and the community can be very important to the business enterprise and deserves serious consideration. Companies seeking marketplace name recognition need to be located in areas that expose the company's name and presence to the public at large.

12. *Community resources.* Community services, such as adequate police and fire departments, community attitude, availability of schools and professional education, lack of environmental dangers, public transportation, and availability of affordable housing for employees, are also critical factors in location selection.

To effectively utilize these factors, a location project methodology should be employed. Schmenner [18] has developed an eight-phase methodology that consists of the following steps:

1. Formally propose a project to search for a new warehouse location, and solicit company feedback.

2. Form a project team, and divide tasks among the team associated with land availability, labor requirements, finances, transportation, warehouse and stocked inventory size, utilities, and governmental and environmental issues.

3. Constitute an engineering team responsible for external and internal facility design, topology, and geology.

4. Develop essential criteria for the new warehouse. Included is alignment of business and functional area objectives and strategies.

5. Identify potential geographical regions and warehouse locations supportive of enterprise goals.

6. Select specific sites for evaluation.
7. Evaluate the benefits and disadvantages of each proposed location.
8. Select a specific location.

During the course of this or any similar methodology, project teams and company executives must make the search a formal process and guide the project along each step to ensure that critical decisions are not made without the concurrence of the entire team. In some cases, planners can also utilize several location strategy models to assist in determining warehouse location. An easy to apply technique, the *factor weighting method*, attempts to utilize location tangible costs, such as taxes, labor, and intangible costs, such as community attitude or quality of life, to determine location. By assigning weights and points to each factor, the method can provide a quantitative means of site selection. An example of this technique appears in Table 11.1. The advantages of this approach are that it provides an objective method of identifying hard to evaluate costs related to each location and the ability to compute *qualitative* factors into the analysis. Other techniques that could be used to determine the optimal warehouse location include *location break-even methods, center of gravity method* (a mathematical technique for determining the location of a warehouse servicing a number of satellites), and *transportation method* (a linear programming method that attempts to determine the best pattern of shipments from several supply warehouses to several receiving warehouses so as to minimize transportation costs) [19].

TABLE 11.1 Factor Weighting Method

Factor	Weight	Site Scores (100 points) Chicago	Atlanta	Weighted Scores Chicago	Atlanta
Labor costs	24%	55	65	.24x55 = 13.2	.24x65 = 15.6
Transportation costs	7%	85	55	= 5.95	= 3.85
Taxes	35%	50	65	= 17.5	= 22.75
Quality of life	11%	65	75	= 7.15	= 8.25
Utilities and facilities cost	22%	75	60	= 16.5	= 13.2
			Totals	*60.3*	*63.65*

WAREHOUSE LAYOUT AND EQUIPMENT

The design, layout, and selection of equipment for a warehouse is a complex process requiring detailed knowledge of the requirements of customer service, product stocking characteristics, material handling, receiving and loading technologies, transportation capacities and capabilities, and the availability of state-of-the-art storage and retrieval equipment. An effective warehouse design and layout is one in which the physical facilities, equipment, and labor can be optimized and are in alignment with overall corporate strategies. If these elements could be ranked, warehouse designers should first have a firm definition of warehouse strategic objectives; second, the proper equipment should be selected and operational parameters established; and, finally, the facility should be designed to satisfy operational goals while acknowledging the physical constraints of the equipment.

Some of the critical physical characteristics of a proposed warehouse have already been discussed in the previous section. Before construction of a new warehouse can begin, architects and engineers must determine the overall suitability of the land. This step includes knowledge of the terrain, the degree of land preparation, and the cost of further site improvements, including sewer, electricity, gas, water, and police and fire protection. The actual design of the building will depend on the nature of the storage environment. When material handling and storage requirements are uncomplicated, the level of architectural and engineering design will be relatively simple and inexpensive, stressing flexibility of storage areas and equipment. On the other hand, if the warehouse contains products that require environmental control such as cooling or dry storage, specialized material handling equipment for bulk products or cross-docking, and other requirements, the architectural design of the facility will reflect an increasing degree of complexity and cost.

WAREHOUSE LAYOUT

Once the general physical structure of the warehouse has been determined, the next decision relates to the type and layout of storage equipment to be installed. In reality, the warehouse is nothing more than a materials handling system whose purpose is to act as a repository facilitating the efficient and cost effective movement of products through the channel network and out to the customer. Analogous to the processing equipment necessary to run a manufacturing company, material handling systems are a manifestation of the objectives pursued by the distribution strategy, and their capabilities and capacities determine the competitive boundaries available to the each supply chain node. In general, the principles of effective warehouse design are as follows:

1. The efficient and cost-effective use of warehouse space
2. The efficient and cost-effective utilization of material handling equipment and labor

3. Maximum warehouse flexibility in order to meet changing storage and material handling requirements
4. Good housekeeping
5. Agility to respond to the changing, competitive needs of customer service

The actual arrangement of a warehouse can take several forms depending on the facility's products, service objectives, and physical characteristics. A traditional model appears in Figure 11.13. This layout has been designed to

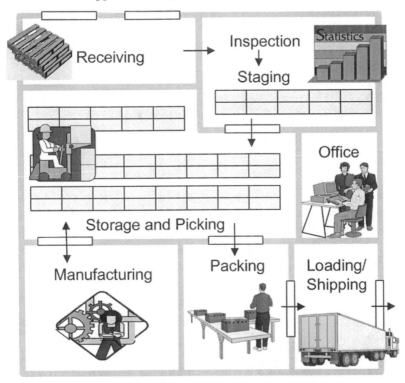

FIGURE 11.13 Basic warehouse layout.

simulate the movement of product from the point of receiving to the point of shipment. On the other hand, the warehouse layout illustrated in Figure 11.14 attempts to employ an item ABC Classification methodology in warehouse design. Here, receiving and shipping utilize the same docking facilities with inventory storage location stratified by usage. The fast-selling products are located closest to receiving and shipping, and slower-moving items progressively to the rear of the building. Finally, Figure 11.15 portrays a schema of a warehouse that contains multiple types of storage facilities. In this case, the warehouse has been divided into receiving and shipping *zones* servicing small parts, bulk parts, and automated stocking areas. In selecting the general de-

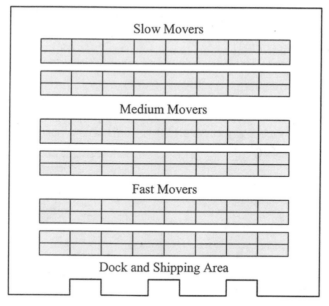

FIGURE 11.14 ABC storage technique

sign of the warehouse, planners must be careful to utilize storage techniques that effectively leverage product and conveyance equipment and minimize labor and investment costs while facilitating product throughput and service targets.

Zone 1 Ship & Receive		Zone 2 Ship & Receive		Zone 3 Ship & Receive
Bins & Drawers	Small Racks	Large Racks	Semi-Automated Storage & Retrieval	Automated Storage & Retrieval

FIGURE 11.15 Mixed-storage mode.

Establishing an effective warehouse layout is a multistep approach requiring detail knowledge of products, facilities capacities, and customer service objectives. The actual storage area and the space necessary to perform related activities constitutes, by far, the largest element in warehouse space allocation. A poorly structured plan can result in a warehouse that is either too large or too small for normal operations. Too much space will result in excess cost arising from underutilized land, construction, equipment, and energy. Too little space, on the other hand, can result in a host of operational problems, such as excessive expediting, inaccessible products, damaged goods, poor housekeeping, and loss of productivity. In order to develop an optimum warehouse layout, the following steps should be performed:

1. *Establish a comprehensive warehouse planning process.* Determining an effective warehouse layout is a multitasked process that requires detailed project management. A successful project is one that is governed by a task schedule outlining due dates, responsible roles, and costs.

2. *Define layout objectives.* Although many managers may feel that the objectives of the warehouse are intuitive, it is best that objectives be precisely defined. Examples of such objectives might be as follows:

   - Provide minimum cost warehousing while maintaining established customer service levels
   - Improve space utilization by 25 percent over last year's average without reducing operating efficiency
   - Optimize space utilization in relation to the costs of equipment, space, and labor
   - Make the warehouse a "showcase" of efficiency and good housekeeping

3. *Define warehouse profiles.* In this step, planners should detail the requirements of the following elements: (1) what products are to be stored; (2) what is the storage size necessary to stock these products; (3) exact dimensions of the warehouse; (4) capacities of the storage area racks, pallets, bins, and so on; and, (5) capacities of planned material handling equipment.

4. *Generate a series of layout alternatives.* In this step, planners must "juggle" physical restrictions, such as the location of fixed objects like pillars and walls, the placement of receiving and shipping functions, storage areas and aisles necessary for equipment maneuverability, assignment of product storage requirements to stocking areas, stock putaway and packing runs, and equipment storage areas. A critical part of this process is determining layout constraints. Besides column spacing and size, an effective plan must also consider bay size and direction, the ceiling height, door and dock locations, building shape and land conditions, geographic area (climate), and local building codes.

5. *Layout evaluation.* Several philosophies can be employed in determining the optimal warehouse layout. The use of ABC Analysis can assist in pinpointing high-turnover items so that they can be located close to receiving and shipping areas. Another philosophy states that items commonly received and/or shipped together should be stored together. In a similar vein, another theory states that products with similar characteristics, such as chemicals, heavy and oddly shaped items,

items subject to shelf life, hazardous items, easily damaged items, and high-value items should be stored together. Yet another suggests that heavy, bulky, hard-to-handle products should be stored close to their point of use in order to minimize costly material handling. Finally, the space utilization principle asserts that the total cube of available warehouse space should be accentuated while optimizing product accessibility and good housekeeping.

6. *Layout implementation.* Once the alternatives have been evaluated, a specific layout must be chosen and implemented. At this point, project activities should be structured around tasks, schedules, and costs necessary for warehouse layout actualization [20].

TYPES OF STORAGE

The process of warehouse design requires detailed review and selection of the necessary types of product storage equipment. Obviously, the selection process depends on the nature of the products to be warehoused. Product characteristics can be described as the number of units to be stocked, throughput targets, weight, cubic volume, width, depth, stacking limitations, association with related products, packaging, dangerous and hazardous substances, temperature control and shelf life. A useful way to view storage types is to divide them into two classes: large-item or large-volume product storage and small-item or small-volume storage. The use of either or both classes in a given warehouse requires an expert knowledge of product and stocking balance requirements as well as the capacities and capabilities of available storage types.

Large-item or large-volume product storage is used to handle products whose unit size is significant or whose planned inventories quantities are large. Examples of storage types in this class include the following:

- *Open floor storage.* This type of storage would be most applicable for large products whose physical characteristics make it difficult for them to be easily stored on pallets or placed on racks. Another application would be the storage of products whose stocked quantity and volume permit stockmen and order picking personnel to cost-effectively stack, service, and fill items directly from open floor storage areas. "Cost-effectively" means that the trade-off for consuming open warehouse space is justified by ease of product throughput.

- *Pallet racks.* This type of storage structure has been designed to facilitate the maximum storage and handling of a product by placing it on pallets. Normally, both the pallet and the storage structure sizes are standardized. When product is received, it is stacked to meet the maximum pallet storage capacity. The pallet is then staged in the rack through the use of material handling equipment such as a fork lift (Figure 11.16) The advantages of this storage type is ease of material

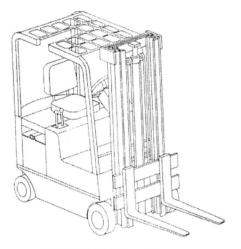

FIGURE 11.16 Fork lift.

handling in put-away and the ability to pick case lots or whole pallets to meet customer demand. The height of pallet structures is governed by the height and load capacities of the lift vehicles possessed by the warehouse. Figure 11.17 illustrates an example of a stacker vehicle used to stage pallets in open-pallet rack structures.

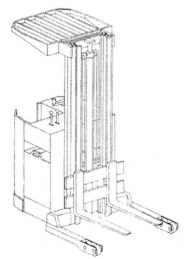

FIGURE 11.17 Stacker vehicle.

- *Drive-in/back-to-back pallet racks*. Through the use of special storage and lift truck equipment, pallet racks can be designed to store

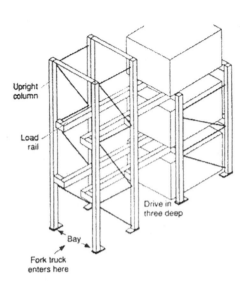

FIGURE 11.18 Drive-in racks.

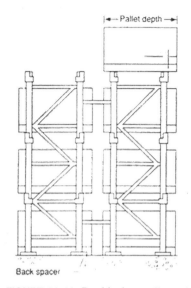

FIGURE 11.19 Double deep pallet racks.

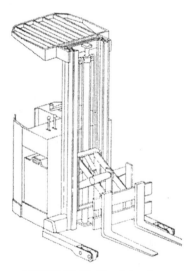

FIGURE 11.20 Reach truck.

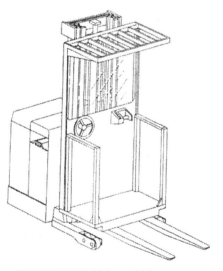

FIGURE 11.21 Picker vehicle.

two or more pallets deep as well as multiple pallets high. Drive-in racks are designed so that forklifts or other equipment can "drive-in" to the racks between structure uprights and pallet support rails (Figure 11.18). Back-to-back pallet racks (Figure 11.19) require a special reach lift truck that has the capability to position pallets two to three levels deep (Figure 11.20). These types of storage provides maximum utilization of warehouse space by eliminating wasted aisle and vehicle maneuvering space.

- *Storage racks.* Often product stocking quantities are too small to warrant pallet storage but whose stock or physical size disqualifies them for small parts storage. These items are best warehoused in storage racks. These racks consist of structure uprights, cross rails, shelving (usually wooden), and shelving cross rail supports. Normally, the storage shelf is standardized into several heights to accommodate product inventory requirements. The height of the rack is determined by the capacity of manned picking vehicles (Figure 11.21).

- *Cantilever racks.* This type of storage rack is named for the leverage technique used to support the load-bearing arms (Figure 11.22). Canti-

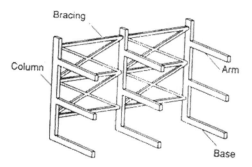

FIGURE 11.22 Cantilever rack.

lever racks normally consist of a row of single upright columns, spaced several feet apart, with arms extending from one or both sides of the upright to form supports for product storage. The columns rest on the warehouse floor, preventing the structure from toppling backward or forward, and horizontal and diagonal bracing between uprights prevents the structure from collapsing inside or out. Because of their long, unobstructed support, these types of racks are best used to store metal rods, tubes, pipes, bar stock, wood poles, and other products of comparable shapes.

- *Flow racks.* The single characteristic of this storage type is the use of conveyors positioned within a rack. By tilting up the back end of the conveyor, gravity draws individual products or pallets serviced from the rear forward so that they can be easily picked (Figure 12.23). Each flow run is dedicated to a single product. The advantages of flow racks over pallet and shelf racks are that they permit easy FIFO inventory control, reduce the need for aisles, minimize handling by having one input and discharge point, and reduce damage and pilferage. Disadvantages are cost of structure materials, required quality of pallet, flexibility, and downtime due to equipment failure.

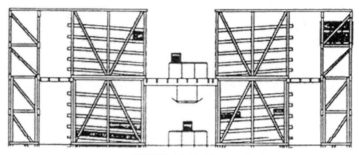

FIGURE 11.23 Flow rack.

- *Specialized racks.* Because of their shape characteristics, some products require specialized storage racking. One example is the use of tilted barrels staged in racks to store casters, metal ingots, and short metal rods. Another is special racks constructed to hold "D" handled shovels, rakes, and ladles [21].

Small-parts or small-volume storage is used to warehouse items whose size and/or volume permit them to be warehoused in small-capacity storage equipment. Small-parts storage systems can be generally classified into two categories: static and dynamic [22]. The difference between the two is how the storage systems permit access to parts. In *static systems,* stock keepers and pickers must travel to stationary storage locations to service and retrieve inventory. For the most part, stationary systems are relatively inexpensive as compared to large-item or large-volume product storage or small-part dynamic systems. In fact, their lack of sophisticated automation and complexity often render them the most efficient and economical type of storage when handling a wide range of items subject to low to moderate throughput. Examples of static storage systems are the following:

- *Shelving.* Shelving is perhaps the most basic type of static storage available. Normally, shelving structures are constructed of light-gauge cold-rolled steel and consist of a number of different type of posts or sides, shelving that is secured through bolts or special brackets, and optional steel backings. Standard widths are generally 36, 42 and 48 inches, depths from 9 to 36 inches, and posts or sides up to 84 inches. In order to provide for stocking integrity and the ability to position more than one item on a shelf, parts can be also be stored in standardized bin boxes or metal dividers located on the shelf. Because of its flexibility, shelving can be used to store a wide range of types and quantity of product. Other advantages are low equipment and maintenance costs and ease of erection, modification, and removal. Drawbacks center on space inefficiencies. Shelving makes poor use of vertical space between the ceiling and the top of the shelf facing, as well as wasted space on the shelf due to the size of the stored item. For example, a product two foot in depth and width would waste significant space on a standard shelf three foot in depth and width. Possible solutions to more effectively utilizing vertical warehouse space are to create mezzanines or high-rise shelving structures. Use of these techniques must, however, be balanced against the cost of additional equipment. Examples of storage shelves appear in Figure 11.24.

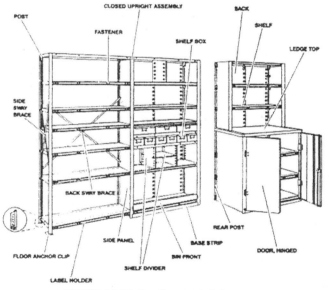

FIGURE 11.24 Small parts shelving.

- *Modular storage drawers.* An alternative method to better utilize shelving space is to use compartmentalized drawers mounted in storage shelving or cabinets. As the size and quantity of items grows smaller, the use of shelving becomes less and less an economical storage choice. However, by dividing the drawer space into small compartments consisting of a variety of sizes, product stocking requirements can be matched to the proper compartment, thereby increasing space utilization. Similar to shelving, modular storage drawers can also be stacked or mezzanined to utilize vertical warehouse space. The major disadvantage of this type of stocking is its relatively high investment cost.

While static storage types have dominated the warehousing of small parts, *dynamic storage systems* have been growing in popularity. Due to the declining costs of computerized systems, the application of automated storage/retrieval and dynamic systems have significantly increased their capabilities and have provided dramatic savings in labor and reductions in inventory levels. The following is a discussion of available dynamic storage systems.

- *Carousels.* This type of storage can be defined as a series of modular, movable shelved or compartmentalized bin facings linked together by means of a motorized oval track. The basic concept is that inventory is brought to the stock person rather than the stock person moving to the bin. Carousels consist of two types: vertical and horizontal. *Vertical carousels* revolve on a vertical oval track and are either top-driven or bottom-driven. The benefit of a vertical carousel is utilization of vertical warehouse space. Drawbacks are limitations on widths, depths, and weights, and they normally cost more than horizontal carrousels. In contrast, *horizontal carousels* revolve around a horizontal track. A motor, mounted in the center of the oval, moves the bins along the track. Horizontal carousels can be configured into a much greater variety of heights, widths, depths, and weight capacities than vertical types, and they can be used for many different warehouse storage applications. The most significant negative features are waste of vertical warehouse space. Normally, an operator activates either type of carousel through manual, microprocessor, or computer controls, bringing the desired bin to the stocking and picking position. Benefits of using carousals are greater labor utilization, increased throughput, improved control, space utilization, simplified inventory control and replenishment, and integration with other warehouse systems. An example of a horizontal carousel appears in Figure 11.25.

FIGURE 11.25 Horizontal carousel.

- *Moveable-aisle systems.* This type of storage is characterized by shelving cabinets or bins placed on movable carriages that either glide or roll on stationary tracks. The major advantage of moveable-aisle systems is the elimination of aisle space between stocking rows. Basically there are three types of movable-aisle systems determined by the type and weight of products stored. *Manual systems* are characterized by the ability of the operator to manually push rows when accessing the necessary storage area. The number of rows in this systems are limited and stocked products are light weight. *Mechanically assisted systems* normally consist of gear systems that facilitate movement of the rows and are used for systems approaching thirty feet in length and for products of medium weight. Finally, *electric systems* utilize electric motors to move rows. This type is most useful for controlling large racking systems and for heavy products.

- *Miniload AS/RS systems.* Miniload systems can be defined as a fully enclosed, automatic storage system that brings parts and materials to an operator for picking, kitting, and so on, and automatically returns the material into the system [23]. Similar to the much larger systems discussed in the next section, this type of small parts storage system depends on an automatic storage container insertion and extraction mechanism that traverses vertically and horizontally a stocking aisle. Mini-load systems can be controlled from keyboards or integrated with warehouse management systems. Benefits of this type of storage are floor space reduction, stocking space cube utilization, increased throughput, reduced labor costs, increased security, and increased control of parts (Figure 11.26).

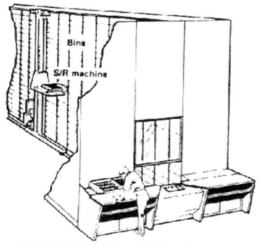

FIGURE 11.26 Miniload AS/RS system.

WAREHOUSE AUTOMATION

The demands of warehousing in the twenty-first century require companies to have an optimal mix of manual and automated material handling systems. To be effective, warehouse automation must be designed and implemented to maximize the use of the enterprise's critical resources--space, labor, capital, equipment, and inventory--while providing a high level of customer service. The best choices are made when managers weigh critical ratios such as cash liquidity, productivity, and profitability when deciding on warehouse automation systems. Generally, the prime reasons driving automation are a desire to decrease labor and logistics costs, increase output rates, increase accuracy of services, and accelerate the speed of customer order turnaround times. Warehouse automation, however, is not without its disadvantages. Drawbacks include high equipment and implementation costs, requirements for modification, lack of flexibility, increased maintenance, and employee training and acceptance.

Speeding DC Productivity

Completed in 2001, Saks, Inc., the parent company of Saks Fifth Avenue and other high-end retail stores, decided to build a new $25 million, 180,000-square-foot state-of-the-art flow-through distribution center in Steele, Alabama.

Thanks to the its robust capabilities, products can be processed through the DC with little human intervention. Product is received on the first floor of the facility through 20 shipping doors. The cartons are unloaded onto conveyors and immediately scanned for correct supplier identification. Correctly identified material moves up the conveyors to the second floor where Cartons are sorted, scanned, marked, and processed to shipping by a completely automated operation.

The goods are then passed to 126 shipping doors where they marked for delivery to specific retail stores.

The new DC can move a single carton through the system in les than four minutes, with a shipping accuracy of 99.9 percent. Altogether, the new system has enabled Saks to triple its throughput, from 15,000 boxes per shift to around 43,000.

Originally, Saks envisioned a DC where no merchandise would be stored. Today, 94% of merchandise is cross-docked, with the goal reaching 100 percent in the near future.

Source: Johnson, John R., "Speed Thrills," *DC Velocity*, 1, 2, (2003), pp. 32-36.

The decision to automate warehouse functions requires thorough strategic as well as operational planning. As with other enterprise projects, the initiative involves weighing costs and potential benefits, as well as considering the risk of failure versus the anticipated productivity. Some of the *strategic* questions that must be addressed are as follows:

- To what degree will warehouse automation increase the company's competitive advantage?
- Are the plans for warehouse automation in alignment with the company's other strategic objectives?
- What impact will warehouse automation have on the firm's marketing objectives?
- Can the proposed automation be transported to other parts of the supply chain?
- What changes in products and markets could render the planned warehouse automation obsolete or redundant?

Operational issues to be considered are as follows:

- What is the increased percentage of space utilization to be expected from warehouse automation implementation?
- What is the increased percentage of productivity to be expected?
- How will the proposed automation project eliminate work-flow bottlenecks?
- What impact will automation have on warehouse employees and skill sets?
- Can current equipment be applied to the automation project?
- What will be the requirements and costs for equipment maintenance?

While automation can take many forms and can range from low-tech assets such as acquiring a forklift to high-tech intelligent labels, for the most part the three most important types of automation are the use of *automatic identification systems, automated storage and retrieval systems* (AS/AR) and *intelligent tags* and *voice recognition*. Automatic identification systems attempt to minimize or eliminate human operator involvement in the collection of information by using optical and radio technologies that input information directly into warehousing systems. The importance of automatic identifycation systems in modern warehousing is twofold: (1) it minimizes or eliminates the need for human activity in data collection and (2) it significantly increases the accuracy and speed of data entry. Automatic identification systems generally fall into three main categories:

- *Radio Frequency.* This technique utilizes vehicle attached or hand-held devices that transmit information via radio frequency.

- *Magnetic Readers.* This technique uses a magnetic film or strip on which is encoded information. By passing a sensing head over the strip, information is collected and passed back to the database.
- *Optical systems.* Techniques in this category utilize light refracted from a printed pattern. Normally, a wand emitting a light beam is passed over the pattern, information encoded, and then passed to the database.

Of the optical system techniques, bar coding is perhaps the most popular. Bar coding can be described as the use of electronically driven automatic identification generated by moving a beam of light across a band consisting of a set of alternating opaque bars and white spaces. A bar coding system consists of three entities:

- *Bar Code Symbology.* This element refers to the type of bar code employed. Although a firm could develop its own codes, the goal is to use universally accepted codes that apply to specific business functions. The most common bar codes are UPC, Logmars Code 39, Code 2 of 5, and Code 2 of 5 Interleaved.
- *Bar Code Printer.* The reproduction of the bar code is of prime importance in bar code reading. Generally, the main concern is the reproduction of a code clear enough to be easily read by the scanning equipment. In addition to this element are possible requirements for packaging aesthetics. Bar codes can be printed in-house through the use of several commercial printers, or by an outside professional printing company.
- *Bar Code Readers.* Readers or scanners come in a wide variety based on warehouse need. The following are possible examples of commercially available bar code readers: hand-held, moving beam readers, fixed-location, fixed-beam readers, fixed-location, moving-beam readers, and photodiode array (PDA) readers.

An effective bar coding system can be a significant assistance to warehouse operations. The advantages of bar coding are accuracy, speed, cost, reliability, simplicity, negligible space requirements, and ease of acceptance by employees.

The use of automated storage/retrieval systems can be divided into two groupings: miniload systems and unit-load systems. *Miniload systems* have already been discussed relative to small-parts dynamic storage systems. In contrast, *unit-load systems* can be defined as the automation of the stock keeping and picking functions associated with pallet or standard container loads. In designing unit-load AS/RS systems, the key is the size and storage cube of the material. Characteristically, an AS/RS system consists of two elements. The first is the rack structure that is to hold the pallets or containers. For the most part, free-standing or building-supported drive-through-type racks are employed. Normally, the aisles separating each row in the rack cluster is wide enough only to permit the movement of the storage/retrieval machine.

The second element of an AS/RS system is the *storage/retrieval machine.* Whereas the rack system provides the storage environment, the storage/retrieval machine provides the material handling function of the AS/RS system. The machine must have the ability to perform vertical, horizontal, and shuttle subcycle (extension, pickup, and retraction) activities. Normally, the machine, called a "crane," resides on wheels and moves up and down each row in the rack cluster. Cranes can be dedicated to just one row or service a group of rows. For the most part, AS/RS cranes today are controlled through the use of computer systems that stock keep and pick based on computer databases that are integrated with sales order, receiving, and inventory management systems. Finally, AS/RS systems are often accompanied by other forms of warehouse automation. Conveyor systems are used to transport product to and from storage clusters. Automated sizing and weighing stations can also be employed to ensure storage loads conform to weight and size requirements. In addition, *automated guided vehicle* (AGV) systems can be used to convey material from and to stocking points and AR/RS pickup stations. Benefits arising from AS/RS systems include enhancement of inventory accuracy, reduction of labor costs, increased warehouse space utilization, and reduced product damage.

The use of intelligent tags and voice recognition constitutes the third major area of warehouse automation. These technologies are today on the cutting-edge of warehousing automation. While still too expensive for general use, several companies are beginning to deploy intelligent tags equipped with RFID chips that have the ability to actually transmit signals to warehouse systems. These signals can be broadcast to tracking devices that will allow companies to trace inventories as they move from manufacturing to storage, picking, palletizing and shipment. The goal is to not only use these intelligent tags to control internal movements but also to persuade supply chain partners to RFID-enable their receiving docks and distribution centers.

Even more radical is the view of Downes who, in an article entitled "The Metamorphosis of Information" [24], details how Wal-Mart and its supply and logistics partners are attempting to move the concept of RFID to its next evolutionary step by installing a Electronic Product Code, similar to a bar code but one that does not need to be scanned and contains its own power source and antenna, to Bounty paper towels. The tag broadcasts by means of radio frequencies to receivers in the warehouse and on store shelves the location of pallets of individually labeled Bounty paper towels. The tracking data is also transmitted up the supply chain to distributors and finally the manufacturer. While the cost of these miniature computers today severely limits their application to experiments only, if Moore's Law is true, perhaps in the next few of years it will not be surprising to find that manufacturers from Procter & Gamble to the Gap will be able to label all their products with such information devices. "Imagine," concludes Downes, "a trillion new intelligent devices, each with its own Internet address, sending and receiving data through their life spans, creating increasingly complete snapshots of every transaction in every supply chain."

RFID Tags at Gillette

Until just recently RFID tags were reserved for use of big objects like railcars. They were bulky and expensive and the idea of tags small and cheap enough to use on individual items seemed futuristic.

Beginning in January of 2003, Gillette, will attach RFID tags to Mach 3 Turbo razor blades that ship to two Wal-Mart stores equipped with "smart shelves" capable of reading signals from the chips and tracking the merchandise's location. The innovation is that these tags are small, measured in microns. Suspended in a fluid, they look to the naked eye like the flakes in a snow globe. What is more, they tags are produced in quantity for as little as five cents each.

Gillette believes the tags will make it possible to follow products through their life cycle from manufacturing through distribution to the point of sale. It hopes the technology will help reduce losses from theft or from stockouts, and will make its entire supply chain more efficient by enabling the collection of real-time data on the status and location of its products, where ever they may be in the supply chain.

Source: Ewalt, David M., "Gillette Razors Get New Edge: RFID Tags," *Information Week*, (January 13, 2003), p.22.

An extension of intelligent RFID tags is the application of a new technology, voice recognition. Begun over a half century ago, software companies have been working steadily to develop applications that can recognize and reproduce the human voice. In 2000 the three main types of speech technology (speech recognition, speaker verification, and text-to-speech) accounted for $153 million in sales and is expected to exceed $1.5 billion by 2005. The first applications to warehouse management occurred in the early 1990s and today are closely integrated with warehouse management systems. They work by first synthesizing data (say, a sales order pick) into speech. This data is then received by operators equipped with headsets to receive oral instruction from the computer. In turn, workers can use their microphones to report task completion to the computer. Rather than pressing keys or scanning bar codes, the operator speaks into the headset to provide data such as order numbers and quantities picked (25).

WAREHOUSE MANAGEMENT SYSTEMS

As the complexity and speed of warehouse operations accelerates in today's business environment, many companies with distribution facilities are implementing computerized *warehouse management systems* (WMS). In all too many warehouse environments sophisticated business systems feed vital information to functions, such as receiving, stock put-away, picking, and transportation, only to have control and feedback of these activities disappear into manually performed tasks that are generally unconnected to each other and to the business system. A WMS attempts to fill in this gap in information communication and planning by providing computerized solutions that seek to fully integrate the various functions of warehousing, ranging from inventory control to yard management. These systems also can be easily linked with the ERP business system as well as logistics transportation and supply chain process management solutions to provide companies with a totally integrated real-time fulfillment system.

Today's WMS offers a wide-range of applications. These solutions can be grouped into seven general areas:

- *Receiving*: In this area WMS toolsets consist of several functions associated with pre-receiving and receiving. Often these applications are EDI or Web-enabled. Among pre-receiving functions can be found inbound product tracking, *advanced shipping notice* (ASN) planning, delivery appointment scheduling and cross-docking, and forward picking planning. Receiving functions include PO verification, label printing, repacking, unitization, inspection, returns, and supplier audit.

- *Warehousing*: In this area can be found functions associated with material handling such as cross docking, put-away, and location and storage. Critical system functionality in this area includes palletizing, containerization, packaging, zone and random storage location selection, off-site storage support, location capacity and utilization management, bar-coding locator, serial and lot control, quarantine management, cycle counting, yard management, and interbranch transfer. The goal of these functions is to improve the accuracy of inventory storage.

- *Order management*: WMS functions in this area are focused at increasing customer service by automating picking and shipping functions, shrinking processing times, and improving service accuracy. Among the activities can be found order allocation, checking and grouping/batching, auto-replenishment of picking locations, pick list

604 DISTRIBUTION OPERATIONS EXECUTION

printing, FIFO, zone, and wave picking, product substitution, pallet layering, assembly and kitting, and scanning.

- *Labeling and floor ready*: Today's WMS must be able to handle complex product labeling requirements such as UPC tagging, shipping container marking, price mark tagging, custom label design/printing, international and customs documentation, and bar code and RFID tags.

- *Shipping and transportation*: WHS systems integrate shipping and transportation functions directly with the ERP backbone. Among WMS functions offered are shipment and load planning, pallet scanning, TL and LTL/parcel post carrier linkage, trailer management, freight rating and shopping, traffic routing/scheduling, outbound appointment scheduling, transportation analysis, and in-transit inventory tracking.

- *DC equipment support*: A critical WMS enabler is the capability to link warehouse equipment directly to the warehousing and business systems. Among these toolsets can be found auto-sortation, conveyors, RF units, speech recognition, picking/putaway equipment and robots, and equipment/vehicle maintenance management.

- *Billing*: WMS applications can also facilitate billing, time reporting, and surcharges and chargebacks.

The benefits of an effective WMS system are obvious. By automating and linking warehouse functions, companies can significantly increase warehouse productivity, efficiency and accuracy. WMS applications can reduce the past manual efforts expended on tracking locations and warehouse space recording, tracking item storage and balance accuracies, reducing stock keeping and picking personnel, and improving order management accuracy and speed. In addition, a WMS helps in performance management through effective cycle counting, automated data collection, accountability, and simulation. Finally, WMS applications enable warehousing equipment to be truly automated by integrating it with business system purchasing, receiving, order management, and shipping and transportation databases.

SUMMARY

Like other functions in the modern supply chain-focused enterprise, the goals and operating objectives of today's warehousing functions continue to undergo significant change. In the past, warehousing's role in the organization was purely operational and consisted of activities associated with receiving, storage, order picking, product sorting, traffic management, production order picking, and value-added processing. The warehouse was perceived merely as a place where inventory was stockpiled, consolidated, assorted into kitted products, and shipped to the customer. In contrast to this view, it is evident that today warehousing itself has begun to be viewed as a fundamental source of competitiveness differentiation and marketplace leadership. Through the use of such tools as the Internet, storage automation, and Lean philosophies accentuating organizational integration, quality, and elimination of all forms of waste and impediments to service leadership, the development of a comprehensive warehouse strategy has become an essential element of a successful supply chain strategy.

There are several types of warehousing alternatives that can pursue. The choice of warehouse type is governed by the ability of the decision to efficiently and effectively execute logistics functions while facilitating attainment of customer service performance targets. The optimal warehouse should permit the enterprise to leverage inventory levels, operations, and transportation modes that effectively support marketing, sales, order processing, and inventory planning in the quest for competitive advantage. In addition, the warehouse system should promote the efficient management of warehouse activities centering on the receipt, storage, picking, and shipping of inventory.

Other critical decisions facing supply chain strategists are selecting the optimal geographic location of warehouses, and effective storage and equipment design. In determining the location or scope of the channel network, planners must reconcile the firm's strategic objectives with product and competitive strategies, channel assets, working capital, and operating budgets, and marketplace strengths in delivery, price, information technology, value-added processing, and business skills. When deciding on warehouse locations, planners have the choice of using several macro or micro approaches that basically search to position facilities in locations that optimize transportation costs, proximity to suppliers and customers, and profitability.

In determining the size of the warehouse, managers must understand inventory and throughput requirements, balance the fixed and current costs associated with plant and equipment with transportation, and target the customer service level to be provided. The design, layout, and selection of equipment for a warehouse is a complex process requiring a detailed knowledge of the requirements of customer service, product stocking characteristics, material handling, receiving and loading, transportation capacities and capabilities, and the availability of automated storage and retrieval equipment. The most effective warehouse layout is the one where the physical facilities, equipment, and operational objectives are supportive of one another. The general objectives of the warehouse layout are to maximize warehouse space, labor, and equipment and to provide for good housekeeping and the ability to respond competitively to the needs of the customer.

QUESTIONS FOR REVIEW

1. Discuss the three basic functions of the modern warehouse. Why do distributors need to have warehouses?
2. How is warehousing integrated with the other major function of the enterprise?
3. Compare and contrast the advantages/disadvantages of using private or public warehousing.
4. What are the different types of warehouse? Discuss what each would be used for, and what kinds of products would best be warehoused in each type.
5. During the first decade of the twenty-first century will distributors be adding or eliminating warehouses in their supply channel structures? Discuss your reasons.
6. Why must distributors develop effective warehouse plans? Detail the planning process.
7. If productivity can be defined as the ratio of real output to real input, how could a firm measure the productivity of its storage facilities?
8. Why is the development of detailed standards so important for effective warehousing?
9. Describe the various methods of performing warehouse picking.
10. Discuss the steps necessary when determining the geographical location and size of a proposed warehouse.
11. Detail the steps required when designing a warehouse layout.

REFERENCES

1. Delaney, Robert V., "Understanding Inventory – Stay Curious," 13th Annual "State of logistics Report." Cass Information Systems, June10, 2002, Figure #10.

2. Foster, Thomas A., "The Logistics Factor," *Global Logistics and Supply Chain Strategies,* 6, 12 (2002), pp. 46-49.

3. See the discussion on developing warehouse strategies in Ackerman, Kenneth B., *Practical Handbook of Warehousing.* New York: Van Nostrand Reinhold, 1990, pp. 205-209.

4. Tompkins, James A., "The Challenge of Warehousing," in *The Warehouse Management Handbook.* New York: McGraw-Hill, 1988, p. 6.

5. Ibid., pp. 9-10.

6. Bowersox, Donald J. and Closs, David J., *Logistical Management: The Integrated Supply Chain Process.* New York: McGraw-Hill, 1996, p. 403.

7. Jenkins, Creed H., *Complete Guide to Modern Warehousing.* Englewood Cliffs, NJ: Prentice-Hall, 1990, pp. 34-48.

8. These definitions have been summarized from Appel, James M. and Ballard, Randall M., "Receiving Systems," in *The Warehouse Management Handbook.* New York: McGraw-Hill, 1988, p. 561; Jenkins, pp. 184-197, 379-384; and, Ackerman, pp. 451-453.

9. Jenkins, p. 320.

10. These figures have been gathered from Robert V. Delaney's various "State of Logistics Report" for the years cited.

11. These figures were cited by Jedd, Marcia, "The Regional Difference." *DC Velocity,* 1, 1, 2003, pp.62-65.

12. Tompkins, James A., "Distribution Today and Tomorrow." *APICS: The Performance Advantage,* 4, 4 (1994), pp. 22-28.

13. Hoover, Edger M., *The Location of Economic Activity.* New York: McGraw-Hill, 1948.

14. Schmenner, Roger W., *Making Business Location Decisions.* Englewood Cliffs, N.J.: Prentice Hall, 1982.

15. Greenhut, Melvin L., *Plant Location in Theory and in Practice.* Chapel Hill: University of North Carolina Press, 1956.

16. Harmon, Roy L., *Reinventing the Warehouse.* New York: The Free Press, 1993, pp. 66-69.

17. Jenkins, pp. 57-76. See also Gardner, R. William, "Distribution Facility Design and Construction," in *The Distribution Handbook.* Robeson, James, F. and House, Robert G., eds. New York: The Free Press 1985, pp. 584-599 and Foster, Thomas A., "Site Location Today," *Global Logistics and Supply Chain Strategies,* 6, 12, 2002, pp. 30-36.

18. Schmenner, pp. 16-21. See also Ackerman, Kenneth B., "Site Selection," in *The Warehouse Management Handbook.* New York: McGraw-Hill, 1988, pp. 82-90.

19. For more information on these techniques see Heizer, Jay and Render, Barry, *Production and Operations Management,* 3rd ed. Boston: Allyn and Bacon, 1993, pp. 344-356.

20. For more information on warehouse layout see Jenkins, pp. 156-166; Smith, Jerry D. and Peters, J. Eric, "Warehouse Space and Layout Planning," in *The Warehouse Management Handbook.* New York: McGraw-Hill, 1988, pp. 101-114; Smith, Jerry D. and Nixon, Kenneth L., "Warehouse Space and Layout Planning," in *The Distribution Management Handbook.* Tompkins, James A. and Harmelink, Dale A, eds. New York: McGraw-Hill, 1994, pp. 16.3-16.26; Mulcahy, David E., *Warehouse Distribution and Operations Handbook.* New York: McGraw-Hill, 1994, pp. 3.1-3.42; Coyle, John, J., Bardi, Edward J., and Langley, C. John Jr., *The Management of Business Logistics: A Supply Chain Perspective.* 7th ed., Mason, OH: South-Western, 2003, pp. 304-308; and Bowersox and Close, pp. 407-416.

21. For more information on storage racks see Jenkins, pp. 253-278; Donnon, J. Henry and Hammond, Ted, "Large-Parts Storage Systems," in *The Warehouse Management Handbook.* New York: McGraw-Hill, 1988, pp. 237-262; Nofsinger, John B., "Storage Equipment," in *The Distribution Management Handbook.* Tompkins, James A. and Harmelink, Dale A., eds. New York: McGraw-Hill, 1994, pp. 18.3-18.9; David R. Olson, "Material Handling Equipment," in *The Distribution Management Handbook.* Tompkins, James A. and Harmelink, Dale A., eds. New York: McGraw-Hill, 1994, p. 19.11.

22. Weiss, Donald J. and Cramer, Michael A., "Small-Parts Storage Systems," in *The Warehouse Management Handbook.* New York: McGraw-Hill, 1988, p. 263. See also Mulcahy, pp. 6.1-6.118.

23. Weiss and Cramer, p. 287.

24. Downes, Larry, "The Metamorphosis of Information," *Optimize Magazine,* June 2002, 37-43.

25. See Cooke, James A, "Vocal Minority," *Logistics Management Magazine,* 41, 10, 2002, pp. 45-48 and Douglas, Merrill, "Adding a Dash of SALT to Logistics," *Inbound Logistics,* 22, 11, 2002, pp. 80-82.

12

TRANSPORTATION

When asked to provide a functional definition of distribution, both the public and professionals alike will most likely structure their response around two general topics: *warehousing* and *transportation*. As was discussed in the previous chapter, *warehousing* is concerned with the storage and handling of inventories. Warehousing provides value by satisfying marketplace time and place utilities. *Transportation*, on the other hand, is normally associated with the movement of product from one node in the supply channel network to another. This ability to provide purposeful movement of goods in the supply chain is fundamental in assisting companies achieve time and place utilities. No matter how sophisticated the warehouse system, if a product is not available at the specific time and place it is wanted, the firm risks lost sales, faltering customer satisfaction, and increased costs resulting from order expediting. Transportation attempts to solve this problem by ensuring that product is moved as efficiently and cost-effectively as is possible from the point of origin to the point of consumption. Basically, transportation creates value by changing the location of inventory. In this sense, to conceive of a "world-class" supply chain without an efficient transportation system to support it is clearly an impossibility. Transportation's ability to create place utility by ensuring that product will be available at the time the customer wants it defines a fundamental pillar in the search for competitive advantage.

This chapter details the principles and functions of today's transportation industry. The chapter begins with a discussion of the principles and statistical scope of transportation as well as the interaction of transportation with other enterprise functions. Following this discussion, the various legal forms, performance characteristics, modes, and types of transportation are examined in depth. The chapter then proceeds to outline the transportation management process, beginning with the determination of internal transportation costs and public carrier rate standards and concluding with a review of transportation performance measurements. Following, the critical challenges confronting the transportation industry are discussed. Included is a review of today's physical transportation systems, regulation past and present, and a short analysis of today's *transportation management systems* (TMS). The chapter concludes with a detailed review of the role and activities of today's *logistics service provider* (LSP) in the management of the transportation function.

THE SCOPE OF TRANSPORTATION

The capacities and capabilities of the transportation system serving not only a particular enterprise but also the entire supply chain determine the boundaries of the market system in which both participate. The availability of inexpensive, efficient, and easily accessed transportation services activates several critical drivers of economic activity. To begin with, transportation enables companies to bridge the geographical gap between the place where products are produced and inventoried from the point where they are consumed. It is virtually impossible in modern economies for companies to function without the ability of transportation to move products from point-to-point across the supply chain. Second, transportation provides for the growth of competition. The more mature the transportation system, the greater the ability of businesses to compete with other companies in distant markets on an equal footing. Third, the wider the product distribution and the greater the demand, the more producers can leverage economies of scale in production and channel transportation costs. Finally, the more efficient and the lower the cost of transportation, the lower the selling price. Because transportation costs to the producer are normally calculated into the price of products, as costs decline and delivery capabilities rise, producers and distributors normally pass on the savings to their customers in the form of lower prices, thereby increasing marketplace advantage.

PRINCIPLES OF TRANSPORTATION

While the impact of transportation on the economic environment can be clearly defined, a detailed understanding can perhaps best be attained by a review of the principles constituting the transportation function. Overall, these principles can be broken down into three fundamental components: *economy of scale, economy of distance,* and *cost of velocity.* The principle of economy of scale states that as the volume and weight of the load increases the cost of transport decreases. For example, the cost of full truckloads (TL) shipments costs less per pound than less-than-truckload (LTL) shipments. The economy exists because the fixed cost of the transportation asset can be spread over the load's weight. The principle of the economy of distance relates to the fact that transportation cost per unit of weight decreases as distance increases. Referred to as the *tapering principle,* the longer in distance a load travels the more the fixed expenses are spread over the distance, resulting in lower overall changes. Finally, the principle of cost of velocity states that as the speed of the movement of the load increases the cost of the transportation increases. Simply, as the velocity of the load increases, the cost of transportation services, such as equipment and fuels, handling, tracking, and loss of scale economies, dramatically increases [1].

In their analysis of transportation, Fair and Williams [2] have elaborated on these three basic principles as such:

- *Continuous flow.* One of transportation's prime objectives is to provide for the uninterrupted flow of products from the producer through each node in the distribution network, concluding at the point of consumption. In pursuing this objective, transportation must continually seek ways to increase in-transit velocities by minimizing material handling, use of modal equipment, and the transfer of product while reducing costs of service.

- *Optimize unit of cargo.* The proper use of transportation requires that the cargo being transported effectively optimizes transportation vehicle capacities. This principle seeks to ensure that transporters are utilizing the best choice of vehicles, material handling equipment, and manpower that provide the best service for the price.

- *Maximum vehicle unit.* As the size of the shipping load grows larger, the capacity of the transport vehicle utilized should grow accordingly. Splitting a large load into smaller loads because of limitations in vehicle capacity will result in increased costs and loss of efficiency. This principle is based on two assumptions: (1) The operating costs of the transportation vehicle do not increase in proportion to the size; (2) service costs, such as material handling, routing and dispatching, and shipment documentation, remain unchanged regardless of the size.

- *Adaptation of vehicle unit to volume and nature of traffic.* Shippers must continually search for techniques to match vehicle transport characteristics and capacities with the transit environment. This principle requires that transportation vehicle size, weight, storage capacity, and speed be optimized to permit as free as possible a flow through the traffic medium. For example, the development of equipment such as two-level rack carriers for automobiles pulled by trucks is targeted at optimizing transport that minimizes costs and facilitates transit through the highway system.

- *Standardization.* Although specialized vehicles are often necessary to meet the shipping requirements of certain goods, the existence of standardized truck trailers, railcars, cargo ships, and air containers offer economical methods to transport products. Because of their general availability, capacity to handle a wide variety of products, and ability to be utilized for backhaul, standardized vehicles often can provide lowest cost transport. This principle also applies to the standardization of docking facilities, material handling equipment, and methods of operation.

- *Compatibility of unit-load equipment.* This principle emphasizes the requirement that material handling equipment placed in transport vehicles and containers should readily fit and maximize cube space. In addition, equipment should be positioned so as to minimize damage to cargo and reduce load shift during transport.

- *Minimization of deadweight to total weight.* The cost of fuel when transporting products is directly derived by combining the weight of the load (payload) and the weight (deadweight) of the vehicle, containers, and material handling equipment. Normally, the larger the transportation vehicle, the more favorable the ratio of payload to total weight. The use of lightweight materials and vehicle design can assist transporters decrease the deadweight of containers and transport vehicles.

- *Maximum utilization of capital, equipment, and personnel.* Transport vehicle design, routing and scheduling, and operational practices can significantly impact the effective utilization of transport resources. Utilization in transport refers to the percentage of time equipment and personnel are in use. The objective of transportation management is to reduce utilization imbalances caused by seasonality, the lack of operational practices such as backhaul, and poor scheduling of vehicle loading and unloading.

A thorough understanding of these principles is essential in developing transportation strategies. The object is to establish transportation selection processes that maximize on transportation economies while minimizing premium carrier modes.

Transportation services. The role of transportation is to offer supply chains participants a variety of critical services. In general, these services can be grouped into two main areas: *load transport* and *product storage.* Load transport services are concerned with the movement of product from an origin location to a geographical receiving point. During this process, the goal is to enhance the value of the product by positioning it in a more advantageous marketing location while minimizing the cost of in-transit inventories, expenditures for transportation and labor assets, and impact on environmental factors such as air pollution, energy consumption, and congestion. In general transport services can be described as follows:

- *Freight services.* The obvious function performed by transportation is the movement of goods through the supply chain network. These services can be performed internally or through the use of a third party provider. Among the transport types can be found direct delivery from origin to the customer, the use of air transport for next day delivery, third party ground delivery within a certain shipment radius, delivery of items requiring special storage such as refrigeration or perishability, freight service for heavy and/or bulky items, LTL/parcel post delivery of small/light items, and global package delivery by air or by freight.

- *Terminal Services.* Whether performed in-house or by a third party carrier, transportation terminals provide several critical services. The most obvious is the pickup and delivery of products from and to channel warehouses. Another critical service involves the performance of value-added processing functions. Among these can be found *consoli-*

dation of many small shipments into full vehicle/container shipments that will optimize transportation costs. Another service is *bulkbreak* whereby large quantities to be shipped are broken down by customer order into smaller deliveries. A third is *shipment service* where normally a third-party provides freight-handling services and performs billing, routing, and other clerical functions. A final terminal service performed by transportation is product and ownership *interchange* [3].

- *Loading and unloading.* When transit is performed by a third party carrier, responsibility for the loading and unloading of transport vehicles varies by type of shipment. For example, when parcel post is used the carrier normally performs the function. For TL shipments, the shipper is required to load and the receiver is required to unload the vehicle. Also, the carrier may perform these services for a charge. The receiver is permitted a specified amount of time (normally one or two days) to unload the vehicle. After that grace period, the carrier normally will charge a fee (termed *demurrage* in rail transport or *detention* in motor transport) per storage vehicle for each day the equipment remains at the receiving location.

- *Value-added services.* Transportation also provides a number of value-added services beyond material handling and transport. Among these can be found electronic tracking of shipments from pickup to delivery, availability of label imaging systems such as UPC or Bar Code, delivery confirmation, management and control of inbound customer transportation charges, expediting of shipments to rush delivery, and line-haul services that permit shippers to change a shipment's destination (*reconsignment/diversion*) or to perform some function that physically changes product characteristics (*transit privilege*).

- *Documentation.* Transportation is normally responsible for the processing, control, and transmission of all shipping documentation. Documentation can consist of domestic documents, such as the *bill of lading, freight bills, F.O.B. terms of sale,* and *claims,* and international documents, such as *sales contracts, terms of sale,* and *export documents.*

- *Transportation rates.* In most organizations the transportation function is responsible for establishing shipping rates when third party transport carriers are contracted. Several factors are used in the determination of transportation services rates. The process begins with the calculation of the actual cost of the needed services. This cost will act as the basis price to be used in carrier selection. Next, planners must factor in additional prices due to the nature of the product to be transported. Based on the principle of the *value of service,* as the value of products increases, so do the transportation charges. Besides the value of the product, the amount of distance to be transported needs to be considered when developing the price. Normally, the greater the distance the product is moved, the greater the transportation rate. This increase in cost due to distance, however, is not directly proportional. Because of the *tapering rate principle*, the rate structure tapers due to the fact that the greater the distance, the more carriers can spread costs, such as handling and shipping monitoring, over a greater mileage base. Finally, the calculation of the full price must consider the weight. For the most part, the price of transport will decline as the weight and volume increases.

The second major area of transportation services is product storage. While the role of transportation is to move products from destination to delivery point, often transporters must perform temporary in-transit storage functions. The following types of storage can be found:

- *Transport mode.* A common type of in-transit storage is to temporarily store products in their mode of shipment, such as trailers, containers, or tank cars. While the cost of this type of storage is high and is normally used to span a very short period, it can be profitably deployed when the cost is lower than the cost of unloading, warehousing, and reloading transport vehicles.

- *In-transit storage.* A variation of in-transit storage is to select a transportation method that would take longer than a more direct or expensive mode to reach its destination. The objective of this delaying option would be to use the transportation mode as a sort of rolling storage facility to solve space shortage problems at the receiver's warehouse.

- *Diversion and reconsignment.* Often companies will postpone shipment receipt by changing the shipment's destination and/or consignee while in transit. Diversion permits the shipper to divert a shipment from its original destination to an alternative destination while en route. Reconsignment provides a similar capability by allowing designation of an alternative destination after it has reached its original destination, but before it has been delivered to its original consignee.

The services transportation can render to the organization are a critical and often overlooked component of competitive strategy. Effective transportation requires a thorough understanding of such functions as pricing, use of third party carriers for terminal services associated with loading and unloading, consolidation, and bulkbreak, transportation regulations governing domestic and international transport, and the selection of in-transit storage. An in-depth knowledge of transportation services and principles is fundamental to the effective cost management and optimization of the logistics system.

Transportation statistics.   The importance of transportation in the deployment of inventory in the manufacturing, wholesale, and retail sectors of the economy can be best understood when the annual expenditure for transportation is matched against the Gross National Product (GNP).   According to Delaney [4], the cost of transportation and shipper related costs in 2002 totaled $577 billion, or 5.5 percent of GNP. When compared with figures since 1981, the transportation side of total physical distribution costs has declined some 21 percent as deregulation enabled more efficient use of all forms of transportation. 2002 saw a dramatic drop in transportation costs, but this is attributable more to the poor economic conditions than to improvement in cost management and will most likely be an anomaly. Since 1990, the ratio between transportation cost and GNP has remained fairly stable and has plateaued around 6 percent of GDP (Table 12.1).

TABLE 12.1 **Cost of Transportation in Relation to GNP (1981 – 2002)**

Year	GNP $ Trillion	Transportation Costs	% of GNP
1981	3.13	$228	7.2
1985	4.21	274	6.5
1990	5.80	351	6.0
1995	7.40	441	5.9
1998	8.78	529	6.0
2000	9.87	590	5.9
2001	10.08	605	6.0
2002	10.47	577	5.5

As is illustrated in Figure 12.1, the cost-side of the transportation system can be essentially broken up into five main areas. Of the five, two are dominated by motor transportation. Without a doubt, it is the motor carrier that drives the U.S. business logistics system. By referencing Figure 12.1, highway transport in 2002 accounted for 80 percent of the total cost of transportation. In terms of the sheer size of shipments in 2001, U.S. carriers shipped 20.1 billion ton miles, with domestic carriers accounting for 7.5 billion and international carriers accounting for 12.6 billion [Table 12.2].

RELATIONSHIP OF TRANSPORTATION TO OTHER BUSINESS FUNCTIONS

As was pointed out in Chapter 2, transportation is one of the key functions constituting business logistics. Although some may argue that warehousing is the pivotal logistics element, a warehouse cannot remain functional for

Transportation Costs		$ Billions
Motor Carriers:		
Truck – Intercity...		300
Truck – Local..		162
	Subtotal	462
Other Carriers:		
Railroads..		37
Water...........(International 19, Domestic 9)............		27
Oil Pipelines..		9
Air...............(International 7, Domestic 17)...........		27
Forwarders...		9
	Subtotal	109
Shipping Related Costs...		6
	Total Transportation Costs	577

FIGURE 12.1 Total transportation costs - 2001

long without transportation. It is transportation's role to deliver products to the warehouse from supply points in the distribution channel. It is also transportation's responsibility to provide the services necessary to move product from the warehouse to the customer in as efficient and cost-effective a manner as possible. Whereas warehousing may rightfully be called the "heart" of the supply chain function, transportation forms the veins and arteries through which the heart pumps products and value-added services from one channel member to another.

TABLE 12.2 Freight and Express Services

Figures in millions of ton miles

Date	Domestic	International	Total
1991	4,946	5,279	10,225
1993	5,458	6,486	11,944
1995	6,397	8,181	14,578
1997	7,169	10,789	17,959
1999	7,289	12,028	19,317
2000	7,953	13,490	21,443
2001	7,452	12,657	20,109

Source: U.S. Department of Transportation, 2002

The transportation and handling of inventories provides other business functions with essential information concerning products, marketing place and time utilities, and transit costs and capabilities necessary for effective supply chain planning and operations execution. Some of these functions interact directly with transportation; others are indirectly impacted. The relationship between transportation and other business functions can be described as follows:

- *Strategic planning.* As enterprises design and improve on their product and service value portfolios, the capabilities and costs associated with the transportation network serve as key inputs to business decisions. Whether it be expanding their geographical footprint or acquiring new companies, strategists must consider how leveraging transportation can optimize their proposed networks. Perhaps the most critical factor is reducing their "cost to serve" by ensuring transportation enablers can cost effectively link re-deployed manufacturing and distribution channel nodes while increasing flexibility and service.

- *Traffic management.* Many logistics functions have a traffic management department that is responsible for monitoring the appropriate transportation modes necessary to move products through the channel pipeline. Figure 12.2 examines the different responsibilities of the modern traffic manager. Over the past decade, warehouse and traffic management have been working closely to reduce the cost of transportation while improving delivery service. Most major freight traffic movement in the United States is governed by master contracts thoroughly negotiated with fine-tuned precision. If the firm possesses its own transportation vehicles, traffic management needs to work closely with warehousing in planning and selecting the optimal mix of private, public, and transport services.

FIGURE 12.2 Administrative functions of the traffic manager.

- *Warehouse receiving and shipping.* The effective scheduling of product receiving and shipping is fundamental to the smooth flow of both warehousing and transportation. For example, instead of planning with carriers to have product delivery synchronized, vehicles haphazardly arrive in bunches. The result is that vehicles have to wait their turn to be loaded and unloaded, costing the company or the private carrier dearly in lost productivity. In addition, inadequate scheduling forces the warehouse to staff excess receivers and shippers than would be unnecessary if the work flow was evened out. Poor scheduling also causes daily periods of intense activity followed by periods of expensive idleness. Finally, poor scheduling causes the warehouse to digest uneven flows of material, requiring unnecessary material handling equipment, and overflow staging areas.
- *Purchasing.* Purchasing decisions have a direct impact on transportation. The physical attributes, quantity, and volume of purchased products require purchasers and transportation to work together to ensure that the cost, availability, and adequacy of transport vehicles are sufficient. In addition, purchasing can positively influence efficient supplier delivery that can facilitate receiving activities. Areas of cooperation include the following:
  - Working with suppliers in determining the most efficient containerization methods for inbound products. Possible options include selecting the best method to package, unitize, or palletize purchased goods that will minimize damage, optimize carrier capacities, and speed shipment and receiving.
  - Selecting the best transport equipment. This factor is particularly important for firms that possess their own carrier services.
  - Determining the timing and location of supplier deliveries.
- *Customer service.* Customer service delivery policy will have a significant affect on outbound transportation. When customers place orders, the price of the shipping and expected delivery can be as important as the product price. Service reps will need access to negotiated shipping rates and lead times to not only provide key information, but also to assist them in the selection of the appropriate service level and cost that meets customers' requirements. Today's technology-enabled customer is also demanding the ability to leverage EDI and Internet tools to increase in-transit inventory visibility as well as accurate freight cost allocation for their orders.
- *Product pricing.* The transportation decision has a direct bearing on product pricing. Because transportation is a significant component of total operations costs, transportation expense must be factored along

with purchasing, labor, and overhead costs when determining product selling prices. Generally, the importance of transportation in price determination grows as transportation's share of product costs increases. Transportation costs can be as high as 50 percent or more of the selling price of bulk commodities such as coal or wood and may be less that 1 percent for small-volume hard goods.

- *Supply channel locations.* As was pointed out in Chapter 11, deciding where to locate new channel warehouses is a complex affair, requiring detailed analysis. Among the key factors in the planning process is determining the cost, availability, and adequacy of modes of transportation. For example, if a distributor depends heavily on railroads for product delivery, any decision concerning the location of a new warehouse will be influenced by close proximity to rail transport.

- *Inventory planning.* One of the areas of critical importance to inventory planning is the comprehensive and timely maintenance of in-transit inventory information. Whether statistical replenishment or MRP/DRP techniques are employed, accurate information relating to in-transit quantities and delivery dates is essential to effective inventory planning and order promising.

MODES OF TRANSPORTATION

There are essentially five *modes* of transportation that may be used to move goods through the supply channel and out to the customer. These five methods are as follows: motor, railroad, water, pipeline, and air transport. Each provides the supply chain with certain advantages and each has its own particular limitation. In addition, certain combinations, or *intermodal*, variations are possible. These include railroad-motor, motor-water, motor-air and rail-water. *Intermodal* combinations of transport will be discussed at the end of this section. Each of these transportation modes is described in detail below.

MOTOR TRANSPORT

As was mentioned above, highway motor transport is by far the most popular mode of transportation today, accounting in 2001 for 80 percent of all transportation revenues. The characteristic feature of this mode is that transit occurs on the nation's highway network over which different types of carriers operate a variety of motorized vehicles capable of carrying a wide range of loads. Unlike the railroads, which must own and maintain tracks, line equipment, and structures, the motor industry has the ability to move products freely over 4 million miles of roads in the U.S. alone. It is estimated that the U.S.

interstate highway system carries more than one-fifth of the total motor transport each year. As such, motor carrier capital investment is normally confined to transport equipment, terminals, and related repair and storage facilities.

The cost structure of the trucking industry is highly direct-cost intensive. Although the fixed costs for trucks, trailer rigs, and material handling equipment are significant, variable costs involved in labor, taxes and tolls for use of public highways, terminal expenses, fuel, taxes, licenses, and insurance account for 80 percent to 90 percent of total motor transport costs. Of these costs, labor accounts for about 60 percent of each cost dollar. Generally speaking, about $0.97 cents of every operating dollar is consumed by operating expenses, with the balance going to cover interest costs and return to investors. As a result, the trucking industry cannot operate for very long with rates below costs. In 2001, there were approximately 593,000 interstate motor carriers registered with the U.S. Department of Transportation employing over 4.7 million drivers, deliverymen, and couriers. Less than full truckload (LTL) carrier leaders in 2002 were United Parcel Service with revenues of $16 billion, Yellow Freight ($3.3 billion), Roadway Express ($2.8 billion), North American Logistics ($2.2 billion), and Con-Way Transportation ($2.0 billion). Bulk transportation leaders were Schneider National with 2001 revenues of $2.4 billion, J.B. Hunt ($2.2 billion), Swift Transportation ($1.3 billion) and Werner Enterprises (1.3 billion) [5].

Traditionally, motor transportation equipment has been divided into two categories: intercity over-the-road equipment and specialized short-haul equipment. The former category generates the majority of all motor transport revenues. Equipment-wise, intercity freight carriers are usually characterized by the familiar tractor-trailer rig, but it also can consist of special equipment to haul products such as automobiles, liquids, tandem or double bottoms, refrigerated, and large storage containers. Specialized short-haul equipment is normally much smaller in volume capacity and more flexible in order to handle a wider variety of products than intercity equipment. This category of motor transport is used for pick-up and delivery of products over short distances (up to a maximum of 20-30 miles). Automobiles, vans, trucks, and short tractor-trailer rigs are examples of short-haul equipment.

The growth of motor transportation can be traced to several factors. To begin with, the speed, flexibility, and relative cost of motor transport are more in alignment with today's strategies aimed at high customer service and Quick Response. These attributes have made motor transport over the past half century the favored choice for manufacturers, distributors, and retailers to haul high-value products over short distances. Unlike the other modes of transportation, motor carriers can provide supply-point-to-supply-point service. Furthermore, equipment versatility permits companies to ship almost any weight or quantity easily and cost-effectively. Motor carriers also provide faster service than railroads and can successful compete with air transport for short hauls. Finally, product loss and damage ratios for motor carriers are substantially less than for most rail shipments.

Still, despite its overwhelming benefits, motor transport will be facing significant challenges in the twenty-first century. Perhaps the foremost is surviving the difficult economic climate. Because of high terminal costs and marketing expenses, LTL carriers in particular, are experiencing extensive consolidation. The bankruptcy in 2002 of 73-year-old Consolidated Freightways, who in 2001 controlled 14 percent of the LTL market, bears evidence of the volatility of the industry. Furthermore, motor transport must assist government and industry find solutions to such issues as shipment security, congestion, pollution, fuel taxes, changes in the workforce and technology, and the globalization of competition.

RAILROAD TRANSPORT

Historically, transportation in the U.S. was dominated by the railroad. From the mid-nineteenth century to the conclusion of World War II, the continental U.S. was linked by a network of rails that provided for the economic and speedy transport of products and travel services. Today, while motor transport accounts for the bulk of transportation revenues, railroads surpass all other modes in terms of shipping tonnage, accounting for almost half of the freight shipped in the United States. This leadership is due primarily to rail's ability to transport large volumes of freight over long distances. In 2000, railroads carried over 1.4 trillion ton-miles of freight (non-commuter) over a track network totaling over 100,000 miles. In 2000, there were 8 major freight-carrying railroads in the United States, employing 168,000 people and operating over 1 million freight cars [6]. For the most part, railroad usage had been declining since the end of World War II, when rail accounted for about two-thirds of the ton-mile traffic. The growth of motor transport has generally absorbed a good deal of the small haulage while water and pipeline carriers have been eroding away the shipment of bulk commodities.

All for-hire railroads in the U.S. are classified as *common carriers*. After deregulation, railroads can legally offer their services to all shippers and are not restricted as to cargo type. The railroad industry consists of a small number of large firms. Altogether, there are about 360 railroads, of which fewer than ten have revenues that exceed $250 million [7]. The reason for the limited number of rail carriers is explained by the nature of the industry. One of the most visible characteristic of rail transport is the enormous physical plant consisting of track and accompanying rolling stock, terminals, miscellaneous facilities, and administrative and management support. Unlike motor transport that uses the public highway system, rail must maintain its own facilities. Because of this very large *fixed* expense, the costs associated with rights-of-way (tunnels and bridges), equipment maintenance, interest, depreciation, taxation, and other costs must be absorbed by the carrier. Unlike other modes of transportation whose life cycles are considerably shorter, the cost of rail maintenance and physical plant remains fairly stable over the life of the equipment and has a minimal impact on transport rates. This means that railroads can take significant advantage of economies of scale. The average freight train hauls a load of 2500 tons and pulls an average of 71.5 cars per freight train. Over the past 10 years, the trend has been greater load per rail car, greater average daily car mileage, and faster trains [8]. Simply stated, as the volume of freight increases, the total cost of transport decreases on a per-unit basis.

Although the most significant advantage enjoyed by rail carriers is that they can transport larger volumes of goods over great distances at a cost generally less than air and motor carriage, there are some distinct disadvantages. To begin with, rail compares unfavorably to motor cartage when it comes to transit time and frequency of service. Trains run on specific timetable schedules dictating departure and arrival. In addition, rail provides terminal-to-terminal service rather than stocking point-to-point service as does motor transit. Unless the shipper has a railroad siding, product must be unloaded and reloaded using other transit modes before it arrives at the stocking point. Finally, rail carriers have not been able to guarantee the same general equipment availability as motor carriers. Part of the problem is that the proper storage car may not be physically present at the shipment location when needed. In order to overcome poor utilization or have rolling stock lost in the cross-country rail network, the rail industry has been turning to a number of advancements in car and information systems designs. Such developments as computerized routing and scheduling, railcar identification systems, development of specialized cars, upgrading of equipment, roadbeds, and terminals, and nonstop shipments between metropolitan areas have enabled the rail industry not only to hold its own but to enjoy the opportunity for growth in the twenty-first century.

AIR TRANSPORT

Outside of pipelines, air carriers account for the smallest proportion of ton-mile traffic. In 2001 air transport revenues amount to $24 billion and accounted for only 4 percent of all transportation revenues. Although the Industry grew during the late 1990s, the sagging economy, airline bankruptcies, terrorist attacks, and war in the Persian Gulf during the first three years of the new century dramatically hurt air transport. Revenues declines over 11 percent as compared to the previous year ($27 billion). Overall ton miles declined 9.2 percent in 2001 to 14.01 billion revenue ton miles; overall shipments declined some 19 percent in 2002 to 2.58 billion from the peak of nearly 3 billion in 2000. It has been estimated that altogether the industry has lost from three to five years of growth. Returning to positive growth will require air cargo companies to successfully meet new security and safety provisions, increased customer expectations, and internal pressures to be profitable and competitive.

For most airlines, providing freight transport is incidental to carrying passengers which is treated on a space-available basis. In 2002, of the 1.6 billion tons of cargo shipped by air, 1.4 billion tons was carried by cargo airlines and 200.8 million tons was carried by passenger airlines. The air carrier industry, furthermore, is highly concentrated into a small number of carriers that account for nearly 90 percent of the industry's revenues. While passenger airlines dominate, freight service companies, like UPS, Airborne, Federal Express, and Emery have their own fleets dedicated solely to transporting freight. These carriers transport approximately 50 percent of all domestic air transport freight.

Air transport equipment costs are associated with the aircraft and supporting ground equipment and labor. For the most part, these variable costs are high, accounting for over 80 percent of every airline expense dollar. Support equipment is used mostly for transporting people, freight, baggage, and fuels to and from the aircraft. Although the military does possess special aircraft used exclusively for freight and troop transport, commercial aircraft, even those used only for freight, is designed around the passenger business. In addition, the standard cargo bays in most aircraft are suitable only for freight that is not subject to special requirements, such as refrigeration, gases and flammable liquids, and dry-bulk storage.

The use of air transport provides shippers with some significant advantages. The most obvious is the speed of service. Aircraft can deliver goods in a fraction of the time required by the other four modes of transportation. In addition, air carriers generally offer excellent frequency and reliability of service, particularly to major metropolitan areas. Air carriers are most profitably used under the following circumstances:

1. Speedy transportation of high-value, low-weight products that need to traverse long distances
2. Emergency transport of critical repair parts
3. Emergency transport of products from stocking point to stocking point in the supply channel to prevent loss of sales

4. Emergency shipments of components necessary to eliminate interruptions in production processes

5. Speedy transport of perishables and seasonal products such as exotic flowers, foodstuffs, and fashion apparel

The foremost disadvantage to the use of air transport is the high cost of service in comparison to the other four transport modes. In addition, the limited cargo capacities of aircraft make it unsuitable for most classes of product. Finally, like rail transport, air carriers function terminal-to-terminal rather than stocking point to stocking point. This means that product must be unloaded from aircraft and then reloaded onto motor transport which then delivers the cargo to the receiving company. Another significant drawback is weather. While modern day navigation equipment has enabled air carriers to cut back on disruptions to service caused by minor weather problems, of the five transport methods air transport is the most susceptible to weather conditions.

WATER TRANSPORT

Historically, water transportation was the earliest form of mass transportation in North America. Although during the colonial period there were a few common carriers that transported goods by ferries, stagecoaches, and wagon lines, the almost nonexistent state of the nation's roads made water transport the only economical means of moving products from place to place until the arrival of the railroad starting in the 1840s. The most important forms of water transport were the trans-Atlantic trade, rivers, lakes, and bays, and the canal systems that were begun in the 1820s and 1830s. Then as now, water transport is particularly suited to the movement of large, heavy, low-value-per-unit goods that can be unloaded and loaded efficiently by mechanical means. Water transport lends itself particularly well to commodity-type products, such as iron ore, grains, building materials, and fuels, which do not require quick delivery and are not particularly subject to shipping theft or damage.

Today, with the explosion in global trade, water transport has grown into a significant industry. In 2001 the U.S. water cargo industry showed revenues of $19 billion for international and $9 billion for domestic trade, a growth of over 6 and 12 percent respectively over 2000 totals. While in 2001 water transportation accounted for only about 4.7 percent of all transportation revenues, its importance is expanding. According to a report by the Colography Group in April of 2003, global water transportation is expected to outpace air transport in growth. Total international shipping is forecasted to reach 10.98 trillion pounds with about 52 billion pounds moving by air. Of the estimated $5.9 trillion in total international goods shipped in 2003, $2.3 trillion will move by air and $3.6 trillion will move by sea, a 4.3 percent increase over 2002 levels.

Most texts on transportation divide water transportation into two major categories: *domestic* and *international*. U.S. domestic water carriers operations can be broken down into three major areas. The first, *internal water transport*, consists of the various inland rivers and canals crisscrossing the nation. Excluding the Great Lakes and seacoasts, this category consists of approximately 26,000 miles of waterway, the heaviest utilized being the rivers and canals associated with the Mississippi Basin. About 55 percent of the inland waterway traffic moves in this river system. The second water transportation category, the *Great Lakes System*, comprises some 95,000 square miles of natural waterways, with a coastline of 8300 miles. About 10 percent of the total of the nation's inland waterway traffic in tons ($545 million in 1999) navigates on the Great Lakes. In addition, continuing improvements in Great Lakes facilities has provided access to the Atlantic Ocean and connection with the Mississippi River system through canals. *Coastal* and *inter-costal transport* is the third category of water transport. Comprised of the many rivers, canals, bays, inlets, and channels that are connected to the Atlantic and Pacific oceans and the Gulf of Mexico, coastal transport accounts for the remaining 35 percent of domestic water transport. Companies in this trade belong to one of four modes: private, contract, regulated, or exempt.

On domestic waterways can be found large ships used on the Great Lakes called *lakers*. Although they are similar to ocean vessels, their long, low profiles render them unseaworthy in the face of weather conditions characteristic of ocean waters. In contrast, on the inland water systems, barges propelled by towboats are the most common equipment. There are primarily three types of barge. *Open-hopper barges* carry dry bulk cargoes such as coal, sand, gravel, and limestone. *Covered dry cargo barges* primarily transport grains. Finally, *tank barges* provide sealed storage environments for transporting petroleum, liquids, or gases. Because of their shallow draft and ability to be linked together as a single unit or *tow*, barges are ideal for navigating the shallow depths of rivers and canals.

The second major category is international water transportation. This method is by far the most popular international shipping method and accounts for over 70 percent of all U.S. international freight. U.S. companies can utilize water to transport almost any product across the globe, but, for the most part, this method is used primarily for low weight-to-value commodities such as petroleum, minerals, dry bulk items, and commodities that are easily containerized. The type of equipment used is governed by the commodity carried and the category of waterway to be navigated. On the world's oceans, large sea-going vessels are used. These ships normally are specifically designed to transport various types of bulk cargos and can be described as *bulk carriers* used for ores, grains, and metals; *tankers* used for petroleum and natural gas; *containers* used for packaged commodities and food-stuffs; *roll-on-roll-off* (RO-RO) used for automobiles and motor transport; and *ocean-going barges* used to carry a wide-variety of products that are pulled by tugs over short ocean voyages to places like Puerto Rico and the Hawaiian islands.

The major disadvantages to water transport are its relative slowness as compared to other transport modes, dependence on water terminals and ports, and low frequency of movement. Advantages possessed by water transport are that of all the transport modes with the exception, perhaps, of pipelines, it is the least expensive and is the most capable. Virtually anything can be shipped by water, especially bulk-type products. For example, a single barge tow comprised of 15 barges each with a capacity of 1500 tons, is the equivalent of 2.25, 100-car train units or 900 large semi truck rigs.

PIPELINES

Compared to the other modes, pipelines are one of the oldest forms of transportation. Perhaps the most unique feature of pipelines is their physical plant. Other than pipes, pumping stations, storage tanks, input and dispersal facilities, and land, pipeline transport is not dependent on roads or facilities and is barely visible to the public at large. As pipelines have no vehicles, maintenance and investment are minimal and no backhaul problem exists. In addition, the pipeline industry is highly automated. The movement of product within the pipeline system can be controlled from pumping stations hundreds of miles away, where computers are used to schedule and monitor operations. Pipelines are very capital-intensive. In 1977, it was estimated that $21 billion had been invested in the pipeline industry. In the late 1980s, it was estimated that it would cost about $70 billion to replace the existing pipeline system. That cost would be dramatically much higher today. The pipeline industry operates (1999) over 177,000 miles of oil pipelines, and (2000) over 1.4 million miles of gas pipelines. In 1990, approximately 22 percent of all domestic intercity ton-mile freight was transported using pipelines [9]. In relationship to the other four transportation modes, pipelines revenues accounted for $9 billion in 2001, or about 1.5 of total U.S. transportation.

The use of pipeline transport is governed by the types of products that can be carried by this mode. There are three basic types of pipeline associated with certain products: oil, natural gas, and slurry. In transporting these products, pipelines can be mounted above or buried beneath the ground. For the most part, pipelines can only be used with commodities that are in liquid or gaseous form. Petroleum products, crude oil, kerosene, water, chemicals, and natural gas are excellent products for pipeline transport. In the oil industry for example, pipelines are used to gather crude oil from the field, which flows to the refinery. Product lines then distribute the finished goods from refineries to consuming centers. Another important type of pipeline product is slurry. Often, solid products can be ground and added to water for pipeline transport. For instance, coal can be reduced to a powdered state, combined with water, transported via pipeline, and converted back into a solid at the receiving point by removing the water component. By far, the predominant users of pipelines are the oil and natural gas industries, with slurry products constituting a very small percentage.

Advantages associated with the use of pipeline transport are significant for liquefied types of products. Pipelines provide an extremely high level of service dependability at a relatively low cost. Pipelines can move large volumes of product, are not labor-intensive, can be easily monitored through automated computer control, are almost free of the chance of loss or damage to product due to leaks or breaks, and are impervious to climatic conditions. On the negative side, pipelines are extremely limited to the products they can transport, have no geographical flexibility, are comparatively slow in speed, and require the use of other transport modes as finished product moves closer to ultimate consumers or retail outlets.

Each of the five transport modes has specific performance characteristic strengths and weaknesses. As detailed above, when making transportation decisions, managers must consider speed, completeness, dependability, capability, frequency, and cost associated with the performance characteristic of each transport mode. Table 12.3 ranks the performance characteristic of each of the five modes of transportation according to these criteria.

INTERMODAL TRANSPORTATION

One of the most debated topics in the field of transportation is the proper allocation of freight traffic among the five transport modes. The issue revolves around the supposition that shippers do not always use the most appropriate carrier mode to transport products and that too much or too little traffic is being carrier by one mode, resulting in loss of efficiencies and possible injuries to the environment. One of the methods to combat possible inequalities in transport mode use is the application of *intermodal* methods. The basis of intermodal forms of transportation resides in the development of systems that integrate or combine together various elements of the five modes of transportation. For the most part, intermodal transportation has focused around variations in the following two methods: *truck trailer on a rail flatcar* (TOFC) and *container on a rail flat car* (COFC).

TABLE 12.3 Transportation Performance Characteristics

Transport Mode	Speed	Completeness	Dependability	Capability	Frequency	Cost
Motor	2	1	3	3	1	2
Rail	3	3	4	4	3	3
Air	1	2	1	2	2	1
Water	5	5	5	5	5	5
Pipeline	4	4	2	1	4	4

Note: 1 = highest

TOFC. The basis of intermodalism in transport is how to facilitate the transfer of unitized loads from one form of transport to another. TOFC, often called the *piggyback system*, is a method by which a truck trailer load is transferred in-transit from the truck carrier to another transit mode without unloading and reloading product. An example would be the use of a motor tractor and trailer for local pick up. When the route is completed, the tractor-trailer would then be loaded intact onto a rail flatbed, which would then execute a long-distance haul. Upon arrival, the rig would be unloaded and would proceed to carry out delivery to the customer. In this TOFC example the low-cost advantages of long-haul rail transport is combined with the flexibility and convenience of the motor carrier. There are several possible forms of TOFC systems. Piggyback methods can be used between motor carrier and rail or between motor carrier and transoceanic vessels or barge (*fishyback*).

COFC. The transfer of containers from one mode of transport to another is a key component of intermodal transportation. A container system is characterized by the storage of products in a box or similar form of container. Normally, the container size has been standardized to facilitate loading and unloading across several transportation modes. In addition to ease of movement, containers also inhibit theft and decrease the possibility of damage. Operationally, COFC methods function similarly to TOFC methods. Procedurally, the container(s) are first loaded onto motor flat bed trailers at the shipping point. After what is usually a short haul, the containers are then unloaded onto flatbed railcars, waterway carriers, or even special air cargo planes for delivery. Upon arrival, the containers are loaded back onto motor carriers for customer delivery.

A variation on the intermodal forms of transport discussed above is the use of an innovative intermodal vehicle called a *railroader* or a *trailertrain*. A railroader is a special form of vehicle that combines motor and rail transport in a single piece of equipment. The railroader resembles a conventional motor trailer that has been specially equipped with both road tires and railroad track wheels that can be rotated as necessary. When the vehicle is used as a railcar, the road tires are retracted and the vehicle rides directly on the steel rail wheels. The advantage of a railroader is savings in time and handling costs to mount conventional semi-truck systems onto railcars. The disadvantage is obviously the excess weight and added costs caused by hauling the steel wheels when the trailer is on the highway.

The use of intermodal methods of transportation promises great benefits to shippers. It can provide better and more flexible services as well as wider area coverage at lower rates. Furthermore, by combining the optimum transportation modes to fit the transportation task, it offers shippers the ability to tailor a transportation package for each system that maximizes transport efficiencies. Still, although intermodal methods offer significant cost advantages and their use has grown over the last four decades, intermodal shares a very small portion of total transportation revenues. According to Delaney [10], intermodal transportation in 1992 accounted for only about $6-8 billion of the $297 billion trucking and $30 billion railroad industries. Despite the fact that the U.S. government has actually established an Intermodal Agency and passed legislation (the Intermodal Surface Transportation Efficiency Act of 1991) designed to promote intermodal transportation, it is evident that manufacturers and distributors prefer to focus their expenditures on trucking services. Undoubtedly, the efficiency, reliability, and faster delivery service provided by the trucking industry is perceived as enabling firms to hold less inventory, hold it in fewer locations, and consolidate shipments from different origins into a single delivery.

TYPES OF TRANSPORTATION

There are several different legal modes of transportation that can be employed by traffic management. Choosing the appropriate type of transportation consists of a number of marketing, product, warehouse location, customer service, and financial decisions. The goal is to develop operational methods that consistently provide for the selection of the best transport carrier system that efficiently and effectively executes transportation requirements while simultaneously facilitating the attainment of customer service performance targets. Factors influencing transportation selection include the type of distribution environment to be serviced, supply chain strategic goals, required delivery lead time, financial capacities, product characteristics such as order quantity size, physical characteristics such as size, perishability, seasonality, potential for obsolescence and theft, and intrinsic value, geographic size of the channel network, carrier-type availability, and strength of the competition.

LEGAL FORMS OF TRANSPORTATION

Before transportation modes are discussed, it is necessary to review how the various types of transportation are legally owned and organized. As a result of the Interstate Commerce Commission (ICC) Termination Act of 1995, essentially five basic types of carrier have emerged: common, regulated, contract, exempt, and private. The first four types are owned more or less by for-hire freight companies and are subject to various federal, state, and local statutes and regulations. In contrast, the fifth type, private carrier, consists of company-owned equipment that is used to transport company products and supplies through proprietary channel networks. The following is a brief review of the five legal types of transportation:

- *Common Carriers.* A common carrier provides transport services to the general public according to a published rates schedule. Although, common carriers no longer have to file their rates with the Interstate ICC, they are still, nevertheless, the most heavily regulated of the five types of carrier. The purpose of this level of control is to protect the shipping public and ensure cost effective service within reasonable limits. In order to operate legally, common carriers must be granted authority from the appropriate federal regulatory agency. Normally, this authority also defines the type of product or commodity that can be carried and the geographical area or terminal points to be served. As part of their legal obligation, common carriers must service all comers, provide rates, classifications, rules, or practices if requested by the shipper, provide service to all points prescribed in their certificates of authority, and deliver products within a reasonable time even if the shipment is not profitable.

- *Regulated Carriers.* This class of carrier provides basically the same functions as a common carrier, but with a few exceptions. They have the same responsibility to provide safe and adequate service, but without the requirement to serve all comers. In addition, while regulated carriers have basically the same immunity from government regulation as other carrier types, they must provide rates to shippers on request and they have the ability to collectively establish rates without antitrust prosecution. A benefit of employing regulated carriers is that they can be held liable for damages to transported goods. The extent of the liability, however, can be limited through the use of tariff rules and released value rates.

- *Contract Carriers.* Similar to common carriers, contract carriers are regulated by the federal government and are authorized to transport certain types of products in certain geographical areas. Contract carriers are not required to offer their services to the general public, but, instead, provide transport services for a negotiated price to selected customers defined by contractual agreement. Normally, contract carrier rates are less than common carrier rates for two reasons:
  1. Contract carriers select customers that wish to transport products that optimize the capacities and capabilities of their vehicle and material handling equipment.
  2. Because customers provide contract carriers with defined contracts that specify products transit and delivery schedules, they can plan better and budget for equipment resources.

- *Exempt Carriers.* This type of for-hire carrier differs from common and contract carriers in that it is not regulated with respect to routes, areas served, and rates. The exempt status is determined by the type of product transported and the nature of the operation. Examples include a variety of land and water carriers that transport commodities such as agricultural products, livestock, poultry, newspapers, and other specialized products. Probably the most important class of carrier belonging to this type is delivery and cartage firms that operate in a local municipality or "commercial zone" surrounding a municipality. Although exempt carriers charge lower rates than common or contract carriers, limitations on the kinds of products that are exempt render their use inappropriate for the transport of most industrial products.

- *Private Carriers.* This final type of carrier is distinguished by the fact that it is wholly owned or leased by the firm and is incidental to the company's main line of business. Private carriers are not subject to federal government regulation regarding costs or scope of service. Private carriers are not allowed to transport the goods of other companies and, as determined by law, must be the sole owner of the cargo. After the passage of the Motor Carrier Act in 1980, permission was granted to companies with private fleets to transport products for wholly owned subsidiaries or backhaul loads from nonaffiliated companies. The decision to acquire a private transport fleet or use for-hire types of transportation must be examined. Wholly-owned transport provides companies with a significant level of control and flexibility to respond directly to customer and internal channel requirements. On the other hand, since deregulation, many for-hire carriers can offer services that are more cost and operationally effective than private fleets.

In addition to these types of carriers, new forms of transport services have grown dramatically since deregulation. These companies purchase transport services from primary carriers, which they in turn retail to their customers by providing services for handling small packages, consolidation and bulk breaking, and local pickup and delivery. These *transportation agencies* can be described as follows:

- *Freight Forwarders.* A freight forwarder, as defined by law, provides the general public with transportation services and, in the ordinary course of business, assembles and consolidates, or provides for assembly and consolidation of, shipments at origin and performs or provides for break bulk and distribution of shipments at the delivery destination. In addition, freight forwarders must assume responsibility for the transportation of a shipment, incur liability for loss or damage to cargo, and must use, for any part of the cartage, a carrier subject to the jurisdiction of the ICC. Finally, according to the Forwarder Deregulation Act of 1986, this type of carrier can operate exempt from ICC jurisdiction.

- *Parcel Post.* Companies engaged in this type of transport focus on the rapid shipment of small (weight and volume) goods and are designed for general public use. Parcel post shippers use all types of air and surface line-haul modes except for pipeline and can consist of bus, motor, or air cartage. The U.S. Post Office, Federal Express, and United Parcel Service are examples of companies in this group. The main advantage of using small-package carriers is *speed of delivery*, especially for emergency situation. The high cost, however, generally prohibits use of this mode for low-value, high-density commodities.

- *Shippers' Associations.* This group is composed of nonprofit shippers' cooperatives whose primary function is freight consolidation. These associations will consolidate smaller shipments from members, search for carriers, and execute low-rate shipment the savings from which can be passed back to association members.

- *Shippers' Agents.* This group is composed of transportation brokers who provide ramp-to-ramp transit from railroads and motor vehicles at origin and destination using truckers as needed under a single bill of lading. They do not provide transport requiring consolidation or bulk-breaking functions. Shippers' agents are exempt from government regulation.

- *Brokers.* The broker is a third-party agent who is neither a shipper nor a carrier but rather an intermediary that arranges a match between the shipper's transportation need and a specific carrier from a pool of carriers they represent. Brokers can be licensed by the *Surface Trade Board* (STB) or unlicensed, but both work under a commission arrangement. Since deregulation that use of brokers has dramatically increased. In addition, brokers are generally not liable for cargo loss and damage. Issues regarding brokers' assistance in pursuing damaged goods claims, rate negotiation, billing, and tracing are normally determined during the contracting process.

When selecting from the above list of transportation carriers, the actual distinctions are slight. The real issues revolve around operating restrictions, financial commitment, and operating flexibility. The dramatic changes brought about by deregulation have lifted the heavy restrictions on the way carriers operate and the way they can be used. Still, there are several critical elements, such as service requirements, type of product, pricing, and level of carrier commitment that must be reviewed during selection.

TRANSPORTATION PERFORMANCE CHARACTERISTICS

There are a number of performance characteristics that shippers must consider when selecting the appropriate mode of transportation. These characteristics must be matched with the type and quantity of product to be shipped, the capacities and capabilities of the transportation mode, and relevant cost issues. According to Bowersox *et al.* [11], there are six transport mode performance characteristics (Figure 12.3) driving any transportation selection decision.

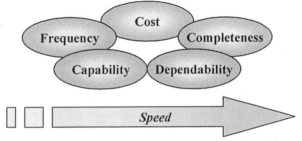

FIGURE 12.3 Performance characteristics of transportation.

1. *Speed.* The ability to transport products from one point in the supply chain to another as quickly as possible is, by far, the fundamental performance characteristic of transportation. Speed provides the marketing utility of *time* and ensures *place* utility. In detail, transportation speed can be defined as the time required to move products from the production source to a terminal, load the products onto the transport

vehicle, traverse terminal points, and deliver the products to the receiving terminal.

2. *Completeness.* This performance characteristic refers to the ability of the transport mode to move inventory from one location to another *without* the use of other modes. This is critical because the less material has to be handled between the point of origin and the point of destination, the lower the transport cost and the short the delivery time. For example, if material was shipped by rail and the company did not have a rail siding, a second mode, most likely motor carrier, would have to receive the load from the rail carrier, and then transport it to the company where it would have to be unloaded again for final receipt.

3. *Dependability.* The degree of transport dependability is measured by the performance of a given mode in meeting anticipated on-time delivery. Dependability is critical in ensuring that planned inventory availability to meet *place* utility is realized to schedule. Poor dependability adds cost in the form of excess inventories and poor customer service.

4. *Capability.* Capability refers to the ability of a given transport mode to accommodate a specific transport load. The driving factor is the nature of the product. Characteristics such as product type (liquid, solid, bulk, or package), load weight, and load dimensions will have an effect when deciding on the necessary capabilities of material handling equipment and mode of transport. For example, when moving liquids, tank cars and pipelines would be the most appropriate methods of transport.

5. *Frequency.* This performance factor is a measure of the frequency a given transport mode can pick up and deliver goods. Generally, the shorter the transport interval the greater the flexibility of the mode to respond to channel requirements. More frequent transport also decreases the required modal size and the magnitude of the inventory to be transported.

6. *Cost.* Although marketing *time* and *place* utilities are critical elements of transport mode selection, the cost the shipper must pay for the transport service is equally important to the survival and competitiveness of the supply channel. There are several costs in transportation. The most obvious cost is the rate paid to the carrier for use of the mode itself. Other indirect costs are labor and material handling to load and unload the transport medium, occurrence of spoilage and damage, insurance to protect against possible loss, and in-transit inventory carrying costs.

TRANSPORTATION MANAGEMENT PROCESS

The effective day-to-day management of transportation activities is absolutely necessary for the smooth functioning of the supply chain. It is the responsibility of the transportation function to perform such tasks as the selection of proper carriers, monitoring and executing inbound and outbound logistics activities, pricing, scheduling, and transport routing. The every-day functions of transportation management are illustrated in Figure 12.4. In planning and

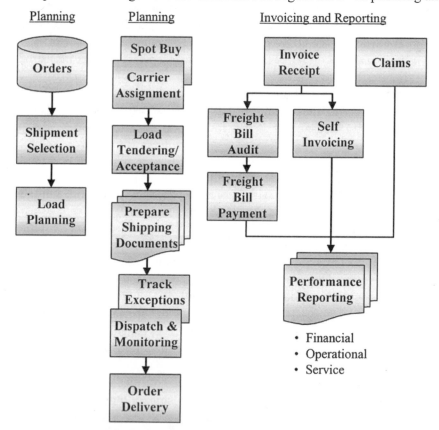

FIGURE 12.4 Transportation planning functions

executing these functions, transportation planners are concerned with such questions as:

- How will customer service objectives influence carrier selection and cost?

- If the firm possesses its own transportation equipment, what should be the mix of shipping carried privately and contracted out to public companies?

- What is the cost in labor, equipment, and maintenance to run the private carrier fleet, and is it cost-effective?
- What transportation capacities are required to handle expected customer demands?
- How much will transportation cost to support current and projected levels of inbound and outbound shipping cost?
- Does transportation possess a formal process for public carrier selection?
- Are there formal procedures in place to ensure transportation is receiving the best freight rates possible?
- Should the company use a freight rating service?
- Can the transportation function benefit by the implementation of software support tools?
- What should be the performance measurements to ensure that transportation is achieving optimal efficiency and productivity?

Whether it is the development of the enterprise's transportation strategy or the daily requirement to service customers and purchase from suppliers, responses to the above questions revolve around an effective understanding of transportation economics and carrier pricing. Surrounding all transportation decisions are seven possible factors that must be used as the foundation driving all transportation planning activities. Failure to understand the below principles will result in excess costs and poor utilization of transportation capabilities [12]:

- *Distance.* The distance products travel from point of origin to the destination will have a critical impact on the transportation decision. Because of the *tapering principle*, the longer the distance the more the fixed and variable costs of transport can be spread out over the total trip. Since more distance can be covered with the same fuel and labor and there are less stops, the cost will decrease.
- *Volume.* Economies of scale can be gained in this factor from the fact that transport cost per unit of weight decreases as volume increases. Leveraging distance and weight factors will drive planners to seek to gather full truck load shipments, especially as the distance grows longer, during shipment planning.
- *Density.* This factor attempts to utilize weight and space considerations when planning for transportation. As a principle, as product weight increases, the cost will generally decrease. The reason for this is that higher density products will have a minimum impact on price because variable costs are not greatly impacted and remain relatively unchanged as weight increases. In contrast, once a transport vehicle's volume is filled, it is completed regardless of the actual weight of the cargo.

- *Stowability.* This factor relates to the actual volume cube of the product to be shipped and how easily it can optimize standard transport vehicle capacities. Simply, size and storage restrictions for some products, such as heavy wheel products, steel rods, and trash cans, can significantly increase transport cost due to use of specialized vehicles or inability to optimize vehicle shipping volumes.
- *Handling.* The loading, unloading, and storage of some products may require shipping planners to utilize costly handling or equipment.
- *Liability.* Many products will require shippers to plan for special modes of transport because of product perishability or damage prevention, the use of insurance to guard against damage or theft, or the use of containers or special marking and handling to ensure transport safety. These types of considerations will increase transportation costs.
- *Vehicle profitability.* Perhaps one of the oldest problems in transportation management is vehicle return. Often when products are transported to a destination, the return trip is made without any cargo, or *deadhead.* This condition is purely a waste of assets and variable costs which are simply added to the original price. Such a condition occurs when there are imbalances in the direction of transport. The ideal is to have a balanced transport environment where once a load is delivered the transport vehicle can pick up another load, or *back-haul*, to the point of origin.

ESTABLISHING COSTS AND RATES

Against the back-drop of the above seven transportation decision factors, there are several critical management steps performed by transport planners. As is illustrated in Figure 12.5, establishing costs and rates for shipments is the first step in the transportation management process. In regard to terminology, the price to move a specific product between two supply channel locations is defined as the *rate.* When this rate (normally expressed in terms of value of service performed, weight, and distance) is listed on a price sheet, it is known as a *tariff.* It is important at this point to separate the cost incurred to operate a private fleet from the price (rate) public carriers charge for transport. The cost for privately owned transport can be measured several ways. Among the expenses to be considered are fixed costs, such a buying and leasing equipment, maintenance, and terminal facilities. Other costs fall into the category of variable expenses associated with fuel, labor, insurance, license fees, supervision, and administration. There is also *marginal cost* which is the cost associated with each product shipped. A private fleet must achieve average revenue that must at least cover the average total cost. If a private fleet does not generate enough revenue to meet costs, the firm might seek to cut the fleet size or abandon it altogether in favor of public carriers.

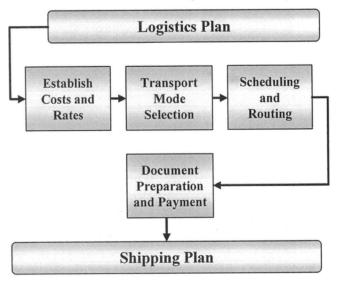

FIGURE 12.5 Transportation management process.

When using public carriers, critical issues revolve around negotiation and calculation of rates. Before deregulation, the tariffs charged by public carriers were established by rate bureaus composed of carrier representatives. Shippers could appear before these bureaus and petition for lower rates on specific commodities or transit routes. Today, although rate bureaus still exist, most rates are the result of direct negotiation between the shipper and the carrier. Although each public carrier publishes transport rates, few shippers pay them. Instead, through a series of negotiations, a discount off the rate is agreed on which then serves as the actual price. Before rate analysis can begin, however, transportation planners must perform two steps. The first is to perform a *classification* of the products to be shipped. Basically this activity requires grouping of shippable products by such criteria as density, stowability, handling, liability and other value characteristics. Once this step is performed, it would be possible to then progress to a determination of the rate. This activity is termed *rate administration*.

Rate negotiation is a four-step process [13]. To begin with, shippers must assess the past, present, and expected shipping volumes. The goal is to quantify the volume, and origin and destination regularity of shipments that can be used during negotiations. The second step is to contact carriers, present the relevant requirements, and solicit bids. In reviewing responses, some of the possible criteria shippers could use include the following:

- The carrier's financial stability

- The carrier's reputation for reliable service
- Billing accuracy of the carrier
- The discount percent off the published rate proposed by the carrier
- Whether the carrier charges for notifying consignee prior to delivery
- The carrier's procedures for handling loss and damage claims
- Availability of special equipment, such as material handling facilities, refrigeration, containerization, intermodal equipment, and others
- The location of the carrier's terminals
- The carrier's level of customer service responsiveness
- Copy of the carrier's insurance certificate.

The final selection of carriers is determined normally by a combination of the price of the service and other quantifiable elements, as well as subjective predilection.

The third step in the carrier negotiation process is the execution of any final discussions between shipper and carrier, mostly relating to negotiating for prices below the formal bid and award of the contract. At this point, a legal contract is drafted, describing the extent of the criteria stated above, plus other clauses relating to performance penalties and incentives. In addition, the contract should include the time limit of the contract, products, and volumes to be shipped, assignment of liability, payment schedule, and the rates to be charged. An example of a motor carrier contract appears in the appendix at the end of this chapter. The final step in the negotiation process is the ongoing administration of the contract after it has been awarded. The results of the negotiation process should result in a contract that includes the following:

1. A pricing system that is simple to understand and execute for all of the shipper's/receiver's locations and commodities
2. Price stability for the shipper during the life of the contract
3. Shipping volume stability for the carrier during the life of the contract
4. A simple and understandable freight bill payment process
5. Capacity of the carrier to use computer technology such as EDI, rating, and scheduling systems
6. Availability of data for auditing and performance measurement.

TRANSPORTATION MODE SELECTION

The choice of carrier shipping mode is the second step in the transportation management process. The goal is to achieve the lowest possible transit cost for the maximum service. In addition, in selecting a carrier, transportation management must be able to address specific shipping issues relating to any required special shipping needs, the rates and services offered by competing carriers, and the probability of loss, damage, or delivery delay. Although the everyday selection of carriers does not necessitate significant and time-consuming analysis, the relative advantages and disadvantages of the various modes and carriers normally employed must be constantly reviewed as conditions change or exceptions arise.

Carrier selection follows five general principles. In the first, *carrier reduction*, transportation management must focus on reducing the carrier database. Concentrating the number of carriers into a few select suppliers permits shippers to develop a collaborative relationship that enhances mutual partnership, increases negotiating power, reduces rates and increases service due to increased volumes and revenues enjoyed by a dedicated carrier, and reduces other logistics costs such as information technology, inventory, and warehousing.

Once carriers have been identified, traffic managers can progress to the next step: *comparing available alternatives*. The goal of this step is to match the shipment with the most appropriate mode of transport. This means, first of all, selecting a carrier that offers the best rate for the service. Second, a carrier should be selected with documented performance regarding speed and reliability. Comparing possible carrier alternatives can be a difficult task: Some transport modes have markedly different attributes not shared by other modes, rendering them not easily substitutable. Studies have shown that most selection is based on a number of criteria including rates, loss and damage record, claims processing experience, transit-time reliability, past negotiations experience, quality of on-time pick-up and delivery, and equipment availability.

The third principle of carrier selection is for traffic management to *continually review* their carrier selection processes with an eye toward continuous cost reduction and service improvement. For the most part, recent studies have shown that firms have been reluctant to change their carriers in the short run. In cases where the transportation fleet is privately owned, the firm is naturally averse to using public carriers, preferring to search for every opportunity to optimize internal resources. In other cases, the carrier selection process is the result of a strategic decision made at the time the supply channel network was being structured, and there is resistance to change. In any case, traffic managers must continually search for ways to buy cost-effective transportation. Some of the methods which can be employed are as follows:

- *Freight Bill audit.* Freight bills must be continually audited to ensure accuracy of the negotiated rate as well as the correct charges. Audits will ensure that traffic management is aware of possible adverse rate changes occurring over time.

- *Monitoring demurrage.* Shippers need to be aware of demurrage charges. Proper internal scheduling reduces the time railcars, trailers, barges, and so on sit idle at the company site.
- *Packaging review.* Changes in containerization or packaging can affect the choice of carrier. Reusable, lighter, or more efficient packing methods could result in easier to handle loads that might warrant a change in carrier.
- *Carrier relations.* Traffic management should always be working with carriers to mutually discover methods of improving service and reducing costs.
- *Outsourcing.* One method to handle all or part of a firm's transportation needs is to outsource them to a third-party logistics services company. Some of the advantages are (1) keeping internal costs low by outsourcing tasks, (2) more customized services, (3) transportation cost reduction, and (4) acquisition of computerized capabilities, such as EDI and Internet, without have to acquire them [14].

Developing *selection criteria* constitutes the fourth principle of carrier selection. Selection criteria can be broadly divided into three areas: traffic related, shipper related, and service related. These three areas have been detailed in Table 12.4. In using this list of criteria, most traffic planners use a

TABLE 12.4 Factors Affecting Modal Choices

Traffic-Related	Shipper-Related	Service-Related
Length of haul	Size of firm	Speed (transit time)
Consignment of weight	Investment priorities	Reliability
Dimensions	Marketing strategies	Cost
Value	Spatial structure of	Customer relations
Value density (weight	production and	Geographical coverage
and cube)	distribution systems	Accessibility
Urgency	Availability of rail	Availability of special
Regularity of shipment	sidings	vehicles/equipment
Fragility	Stockholder policies	Monitoring of goods
Toxicity	Management structure	Unitization
Perishability	System of carrier	Ancillary services (bulk
Packaging type	evaluation	breaking, storage, etc.)
Special handling		Computer capabilities/
characteristics		compatibilities

Source: Adapted from Ref. 15.

weighting method. For the most part, size of shipment, length of haul, transit time, and cost are the key factors employed. In making carrier selection choices, planners usually trade off one factor against another, rather than consider each separately in an ordered sequence.

The formulation of a rigorous *selection procedure* is the final principle of carrier selection. Normally, it is feasible that a shipper could use one of several modes of transport. Each mode will possess strengths and weaknesses when matched against a particular shipment requirement. In practice, the process for selecting the best mode and carrier must be one that meets the company's shipping and cost objectives. This does not mean that any form can be used just to meet or exceed service targets nor does it means that the cheapest mode should be chosen to meet cost objectives. Similar to carrying inventory, traffic planners must plot cost and quality of service and establish the optimum trade-off. The criteria most likely to be used in any optimization analysis are cost, speed, and reliability. As is exhibited in Figure 12.6, a decision model can be constructed using costs and transit times, several different types of carrier marked A, B, C, and D, and their x and y coordinates corresponding to particular combinations of cost and transit time. Shippers would prefer carriers above the curve, and when two modes lay on or close to the curve, other factors would then be applied. Another method would be the use of a computerized transportation modeling application that would calculate the optimum transportation mode based on user-defined and weighted parameters.

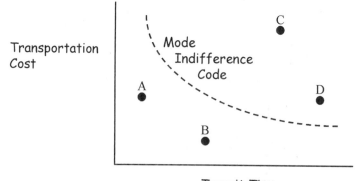

Transportation Cost

Mode Indifference Code

Transit Time

FIGURE 12.6 Plotting cost and transit time.

Traffic planners often find it advantageous to use more than one transportation mode to ship product. This can occur when the shipper uses intermodal methods, a given mode is regularly used for specific products, geographical locations, and types of customers, or emergency shipments or peak transit periods require different modes. Developments facilitating the use of multimode strategies include diversification of product ranges, growth in market areas, reduced dependence on a single mode, inventory reduction pressures, and innovations in intermodal systems. Such a strategy has shifted transportation's concern from choosing the best mode, to an emphasis on deciding on the optimum allocation of traffic among several modes [16].

SCHEDULING AND ROUTING

Scheduling and routing are two functions associated with shipping. *Vehicle scheduling* can be defined as the selection of which customer orders are to be delivered by a single vehicle. *Vehicle routing*, on the other hand, establishes the sequence in which selected customer orders are to be delivered during the route. Most shippers are more concerned with scheduling than with routing. The selection of orders for the shipping schedule is normally the responsibility of a load planner or dispatch clerk. After orders have been chosen, scheduling is normally executed based on zones containing clusters of customers, with the routing indicating the sequence of delivery within each zone. In motor transport, the driver is usually empowered to select the routing within each zone. When customers within a route are stretched across zones, the usual practice is to treat groups of customers in different zones as nodes to be serviced along the route. Once these nodes are reached by the vehicle, the driver chooses the delivery sequence based on knowledge of local roads and customer preferences.

The routing and scheduling of deliveries is a critical task. For small firms with a limited number of products, shipment routing is a repetitive affair with minimal variation. Larger firms, on the other hand, who ship a wide variety and volume of products to a widely spaced geographical customer base, must perform detailed routing analysis. For companies with their own fleets, effective scheduling and routing of transportation has long been recognized as pivotal in fully leveraging the significant capital investment in transportation equipment and facilities and operating expenses made by the firm necessary to achieve service level and cost objectives. The key topics relating to routing and scheduling are single versus multiple deliveries, value of load consolidation, routing methods, and vehicle scheduling.

One of the fundamental elements of mode transport routing is the relationship between the number of delivery loads per vehicle and the number of delivery points constituting the route. Basically, as the number of load deliveries to be transported by a single vehicle declines, the complexity of the routing correspondingly declines. For example, if the customer shipment filled the total capacity of the vehicle, the routing would consist of only one route and one delivery. On the other hand, as the number of load deliveries per vehicle increases, the number of delivery locations normally increases, and the more difficult it becomes to define a route that maximizes vehicle capacities and operating expense. Alongside the issue of routing complexity, the number of loads per vehicle also has an impact on the distance the vehicle will traverse en route to the customer. As a rule, as the number of deliveries increase per route, the overall distance of the route declines. While the multiple delivery routes may indeed be more complex, the round distance is normally shorter than a straight radial distance that also entails vehicle backhaul.

In the past, the relation of load size and the routing favored direct radial deliveries. The reason for this stemmed from two factors. The first related to transportation cost per unit. Simply, the larger the load in relation to vehicle capacity, the lower the transport cost. Full load delivery, although it did, indeed, require running empty return vehicles, was more efficient than multiple delivery methods. The second reason can be found in the assumption that customers preferred to have their inventory requirements met by shipping as large a lot size as possible. In the past inventory planning systems focused on ordering stock according to EOQs, max inventory levels, or other lot-sizing rules. The result was that transit practices using small, more frequent stops could deliver only a portion of customer demand, whereas a full truckload could perhaps meet customer lot-size requirements in full. In addition, the larger the lot size, the larger the vehicle. On routes subject to multiple deliveries, so much time is spent in repeating delivery activities that only a relatively small payload can be delivered in the time allotted. As the distance between delivery sites decreases, payload can increase, but it cannot match the economies achieved by singe delivery routes.

As the era of JIT arrived, the pendulum between single and multiple deliveries began to swing dramatically in favor of multiple-delivery, LTL methods. Whereas unit-cost transport is still best served by as large a truckload as is possible, customer requirements for smaller lot sizes and more frequent deliveries has caused a renewed interest in complex routing. Industrial customers who use flow manufacturing in their plants are requiring a corresponding *flow of materials* to the process floor. Automotive giants like Ford and GM, for example, require multiple daily deliveries of products. One transport technique, called a *milk run*, consists of the pick up and delivery of empty containers and product beginning at the customer's plant, progressing through the channel supply points, and ending up finally with delivery at the customer plant daily or several times during the day. For deliveries which must traverse long distances, milk runs can be combined with long-haul carriers to provide effective mixed-mode transportation [17].

Another method that can be utilized is to increase load volume and minimize the number of delivery points through order consolidation. Shipment consolidation can take place on the loading dock, externally through intercompany collaboration, or through the use of a common carrier. Internally, traffic planners can suspend delivery of orders to a customer until a sufficiently large enough load has accumulated. The negative side of this practice is that it lengthens lead times, increases cycle stocks, and requires the customer to hold more safety stock to account for possible delivery variation. Externally, consolidation services can be used that will group orders from multiple suppliers for shipment to a common customer. An example of cost reduction using consolidation appears in Table 12.5. In the table, four orders to be shipped each day starting on Monday have been delayed due to consolidation. If the cost per hundred weight (CWT) was $2.00 for shipments above 25,000 pounds, by consolidating the orders the shipper would save $490.00 or 40% over the charges if each order had been shipped separately. Besides carrier cost savings, multi-company consolidation also assists in environmental issues such as declines in traffic congestion, fuel consumption, and pollution.

TABLE 12.5 Consolidated Shipments

Order	Ship Date	Weight (lbs.)	Rate (CWT)	Cost
1	Monday	6,000	$4.00	$240.00
2	Tuesday	7,000	$4.00	$280.00
3	Wednesday	12,000	$3.00	$360.00
4	Thursday	11,000	$3.00	$330.00
	Total	36,000		$1,210.00
	Consolidated	36,000	$2.00	$720.00
	Savings			$490.00

When planning multiple delivery routes, transportation planners are faced with the problem of maximizing two related but constrained elements: the distance a vehicle can travel on a single route and the load capacity of the vehicle. Obviously, if a vehicle had unlimited capacity to deliver all customer orders on a single route, these constraints would not apply. Because this is impossible, planners must then be able to determine specific routes that are to serve specific customers as well as the order in which they are to be visited.

This conundrum has been termed the *vehicle dispatching problem* and is defined as the process of establishing a route serving a number of customers which minimizes delivery costs within vehicle payload and distance (or travel time) constraints. A number of routing algorithms have been developed to solve this problem that can essentially be divided into two classes. In the first, *simultaneous methods*, solutions are determined by computing all feasible routes to satisfy specific customer shipping requirements, and then planners select the one that collectively yields the lowest cost. The problem with this method is the complex mathematical calculation that must be performed. As the number of delivery points increase, the solution is more difficult to compute. The second type of vehicle routing algorithms, *sequential approaches*, attempts to overcome the problems associated with simultaneous methods by either dividing delivery into smaller geographical regions of customers that can be connected in a feasible route, or by constructing routes one at a time, adding contiguous links to a single route until distance and vehicle capacity constraints are reached. Many of the complexities of vehicle routing have been facilitated by the introduction of *warehouse management systems* (WMS) that contain applications for freight rating, rate shopping, traffic routing/scheduling, outbound appointment scheduling, transportation analysis, and in-transit inventory tracking. Computerization has assisted traffic planners reduce costs, improve customer service, reduce clerical work, facilitate tracing of shipments, and collect data for performance measurement [18].

DOCUMENTATION PREPARATION AND PAYMENT

The final step in the transportation management process is the preparation of all necessary shipping documentation and payment of carrier invoices. Domestic transportation (*international transport* will be discussed in the Chapter 13) utilizes several key documents to record, direct, and control shipments. Perhaps the most important is the *bill of lading*. Normally, this document is prepared in the shipper's traffic department and signed by the carrier. The bill of lading is a legal document by which the carrier acknowledges receipt of the shipment and provides evidence of title to the goods. In addition, it also constitutes the basic contract of carriage between shipper and carrier, setting forth the rights and responsibilities of each party. The front side of the document is completed by the shipper or carrier. It contains information such as the names and addresses of the consignor and consignee, routing instructions, the shipping rate, a description of the goods and the quantities to be shipped, payment method, and other information. On the back of the document will be found the contract terms, degree of carrier's liability, and other legal points. Railroads and truck carriers use standardized bills similar to the standard bill of lading. Freight forwarders, on the other hand, often use the bills of the mode of transport hauling the product. Both ocean vessels and air freight shipments use special air bills and ocean bills. Because of their uniqueness, pipelines use a *tender of shipment* form in lieu of a bill of lading. Finally, all contract shipping is subject to the terms of the individual carrier contract executed between shipper and carrier.

There are three classes of bills of lading: government, livestock, and commercial. The first two are related to specific transactions; the third is used for all other ordinary business or personal shipments. *Commercial bills of lading* can be used either for domestic or for international shipping. Domestic commercial bills of lading may be either an *order* or a *straight bill*. The former is a negotiable instrument in which the title of goods can be endorsed over to other parties. In contrast, a straight bill is non-negotiable. Receivers are within their right to reject shipment of an improperly endorsed bill.

In addition to the bill of lading, there are a host of other pieces of shipping documentation. *Freight bills* are tendered by the carrier to the shipper using the bill of lading and indicate the price for the transport services performed and data such as the carrier's credit payment terms. A *prepaid shipment* means that the carrier presents the freight bill on the day of shipment. In comparison, a *collect shipment* means that the bill is presented on the day of delivery. Both must be paid according to the terms of the agreement. Another document, the *freight claim* is used by the shipper to file a record of reimbursable losses with the carrier for such events as loss, damage, loss due to delay, and over-charging. The filing of claims is governed by law and the terms specified on the original Bill of Lading. Transportation departments must be routinely concerned with other documents such as arrival notices, delivery receipts, inspection reports, claims reports, and others.

As critical as documentation preparation is the receipt and payment of carrier invoices after transport services have been completed. As is illustrated in Figure 12.4, this process consists of the receipt of the carrier invoice, invoice audit and possible adjustment, decision to pay, invoice payment, and, finally, performance measurement reporting. In today's tight economic times, the speedy performance of these steps has become of great importance to carriers. According a study by Ernst & Young (October 2002), it was found that 2 to 4 percent of the total carrier invoice was consumed in administrative and financial costs. Administrative costs are composed of pure processing costs of creating and delivering invoices, receiving payment, applying payment, resolving disputes with the shipper, and collections. Financial costs include two components: day sales outstanding (DSO) carrying costs and bad debt expenses [19].

Carriers have recently been looking to logistics partners and technology to accelerate the payment process. A widely used technique is to employ the services of third party payment providers (3PPs), which approach the problem from the shipper's A/P. These providers typically will assume management of invoices and bill the shipper either a percent of the payment processed or a per-invoice fee. For freight carriers, software applications providing direct connectivity to shippers through technologies, such as EDI, that can significantly automate the processing of BOLs and the generation of freight invoices. The most advanced carriers have turned to the Internet and implemented *electronic bill presentment and payment* (EBPP) extensions to their web-enabled systems. The advantage of Internet-based tools is that they can provide carriers with real-time communication as well as collaborative approaches to document management, payment processing, and exception handling.

PERFORMANCE MEASUREMENT

Transportation performance measurements provide traffic managers with quantifiable data to track shipping metrics as well as illuminate regions for increased productivity and competitive advantage. Improvement programs require transportation planners to work closely with other business functions. In fact, it is really customer service priorities and objectives, inventory position, operational philosophies, and channel configurations, rather than purely transportation activities themselves that contribute the most to overall transportation performance. Once the enterprise is functioning as a unified organization with a common set of objectives, transportation management can formulate valid performance criteria and focus on continuous improvement tools to reduce cost, improve flexibility, and increase productivity.

Designing effective performance measurements requires dividing transportation into two separate entities: transportation services that are purchased and transportation that is provided by internal (private) equipment. Although both the cost and benefits of any performance measurement program will vary by business, in general when transportation is purchased, performance is determined by managing transport mix, quantity, and cost (price). In contrast, in companies that possess their own transportation fleets, performance is measured by managing input factors associated with fixed costs (vehicles, maintenance facilities, terminals, computer systems, etc.) and variable costs (labor, repair and service, fuel, administrative staff, etc.).

Performance measurements associated with purchased transportation focus on two elements: purchase cost (price) and carrier delivery performance. Because the service is purchased, the shipper is unconcerned with operational measurements associated with fixed and variable costs. On the other hand, shippers can influence cost (price) through the following three inputs:

- *Price.* Depending on the scope of the transportation requirement, shippers can influence price either through competitive shopping or through negotiation. Shipment destination, required date of delivery, shipment size, mode of transport, nature and shape of the product, availability of transport equipment, and other factors will have a direct impact on price.
- *Quantity.* Based on the size (volume) of the shipment, shippers can work with carriers to arrive at advantageous prices. The larger the volume and regularity of the shipment, the greater the ability of the shipper to control pricing.
- *Transport mix.* The nature, size, and shipment quantity of the product provide shippers with the ability to select modes of transportation

(truck, rail, air) that more economically match the shipment requirement.

The best single measurement in charting transportation performance is the *ton-mile*. A ton-mile can be defined as the cost required to move 1 ton of goods 1 mile. A ton-mile is calculated by multiplying the shipment weight by the number of miles from point of origin to delivery, divided by 2000. If, for example, a shipment weighed 2500 pounds and the delivery spanned 1500 miles, the ton-mile (TM) would be calculated as follows:

$$TM = 2500 \times 1500 / 2000 = 1875.$$

From this figure, the price paid for the ton-mile can then be obtained by dividing the price ($$P) paid to the carrier by the ton-mile (TM), or $$P/TM. Shipment productivity can then be computed by inverting the factors, TM/$$P. By comparing the ratio as a function of price charged by each carrier, it would then be possible to determine the best transportation productivity for the price. When a mix of transport modes is used, the TM and $$P would have to be calculated for each mode. Another variable to the ton-mile ratio is produced by load scale factors. Prices can change depending on the ratio of partial to full loads, average length of haul, and average weight of partial loads [20].

Keeping transportation price and mix on target can be assisted by reporting and adherence to shipping budgets. Through a system of thorough reporting that collects information relating to ton-miles, cost per ton-mile, service mix, product mix, and others, transportation managers can examine costs and changes to costs. In addition, a shipping budget can be developed that will provide shippers with price and mix targets (Table 12.6). In the final analy-

TABLE 12.6 Simple Transportation Budget

Service Type	Planned Mix %	Estimated Ton Miles (Vol x Mix %)	Cost per T/M	Budgeted Transportation Cost
Truck	40	3,200,00	$0.11	$252,000
Rail	25	1,500,000	$0.12	$180,000
LTL	13	450,000	$0.45	$202,000
Piggyback	17	1,250,000	$0.15	$187,500
Air	0.05	65,000	$6.00	$390,000

sis, performance for purchased services is measured by controlling transport mix and price. Mix is optimized by ensuring that shipment utilization is high per mix and by avoiding premium-priced carriers. Price optimization is attained through effective carrier negotiation. In both cases, pursuing the best transportation for the dollar is really an entire company effort, requiring the cooperation of sales, warehousing, and transportation departments.

When developing performance measurements for internal or private transportation, three questions must be addressed:

1. Does owning and operating a fleet provide a more cost-effective advantage than if the same service was contracted from a public carrier?
2. What should be the performance measurements used to examine internal fleet productivity and how should those metrics be collected?
3. Considering the multitude of changes due to costs and opportunities for new equipment and technology alternatives, what are the appropriate metrics to be employed for improving or at least maintaining the initial cost level?

The first step in measurement identification is to detail the major components and percent usage of transport cost. A possible breakdown appears in Table 12.7. This breakdown should help traffic planners isolate areas where

TABLE 12.7 Cost by Major Activity

Activity	Percentage of Total Cost (%)
Linehaul	84.6
Pick-up/Delivery	1.6
Platform	4.0
Maintenance	2.4
Indirect, others	11.0

cost improvements can have the most significant impact. The next step would be to associate with each major cost component, such as employee compensation, vehicle costs (fixed as well as operating costs like depreciation and fuel), support expenses (facilities and equipment), and other expenses (cargo insurance, travel expense, general supplies and expenses) a productivity value. The value source would include such elements as miles per road driver-hour worked, miles per gallon fuel, miles per trailer, weight handled per platform-employee hour, and fleet miles per maintenance employee-hour. For example, when analyzing vehicle costs by using the *activities* expressed in Table 12.7, *value sources* such as ton miles per road driver worked, customer stops per local driver-hour, and shipments handled per platform-employee hour could be calculated by each activity. The goal of the process would be to chart through time changes occurring in each expense value. Opportunity for improvements would focus on reversing an upward trend or decreasing a fairly stagnant cost. Possible examples for performance improvement include the following: usage of vehicles on second and third shifts, reduce empty backhaul mileage, increase vehicle space utilization, alter routes to reduce mileage and/or driving time, effectively mix private and public transport to maximize on private fleet utilization, improve equipment utilization, and others.

ISSUES CONFRONTING TRANSPORTATION

Transportation, like all business functions in the first decade of the 2000s, is grappling with an accelerating rate of change and operational complexity. In the past, transportation was a fairly straightforward process concerned with rate and route calculations and carrier selection. Today, as the demands of global competition, new paradigms of customer services, and growth of computerization and Internet interoperability, architecting a successful logistics strategy requires coming to grips with a number of critical issues. The first relates to the physical transportation environment in the first decade of the twenty-first century. The second concentrates on the issues surrounding government regulation of transportation. Finally, the last issue is concerned with the application of computer systems capable of automating all areas of transportation management.

TRANSPORTATION INFRASTRUCTURE

While today's shippers and carriers have made enormous strides in improving efficiency, reliability, and security of supply chain systems through the implementation of JIT/Lean operations philosophies and computerized technologies, some experts feels that the nation's infrastructure is not growing fast enough to facilitate the output of the available logistics planning tools. Although it is true that the existing infrastructure is providing an extremely competitive and cost efficient foundation, as the decade of the 2000s proceeds there is worry in some quarters that the technologies by themselves will increasingly become unable to overcome infrastructure shortcomings. With funding for the reauthorization of the U.S. government's transportation infrastructure funding mechanism, TEA-21 (the Transportation Equity Act for the 21st Century), currently up for review, transportation functions are deeply concerned. How Congress answers this issue will determine the nature of transportation in the U.S. for years to come.

According to the data currently being assembled about the condition of U.S. surface, air, and water systems, it is clear that major upgrades and new development to increase capacity is warranted. According to the Texas Transportation Institute's (TTI) Urban Mobility Study, traffic congestion alone cost U.S. companies $67.4 billion in 2002, including the cost of 3.6 billion hours of extra travel time and 5.7 billion gallons of wasted fuel. What is more, the level of "undesirable" congestion in urban areas rose to 56 per-cent, up from 7 percent in 1982 and 29 percent in 1990. According to the U.S. Department of Transportation's (USDOT) Bureau of Transportation Statistics, on-time air travel fell to 77.4 percent in 2002, down from 82.1 percent in 2001 even as air travel plummeted in the wake of terrorism and economic slowdown. U.S. railroads and water transport infrastructures, historically stuck on the short side of funding, are slowly falling each day farther behind modern day requirements. One expert cites a study performed on a single segment of the rail network on the I-95 corridor between Richmond, Va. and New York City identifying $6 billion of needed improvements over the next twenty years to reduce bottlenecks. On the nation's waterways, more than 53 percent of dams and locks are now older than their design life. As a result, the locks are too short for modern vessels, causing excessive congestion and loss of efficiency.

These problems are expected to spiral over the next twenty years. USDOT estimates that by 2020 the nation's transportation system will transport cargo valued at almost $30 trillion compared to $9 trillion in 2003. In addition, volumes in tons will increase by nearly 70 percent over current levels of 15 billion tons. International transportation requirements are also expected to double during this period. Finally, USDOT estimates that annual expenditures of almost $76 billion will be required 2001-2020 just to maintain the existing infrastructure at year 2000 capabilities and capacities [21].

While solutions to these problems are forthcoming, shippers and carriers are gearing their strategies and transport assets to respond today. One key area to performance enhancement is the growth and integration of technologies with transportation management processes and infrastructure. This merger of information and process should assist in the development of more effective transport strategies and practices that will enable system optimization. Another area is the growth of *intermodalism*. Through the design of compatible vehicles and containers, intermodal transport will optimize mode utilization and efficiency by providing for quick loading and unloading to ensure that at the various points of delivery and shipment transport activities are performed as cost-effectively and quickly as possible. In detail, carriers can assist in removing transport bottlenecks by converting to equipment such as smaller, faster, lower cost locomotives that speed up rail movement; enhancement of loading equipment and rolling stock that facilitates the "piggybacking" of motorized vehicles and containers; the use of side-loading trailers that permit quick loading and unloading; and the installation of docking bays that facilitate tailer cargo handling, application of conveyor systems, and cross-docking. These and other innovations will support the new view of logistics as a continuous flow pipeline rather than as a stagnant system of warehouses connected by modes of transit.

TRANSPORTATION REGULATION

Government has long been involved in the regulation of transportation. Regulation has traditionally involved two key objectives: the promotion of transportation and regulation to ensure safety and competition. During the early history of the U.S., the country was more focused on developing adequate transportation than imposing restrictions. During this promotional period, although monopolistic excesses and other abuses took place, government was more concerned with the building of an effective transportation system that would support the economic growth of the young republic than imposing legislation targeted at safety or the promotion of competition. It was not until after the Civil War that government began to turn its attention to growing abuses arising from monopolistic control, particularly the railroads.

The first real government regulation, The Act to Regulate Commerce, occurred in 1887. This legislation placed all railroad common carrier service engaged in interstate and foreign transport under federal government regulation. In addition, the act also established the Interstate Commerce Commission (ICC) which was invested with the administration of the act. The ICC could hear complaints, issue cease-and-desist orders, determine awards for damages, and recommend new legislation to Congress. In 1920, the act was superseded by the Esch-Cummins Act (the Interstate Commerce Act). The act marked a new era in regulatory control. Previous legislation had attempted to enforce competition among transport companies; this act, on the other hand, focused on guaranteeing a strong transportation industry through positive regulatory controls on rates, service, carrier consolidations, securities, and labor. Other acts, such as the Hepburn Act (1906) and the Shipping Act of 1916, focused on protecting the pipeline and ocean carrier industries from monopoly.

Government regulation up to 1930 was targeted at one objective: prevention of monopoly by increasing control over service routes, labor disputes, consolidations and mergers, and issuance of securities. During this period, regulation was focused on the emerging motor transport industry. One of the results of the burst of activity focused on public works during the Great Depression was the growth of the nation's highway system. Although some states did, indeed, exercise some control over motor transport safety, during the late 1920s and early 1930s the ICC and other groups recommended the federal regulation of motor carriers. It was not, however, until the passage of the Motor Carrier Act of 1935 that the ICC gained control of the motor carriers and extended the same type of regulation to trucking that had been applied to the railroad industry. The main provisions of the act were to establish three classes of carrier (common, contract, and private), control carrier entry by requiring an ICC certificate, institute strict rate control by the ICC, oversee consolidation and merger regulations, and structure securities and accounts provisions. The Civil Aeronautics Act of 1938 extended competition protection to the newly emerging airline industry. Similarly, the Transportation Act of 1940 placed all domestic water carriers under ICC rate and service regulation.

With the act of 1940, nearly all modes of the nation's transportation system were now under government regulation. The act, however, also marked a critical change of government policy away from a focus on preventing monopoly and toward recognition of the place of competition in the transportation industry. The critical concept embodied in the act was that a healthy transportation system is based on a new idea that each mode of transport is an integral part of an entire transportation system and that it is the responsibility of government to preserve the competitive existence of each mode. The essential accomplishment of the act was the recognition that the fundamental problem facing transportation was no longer monopoly, but the lack of intermodal competition.

Following the act of 1940, there were three additional pieces of government regulation. The first, the Freight Forwarder Act of 1942, declared that freight forwarders were now subject to the Interstate Commerce Act. The Reed-Bulwinkle Act of 1948 amended the Interstate Commerce Act by authorizing the use of rate bureaus. A rate bureau can be defined as a price-setting body, governed by the ICC, consisting of carriers who decide among themselves what rates are to be charged. The act did allow for the right of independent action on the part of a carrier. This act was critical in that it still left the ICC with control over rate-making, yet it did provide for recognition of competition among carriers. Finally, the Transportation Act of 1958, sought further clarification of the policy of competition. Perhaps the most significant part of the act was an amendment to rate-making rules by adding the phrase, "Rates of a carrier shall not be held up to a particular level to protect the traffic of any other mode." This meant that the federal government was clearly at the same time protecting and calling for more intermodal competition.

The era of deregulation began with President Kennedy's Transportation Message in April, 1962. In the message, Kennedy talked about the deadening effect regulation had had on transportation and ended by calling for "greater reliance on the forces of competition and less reliance on the restraints of regulation." Although no congressional action ensued, the initiative clearly was pointing at responding to the problems that had been arising as a result of regulation. As shifts in the population and industry from the Northeast to the South and Southwest occurred in the 1960s and 1970s, regulated carriers found it difficult to redeploy assets to meet more favorable markets. The situation was further worsened by the growth of carriers exempt from regulation, such as company-owned truck fleets, that quickly absorbed the business of these new areas. In addition, the ICC literally prescribed the level of competition, and some carriers found themselves caught in legal contradictions permitting them to haul freight in one direction but not on the backhaul, serving terminal points but not intermediate points, serving between some cities only on a circuitous route, and being able to carry some goods but not others. Finally, the cost of supporting carriers facing bankruptcy as well as the whole regulatory structure was costing the U.S. anywhere from $6 billion to $12 billion annually.

The first salvo targeted at regulation was fired with the Railroad Revitalization and Regulatory Reform Act of 1976. Serving as a prototype for deregulation legislation to follow, the act permitted railroads to charge discretionary rates within certain limits without ICC approval, rates were allowed to at least cover variable costs, upper level of rates were unlimited unless the carrier possessed "market dominance," and speedier action was to be taken by rate bureaus. The first real deregulation legislation was soon to follow in 1977 with the passage of the Air Cargo Deregulation Act. The act essentially permitted airlines to charge any rate they wished as long as it was not discriminatory and removed restrictions on cargo aircraft size. In 1980, the Motor Carrier Act and Staggers Rail Act extended regulatory reform to the trucking and railroad industries, respectively. These acts gave both Industries substantial price-setting freedoms, established broader provisions for geographic, route, and commodity authority for common and contract carriers, eliminated one-way provisions and other restrictions, significantly increased opportunities for privately held carriage, permitted railroads to act as contract carriers, and facilitated mergers and consolidations. Perhaps the "final chapter" in the history of motor carrier deregulation occurred with the signing of the Trucking Regulatory Reform Act of 1994. Effectively, the bill eliminated the requirement that for-hire motor carriers file tariffs with the ICC.

With the terrorist attacks of 9/11 and initiatives to provide for homeland security, the U.S. transportation system has become subject to a new round of regulation designed to make America's boarders safer. For the most part, these regulations are targeted at a much closer scrutiny of import/export operations. Such legislation as the Customer-Trade partnership Against Terrorism (C-TPAT) and the Container Security Initiative (CSI) are designed to identify high-risk cargo and container shipments and mandate pre-approval of shipments at foreign ports. Food imports are required to submit to FDA prior notice of food importations; regulations for tightening security on international air cargo are pending. Domestically, the Department of Homeland Security's Operation Liberty Shield is seeking new powers to ensure security at U.S. boarders and protect transportation and vital infrastructure. Security has been stepped up at rail facilities and key rail hubs; motor travel has been subjected to more intense control over the shipment of hazardous materials, the use of additional checklists, and checking employee identification. Such legislative initiatives are sure to provoke fresh debate between the needs of security and threats to the nation's competitiveness.

TRANSPORTATION MANAGEMENT SYSTEMS

Many traffic management functions are utilizing *transportation management systems* (TMS) to assist in the transportation management process. Instead of a mixture of a variety of manual and interfaced transportation applications, the purpose of as TMS is to provide a single integrated solution that spans the transportation management cycle from order selection and carrier bid to delivery and performance measurement. With the information provided by a TMS, traffic planners can implement new transportation management practices that integrate and streamline every aspect of the distribution system, wringing costs from and adding value to every step of the distribution process. What is more, as requirements for shipment accountability stemming from legislation designed to ensure Homeland Security expand, the need for systems capable of handling global logistics planning and documentation is expected to expand concomitantly. According to AMR Research, TMS applications are expected grow at a five-year compound annual growth rate of 14 percent from 2002 to 2006, representing a jump from around $750 million to $1.5 billion in sales.

Overall, a TMS will assist traffic planners to perform the following four functions [22]:

- *Transportation procurement* for automating and optimizing everything from carrier and mode search and selection to rate quotation and final negotiation.
- *Transportation planning* for designing the transportation network, running simulation analysis, load building, fleet management, parcel management, structuring lanes, and identifying opportunities for improvement.
- *Transportation execution* for managing the entire in-transit life cycle, from route planning to load tendering, the confirmation process, and freight audit and payment.
- *Visibility and reporting* for access to real time shipment status information, track and trace, proactive exception-based alerting, cost analysis, and post-shipment analysis processes.

658 DISTRIBUTION OPERATIONS EXECUTION

As trading partners and logistics service providers become linked real-time into the logistics network web, companies can freely retrieve shipping, service, and contact information to identify carriers, transit times, and compliance issues such as Certificate of Origin, customs invoice, global settlement of freight payment and billing, allocating the true cost of transportation based on actual charges, and electronic notice of consignment and statements of revised charges for change of destination of an in-transit shipment.

While these stand-alone applications provide significant benefits, the real value of a TMS is found when it is combined with enterprise business and supply chain management systems. By linking together a TMS and WMS, demand management, and inventory systems, traffic planners have access to a suite of supporting systems that can create a seamless flow of information up and down the supply channel. For example, by linking a TMS system into a WMS, planners can assign carriers as products are picked and moved to the shipping point. Interfacing a TMS with a *supply chain event management* system can provide order visibility from the point of shipment all the way to customer receipt. An effective TMS is so critical to fulfillment that many experts consider a supply chain management system to be incomplete without it.

Finally, when the enabling power of the Internet is applied to a TMS, shippers have the ability to share information across logistics e-marketplaces. Among the new opportunities available for shippers and carriers is software for consolidating, cost optimizing, and collaborating in real-time on load planning. These applications can also optimize orders into loads for tendering, matching loads across service providers, meeting hazardous materials requirements, optimizing available assets, and more effectively managing and measuring relationships and contracts. Finally, e-TMS assists carriers to optimize fleet management through interactive tools providing for dynamic routing, real-time dispatch, and wireless application integration.

LOGISTICS SERVICE PROVIDERS

Of the trends impacting today's management of transportation, the use of *logistics service providers* (LSPs) is perhaps the most dramatic. In today's fast paced, complex business environment, companies are finding that they simply can not provide effective supply chain end-to-end management. Increasingly, logistics departments are struggling to cope with the task of responding to continuously morphing supply channel networks characterized by frequent new product introductions, the presence of Internet-based sales channels, the impact of regulations surrounding home security, information technologies that provide for real time information, transaction control, and delivery visibility management, and an unquenchable thirst for speed in the movement of goods and services through the supply chain. Effectively responding to these challenges has driven many logistics planners to turn to a relatively new channel partner facilitator, the LSP or, as it is often termed, the *third-party logistics* (3PL) provider.

ORIGINS AND GROWTH OF THE LSP INDUSTRY

While companies providing logistics services have always existed, a watershed in their growth occurred with the deregulation of transportation. For example, in 1980, Leaseway Transportation Corporation was the largest provider of contract services in the U.S. with revenues of $250 million. Through its subsidiary, Signal Delivery Services, Inc., the company provided contract trucking, home delivery, cross docking, and warehouse services for Sears Roebuck & Co. and Whirlpool Corporation. As deregulation took hold, the use of Leaseway and other budding LSPs mushroomed by providing customized services and offering an alternative to regulated carriers. Today, there are more than 1000 LSPs offering services in North America alone, each vying for survival through service innovation and intense competition.

Businesses in the twenty-first century are turning to LSPs to solve increasingly sophisticated requirements for technology-based and strategic supply-chain services. In a survey conducted in mid-2002 [23], more than 75 percent of the respondents used outsourcing as part of their logistics strategies. The top five areas outsourced were warehouse/DC management (77 percent), web-enabled communications (64 percent), transportation management (64 percent) shipment tracking/event management (62 percent), and export/import/customs clearance (62 percent). According to Delaney [24], the revenues of the LSP industry in 2001 exceeded $60 billion [Table 12.8], up

Table 12.8: LSP Revenues (2001)

Figures in billions of dollars

Third Party Service Providers	Gross Revenues	Growth Rate (%)
Dedicated Contract Cartage	8.3	2.5
Domestic Transportation Mgmt.	17.5	3.6
Value-Added Warehouse/Distribution	15.3	13.3
U.S. Based with International Operations	15.7	7.5
3PL Software	4.0	
Total Contract Logistics Market	60.8	7.4%

from $56.4 billion in 2000. While the industry exhibited a slowing of growth from the 24 percent recorded in 2000, to 7.4 percent in 2001, the decline is seen as temporary due to the economic slowdown of the period. All in all, utilizing LSPs enable transportation planners to shrink dramatically physical logistics assets, such as delivery and accounts payable systems and personnel. Additionally, logistics outsourcing enables shippers to leverage LSP invest-ments in information, material handling, and operating equipment. Finally, the need to optimize the constantly shifting parameters of supply chain opera-tions requires companies to possess a degree of agility that can only be found in logistics organizations that are totally dedicated to logistics management.

While use of LSPs have been growing, there are, however, a number of hurdles that transportation planners must solve before a more strategic ap-proach to outsourcing can be pursued. To begin with, LSP relationships re-quires a significant level of collaboration between two companies that often possess separate objectives, information capabilities, financial targets, op-erating philosophies, and work cultures. In addition, LSP partnerships, while intended to be long-term, have a tendency to erode quickly as partners change business priorities, levels of urgency, and strategic direction. In the survey mentioned above, nearly half of respondents admitted to a fear of losing op-erational control. Others cited cultural barriers, costs, risks of long-term de-pendency on a LSP, and unreasonable expectations regarding return on in-vestment. Finally, LSPs must find better ways to work with clients and streamline processes. If a client spends as much time managing an out-sourced process as they spent managing the process in-house, then that defeats one of the main reasons for outsourcing. Responding to these hurdles requires transportation planners to develop a comprehensive outsourcing strategy complete with a project team assigned the task of identifying realistic outsourcing service, operations, and financial objectives and determining how the outsourcing relationship is to be managed.

Suite of LSP Services

As the utilization of LSPs grows in the current decade, providers have begun expanding their suite of services to encompass greater functionality in finance, inventory, technology, and data management. In the past, businesses often sought to utilize LSPs to outsource non-core functions that were com-moditized and could realize quick cost savings. Today, logistic executives utilize LSPs as part of their logistics strategies. The fact of the matter is that the continuous squeeze on all elements of the supply cycle are simply pushed executives to explore LSPs to realize added value. According to experts in the field of outsourced logistics services, companies today are looking to LSPs to provide four key sources of logistics value.

- *Trust.* The goal of this value is to find a competent LSP partner that can relieve the company from the task of managing the supply channel.
- *Information.* The objective of this value is to leverage the technology capabilities of LSPs to provide logistics information accuracy, quality, and timeliness of the operations they deliver.
- *Capital utilization.* The reduction of fixed assets in the form of physical plant and equipment is a major source of LSP value. Less fixed expense can expect to be returned in the form of better working capital.
- *Expense control.* The overall reduction of logistics channel costs is by far the primary objective of using a LSP provider. Increase in customer service combined with lower logistics costs is seen by savvy CEOs as a critical path to survival [25].

LSP services can essentially be divided into the following five areas [26]:

- *Logistics.* Services in this area are designed to provide shippers with outsourced expertise in the management of a variety of tasks ranging from the application of strategic management tools to on-going operational functions. Among the services can be found assistance with the implementation and execution of JIT/Lean philosophies, global trade services, management of inbound logistics functions, warehousing, performance of payment audit and processing functions, inventory management, supplier management, and product life cycle management.
- *Transportation.* The execution of carrier functions is at the core of all LSP partnerships. The role of LSPs in this area is to absorb all of the core functions associated with product transport including: small package delivery, air cargo management, all types of LTL and TL motor cartage, intermodal transportation management, ocean, rail, and bulk transport, track and trace, fleet acquisition consulting, and the leasing of transport equipment and drivers.
- *Warehousing.* While most businesses maintain their own warehousing functions, often demand events, such as seasonality, requirements for new geographic market penetration, the use of *vendor managed inventory* (VMI) programs, and specialized delivery requirements, will necessitate the use of an LSP. Among the warehousing services provided are pick/pack and assembly, cross-docking, DC management, warehouse location services, and fulfillment.
- *Special services.* As the marketplace grows, companies often find themselves with the task of performing specialized services for their supply chains. Among the services LSPs can perform in this area are delivery direct to the retail environment, delivery direct to the consumer's home, import/export/customs functions for international sales,

reverse logistics for the management of waste and damaged goods returns, marketing and customer management, and logistics/transportation consulting.

- *Technology.* In today's increasingly computerize environments, companies may find themselves having to acquire technologies and technical personnel for which they are unable or reluctant to build in-house. LSPs solve this dilemma by offering rented services and equipment to manage applications such as EDI, satellite/wireless communications, and enterprise web enablement.

According to a 2001 third-party logistics services study, the detail of the services by percent contracted from LSPs can be seen in Table 12.9.

TABLE 12.9 Outsourced Logistics Services, 2001

Type of Service	Percent Outsourced
Warehousing	73.7%
Outbound transportation	68.4
Freight bill auditing/payment	61.4
Inbound transportation	56.1
Freight consolidation/distribution	40.4
Cross-docking	38.6
Product marking/labeling/packaging	33.3
Selected manufacturing activities	29.8
Product returns and repair	22.8
Inventory management	21.0
Traffic management/fleet operations	19.3
Information technology	17.5
Product assembly/installation	17.5
Order fulfillment	15.8
Order entry/order processing	5.3
Customer service	3.5

Source: Langley, C. John Jr., Allen, Gary R. Allen, and Tyndall, Gene R. Tyndall, *Third-Party-Logistics Services: Views from the Customers.* (Atlanta, GA: Georgia Institute of Technology, Gap Gemini Ernst & Young and Ryder System, Inc., 2001).

Responding to these and other service needs have driven many LSPs to architect strategies that are reshaping the nature of logistics outsourcing. While the number of possible permutations is large, today's LSPs can be separated into two camps. On the one side can be found LSPs that are focused on offering a limited selection of cost-driven, standardized services through an owned network of transportation and warehouse functions. They provide value to their customers by leveraging their logistics assets to cut supply chain costs, manage non-asset cost factors, and drive process innovation. In the other camp stands a much more aggressive type of LSP that seeks to manage their customers' logistics needs from end-to-end. Termed *fourth party logistics* (4PLs) or *lead logistics providers* (LLPs), LSPs in this category can be defined as supply chain integrators whose strategy is to assemble and manage dynamic organizations composed of a wide range of resources, capabilities, and technologies either within the organization or in partnership with complementary LSPs to deliver a comprehensive, customized logistics solution to the customer through a central point of contact. Most LSP arrangements fail to deliver benefits beyond one-time operating cost reductions and asset transfers: LLPs, on the other hand, are dedicated to long-term strategic logistics partnership and continuous growth in revenues and reductions in operating cost and fixed and working capital for the customer.

While providing a host of new and critical services, the use of an LLP for strategic partnership is mostly on the horizon for most companies. While the 2001 LSP services survey mentioned above indicated that over 93 percent of the companies responding felt LSP services provided a "strategic, competitive advantage," few viewed their LSP relations as playing a dominant role. In the multiple variable survey over 75 percent saw their LSP as purely an alternative resource provider; 68 percent saw them as "Problem solvers" and "Resource managers." In contrast, only 13 percent felt their LSPs to be an "Orchestrator," 7 percent as a "Supply chain strategist," and 13 percent as a "Distribution strategist [27]."

INTERNET-DRIVEN LSPS

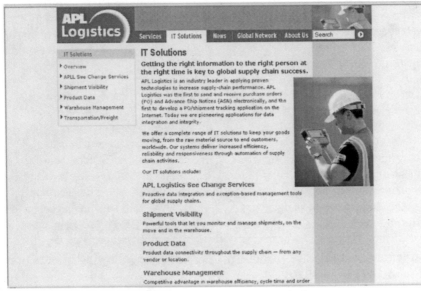

FIGURE 12.8 APL Logistics web-site.

As the utilization of the Internet has expanded into the realm of logistics management, companies have increasingly turned to their LSP partners for access to Web-based technologies. Many companies simply do not have the financial and people resources to hook-up to today's fast-paced Internet applications and are increasingly looking to their LSPs to provide the expertise to collect and scrub data and drive it directly into their backbone systems, perform e-commerce functions, provide proactive exception management, and enable participation in the Web-driven supply chain [Figure 12.8]. This growth in Web-based LRM services caused several of logistics experts to dub these LSPs *.comLLPs* [28]. The purpose of the description is to convey the critical competitive advantage available to customers through LLPs who have deep Internet capabilities.

APL Logistics and the Internet	
APL Logistics provides not only core logistics services, but also advanced technology capabilities to its customers. APL has an entire division devoted to developing and integrating the latest in proprietary and industry-standard supply chain technologies for product visibility, exception management, execution systems optimizing shipping and warehouse decisions, Web-based decision tools, and performance reporting. Customers have the capability to then turn-up or phase down their use of these services depending upon on-going needs and level of internal expertise. For example, NetTrac XL is an end-to-end supply chain visibility tool for international shipments. It gives logistics and procurement managers real-time, web-based visibility to	APL Logistics managed shipments. *Pipeline View* is a proprietary system offering customers an integrated view of their warehousing and distribution "pipeline" in North America. Through an easy-to-use Web interface, customers can conduct real-time inquiries about the status of APL Logistics handled inventory and shipments and get immediate answers, 24 hours a day, seven days a week. APL's international services are supported by a web-enabled operating system designed for real-time shipment management and customer service. Features include on-line booking, tracking and tracing, and integration with APL Logistics' suite of visibility and data management tools.

Internet-driven LSP have the ability to provide the following information-based services [Figure 12.9]:

- *Comprehensive solutions.* Perhaps the critical advantage of a *.comLLP* is to use technology to reverse the increased propensity for logistics

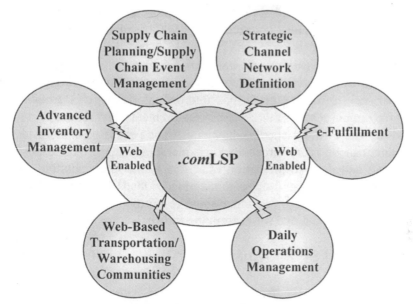

FIGURE 12.9 *.com*LSP functions.

fragmentation as products make their way through the supply channel. *.com*LLPs possess the capability to offer customers a centralized, comprehensive logistics management point that can facilitate the merger of a community of functional logistics providers with the enabling power of a customized, client optimized, uniform technology strategy. Such a technology-based solution has the capability of leveraging networking tools like the Internet to drive the synchronization of real-time logistics planning and execution across trading partners while increasing ever-widening collaborative cooperation.

• *Improved information flows.* The Internet provides LSPs with supply chain event applications that enable real-time visibility to shipments anywhere, at anytime in the supply chain. In addition, Web-based workflow tools render the transfer of information, such as freight tenders and bookings, a simple process. Also, by significantly accelerating the flow of shipping information and providing electronic funds transfer capabilities the payment cycle can be considerably shortened.

• *Enhanced fulfillment capabilities.* Today's companies are being faced with steep challenges when it comes to Internet-driven fulfillment. Historically, most companies have developed logistics practices and infrastructure geared to handle the bulk storage and movement of products through the supply network. Increasingly, companies are requiring order picking and fulfillment in smaller, more frequently delivered lot sizes and are turning to their LSPs for the answer. Responding to these fulfillment needs will require nimble LSPs equipped with both the necessary infrastructure and access to Web-based logistics communities that can make delivery of any order size at anytime a reality.

- *Supply chain inventory management.* Computerized supply chain applications provide *.com*LLPs with a range of inventory throughput tools that seek to replace, when possible, inventories with information, enable nimble response to customer requirements, and reduce cycle times everywhere in the supply channel. Among these computerized functions can be found cross-docking, merge-in-transit, remote postponement, and delayed allocation of orders to the latest possible moment before shipment, and the commingling of loads from multiple service providers in order to maximize shipment, provide pricing advantages to shippers, and remove waste from the fulfillment process [29].

CHOOSING AN LSP PROVIDER

Developing a logistics outsourcing partnership requires a comprehensive strategy and a well conceived and executed implementation plan. Overall, an LSP strategy is focused around attaining two major benefits: enabling the businesses to shed costly transportation assets and activities that are normally beyond the core competencies and traditional hard asset investments that are at the heart of the company. Secondly, by outsourcing these functions to third-party experts, firms can take advantage of world-class resources and processes without developing them in house. When designing a logistics outsourcing strategy, it might be helpful to start by describing the array of possible LSP arrangements that are available. On the low end of the spectrum of strategies can be found the *traditional model* where internal company functions totally control logistics resources. When LSP activities do occur, these would be for one-time spot buys to solve a temporary weakness in internal capabilities. In the next model, *classic LSP,* logistics planners utilize LSPs to service logistics functions that are on the periphery or are poorly performed by the internal logistics group. An example would be using an LSP to handle international distribution functions. For the most part, in both of these models control of strategic logistics functions and design and execution of supply chain strategies is retained by the company.

In contrast to the first two strategies, which are focused strictly on operational objectives, a *partial LLP model,* is characterized by a partial surrender of logistics control to the LSP. While the shipper still acts in the role of logistics integrator and retains control of channel design, LLPs are given responsibility for managing entire portions of the supply chain. Normally, the shipper plays an active part in assisting the LLP to assemble the team of LSP service providers, is responsible for enforcing LSP adherence to the channel strategy, and oversees operational logistics function execution. In the final LSP model, a *full LLP*, the shipper selects a LLP who assumes full responsibility for logistics management. While the shipper is still an active partner in the architecting and maintenance of both the logistics strategy and the LSP community of providers, full responsibility for the total logistics solution is given to the LLP. The LLP assumes ownership for channel design, LSP partner selection, and detail operations execution.

Whether committing to a full LLP or using a portfolio approach to LSP services, transportation strategists need to consider the following factors in their decisions:

- *LSP flexibility.* The only thing known for sure about a logistics partnerhip is that the circumstances driving its inception will change through time. When structuring the LSP contract, logistics planners must be careful to draft a document that provides for flexibility to respond to service changes due to new technologies, remapping of the supply channel, new products, new competitors, change of management, and other issues. Open dialogue is critical in ensuring both parties have commonly accepted definitions and terms, detailed performance measurements, and a methodology to adjust logistics functions and expectations to meet current realities.

- *Defined cost of services.* In spite of the best constructed contract, rarely are all possible permutations of costs and scope of services fully defined. Once actual services begin, timeliness, accuracy, thoroughness, and level of service detail can often vary widely from agreed upon contracted standards. An effective method to cope with these issues is to plan for high, medium, and low costs in the contract. Consistently enforcing the low cost solution will unsettle even the best relationship.

- *Managing the human side of outsourcing.* The introduction of a LSP into the supply chain equation requires the effective education and concurrence of the people side of an organization. Outsourcing what were once internal functions to an outsider can cause friction and uneasiness among affected employees. A plan that integrates managers, supervisors, and staff into the process will ensure their feedback and support are a critical factor in reaching the outsource decision.

- *Realistic expectations.* False expectations about savings and effectiveness of outsourced services can sink even the most finely tuned LSP relationship. In reality, both parties must work closely together to establish realistic expectations and then structure a program to guide continuous improvement through time. From the beginning and throughout the life of the relationship, both parties must be prepared to work through practical examples, step-by-step, testing baseline and every possible type of exception process to remove false expectations and uncover real measurable benefits.

- *Technology misunderstandings.* All too often customers and LSPs exaggerate their technologies capabilities as well as down-play what technology expertise is required of each other. Solving this problem requires both parties to come to the table with realistic technology statements of their capabilities that can act as a baseline to initiate technology improvements that enhance the partnership and drive new benefits.

- *Partnership commitment.* Similar to a corporate strategy, it is essential to secure the firm commitment of top and middle management to the proposed outsourced arrangement. The executive team must be apprised of their role as leaders and supporters in the on-going management of the relationship, both from a change management and an expanding collaborative partnership perspective.

- *Retain core skills.* Companies seeking outsourced logistics functions must be vigilant to ensure that critical skills and processes are not contracted away. A fine line must be preserved between outsourcing the expense while retaining the skill set to be able to re-evaluate the arrangement, recapture the outsourced function, or rethink the entire outsourced strategy.

Once these elements are incorporated into the LSP strategy, planners can then begin the process of effectively identifying the services they really need from an LSP, present and gain support for the project from management and staff, search and locate LSPs possessed of the necessary competencies from fixed assets to information technologies, execute a viable contract, and determine the performance measurements to guide the on-going strengths and benefits of the partnership.

TODAY'S LSP CHALLENGES

While the slowing of growth and continued consolidation in third party services in 2001 indicates that the industry is still evolving in the current economic environment, the real challenges confronting the development of the LSP model revolve around a variety of issues, from strategic to technological. One thing is certain: shippers are demanding that LSPs possess the capability to support increasingly complex business processes and accelerate value-added performance even as fragmentation of supply chains and resulting coordination requirements escalates. These challenges can be organized into the following points [30]:

- *Enhanced logistics functions.* The foundation of the LSP industry rests on the ability to provide logistics functions that individual compa-nies can not effectively perform with their own resources. LSPs must continue to shape their service offerings around the dramatic changes driven by growth in channel complexity, the need for ever smaller and quicker LTL delivery, requirements for cross-docking or merge-in-transit operations, and the migration of supply chains from large super-DC consolidators in favor of flexible, agile networks of regional DCs characterized by an optimum mix of strategically located inventory and short-haul distribution. LSP functions should facilitate the growing use of "pull" replenishment systems, whereby demand is driven through networks of regional DCs.

- *Partnership functions.* Beyond simple transaction-based functions, LSPs are being asked to perform a host of specialized functions. For example, LSPs are being asked to co-locate their activities at the shipper's location, serving as an extension of the shipper's processes and performing activities normally belonging to the shipper. Alternatively, LSPs may perform additional activities at their own or partner site focused at reducing processing costs, reducing supply chain inventories by postponing product final configuration, or facilitating customer returns or product recycling. Then again, LSPs might be contracted to perform order processing, procurement, and financial processes, such as invoicing, credit management, and collections.

- *From transaction to process management.* As logistics outsourcing emerged during the period of deregulation, the use of LSPs has evolved from a concern with simply performing transaction based services, like warehousing and spot transport buys, to managing whole logistics processes. Because of their core competencies, operational economies of scale, and ability to leverage technologies tools, LSPs were easily able to outperform the logistics departments of their customers. Regardless of the nature of the outsourcing engagement, this has meant that LSPs could take a systems approach to managing their client's logistics needs and have an impact on *process* instead of simply providing one-time solutions in isolation. LSPs can respond to this challenge by pursuing either a basic *focused strategy* that limits capabilities to offering standardized services through an owned network of transportation and/or warehousing assets, or a dynamic *strategic solutions* strategy that provides a more innovative and systemic approach to customer needs by architecting customized, collaborative logistics channels composed of a portfolio of multiple-focused service providers.

- *Technology facilitators.* With the rise of Internet real-time connectivity, LSPs are increasingly being asked to shoulder the burden of providing advanced supply chain technologies. In the past, LSPs focused on providing toolsets like EDI that provided transaction support. With the advent of Internet networking, LSPs are now being required to provide a much broader set of information solutions that enable a supply chain node to work directly with any other node in the channel network. Major LSPs are now licensing their Internet systems with customers and other partnered LSPs.

- *Increased globalization.* A critical challenge before LSPs is responding to need for global logistics coverage in an age of increasing international outsourcing. As outsourced manufacturing makes its way across the globe, supply chains have become extended and increasingly complex. Shippers simply can not be hamstrung by unconnected logistics functions. Instead, LSPs are being asked to assist in the assembly of resources to operate highly integrated logistics management systems stretching across a global network.

- *Homeland security.* A new and potentially fertile field for LSP support is the area of logistics security. Since the attacks of September 11, 2001, the U.S. and other nations have begun the process of passing legislation designed to eliminate the possibility of terrorist attacks. As the opening salvos of this round of new regulation are applied to logistics activities, global companies can expect to see increases in supply chain transit times and increased documentation. The role of LSPs in minimizing the impact of security legislation is destined to become of the utmost importance as the decade of the 2000s unfolds.

SUMMARY

Although warehousing has often been called the "heart" of the distribution channel function, transportation can justly be described as the veins and arteries by which products are moved through the supply chain pipeline. By providing for the swift and uninterrupted flow of products, transportation provides companies with the ability to compete with other businesses in distant markets on an equal footing. Transportation also permits wider and deeper penetration of new markets far from the point of production. In addition, by maximizing vehicle and materials handling capacities and cargo requirements, effective transportation permits enterprises to leverage economies of scale by lowering the per-unit cost of transporting product. Efficient transportation enables firms to reduce the selling price by holding costs down, thereby providing for more competitive product positioning. Finally, transportation provides other business functions with essential information concerning products, marketing place and time utilities, and transit costs and capabilities necessary for effective supply chain planning and operational execution.

There are several legal forms and modes of transportation. Factors influencing transportation selection include the type of distribution environment to be serviced, enterprise strategic goals, financial capabilities, product order volumes, required delivery lead time, physical characteristics such as size, perishability, seasonality, potential for obsolescence and theft, and intrinsic value, geographical size of the distribution channel, carrier type availability, and strength of the competition. Shippers have the choice of using four possible legal types of transportation. The first three types, common carriers, contract carriers, and exempt carriers, are operated by for-hire freight companies and are subject to various federal, state, and local statutes and regulations. In contrast, the fourth type, private carriers, are normally owned by the company who uses their own equipment to transport products and supplies through internal channel networks to the customer. There are essentially five modes of transportation: motor carrier, railroad, water, pipeline, and air transport. Selection of transportation mode is governed by performance characteristics such as speed of delivery, minimization of changing modes during transport, dependability, capacity, frequency, and cost.

The effective day-to-day management of transportation activities is absolutely necessary for the smooth functioning of the business. The first step in the management process is to establish the cost-effectiveness of private transportation fleets and, as necessary, search for and select public carriers. The goal is to ensure the highest level of customer service at the lowest possible price. The selection of a carrier is normally based on a combination of factors including the price of the service, carrier financial stability, reliability, mode availability, and subjective elements. The second step involves the ongoing choice of selected transport modes to meet daily shipment requirements. Modes should be chosen that will best perform the service for the cost, satisfy any special shipping requirements, exceed the services offered by competing carriers and minimize the likelihood of loss, damage, or delivery delay. Once the mode and carrier have been selected, shippers must work with their *logistics service provider* (LSP) to establish an effective schedule and the proper vehicle routing to ensure timely customer delivery. The fourth step of the process is the preparation and completion of the necessary shipping documentation. Finally, mangers must be diligent in developing transportation performance measurements that will provide them with quantifiable data necessary for increased productivity and competitive advantage. Metrics should be developed for both purchased and internal transportation and should consist of price and carrier delivery performance.

The transportation industry in the twenty-first century is having to grapple with a host of radically new domestic and international issues. These challenges can probably best be summarized into three areas. The first, challenges posed by the need to renew the nation's aging transportation infrastructure and problems in each transport mode, strikes at the very heart of transport capabilities and efficiencies. The second area consists of managing the challenges posed by regulation. While deregulation of the transport Industry in the early 1980's dramatically freed transportation from outdated and inefficient legislation, the threat of terrorism in the early part of the 2000s is requiring transport managers and carriers to alter JIT/Lean assumptions about the supply chain that had grown over a twenty year period. Finally, transportation functions are having to implement and utilize a number of new information technologies. Today's Internet-enabled *transportation management systems* (TMS) provide traffic managers with integrated applications for transportation procurement, planning, and execution and tools enabling in-transit visibility and reporting.

Finally, of the trends impacting today's management of transportation, the use of *logistics service providers* (LSPs) is potentially the most revolutionary. In today's complex, global logistics environments, companies are finding that they simply do not have the capability to provide the full range of services to effectively execute end-to-end supply chain management requirements. LSPs fill this gap in non-core functions by providing the following critical services: *logistics services* associated with strategic management of JIT/Lean initiatives, global trade, supplier management, payment and auditing, and product life cycle management; *transportation services* including all forms of transport from LTL and intermodal to fleet acquisition consulting and equipment leasing; *warehousing services* focused on warehouse outsourcing and management, VMI programs, and fulfillment; *special services* required for such activities as home delivery, international sales, reverse logistics, and transportation consulting; and, *technology services* providing access to computerized tools such as the Internet or EDI. Choosing an effective LSP partner has become a critical strategy for most transportation departments requiring a firm understanding of partnership objectives, depth of the relationship, defined cost, benefits, and expectations, and flexibility of services available.

APPENDIX: MOTOR CARRIER CONTRACT

This contract is entered into this _____ th day of
_____, 19____, between

_____, and **ABC TRUCK LINES, INC.**, having its place of
business at 500 West Madison St., Chicago, IL 60068, (hereinafter
called "Carrier").

Carrier is engaged in the business of transporting property by motor
vehicle as a contract carrier in interstate and foreign commerce, holding
authority issued to it by the Interstate Commerce Commission under Permit
No. 59367 (Sub No. 150).

Customer requires motor carrier transportation services designed to
meet Customer's distinct needs.

Customer desires to utilize the services of Carrier and Carrier is
willing to provide such services to Customer, as a contract carrier, in
accordance with all the terms and conditions set forth below.

NOW, THEREFORE, in consideration of the mutual covenants and
agreements contained herein, the parties hereto agree, as follows:

1. **Term**. The term of this Contract shall be one year beginning on the date set forth
above. The Contract shall renew automatically for additional periods of one year
each; provided, however, that either party may terminate this Contract by giving a
minimum of thirty days' advance written notice of termination to the other party.

2. **Minimum Shipping Requirement**. Customer agrees to tender to Carrier a series
of shipments under this Contract, which shall include a minimum of three shipments
during the initial term and a minimum of three shipments during each renewal terms of
the Contract.

3. **Carrier's Obligations**. Carrier shall transport the minimum number of shipments
required to be tendered by Customer, and such additional shipments tendered by Customer from time to time, subject to the capacity and availability of Carrier's equipment. Nothing contained in this Contract shall require Customer to exclusively use
Carrier's service, or Carrier to exclusively serve Customer, and the failure of Carrier
to provide transportation service for any particular shipment, or the failure of Customer to tender any particular shipment to Carrier, shall not be deemed to be a breach
of this Contract.

4. **Relationship of Parties**. Each party is an independent contractor and neither
party hereto is the agent of the other party. Employees or independent contractors utilized by either party shall not be deemed to be employees or agents of the other party.

5. **Customer's Distinct Needs**. Customer represents and Carrier acknowledges that
Customer has distinct transportation needs which can be fulfilled by the contract carrier service to be performed by Carrier under this Contract.

6. **Equipment and Costs**. Carrier shall provide equipment in good condition and
repair which shall be suitable for the transportation of the commodities to be transported hereunder. Carrier shall assume and pay all costs and expenses incident to the

transportation of commodities tendered under this Contract, including, but not limited to, all costs and expenses arising out of the maintenance, repair or operation of its equipment, labor, supplies and insurance.

7. **Rates and Charges.** The rates, charges and specific terms of transportation covering all shipments moving under this Contract are set forth in Schedule A attached hereto and incorporated herein by reference. The rates, charges and terms specified in Schedule A may be amended from time to time, but only if such amendment is in writing, signed by both parties, prior to the effective time of such amendment. Such amendments containing copies of signatures of individuals representing both parties shall be binding, without the necessity of producing original signatures.

8. **Payment.** The charges to be paid by Customer for services rendered under this Contract shall be paid in the manner and at the times set forth in Schedule A. Customer guarantees the payment of all freight charges lawfully charged by Carrier under the terms of this Contract, regardless of whether such shipments are designated a prepaid or collect, and notwithstanding any notation to the contrary contained on the bill of lading governing the shipments transported under this Contract by Carrier for Customer.

9. **Identification.** Carrier shall indemnify and hold harmless Customer from and against all loss, damage, fines, expense, actions, and claims for injury to persons (including injury resulting in death) and damage to property wherein such loss, damage or injury is proximately caused by acts or omissions of Carrier, its agents or employees, and arising out of or in connection with Carrier's discharge of duties and responsibilities as specified in this Contract; provided, however, that such indemnification and agreement to hold Customer harmless shall not extend to the amount of any loss, damage or injury resulting from negligent or intentional acts or omissions of Customer, its employees and agents.

10. **Insurance.** Carrier shall procure public liability and property damage insurance with a combined single limit of not less than $1,000,000 per occurrence, and all-risk cargo insurance with liability limits sufficient to cover shipments having a value of $50,000.00 with a rider or other endorsement adequate to insure shipments having a value not to exceed $100,000.00. Carrier shall immediately notify Customer in writing if said insurance is canceled or modified in any material respect. Carrier shall, at the request of Customer, provide to Customer a certificate evidencing such insurance.

11. **Freight Loss or Damage.** Carrier shall be liable and responsible for loss, theft, damage, or injury to shipments occurring while in the custody, possession or control of Carrier under this Contract. The extent of Carrier's liability shall be governed by Section 11707 of the Interstate Commerce Act, in the same manner that liability is determined for common carriers. All claims for cargo loss or damage shall be governed by the rules and regulations contained in Part 1005 of Title 49 of the Code of Federal Regulations.

12. **Allowance.** It is mutually agreed that if Carrier's rates and charges set forth in Schedule A provide for allowances (whether directly stated or not) to Customer for services it provides, which services Carrier would ordinarily provide, such as loading or unloading, such allowances are reasonably related to the actual costs of such services.

13. **Freight Bill Notations.** If the rates and charges set forth in Schedule A are subject to any subsequent reduction, allowance or adjustment under any other provisions contained in Schedule A, Carrier shall so indicate in its initial freight bill submitted to Customer.

14. **Successors and Assigns.** This Contract shall be binding upon successors and assigns of the parties hereto, provided, however, that no such assignment shall be effective without the written consent of the non-assigning party.

15. **Entire Agreement.** This Contract, including Schedule A and any written amendments thereto, shall constitute the entire agreement between the parties, and no oral representations, agreements, understandings or waivers shall be binding upon the parties to this Contract.

16. **Notices.** All notices given under this Contract shall be in writing, signed by or on behalf of the party giving the same and sent via mail or telefax to the other party; provided, however, that requests for service and confirmation thereof may be communicated in person or by means of telephone or computer.

17. **Applicable Law.** The terms of this Contract shall be governed by the laws of the State of xxxxxx.

18. **Confidentiality.** Except as required by law, the terms and conditions of this Contract shall not be disclosed by either party to persons other than each party's own affiliates, officers, directors, employees and agents; provided, however, that Customer may disclose the contents of this Contract to its vendors and customers which might be affected thereby.

IN WITNESS WHEREOF, this Contract has been signed by authorized representatives of Carrier and Customer.

CARRIER: **CUSTOMER:**

ABC TRUCK LINES, INC.   _____
500 West Madison   _____
P.O. Box 915   _____
Chicago, Illinois 60068   _____
Telephone: (312)474-7350   Telephone: _____
Telefax: (312)474-7300   Telefax: _____

By: Sam Smith   By: _____
Title: Director of Operations Title: _____
Date: July 7, 20xx   Date: ____/____/20__

QUESTIONS FOR REVIEW

1. Describe the fundamental principles of transportation.
2. Why must purchasing, warehousing, and transportation functions work closely together?
3. What are the legal forms of transportation?
4. Detail the performance characteristics associated with transportation. How would companies use these characteristics to plan for transportation requirements?
5. Compare and contrast the five modes of transportation.
6. What is intermodal transportation? Point out some applications of intermodal transport.
7. How have requirements for JIT and Quick Response deliveries changed the face of transportation?
8. Why is transportation scheduling and routing so important to the efficient running of the business?
9. In what ways has the U.S. government used regulation to control transportation?
10. Describe the nature of the *logistics service provider* (LSP) and why have they become so important to logistics management?

REFERENCES

1. See the comments of Bowersox, Donald J. and Closs, David J., *Logistical Management: The Integrated Supply Chain Process.* New York: McGraw-Hill, 1996, p. 314.

2. Fair, Marvin L. and Williams, Ernest W., *Transportation and Logistics.* Plano, Texas: Business Publications, 1981, pp. 90-100.

3. See the discussion in Coyle, John, J., Bardi, Edward J., and Langley, C. John Jr., *The Management of Business Logistics: A Supply Chain Perspective.* 7th ed., Mason, OH: South-Western, 2003, pp. 397.

4. Delaney, Robert V., *Fourteenth Annual State Of Logistics Report.* St. Louis, MO: Cass Business Logistics, 2003, Figure #7.

5. These figures were taken from Editor, "Trucking 2002," *Inbound Logistics*, 22, 9, 2002, pp. 49-59.

6. Bureau of Transportation Statistics, U.S. Department of Transportation, *National Transportation Statistics, 2002.* Washington D.C.: U.S. Government Printing Office, 2002.

7. Coyle, *et al*, p. 346.

8. Sampson, Roy J., Farris, Martin T., and Shrock, David L., *Domestic Transportation: Practice, Theory and Policy.* Boston: Houghton Mifflin Company, 1985, pp. 62-63.

9. Wood, Donald F. and Johnson, James C., *Contemporary Logistics.* New York: Macmillan & Co., 1993, p. 147 and U.S. Bureau of the Census, *Statistical Abstract of the United States: 1990*, 110th ed. Washington, DC: U.S. Government Printing Office, 1990, p. 597.

10. Delaney, Robert V., *Fourth Annual State of Logistics Report.* St. Louis MO: Cass Business Logistics, 1993, p. 4.

11. Bowersox, Donald J., Calabro, Pat J., and Wagenheim, George D., *Introduction to Transportation.* New York: Macmillan Publishing Co., 1981, pp. 56-57.

12. These factors have been abstracted from Bowersox and Close, pp. 365-367.

13. Cavinato, Joseph, "Tips for Negotiating Rates," *Distribution* 66-68 (February 1991); Patton, Edwin P., "Carrier Rates and Tariffs," in *The Distribution Management Handbook.* Tompkins, James and Harmelink, Dale A., eds. New York: McGraw-Hill, 1994, pp. 12.11-12.18; Coyle *et al*, pp. 393-396; and, Bowersox and Close, pp. 370-378.

14. These fundamental methods have been abstracted from Dillion, Thomas F., "Outsourcing--More Than Another Buzzword." *Purchasing World*, (February 1989).

15. McKinnon, Alan C., *Physical Distribution Systems.* New York: Routledge, 1989, p. 173.

16. See the comments in Ibid., p. 178.

17. For the implications of JIT/Lean Manufacturing on traffic management see Wantuck, Kenneth A., *Just-In Time For America.* Milwaukee, WI: The Forum Ltd., 1989, pp. 333-336.

18. For more information on these methods see McKinnon, pp 195-205.

19. Bass, Howard K., Garg, Ashish, and Iijima, T.J., "What is the 'True' Cost of Processing a Freight Bill?" *Global Logistics and Supply Chain Management*, 6, 10, 2002, pp. 54-57.
20. For more information see Kreitner, John, "Managing Transportation Productivity," in *The Distribution Handbook*. James F. Robeson and Robert G. House, eds. New York: The Free Press, 1985, pp. 512-518.
21. These comments can be found in Panchak, Patricia, "Stuck in the Slow Lane," *Industry Week*, 252, 5, (May 2003), pp. 47-50.
22. For information on TMSs see Bradley, Peter, "Turn on the Power," *DC Velocity*, 1, 3, 2003, 46-48; Gaines, Stephen, "Tips for Choosing the Right TMS Package," *dot.com Distribution*, 2, 2, 2001, pp. 3-8; and Ross, *Introduction to e-Supply Chain Management*, pp. 295-296.
23. This survey was conducted jointly by Cap Gemini Ernst & Young, Georgia Tech, and Ryder System and reported in *Global Logistics and Supply Chain Strategies*. 6, 11, 2002, p. 16.
24. Delaney, Robert V., *Thirteenth Annual State Of Logistics Report*. St. Louis, MO: Cass Business Logistics, 2002, Figure #13.
25. Sutherland, Joel and Speh, Thomas W., "Using 3PL Service Providers to Create and Deliver Significant Supply Chain Value," in *Achieving Supply Chain Excellence Through Technology*, 4, Mulani, Narendra, ed., Montgomery Research, San Francisco, CA, 2002, pp. 176-178.
26. See Kuglin, Fred A. and Rosenbaum, Barbara A., *The Supply Chain Network @ Internet Speed: Preparing Your Company for the E-Commerce Revolution*, AMACOM, New York, 2001, p. 129; Schryver, Rob, "The Trade Tsunami: Traditional 3PLs Expand Roles," *Inbound Logistics*, 21, 9, 2001, 71-76; and, Editors, "Top 100 3PLs," *Inbound Logistics*, 22, 7, 2002, pp. 65-75.
27. Langley, C. John Jr., Allen, Gary R. Allen, and Tyndall, Gene R. Tyndall, *Third-Party-Logistics Services: Views from the Customers*. (Atlanta, GA: Georgia Institute of Technology, Gap Gemini Ernst & Young and Ryder System, Inc., 2001).
28. See Kuglin and Rosenbaum, p. 138.
29. This section is abstracted from Ross, David F., *Introduction to e-Supply Chain Management: Engaging Technology to Build Market-Winning Business Partnerships*. Boca Raton, FL: St. Lucie Press, 2003, p. 301.
30. See the comments in Kopczak, Laura Rock, "Trends in Third Party Logistics," in *Achieving Supply Chain Excellence Through Technology*, 1, Anderson, David, ed., Montgomery Research, San Francisco, CA, 1999, 268-272; and Truncik, Perry A., "4 Logistics Trends Driving and Driven by 3PLs," *Chief Logistics Officer*, 10, 2002, pp. 7-11.

UNIT 5

INTERNATIONAL DISTRIBUTION AND DISTRIBUTION INFORMATION TECHNOLOGY

CHAPTERS:

13. International Distribution
14. Information Technology and Supply Chain Management

Unit 4 focused on the *distribution operations execution* processes. Planning and control activities in this area centered on the short- to immediate-range activities associated with servicing the customer, acquiring and warehousing inventory in the supply channel network, and transportation and delivery. The goal of the execution processes discussed was to ensure that the entire supply chain possesses sufficient inventories and warehousing and delivery capabilities to achieve total customer service at the lowest possible cost. Unit 4 concluded the *enterprise management planning process* that had begin in Unit 2.

Unit 5 is concerned with a discussion of two areas that are integral elements of today's supply chain environment. The first focuses on the management of international trade. The growth of global trade is the result of a number of marketplace trends. Some relate to the convergence of several information process technologies, particularly the Internet, and their ability to network companies from across the globe in a common community. Other factors focus on the maturing of the economies of today's industrialized nations and their need to explore foreign markets as a source of both competitive advantage as well as of basic materials, cost-effective components, and low labor costs.

The rise of international competition and global trading blocks has also occurred because of fundamental changes in the marketplace. Of prime importance is the end of the long-standing international predominance of U.S. manufacturing and distribution. The rise of Japan, China, and the Pacific Rim and the solidification of European Union have altered the balance of trade and necessitated the establishment of new global partnerships and logistics techniques. Finally, the growth in incomes worldwide, the development of logistics infrastructures, and the speed of communications have created new marketplace opportunities. To respond to these changes, companies have had to alter fundamentally their inventory and delivery systems. The goal of today's international company is to attain the best cost and customer service possible while welding enterprise and worldwide partner logistics resources together with global markets, capital, and manufacturing to maximize competitive advantage.

The final chapter in the text is concerned with the second critical area facing today's supply chain manager: the implementation of information technology. As it has had in all elements of today's business environment, the availability of computerized tools that not only facilitate and accelerate the speed of information processing but also provide the framework for the integration and interoperability of companies regardless of time and geography has had an enormous impact on supply network management. In harnessing the power of today's software applications, open-system architectures, and Internet networking capabilities, companies must be prepared to conduct an effective computerized application solution search and then possess the necessary project management skills to successfully implement the software. Such a task requires implementers to have a full grasp of the strategic and tactical objectives to be attained by the software, the impact system changes will have on the organization and its capabilities, the costs, manpower, and time it will take to implement the software, and the expected improvements in productivity and competitive advantage resulting from the implementation. Finally, effectively leveraging information technology requires supply chain professionals on all levels to develop performance measurements targeted at continuous improvement in information technology tools and organizational capabilities.

13

INTERNATIONAL DISTRIBUTION

When business historians look back at the period of the last 25 years of the 20th century and the opening of the new millennium, one of the most salient developments will be the emergence of the global economy. For several decades after the Second World War most manufacturing and distribution companies remained within their own national boundaries. Although some of the world's largest corporations, such as Coca-Cola, Ford Motor, and Procter & Gamble, had historically engaged in a significant international trade, governments were fearful of exporting technology and wealth that might drain national resources in the face of the Cold War. In many cases, whole markets, such as Eastern Europe and China, were closed to U.S. and European companies. Today, the end of the Cold War, the connective capabilities of information technologies like the Internet, and the deployment of global outsourcing strategies has accelerated the growth of the international marketplace and the integration of the world's economic activities. The old Soviet Union and the emerging nations of Eastern Europe are now openly soliciting political alliances, economic assistance, trading status, and investment from the West. The European Union has a common currency and is moving closer to full elimination of trade barriers. Perhaps the most fertile area of economic growth, the Pacific Rim, is seeking favorable trading status and the import of foreign goods.

Fundamental to sustaining this growth is efficient and cost-effective global supply chain management strategies and processes. Beyond the manufacturing, financial, and marketing aspects of international trade, distribution channel issues relating to global materials and product sourcing, cost-effective storage, fulfillment management, and speedy transportation have become the foremost frontiers of competition. As the world's industrialized nations intensify their search for new markets and new sources of products and services abroad, the state of logistics functions have become increasingly pivotal for success. Nations that have substandard systems of roads, waterways, and rail, poorly trained labor pools, inadequate distribution support systems, and protectionist governments will be more costly to penetrate and by-passed by global strategists. As internationalization expands, it will be the responsibility of supply chain planners to design the logistics networks of the future, determine cost versus benefit, and engineer the sourcing, manufacturing, inventory control, warehousing, and transportation functions that will propel the global economy into the 21st century.

Understanding global distribution is the focus of this chapter. After considering the economic, competitive, and supply chain trends fueling globalization at the dawn of the twenty-first century, the chapter proceeds to a discussion of the major features of an effective international distribution strategy. Next, the chapter explores the options available to international firms in the search to effectively penetrate global markets and position products. Critical to the success of a channel strategy is the development of an international distribution network. Topics discussed in this section are managing the service and cost of the distribution network, structuring the global channel, international marketing considerations such as price, promotion and sales terms, international financial issues, and export documentation. The chapter then proceeds to discuss in detail the transportation and warehousing requirements of global channel management. An analysis of international purchasing and product importing forms the basis of the next section. Topics discussed are advantages of international sourcing, countertrade purchasing, and the international purchasing management process. The chapter concludes with a short review of the nature of today's international environment.

FORCES DRIVING GLOBALIZATION

Over the past 30 years, the growth of global trade has been dramatic. In 1970 the U.S. exported over $56.6 billion and imported over $54.3 billion. In 1990, exports reached $535 billion and imports $616 billion. By 1995 exports stood at $794 billion and imports at 890 billion. Finally, in 2002 exports reached $971 billion ($682 billion in goods and $289 billion in services) and imports stood at $1.4 trillion ($1.16 trillion in goods and $240 billion in services). By the year 2005, the World Trade Organization (WTO) estimates the totally of International trade to grow to over $9 trillion (1). Although the U.S. trade deficit amounted to $435.6 billion in 2002, global trade, according to the U.S. Department of Transportation, supports over 11 million jobs and has accounted for one-third of economic growth since 1993.

This explosion in foreign trade and increasing inter-dependence of global markets is the result of a number of trends, such as continued world economic growth and the connective power of technology that are expected to accelerate the growth of globalization in the twenty-first century. This growing economic internationalism, however, is not assured nor universally accepted as evidenced by the recent violent protests accompanying the meetings of international bodies like the International Monetary Fund and the WTO. Among the barriers are to be found political and economic regulations, financial barriers, and poor logistics infrastructures

TRENDS ACCELERATING GLOBALIZATION

There are a variety of forces driving today's growth in international trade. Among the key factors are the following: maturing of the U.S. economy, growing foreign competition, acceleration in global deregulation, growth of strategic alliances, and closer integration of domestic and international distribution systems. Each of these topics is discussed below.

Maturing of the U.S. Economy. The maturing of the U.S. economy has fundamentally altered traditional thinking about global trade. For over a decade before the new millennium, it had become clearly evident that the era of high growth was over as business consolidations, shrinking margins, declining profitability, and overcapacity indicated that many sectors of the economy had slipped from growth to maturity. While it is true that the U.S. occupies a position of unsurpassed global economic hegemony, it had become clear that continued economic growth can only take place in the context of increased dependence on international partnerships. Today, some of the largest global corporations, such as Daimler/Chrysler, are combinations of once solely owned U.S. companies and foreign companies.

As markets at home have stagnated, U.S. enterprises have turned to the newly opening markets of the Pacific Rim, Central and South America, and Eastern Europe. The decline in global tensions, the explosion in communications technologies, the movement of former communist countries toward market economies, and the easing of protectionist attitudes have made foreign trade of critical importance in sustaining competitive advantage. In addition, the U.S. can no longer avoid the fact that continued economic success is predicated on international trade. Many products, such as oil and other basic raw materials, must be imported; often cost-effective components assembled in foreign countries are critical for the production of domestic finished goods. Finally, there can be no denying that certain imported products are here to stay. China's growing capacities in the production of high-labor, low cost commodities and textiles can only expect to expand; Japanese leadership in television sets and low-priced microelectronics and parity in the automobile market are testimony of the impact of foreign products on American purchasing habits.

Growing Foreign Competition. Over the past decade, the expanding internationalization of foreign companies, as well as the coalescence of trading blocks in Europe and Asia, have dramatically impacted U.S. manufacturing and distribution and altered the balance of trade. This globalization of competition has accelerated sharply in just the past few years. The market value of U.S. direct investment abroad rose 35 percent, to $776 billion, from 1987 to 1992 while the value of direct foreign investment in the U.S. more than doubled to $692 billion. Similar to the growing maturation of domestic markets in the United States, the advanced industrialized nations in Western Europe, China, and Japan have long looked to the U.S. import marketplace to sustain their growing economies and to gain trade parity. In addition, many second-tier countries, such as Brazil, Mexico, and South Korea, who enjoy lower operating costs, are also seeking to catapult their economies to "world-class" status by supporting domestic companies with leadership in textiles, apparel, and electronics. The U.S. has countered by refocusing its efforts at increasing exports, not only with the major industrialized nations, but also with developing countries on a bi-lateral basis. The result has been a clear-cut requirement for American businesses to decrease production and distribution costs to remain competitive.

In addition, many nations have come to realize that deregulation and opening avenues of foreign trade, reducing tariffs, and fostering free trade are necessary to their continued expansion. The growth in incomes worldwide, the development of distribution channel infrastructures, and the speed of communications have increased global demand for new products and market opportunities. The initiatives targeted at dividing the industrialized world into three massive trading blocs in Europe, Asia, and North America can also have an enormous impact on U.S. trade and logistics. The surprisingly easy successes enjoyed by the European Union to effect continental economic unification and a common currency (2002) are providing Europe with the potential to assemble a powerful economic engine.

A critical development has been the emergence of the Pacific Rim countries. Despite over a decade of recession, Japan still possesses the world's second largest economy. As a single nation, China is expected to be the third largest economy before long and, if the current rate of growth is sustained, will be the world's largest economy in 20 years. Despite many original misgivings, Beijing, Hong Kong, and Taiwan are becoming one China from the standpoint of trade. In 1993, the United States, Canada, and Mexico took the first step in signing the North American Free Trade Agreement (NAFTA) as a counterbalance to the emergence of the trading blocks in Europe and Asia. While much of the early fears of massive loss of jobs and industries to Mexico have proven baseless as the agreement completes its first decade, NAFTA has helped to expedite trade between the U.S.'s largest (Canada) and second largest (Mexico) trading partners.

In order to manage the new era of global competition, the efficient operation of logistics functions is fundamental. As companies seek to export products not only to major trading partners but also to markets dispersed throughout the world, logistics costs involved in international warehousing and transportation will become critical in holding down prices and assuring tolerable margins. In addition, as many U.S. companies seek to source components or even to relocate their operations overseas, corporate planners are having to formulate logistics strategies that will guarantee the smooth and efficient flow of materials and products through the domestic and international distribution pipeline. In summary, the goal of these movements toward regional trading blocs is to reduce tariffs and customs requirements, develop common shipping documentation, and establish compatible transportation and material handling systems that enable countries belonging to a regional trade union to act as if they were a single commercial entity.

Deregulation. A fundamental condition for the growth of global trade is the lessening and/or elimination of legal barriers to international trade. There are two major areas driving this trend: *financial* and *logistics deregulation* [2]. The massive changes brought about by such events as the creation of the U.S. Export-Import Bank and the International Monetary Market (IMM), have enabled establishment of global financial standards, the extension and guarantee of long-term import/export credits beyond individual bank capabilities, and the mechanism to exchange currencies and trade futures at market rates. The decision of the U.S. to drop the gold standard in the early 1970s has assisted in removing previous restrictions on the setting of monetary rates. In addition, the adoption of the Euro in 2002 has greatly facilitated the flow of global trade by providing yet another source of stable mediums for exchange. In fact, one commentator recently felt that the use of the Euro would eventually surpass the dollar as the global standard of exchange.

The second area of global trade deregulation is occurring in transportation. The decision of the U.S. in the early 1980s to deregulate transportation has been slowly but steadily expanding across the globe. Historically, governments rather than market forces determined the scope and price of transportation. Many nations did not allow foreign-owned carriers to operate within their boarders. Many transport modes, such as the current rail system in Mexico, were state owned or, as in Germany, subsidized by the government. Today, removal of these barriers to free-market drivers in most industrialized nations have followed U.S. example. UPS, for example, currently operates via any combination of rail, motor, air, or water in over 190 countries in a seamless manner via ownership, joint marketing, and operating agreements. Beyond operating privileges and privatization, changes in *cabotage* (requirements that goods and passengers between two domestic ports must use only domestic carriers) have been gradually relaxed, especially between countries in the European Union and the partners to NAFTA.

Strategic Alliances. The fourth major trend driving globalization is the continued expansion of strategic alliances and joint ventures. In the past, most companies pursued a strategy of *vertical integration*. The argument ran that if the enterprise owned not only the production and distribution processes but also the source of raw materials, then corporate control over material fabrication, product design and marketing, and supply sources, market share and profits would be assured. By removing dependence on other companies, the enterprise would be self-sustaining and free of disruptions to the flow of material, labor, and transportation. Today, the vertically integrated company has become a strategic objective of the past. No one firm can possibly hope to be the leader in all aspects of their industries. With the growth of competitors, both domestic and foreign, focused on price parity and value-added features such as quality and service, vertical organizations could not hope to sustain their previous market dominance. One by one, leadership in steel, auto, computer, and other markets was lost to more streamlined foreign enterprises that focused on core competencies.

This refocusing of the strategies and detail operations of the enterprise on core competencies has also been accelerated by the needs of today's products and markets. Global competition, high product and service quality expectations, short product life cycles, and rapidly shifting markets have motivated firms to seek partnerships and alliances both domestically and internationally. Partnerships provide the benefits of vertical integration without the risks. Joint ventures permit all participating companies to leverage the competencies of other partners to increase the speed of product design, and process, quality and service flexibility. In addition, other partnering advantages include access to capital, communications, and markets that businesses acting on their own could not attain or which are closed by foreign governments or restricted by trade barriers.

One of the best examples of global partnering can be found in the auto industry. Auto dealers both in the U.S. and abroad often buy vehicles from other countries to satisfy customer requirements for imports. Many a U.S. Ford or GM dealer that formerly sold only domestic models often today have foreign import divisions for sales and services. Recent trends among global auto makers have indicated a flourish of joint ventures. The merger of German automaker Daimler with Chrysler, GM partnerships with Saab, Toyota in Australia, Isuzu in Japan, and Daewoo in Korea are examples. In addition, GM has foreign-owned subsidiaries in Europe (Opel), the United Kingdom (Lotus and Vauxhall), and South America (GM do Brasil). As the world moves closer to three trading blocks in North America, Europe, and Asia, U.S. firms that do not have either foreign subsidiaries or joint ventures might find themselves excluded from free trade with the European and Asian blocks.

Integration of Global Distribution Systems. The final area driving globalization is the use of international logistics service providers, transportation functions, and information technologies to link companies spanning several continents. The objective of end-to-end service with real time order visibility and order tracking has become the mantra of today's LSPs as they search to expand their international footprint. These global LSPs provide continuity and visibility to the logistics needs of customers across the entire supply chain, rather than dependence on individual players who perform narrow local transactions and then pass shipments on to the next channel partner. The goal is to provide customers with technology tools to control the global supply chain by enabling them to change both the velocity and delivery points of goods as they move across global networks. Such a capability is critical for companies utilizing forms of intermodalism that utilize combinations of ocean-land bridge (ocean, rail or motor, and ocean), all water, or ocean/mini-land bridge (ocean and rail or motor) transport.

The key driver of global logistics integration is today's information technology tools, particularly the Internet. Through Internet Marketing sites customers can search the globe for competitive suppliers who can provide as well as stimulate interest in products and services without regard for time or geographical limitations. e-Business Web sites also provide anyone, anywhere on the earth the ability to buy products and participate in trading exchanges. Such tools enable companies to open real-time communication with global suppliers as well as eliminate cumbersome paper documentation relating to contracts, orders, delivery requirements, and customs forms. Finally, these systems are providing planners with real-time visibility to a range of critical functions from forecasting requirements to on-line track-and-trace of products in-transit and electronic bill payment.

BARRIERS TO GLOBALIZATION

While the above factors are enabling companies world-wide to expand their international trade strategies, there remain significant barriers that threaten growth. Among these barriers can be found tariffs and trade practices, cultural issues, financial restrictions, security, and logistics infrastructure weaknesses. Each of these barriers to globalization is detailed below.

Tariffs and Trade Practices. As companies draft a globalization strategy, they are soon confronted with a critical barrier: international taxes, tariffs, and duties. Originally these charges were designed by governments to protect domestic industries by making imported goods more expensive. As such, they must be considered primarily as political instruments devised for the purpose of governing the practice of foreign trade within national boarders. These costs not only can greatly fluctuate by country and region, they are often difficult to ascertain, complex, and continuously changing. While such data is compiled by every country's department of commerce, it is published in widely different formats, taxonomies, and languages. As one expert put it

> Traditionally, the only accurate way to access this information is through customs brokers, who must often research the intended shipment before they can estimate the cost. This process is painful, slow, manual, error-prone, and often outdated

by the time it's completed. It does not lend itself to rapid iteration, let alone optimization [3].

What is more, as the world grows smaller, countries and trading communities can utilize threats of increased tariffs, duties, or other restrictions as a powerful diplomatic tool. Retaliation is often swift, with talk of looming trade wars. For example, President George W. Bush's decision in 2002 to increase protective tariffs on U.S. steel brought a storm of protest from the European Union who in turn appealed to the WTO for punitive action.

Beyond the use of tariffs and restrictions to control trade, countries often promote national practices that give domestic industries an unfair advantage. Sometimes these practices are administrative and consist of unnecessary technicalities or regulatory requirements that simply add cost and retard trade. Many countries require that a portion of the material composition of the product and the labor force originate from the home country. More serious are license requirements and import quotas that limit trade and protect local immature industries. Perhaps the biggest barrier is global competitors that are supported by local governments. For example, even giant UPS cannot compete with global shipping concern Deutsche Post that draws financial support from the German government.

Cultural Barriers. Building a successful global trade strategy requires bridging cultural complexities that can add new dimensions to the challenges of international channel management. While trade laws, exchange rates, tariffs and restrictions, coping with managing transit distance, global finance, and political risk are difficult enough for the international planner, cultural differences pose a serious threat to success. A failure to understand local customs or an unintentional violation of social taboos can create a veiled resistance on the part of nationals to do business with offending outside traders. While many practices and the use of logistics assets are uniform across the world, global companies must be able to manage the following cultural issues [4].

- *Trade relationships.* The personal elements necessary to develop trade relationships can vary widely by nation. For example, in the U.S. business can be conducted over the phone or by e-mail. In Asia, face-to-face contact is a requirement.
- *Use of LSPs.* The use of outside service providers is perceived in some countries as a negative factor, indicating that a trading partner does not possess sufficient competencies.
- *Contracts.* Many cultures have different views regarding the binding power of contracts. In the U.S., contracts are perceived as legal and moral documents that posses the force of law and personal commit-

ment. In some countries a contract is understood as a statement of intent, and if the environment in which the contract was originally drafted changes drastically, parties are justified in abandoning their commitment to the contract.

- *Working styles.* The work ethic and considerations of holidays and pay may differ greatly in many countries. In Europe, for example, many nationals expect lengthy vacation and holiday seasons. The best way to manage local workers is to have local or regional managers guiding employee decisions. The golden rule is to strategize globally, but execute regionally using the local language and culture.

- *Speed.* In many cultures the signing of contracts or commitment to strategic decisions can be a lengthy affair. While U.S. strategists are accustomed to quick deals and rapid decision deployment, many cultures often wish to deliberate over alternatives before making a decision.

Differences in national management, work ethics, and decision styles can cause considerable friction and frustration when developing international strategies. Besides possessing the skill to execute the proper number crunching and legal deliberations, effective global planning teams must also possess a deep familiarity with the cultural and linguistic sensibilities of proposed local partners.

Financial Restrictions [5]. Financial barriers to global trade consist of two critical areas: generating effective financial forecasts and charting the capabilities of institutional and monetary infrastructures. The ability to forecast financial positioning is critical to effective business management. It is the responsibility of financial managers to forecast company investment (earnings, growth, and ROI), profits (revenues, margins, and profits), assets (cash, receivables, and plant), and capital (debt) in order to chart business strategy. Domestically, creating forecasts for these elements is a challenge in itself. When combined with a global perspective, computing in additional factors such as exchange rates, customs and tariffs, inflation, and local government policies render the tasks of financial forecasting even more complex.

Financial infrastructure barriers arise out of the practices found in every country governing how facilitating institutions, such as banks, insurance, law courts and the legal practice, and transportation carriers, operate. Often, many of the financial and legal services found in the highly industrialized nations are in their infancy or simply not available in many parts of the world. For example, Hewlet-Packard found out early that legal and operating expectations with LSPs varied greatly by region. HP has solved the problem by having each LSP sign a base agreement, but then tacks-on addendums that contain regional specifics. Through this approach, HP is able to standardize its processes on a global basis as much as possible, while structuring the business to accommodate local and regional differences. The lack of financial and institutional structure can add a significant degree of uncertainty and pose critical challenges to the development of competitive global trading strategies.

Security. While historically a complex process, international trade has become exponentially more difficult as nations grapple with the growing problem of security and international terrorism. In fact, since the terrorist attack of 11 September 2001, governments have been erecting compliance and security restrictions on passengers and cargo that have the potential to seriously impede global trade. Global transportation costs are rising as carriers add security surcharges and delays elongate transit times. For example, Con-Way Transportation Services began charging an $8 per shipment Homeland Security tax on January 1, 2003. The extra fee is used to pay the cost of U.S. government-mandated changes regarding registration of equipment, drivers, customs documentation, and security inspections at the U.S./Canadian boarder.

Several U.S. government initiatives have been passed that impact import/export operations directly. The Customs-Trade Partnership Against Terrorism (C-TPAT) and the Container Security Initiative (CSI), both passed in the first half of 2002, are designed to protect the security of cargo entering the U.S. Other security measures are aimed at protecting the nation's seaports (Operation Safe Commerce – OSC) by making it mandatory for carriers to file electronic manifests information in advance of arrival. Such regulations are also to be enacted on international air cargo movements by October of 2003. U.S. customs will require that all carriers, deconsolidators, freight forwarders, and some consignment couriers use the Automated Manifest System (AAMS) to provide advance electronic cargo declaration information to U.S. customs.

The impact of these and other measures on global trade is potentially far-reaching. Already companies have begun to revisit their JIT strategies and alter assumptions about inventory as lead times and delays elongate. Rules requiring transmission of shipment-level detail could add 24 to 72 hours to inventory cycles, threatening to reverse decades of logistics productivity improvement overnight. These security measures have also generated a great deal more documentation which is often slower than the speed of the goods shipped, causing deliveries to languish while freight clears an increasingly entangled customs system. What is worse, as the outbreak of Severe Acute Respiratory Syndrome (SARS) in China during the first half of 2003 bares witness, security measures have to grapple with non-terrorist attacks on the general health, food supplies, and well-being of trading nations.

Infrastructure Weaknesses. Besides government policy, legal, cultural, and financial barriers, the lack of physical distribution infrastructure is perhaps the most critical impediment to global trade. Part of the problem resides in the lack of standardized transportation, material-handling equipment, containerization, warehousing, port facilities, and communications and technology that renders inter-country movement of goods difficult. Such barriers require products to be loaded and unloaded, sometimes by hand, from vehicles/containers as they cross national boundaries. What is worse, many developing nations do not have sufficient logistics infrastructures. Often basic transportation infrastructure, such as roads, rail lines, fuel depots, and customs agencies are rudimentary or, in some cases, non-existent. When it is considered that an average of 17 to 20 parties touch a typical international shipment in one way or another as it moves between carriers, brokers, forwarders, across boarders, and through customs and financial institutions, even minor problems in the global supply chain can cause major shipment delays.

Summary. Companies are faced with many opportunities as well as challenges in the pursuit of global trade. Each year, an increasing number of products from steel to toys and jewelry are imported, whereas at the same time, more U.S. goods are finding their way to new foreign markets. Few businesses today can feel immune from the threat of foreign competition. Bender [6] has succinctly described the conditions propelling globalization as composed of three interconnected areas. The first consists of *strategic* reasons such as the following:

- Attempting to leveraging shrinking product and process life cycles and recovering development costs by selling products on a global basis.
- Denying marketplace sanctuaries to competitors. Companies can sell at a high profit margin to captive markets, making it affordable to sell at a lower margin to more markets.
- Avoiding government-directed protectionism as found in many developing countries.
- Balancing production and investment with the differing economic growth patterns and economic cycles occurring across the globe.
- Profiting from global financial systems, communications and media, and market demand homogenization.
- Establishing early presence in emerging markets.
- Maximizing opportunities arising from symbiotic relations between suppliers and customers based on long-term commitments and close relationships.

The second area fostering business globalization is associated with the following *tactical* issues:

- Capitalizing on foreign trade to increase profits. Companies participating in international trade are likely to grow faster and be more profitable than companies focusing on national or regional markets.
- Participating in countertrade agreements. About one-third of all international trade involves countertrade (bartering), rather than cash transactions.
- Achieving stabilization by matching product and investment with global business cycles.
- Obtaining economies of scope by maximizing marketing, production, and logistics advantages through international trade.
- Reducing costs by transferring products across national boundaries that reduces taxes.

The final area focuses on *operational* issues and is concerned with the following:

- Reallocating manufacturing and distribution capacities to match global market demand.
- Reassigning production, purchasing, processing, sales, and financing to take advantage of different rates of international exchange.
- Accelerating the learning effect. As a company learns more about the global marketplace, costs associated with manufacturing and distribution processes decrease.
- Exploiting automation's declining breakeven point. As the volume of product and processes increase, technology costs are recovered much quicker.

DEVELOPING GLOBAL STRATEGIES

Although it is critical for today's enterprise to explore international trade alternatives if they are to maintain and expand competitive advantage, there are a number of questions that must be addressed before engaging in international operations. Among those questions are the following:

- What is the scope and objective of the current international trade initiatives?
- What should be the firm's strategies in pursuing foreign trade, given the available logistics alternatives and assessment of opportunity, risk, and enterprise capability?
- What are the competitive pressures currently being experienced from foreign imports?
- What foreign markets are to be targeted, and what global strategies should be formulated to penetrate those markets?

- What are the firm's logistics strengths and weaknesses relative to proposed foreign markets?
- Who should make domestic and international trade decisions?
- How are domestic and international logistics functions to be structured and integrated to ensure optimization of objectives, costs, skills, and resources?
- What customer service, inventory, warehousing, and transportation operational strategies are to be established for each target market?
- How are global logistics strategies and operations to be measured to ensure the supply channel is achieving optimal performance?

Without a thorough evaluation of these and other strategic questions, firms searching for definition of their involvement in foreign markets cannot possibly hope to succeed.

GLOBAL STRATEGY DEVELOPMENT

When embarking on an international trade initiative companies normally will pursue one of three possible strategies [7]. The first, and most common, strategy is concerned with the simple export and import of products and services as part of a general effort to penetrate the global market. Normally, companies pursuing this strategy will turn over the entire effort to a broker, freight forwarder, or LSP rather than establish an internal international organization to perform these activities. In this model the global initiative is more concentrated on transaction management than building a comprehensive strategy. In the second strategy, companies are pursuing a limited form of international business. While they may be working through distributors or subsidiaries, the firm will actually be conducting some form of regional production and sourcing as a separate function within the company. In the final, and most advanced strategy, companies are truly conducting international trade and possess international brands. They possess global, centralized planning functions that are responsible for conducting international sourcing and distribution functions. Companies pursuing such a strategy think globally and are really integrated networks where channel distribution and manufacturing nodes pursue local objectives built around standardized processes.

Regardless of the approach taken, an effective strategy must identify the nature and scope of the international trade initiative, define the appropriate marketing and logistics strategies, design operational objectives and structures, and, finally, develop the appropriate performance metrics to measure success and uncover regions for improvement. According to Keegan [8], an effective international trade strategy is composed of the following five elements: (1) environmental analysis, (2) global strategic planning, (3) organizational infrastructure, (4) implementation, and (5) performance measurement [Figure 13.1]. The goal of the exercise is to develop "world-class" international trade operations that provide global companies with the mechanics to optimize and align the distribution system with each international target market.

FIGURE 13.1. Global Strategy Development

Environmental Analysis. The first step in global strategy development is defining the strategic dimensions of the enterprise. There are essentially three areas to consider. The first is concerned with detailing the *external business environment*. This environmental analysis should be divided into *macro* economic, sociocultural, political, and technical factors, and then into *micro* factors such as markets, costs, competitors, and governments. An effective analysis should cover the whole world, ensuring that no relevant market, competitor, or trend is overlooked. The second strategic dimension involves assessing the *strengths and weaknesses of supporting infrastructure*. A firm understanding of this strategic area is essential in dealing with identified opportunities, threats, and global trends. In addition, the firm should identify its own particular area of distinctive competence. This means that planners should know the products to be offered and the markets served, technological, sales, distribution and resource capabilities, and growth and profitability targets.

The final strategic dimension is coming to terms with and matching stakeholder values with perceived enterprise objectives. Stockholders, managers, employees, customers, and others often have conflicting values and interests regarding enterprise size and growth, profitability and return on investment (ROI), sense of social responsibility, and ethics. Before a global strategy can be constructed, planners formulating the direction of the company must be sure that objectives are in alignment with the realities of the external environment, the capabilities of the organization, and the desires and assumptions of the stakeholders.

Global Strategic Planning. Once the strategic environmental dimensions have been identified, planners can proceed to detail the nature and scope of the overall global channel strategy and define in detail the unique characteristics of each national market. Normally, a company begins to explore the possibility of entering foreign markets either because it feels it must in order to sustain competitive' advantage or it is solicited by an importer or a foreign government. Before detailed market analysis can begin, however, it is important that the firm defines its international marketing objectives and policies. This process normally consists of three parts. To begin with, planners must determine the desired proportion of foreign sales to total sales. This ratio depends on product, competition, logistics channel requirements, and marketplace aspirations. Second, planners must choose between marketing and distributing to a few countries or to many countries. Generally, it makes sense to begin first by selecting a few countries in which a strong commitment and significant product penetration can occur. Finally, the firm must decide on the types of countries with which they would like to do business with. Issues relating to political stability, product fit, income, transportation substructure, geography, and others are possible elements to consider.

Once the global strategy has been determined, marketing and logistics planners must turn their attention to pinpointing which national markets are to be selected. Kotler [9] feels that candidate countries should be rated on three major criteria: market attractiveness, competitive advantage, and risk. *Market attractiveness* consists of such factors as language, laws, geographical proximity, stability, cultural similarity, and other micro factors. *Competitive advantage* focuses on overall marketplace strategies, presence of competitors, product life cycles, and such. *Risk* is divided into two types: asset protection/investment recovery risk, which is concerned with the possibility of foreign government nationalization or limits to the transfer of invested resources, and operational profitability/cash flow risk, which arises from local economic depression, currency devaluation, strikes and other factors. Once these criteria have been reviewed, choices must be made based on estimated return on investment. This step includes estimating market potential and possible risk, forecasting sales potential, estimating costs and profits, and, finally, determining the rate of return on investment.

Organizational Infrastructure. In the past, global logistics has often suffered from poor organization, a lack of training, and the absence of interorganzational power and influence. Physical distribution is normally considered as playing a supporting role and not regarded as a key element in the enterprise's global marketing strategy. What is more, often the responsibilities of both domestic and global logistics are divided between competing business departments. Such infrastructures have resulted in limited opportunities for integrating the two functions and pursuing simultaneously improvements in cost, efficiency, and productivity. Without effective global logistics organizations, the enterprise cannot hope to optimize on global opportunities and deter possible competitive threats.

The architecture of an effective global logistics organization can vary. For firms whose global effort is focused on a single country or homogeneous region, a centralized organization can be particularly effective. When, however, the scope of the logistics effort traverses many countries and diverse regions, the best form of organization is one in which the planning and control functions are centralized and integrated with other enterprise departments but the actual operations functions are decentralized. Simply, as the variety of differences in culture, governmental regulations, and knowledge of trends in local economic conditions expands, centralized global organizations become increasingly ineffective. In such environments, personal familiarity with the countries composing the international marketplace becomes invaluable.

Implementation. Once the global strategy has been completely structured, it must be implemented. This step entails obtaining and committing current resources to executing regional market, market cluster, and product life cycle plans. The key element in implementation is the presence of effective organizational infrastructures for ongoing logistics resource management.

Performance Measurement. Once the global strategy has been put in place, strategists must be careful to have a comprehensive program of performance measurements in place. In this step, actual results are constantly compared with expected output. To the extent that the results of the strategy are consistent with original goals and assumptions, it can remain unaltered. If, however, wide performance variances occur, planners must adjust the strategy by isolating specific areas for improvement. In addition, performance measurement must provide information that enables continuous strategic alignment with the external environment and organizational and value assessment assumptions established at the beginning of the strategy formulation process.

STRATEGY DEVELOPMENT SUMMARY

As the requirements for globalization increase in the twenty-first century, strategists must change fundamental methods of planning and operating the logistics functions of their companies. Firms with minimal involvement in foreign trade can defer logistics complexities to intermediaries who will handle the problems associated with shipping, insurance, pricing, trade restrictions and licensing, warehouse storage, and transport mode selection. For multinational corporations, however, a unified global strategy is necessary to ensure the smooth flow of product through the international pipeline. In responding to global strategies, Gopal and Cypress [10] feel that companies must find solutions to the following issues:

1. Ability to balance company resources (capital and inventories) and organizational structure with the needs of the global marketplace.
2. Monitoring and managing the constant changes occurring in global trade. Trends include shifting attitudes toward tariffs, administrative procedures, restrictions on intercountry transportation modes, and warehouse storage, as well as managing the pace of rapidly changing marketing and logistics strategies, new product introduction, and increased information linkages. By responding effectively to change, multinational firms can increase the speed and reliability of global delivery, reduce overall transportation costs, and reduce the size (quantity) of shipments.
3. Extending and tailoring the supply chain to meet the distribution structure of each foreign nation or geographical region. Distribution channels in Europe, for example, are very mature and require local distribution centers, local management of transportation owing to the number of transit countries, knowledge of local customs, and all regulations dealing with the European Union. Trade with Japan requires short delivery cycles and local inventory to meet planned and random demand patterns. Distribution in the Pacific Rim, on the other hand, requires using local freight forwarders and lead time planning to counter delays due to the lack of a fully developed logistics infrastructure and protected local industries.
4. Ability to execute distribution for simultaneous multicountry, multiproduct introductions.
5. Ability to work with value-added taxing found in many foreign countries and transfer price regulations both domestic and foreign.
6. Implementation of information systems that provide for worldwide inventory planning and stock availability and customer order status.
7. Benchmarking global channel performance with that of international competitors.

Effectively managing these and other global trade issues is more operational than strategic. The companies that will succeed in the highly competitive international marketplace of the twenty-first century will be those that can leverage information and decision support technology tools to solve global differences in market preferences, logistics structures, perceptions of quality and service, and performance measurement.

CHANNEL STRATEGIES

In defining the strategic approach to the global marketplace, firms have four possible alternatives available. A company may choose to follow one or combine several together to match particular objectives or marketplace conditions. The four strategies are exporting, licensing, joint venture, and direct foreign investment (ownership). Of the four, exporting is the easiest to execute. The remaining three strategies, licensing, joint venture, and ownership, are in order increasingly more complex because they involve the establishment of manufacturing or warehousing facilities *within* foreign countries and the integration of company-owned domestic and foreign distribution channels (Figure 13.2).

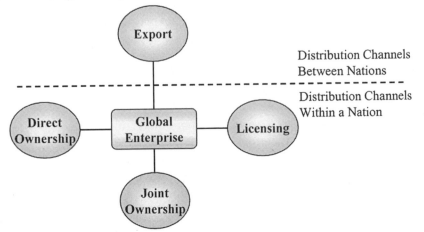

FIGURE 13.2 Alternative international strategies.

EXPORTING

The most common form of global trade is the export of products into foreign markets from domestic facilities. Exporting requires the least involvement because the actual marketing and logistics activities are carried out by some form of international trading house or intermediary. Exporting can be pursued as either a *passive* or an *active* strategy. In a passive strategy, companies might engage in exporting products to foreign markets from time to time, or in response to an unsolicited order from a foreign customer. Active exporting, on the other hand, occurs as part of a strategic decision to expand sales into foreign markets. Regardless of the policy, exporting as a method of approaching foreign markets involves the least change in product lines, distribution channels, internal organization, investment, and enterprise mission.

Exporting can take two forms, depending on how involved the firm wants to become in the export process. Exporting can be executed *indirectly* through a variety of specialized brokers or *directly* through foreign merchants or wholesalers.

Indirect Exporting. Indirect exporting involves the least amount of effort and is the method normally recommended to firms that are taking their first steps toward developing international trade. This type of exporting is *indirect* because the company deals with some form of intermediary that is located in the same domestic market. The major advantage of indirect exporting is that the business can engage in foreign trade without having to deal with the complexities of global logistics, tariffs and taxes, international marketing contacts, and accompanying paperwork and legal issues. In addition, it requires little risk or investment, the bulk of the work for transaction management falling upon the intermediary. Finally, indirect exporting renders the firm immune to possible foreign political and economic upheavals, as well as permits easy exit from a foreign market that fails over time to realize sales or profit targets. Negatives surround the company's loss of control over the ultimate cost and delivery of its products. The various types of indirect export intermediaries are described below.

- *International Trading Company.* This type of intermediary performs many functions. Among them are the purchasing and selling of goods, arrangement for the transportation and warehousing of goods from the export company to the foreign customer, financing currency conversion and absorbing rate fluctuations, assisting with consulting advice, and other logistics issues.

- *Export Merchants.* Export merchants act as a form of international wholesaler. Similar to domestic wholesalers, they purchase goods from domestic manufacturers and distributors and then pack and ship them to foreign markets. Although some export merchants may have facilities located in foreign countries close to the target market, they mostly deal with foreign intermediaries in the country of destination.

- *Resident Buyers.* Foreign firms and governments will often locate buyers directly in the export country. Their responsibility is to locate, purchase, and ship goods to their home countries. Sears, for example, maintains buyers in foreign countries who buy direct from manufacturers for resale in the United States.

- *Export Commission House.* This type of intermediary performs the same functions as a *resident buyer* except that the buyer is not an employee but rather of an agent empowered to negotiate, buy, and ship from firms in the exporting country. In return, the commission house is normally paid a commission by the foreign buyer.
- *Allied Manufacturer.* Exporting through a business partner is an easy, cost-effective way of shipping overseas. In the arrangement, a company with well-established foreign trade activities negotiates to "piggyback" the products of other domestic firms with shipments of their own products to foreign countries. The advantage is mutual. For the shipping company, carrying other products can assist in presenting foreign markets with extended product lines or achieving a higher utilization of transportation and warehousing capacities. For the exporting firm, the arrangement provides them a good deal of the benefits of a mature foreign trade system without the investment.
- *Export Management Company.* An export management company is a product line or foreign market specialist who works that export for one or a group of noncompeting manufacturers. Although most act as selling agents directly for their manufacturers, some of the larger firms do purchase products for resale.

Direct Exporting. Despite the advantages offered by indirect marketing, some firms choose to export directly to intermediaries located in foreign nations. The choice of this strategy requires the establishment of an export department whose responsibility it is to establish the necessary distribution channels appropriate to each trading nation; find, maintain, and motivate intermediaries in targeted foreign countries; plan and execute all international shipping requirements; and, execute all export documentation. The major advantage of direct exporting is increased control over products sent to foreign markets. Disadvantages are found in the extra costs and overheads that arise from shipping directly to a foreign nation. The various types of direct export intermediary are described below.

- *Domestic-Based Export Department or Division.* Many companies have an export department or division in their organizations manned by an export manager and staff. This group executes actual selling and, in some instances, will perform other tasks associated with shipping, establishing logistics channels, and export documentation.
- *Foreign Sales Branch/Subsidiary.* Companies with a significant presence in certain foreign countries might elect to locate a sales branch or

subsidiary in each country. Overseas branches permit the exporter a much greater control over marketing decisions and product positioning and can provide on-site skills and services necessary for effective sales or marketing activities. In addition, branches may handle warehousing issues and promotions.

- *Traveling Export Sales Representatives.* Export firms may send sales representatives directly to foreign nations to solicit and execute export arrangements and sales.
- *Foreign Wholesale Agents and Merchants.* There are several types of intermediaries in this class. A *foreign sales agent* is an independent contract sales representative that promotes and sells for an export company. The agent is generally compensated through commissions. The actual sale is shipped and paid for by the exporter and the foreign buyer. On the other hand, *foreign merchant distributors* buy the goods directly from the exporter and establish their own pricing, promotions, and other marketing strategies except where prohibited by contract.
- *Direct Sales.* This is the least used form of direct export. In this technique, exporters seek to sell products directly to foreign retailers or even end customers. Normally, this type of exporting is used only for high-ticket and specialty items sold to foreign governments, businesses, or institutions.

LICENSING

Similar to exporting, licensing manufacturing processes and distribution of products is a relatively simple, cost-effective method of entering global markets. Licensing can be defined as a contractual arrangement by which a firm (the licensor) in one country agrees to permit a company in another country (the licensee) the right to use a manufacturing process, trademark, patent, technical assistance, trade secret, merchandising knowledge, or other skills. In exchange for these rights, the licensor will receive a fee or royalty. The objectives of a licensing agreement are straightforward: The licensor is able to gain access to a foreign market with a minimum of risk and capital expense; in turn, the licensee receives the right to distribute brand name products or access to proprietary processes either to found a business or to add to existing product lines. The best known examples of licensing are Coca-Cola and McDonald's. Both firms penetrate foreign markets by licensing (franchising) product name, processes, and products to bottlers and food service companies across the globe.

There are several advantages licensing has over exporting. To begin with, licensing provides the licensor with a greater degree of control over how the product is marketed and distributed. Also, licensing normally does not require a great deal of capital investment. Like exporting strategies, licensing provides licensors with a less risky method of gaining access to foreign markets than direct ownership, while providing sufficient flexibility to cancel unprofitable arrangements. On the negative side, the licensor has less control over the licensee than if the firm had established a directly owned business. If the licensee does not live up to the terms of the contract, all the licensor can do is threaten to end the agreement. Finally, if the licensor decides to cancel the contract, they might find that they have not only lost control but have created a competitor with a strong market position in a foreign country where the licensor might subsequently find it difficult to penetrate on their own.

There are several forms of licensing in foreign markets. One is to execute a *management contract* in which a licensor sells management services for a fee to a foreign company to assist in managing a factory, distribution center, hospital, or other organizations. Management contracts are low-risk methods of gaining entrance to a foreign market, especially if the contracting firm provides an option to purchase a portion of the business. Another method is *contract manufacturing*. In this method a firm licenses and agrees to assist a foreign company produce or distribute its products. Although licensing has the drawback of potential loss of control over processes, it does provide the firm with the opportunity of partnership or acquisition if the market matures.

JOINT VENTURES

Unlike the first two strategies, the decision to execute a joint venture with a foreign company directly involves a company in the management of a foreign enterprise. Normally, a joint venture occurs when a firm decides to join with a foreign company for the purpose of exercising joint ownership and control over a business. Joint ventures may occur when a firm invests in the manufacturing and distribution operations of an existing foreign company, or the two parties may join together to found an entirely new company.

Companies decide to enter into joint ventures for several reasons. The most obvious is to significantly increase local control over the product, distribution, and marketing strategies of the foreign company due to its financial partnership. A firm may also enter into a joint venture to utilize the specialized skills or gain access to the physical distribution system possessed by a foreign partner. Companies are sometimes prohibited by foreign governments from entering alone into a local marketplace. Such restrictions often occur in less developed countries where government is actively promoting the growth of home industries. A partnership with a local firm may provide an avenue around this difficulty. Finally, a firm may lack the capital, managerial, and personnel capabilities to enter a foreign market on its own without the assistance of an established foreign company.

There are a number of drawbacks associated with joint ventures. The most obvious is the significant degree of risk involved. Outside firms normally invest capital in foreign ventures that they wish to convert to profits that can be returned to the home country. Disagreements with the partner or even government restrictions may inhibit return on investment expectations. In addition, disagreements might also arise over product, marketing, and distribution channel strategies. Settling these differences might be a difficult affair requiring some compromise on the part of both parties. Finally, joint ventures might even impede a multinational company from executing specific marketing and distribution strategies on a worldwide basis.

DIRECT OWNERSHIP

The direct ownership of manufacturing and distribution companies in a foreign country represents the highest level of control and involvement an enterprise can have in the pursuit of foreign trade. Instead of working through an intermediary or a venture partner, the firm assumes all the responsibilities for facilities, personnel, marketing, and product distribution. Ownership can occur through two methods. In the first, a company may seek to build a new facility. This method is the more difficult of the two. The company must establish marketing contacts and distribution channels, select the site, hire personnel, acquire equipment, and provide for capital funding among other things. A far more cost-effective method is to acquire an established foreign firm. All the company has to do is to buy into the preexisting structure, making alterations as required to meet changes in product and marketplace emphasis.

There are some significant advantages to direct ownership. As the company now controls the foreign venture, it can determine the marketing, product positioning, and distribution strategies to be pursued in the local market without interference. This point is critical for multinational enterprises seeking to develop long-term, unified strategies throughout the globe. Second, direct ownership provides the ability to compete more effectively on price. Because the cost, in some cases, of transportation of the product from the home country is eliminated along with import taxes and customs duties, the foreign subsidiary can become more price competitive. Third, the new venture might be able to achieve cost economies in the form of cheaper labor or raw materials, foreign government incentives, or process improvements. Fourth, the company's image may improve in the foreign country due to its commitment to the local economy. Finally, as the company's knowledge of the foreign country grows, it might be able to improve on its marketing techniques and product offerings to match the ongoing needs of the local community.

Although the benefits of direct ownership are substantial, so are the drawbacks. The most obvious negative is the enormous risk a company takes in investing in a wholly-owned foreign venture. Some of the concerns are currency devaluation, political unrest, declining markets, and nationalization. In addition, the investor company can find its flexibility to respond to home or other foreign markets circumstances curtailed because of the financial commitment involved. In addition, if the company decides to discontinue the operation, it may involve not only forfeiting the cost of the plant, equipment, and personnel but also the company's reputation in that region. Finally, reorienting the product and the sales environment in response to overall changes in the company's internal objectives might be more difficult to implement due to governmental and regional regulations.

MANAGING GLOBAL DISTRIBUTION NETWORKS

The establishment and maintenance of a global distribution network is a complex affair involving most of the functions of domestic distribution, plus additional requirements associated with global market channels, terms of sale, pricing, transportation, and warehousing. What is more, whereas the functions of distribution are universal, the structure and performance criteria of channels of distribution vary throughout the world. It used to be assumed that the level of distribution channel structure development found in one country paralleled the structures of other countries that had attained the same degree of economic and technological development. As Bowersox and Cooper [11] have pointed out, however, actual global distribution structures are "so closely intertwined with a country's social, cultural, economic, technological, and political conditions and development that it is impossible to generalize about one specific form or structure throughout the world." As a result, firms aspiring to participate in global trade must constantly seek to understand and adjust to the marketing and logistics channel structures of their trading partners if effective global strategies are to be realized.

In general, structuring a global distribution channel requires making many of the same decisions concerning cost, product positioning, sales and profitability, channel control, and flexibility that are made when defining the objectives for domestic channels. There are, however, a number of issues that are specific only to global channels. These refer to sales, marketing, pricing, investment and payment, and documentation. Managing these issues will be the subject of the sections below.

MANAGING THE GLOBAL DISTRIBUTION CHANNEL

Establishing and maintaining a global distribution channel requires working with marketing functions to design an effective distribution network, monitor costs and benefits, and tirelessly search for avenues of constant improvement in customer services. The following points explore these topics.

Service/Cost Elements. In the creation of any marketing channel, the enterprise must chart out the desired product and service targets and the cost of meeting those objectives. This is particularly true when it comes to structuring a global distribution channel. Because of the increased number of variables and constraints, however, clearly understanding service and cost ratios can be a difficult exercise. The flow of communications can be easily interrupted by distance and differences in language, culture, and legal factors. Documentation is more extensive, often resulting in long delays. Financial flows are full of roadblocks in the form of cash and payment transaction conversions, pricing, credit management, insurance, and liability. Furthermore, the presence of legal and regulatory restrictions, duties and taxes, export and import restrictions, and local laws and customs make measurement difficult. Finally, the number of channel levels in the pipeline, the use of intermodal freight carriers over long distances, and packaging and labeling can make it difficult to create precise metrics to weigh the cost versus the level of service.

In effectively mapping service versus cost elements, Bender [12] feels that four service criteria (response time, order completeness, shipping accuracy, and shipment condition) are critical in making any evaluation. *Response time* refers to the time elapsed from receipt of a customer order until goods are received by the customer. When it comes to global distribution, the market is less sensitive to long lead times. Owing to the size and complexity of the channel, most foreign customers normally will increase lead times and inventories to compensate for slower service. Still, a global distributor must constantly search for methods of increasing delivery service while maintaining or lowering costs. Developing alternate distribution systems, streamlining paperwork flows and operations, the use of computerized supply chain management applications, and others are possible avenues for improvement.

Due to the length of the channel and the time required for order delivery, the last three service elements are of much greater importance. Probably the most critical of these elements is *order completeness*. Order completeness can be defined as the percentage of how close the actual shipment satisfies the product and quantity requirements of the original order. As the percentage of order completeness grows, logistics costs decline correspondingly. Simply, the less a company has to handle backorders and expediting, the less the cost for order completion processing and shipping. *Shipping accuracy* is the ratio between the number of deliveries that have the correct products, quantities, and so forth, and the total number of deliveries for a specific time period. The level of accuracy depends normally on the level of control, and the higher the level of control the higher the expense. The cost of poor accuracy in global distribution is excessive, including paying for and processing returns, reshipping orders, canceling orders, and loss of customer goodwill. The final service/cost element is *shipment condition.* This measurement can be defined as the ratio between the number of orders delivered in good condition and the total number of orders shipped. Unlike domestic shipments, international orders are often handled many times as they move through the pipeline. At each occasion, the order is exposed to the possibility of damage. Considering the cost of backorders, packaging, and time spent in order replacement, undamaged orders are a significant service/cost element. Similar to response time improvement, global distributors must constantly search for ways to improve these service elements while reducing costs.

The Distribution Channel. Whether domestic or global distribution, the goal is identical: how to transport product from supplier to customer as quickly and cost-effectively as possible. Beyond this goal, however, domestic and global distribution differ significantly as to channel structure and techniques. Perhaps the most obvious distinction is the explosion of the number of levels in a typical global channel. On a high level, a global channel can be broken up into four distinct sections: the domestic channel, channels between nations, channels within nations, and the buyer (Figure 13.3). The domestic

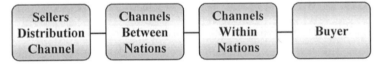

FIGURE 13.3 Overview of international channels.

portion of the channel is fairly homogeneous. Once, however, the shipment begins its transit through foreign ports to the customer, it can pass through several iterations of unloading and reloading, transport consolidation, and warehousing occurring in different foreign countries. These distribution nodes can represent an intermediary, government customs and tariffs check point, or stocking location. In addition, because of the relative size of the distribution channel, there are a significant number of options available to suppliers and customers. For example, orders can be filled from several locations in the channel. Because of the size and flexibility of the global network, it is of critical importance that planners structure a channel that optimizes cost and service objectives and is in alignment with marketing, product, and financial strategies.

mizes cost and service objectives and is in alignment with marketing, product, and financial strategies.

In a classic article, Picard [13] segmented global channels into four systems. These systems cut across the four channel strategies described above. In the first system, as illustrated in Figure 13.4, products are shipped directly

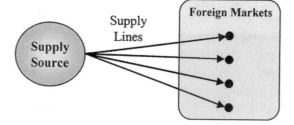

FIGURE 13.4 Direct system of global trade.

from the home country to intermediaries or customers in a single foreign market. The advantages of this system are that there is no need for foreign warehousing or consolidation and there is less product in the distribution channel. A serious drawback of this system is the accompanying long lead times for customer delivery. In addition, the length of the supply line renders the shipment subject to possible disruption and delay. Finally, the packaging and documentation costs associated with this system are normally higher than for the other three systems. The second channel system (Figure 13.5) attempts to

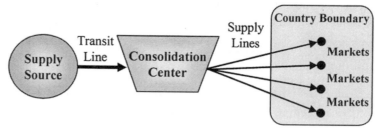

FIGURE 13.5 Consolidation strategy.

solve some of the problems of the direct system by interposing a consolidation center in between the domestic warehouse and the customer. The purpose of the consolidation center is to decrease the overall cost of transport. Product can be shipped from the home country in bulk and then converted (bulk break) into individual customer orders and stocking units and distributed within the foreign market.

The last two global channel systems are distinguished from the first two by the fact that they both require the creation of a stocking warehouse in the foreign market. In the third system (Figure 13.6), inventory is shipped from the home country to a stocking warehouse located within the foreign market. The benefits of this arrangement are obvious. Delivery to the foreign warehouse can be done in bulk and with slower transportation modes, thereby decreasing shipping costs; order lead times are shorter that in the first two systems; customers have greater flexibility in product and quantity selection; and, because the shipment is really an intracompany transfer, the costs associated with tariffs and documentation are reduced. Negatives to the system are the cost associated with maintaining a foreign facility and higher levels of pipeline inventory.

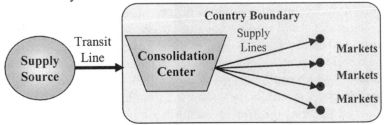

FIGURE 13.6 Consolidation strategy within a country.

The final global channel system (Figure 13.7) expands on the concept of foreign warehousing by enabling product sales to multiple foreign markets from a single strategically positioned warehouse. The most significant advantage of this system is reduction in facilities and inventory stocking costs while preserving shorter lead times and customer flexibility. Benefits, however, might be compromised by transport and administrative costs as shipments are sent to other foreign countries. Multicountry warehouses should ideally be located in a free-trade zone, thereby eliminating costs arising from local tariffs and taxes.

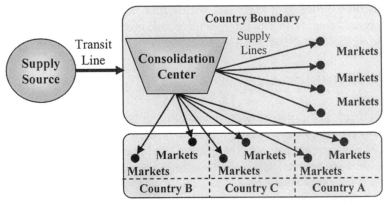

FIGURE 13.7 Consolidation strategy for multiple countries.

In deciding which channel system or combination of systems to implement, channel planners must carefully review a number of key factors relating to the nature of the product, market, export requirements, and foreign environment. *Product*-related issues focus on such attributes as value density, product line variability, perishability, obsolescence, position in the product life cycle, and expected turnover rate. *Market*-related issues refer to the number and size of the foreign customer base, level of expected service, sales volume, quality of foreign intermediary or company-owned distribution channels, fitness of product, and prospects for growth. *Export*-related factors center around export marketing strategy, sophistication of intermediaries, and firm size. *Foreign environment* issues focus on sophistication of global channel infrastructure, political and economic stability, degree of government regulation and customs constraints, and the presence of strong, cost-effective foreign partners and transit contractors. By using these key factors, planners have the ability to develop several different global channel systems. For instance, a direct channel system could be used to supply bulk shipments to large foreign customers, whereas a multicountry approach could be employed simultaneously to penetrate several different countries supplied from a central foreign warehouse [14].

Distribution Operations Costs. Effective management of a global distribution network also requires close supervision of channel operations costs. Some of these costs are the same whether they are associated with domestic or foreign distribution channels. Among these are costs for administrative facilities and warehouses, transportation rates and fleet maintenance, purchasing, value-added processing, inventory, and information processing. In addition, foreign distribution channels can have other significant costs. The expense of developing new marketing channels, maintaining an internal international department, carrying in-transit inventory, insurance, product packaging, customs duties, and taxes fall within this category. As a result, areas for cost controls and potential improvement will grow significantly as the size and scope of the global channel expands.

GLOBAL MARKETING CONSIDERATIONS

Although there are great similarities among domestic and global channel costs, network design, and management systems, there are also a number of differences regarding terms of sale, pricing, and marketing that are unique to international transactions. These features are described below.

Marketing Issues. An effective global distribution system requires several decisions regarding the marketing approach to be taken by the firm in regard to product positioning, promotions, and organization. The marketing approach pursued can take one of two approaches. In one option strategists might choose to follow a *standardized approach* by offering the same products, prices, advertising, promotions, distribution channels, and value-added services to all foreign market segments. This option is the less costly, as little or no modification is made to the marketing offering. On the other hand, strategists might pursue a *customized approach* in which the marketing offering is tailored to meet the needs of each target market. Many companies develop a strategy somewhere in between these two extremes, searching for ways to optimize sales and profits while reducing costs.

Among the marketing decisions, probably the most important relates to *product*. When offering a product to a global buyer, the seller must determine how closely existing product characteristics fit local marketplace requirements. Keegan [15] has identified five possible options. In the first, *straight extension*, the product is offered to the marketplace without modification to local needs. This is the least expensive of the options and can be successfully used for most durable goods such as appliances, cameras, consumer electronics, tools, and machinery. Still, whatever the level of success, marketers must be constantly searching for new ways to market the product in foreign countries. The second product option is *product extension-communications adaptation*. In this strategy, the product is offered to the marketplace essentially unchanged; the only adjustment required is in marketing communications. Bicycles and motor scooters are examples of products that fit this approach. The third product management approach is *product adaptation*. This strategy requires changing the existing product in some way to meet the standards or tastes of local customers. This option is particularly important for food distributors who must change seasonings, textures, and colors to meet local preferences. Durable goods, such as automobiles, sometimes must be modified to fit the safety requirements of foreign countries. The fourth strategy involves both *product* and *communications adaptation*. The final option, *product invention*, occurs when a firm decides to reintroduce an obsolete product into a less developed foreign market or create a new product just for the target market. This option is a costly strategy, the benefits of which must be closely analyzed.

Advertising and promoting products in foreign lands is a critical activity that requires an intimate knowledge of the cultures, languages, and histories of each target market. Even small things such as name, color, and nuance can have an enormous impact on foreign market acceptance. One alternative is to promote products using the same messages as those used in the domestic market. The familiar sight of the Coca-Cola logo and MacDonald's "Golden Arches" are good examples. However, sometimes product names, advertising media, and labeling need to be changed because of local customs and language. For example, the color purple is associated with death in most of Latin America, and white in Japan with mourning. Finally, the utility of advertising media throughout the world varies. Television is a critical medium in the U.S. but limited by country in Europe and almost nonexistent in poor countries. The same variance in global audience can occur for ads placed on the radio, in newspapers or magazines, or available through the Internet.

The final global marketing decision that must be made refers to the type of marketing channel organization used by the firm. Often large multinational companies may pursue several types based on their global channel strategies. The least complicated type of organization is the domestically based *export department.* Such a department can consist of an export clerk, a sales manager, and a few assistants, or a complex business unit with expanded roles and service offerings. Exporting departments can be *indirect,* contracting with domestic or foreign wholesalers or distributors, or *direct,* shipping product directly to foreign buyers. If a company is involved in licensing, joint ventures, or direct ownership, normally these affairs are conducted by an *international division.* This function could be organized around geographical or regional managers and sales representatives, product groups, and global subsidiaries and branch sales offices. Finally, some organizations have become so big that they consider themselves more as *global marketers* rather than national marketers. Companies like IBM, Black and Decker, Xerox, Warner Lambert, and others are involved in the planning and execution of global distribution channels, manufacturing, marketing strategies, and financial systems.

Terms of Sale. Beyond issues associated with advertising, promotions, and channel organization, global marketing must consider issues associated with the following range of fees, duties, and terms of sales:

- *Harmonized system* (HS) *codes.* These codes, which vary by country and number in the hundreds of thousands, detail the fees and restrictions associated with the transport of goods across national borders. These codes must be defined and harmonized for all goods crossing a border.

- *Incoterms.* When selling goods across international boundaries it is critical to determine when and where the physical transfer, payment, and legal transfer of the goods, and responsibility for such things as insurance, payment for transportation, and controlling (preserving) the goods occurs between seller and international buyer. The below terms define the roles and responsibilities associated with any given cross-border transaction.
    1. At the seller's dock (or "ex works"). The sale is executed at the price quoted at the domestic warehouse or factory.
    2. Free carrier (at a named point). In this method, the sale is completed with the delivery of the goods to a carrier at a specific ware-

house or consolidation point. This method is common used when intermodal carriers are employed.

3. Free on rail. Sale occurs usually when the goods are loaded aboard rail cars near the shipper's dock.
4. FOB (free on board) airport. Transfer occurs with delivery to the airport of export.
5. FOB a vessel. The shipper is responsible for obtaining export clearance and for loading the ship.
6. FAS (free alongside ship) at port of export. The buyer is responsible for clearing the goods for export and loading them aboard a vessel.
7. FRC (free carrier). This term applies to overland movements between adjoining states. The shipper has responsibility for transport until the goods are transferred to the buyer at the international boundary.
8. C & F (cost and freight). The shipper pays costs and freight to a specified destination, making the buyer responsible once goods have been loaded.
9. CIF (cost, insurance, freight). This method is similar to C & F, except that the seller is also responsible for insurance.
10. Freight and carriage paid to a specific point. Responsibility in this method is placed on the buyer at the point where the goods are tendered to the first carrier.
11. Freight or carriage and insurance paid to a specific point. This is the same as the previous method, except that the shipper also insures the goods during shipment.
12. Ex ship. The shipper transfers the goods to the buyer aboard the ship at the port of import.
13. Ex quay. The shipper transfers the goods to the buyer alongside the ship at the port of import.
14. Delivered at frontier. The shipper transports the goods up to the location of the buyer's national customs.
15. Delivered, with duty paid. The shipper delivers the goods to the buyer's facility.

Collectively, these various terms are referred to as *incoterms*. In addition, sellers and buyers might agree on variations in these terms to accommodate the many special services and charges associated with the movement of goods.

- *Preferential fees, duties, and taxes.* Import tariffs are normally comprised of *general* and *preferential duty rates*, in additional to other fees and charges. Preferentially duties are influenced by such elements as *most favored nation's* (MFN) status and duty rates based on specific certain countries to offset unfair pricing of the imported product. Finally, marketing must be aware of taxes, such as *valued-added tax* (VAT), *general services tax* (GST), and *merchandise processing fee* (MPF) and a host of fees collected for *other government agencies* (OGA), including excise taxes, harbor fees, trade promotion fees, control taxes, and others, that can impact a global trade initiative.

Pricing. Closely aligned with terms of sale is global pricing. Similar to the process of determining domestic prices, global prices must be set in accordance with price-setting behavior of competitors, customer's ability to buy in various national markets, strategic cost and profit goals, place of product in the product life cycle, and local legal and pricing regulatory environments. Firms have three options in fashioning global pricing policies. A company may, first of all, establish a uniform price for all markets. When pursuing this policy, all nations, whether rich or poor, would pay the same price. A second method would be to set a market-based price in each trading country. In this strategy, the firm would charge what each country could bear. Finally, a firm may pursue a cost-based price in each country. Selling price would be cost plus a standard markup. In any case, prices for products sold in foreign countries are likely to be higher than in domestic markets. Much of the reason resides in the fact that shippers must add the cost of administrative overheads, transportation, tariffs, intermediary, wholesaler, and retailer margins to the factory price.

Once a pricing policy has been determined, actual pricing is governed by the terms of sale. The pricing set by the terms of sale differs in the way transportation, insurance, tariffs, and other costs are incorporated into the total price. Prices charged at the point of origin are normally the domestic selling price minus any export discounts. Beyond *Ex* (point of origin) pricing, pricing schemes normally fall somewhere in between two basic methods: *ex works*, where the foreign customer must bear the freight and insurance costs, and *delivered* pricing. When using delivered pricing, the shipper's price includes not only the price of the goods but the cost of all transport, customs, tariffs, insurance, documentation, and other expenses. Delivered price provides certain advantages. To begin with, the seller gains control over the distribution process, thereby ensuring customer service and pricing competitiveness. Second, the seller may be able to obtain bulk discounts, which ultimately allows price reduction. Finally, delivered pricing has the effect of increasing the nation's balance of trade and utilization of domestic logistics services.

There are several forms of *FOB* pricing depending on the type of carrier. The price is basically a composite of the transportation costs associated with packing, marking, loading, and transit freight costs. To this price is added

There are several forms of *FOB* pricing depending on the type of carrier. The price is basically a composite of the transportation costs associated with packing, marking, loading, and transit freight costs. To this price is added other charges for unloading/loading, material handling, and transit duties. *C & F* pricing includes the FOB cost plus the ocean freight charge, export license, and export duties and taxes. *CIF* pricing consists of *C & F* cost plus marine insurance. *Ex ship* and *ex quay* pricing consists of CIF costs plus expenses for consular invoices, certificate of origin, unloading, import licenses, tariffs and taxes, customs clearance, and additional marine and war risk insurance coverage.

INTERNATIONAL FINANCIAL ISSUES

An enterprise involved in global trade is faced with a number of financial issues that are not present in the domestic market. These issues are concerned with such factors as cash flow and currency conversion, inventory cost, the role of government, and methods of payment. Without a doubt, cash flow is of prime importance. Typically, global companies need a great deal of working capital to pay for plant and equipment, transportation services, inventories, and credit. Much of the reason lies in the great distances goods have to travel and the normal administrative delays encountered in foreign trade. Even when the transactions are relatively simple, customs clearance, the transfer of international payment documents, government restrictions, and shipment disputes can hold up payment. In addition, variations in the rate of currency exchange can severely impact capital planning. This is particularly true when it is considered that the value of the currency upon which the price was based could devalue between the time of shipment and the time of delivery. Besides cash flow issues, currency variation will have an effect on local costs associated with warehousing, labor, transportation, information processing, and other costs. Finally, there are also potential collection issues arising from inadequate credit reports on customers, problems of currency exchange controls, distance, different legal systems, and the cost and difficulty of collecting delinquent accounts.

The management of inventories is also a critical aspect of international finance. Because of the size and variability of global distribution channels, the flow of inventory is subject to delays and unexpected stoppages. In general, these variances in inventory availability require global firms to carry high levels of safety stock in each foreign market. A significant risk is the potential for high carrying costs due to monetary fluctuations due to inflation. In such environments, LIFO (last-in-first-out) methods of inventory valuation are preferred in order to keep inventory value as close as possible to the current market cost of replacement. Although modern computer systems can significantly assist firms to monitor the value of their inventories and the costs associated with duties and tariffs, international inventory managers must be ever vigilant in controlling global inventories.

The flow of cash can also be impacted by the wide variety of methods of payment common in international trade. In the U.S. order value is normally first reviewed against the customer's credit, with actual billing occurring on shipment. Although this method is commonly employed in international transactions as well, letters of credit and drafts are also used. A *letter of credit* is a document issued by foreign banks on behalf of a company in that country assuring the seller that the company possesses sufficient capital to effect payment for products received. There are three types of letters of credit:

- *Irrevocable.* This form of credit can be opened at either the domestic or foreign company's bank at the request of a foreign correspondent in favor of the exporter. This type of letter of credit cannot be canceled without the consent of the exporter.
- *Confirmed irrevocable.* In this situation, a foreign bank opens the letter of credit and it is guaranteed by a U.S. bank in favor of the shipper.
- *Revocable.* Normally, this letter of credit is really a pro forma document to be used as a basis when preparing irrevocable letters of credit.

Besides letters of credit, international payments can occur through the use of *drafts.* One type, a *sight draft*, permits the foreign buyer to defer payment until the actual draft is presented at the time goods are delivered. Actual ownership is not transferred until after the draft is paid. The second type, a *time draft*, permits the foreign buyer to assume ownership of a shipment upon receipt of the draft but may defer payment for 30, 60, or 90 days.

DOCUMENTATION

Another aspect differentiating international from domestic distribution is the number of additional pieces of documentation necessary to execute the transaction. Global documentation is determined by the product being shipped, its origin, and its destination. The major types of documentation surrounding product export are the following:

- Bill of Lading. This document is executed upon acceptance of a shipment by a carrier. As such, it is both a receipt for the shipment and a contract detailing the agreed upon transportation services. There are several types of global Bills of Lading. An *Order Bill of Lading* is a unique type that may be used as a negotiable instrument of ownership and can be sold, bought, or traded while the goods are in transit. A *Clean Bill of Lading* is issued when the shipment is received complete and in good condition. An *On Board Bill of Lading* certifies that the cargo has been placed aboard the named vessel and is signed by the master of the vessel. On letter-of-credit transactions, an On Board Bill of Lading is usually necessary for the shipper to obtain payment from the bank. An Inland Bill of Lading, also known as a *Waybill* for rail or a Pro Forma Bill of Lading in trucking, is used to document the transportation of the goods between the port and the point of origin or destination.

- Dock receipt. This document is used to transfer responsibility for the cargo between the domestic shipper and the carrier at the terminal where the transaction occurs. The dock receipt is prepared by the shipper and is signed by the carrier acknowledging receipt of the cargo.
- Delivery instructions. This document provides specific information to the inland carrier concerning the arrangement made by the shipper to deliver the merchandise to a particular pier or steamship line.
- Export declaration. Required by the U.S. Department of Commerce, this document controls exports, in compliance with export licensing, and acts as a source document for export statistics. It includes complete particulars on the shipment.
- Letter of credit. A financial document issued by a bank at the request of the consignee guaranteeing payment to the shipper for the cargo if certain terms and conditions are fulfilled. It normally contains a brief description of the goods, documents required, a shipping date, and an expiration date after which payment will no longer be made.
- Consular invoice. Required by some countries, this document is used to control and identify goods shipped into their country. It usually must be prepared on special forms and may require legalization by the purchasing nation's diplomatic consul.
- Commercial invoice. A bill for the shipment from the seller to the buyer. It is often used by governments to determine the true value of goods for the assessment of customs duties and consular documentation.
- Certificate of origin. This document is affirms for the buyer the country of origin where the shipped goods were produced. The certification is usually performed by a recognized chamber of commerce.
- Insurance certificate. This document assures the consignee that insurance is provided to cover loss or damage to the cargo while in transit.
- Transmittal letter. This document provides a list of the particulars of the shipment and a record of the documents being transmitted together with instructions for disposition of documents. It also includes any special instructions [16].

Over the last couple of decades, the paperwork associated with international trade has been significantly simplified. As Bender points out [17], this movement

> was prompted by the complexity and cost that was involved in preparing the necessary forms to support international logistics operations. By the early 1970s, the situation had reached a point where common international shipments might involve up to 28 different parties, originating more than 120 different documents to move the cargo. Documentation costs amounted to as much as 10% of the dollar value of the trade itself - enough to eliminate a substantial part of the profits.

Since that time, a number of developments have occurred targeted at reducing the volume of paperwork. One of those developments has been the creation of several national and international bodies, such as the U.S. National Committee on International Trade Documentation (NCITD), the Canadian Organization for the Simplification of Trade Procedures (COSTPRO), and the United Nations Economic Commission for Europe (ECE), to eliminate and simplify trade documentation. Another has been the development of Internet and EDI systems for international transportation. In the United States the Transportation Data Coordinating Committee (TDCC) and the ECE have developed extensive sets of electronic transmission standards to cover both domestic and international transportation. Finally, a number of specialized firms have grown that handle the requirements of international trade documentation. For example, international freight forwarders assume complete responsibility for documenting all of a customer's export shipments.

INTERNATIONAL TRANSPORTATION AND WAREHOUSING

The scope of an enterprise's global supply channel dictates the structure and defines the boundaries of its international trade strategy. The *execution* of the global channel process is the function of transportation and warehousing. As is the case with other elements of the supply chain, international transportation and warehousing have a number of distinguishing factors that require them to perform different functions than their domestic counterparts. The most obvious differences stem from the long distances goods are transported, heavy reliance on intermodal transport methods, and interaction with foreign governments. More subtle differences can be found in political issues revolving around "balance of payments," the right of nations to use their own carriers for all domestic trade (known as *cabotage)*, and arrangements made by nations to facilitate and make international transportation more affordable.

OPENING ISSUES

All nations engaging in global trade are concerned about their balance-of-payments position. When it is considered that in 2000 transport buyers paid $1.5 trillion for international transportation, controlling costs is critical. A favorable balance of payments occurs when more goods are exported than imported into a country. The objective is to ensure that more "hard" cash is entering the country than leaving it. Beyond fiscal concerns about product, pivotal to this strategy is the possession of viable transportation modes that span boarders. Nations possessing international transportation capabilities can significantly assist in reducing their out-going cash flow. To this end, governments will subsidize the growth of local carriers to ensure that as large a portion as possible of exports and imports are carried in domestic transport modes. Also, nations will sometimes have cargo preference laws requiring that certain types of goods can only be carried by domestic carriers. For example, all military supplies and cargoes arising from U.S. government appropriations, such as charitable foodstuffs being sent to foreign lands, must be carried in U.S. vessels.

Transportation services may even themselves be considered an export product that is offered to the global community. For nations wishing to engage in cross-trading, the possession of a diverse transportation fleet is a requirement. Cross-trading occurs when a country's maritime vessels or aircraft is engaged to transport products of other nations. Some nations have attempted to control cross-trading by a pooling agreement. Such agreements require that all or part of the products moving between the agreeing countries must be transported by their own international carriers.

INTERMODAL TRANSPORT OPTIONS

Companies wishing to either export or import products have a wide range of transportation mode options available. Trade flowing from the U.S. to Canada and Mexico might use just one mode, such as a motor carrier, to move goods. Most international shipments, however, must traverse large distances and overcome oceans and other natural obstacles. In such cases, the shipment will require the use of more than one of the following carrier modes.
1. Ocean and air transport as the international/intercontinental medium
2. Motor, rail, and canal networks for inland feeder services
3. Numerous systems of intermodal transfer

The selection of the most efficient and cost-effective intermodal combination is a complex affair requiring an expert knowledge of intercontinental transport mediums and the internal transport systems of foreign nations. Many exporters will use the services of a freight forwarder in structuring the proper mix of transportation modes for foreign shipments.

A critical part of intermodal selection is the ability of the transport type to handle *unitized* loads. Although the transfer of products in bulk, such as petroleum and grains, comprises an enormous portion of the world's international trade, specialized vessels and equipment are usually employed. Nonbulk products, on the other hand, are best handled through unitization. Whether packed in a container, rigid boxes, shrink wrapped pallets, or other packing forms, unitization is significantly more efficient than handling loose individual products. It facilitates loading, marking, and shipment identification as well as intermodal product transfer. Furthermore, it removes the need for enclosed storage space at ports, consolidation points, and freight terminals. Finally, it also reduces the chance of damage or theft while in transit.

The two most popular forms of unitization are standard containers and tractor trailers. Containers come in a variety of sizes and can be used for all types of transport from aircraft to ocean vessel. Containers have been designed to realize two goals: (1) maximization of the cubic capacity within the container and (2) maximization of the cubic capacity within the transport equipment. The great advantage of containers is that they can be used practically with any transportation mode. In addition, they can easily be loaded and unloaded and stored in freight terminals. Finally, containerization reduces the risk of damage and theft and facilitates documentation flows. Drawbacks to using containers include their relatively high handling cost, limited storage capacity because of their cubic dimensions, and reduction of maximum payload due to tare weight.

Tractor trailers are, in essence, a form of self-mobile or partially mobile container. When used in an intermodal fashion, trailers can be accompanied by a tractor or shipped alone. In the latter case, the trailer is usually loaded aboard a rail car or canal or ocean vessel and sent "piggyback" to the next terminal, where it can then be transferred to another form of transportation. Besides advantages associated with handling, trailers are relatively easy to pass through customs, thereby reducing lead times and speeding overall trailer utilization. Disadvantages to utilizing trailers are found in the cost for tractors and having to pay for drivers during transport along with the goods. Unaccompanied trailers normally take longer to move from terminal point to terminal point and require a high level of organizational control.

OCEAN TRANSPORT

Ocean transport varies from domestic water transportation in the variety and sizes of the vessels used and in the required services provided. In 1994 total revenues for ocean transport was approximately $960 billion. Domestic water carriage, except Great Lakes carriage, is normally performed by barge. Although barges do differ, they are wholly different than the types of oceangoing vessels used in international transportation. According to Sampson *et al.* [18], there are at least five different types of ocean vessel, which can be further divided into several subtypes based on size, intended use, and specialization. The five types are described as follows:

- *Break-bulk freighters.* These vessels primarily transport individually packaged or crated cargoes, each of which is loaded one piece at a time. Often these vessels can carry cargoes for dozens even hundreds of individual shippers at a time. Sometimes these vessels may specialize in carrying products that require refrigeration or other services.

- Container vessels. These vessels primarily transport products stored in containers. The containers are brought to the seaport by other modes of carriage, loaded aboard ship, and distributed at destination seaports by other modes of carriage. Container ships normally stow all types of containers. Containers moving between the Far East and Europe often make use of the *landbridge route* across the United States. In this process, containers are unloaded in western ports, then moved by railroad across the country to the east cost, and then reloaded aboard vessels for the voyage across the Atlantic. Landbridges have the advantage of dramatically reducing transit time by avoiding much slower and often circuitous water routes, and increasing the utilization of containerships. A variation of container vessels are *Lighter Aboard Ship* (LASH) and *Roll-on/Roll-Off* (RO/RO) vessels. LASH vessels handle floating containers and can be used most advantageously in areas where the central port is connected to inland areas by shallow waterways. RO/RO vessels are designed to transport trucks, tractor trailers, and other self-propelled vehicles that roll on and off when loading or unloading.

- *Bulk vessels.* These vessels are designed for transporting nonpackaged dry goods commodities such as grain, coal, and ores. They rarely carry more than one type of product at a time and usually service only one shipper, or a few shippers, on one voyage.

- *Tankers.* These vessels have been designed to transport liquified products. Among these products can be found crude and refined petroleum, liquified gases, chemicals, wine, molasses, and other goods. Much of the world's total shipping tonnage is the transportation of petroleum.

- *Seagoing barges.* These types of vessels are carriers involved with small cargoes, short hauls, or routes with narrow or shallow channels. These vessels are much larger and built sturdier than river barges.

Normally seagoing barges can handle bulk, bulk break, containerized, and liquid cargoes.

Usage of these types of oceangoing vessels varies. The unit of capacity measurement for ocean vessels is *deadweight tonnage*. According to figures gathered in 1991, 39% of the total ocean going tonnage was transported by oil tankers, 30% by ore and dry goods carriers, 6% by vessels carrying either liquid or dry bulk cargo, 16% by break bulk general cargo, and 4% by containerships.

There are three basic types of service provided by ocean vessels: liner, tramp, and industrial carriage. These services roughly correspond to common, contract, and private carriage in land transportation. *Liner service* provides scheduled for-hire carriage for general goods between ports based on published freight rates. Ocean general cargo (or break-bulk liner) rates are set by *shipping conferences*. A conference is an organization consisting of all vessel owners operating in certain regions who agree to offer regular service and lower rates to shippers who agree to use the service exclusively. *Tramp services* are offered by vessels that literally "tramp" from port to port looking for freight. Tramp vessels do not follow established schedules or routes, and rates are established by individual charters with shippers. This type of service is used by most of the world's bulk freighters, tankers, and seagoing barges. The final type of service is *industrial carriage*. Here the shipper uses its own, or a leased vessel, to transport its own goods [19].

INTERNATIONAL AIR TRANSPORT

Whereas air transportation accounts for only a small fraction of the total international freight, it has become, nevertheless, the fastest growing mode of transportation. Revenues for international air transportation in 1994 totaled approximately $40 billion. Nations big and small have the ability to open lanes of international trade simply by buying aircraft and opening an airport. In many nations, the air transport industry is either wholly- or partially-owned by the country. Also, air transport and facilities normally used for passenger service can easily be used to carry and handle freight as well.

The main advantage of air transport lies in the speed by which goods can traverse the globe in comparison to other carrier modes. Although even the largest cargo aircraft has a tonnage-carrying capacity of about 1 percent of a fairly small break-bulk ocean vessel, it can make a delivery within a few hours or a few days that would take an ocean vessel several weeks. International air carriers are normally used to transporting small shipments of products, characterized by high value, extreme seasonality, perishability, and sensitivity to fashion, over long distances. Often, such products would never be able to find their way into foreign markets without air transportation. The negative side to air transport is obviously the cost for aircraft, maintenance and repair, and airport facilities. In addition, the limited storage capacity of aircraft and the inability to carry many types of products limit its use to all but emergency-type deliveries.

International air transportation consists of two types: *chartered* and *scheduled*. Companies can charter an aircraft from a variety of private and commercial services. Although chartering an aircraft is expensive, it could be justified for the shipment of a product whose nature or demand requires extreme reduction in transit time over other forms of carriage. Regularly scheduled flights by major commercial airlines offer companies who wish to ship by air a cheaper alternative. Shippers have the benefit of planning delivery almost anywhere in the world by consulting the published routes of commercial airlines. Rates are established by the International Air Transport Association (IATA), a cartel consisting of almost all of the world's airlines.

SURFACE TRANSPORT

When nations are not divided by oceans, inhospitable terrain, and political conditions, they may be able to use rail and motor carriers to transport goods across international boundaries. In North America, for example, trade between Canada, the United States and Mexico is unimpeded by natural barriers. In fact, the equipment of the three nations has been designed to be interchangeable. Railroads and highways interconnect at various border points. The railroad gauge is the same for all three countries and they all use similar rolling stock. The same can be said about highway structures and tractor and trailer equipment. Actually, the only barriers inhibiting the free flow of goods in North America are associated with motor transport and consist of customs requirements, operating rights, and other restrictions. The passage in 1994 of NAFTA should remove the last impediments to free transportation throughout North America. The trading blocks in Europe and Asia are focusing on the same liberalization of transportation within their own trading communities.

When using foreign surface transportation, global companies must be thoroughly apprised of conditions within individual nations. With the exception of the U.S., the railroad systems throughout the world are owned or controlled by the state for the common good of the nation. Rates are not published but rather are negotiable. Finally, although railroads are critical for intermodal transportation, the rail systems of many poorer nations do not possess the equipment to effectively work with containerization or "piggyback" operations. Effective motor transport is also critical for intermodalism. In

North America and Western Europe, the road systems and availability of motor transport is excellent. In most Eastern Bloc countries, motor transport is run by the state. In the rest of the world, road transit is carried on with small companies or individual operators on a contract basis.

INTERNATIONAL WAREHOUSING

International warehousing can be divided into two basic categories. The first consists of a variety of different types of consolidation warehouse. These facilities can be privately owned by the exporting firm or offered for public use by local transit companies and can be found at seaports, airports, and in most large cities. The basic purpose of consolidation warehousing is to receive foreign shipments and prepare them for the next leg through the distribution channel as they move toward the end customer. The functions of international consolidation centers are similar to those performed by domestic counterparts. Operations may consist of such activities as bulk breaking, conversion of the shipment to other modal means of transport, repacking, labeling, and marking. Among this type of warehouse can be found the following:

- *Transit Sheds.* This is perhaps the most basic form of international warehousing. Transit sheds are normally enclosed facilities at piers used to temporarily store shipments. The shed provides sufficient protection against weather conditions and assists in organizing the shipment for the next carrier. Transit sheds usually contain cargo, such as containers and trailers that have been unloaded from an ocean vessel and are waiting to be loaded onto a rail or motor carrier.
- *In-Transit Storage.* Often, international shippers need to temporarily store inventory while performing consolidation activities and negotiating rates with local carriers. In-transit storage warehousing provides this service. These warehouses are normally provided by the nation's railroad system and are located at seaports and airports.
- *Hold-on-Dock Storage.* This type of storage is offered by ocean carriers who permit shippers to warehouse cargoes in their facilities, usually at no charge, until the next scheduled sailing. Often shippers take advantage of the free storage to warehouse goods and to perform consolidation activities.
- *Public Warehousing.* When shipments are delayed or are held by the customer or government regulation, shippers may have to contract with a public warehouse to store the cargoes. Practically all international ports offer public warehousing to foreign shippers.
- *Shared Warehousing.* It is not uncommon for foreign shippers to pool their resources and contract as a co-operative for public warehousing.

This practice enables companies to retain public warehouse storage at lower costs.

- *Bonded Warehouse.* This type of warehouse is operated under government customs supervision for the express purpose of storing imported goods. Bonded warehouses can be owned directly by the government, by private companies for their imported goods only, or by public warehousing LSPs. All shipments to and from bonded warehouses must be handled by government-licensed bonded carriers. While they are stored in a bonded warehouse, goods cannot be further processed or manufactured

- *Foreign Trade Zones.* This is a special type of warehousing in which imported goods can be stored duty free until they are sold in the foreign market. In addition, goods marked for reexport do not pay any duties as long as they remain in the free-trade-zone location. While in storage, goods can be further processed or manufactured. Shippers must be thoroughly familiar with the regulations affecting both bonded and free-trade-zone warehouses [20].

The second category of international warehousing is concerned with privately owned warehousing. The decision criteria for building and maintaining a foreign warehouse is fairly close to that for domestic warehousing. Criteria can be broken up into two sets of elements: macro and micro. *Macro* elements can be divided into five major factors.

- *Transportation.* One of the most critical factors when making a decision to locate a warehouse in a foreign country is the availability of transportation. The site should provide easy access to foreign terminals, such as sea docks and airports. Also, the state of local land transportation is critical. Quality and accessibility of the road system, availability of local carriers, and ability to use a private fleet must be determined before site selection.

- *Labor.* Once a warehouse has been built, it will need to be staffed. Issues to be considered are the level of education and skill possessed by the local work force, requirements for training, ability to recruit local management, attitudes and customs of the local populace, and government restrictions and labor laws.

- *Land.* The property occupied by the warehouse must be thoroughly investigated. Key issues are the existence of public services such as sewers, water, roads, refuse pick-up, police and fire protection, governmental construction requirements, terrain, and possibility for expansion.

- *Energy and utilities.* A constant and uninterrupted source of power is crucial for effective warehouse operations. In regions were utilities are inadequate, companies may have to construct and operate their own power plants.

- *Taxes and incentives.* When looking for an off-shore warehouse site, companies often can get local governments to assist in construction and operation, as well as to give special tax breaks. The reverse can just as easily be the case, with some nations placing high taxes and restrictions on foreign operations in an endeavor to protect local businesses.

Once these macro factors have been addressed, the firm must consider a host of *micro* concerns. Some of these issues relate to the following:

- Currency exchange rates
- Government and social stability
- Currency stability
- Ability to take profits out of the country and availability of barter agreements
- Popular attitude of the locale toward the company
- Government attitude toward the company
- Depth and complexity of import and export regulations
- Availability of required materials handling equipment
- Free trade or most-favored nation status
- Culture and customs of the host country

INTERNATIONAL PURCHASING

As was discussed in Chapter 10, purchasing has become of a critical strategic function in the quest for competitive advantage in the twenty-first century. Increasingly, global purchasing decisions are having an enormous impact on product quality, delivery reliability, increased flexibility, and cost competitiveness as companies intensify their implementation of JIT/Lean and Internet approaches to suppliers, internal operations, and customer service. This search for continuous improvement in products and services has led purchasing functions in increasing numbers from both domestic and international firms to search for new sources of supply outside the domestic market. The effective management of this movement toward international sourcing is pivotal to the acquisition of the best products to meet ever-accelerating levels of customer service.

OVERVIEW

Historically, U.S. firms first embarked on a serious concern with importing products and raw materials as far back as the 1960s. At that time, the motive was purely to reduce the cost of labor. By the 1980s, this central concern with cost reduction, a somewhat negative approach to foreign sourcing, began to be replaced by the realization that a number of dramatic changes in the global economy had altered the traditional view of international sourcing. According to Carter [21], there have been several changes in the basic business mechanics of nations that have facilitated the emergence of international purchasing as a strategic weapon.

To begin with, the growing competitive intensity and interdependence of the global marketplace, complicated by pressures to reverse the trade deficit, has "internationalized" the purchasing function. Second, the pressure to reduce costs while simultaneously increasing quality and customer satisfaction in mature markets with little product differentiation has pushed purchasers to look for the best sources of supply, either domestic or foreign. Third, purchasers have looked at importing foreign components as a way to increase marketplace flexibility. Capital invested in new products and process equipment is expensive and restricts the firm's ability to respond to the market. Importing components permits them to sustain "world-class" leadership by purchasing demonstrated foreign engineering, technological, and process capabilities. These capabilities provide reduced cycle times for new product development and increased quality. Finally, importing provides purchasers with the ability to leverage the technology of other nations for products such as industrial machinery and consumer electronics. Instead of being merely a market for cheap labor, overseas suppliers are now viewed as prime sources of new technology for manufacturing and global distribution.

ADVANTAGES OF INTERNATIONAL SOURCING

There are many valid reasons for today's purchasing function to explore international sources of supply. Among these reasons can be found the following:

- *Availability*. Due to the growth of foreign competition, many products that were once made domestically are now available only through international sources. Among such products can be found many electronic components, machine tools, capital equipment, specialty metals and alloys, and electromechanical goods.
- *Quality*. Many buyers have had to look to global sources for products that will meet the levels of quality demanded by the marketplace. Although the quality and JIT/Lean movements in U.S. manufacturing have enabled many domestic producers to quickly close the "quality gap," the lead in quality seized by some foreign companies provides buyers with little alternative but to purchase from them.
- *Timeliness*. As JIT/Lean techniques continue to decrease inventories, the need for reliability in meeting schedule requirements correspond-

ingly has grown in proportion. Many purchasers have had to import products from global companies who have developed philosophies and techniques focusing on 100 percent customer satisfaction.

- *Continuity of supply.* Increased demand and competition for goods worldwide has made purchasers sharply aware of possible shortages in raw materials and finished components due to strikes, economic downturns, or even political unrest. Today's purchasers must be aware of and cultivate alternative sources of supply to ensure continuity of product.
- *Cost/price.* Generally, foreign companies have been able to offer international buyers lower prices on goods because of lower material, labor, and overhead costs. This is particularly true of products, such as textiles, apparel, shoes, molds and dies, assembled components, and automobiles. Coupled with this advantage, some foreign producers also may possess specialized skills, technologies, or patent rights that provide them with a overwhelming competitive advantage. In exploring cost advantages, buyers must be careful to calculate the total landed cost, including transportation, communication, import duties, source investigation and so forth, when executing foreign purchasing.
- *Technology.* Many foreign nations historically have prided themselves on the high level of craftsmanship and quality that characterizes their products. Today, there are many foreign nations, particularly Japan and Germany, which now possess technologies in some industries far in advance of comparable U.S. companies who often are charging a higher price. Buyers who do not take advantage of this technological leadership to acquire superior products might find themselves losing to competitors who do. In addition, the superior technology of some foreign companies may permit other firms to "acquire" the technology without investing in the development of the process itself. Importing the products of these technologies permits companies to remain focused on core competencies while leveraging imported components to offer to the market a wide variety of highly competitive products.
- *Market entry.* Some nations require foreign exporters to also buy from their country, or have a certain percentage of the export product be manufactured from materials or components originating from the home country. International purchasing also requires buyers to know the overall sources of products if they are to effectively procure components or finished goods in support of marketing, manufacturing, and sales plans.

COUNTERTRADE PURCHASING

Countertrade is a generic term used to describe any transaction in which payment is made partially or fully with goods instead of money. Countertrade links together two normally independent functions: the export of sold goods to a specific country and the import of purchased goods from the same country. Countertrade can occur for a number of reasons. For example, the importing country has balance-of-payments, currency exchange, or political restrictions preventing cash purchase. Sometimes it is imposed by governments in an effort to promote local products or to gain imports while also keeping currencies inconvertible. Countertrade provides certain advantages such as facilitating sales, expanding competition, improving profit potential, opening responsive markets, developing new capabilities, and retarding inflation. There are, however, drawbacks. It complicates purchasing, adds administrative costs, extends transportation time and cost, incurs duties and taxes, drains home technology resources, and imposes unfamiliar requirements to be performed.

There are five types of countertrade. These types, in turn, are driven by four variables: (1) the nature of the goods, (2) the percent of payment made in goods, (3) length of time before full payment is to be made, and (4) the number of parties involved [22]. The five major types of countertrade are as follows:

- *Barter.* This is probably the oldest form of transaction. Barter is the direct exchange of goods or services or both between two parties without the exchange of cash. Problems with this type of countertrade are the normal lag in time before goods are fully received, the possibility that one party may receive goods they cannot use, or one party receives goods that are less than the expected value.
- *Counterpurchase.* Many times two companies will agree upon reciprocal buying arrangements. Both companies agree to buy the products of each, pay for the majority of their purchases in cash, and fulfill their mutual sales obligations within a specified time period.
- *Offset.* This type of countertrade is similar to counterpurchase. The difference is that some or 100% of the counterpurchase obligation can be offset by buying from any company in the foreign country. Offset countertrade agreements are normally executed with countries that have centrally planned economies. As an example, McDonnell Douglas agreed to buy aircraft components from Canada in exchange for a $2.4 billion commitment by Canada to buy aircraft over a 15 year span [23].
- *Compensation or Buy-Back.* In this type of countertrade a company agrees to build a plant or supply technology, equipment, and/or

technical advise to a foreign country, and takes a percentage of the output from the facility as payment. Occidental Petroleum, for example, negotiated a $20 million deal with Russia to build several plants there and receive ammonia over a 20-year period as partial payment. Normally, the host country receives ownership when the terms of the agreement have been completed.

- *Switch-Trading.* This countertrade method utilizes a third-party trading house that buys the selling company's counterpurchase goods, services, or trade credits, and sells them to another company that requires them.

In a survey conducted by Carter *offset* was practiced by 73 percent of the businesses engaged in countertrade. This type was followed by counterpurchase at 60 percent, buy-back at 22 percent, barter at 19 percent, and switch trading at 3 percent [24].

The purchasing function plays a key role in countertrade. On the strategic side, a successful global countertrade system requires effective global purchasing planning. It is purchasing's role to develop the long-term relationships with foreign suppliers necessary for the effective execution and transfer of products, skills, and technologies across the globe in support of enterprise manufacturing and distribution competitive advantage. In detail, it is purchasing's responsibility, along with marketing, to pursue, negotiate, and schedule those products whose value will assist in competitive sourcing. Also, its is purchasing's role to monitor and control the costs involved in countertrade transactions. These costs are comprised of the cost of fees paid to trading agents and companies and the discount from the perceived or fair-market value of the goods versus the value actually received.

INTERNATIONAL PURCHASING MANAGEMENT PROCESS

Perhaps the best way to look at the process of international purchasing is to divide it into several critical activities. As illustrated in Figure 13.8, the first step in the process is to identify that a foreign source is necessary or economically feasible for the procurement of raw materials, a component, or family of components. This step could be undertaken for a variety of reasons: product unavailability in the domestic market, requirements for a higher level of quality than can be found from domestic suppliers, search for alternate suppliers other than domestic sources, and search for lower-cost alternatives. In addition, more detailed criteria, such as the length of the supply line, desire for supplier partnership and involvement, stability of product design, completeness of engineering documentation, length of the product life cycle, superiority of manufacturing methods, necessary materials and tooling, and terms and conditions of contracts, are also critical criteria that must be determined ahead of any outsourcing negotiation.

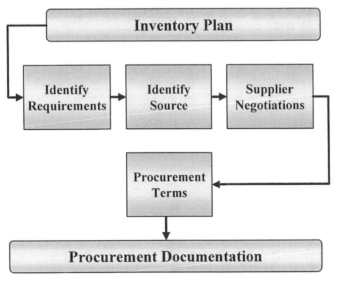

FIGURE 13.8 International procurement process.

As planners begin to map out the first leg of the process, it is critical that they also detail the drawbacks as well as the advantages of international sourcing. In most cases, purchasing from foreign sources is a good deal more difficult than buying from domestic sources, requiring the ability to solve not only the same kind of problems encountered in domestic procurement but also problems accentuated by language, culture, currency, transportation, and government regulations. The contrast between domestic and global purchasing are illustrated in Table 13.1. In managing these and other differences, global purchasers must continually review foreign sourcing to ensure that anticipated advantages associated with lower prices, better service, exceptional quality, and technological innovation do not evaporate over time.

Once the determination to use a foreign source has been made, the next step is to begin the search for a global partner. This step can be as easy as making a phone call or as complex as a small project. Information concerning prospective suppliers can be gathered from trade journals and newspapers, directories of manufacturers and distributors, government trade lists and surveys conducted by the U.S. Department of Commerce, professional purchasing associations, and word of mouth. A critical part of the process is deciding whether the goods are to be purchased directly from a foreign supplier or indirectly through a trading intermediary. If the latter is chosen, purchasing will have the choice of working with import merchants, commission houses, manufacturer's/distributor's agents, import brokers, or trading companies. Some of these intermediaries assume financial risk and carry inventory; brokers and agents, on the other hand, do not.

TABLE 13.1 Comparison Between Global and Domestic Purchasing

Domestic Purchasing	Global Purchasing
Culture	
Single nation and culture	Multinational/multilingual factors
Communications	
Single language; short lines of communication	Multilingual; long, complex lines of communications
Currency exchange	
Single currency	Currencies differing in stability and value
Customs regulations	
Relative freedom	Complex customs and tariff requirements
Lead times and inventories	
Stable/decreasing lead times and inventories	Long lead times and large safety stocks; need for repackaging and relabeling
Payment	
Cash and credit transactions	Letters of credit, electronic payment, and countertrade
Quality	
Common quality standards and specifications	Different standards of quality
Government involvement	
Minimal interference	Direct involvement in national economic plans
Economic stability	
Uniform economic environment	Variety of financial climates ranging from over conservative to wildly inflationary
Operational coordination	
Easy access to plant visits and technical assistance	Long-distance coordination with local managers

Firms that choose to buy direct must perform the services normally executed by intermediaries. Besides administrative functions, the most important of these services is qualifying the prospective supplier. Intermediaries, through long experience, know the international market and can make arrangements with the best foreign companies. When buying direct, the importing company must verify the supplier on its own. Among the criteria that should be used are (1) evaluation of the supplier's experience and management expertise, (2) financial strength and capability to meet requirements for new equipment and inventories, (3) availability of excellent communications for speedy decision-making on markets, equipment, and inventory control, (4) ability to maintain levels of inventory necessary to meet longer lead times and faster delivery, and (5) willingness of the supplier to enter into a long-term partnership. Sometimes firms with strong global purchasing functions will establish foreign offices to assist in supplier relations. Such offices normally cost less than intermediary fees, provide purchasing with better controls over price, quality, and delivery, provide more current information, and encourage better understanding with the supplier [25].

With the selection of prospective suppliers, the next step in the purchasing process is *request for quotation* (RFQ). The purpose of this step is to detail the purchase requirements and evaluate the total cost of the proposed purchase. The former consists of such elements as submission of necessary specifications and drawings, statement of quality requirements, special packaging needs, likely lead times, and estimated annual volume and quantities. Calculating the total cost also requires extensive analysis. Closely monitored costs will ensure that price advantages are not lost over time due to cost changes. Among the cost elements to be considered are standard elements such as transportation, customs, duties, and taxes, insurance and broker costs, inventory carrying costs, risk of damage or spoilage, fees for documentation, terminal and port costs, letters of credit, and others.

Of particular importance in price negotiation is currency valuation management. One of the realities in international purchasing is that no matter what currency is used for the base price, fluctuation in exchange rates will ultimately shift currency values. Currency fluctuation is influenced by such factors as domestic interest rates, inflation or deflation, and relative balance of trade. There are several strategies purchasers can use to counter currency fluctuations. The most radical approach is to insist that negotiation and payment be executed in the home currency. Another alternative is for buyer and seller to split fluctuations in value either fifty/fifty or by some other agreed upon formula. Many buyers will negotiate a price along with a variance, say of plus or minus 5%. If the price exceeds the variance threshold, buyer and seller would equally share in the variance. Finally, some companies can hedge currency fluctuations by purchasing fixed rates via currency futures or forward contracts [26].

Negotiations with prospective foreign suppliers, once price and product issues have been resolved, require purchasers to acquire a good deal of understanding and insight about the supplier's country and customs. Although the normal planning activities associated with a negotiation, such as team membership, establishment of objectives, and issues up for compromise, are critical, purchasers must be prepared to tailor the process to meet the often very different practices and perceptions of foreign negotiators.

One of the most critical decisions that must be resolved during negotiations revolves around shipping terms and method of payment. Most of the terms reviewed earlier in this chapter relating to exports also apply to product imports. Among the most common are FOB, Ex Works, FAS, C&F, CIF and

Delivered Duty Paid. Traditionally, a number of payment methods are used when transacting international trade including the following:

- *Cash in Advance.* Often when buyers do not have a good credit rating or are unknown, or when the buyer's country is politically or economically unstable, sellers will require them to pay for purchased material in advance.
- *Open Account.* Although this is the preferred method of payment for domestic business in the U.S., it is not often used in international purchasing. The reason stems mostly from the uncertainties in currencies and international political conditions.
- *Drafts.* This is currently the most widely used of the payment methods. A draft is a negotiable instrument that contains an order to pay. When a sale takes place, the seller forwards the transfer documentation and draft through its bank to the buyer's bank for payment. A *sight draft* is executed when the buyer pays the draft. A *time draft* requires that the buyer pay the draft on a specific due date. In a *clean draft*, the seller presents its draft to the buyer for collection and the transaction documents are delivered directly to the buyer.
- *Letters of Credit.* In this method, letters of credit are arranged by the buyer with a bank, and the supplier can draw payment against the credit with the submittal of the appropriate transaction documents. Letters of credit can be *irrevocable,* meaning that they cannot be changed without the prior agreement of all parties, or *revocable*, meaning that they can be changed without the seller's consent.

The final area relating to pricing and terms is the payment of tariffs or duties on imported goods. Tariffs can be used as a method for revenue generation, as a devise to protect domestic industries and/or to discourage the importation of certain products. There are three major types of tariffs: Ad valorem, specific, and compound. *Ad valorem*, the type of tariff most applied, is calculated as a percentage of the appraised value of the goods received. A *specific* tariff is defined as a specified amount per unit weight or other unit of measurement. For example, $0.20 per gross. Finally, a *compound* tariff is calculated as a combination of both an ad valorem and a specific rate. The payment of tariffs can be delayed by warehousing goods in a *free-trade zone.* Tariffs are not paid on the goods until they are removed from the free-trade zone and sold. Another method used by firms that reexport products is a duty *drawback.* The drawback provides for a 99 percent refund of ordinary customs duties paid when the goods were originally received [27].

The last step in the international purchasing process is the completion of the trade documentation. Whether handled by an international freight forwarder, customshouse broker, or the company's own agents, the proper execution of documentation is critical. The following represents the key import documents:

- *Arrival Notice.* This document is sent by the carrier and informs the buyer of the estimated arrival date of the transport mode, identifies the shipment with details such as number of packages and weight, and indicates when "free time" will expire. The notice is often used as a freight bill.

- *Customs Entries.* There are several different types of forms used when entering imported goods into the U.S. The first type, *consumption entry*, is required of all entering goods by U.S. Customs. The form contains information as to the origin of the cargo, a description of the merchandise, and estimated duties applicable to the particular commodity. Estimated duties must be paid when the entry is filed. The second type of entry form, an *immediate delivery entry*, is used to expedite the delivery of cargo. It allows up to 10 days for the payment of estimated duty and processing of the consumption entry. In addition, it permits delivery of the cargo prior to payment of the estimated duty and then allows subsequent filing of the consumption entry and duty. It is also known as "I.D. entry." The third type of customs entry, *immediate transportation entry*, allows the cargo to be moved from the pier to an inland destination via a bonded carrier without the payment of duties or finalization of the entry at the port of arrival. It is also known as an "I.T. entry." The final type of customs entry, *transportation and exportation entry*, permits goods coming from or going to a third country to enter the U.S. for the purpose of transshipment. It is also known as "T&E entry."

- *Carrier's Certificate and Release Order.* This document is used to advise U.S. Customs of shipment details, ownership, port of lading, and other information. By means of this document, the carrier certifies that the company or individual named in the certificate is the owner or consignee of the cargo. It is commonly known as the "Carrier Certificate."

- *Delivery Order.* This document is issued by the consignee or authorized customs broker to the ocean carrier providing authority to release the cargo to the inland carrier. It includes all data necessary for the pier delivery clerk to determine that the cargo can be released to the domestic carrier. This document is also known as a "Pier Release."

- *Freight Release.* This document provides evidence that the freight charges for the cargo have been paid. If in writing, it may be presented at the pier to obtain release of the cargo. (Normally, once the freight is paid, releases are usually arranged without additional documentation.) It is also known as a "Freight Bill Receipt."

- *Special Customs Invoice.* This is an official form usually required by U.S. Customs where the rate of duty is based on value and the shipment value exceeds $500. The document is usually prepared by the foreign exporter or authorized forwarder and is used by Customs in determining the value of the shipment. The exporter or designated agent must attest to the authenticity of the data furnished [28].

The execution of the international purchasing process is significantly different than domestic purchasing and must be effectively managed if it is to be successful. As illustrated in Figure 13.9, the first step is the development of a

FIGURE 13.9 Managing the global procurement process

formal global purchasing plan. This exercise should detail international sourcing requirements, the methods to be followed for achieving these requirements, and how the strategy is to be aligned with and supportive of overall enterprise goals. The second step is the organization of an international purchasing function whose role it is to gather information and evaluate opportunities, as well as execute the activities associated with managing global channel inventories, foreign negotiations, pricing, and delivery issues. This department can be organized several ways, including the use of a resident foreign purchasing office, import broker, merchant or international trading company, or formal structure within the corporate purchasing function. Third, the international purchasing organization needs to be closely integrated with other company and channel functions. This will assure that individual departmental objectives as well as the supply chain strategy are effectively supported. Finally, the purchasing planners must devise detailed procedures that can assist in international sourcing program evaluation. Among the key elements are review of cost-reduction strategies, pursuance of targeted value-added services, maintenance of quality levels, and others.

TODAY'S GLOBAL TRADE ENVIRONMENT

As the last years of the twentieth century drew to a close, the global economy appeared to be steaming forward to new heights. The fall of communism and the end of the Cold War, the rise of an independent Eastern Europe, the explosion of commerce in the Pacific Rim, and the apparent movement of controlled economies toward the market system and free trade seemed to portend a golden age of global wealth. As the new century dawned, however, global events have dampened what was once an unbridled enthusiasm. To begin with, a stubborn recessionary period was ushered in with the new century, drying up global capital investment and forcing companies to approach the marketplace with extreme caution. The terrorist attacks of 9/11, continued unrest in the Middle East, the second Gulf War, and sporadic attacks by global terrorists like al-Qaida have ushered in a new era of restrictions on trade, increased vigilance, and a general wariness of foreign trade. If economic and political traumas were not enough, the outbreak of Severe Acute Respiratory Syndrome (SARS) in China and Mad Cow disease in Canada in early 2003 threaten to curtail global trade from yet another direction. In the 1990's the concern was that they newly emerging world economy would be stymied by protectionist trading blocks. As the new century proceeds, that fear has switched from protectionism to security from terrorism and fears regarding the spread of potentially lethal diseases.

Although what specific avenues global trade will take in the 2000s is still uncertain, there are, nevertheless, three main themes governing overall development. The first is the growing importance of supply chain management as a global competitive weapon. There are two critical components: one *tactical* (associated with the operational acceleration of the velocity of products and information through the global pipeline) and the other *strategic* (associated with the architecting of collaborative partnerships designed to make global enterprises more flexible and agile to capitalize on new vistas of competitive advantage). The second theme points to the fact that although barriers to trade are falling globally, the international market will still be fragmented. This is particularly true in the case of emerging nations with strong cultural, socioeconomic, and political differences. International companies who wish to exceed will not only have to develop a clear understanding of national differences but also be able to leverage them if competitive advantage is to be gained. The final theme is developing effective global security systems that can protect individual countries and infrastructures from armed and bioterrorism while providing for the progressive expansion of trade among all the nations of the earth.

NORTH AMERICA

With the activation of the North American Free Trade Act (NAFTA) on January 1, 1994 between the U.S., Canada, and Mexico, the globe's richest trading was established. Altogether, the North American bloc contains a population exceeding 365 million people and accounts for a Gross Domestic Product (GDP) of over $6.5 trillion and a total merchandise trade of $250 billion. NAFTA will phase out tariffs between the three nations on more than 10,000 commodities over the next fifteen-year period and will create a free trade zone that stretches from Alaska to the borders of Central America. For example, in 1993, U.S. goods faced an average tariff barrier at the Mexican border of about 10 percent, five times the 2.07 percent rate that the U.S. imposed on Mexican goods. With NAFTA, Mexico's average tariff has already fallen to about 2 percent. Import licensing and other non-tariff barriers have been eliminated and more than two-thirds of U.S. exports now enter duty-free.

The purpose of NAFTA was to create the opportunity for the countries of North America to create an environment conducive to mutual trade and economic development as well as pose as an alternative to the trade blocks forming in Europe and Asia. Essentially, the goals of the alliance are to facilitate cross-border investment and trade; reduce or eliminate tariffs, administrative costs, infrastructure incompatibilities and other barriers; and, finally, to foster between the three nations an attitude of economic creativity, innovation, and development. In 2002 the trade statistics between the partners demonstrates the potential of NAFTA. U.S. exports in industrial and agricultural products and services to Canada in 2002 stood at $16 billion and Mexico at $9.7 billion. Imports from Canada were posted at $21 billion and Mexico at $13.4 billion (29).

The challenges to NAFTA in regard to implementing the kinds of logistics, legal, and commercial environment necessary for a truly borderless trade community are uneven. Since 1989 the U.S. and Canada already had in effect a Free Trade Agreement that eliminated protective tariffs and government restrictions. Also, the political and economic environment in Canada is highly advanced and very receptive to trade partnership. The same issues with Mexico are quire different. After decades of controlled economies, Mexico has only recently undergone dramatic change in the direction of currency stabilization, social accord among workers, employers, and the government, trade liberalization, growth of privatization, and government deregulation.

Mexican law still strictly enforces its *cabotage* laws and prohibits U.S. and Canadian motor carriers from operating domestically. There is only one railroad, which is owned and operated by the Mexican government. Finally, Mexico has no LTL trucking companies, and air cargo transport is limited to just a few airports.

While there are still many barriers inhibiting truly free trade between the NAFTA countries, they will diminish with time as infrastructure improvements, political change, and the implementation of new systems facilitate documentation, procedures, transportation, and the identification of new markets and trading intermediaries. One thing is clear: the challenges of European and Asian trading blocks will only intensify. Already Mexican *maquiladoras*, manufacturing and distribution plants located along the U.S.-Mexican border that pay no duty on imported semi-finished goods and only a value-added export duty, are reeling from competition from China. As a community, supply chain strategists from all three countries must continue to refine their efforts to create a highly competitive borderless trade network capable of competing globally.

EUROPEAN COMMUNITY

The European marketplace is a densely populated region of 320 million consumers packed into a relatively small and compact geographical area, with mature economies and logistics systems. It is also the gateway to Eastern Europe and the old Soviet Union. At the dawn of the twenty-first century this community of nations (Austria, Belgium, Denmark, Finland, France, Germany, Greece, Ireland, Italy, Luxembourg, the Netherlands, Portugal, Spain, Sweden, and the United Kingdom) has been welded together into an integrated economic entity (with the faint glimmerings of political overtones looking towards a "United States of Europe") called the European Economic Community (EEC), popularly known as the European Union (EU). The goals of the EU are straightforward and call for the eventual removal of all trade barriers associated with

- *Political barriers,* such as restrictions due to border checks, goods inspection, customs controls, national brands and markets, cabotage, and documentation
- *Governmental barriers,* such as focused around welfare, pensions, health, safety, and labor migration
- *Fiscal barriers*, such as customs duties, taxes, excise duties, and currency fluctuations.

As political and economic conditions continue, the EU is likely to emerge as a tightly knit trade network. A significant step towards European economic and political integration was achieved with the acceptance in 2002 by most EU countries of the *Euro* as the common currency for all EU transactions. Politically, the acceptance of most of the former Soviet block into NATO, including Russia, which recently became a "junior" member, has also eased the concern of so many countries, their economies anything but equal in size and influence. The impact of a united Europe is sure to have both an economic and, as witnessed during the Second Gulf War (2003), political implication. For example, trade between the U.S. and the EU in 2002 was dramatic. The U.S. exported $14.3 billion in goods and services while importing $22.6 billion.

Despite all of the positive signs, there have been some persistent troubles. Some nations, notably the UK, Sweden, and Denmark, elected not to adopt the *Euro* as their currencies, preferring to hold on to national fiscal decisions. The continued threat of terrorism has distracted many European governments from seeking even closer business ties. The continuing recession of 2000 has exposed problems caused by the inequality of national economies. The EU desperately needs to reduce interest rates to stimulate the economies of the wealthier nations, such as Germany (the flagship of the EU) which has shown stagnant growth for years and is saddled with an unemployment rate that exceeds 10 percent unemployment, but cannot do so without EU concurrence. Finally, many differences, ranging from tax policies to transport access remain to be resolved.

ASIA AND THE PACIFIC RIM

Although the most disorganized of the major global trading blocks, Asia and the Pacific Rim has been described as potentially the world's largest market. For many decades Japan has been the key player in the region with the world's second largest national economy. Other countries, notably Hong Kong, South Korea, Singapore, Taiwan, and most importantly, China, account for significant portions of global trade. During the mid-1990's the region was considered the hot-bed of future economic development. By the late-1990s reality had set in. Talk of the Asian miracle and of Japanese banks dominating global finance has been silenced in the near collapse of hyper-extended economies and a prolonged Japanese recession. Instead of unlimited development, the problems of the region, huge foreign debt, unstable governments, non-standard commercial practices, a still-emerging middle-class, and woefully inadequate logistics infrastructures, have become all too evident.

U.S. trade with the region has been growing unevenly. In 1999, Japan was the largest exporter of goods to the U.S., accounting for over $130.8 billion, with $57.4 billion in imports. By 2002, U.S. trade with Japan had slipped to

$121.4 in imports and $51.4 in exports. Much the same results were evident with trade with the U.S.'s two other large regional trading partners, Taiwan, which has experienced a 9 and 4 percent decline respectively in exports and imports, and South Korea, which during the same period saw exports to the U.S. grow from $31.1 to $35.5 billion, with imports from the U.S. remaining flat. The big exception has been China which has emerged as a legitimate economic player with a $4.5 trillion economy, the world's sixth largest. In 1999 the U.S. imported $81.7 billion while exporting $13.1 billion in trade with China. In 2002, those figures had increased dramatically to $125.1 billion in imports with exports reaching $22 billion [30].

China Syndrome

An executive from a large U.S. retailer sourcing in China was mystified: Why were all the goods in ocean containers arriving depalletized? The goods had left the factories in China on pallets. A visit to the port revealed the answer. Warehouse equipment is expensive and labor is cheap. It was simply more cost effective to load the containers by hand than make use of a fork truck.

This example bears witness to the fact that while China economy is exploding and the country has invested heavily on supporting infrastructure, logistics is still in its infancy.

According to a survey conducted by The Logistics Institute-Asia Pacific, a joint venture between Georgia Tech's Logistics Institute, the National University of Singapore, and the Institute of Logistics and Transportation, China's logistics System can be described as backward, even chaotic. As example, the report stated that most warehousing facilities are fairly rudimentary and make little use of information technology. The survey also identified other serious impediments to Chinese logistics development. Both foreign and domestic logistics providers say that the shortage of logistics professionals is a critical concern. Domestic companies also worry whether sufficient resources are available for future development. Foreign companies cite policy restrictions and regulation in China as their biggest challenge.

Source: Bradley, Peter, "The China Syndrome: Logistics is Hot, Performance is Not," *DC Velocity,* April, 2003, p. 43.

Logistically, the Pacific Rim contains a block of highly developed infrastructures located in Japan, South Korea, Hong Kong, and a few other industrialized areas. Although languages and cultures are different, international companies have found sophisticated transportation systems, a variety of warehousing options, high use of automated material handling systems, and familiar standards of customer service. In less developed nations, on the other hand, logistics systems are woefully inadequate and slow to develop, requiring a great deal of capital investment and management skill. In addition, in countries such as China, the government is responsible for executing logistics activities. In fact, many analysts feel that China's slowness to respond to necessary changes in the transportation infrastructure is holding back progress. The country's GDP has grown approximately 8 percent over the past ten years, but the growth rate for railway and highway construction has never reach 5 percent a year and total demand for transportation exceeds the current capacity of road, railway, and water systems. The World Bank estimates that China will not be able to meet its logistics requirements until at least 2020. Chinese planners, however, have been concerned with expansion that is too rapid and misdirected, resulting in transportation imbalances and overcapacity. In any case, global firms can only be expected to accelerate their investment in China and other Pacific Rim countries. Already these countries have become the preferred sources for raw materials and manufactured components. With their almost unlimited reservoirs of cheap labor (China's manufacturing labor cost averages just 5 percent of the average U.S. manufacturing wage) and reputation for quality, these countries are expected to expand their capacities as global suppliers of commodity goods such as apparel, furniture, consumer electronics, and automobiles.

SUMMARY

At the dawn of the twenty-first century, the globalization of the marketplace has become one of the most critical components shaping today's business climate. This explosion in international trade is the result of the maturing of the economies of the highly industrialized nations, growing global competition, the establishment of strategic alliances and joint ventures with foreign companies, and the development of a single logistics system focused on attaining the best cost and service possible while welding enterprise and partner logistics resources with global markets, capital, and manufacturing to maximize competitive advantage. While global trade offers many advantages, companies need to be aware of the many barriers that render an international trade initiative difficult. Global strategists must be prepared to find solutions to such barriers as tariffs and trade practices, cultural issues, financial restrictions, security requirements, and logistics infrastructure weaknesses.

An effective global initiative requires the development of a comprehensive global business strategy to effectively guide the effort. The construction of such a strategy is composed of five steps. In the first, planners must identify the three strategic dimensions of the internal and external business environment. The goal of this step is to isolate the macro economic, political, and governmental environments as well as the micro factors of markets, costs, and customers, and determine how well the organization is posed to handle identified opportunities, threats, and trends. In the second step, planners must select those markets that match enterprise aspirations and capacities. The third step consists of defining the structure of the organization to optimize objectives given existing skills and resources. The fourth step is implementing the product, marketing, communications, and logistics channels detailed in the third step. The final step is concerned with the measurement and monitoring of the success of the strategy.

In defining the strategic approach to the global marketplace, firms have four possible alternatives. One strategy is to export products into foreign markets from domestic sources passively through the use of a domestic intermediary, or actively by seeking out intermediaries in foreign countries. Another strategy, joint venture, differs from exporting in that the firm invests and is directly involved in the management of a foreign enterprise. The final strategy is direct ownership of a company located in a foreign country. Once the international channel strategy has been defined, it must be effectively managed. Maintenance of a global channel is a complex affair involving most of the decisions required to run domestic functions, plus new requirements associated with the realities of international trade. Of critical importance is the execution of the functions of transportation and warehousing. Transportation is essential in delivering the product through the distribution channel to foreign destinations and warehousing with consolidating and storing it on its way to the customer.

Enterprises have also turned to global purchasing as a critical source of competitive advantage. Historically, foreign sourcing has been used for decades as a method of acquiring products at prices cheaper than what could be purchasing in the U.S. domestic market. Today, importing products from international sources is considered as a means to increase marketplace flexibility by acquiring the products manufactured by advanced engineering, technological, and production processes without investing in those resources. Fundamental to effective global sourcing is the execution of the international purchasing management process. The first step in the process is to identify the feasibility of using a foreign source for the procurement of a component or finished good. Once the decision to outsource has been made appropriate suppliers have been identifies, the second step is request for quotation. The purpose of this step is to detail the purchase requirements and evaluate the total cost of the proposed purchase. After the list of perspective suppliers has been finalized, purchasers must then negotiate for prices, delivery schedules, and contracts detailing the scope and length of the proposed partnership. The final step in the process is the completion of the importing documentation.

QUESTIONS FOR REVIEW

1. List some of the key trends in today's business environment accelerating the growth of international trade.
2. What are some of the reasons why a domestic-based manufacturer or wholesaler would seek to engage in foreign trade?
3. Why is an international distribution strategy so important to an enterprise seeking to enter global markets?
4. Compare and contrast the four possible alternatives a firm would implement to enter foreign markets.
5. It used to be assumed that the level of distribution channel structure development found in a country paralleled the structures of other countries that had attained the same degree of economic and technological development. Why is this assumption incorrect in today's marketplace?
6. Describe the performance tools companies can use to measure the cost/service trade-offs of their international marketing effort.
7. Describe the four basic marketing channel structures. What are the factors influencing a company to choose a given strategy?
8. What are some of the product marketing decisions that an international company must make?
9. List some of the reasons why international marketing and logistics is so much more complex than performing the same functions domestically.
10. Discuss the impact of international trade on the development of an effective transportation policy.
11. Describe the advantages companies can gain by engaging in global purchasing.
12. What is countertrade purchasing, and why is it so important?

REFERENCES

1. These trade figures are from the U.S. Census Bureau, Foreign Trade Bureau.
2. These points have been summarized from Bowersox, Donald J. and Closs, David J., *Logistical Management: The Integrated Supply Chain Process.* New York: The McGraw-Hill Companies, Inc., 1996, pp. 133-135.
3. Horne, David J., "Global Sourcing Scenario," *APICS: The Performance Advantage,* 13, 5, 2003, pp. 21-24.
4. See the discussion in Harps, Leslie Hansen, "Bridging the Cultural Divide," *Inbound Logistics,* 23, 3, 2003, pp. 34-40.
5. For more information see Bowersox and Closs, pp. 138.
6. Paul S. Bender, "International Logistics," in *The Distribution Management Handbook,* Tompkins, James A. and Harmelink, Dale A. eds. New York: McGraw-Hill, 1994, pp. 8.2-8.4.
7. For a more detailed discussion see Tyndall, Gene, Gopal, Christopher, and Partsch, Wolfgang, *Supercharging Supply Chains.* New York: John Wiley and Sons, 1998.
8. Keegan, Warren J., *Global Marketing Management,* 4th ed. Englewood Cliffs, NJ: Prentice-Hall, 1989, pp. 41-49.
9. Kotler, Philip, *Marketing Management,* 6th ed. Englewood Cliffs, NJ: Prentice-Hall, 1988, pp. 388-389.
10. Gopal, Christopher and Cypress, Harold, *Integrated Distribution Management.* Homewood, IL: Business One Irwin, 1993, pp. 209-210.
11. Bowersox, Donald J. and Cooper, M. Bixby, *Strategic Marketing Channel Management.* New York: McGraw-Hill, 1992, p. 415.
12. Bender, Paul S., "The International Dimensions of Physical Distribution Management," in *The Distribution Handbook,* Robeson, James F., and House, Robert G., eds. New York: The Free Press, 1985, pp. 784-786.
13. Picard, J., "Topology of Physical Distribution Systems in Multi-National Corporations." *International Journal of Physical Distribution and Materials Management,* 12, (6), 26-39 (1982).
14. For more discussion see McKinnon, Alan C., *Physical Distribution Systems.* New York: Routledge, 1989, p. 220.
15. Keegan, Warren J., *Global Marketing Management,* 4th ed. Englewood Cliffs, NJ: Prentice-Hall, 1989, pp. 378-382.
16. For more information on these documents see Johnson, James C. and Wood, Donald F., *Contemporary Transportation,* 3rd ed. New York: Macmillan, 1993, p. 472.
17. Paul S. Bender, "The International Dimensions of Physical Distribution Management," p. 808.
18. Sampson, Roy J., Farris, Martin T., and Shrock, David L., *Domestic Transportation: Practice, Theory, and Policy.* Boston: Houghton Mifflin Co., 1985, pp. 99-102.
19. See the discussion in Sampson, *et al.,* pp. 100-101; and, Paul S. Bender, "The International Dimensions of Physical Distribution Management," p. 793.

20. See the discussion in Bender, "The International Dimensions of Physical Distribution Management," pp. 799-802.
21. Carter, Joseph R., *Purchasing: Continued Improvement Through Integration.* Homewood, IL: Business One Irwin, 1993, pp. 110-116.
22. See the discussion in Norquist, Warren E., Lees, Robert H., Morton, James E., and Tahmoush, Frank, "Global Purchasing," in *The Purchasing Handbook,* Fearon, Harold E., Dobler, Donald W., and Killen, Kenneth H., eds. New York: McGraw-Hill, 1993, p. 194.
23. Carter, p. 134.
24. Ibid, p. 136.
25. See the discussion in Ibid, pp. 121-122.
26. For more information on currency issues see Heinritz, Stuart, Farrell, Paul V., Giunipero, Larry C., and Kolchin, Michael G., *Purchasing: Principles and Applications*, 8th ed. Englewood Cliffs, NJ: Prentice-Hall, 1991, pp. 196-198.
27. For additional information see Heinritz, *et al.,* pp. 201-202; and, Cateora, Philip, *International Marketing*, 8th ed. Homewood, IL: Irwin, 1993, pp. 41-44.
28. For a full treatment of these documents see Johnson and Wood, p. 47.
29. These trade figures are from the U.S. Census Bureau, Foreign Trade Bureau.
30. These trade figures are from the U.S. Census Bureau, Foreign Trade Bureau.

14

INFORMATION TECHNOLOGY AND SUPPLY CHAIN MANAGEMENT

As it has in all areas of today's business environment, the application of information technology has caused a revolution in the concept and practice of *Supply Chain Management* (SCM). As the complexity of managing today's global enterprise expands and the speed by which information concerning products, customers, and processes accelerates, companies can have little hope of responding effectively without applying computerized information systems. Many areas impacted by the computer have already been discussed in previous chapters: the integration of the operating functions of the enterprise, solutions accelerating ordering processes and shrinking delivery times to customers, Internet and *electronic data interchange* (EDI) applications providing connectivity between companies, planning systems that facilitate channel inventory management, simulation programs eliminating the guesswork involved in transportation routing and scheduling, and many others. The use and complexity of such computerized tools can only be expected to grow, changing the way companies have traditionally serviced their customers and how they communicate with supply channel partners.

Exploring the impact of information technology on supply chain management is the subject of this chapter. Discussion begins by exploring how computer technologies have reshaped the way companies utilize information to plan and control internal functions and create interactive, collaborative relationships with their customers and trading partners out in the supply channel network. Among the topics defined are the principles of information processing, integration, and networking. Following, the chapter focuses on an in-depth exploration of the basic architectural elements of today's *enterprise information system* (EIS). Included is a review of how the EIS architecture can be adapted to respond to the needs of the distribution industry. Next, the various forms of connectivity made available by the Internet are examined. Topics detailed are Web-based marketing, e-commerce, e-business, and e-collaboration. The chapter concludes with a discussion of the processes necessary to properly identify and evaluate today's range of information technology solutions, making technology choices, and implementation and continuous improvement issues.

FOUNDATIONS OF ENTERPRISE INFORMATION TECHNOLOGIES

As the importance of timely, accurate, and complete information increases in the supply channel environment, information technologies have progressively become the key enabler integrating the supply network environment. What this means is that today's marketplace leaders must view computerized technologies not only as a tool to accelerate the speed and productivity of business functions through automation, but also as a key driver that enhances the opportunity for supply chains to continually activate new relationships and operating structures that change the way they compete in the marketplace. *Internally,* information technologies enable companies to develop databases and implement applications that provide for the efficient management of transactions and the timely collection, analysis, and generation of information about customers, processes, products, services, and markets necessary for effective decision making. Building a real-time knowledge repository can create the pathway necessary to seamlessly synchronize the capabilities of individual companies with their customers and trading partners. *Externally,* information technologies enable supply chain strategists to architect channel networks that are collaborative, agile, scalable, fast flow, and Web-enabled. The goal is to present customers anywhere in the supply chain a single, integrated response to their wants and needs by creating a unique network of value-creating relationships. Connectivity and synchronization at this level require the elimination of channel information silos and the construction of collaborative, channel-wide communication and information enablers directed at a single point: total customer satisfaction.

There can be little doubt that while it can be said that the *supply chain management* is perhaps the single most important driving force in today's global business environment, at the heart of SCM can be found the integrative power of information technologies. Employing this power, however, requires both planners and technologists to rethink their use of the computer. Actualizing the potential of today's information systems will require companies to move beyond traditional paradigms that utilize computerization purely as a means to plan and control internal business processes. In fact, connectivity enablers, like the Internet, now permit companies to escape from the narrow boundaries of their own information environments to network with a universe of geographically dispersed channel trading partners and create real-time strategies, operations, and planning systems previously thought unattainable. Today's boundary-spanning technology tools enable companies to harness the explosion of data that continuously emanates from every plane in the supply chain galaxy, integrate it with internal business systems, perform sophisticated analysis of the information, make visible an accurate picture of individual enterprise and supply chain partner performance, and architect revolutionary capabilities and competencies for the generation of new sources of products and services, whole new businesses and marketplaces, and radically new forms of competitive advantage.

BASICS OF SUPPLY CHAIN INFORMATION PROCESSING

It can be stated that the operational and strategic functions of any supply chain consist of two major flows: the flow of *material* from the source of supply to the customer and the flow of *information* from the customer back through each channel node to the origins of supply. As the velocity of the flow of materials is limited in time by the capabilities of channel handling, storage, and transportation, so too is the availability and usefulness of information limited by existing information technologies. Definition of these limits directly defines the physical capabilities of the supply chain and the ability to create, collect, assimilate, access, and transfer information necessary for effective action and decision-making. Historically, the ability of supply chains to not only control physical events, but also to leverage data to achieve operational optimization and exploit the internal and external linkages between activities was inhibited by limitations in information processing. Data could be collected, assimilated, and passed on to other business functions only as fast as human efforts, assisted by crude forms of automation, could process it.

With the advent of the computer, capable of handling information in volumes and at speeds previously thought unimaginable, the heavy information processing constraints of the past were lifted, revealing new horizons of information and obsoleting many of the older methods and organizational processes and structures. Availability of information provided channel managers with a variety of previously unavailable tools to solve critical supply chain problems. To begin with, computers enabled companies to integrate their internal business functions so that strategies and plans could be broadcast to each department. Second, computers provided for the accurate and timely entry and maintenance of business transactions. This data in turn could be used to control processes as well as verify performance. Third, the computer provided customer service with the means to confirm inventory availability, order and delivery status, and payment information. And finally, the computer enabled planners to reduce channel inventories and resource requirements by substituting information about supply and demand in place of redundant physical assets as a means to react to supply chain uncertainties. Effectively utilizing the computer requires a full understanding of the architectural functions and nature of computerized information.

INFORMATION SYSTEM BASICS – INTEGRATION AND NETWORKING

At the core of today's *enterprise information system* (EIS) can be found two fundamental principles. The first is the availability of a technical infrastructure that links computer systems and people. The word commonly used for this process is *integration.* One of the problems with this dimension is understanding exactly what it means. As Savage has pointed out [1], there has been a great deal of confusion concerning the definition of the word *integration.* It is often erroneously used synonymously with *connectivity* and *interfacing.* Connectivity means connecting processes together, such as when a telephone system connects customers and order processing functions. Interfacing means bringing information from one system and presenting it for input to another, such as occurs in an EDI transaction. Although both assemble and transmit information to the enterprise, neither connectivity nor interfacing change the way the organization works. If the organization is really nothing more than a collection of independent functions, each performing separate activities according to their own strategies and performance measurements, then neither connectivity nor interfacing will have much impact on transforming the organization.

In contrast, integration calls for the elimination of the ideological, strategic, and performance barriers that separate functions within an organization. Integration means to come in touch, or to be in touch with itself. Organizationally, integration means leveraging information tools that bring business functions together by facilitating ever closer coordination in the execution of joint business processes. Integration focuses on activating the creative thinking within and between enterprises. Integration attempts to bring into alignment the challenges and opportunities offered by information technologies and the cultures and capabilities of the modern organization.

The second technology dimension at the core of today's EIS is *networking*. In the past, computer system architecture permitted only hierarchical communication. As each processor completed its tasks, the output was then available for the next processing task, which, in turn, passed its output to the next downstream processor. With the advent of client/server architectures and Internet browsers, the process of communicating information has shifted from processing hierarchies to connecting different computers and their databases together in a network. The growing availability of open-system softwares and intranet and extranet networks is targeted at solving the problem of the dissimilarity of hardware operating systems. The advantage of networked systems is that people can now communicate information directly to other people in the network. This peer-to-peer networking enables companies to leverage the capabilities, skills, and experience of people by integrating and directing their talents around focused tasks. What is more, the establishment of focused teams can occur not only inside the enterprise but also can be extended to suppliers, customers, and trading partners constituting the entire value chain [Figure 14.1].

Integration is the process of linking business functions together; networking, on the other hand, is the activation of those links by enabling and empowering people to cut across functional barriers and interweave common and specialized knowledge to solve enterprise problems. Integration and networking are complimentary activities that can be combined and defined as the *integrative process.* According to Savage, this process

> puts us in touch with the whole, with one another, with customers, and with suppliers in ever-changing patterns of relationships. It also puts us in touch with our own wills, emotions and knowledge. The integrative process is a process of

human networking: networking our visions and knowledge so we can take decisive action in concert with other efforts [2].

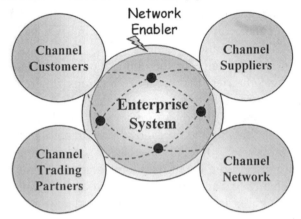

FIGURE 14.1 Basic business universe.

This integrative process is the driving force in the acquisition of computerized technology and is, in turn, governing the development of its topology.

Basic Enterprise System Architectural Functions. While the modern *enterprise information system* has evolved dramatically over the past decades, today's business system architectures are essentially based on a common set of functions. As portrayed in Figure 14.2, there are five critical functions found in every business system:

- *Enterprise database.* The foundation data necessary to operate the business is located in the system database. These records are, for the most part, composed of two types of data. The first, *static data*, consists of core information elements, such as customer and supplier masters, item masters, product structures, product costing, warehouse geography, bills of material (BOMs) and process routings, manufacturing equipment, and channel structures that do not change during the performance of transactions. The second type, *variable data*, consists of databases, such as open order, transaction balance, and accounting that are impacted through transaction management. Today's computing technologies enable companies to have a single database (relational database) that all departments can use jointly. Furthermore, the advent of connectivity tools, like the Internet, provide the capability for *database networking*, where key database files such as forecasts, channel inventories, and open order status, can be viewed by users both external as well as internal to the company.

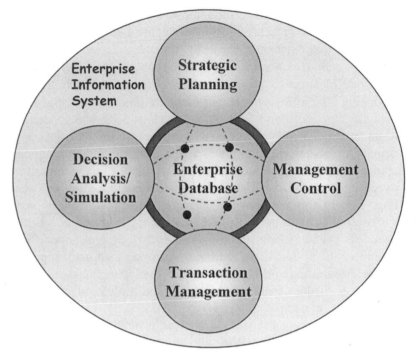

FIGURE 14.2 Enterprise system architecture.

- *Transaction management.* The transaction functions form the foundation applications of every EIS and consist of such activities as order
  entry, inventory balance maintenance, order selection, allocation and
  shipment, payables and receivables, and various data displays. Functions in this area served several purposes. They provide for the accurate and timely entry and collection of transaction data; they automate difficult and time-consuming record-keeping; they enforce rules
  governing transaction data entry and maintenance; and, they enable
  companies to collect large volumes of data that can in turn be used for
  business analysis, management control, and strategic planning. The
  overall goal of transaction management functions is to ensure an accurate record of the firm's day-to-day operations.

- *Management control.* The entry of transactions and the compilation of
  databases are meaningless without defined performance measurements
  to guide decision-making. Applications residing in this function focus
  on toolsets that permit analysts to "mine" enterprise databases in an effort to uncover and detail operational and financial measurements relating to such issues as cost, asset management, customer service, productivities, and quality. Management control has the following goals:
  provide the feedback necessary for the timely reformulation of oper-

ations plans and activities, on-going measurement of the competitive capability of the enterprise, and development of plans providing for continuous improvement.

- *Decision analysis/simulation.* A critical function of today's EIS is the ability of planners to utilize a variety of modeling tools to assist in managing simple to increasingly complex processes during decision-making. Some of these applications, such as MRP and capacity management, provide mature and easy-to-use tools to simulate the impact of demand on inventories and productive capacities. Other computerized applications assist in the identification, evaluation, and comparison between alternative courses of action, such vehicle routing and scheduling. Finally, this area also can consist of powerful *advanced planning systems* (APS) and *supply chain management* (SCM) systems driven by complex mathematical algorithms used to design supply chains, determine plant locations, and aggregate demand and supply data across channel networks. The goal of these functions is to provide planners with the capability to identify and evaluate the best choices from a range of competing alternatives.

- *Strategic planning.* The role of strategic planning functions is to provide managers with the capability to construct long-term plans and forecasts used to determine enterprise financial goals, explore strategic business partner alliances, design marketing approaches, and define and develop productive capacities necessary to support product and ser-vice requirements. The plans developed in this function provide the basis for management control, decision analysis, and performance, and are used to drive the operations plans executed by transaction func-tions. The overall goal of strategic planning functions is to provide the enterprise with competitive advantage.

While the exact structure of the applications used by today's EIS varies by industry, they must all provide the business with a common database, a suite of relevant transaction programs, some form of simulation, and data and functionality for on-going operations management and control as well as long-range planning.

Principles of System Management. Whether it be in the capture of historical data for forecasting or the utilization of inventory transaction balance records, an effective EIS requires databases of the highest integrity and processes easily understood by the user. The following seven principles of system management are fundamental to an effective EIS [3]:

- *Accountability.* While computers provide the functions for the entry and maintenance of data, the quality and integrity of that data resides squarely with the people who use the system and must ultimately be held responsible. Furthermore, while the system generates production schedules and order picking priorities, it is the planner who must be held accountable for approving the schedule. Without accountability, an EIS will quickly spin out of control and lose its ability to provide meaningful information for planning and decision making.

- *Transparency.* One of the fundamental keys to effective EIS architecture is that the logic of how the system works be simple, understandable, and apparent to the user. To the user, the complexity and sophistication of the technical architecture of the system is irrelevant. The issue is simply one of *understanding.* If the logic of a particular application is easy to work with and conforms to best practices, the system will be intelligently and competently used. Transparency means that the system provides the user with answers as to why and how the system requires a particular activity to be performed.

- *Accessibility.* One of fundamental problems of paper-based systems is that data is not readily accessible for decision-making. Effective computer systems remove the difficulties surrounding data retrieval by containing programs that provide for quick access and update of critical information, such as order status, that span company departments, geographical dispersion, or even databases belonging to trading partners.

- *Data integrity.* The usefulness of an EIS is directly dependent upon the accuracy and timeliness of its databases. *Accuracy* can be defined as the degree to which actual physical data matches up against the same data recorded in the system. As a metric, most data in an EIS should be at 99 percent. As the gap between the physical and the system data widens, companies are normally forced to increase inventory levels or safety stocks as a buffer against variance. *Timeliness* can be defined as the spatial delay between the moment a transaction occurs and the point in which it is recorded in the system. The speed of data update is critical in providing managers with current information to guide them in taking corrective action. Similar to accuracy, high levels of timeliness enable companies to remove uncertainties and increase the accuracy of decisions.

- *Valid simulation.* If an EIS is to provide useful information, the transactional and maintenance programs in the system must work the way the business actually works. In effect, a business application is in actuality a *representation,* a simulation of the actual physical action performed during process execution. For example, if the act of physically receiving a product to a location is not mirrored by the transaction entered in the application, data integrity is diminished and the ability of users to keep data records accurately decreases exponentially as invalid data cascade through the system.

- *Flexibility.* An effective EIS must provide the users with the capability to perform transactions or manipulate data to meet the needs of both the business and customers and suppliers out in the supply chain. For example, inventory allocation and shipping functions should permit customer and interbranch transfer orders to be created restricting delivery to a single receiving location or allowing multiple delivery points on a single order. In addition, the software itself should permit easy upgrade capabilities without causing the company undo cost or implementation time.

- *Control versus planning.* A fundamental benefit of an EIS is the ability to control business processes through management by exception. EIS applications provide managers with reporting and exception messaging designed to alert them as early as possible to actual or pending out of control processes. For example, a forecasting method should be able to recognize changes in basic patterns or relationships at an early stage and provide forecasters with warning alarms to take preemptive action. Such functionality is critical for effective planning, which assumes that existing patterns will continue into the future.

The basic architecture and principles of effective system management are fundamental to the establishment of an effective EIS. The basic architecture should contain programs for database management, transaction management, management control, decision analysis/simulation, and strategic planning. Actual operation of the EIS should encompass the seven critical principles of accountability, transparency, accessibility, data integrity, valid simulation, flexibility, and control versus planning.

CONFIGURING THE EIS SOLUTION

Effectively managing today's multi-faceted supply chain requires architecting enterprise solutions that facilitate the management of the linkages existing within the supply chain. The goal of the process is not to create a monolithic, rigid system, but rather to configure scalable, highly flexible information enablers that provide the business with the capability to respond with customized customer value solutions and collaborative relationships at all points in the supply channel network. The software solution that emerges should be able to effectively respond to the various levels of information management to be found within the supply chain. As will be discussed, there are three possible dimensions today's enterprise system must encompass. The first is concerned with solutions that integrate *internal* data and processes. The second is concerned with linking *external* parts of the company together. The third, and final, dimension examines technology tools that link external customers and suppliers to enterprise demand and supply planning functions.

ENTERPRISE INFORMATION SYSTEMS

The fundamental objective of an EIS is to extend the structure and benefits of computer integration and networking to encompass the entire enterprise. In practical terms, this means that not just a portion but all business functions, from purchasing and inventory control to forecasting and general ledger, are integrated together. The goal is to place all internal enterprise processing, decision-making, and performance measurement in a common database system capable of being maintained and referenced in real-time by all company users. The EIS itself is composed of two elements: the *hardware,* consisting of the computer, input/output devices, and data storage/warehousing, and the *software,* the application programs used for processing transactions, displaying the database, printing reports, management control, and operational and strategic planning.

Basic Architectural Issues. A fully integrated EIS enables companies to manage the business from two sets of interrelated activities. As illustrated in Figure 14.3 these activities can be described as *strategic planning* and *opera-*

FIGURE 14.3 Regions of basic EIS activities.

tions execution. The strategic planning area provides company management with the tools to translate strategic objectives into the functional level plans necessary to develop marketing and sales campaigns, construct the fulfillment channel, schedule production and materials acquisition, and identify financial and capacity constraints. The goal of the process is to integrate and synchronize information and plans within each business function and between the entirety of the enterprise. An EIS seeks to link not only homogeneous business areas, such as financials, but also heterogeneous business areas, such as sales, inventory, logistics, purchasing, and manufacturing into a common planning process. Finally, integrated strategic plans enable the effective execution, control, and performance measurement of detail operations activities and databases.

The operations execution functions found in an EIS are broadly grouped around the performance of the transactional activities necessary to generate orders, plan for finished goods acquisition, schedule production, ship product through the supply chain, purchase materials and components, manage costs, and post payables and receivables. There are several objectives pursued in this region. To begin with, it is the role of the EIS to provide for the integration and coordination of business activities driven by enterprise plans by providing process-specific application functionality that enable users to easily and consistently enter, maintain, and view system data. These tools should in turn reduce delays, errors, process redundancies, and bottlenecks and ensure operational flexibility and agility to respond to any circumstance. In addition, the functionality offered by the software provides each business area with new opportunities to engineer process optimization and to promote best practices internally across supply channels and externally with suppliers and customers. Finally, by creating a common community of users, each interdependent on the participation, knowledge, and information inputs found in the system, the enterprise as a whole can move to a higher level of coordination, service, and performance measurement.

The Standard EIS Architecture. As was mentioned at the beginning of this section, today's EIS must be capable of being configured to meet the information solution requirements of various types of players in the typical supply chain. In this section the most common EIS type found in every firm populating the typical supply chain - *applications to manage the internal functions of the firm* - is explored. A common software that has been applied by firms over several decades to manage their internal supply chain is *enterprise resource planning* (ERP). An illustration of the functions of the typical ERP system can be found in Figure 14.4. Depending on the nature of the business, an enterprise may utilize some or all of the applications. For example, the business system solution for a manufacturing company with distribution functions will utilize all of the applications. A wholesaler, on the other hand, will exclude the manufacturing related functions. Regardless of the business environment, every company will at least have to install marketing and sales planning, order management, financial, and asset applications. These core functions would be difficult to outsource without loosing corporate integrity.

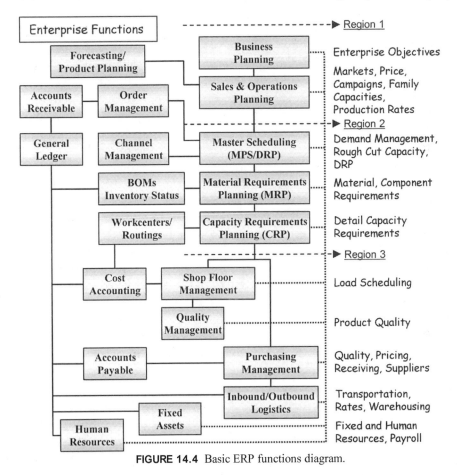

FIGURE 14.4 Basic ERP functions diagram.

The architecture of an EIS system attempts to integrate all of the information processes of the enterprise and use the resulting synergy of planning and control enabled by this integration to continuously improve performance to the customer as well as establish uniform policies and practices across the internal supply chain. An EIS system can be best understood by dividing Figure 14.4 into three regions. In *region 1* can be found applications used for the development and disaggregation of top management plans governing the overall direction of the enterprise, products and market programs, sales and promotions campaigns, and aggregate product family priority and resource capacity planning. *Region 2* is composed of applications for demand management encompassing forecasting finished goods, order management, order promising, and managing inter-company channel demand and inventory replenishment priority and capacity planning. In *region 3* can be found applications focused on operations execution activities such as purchasing, production activity control, transportation and shipping, fixed asset and human resource management, and financial accounting. A short description of these critical applications is as follows [4]:

- *Strategic planning.* Applications in this area provide corporate strategists with tools to develop the overall goals and objectives to be pursued by the enterprise. The output of these applications is focused on determining how the business is going to compete - product lines, financial investment and return, markets, research and development - in the future. Planning in this area begins with the utilization of detail transactional databases from marketing, finance, production, and distribution that in turn are used as the basis for long-range forecasting and decision making. The strategic business plan developed from the process is then used as a framework that determines the goals and objectives for marketing and sales, finance, engineering, production, and logistics departments. Each department translates the plan into their own set of performance objectives necessary to meet the corporate objectives. Finally, the ERP system provides the planning and control tools to ensure the performance of activities in support of departmental goals.

- *Sales and Operations Planning* (S&OP). The goal of application functions in this area is to build consensus teams in sales, operations, finance, and product development that enable the continuous revision of the business strategy and realignment of departmental plans. The process begins with marketing and sales, which are responsible for using the business system database to review the success of the sales plan, assess market potential, and forecast future demand. Plan revisions are then communicated to manufacturing, engineering, and finance who in turn must re-align their operations plans to meet the demands of the new marketing and sales plan.

- *Customer management.* The primary role of these applications is to enable quick and accurate order entry, order promising, and open order status maintenance. Order entry and on-going service maintenance is the gateway to the sales and marketing database. Second, this module should provide the data necessary to perform real-time profitability analysis to assist in calculating costs, revenues, and sales volumes necessary for effective quotation, on-going customer maintenance, and accounts receivable. Third, these applications should provide marketers with tools to design sophisticated pricing schemes and discount models. In addition, the software should permit the performance of miscellaneous functions such as order configuration, bonus and commissions, customer delivery schedules, global tax management, customer returns, and service and rental. Finally, the customer database should be robust enough to permit the generation of sales budgets for forecast management and the generation of statistical reporting illustrating everything from profitability to contributing margins analysis.

- *Inventory planning processes.* At the heart of the modern day EIS can be found the oldest applications of the system: the finished goods, component and raw materials, and distribution channel inventories planning tools. These modules contain functionality to enable the generation and maintenance of inventory database records and parameters, the efficient and timely replenishment of inventories, and inventory planning simulation. The *Master Production Schedule* (MPS) receives demand on finished goods from the production plan, forecasts, actual customer orders, and interbranch demand (DRP) and calculates the replenishment quantities necessary to maintain customer service levels. Once completed, this application sends finished goods requirements down to the *Material Requirements Planning* (MRP) by exploding product *bills of materials* (BOMs) where component and raw materials are then calculated to provide the company's plan for materials and product replenishment.

- *Capacity management.* Once EIS applications have generated the inventory priority plan, it must be reviewed in relation to the available capacities within the firm and outside in the supply channel to manage replenishment proposals. Capacity constraints can arise from a variety of sources including manufacturing capabilities, warehousing, transportation, and labor, and material handling equipment. The goal of the process is to identify process bottlenecks that could constrain the efficient production, storage, and movement of goods. Today's EIS provides planners with the capability to view plant and channel capacities that match aggregate, finished goods, and detail inventory priority plans. If priority and capacity plans are not found to be in balance at any planning level, planners must resolve the imbalance by resource acquisition, outsourcing, or postponement of production or delivery.

- *Manufacturing/Value-Added Processing.* Functions in this application comprise the activities determining manufacturing order release, daily order scheduling and synchronization, overall shop floor control, forms of value-added processing such as labeling and bulk breaking, and cost reporting. Included in these modules is functionality for activities such as inspection, project management, capacity/resource management, and the compilation of production statistics. Finally, advances in technology have enabled the enhancement of these applications with "bolt-on" data collection devices and advanced shop floor planning and optimizing software.

- *Procurement.* Once the materials plan has been authorized, it is the responsibility of purchasing applications to begin the task of acquiring all purchased components and raw materials. Basic management of procurement requires a close integration with internal MRP and *maintenance, repair, and operations supplies* (MRO) systems. Today's EIS contains robust functionality to facilitate purchase order processing, delivery scheduling, open order tracking, receiving, inspection, and supplier statistics and performance reporting. In addition, detailed *request for quotation* (RFQ) must be available that ties back to customer demands and extends out to supplier management, negotiation, and pricing capabilities. Finally, the system architecture must include *electronic data interchange* (EDI) and Internet-enabled capabilities.

- *Logistics.* The logistics applications in an EIS are concerned with coordinating transportation, warehousing, labor, and material handling equipment with the place and time requirements of sales, manufacturing, and inventory management. Today's EIS must provide the mechanism to run the internal supply chain of the business as well as provide the necessary connectivity to external trading partners located on the rim of the supply network. Perhaps the most critical goal of logistics applications is to ensure that overall supply chain requirements are integrated with both capacity constraints at the origins of the channel and with manufacturing, inventory, and delivery capabilities at the ends of the supply network. Critical tools in the module center on distribution channel configuration, warehouse activity management, channel replenishment planning and distribution order management, and the generation of distribution, asset, and profitability reporting. Also, of growing importance is the integration of EIS functions with "bolt-on" *warehouse* (WMS) and *transportation management systems* (TMS), as well as applications supporting Web-based customer and supply chain management systems.

- *Product data.* At the core of manufacturing and distribution information systems reside the databases describing the products that they build and distribute. Often considered highly proprietary, these databases contain information ranging from engineering descriptions to details concerning cost, suppliers, planning data, and product structure details.

Beyond their use for inventory and manufacturing planning and shop floor management, these databases are critical for product life cycle management analysis and costing, engineering product introduction, and financial reporting and analysis. As the speed of new product time-to-market and ever-shortening product life cycles accelerates, progressive companies have been looking to channel partners to implement collaborative technologies through the Internet that can network-in real-time *computer-aided design* (CAD) and design documentation in an effort to compress product development and introduction time, and facilitate the phase-out of obsolete products and services.

- *Finance.* Perhaps the most highly developed applications within an EIS are the suite of financial modules dealing with management accounting. In fact, one of the criticisms leveled at an EIS is that it is really an accounting system requiring everyone in the business to report in real-time each transaction performed with 100 percent accuracy. Today's financial applications provide for the reporting of all transaction information originating from inventory movement, accounts receivable, accounts payable, taxes, foreign currency, cost accounting, and journal entries occurring within the enterprise. The more timely and accurate the posting of data, the more effective are the output reports and budgets that can be used for financial analysis and decision-making at all levels in the business.

- *Assets.* Effective control of an enterprise's fixed assets is essential to ensuring the success of the continuous planning of the supply chain productive resources. EIS applications center on the establishment of equipment profiles, diagnostics and preventive maintenance activities, and financial tracking.

- *Human resources:* Finally, a modern EIS contains applications for the management of an enterprise's people resources. Functions in this area can be broken down into two main areas. The first is concerned with the performance of transaction activities, such as time and attendance reporting, payroll administration, compensation, reimbursable expenses, and recruitment. The second is focused on the creation of databases necessary to support employee profiles, skills and career planning, and employee evaluations and productivity statistics.

EIS Benefits. The applications and management processes constituting an EIS are universal for any type of manufacturer or distributor and truly can be said to be the "backbone" of today's business system. As a planning and control mechanism, an EIS enables whole enterprises to organize, codify, and standardize business processes and data. Achieving such objectives in turn permits strategists and planners to optimize the business's *internal* value chain by integrating all aspects of the business, from purchasing and inventory management to sales and financial accounting. In addition, by providing a common database and the capability to integrate transaction management processes, data is made instantaneously available across business functions, enabling the visibility necessary for effective planning and decision making, while simultaneously eliminating redundant or alternative information management systems and reducing non-value-added tasks.

EIS at Behr Climate Systems Inc.

When Behr Climate Systems, Inc., a supplier of automotive parts started their technology search by looking at a partial solution to integrate customer service, forecasting, and DRP. It quickly became apparent that to attain the level of performance desired, what was needs was an EIS approach that also encompassed financial, distribution, and warehousing into a single comprehensive system.

The implementation of a major EIS solution enabled Behr to realize immediate results due to automation. Table-driven put-away and picking rules significantly assisted warehouse control. In customer service, the system streamlined order promising, parts availability, and fulfillment. All these functions, in turn, sent real-time data to the financial applications.

The real advantage of the EIS, however, was Behr's ability to significantly increase the entire flow of business as it passed through the company. Altogether the EIS is enabling Behr to accomplish the original goals of increase customer service and improved ROI while providing new avenues to total quality management and superior marketplace advantage.

Source: Brooks, Harold, "Computer Overhaul Improves the Warehouse System," *APICS-The Performance Advantage,* 4, 4, 1994, pp. 29-30.

An EIS provides other benefits. As companies grapple with managing continuous change to products, processes, and infrastructure, strategists are looking to the suite of "best practice" process designs embedded in today's EBS business functional work flows to assist in the removal of ill-defined or obsolete processes and the structuring of "best in class" processes by building them around the capabilities of EIS applications. Finally, as enterprises evolve to meet new challenges, companies with standardized processes driven by an EIS are more adaptable to change. A single, logically structured, and common information system platform is far easier to adapt to changing circumstances than a hodge-podge of systems with complex interfaces linking them together.

EIS ARCHITECTURE FOR DISTRIBUTION INDUSTRIES

One of the most crucial aspects of an EIS is its ability to adapt to different supply chain environments. The applications and processes detailed in the previous section can aptly be described as constituting an ERP system primarily used to run the *internal* functions of manufacturing companies. In this section the architecture of an EIS for running an enterprise with *external* functions will be examined. Termed *Distribution Resource Planning* (DRP II) [5], such as system is defined as a

> computer assisted management philosophy for planning the utilization of the totality of a distribution enterprise's resources, while providing for the execution and performance measurement of material procurement, supply chain distribution, and financial accounting to fulfill strategic business requirements for customer service and marketplace leadership.

The DRP II system function flow is illustrated in Figure 14.5.

This model illustrates the integrative, interactive, and closed-loop nature of the typical activities occurring within a distribution enterprise. Similar to the general ERP model detailed in the previous section, DRP II presents a systemic approach. The flow of information begins with business planning functions and proceeds through operations and financial execution and concludes with performance measurement. Besides providing a systems approach to directing and measuring the entire enterprise, from internal functions to the management of supply channels, DRP II provides a solution to the following problems plaguing the distributor:

1. DRP II permits the creation of business plans addressing the strategic decisions defining enterprise mission, market demand, and the allocation of financial, physical assets, and human resources, and then provides the mechanism to disaggregate those plans through *logistics resource planning* (supply chain capacity) and *inventory planning* (*distribution requirements planning* – DRP). The goal is the generation of time-phased plans where the demands of the entire supply chain are balanced against inventory, value-added processing, logistics, and purchasing capabilities.

2. DRP II provides distributors with the capability to be agile and flexible enough to respond to the many changes occurring in the business environment by providing visibility to customer demand and real-time status of the supply chain. Change in market demand, supplier delivery

problems, excess inventories, inventory imbalances within the channel network, marketing promotions, and a host of other events are made visible along with the mechanism to adjust and reallocate critical resources.

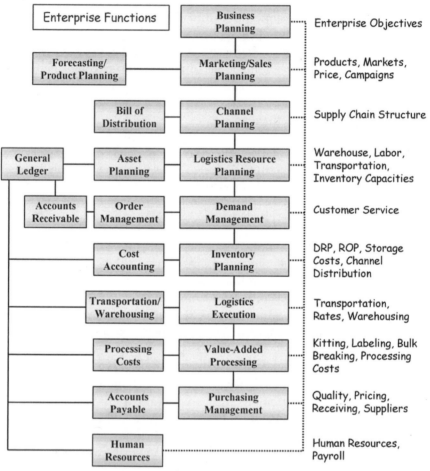

FIGURE 14.5 Distribution enterprise system diagram.

3. By applying the time-phased logic of MRP and the ability to structure an integrated channel planning mechanism through the *bill of distribution* (BOD), DRP II provides planners with a detailed workbench to keep channel inventories low and evenly distributed to meet the demands placed on each channel node, while providing the tools to resupply the supply chain as efficiently and cost effectively as possible. DRP II also enables the design of performance measurement programs

that look beyond local agendas to how well each channel segment is supporting the overall business plan.

4. Finally, when integrated with today's newest supply chain event management and collaborative forecasting and planning toolsets, DRP II provides a catalyst for the application of Internet-based technologies and Lean/JIT principles targeted at removing barriers to time and space as well as to quality and excellence.

DRP II offers wholesalers and distributors a fresh approach to running the supply chain that is fully compatible with today's newest Web-based technologies. Both as a management philosophy and as a suite of integrated business applications, DRP II permits distribution companies to synchronize demand and supply up and down the channel network and link their planning systems with the EIS functions of customers, suppliers, manufacturers, and retailers. Such approaches enable entire supply chains to compete as if they were a single, seamless entity focused on cost reduction and superior customer service.

EIS CONNECTIVITY TOOLS IN THE AGE OF e-BUSINESS

While the various forms of today's EIS provide manufacturers and distributors with effective technology tools for the management of the internal and external functions within the enterprise, the third dimension of information technology, the application of connectivity technologies, is providing companies with the ability to link in real-time demand and supply functions directly with customers and suppliers. In the past, even the most technology savvy company was constrained by the inability of computerized applications to connect and synchronize the vital information passing between customer and suppliers out in the business network. Even simple data components, like inventory balances or forecasts, were communicated with great difficulty to sister warehouses or divisions, let alone to trading partners whose databases resided beyond the barriers of their own information systems.

Electronic Data Interchange (EDI). The first major technology breakthrough was the use of EDI to enable the company-to-company transmission of data. EDI constitutes today's most widely used method of supply chain connectivity. EDI provides for the electronic transmission of such critical supply chain transactions as planning information, customer orders, invoices, shipping notices, and payment. Architecturally, EDI is an *extranet* application consisting of a computer-to-computer linkage whereby information driven by a mutually agreed upon set of data transfer standards is transmitted between trading partners via private *value-added networks* (VANs). A critical advantage of EDI is that the technology permits electronic data transfer between transacting companies that are using EISs running on different software systems and hardware. The EDI standards function like a "translator" the enable disparate systems to "talk to each other."

The importance of the use of EDI as a technology that enables companies to escape from the barriers of their internal EIS solution can be seen in its various benefits [6]:

- *Increased communications and networking.* By enabling channel partners to transmit and receive up-to-date information regarding network business processes electronically, the entire supply chain can begin to leverage the productivities to be found in information networking.
- *Streamlining business transactions.* By eliminating paperwork and maintenance redundancies, EDI can significantly shrink cycle times in a wide spectrum of transaction processing activities.
- *Increased accuracy.* Because transactions are transferred directly from computer-to-computer, the errors that normally occur as data is manually transferred from business to business are virtually eliminated.
- *Reduction in channel information processing.* EDI provides for the removal of duplication of effort and acceleration of information flows that can significantly reduce time and cost between supply channel partners.
- *Increased response.* EDI enables channel members to shrink processsing times for customer and supplier orders and provide for timely information that can be used to update planning schedules throughout the channel.
- *Increased competitive advantage.* EDI enables the entire supply network to shrink pipeline inventories, reduce capital expenditure, improve on return on investment, and actualize continuous improvements in customer service.

While providing obvious benefits, there are, however, some serious drawbacks to EDI. To begin with, the technology is expensive and time-consuming to implement. Companies must agree upon the use of a transmission standard, often in itself a daunting task. Next, companies will have to shoulder the cost for hardware and software, and then they must begin the process of data-mapping and architecture design. Once in place, companies must then be prepared to pay for recurring costs associated with on-going modifications and upgrades to hardware and software. In addition to the costs, there are serious deficiencies in the capability of EDI to support real-time information processing. EDI works by transmitting whole packages of information, versus a continuous data stream, that may often take several days for transmission, translation, and receipt from one trading partner to another. While it enables partners to improve on transactional elements, its high costs and proprietary nature render it a poor channel planning tool.

Rise of Internet Connectivity. By the late 1990's a new technology tool, the Internet, had begun to fully emerge with the potential to achieve the level of information connectivity necessary to link supply chains anywhere, at any time on the globe. Fueled by the explosion in personal computer (PC) ownership, advancements in communications technologies, and the declining cost of computer hardware and software, companies quickly became aware of a new information integration medium that would sweep away the previous limitations governing the flow of supply chain products and data. The rise of modern information system connectivity is portrayed in Figure 14.6 and is briefly described below [7].

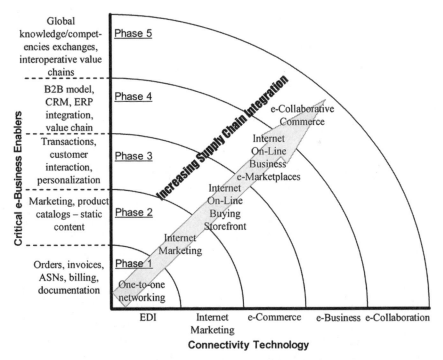

FIGURE 14.6 Phases of Web-enabled e-business.

- *Phase 1: EDI.* The application of the Internet to EDI has enabled a resurrection of traditional EDI, extending its capabilities through the application of Web-based technologies that increase automation and efficiency while augmenting its benefits and overcoming its shortcomings. Simply, Web-based EDI can be defined as using the Internet instead of VANs to send transactions accessed by the receiver using a

PC and browser. There are several advantages. First, using the Internet is a much cheaper technology alterative to implement and maintain. Second, the use of *extensible markup language* (XML) cuts transaction costs by enabling parties to connect directly without VANs, which require both parties to pay for each communication. Third, since tools like Java enable Internet applications to be reusable, Web-based EDI possesses virtually unlimited scalability. Fourth, Web-based EDI is more flexible and easily adapted to different business models and system infrastructures. Fifth, the Web enables the structuring of a centralized many-to-many point of contact that facilitates supply chain collaboration and provides the basis for the creation of new forms of channel models, such as vertical marketplaces and trade networks. While the immaturity of XML standards at this point in time guarantee the use of EDI for the immediate future, it is destined to die as new Internet technologies evolve that yield capabilities and levels of efficiencies beyond their current scope [8].

- *Phase 2: Internet Marketing.* The first pure use of the Internet for business purposes occurred in the early to mid-1990s and took the form of using the Web as a source for marketing products, services, and company stories. In the past, businesses were forced to utilize expensive advertising, printed matter such as catalogs and brochures, trade shows, industry registers, promotions, and direct sales that represented a *physical* and passive approach to marketing. The application of the Internet revolutionized this concept of marketing. Internet marketing enables marketers to place information about their companies on the Web where they can be easily searched for and accessed *actively* by prospects anywhere, at anytime around the world utilizing relatively simple Internet-based multimedia browsing functions. Today it would be hard to find a company, both large and small, that does not have an Internet marketing site.

- *Phase 3: e-Commerce.* While Internet marketing sites provide information about company products and marketing strategies, they were never designed to allow browsers to actually order products and services through the Web site. During the mid- to late-1990s, a new type of Internet site began to emerge - the pure-play Internet storefront or (B2C) - designed specifically to sell and service customers on-line. By the end of the decade, on-line e-tailers like Amazon.com, eBay, and Priceline.com were offering Web sites that combined Internet marketing, on-line catalogs, and advertising with order management functions, such as site personalization, self-service, interactive shopping carts, and credit card payment, that provided actual on-line shopping. While the rise and fall of the dot-com mania severely injured the budding industry and exposed its weaknesses, the pure B2C trading exchange has provided a virtual revolution in customer-supplier connectivity by combining ease of shopping via personal PC with an immediacy, capability for self-service, access to a potentially limitless repository of goods and services, and information far beyond the capacities of traditional business models.

- *Phase 4: e-Business.* By the year 2000, a new Internet approach that sought to utilize the interactive and integrative power of the Web to connect companies began to emerge. The differences between e-commerce and e-business are pointed. To begin with e-business is focused on using the Web to construct e-marketplaces for transactions between businesses (B2B). Second, the business relationship established is different. Instead of a focus on the consumer and creating brand (Internet site) loyalty, B2B resembles traditional purchasing in that the goal is to use the Web to generate long-term, symbiotic, collaborative relations between businesses through the deployment of real-time connectivity. B2B relationships can be divided into three types: *independent trading exchanges* (ITX) composed of buyers and sellers networked through an independent intermediary focused on spot purchasing; *private trading exchanges* (PTX) defined as a single trading community hosted by a single company that requires collaborative membership as a condition of doing business; and *consortia trading exchanges* (CTX) whereby a few powerful companies organized into a consortium establish a trading group consisting of the collective supplier base.

- *Phase 5: e-Collaboration.* For the most part, the e-business solutions that have arisen around the turn of the twenty-first century have been primarily focused on facilitating the flow of information and transactions across the supply chain. In contrast, e-collaboration attempts to extend the capabilities of the Internet to closely network customers, information, core competencies, and people, process, and inventory resources. In place of the traditional linear supply chain, e-collaboration calls for the generation of *value webs* described as any-to-any connections that can drive procurement webs, manufacturing webs, and even linked business strategies. The goal is the architecting of real-time, integrated Web-based connectivity that permits supply chain members to share their planning systems and core competencies directly wherever they are located on the globe.

While the bursting of the dot-com bubble has tempered the once unbridled enthusiasm for e-business, beneath the hype and misunderstandings there are a lot of benefits companies can take directly to the bottom line. The range of benefits can be detailed as

- Increased choices for customers, larger markets, and better prices
- Increased order processing, purchasing, and selling efficiencies
- New forms of customer service customization
- Radically new concepts of market segmentation that seek to match product and service value to specific customers
- Increased collaboration among buyers and suppliers integrating product design, forecasting and planning, marketing campaigns, and product life-cycle management programs
- Generation of synchronized supply chains where total channel demand and supply information can be driven simultaneously across the entire value chain resulting in increased inventory turnover, faster product introduction, lower channel WIP, and lower total channel costs.

While the capabilities of e-collaboration are limited by the scope of today's technologies, there can be little doubt that future e-businesses will possesses tools to effect closer integration and synchronization of value producing resources.

INFORMATION TECHNOLOGY SOLUTIONS

The deployment of JIT/Lean, *quick response* (QR), and Internet-enabled applications to manage supply chains, coupled with the explosion in computerized tools, have provided companies with an array of organizational and information technology choices targeted at increasing supply channel productivity and serviceability while reducing total costs. The ability to properly align information technology and new performance objectives requires strategists to closely match channel management goals with the capabilities of the technologies available. In weighing the decision to acquire new technology, strategists must find answers to such questions as the following:

- What is the nature of the *internal* and *external* information requirements of the enterprise necessitating a change in the manner by which information is currently processed?
- Is the decision to expand information capacities governed by a desire to automate or to activate and empower the whole enterprise?
- Of the many business areas, where should technologies be applied first, and which areas will provide the largest competitive boost for the expense?
- What impact will the implementation of new information technology have on the customer service, logistics, and financial functions of the current organization?
- What will the implementation of new technology cost in terms of resources and operational trauma to the existing organization?

- How is new technology to be integrated with legacy systems?
- What new resources will be required to operate the new technology?
- What new opportunities for competitive advantage will be available to the enterprise?

In responding to these and other questions, strategists must first thoroughly understand the scope and nature of the possible technical solutions available before deciding on the proper solution.

UPS Goes Wire-Free

United Parcel Service Inc. plans to invest in wireless technology for its 1,700 hubs worldwide, including its new $1 billion Worldport air transportation hub at Louisville International Airport in Kentucky, where 304,000 packages are sorted per hour. In June 2003, UPS will start a $20 million project to replace wired scanners, used to record package-tracking data, withy 55,000 devices from Symbol Technologies Inc. that use Bluetooth wireless technology. Smaller hubs will get the devices first, UPS manager Donna Barrett says, so UPS can work out any kinks before deploying the technology at Worldport. The current technology is cumbersome and the wires often break, the carrier says, adding that wireless technology is now mature enough to handle UPS's huge workload.

IDENTIFYING INFORMATION SYSTEM SOLUTIONS

Enterprises seek to acquire information technology to solve a broad range of opportunities for improvement. Most problems experienced by companies are universal and can be found at the core of productivity and performance deficiencies in just about any business system. The requirements are familiar:

- Faster customer order turnaround time
- Continuous reduction in inventories and carrying costs
- Increased information accuracy
- Better equipment utilization and reduced labor costs
- Reduction in transportation costs
- Closer integration of business functions
- Reduction in capital investment
- Closer integration with supply chain partners

Doubtlessly this list could be expanded to cover the myriad of other problems that contribute to rising customer complaints, shrinking profit margins, and loss of business to competitors.

While the implementation of information systems can assist companies solve a host of operational impediments to productivity, it also holds out opportunities for strategic advantage. Several key enablers come to mind.

1. *Lowering cost and improving productivity.* As stated above, information technologies can lower costs and improve productivities in any part of the value chain. Historically, technology has always been applied to reduce the cost of activities subject to repetitive information processing. The advent of networking technologies, however, has empowered technologists to not only search for cost and productivity drivers through activity automation, but also to expand the information content of the activities themselves. In this sense, information systems cannot only help a company function more effectively, it can also exploit advantages in competitive scope.

   This dynamic can perhaps best be seen by contrasting operations in a manual or batch-oriented warehouse and the opportunities offered by a real-time integrated processing system. In a batch environment, customer order processing generates orders which are passed to the warehouse for picking and shipping. Normally, orders arrive with little logic as to how they are to be picked or consolidated. In addition, because receiving and order promising are not integrated, stock could be temporarily located on the dock or in staging areas waiting put-away and is unavailable for order fulfillment. In contrast to this chaos, a warehouse possessed of an integrated, real-time system would have portable terminals that communicate with the central computer via radio frequency. Orders would be released to warehouse pickers based on such criteria as the shipping departure time of the carrier transporting the product to the customer, classification by order quantity or dollar size, and the availability of picking and packing resources. Productivity can be astounding. One company that possesses four distribution centers and processes between 1800 and 2700 orders daily has reported that real-time warehouse tools permit the company to ship 96% of its orders by noon, and every rush order by 3 P.M. Shipping accuracy has approached zero-percent defects, while receiving to put-away time has been reduced by 12 hours [9].

2. *Enhancing strategic differentiation.* Information technology has the power to leverage cost, differentiation, and focus strategies focused on a company's products. By shortening the order processing and delivery cycle and providing customers the ability to customize their product requirements while reducing lead times and increasing the speed of information transfer through EDI or Web functions, companies can improve product positioning. For example, a Fortune 500 manufacturer needed to get inventory to meet customer requirements from its domestic and

foreign warehouses when and where it was needed. The implementation of a logistics system enabled the company to achieve a single delivery solution through an in-transit merge program. Information on the sales order is sent electronically to the system, which, in turn, allocates specified products from different locations as they are ready, "merging" the sales order for delivery at the point closest to the final delivery destination [10]. Technologies can also enhance the performance of value-added services such as inside delivery, installation, kitting, and crating that increase marketplace differentiation.

3. *Broadening competitive scope.* The effective implementation of enabling technologies can also provide the enterprise with an opportunity to broaden the competitive scope of operations and, by extension, alter the reach of competitive advantage. Besides increasing the ability to coordinate activities on a global scope, technologies can assist a company to penetrate new markets and offer value-added services beyond former capabilities. Consider Dell Computer's distribution strategy. By selling to customers directly, building to order rather than to inventory, and integrating its logistics functions with its suppliers, Dell has been able to revolutionize the way PCs are made, marketed, and financed. Dell's competitive advantage rests on an organizational culture that optimizes and streamlines operations and management systems driven by integration, reliability, and high-speed transactions.

EVALUATING INFORMATION TECHNOLOGY SOLUTIONS

While technology can provide the enterprise with the ability to achieve order-of-magnitude breakthroughs in productivity and competitiveness, strategists must be careful to match technology solutions and business scope. Perhaps the first action to be undertaken is identifying clearly the scope of the business problems to be solved. This step will significantly narrow the range of possible solutions. An effective requirements definition will greatly assist companies to avoid critical errors, such as buying technology that is overkill, does not address the critical issues, or narrows future technology options because of hardware or software enhancement limitations. In addition, the requirements definition will determine whether the company wishes to merely automate activities that are currently being done manually or open networking capabilities to a group of business functions or to the whole enterprise. This determination is critical. The cost and impact on the organization to automate activities is significantly less than it is to integrate business functions. The following five steps can assist enterprises in leveraging the range of technology solutions for competitive advantage [11].

1. *Assess information intensity.* Before a solution can be effectively chosen, companies must evaluate the existing and potential information intensity of its products and operations processes. The objective is to determine the *breadth* of the information required both to run the supply chain and manage product and service processes. The former includes the number of customers and suppliers in the channel, scope of marketing and selling information, number of product variations and depth of product variety, and length of cycle times. The latter includes product related issues such as complexity, requirements for buyer knowledge and training, and the ability of the product to service alternative uses. Technology solutions should enable the enterprise to leverage product and process information content to achieve marketplace leadership.

2. *Industry impact.* Companies must closely examine the impact of the introduction of new technologies on marketplace competitive forces. Technology can dramatically alter a firm's bargaining power with suppliers, ability to offer new products and substitute products, and capability to fight off new as well as existing competitors. Effective technology strategies can enable a company to seize marketplace leadership and force competitors to follow. Costco, the chain of warehouse club stores, uses its information systems to track product movement to ensure that new products are integrated with successful existing lines to provide customers with the assortments they want. These data also drive stocking decisions that optimize floor space usage.

3. *Search for ways technology can increase competitive advantage.* By targeting activities that represent a large proportion of supply chain costs, are critical to marketplace differentiation, or compose critical links internally and externally within the supply channel, technology can assist companies to identify new avenues for sustainable competitive advantage. In addition, technology provides the opportunity for strategists to explore changes in competitive scope. Does the solution permit the enterprise to enter new market segments or invade the preserve of strong niche players? Will the solution enable the company to compete globally or to exploit interrelationships with other industries?

4. *Investigate how technologies can spawn new industries.* Information tools can spawn new businesses by diversifying existing organizations. Can a company's technologies provide sources of information or processing capabilities that can be sold? Does the solution enable the development of ancillary products that complement existing product lines? Take, for example, North American Van Lines who has created

an information services and logistics software business that is complimentary to their traditional product and services strategy.

5. *Develop a long-term plan that seeks to continuously leverage new information technologies.* Strategists must be diligent in instituting a formal methodology for the on-going review of new technologies, the strategic alignment of business opportunities and new technology toolsets, the investments necessary to implement new hardware and software, and the impact technologies will have on supply chain linkages. Successfully enhancing competitive positioning can no longer occur simply by entrusting the exploration of new information technologies to the firm's *chief information officer* (CIO). Tomorrow's successful companies will require the participation of all functional levels both within the organization and outside in the partner channel if business technologies tools are to be effectively utilized.

A possible method that can be used to match business information needs and available technologies is to chart out the critical relationships between the level of business functionality and the scope of planning and control information desired. Such a chart can be found in Figure 14.7. Along the verti-

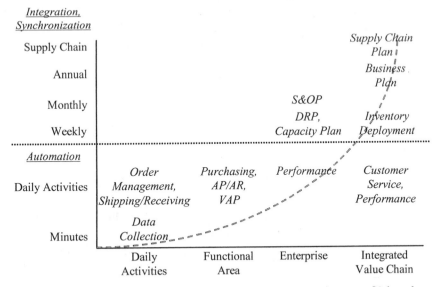

FIGURE 14.7 Charting business and technology solution requirements. [Adapted from Ref. 12]

cal axis can be found the type of information processing required. On the lower end of the scale can be found information that is transaction based, such as order entry or accounts receivable, and occurs in the immediate time frame. As the vertical axis is ascended, information requirements move more into the realm of planning and control, concluding with strategic channel planning. Correspondingly, the information time frame moves from the short term to the long term. The horizontal axis details the level of business function, beginning with technologies seeking to automate and accelerate the processing of daily activities and progressing through functional area, enterprise, and integrated supply chain information management needs. The curve in the diagram represents the relative cost and time required to implement targeted technologies.

MAKING TECHNOLOGY CHOICES

In this section, three possible technology solution choices will be examined. The first examines the application of technology to automate business activities targeted at increasing speed and accuracy. The second examines the application of technology to integrate a group of homogeneous business areas. Finally, the third examines the requirements and ramifications of integrating the entire enterprise with the implementation of a full EIS.

Automation. The idea of applying tools that ease or facilitate work has been in existence since ancient times. Aristotle in his *Politics* dreamed of a world where work could be performed by the object itself on command or in intelligent anticipation. However, the removal of physical drudgery is not the only reason for automation. When human skills are applied to highly repetitive tasks or activities that require a great deal of precision, variation in output quality is inevitable. Automation attempts to solve this problem by substituting technology for humans to perform the work. Machines never tire, are unimpeded by personal concerns, and will faithfully execute their tasks according to their designs. Although it is true that machines suffer from a lack of flexibility and cannot exceed the boundaries of their capabilities, work flows can be redesigned that optimize their functionality. Overall, the decision to implement computer software targeted at automation represents a *tactical* move to either gain additional productivity and quality or to cut the cost of an operation in a workflow process.

An example of the application of the principle of automation can be found in the decision of the Burnham Corporation, a leading manufacturer and supplier of hot water and steam boilers, to install a PC-based item and order verification system. Because of the length of the sales cycle involved, price of the product, and cost of transportation, the company needed a way to reduce or eliminate misshipments and incomplete orders. The company normally processes over 2500 orders yearly, ranging from orders as large as 200 boilers to small replacement parts. In the past, orders had to be pulled, staged, and serial numbers painstakingly recorded before loading. Today, customer orders are downloaded from the company business system into the PC verification system. The PC system, in turn, generates picking lists and bar codes. Picker teams, equipped with handheld radio-frequency (RF) scanners, then scan their own bar-coded badges and the bar-coded order number on the pick list. As each product is picked, it is scanned and loaded. When the loading is complete, the system closes out the order file on the PC and signals the shipping clerk that a final bill of lading can be printed for the freight carrier [13].

The implementation of information technology to automate an activity or group of activities is a fairly straightforward process. The objectives, benefits, and payback period of the project are relatively easy to calculate; so are costs, such as equipment, training, maintenance, and supplies. What was required at Burnham was expenditure for the PC and RF equipment, programming to interface the company's business system and PCs, and a little training. In addition, the impact on business operations was localized in the company's picking and shipping departments.

Partial System Integration. The application of the next level of information technology involves *integrating* a homogenous group of business functions. This level of information technology is significantly more complex than simply automating activities and is designed to propel a targeted group of contiguous business functions and operations onto a new plane of performance. In this sense the application of technology focused on a partial business functional integration is both a tactical decision intended to increase operational productivity and a strategic decision centered on the search for competitive advantage. The functionality of the software will not only increase productivity and/or eliminate the cost of an operation, but it also will provide the business areas affected with the opportunity to change and improve the entire process. By integrating functions, the software will provide users with the ability to link information together to provide new levels of performance and productivity.

Several points need to be discussed at this juncture. Although accelerating the performance of an operation, automation will not significantly impact the performance of a business process as a whole. For example, whereas EDI will enable customers to transmit order information faster, unless the entire organization can respond at the same speed, the customer will most likely not experience any significant decrease in delivery time. Although it is true a targeted business function will enjoy varying levels of increased productivity as a result of automation, the real objective of implementing an integrative technology is to provide a mechanism whereby functions along an information chain can perform not only one particular operation of an activity better but the entirety of the activity better, as well as other activities that intersect it.

This integration of activities enhances connectivity and synchronization, whereby the level of performance of one activity drives information automatically into and increases the level of performance of other activities. Automation provides a business function with the ability to leverage technology to achieve incremental improvements to operations; integration, on the other hand, enables order-of-magnitude breakthroughs in the processes by which the company does business.

An excellent example of partial systems integration is the implementation of applications targeted at computerizing a firm's financial functions. As illustrated in Figure 14.8, the functions to be implemented are general ledger,

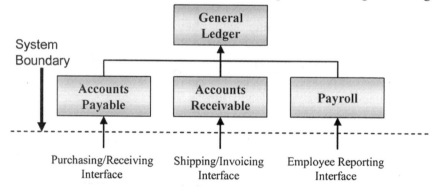

FIGURE 14.8 Financial system implementation.

accounts receivable, accounts payable, and payroll. Architecturally, the four modules are linked together by interactive programs and a common database. Receivables, payables, and payroll information outputs, for instance, are driven directly into the general ledger module. Inputs into receivables, payables, and payroll come from activities occurring in their respective downstream functions. The difference between the information that flows into the general ledger and the information that flows into receivables, payables, and payroll is that the former is *integrated*, whereas the latter is *interfaced*. For example, by running a processor summary account information from receivables will automatically update account values in the general ledger. In contrast, purchasing/receiving information will have to be manually keyed or loaded through a programmed interface into payables.

The benefits of a partially integrated system occur on two levels. In the first, business functions can leverage computer functionality to automate activities. For example, payables personnel can automatically generate checks for supplier payment, review the current payables aging report, check on open account statuses, perform check reconciliation, and execute other functions. The degree of the benefit of the automation depends on the level of a business function's dependence on manual processes. The real value of the system, however, can be found in the ability of the organization to integrate information both within the function (i.e. payables, receivables, etc.), and among the business areas constituting the information system. Instead of a fragmented set of business functions, each bounded by the constraints under which each operates, an integrated system brings individuals and functions together by putting each in touch cross-functionally, by activating and linking together creative thinking within and between people and functions to respond to whole challenges and opportunities. A partially integrated computer solution will provide those business functions involved with the capability to act and make decisions, not as separate entities but as a networked group with a common set of goals and measurements, drawn together by common data and requirements for interactive participation.

The selection and implementation of a partial systems integration project is significantly more difficult that an automation project. To begin with, the benefit and payback period are more difficult to calculate. Because the real benefits arising from the technology are to be achieved from the integration of information and functions, performance metrics are more difficult to establish and measure. Second, because the technology will in some cases dramatically change the way employees have traditionally performed their jobs, the costs associated with conceptual as well as functional training, current operations diagnostics, database loading, systems testing, and policy and procedural development will be high, as much as 50-100 percent or more of the original hardware and software purchase cost. In addition, a high level of disruption in operational productivity and performance is likely to occur during the implementation life cycle. Finally, because a number of the inputs necessary to feed the system will come from areas outside of the system, signifycant attention must be paid to interfacing outside manual or automated business functions.

Business System Integration. The most complex application of information technology is to extend the structure and benefits of business system technology to encompass the entire enterprise. In practical terms, this means that not just a portion but all of the functions of the business, from purchasing and inventory control to forecasting and general ledger, are integrated into a single EIS. The goal is to place enterprise processing and decision-making in a common database that is shared by all users. As such, implementation of an EIS represents a strategic decision on the part of management to provide the enterprise with the potential to catapult the entire organization onto new planes of competitive advantage made possible by a fundamental change in the speed and accuracy by which information in the organization is assembled, processed, and disseminated. A possible schematic of an EIS can be seen in Figure 14.4.

Similar to a partial system implementation, the benefits of a fully integrated EIS occur on two levels. The functionality offered by the software provides each business area with new opportunities to streamline workloads and eliminate wastes and redundancies in information processing through automation. However, the real benefit of the system is found in the utilization of integrated information both within each function and between the entirety of the enterprise. An EIS seeks to link not only homogeneous business areas together, such as financials, but also heterogeneous business areas, such as inventory, sales order, purchasing, and value-added processing. Finally, by creating a common community of users, each interdependent on the participation, knowledge, and information inputs found in the system, the enterprise as a whole can move to a higher level of coordination, service, and performance measurement.

By extending the information system to the whole organization, the selection and implementation of the software becomes exponentially more difficult and contains enormous risks as compared to a partially integrated solution. Besides the cost of the hardware, software, and equipment, the demands placed on the user community during a full business system implementation can be overwhelming. In a partial implementation, normally a horizontally organized group of business functions, such as the financials, are involved. The operating principles and user skills and knowledge represent a fairly focused and homogeneous group that can be readily retrained and quickly oriented to the new system. A full business system implementation, on the other hand, requires training and integrating functions that run *vertically* through the organization. Problems arise when conflicting business area objectives, levels of education and training, and variances in the current level of functional automation must be elevated to a common plane so that the software can link the actions and goals of each area cross-functionally. In addition, the length of most implementations, extending normally a year or longer, can significantly drain the enthusiasm of the user community, divert critical resources, and disrupt the pursuit of other corporate strategic objectives.

IMPLEMENTATION ISSUES

The decision to undertake the implementation of information technology is a critical one for the organization. Whether it is automation, partial system, or full EIS, success depends on thorough planning, design, and commitment from all enterprise professionals from the president to the loading docks. According to Walton [14], there are three fundamental processes essential to the success of any information technology project:

- *Alignment.* This process is concerned with the ongoing alignment of enterprise business, organizational, and technology strategies during the course of the implementation. As the implementation moves successively through each part of the implementation life cycle, the alignment process must focus on developing and sustaining a management context where technology, business, organizational, and operational strategies are kept in alignment.
- *User commitment and ownership.* This process has two closely interwoven themes. The first is establishing and developing a strong sense of commitment on the part of users and management to the system. The second is nurturing a sense of system ownership. Without the existence of these two conditions, an implementation will never achieve the expected improvements nor will it provide the stimulant for the organizational change necessary to engineer fundamental improvement in operational processes.
- *User competence and mastery.* Implementation objectives are met when users utilize the system to create higher levels of operational competencies that permit the broadening and deepening of enterprise capabilities. An acceleration of information flows requires management to continuously reinvestigate and realign original business, operational, and technology strategies that more closely mirror competitive advantages.

Lack of development in any one of the three processes is fatal to the realization of information system potential. Without proper alignment efforts focused on commitment and system mastery, the new system will be misdirected and still-born. Without a sense of full enterprise commitment, system mastery will always lag behind strategic objectives. Finally, without system mastery users will never realize full system potential.

PART 1: ALIGNING INFORMATION TECHNOLOGY AND COMPANY STRATEGIES

The starting point for any information technology project is to, in effect, unfold a broad vision of the *goals* to be pursued and how the integration of technology and organizational strategies will assist in the pursuit of those goals. It is critical, therefore, that before a technology solution search begins, top management clearly articulates a comprehensive strategy to align the enterprise business vision, organizational goals and values, and information systems. The objective is to activate thinking among the management team concerning the development and communication of a coherent strategy detailing the expectations and anticipated opportunities. This strategy should include such elements as a clear definition of enterprise strategic priorities, organizational structure and values, operational implications, and appropriateness of the proposed system to the culture and objectives of the firm.

Perhaps the most difficult task at this juncture is defining business objectives to be achieved by the implementation. Normally, firms begin a software search in response to problems occurring at two levels:

1. *Strategic objectives.* On this level, companies are searching for systems to provide solutions to broad enterprise problems regarding competitive positioning, sales and marketing objectives, products and services, financial capacities, and marketplace realities. These strategic problems influence the performance of the enterprise on the macro level and cut across all business functional areas. An example of a strategic objective would be increasing enterprise profitability by decreasing total logistics costs and increasing sales.

2. *Tactical objectives.* Solutions on this level are focused on increasing functional or business area performance and productivity. These objectives can be attained either through automating activities or integrating members in a business area or group of business areas. Examples of tactical objectives would be decreasing transportation costs, reducing warehousing storage costs, increasing the speed of customer deliveries, and reducing purchasing costs.

As can be seen from the above objectives, in many cases managers can define goals that in reality have conflicting strategic and tactical objectives. No one would disagree that a business strategy whose objective it would be to increase profit while reducing costs constitutes a sound corporate mission. However, on the tactical level, pursuing such a strategy often results in counterpoising tactical objectives. For example, achieving higher sales while reducing costs means that, while sales and service are increasing, the cost of logistics is decreasing. Conflicts can arise as each business function employs the system to realize tactical objectives. Sales and service fear that as inventory, warehouse, and transportation costs decline, so will their ability to respond to customer requirements. On the other hand, logistics assumes that as sales and service pursue higher levels of sales and delivery, they will be forced to increase their operational costs. Resolving these dichotomies between strategic and tactical objectives is critical to a successful system implementation. The goal for implementers is to ensure that enterprise strategic and tactical goals are in alignment with and supportive of one another. If system strategies are directed narrowly on improving the performance only of tactical functions or on too broad of an enterprisewide perspective, the expected value of the technology solution will never be realized.

PART 2: SELECTING TECHNOLOGY SOLUTIONS

Once an effective technology strategy has been designed, the next task will be to find the appropriate system solution. In selecting an information system solution, implementers have two basic alternatives. The first method is to develop the system in-house using internal management information and operational staffs. Whether the solution consists of an automation project or the implementation of a full EIS, there are a number of pros and cons to this approach. To begin with, developing solutions in-house involves a great deal of time. Developing and executing a fully integrated EIS, for example, is a multiyear project that involves a tremendous commitment of organizational resources. In the end, the cost of development and implementation may far exceed the cost of purchasing and implementing a packaged system. Second, a significant danger encountered in in-house development projects is spending enormous resources on functionality that currently can be found in commercial packages. Although in-house development will result in a system that has been custom-fitted to the needs of the organization, design teams may find themselves rediscovering all the mistakes that software suppliers had made and solved years ago. Third, even the best run systems development project may not succeed in realizing the original business objectives. One of the benefits of a commercial package is that it can be seen in operation in existing customer sites. Finally, applications developed in-house reflect the needs of the organization as it exists *today*. As time and the needs of the enterprise move forward, however, software that once answered business information requirements can become obsolete. In addition, home-grown software must be able to change to meet the rapidly developing technology environments of tomorrow.

The second method of acquiring technology systems is to purchase them from a software supplier. In today's current marketplace there are literally hundreds of technology companies marketing products designed to service every industry. They range from very small PC software companies offering low-cost products targeted at specific business needs, such as EDI and freight rating systems, to full-blown integrated manufacturing and distribution resource planning systems that also possess the ability to network with other systems. In today's technology environment, most of these suppliers offer applications that are based on open systems principles and are designed to work through Internet technologies without dependencies on proprietary hardware.

The advantages of using commercial software are the immediate availability of applications that are compliant with today's state-of-the-art technologies, portability of most packages to migrate across hardware platforms and database management systems, and availability of maintenance, support, enhancements, and documentation. The disadvantages are the need to modify applications to fit internal processes or development of whole new functions not supported by the package, high cost of training and implementation due to the number of applications and complexity of functionality, and, finally, the trauma often experienced by internal technology groups who must often learn new programming languages, networking, and system administration functions.

The final activities in software selection revolve around live demonstrations of the software. Some consulting firms recommend the use of sophisticated checklists to compare suppliers' applications with the firm's perceived functionality and technology requirements. A more important part of the search process is gaining insight into the software and the supplier through a series of well-constructed demonstrations. Effective demos consist of both application as well as technical demonstrations. Application demos will reveal such system attributes as easy of navigation, maintenance, entry, inquiry, and reporting. Technical demos should be targeted to reveal system architecture and programming standards. Perhaps the most critical aspect of the demo process is positioning the firm's user base at the forefront of the process. Their acceptance and buy-in are the foundations of implementation success, and it should be their concerns and recommendations that are the determining factors in the final selection.

PART 3: SOFTWARE IMPLEMENTATION

Once the technology solution has been chosen, the organization must turn its attention to the task of system implementation. Many a top executive has assumed that most of the hard work in implementing a system has been completed with the software selection and hardware installation. In reality, implementing a system, and an EIS in particular, is one of the greatest challenges an enterprise can undertake. An implementation project requires a great deal of time, effort, and expense on the part of the company and all of its employees. Many times an implementation project is misperceived as purely a computer system and properly the responsibility of the MIS department. In reality, the implementation of business software presents the enterprise with the opportunity to streamline business processes and activate new levels of competitiveness. To be successful, the implementation should be considered as a formal management process consisting of the following project elements:

- Obtaining top management's commitment to the new system
- Developing a strategic plan detailing project scope and objectives

- Establishing a detailed and achievable project plan and budget
- Executing a full education plan and conference room pilot test of the software
- Defining and performing necessary modifications
- Conducting effective ongoing system performance measurements

The implementation process consists of four interwoven elements: people resources; project control; hardware, software and data; and enterprise structure, policies, and procedures. The central requirement of a successful project is to keep these four elements on track as the organization moves toward successful implementation. In managing this process of alignment, project teams can utilize a number of management tools and techniques. Perhaps the most critical of these is the structuring and publishing of a detailed *project schedule*. The project schedule should consist of all the phases, steps, and activities necessary to complete the implementation on time and within budget. The project schedule should also time-sequence all implementation tasks, specifying start and completion dates, responsible roles for task execution, and all project budgets.

The second essential project management component is the establishment of an effective project organization (Figure 14.9). Overall, it is the responsi-

FIGURE 14.9   Implementation project organization.

bility of the project organization to define the strategic objectives of the system, provide funding and enterprise resources, execute the project schedule, and review performance measurements. The project organization defines all project roles and organizational structures necessary to execute successfully the *project schedule*. The third component of successful project management is the placement of *project milestones* at key junctures in the project's life cycle. The purpose of the project milestone is to provide the project organization with a measuring stick detailing implementation progress. Each milestone contains a set of activities, beginning and completion dates, and project roles. As each milestone is reached, the project organization should review the costs, time, problems, and opportunities that have occurred. After review, a plan detailing the steps necessary to achieve the next milestone should be defined. The final component of project management is developing effective *project management skills and techniques* that will assist in assigning, executing, and evaluating the success of project resources in performing project activities and accomplishing tasks on time and within budget. Types of project management techniques include project tracking, interviewing, analysis, conceptual and technical design, development, and quality assurance.

PART 4: CONTINUOUS IMPROVEMENT

After completion of Part 3 of the implementation framework, the event must be understood more as gateway than as an end point in exploring the use of technology and the opportunities it provides to the enterprise. The availability of a business system does not automatically guarantee that the operational constituents will use it properly nor that it will activate an on-going pro-cess of improvement and competitive advantage. In order to realize the full value of any technology system, implementers need to constantly reexamine and reorient the elements of the implementation management processes stated above.

Alignment. Although a particular technology solution was chosen to respond to particular strategic business and tactical needs, implementers can be assured that the original objectives will shift over time. Change can come from either the firm's strategic or operational sectors. A redirection of the enterprise's business mission, expansion in the distribution channel, or entry into international trade, may require an overall restructuring of the original business system. Just as important, shifting operational requirements may also require system modification. Such things as Internet technologies, interface with third-party applications, and the automation of activities previously performed manually will alter not only the way the system is currently being used but also the level of user mastery and the way the system is applied to enhance user performance.

Finally, the need for realignment may emerge out of the technology environment itself. This need for realignment can be the result of continuous incremental changes or breakthroughs that permit the system to move to new technological planes. For example, incremental functional enhancements to the system may provide constituents with new opportunities to eliminate costs and improve information throughput. On the other hand, advancements in technology, such as the integration of intelligent workstations into a client/server network, may provide new information technology vistas or even obsolete current systems.

User Commitment and Ownership. Ideally, the commitment to and ownership of the system on the part of the user constituency should have been gained during Part 2 of the implementation framework and strengthened during Part 3 with the final design and implementation of a solution that fulfills the needs of users and other stakeholders. In Part 4 of the implementtation framework, management must seek to confirm and extend this commitment and ownership.

IT system implementations are always characterized by a spectrum of user support. In most projects support for the solution proceeds essentially through two stages. In the first, found during the execution of Part 3, the user constituency can be divided into three groups: those who are *committed* to the new system, the mass of the users who are *uncommitted* with a "wait and see" attitude, and a small percentage of *nay-sayers* who feel the initiative will be a failure. By the time Part 4 of the implementation framework is reached this original division should be dramatically altered. The majority of users should be fully committed and prepared to take ownership of the system. *Naysayers* should have completely disappeared. The ability of management to continually expand system commitment and ownership becomes especially important as incremental and technological advancements change original system objectives and the social contract between the user constituency and the enterprise.

User Competency and Mastery. Earlier in this chapter it was stated that as the functionality of the business system becomes more robust, the knowledge and flexibility required of the user constituency to effectively utilize it grows exponentially. With this fact in mind, the critical question then becomes, *"How can system users develop and expand system competency so that it is operationally aligned, progressively owned, and increasing mastered?"* During Part 3 of the implementation framework, users should have been closely involved in system definition, exploration of system capabilities, and assessment of potential system results, as well as determining regions for user learning and self-management. In Part 4 of the implementation framework, managers must be careful to develop metrics illustrating the *skill gap* between the user constituency and the operational requirements and potentialities of the new system. The goal is to close this gap by illuminating the alignment between the system and the business vision, ongoing training and education, performance measurement systems, encouragement of user innovation, and participation in system functional evolution. This developmental process is detailed in Figure 14.10.

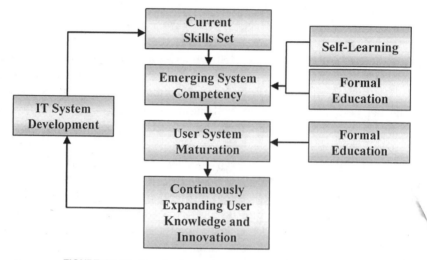

FIGURE 14.10 Developing system mastery and competence.

Regardless of the complexity of a given technology solution, implementers must continually realign technology and the enterprise's strategic and operational objectives. Walton [15] has proposed an iterative process for ensuring the alignment of IT and business requirements. As illustrated in Figure 14.11, the process consists of three elements. In the first, *design/redesign*,

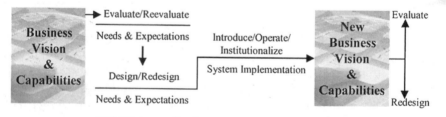

FIGURE 14.11 Business system development process.

implementers must seek to design systems that are in alignment with business realities and enterprise strategic and operational goals. Once designed, the IT system enters the *introduce/operate/institutionalize* phase, in which the solution is applied to the business environment. Because no system design can be considered as definitive, current design must continually be under a process of *evaluation/reevaluation*. This process occurs because of changes to technology, enhancement to system functionality, or even rising user expectations concerning system capabilities. Figure 14.11 is meant to illustrate both the iterative nature of Part 4 of the implementation framework, as well as the objective of attaining ever-expanding business system results.

SUMMARY

The application of computer technologies has caused a virtual revolution in the concept and practice of modern *supply chain management.* In today's business climate, the importance of timely, accurate, and complete information has increasingly become the key enabler for marketplace advantage. *Internally,* information technologies enable companies to develop databases and implement applications that provide for the efficient management of transactions and the timely collection, analysis, and generation of information about customers, processes, products, and markets necessary for effective decision making. *External,* information technologies enable strategists to architect channel networks that are collaborative, agile, scalable, fast flow, and Web-enabled. Actualizing the potential of today's technologies will require companies to move beyond viewing computers as purely a tool for *automating* business functions. Increasingly, the real value of information technology will be found in its ability to enable integration and networking between channel trading partners that will provide for revolutionary capabilities and competencies for the generation of new products and services, whole new businesses and marketplaces, and radically new forms of competitive advantage.

The ability to leverage the power of today's information technologies requires a detailed knowledge of basic system architecture features as well as a thorough grounding in the principles of modern system management. Today's system architectures consist of five basic elements: the *database* (the static and transactional data captured during system processing); *transaction management* (the performance and recording of daily operations); *management control* (the performance feedback necessary for purposeful planning); *decision analysis/simulation* (the use of modeling tools to manage complex processes); and *strategic planning* (the development of long-term forecasts, market approaches, and business partner alliances). Effectively utilizing these general system features requires a firm grasp of the seven principles of system management. Regardless of the scope of the technologies used or their ultimate objectives, the effective operation of today's business applications requires *accountability* for the entry, maintenance, quality, and integrity of data, *transparency* as to how the system works and can be applied to the solution of practical business problems, *accessibility* to data and retrieval utilities for reporting, a *valid simulation* of the way the business actually works, *flexibility* to perform transactions or manipulate data, and the capability to use system exception messaging for the *planning* and *control* of business management processes.

A critical characteristic of today's enterprise business software is its ability to be configured to meet any particular industry or specific business requirement. The goal of the system architecture is to facilitate, either through existing application suites or through software partners, the creation of scalable, highly flexible information enablers that provide the business with the capability to respond with customized customer value solutions and collaborative relationships at all points in the supply channel network. The configured product must be capable of encompassing three possible solutions. The first is concerned with solutions that integrate the *internal* data and processes of an enterprise. The second is concerned with the availability of connectivity tools necessary to link *external* parts of the enterprise together. Finally, the technology solution must link the business with the customers and suppliers constituting the supply chain network.

When exploring the application of technology solutions, implementers must ask several critical questions focused on determining the optimal alignment of information tools and expected increases in enterprise productivity and serviceability. Perhaps the most critical decision to be made at the beginning of the technology search is clearly defining the scope of the business problems to be solved. Successfully completing this step will narrow the range of possible technology solutions and ensure the effort is focused on core business issues. Equally as important is charting the effect the technology will have on the organization and its capabilities. In fact, the more encompassing the implementation, the more robust are the requirements for learning and change management necessary to utilize the solution.

This alignment of the organization with the proposed system impacts the enterprise in three ways. To begin with, the integrative capabilities of today's enterprise systems require implementers to restructure the culture and capabilities of their organizations to promote values fostering continuous improvement and teamwork. Second, enterprise systems enable the organization not only to rethink traditional enterprise information flows but also to leverage new information tools such as graphics, workstation technologies, and Internet-driven network-to-network computer integration. Finally, the effective application of new information technologies requires a redefinition of the goals and skills of the enterprise's people resources.

Besides orchestrating changes to organizational structure and cultural fabrics, implementers must also focus on a detailed framework designed to guide them successfully through the entire technology solution search and installation project. Such a framework should consist of four broad phases. In the first, enterprise management defines the intensity of the automation and process integration objectives to be achieved. The second phase of the framework encompasses the technology search process, culminating in the selection of the optimal solution. There are two possible avenues that can be pursued: legacy software can be enhanced to meet new enterprise information requirements, or a totally new software system is purchased. In phase three, the new information system is introduced, users trained, the software tested, modifications performed, and the final product implemented. In the final phase of the framework, a program targeted at continuous improvement in organizational capabilities and identifying new technology tools is initiated. By far, of the four phases of the implementation framework, the greatest challenges to the organization will be found in planning and controlling the implementation processes found in phase three. Successful technology projects occur when implementers create a functional project organization and run the project according to a detailed project plan and budget.

QUESTIONS FOR REVIEW

1. It has been said that the velocity of a firm's ability to process information defines the boundaries of its business activities. Explain.
2. What is the objective of information technology targeted at *automation*?
3. Explain why IT focused on *integrating* business functions is a more difficult task than automating functions.
4. The implementation of integrative IT systems requires changing the organization and its capabilities. Explain.
5. What are the three fundamental management processes essential to implementation success, and why are they so important?
6. Why is obtaining top management's support for the IT project so important?
7. Outline the structure and discuss the responsibilities of an effective IT implementation team.
8. The use of the Internet can drastically alter the competitive field. Why is this the case?
9. Discuss the five stages of Internet connectivity.
10. How can the implementation of information technologies impact strategic advantage?

REFERENCES

1. Savage, Charles M., *Fifth Generation Management*. Burlington, MA: Digital Press, 1990, p. 70.
2. Ibid, p. 71.
3. There are many descriptions of what constitutes an effective system. One of the most important is Wight, Oliver W., *Manufacturing Resource Planning: MRPII – Unlocking America's Productivity Potential*. Essex Junction, VT: Oliver Wight Limited Publications, Inc., 1982, pp. 100-106. See also Bowersox, Donald J. and Closs, David J., *Logistical Management: The Integrated Supply Chain Process*. New York: The McGraw-Hill Companies, Inc, 1996, pp. 190-193.
4. For a full treatment of these applications see Ross, David F., *Introduction to e-Supply Chain Management: Engaging Technology to Build Market-Winning Business Partnerships*. Boca Raton, FL: St. Lucie Press, 2003, pp. 83-86; Arnold, J.R. Tony, *Introduction to Materials Management*. 3rd ed. Upper Saddle River, NJ: Prentice Hall, 1998, pp. 16-22; and, Bowersox and Closs, pp. 194-201.
5. This term was coined in 1993 by the author in an article entitled "DRP II: The Answer to Connecting the Distribution Enterprise," *APICS-The Performance Advantage*, 3, 3, 1993, pp. 59-62.
6. These points have been abstracted from Ross, *Introduction to e-Supply Chain Management*, pp. 90-91.
7. For a full treatment of this topic see Ross, *Introduction to e-Supply Chain Management*, pp. 92-107.
8. An excellent discussion of Web-based EDI can be found in Gulisano, Vincent, "EDI is Only as Dead as You Want It to Be," *Global Logistics and Supply Chain Strategies*, 5, 2, 2001, pp., 67-68; Davis, Kit, "Web-based EDI Begins to Take Hold," *Consumer Goods Technology*, 10, 4, 2001, 18-19; and Hedrick, Amy, *Reports of EDI's Death Were Premature*, AMR Research, Inc., July 2001.
9. Allen Pinkus and Robert Ericksson, "Maximizing Productivity from Inventory Management," *APICS: The Performance Advantage*, 40-42 (September, 1994).
10. North American Van Lines, "Customized Logistics Solutions," *Inbound Logistics*, 24 December 1994).
11. Porter, Michael E. and Millar, Victor E., "How Information Gives You Competitive Advantage," *Harvard Business Review*, 63, 4, (1985), pp. 148-152.
12. Gopal, Christopher and Cypress, Harold, *Integrated Distribution Management*. Homewood, IL: Business One Irwin, 1993, p. 153.
13. Ritter, Delmar, R., "Verification on the Run," *APICS: The Performance Advantage*, 23-25 (May, 1994).
14. Walton, Richard E. *Up and Running: Integrating Information Technology and the Organization*. Boston, MA: Harvard Business School Press, 1989, pp. 205-218.
15. Ibid, pp. 154-155.

BIBLIOGRAPHY

This bibliography acknowledges those authors who are referenced in the text and whose concepts and ideas contributed to the writing of this book. In addition, the bibliography provides the student of Supply Chain Management and Logistics with a ready source for independent reading and research.

TEXTBOOKS

Bowersox, Donald J. and M. Bixby Cooper. *Strategic Market Channel Management.* New York: McGraw-Hill, 1993.

Bowersox, Donald J. and David J. Closs. *Logistical Management: The Integrated Supply Chain Process.,* New York: The McGraw-Hill Companies, Inc., 1996.

Ballou, Ronald H. *Business Logistics Management: Planning and Control, 4th ed.* Englewood Cliffs, NJ: Prentice-Hall, 1998.

Cateora, Philip. International Marketing. 8th ed. Homewood, IL: Irwin, 1993.

Coyle, John J., Edward J. Bardi, and C. John Langly. *The Management of Business Logistics,* 7th ed. Mason, Ohio: South-Western, 2003.

Dobler, Donald W., David N. Burt, and Lamar Lee. *Purchasing and Materials Management,* 5th ed. New York: McGraw-Hill, 1990.

Fogarty, Donald W., John H. Blackstone, and Thomas R. Hoffmann. *Production and Inventory Management,* 2nd ed. Cincinnati, OH: South-Western Publishing Co., 1991.

Heinritz, Stuart, Paul V. Farrell, Larry C. Giunipero, and Michael G. Kolchin. *Purchasing: Principles and Applications,* 8th ed. Englewood Cliffs, NJ: Prentice Hall, 1991.

Heizer, Jay and Barry Render. *Production and Operations Management,* 3rd ed. Boston: Allyn and Bacon, 1993.

Horngren, Charles T., Foster, George, and Datar, Srikant M. *Cost Accounting: A Managerial Emphasis,* 8th ed.. Englewood Cliffs, NJ: Prentice-Hall, 1994.

Johnson, James C. and Donald F. Wood. *Contemporary Logistics.* New York: MacMillian Publishing Co., 1993.

Keegan, Warren J. *Global Marketing Management,* 4th ed. Englewood Cliffs, NJ: Prentice-Hall, 1989.

Kotler, Philip. *Marketing Management,* 6th ed. Englewood Cliffs, NJ: Prentice-Hall, 1988.

Lambert, Douglas M. and James R. Stock. *Strategic Logistics Management.* 3rd ed. Homewood, IL: Irwin, 1993.

Leenders, Michael, Harold E. Fearon, and Wilbur B. England. *Purchasing and Inventory Management,* 8th ed. Homewood, IL: Irwin, 1989.

Magee, John F., William C. Copacino, and Donald B. Rosenfield. *Modern Logistics Management*. New York: John Wiley & Sons, 1985.

Plossl, George W. *Production and Inventory Control: Principles and Techniques*, 2nd ed. Englewood Cliffs, NJ: Prentice-Hall, 1985.

Sampson, Roy J., Martin T. Farris, and David L. Shrock. *Domestic Transportation: Practice, Theory and Policy*. Boston, MA: Houghton Mifflin Company, 1985.

Silver, Edward A. and Rein Peterson. *Decision Systems for Inventory Management and Production Planning*, 2nd ed. New York: John Wiley & Sons, 1985.

Stern, Louis W. and Adel I. El-Ansary. *Marketing Channels*, 3rd ed. Englewood Cliffs, NJ: Prentice-Hall, 1988.

Terpstra, Vern and Ravi Sarathy. *International Marketing*. New York: Dreyden Press, 1991.

Vollmann, Thomas E., William Lee Berry, and D. Clay Whybark. *Manufacturing Planning and Control Systems*, 2nd ed. Homewood, IL: Dow Jones-Irwin, 1988.

Wood, Donald F. and James C. Johnson. *Contemporary Transportation*. New York: MacMillian Publishing Co., 1993.

SECONDARY WORKS

Ackerman, Kenneth B. *Practical Handbook of Warehousing*. New York: Van Nostrand Reinhold, 1990.

Albrecht, Karl and Lawrence J. Bradford. *The Service Advantage*. Homewood, IL: Dow-Jones Irwin, 1990.

Anderson, David L. and Hau Lee, eds. *Achieving Supply Chain Excellence Through Technology, Vol. 3*. San Francisco, Montgomery Research, 2001.

_____, eds. *Achieving Supply Chain Excellence Through Technology, Vol. 1*. San Francisco, Montgomery Research, 1999.

Ansari, A. and Modarress, B. *Just-In-Time Purchasing*. New York: The Free Press, 1990.

Anthony, Robert N. *The Management Control Function*. Boston, MA: Harvard Business School Press, 1988.

APICS Dictionary, 9th ed. Falls Church, VA: American Production and Inventory Control Society, 1998.

Ayers, James R. *Handbook of Supply Chain Management*. Boca Raton: St. Lucie Press, 2001.

Band, William A. *Creating Value for Customer*. New York: John Wiley & Sons, 1991.

Bovet, Rob and Joseph Martha. *Value Nets: Breaking the Supply Chain to Unlock Hidden Profits*. New York: John Wiley & Sons., 2000.

Bowersox, Donald J. "The Strategic Benefits of Logistics Alliances." *Harvard Business Review* 36-45 (July-August 1990).

Bowersox, Donald J., Pat Calabro, and George D. Wagenheim. *Introduction to Transportation*. New York: Macmillian, 1981.

Bowersox, Donald J. and Patricia J. Daugherty. "Achieving and Maintaining Logistics Leadership: Logistics Organizations of the Future." *Council of Logistics Management Annual Conference Proceedings,* Vol. I, 1989, pp. 59-72.

Bowersox, Donald J., Patricia J. Daugherty, Cornelia L. Droge, Richard N. Germain, and Dale S. Rogers. *Logistical Excellence.* Burlington, MA: Digital Press, 1992.

Bowersox, Donald J., Patricia J. Daugherty, Cornelia L. Droge, Dale S. Rogers, and Daniel L. Wardlow. *Leading Edge Logistics: Competitive Positioning for the 1990's.* Oak Brook, IL: Council of Logistics Management, 1989.

Bowersox, Donald J., Bernard J. LaLonde, Edward W., Smykay, eds. *Readings in Physical Distribution Management: The Logistics of Marketing.* London: Macmillan, 1969.

Brewer, Peter C. and Thomas W. Speh. "Adapting the Balanced Scorecard to Supply Chain Management," *Supply Cain Management Review,* 5, 2, 2001.

Brown, Robert G. *Advanced Service Parts Inventory Control.* Norwich VT: Materials Management Systems, Inc., 1982.

_____. *Decision Rules for Inventory Management.* New York: Holt, Rinehart Winston, 1967.

_____. *Materials Management Systems.* New York: John Wiley & Sons, 1977.

_____. *Statistical Forecasting for Inventory Control.* New York: McGraw-Hill, 1959.

Bucklin, Louis. *Competition and Evolution in the Distribution Trades.* Englewood Cliffs, NJ: Prentice-Hall, 1972.

Carter, Joseph R. *Purchasing: Continued Improvement Through Integration.* Homewood, IL: Business One Irwin, 1993.

Chambers, John C., Satinder K. Mullick, and Donald D. Smith. "How To Choose the Right Forecasting Technique." *Harvard Business Review* 55-64 (August-July 1971).

Chandler, Alfred D. *The Visible Hand: The Managerial Revolution in American Business.* Cambridge, MA: Harvard University Press, 1977.

Dadzie, Kofi Q. and Wesely J. Johnston, "Innovative Automation Technology in Corporate Warehousing Logistics." *Journal of Business Logistics* 12, (1), 74-78 (1991).

Davidow, William H. and Bro Uttal. *Total Customer Service: The Ultimate Weapon.* New York: Harper & Row, 1989.

Delaney, Robert V. *Contract Logistics Service: The Promises and the Pitfalls.* St. Louis, MO: Cass Business Logistics, Inc., 1994.

_____. *Fourteenth Annual State of Logistics Report.* St. Louis, MO: Cass Business Logistics, 2003.

Davenport, Thomas H. *Mission Critical: Realizing the Promise of Enterprise Systems.* Boston: Harvard Business School Press, 2000.

DeLurgio, Stephen, A. and Carl D. Bhame. *Forecasting Systems for Inventory Management.* Homewood, IL: Business One Irwin, 1991.

Downes, Larry and Chunka Mui. *Unleashing the Killer Apps: Digital Strategies for Market Dominance.* Boston: Harvard Business School, 1998.

Drapkin, Michael. *Three Clicks Away: Advice from the Trenches of E-Commerce.* New York: John Wiley & Sons, 2001.

Drucker, Peter F. *Management: Tasks, Responsibilities and Practices.* New York: Harper & Row, 1973.

Dudick, Thomas S. *Cost Accounting Desk Reference Book.* New York: Van Nostrand Reinhold, 1986.

Dyche, Jill. *The CRM Handbook: A Business Guide to Customer Relationship Management.* Boston, MA: Addison-Wesley, 2002.

Elderkin, Kenton, W. and Warren E. Norquist. *Creative Countertrade: A Guide to Doing Business Worldwide.* Cambridge, MA: Ballinger Publishing Co., 1987.

Emmelhainz, Margaret A. *Electronic Data Interchange: A Total Management Guide.* New York: Van Nostrand Reinhold, 1990.

Fearon, Harold E., Donald W. Dobler, and Kenneth H. Killen (eds.). *The Purchasing Handbook.* New York: McGraw-Hill, 1993.

Fine, Charles. *Clockspeed: Winning Industry Control in the Age of Temporary Advantage.* Reading, Massachusetts: Persus Books, 1998.

Fingar, Peter, Harsha Kumar, and Tarun Sharma. *Enterprise E-Commerce.* Tampa, FL: Meghan-Kiffer Press, 2000.

Fredendall, Lawrence D. and Ed Hill. *Basics of Supply Chain Management.* Boca Raton: St. Lucie Press, 2001.

Fuller, Joseph, B. James O'Conner, and Richard Rawlinson. "Tailored Logistics: The Next Advantage." *Harvard Business Review,* 87-98 (May-June 1993).

Gentry, Julie and Martin T. Farris, "The Increasing Importance of Purchasing in Transportation Decision Making." *Transportation Journal,* 61-71 (Fall 1992).

Goddard, Walter E. *Just-In-Time.* Essex Junction, VT: Oliver Wight Publications, 1986.

Gopal, Christopher and Gerard Cahill. *Logistics in Manufacturing.* Homewood, IL: Business One Irwin, 1992.

Gopal, Christopher and Harold Cypress. *Integrated Distribution Management.* Homewood, IL: Business One Irwin, 1993.

Graham, Gordon. *Distribution Management Inventories for the 1990's.* Richardson, TX: Inventory Management Press, 1987.

_____. *Distributor Survival in the 21st Century.* Richardson, TX: Inventory Management Press, 1991.

Green, James H. (ed.). *Production and Inventory Control Handbook.* New York: McGraw-Hill, 1987.

Greenberg, Paul. *CRM at the Speed of Light: Capturing and Keeping Customers in Internet Real Time.* Berkley, CA: McGraw-Hill, 2001.

Hamel, Gary and C.K. Prahalad. *Competing for the Future.* Boston, MA: Harvard Business School Press, 1994.

Hammer, Michael and James Champy. *Reengineering the Corporation.* New York: HarperCollins, 1993.

Handfield, Robert B. and Ernest L. Nichols. *Introduction to Supply Chain Management.* Upper Saddle River, NJ: Prentice Hall, 1999.

Harding, Michael and Mary Lu Harding. *Purchasing.* New York: Barron's Business Library, 1991.

Harmon, Roy L. *Reinventing the Warehouse.* New York: The Free Press, 1993.

Hayes, Robert H. and Steven C. Wheelwright. *Restoring Our Competitive Advantage.* New York: John Wiley & Sons, 1984.

Hayes, Robert H., Steven C. Wheelwright, and Kim B. Clark. *Dynamic Manufacturing.* New York: The Free Press, 1988.

Hill, Terry. *Manufacturing Strategy: Text and Cases*, 2nd ed. Burr Ridge, IL: Irwin, 1994.

Hoque, Faisal, *e-Enterprise: Business Models, Architecture, and Components.* Cambridge, UK: Cambridge University Press, 2000.

Hutchins, Greg. *Purchasing Strategies for Total Quality.* Homewood, IL: Business One Irwin, 1992.

Jenkins, Creed H. *Complete Guide to Modern Warehousing.* Englewood Cliffs, NJ: Prentice-Hall, 1990.

Jordan, James A. and Frederick J. Michel. *Next Generation Manufacturing: Methods and Techniques.* New York: John Wiley & Sons., 2000.

Kaplan, Robert S. and David P. Norton. *The Balanced Scorecard.* Boston, MA: Harvard Business School Press, 1996.

_____. *The Strategy Focused Organization.* Boston, MA: Harvard Business School Press, 2001.

Korabik, Ron. "Get the 'Rock' Out of Your Inventory." *APICS: The Performance Advantage* 39-41 (June, 1992).

Krupp, James A. G. "Are ABC Codes an Obsolete Technology?" *APICS: The Performance Advantage* 34-35 (April 1994).

_____. "JIT in Distribution and Warehousing." *Production and Inventory Management Journal,* 18-21 (Second Quarter 1991).

Kuglin, Fred A. and Barbara A. Rosenbaum. *The Supply Chain Network @ Internet Speed: Preparing Your Company for the E-Commerce Revolution.* New York: AMA-COM, 2001.

LaLonde, Bernard, Martha C. Cooper, and Thomas G. Noordewier. *Customer Service: A Management Perspective.* Chicago: Council of Logistics Management, 1988.

LaLonde, Bernard and Paul H. Zinszer. *Customer Service: Meaning and Measurement.* Chicago: National Council of Physical Distribution Management, 1976.

Magad, Eugene and John M. Amos. *Total Materials Management.* New York: Van Nostrand Reinhold, 1989.

Makridakis, Spyros and Steven Wheelwright. *Forecasting Methods for Management.* New York: John Wiley & Sons, 1989.

Martin, Andre. *DRP: Distribution Requirements Planning.* Essex Junction, VT: Oliver Wight Publications, Inc., 1993.

Martin, John E. "Use Strategic Modeling to Evaluate Warehouse Automation." *APICS: The Performance Advantage,* 19-22 (December 1993).

McKinnon, Alan C. *Physical Distribution Systems.* New York: Routledge, 1989.

Melnyk, Steven A. and Philip L. Carter. *Production Activity Control.* Homewood, IL: Dow Jones-Irwin, 1987.

Melnyk, Steven A., Philip L/ Carter, David M. Dilts, and David M. Lyth. *Shop Floor Control.* Homewood, IL: Dow Jones-Irwin, 1985.

Moore, James F. *The Death of Competition.* New York: HarperBusiness, 1996.

Mulcahy, David E. *Warehouse Distribution and Operations Handbook.* New York: McGraw-Hill, 1994.

Neberling, Michael E. "The Rediscovery of Modern Purchasing." *International Journal of Purchasing and Materials Management* 29, (4) 406-453 (Fall 1993).

Norris, Grant, James R. Hurley, Kenneth M. Hartkey, John R. Dunleavy, and John D. Balls. *E-Business and ERP: Transforming the Enterprise.* New York: John Wiley, 2000.

Orlicky, Joseph. *Material Requirements Planning.* New York: McGraw-Hill, 1975.

Picard, J. "Topology of Physical Distribution Systems in Multi-National Corporations." *International Journal of Physical Distribution and Materials Management,* 12, (6) 26-39 (1982).

Poirier, Charles C. and Michael J. Bauer. *E-Supply Chain: Using the Internet to Revolutionize Your Business..* San Francisco: Berrett-Koehler Publishers, Inc., 2000.

Porter, Michael E. *Competitive Advantage.* New York: The Free Press, 1985.

_____. *Competitive Strategy.* New York: The Free Press, 1980.

Prahalad, C.K. and Venkatram Ramaswamy. "The Collaboration Continuum," *Optimize Magazine,* November, 2001.

Pyke, David F. and Morris A. Cohen, "Push and Pull in Manufacturing and Distribution Systems." *Journal of Operations Management* 9, (1) 24-43 (1990).

Raisch, Warren D. *The E-Marketplace: Strategies for Success in B2B E-Commerce.* New York: McGraw-Hill, 2001.

Rajagopal, Shan and Kenneth N. Bernard. "Strategic Procurement and Competitive Advantage." *International Journal of Purchasing and Materials Management* 29, (4) 65-71 (1993).

Redmond, Jon. "Just-In-Time Inventory Management." *Council of Logistics Management, Annual Conference Proceedings.* Vol. 2, 1989, pp. 301-311.

Riffle, William K. "EDI: Let's Look at the Basics." *APICS: The Performance Advantage 26-28 (*June 1993).

Robeson, James F. and Robert G. House (eds.). *The Distribution Handbook.* New York: The Free Press, 1985.

Ross, David F. "Aligning the Organization for World-Class Manufacturing." *Production and Inventory Management Journal* 22-26 (Second Quarter 1991).

_____. *Competing Through Supply Chain Management: Creating Market-Winning Strategies Through Supply Chain Partnerships.* New York: Chapman & Hall, 1998.

_____. "DRP II: Connecting the Distribution Enterprise." *APICS: The Performance Advantage* 59-62 (March 1993).

_____. *Introduction to e-Supply Chain Management: Engaging Technology to Build Market-Winning Business Partnerships.* Boca Raton: St. Lucie Press, 2003.

Savage, Charles M. *Fifth Generation Management.* Burlington, MA: Digital Press, 1990.

Sawhney, Mohan and Jeff Zabin. *The Seven Steps to Nirvana: Strategic Insights into e-Business Transformation.* New York: McGraw-Hill, 2001.

Schonberger, Richard J. *Building a Chain of Customers.* New York: The Free Press, 1990.

_____. *World Class Manufacturing.* New York: The Free Press, 1986.

Schorr, John. *Purchasing in the 21st Century.* Essex Junction, VT: Oliver Wight Productions, 1992.

Schultz, Terry. *BRP: The Journey to Excellence.* Milwaukee, WI: The Forum, 1986.

Shingo, Shigeo. *Study of Toyota Production System.* Tokyo: Japan Management Association, 1981.

Smith, Bernard T. *Focus Forecasting: Computer Techniques for Inventory Control.* Essex Junction, VT: Oliver Wight Publications, 1984.

_____. *Focus Forecasting and DRP.* New York: Vantage Press, 1991.

Spencer, Michael, Patricia J. Daugherty, and Dales S. Rogers. "Towards a Deeper Understanding of JIT: A Comparison Between APICS and Logistics Managers." *Production and Inventory Management Journal* 23-28 (Third Quarter 1994).

The Standard Industry and Classification Manual. Springfield, VA: National Technical Information Service, 1987.

Taylor, David and Alyse Terhune. *Doing E-Business: Strategies for Thriving in an Electronic Marketplace.* New York: John Wiley, 2001.

Tompkins, James A. "Distribution Today and Tomorrow." *APICS: The Performance Advantage* 22-28 (April 1994).

Tompkins, James A. and Dale A. Harmelink (eds.). *The Distribution Management Handbook.* New York: McGraw-Hill, 1994.

Tompkins, James A. and Jerry D. Smith (eds.). *The Warehouse Management Handbook.* New York: McGraw-Hill, 1988.

Wallace, Thomas F. *MRP II: Making It Happen.* Essex Junction, VT: Oliver Wight Publications, 1985.

Walton, Richard E. *Up and Running.* Boston, MA: Harvard Business School Press, 1989.

Wantuck, Kenneth A. *Just-In-Time for America.* Milwaukee, WI: The Forum, 1989.

Waters, C.D.J. *Inventory Control and Management.* New York: John Wiley & Sons, 1992.

Webster, Frederick. *Industrial Marketing Strategy.* New York: John Wiley & Sons, 1984.

Wemmerlov, Urban. *Capacity Management Techniques.* Falls Church, VA: American Production and Inventory Control Society, 1984.

Wetzer, Michael. "Will Virtual Corporations Design and Manufacture Virtual Products?" *APICS: The Performance Advantage* 27-28 (May 1993).

Wight, Oliver. *Production and Inventory Management in the Computer Age.* Boston: CBI Publishing, 1974.

Wilkins, Robert H. "Cornerstones of Total Quality." *APICS: The Performance Advantage* 56-59 (October 1993).

Woolsey, Gene. "The Never-Fail Spare-Parts Reduction Method: An Editorial." *Production and Inventory Management Journal* 64-66 (4th Quarter 1988).

_____. "A Requiem for the EOQ: An Editorial." *Production and Inventory Management Journal* 68-72 (3rd Quarter 1988).

Zeithaml, Valarie, A. Parasuraman, and Leonard L. Berry. *Delivering Quality Service.* New York: The Free Press, 1990.

_____. "A Conceptual Model of Service Quality and Its Implications for Future Research." *Journal of Marketing* 41-50 (Fall 1985).

Zuboff, Shoshana. *In the Age of the Smart Machine.* New York: Basic Books, 1988.

INDEX